THE COMPLETE
HOME HANDYMAN'S GUIDE

THE COMPLETE
HOME HANDYMAN'S GUIDE

Hundreds of money-saving, helpful suggestions for

making repairs and improvements in and

around your home.

Edited by
HUBBARD COBB

1949
WM. H. WISE & CO., INC.
NEW YORK

INTRODUCTION

The average American home is the most comfortable and efficient dwelling on the earth. It boasts of plumbing, electricity, central heating, and hundreds of other modern improvements which in other countries are found only in the homes of the very wealthy—if at all. On the other hand, this complicated equipment is useless if it is not in proper working order, and like all man-made devices, it does get out of order from time to time and requires care and attention. Light switches cease to work and require replacing. Plumbing drains stop up and glass window panes break. A house needs constant maintenance if it is to be a comfortable and attractive place in which to live. Even the most expensive homes built of the finest materials will require some repair from time to time. If you have ever walked through a house that has been deserted for a year or more, you will have seen how fast it disintegrates when left without proper care for a short time.

Fifty years ago, the upkeep of a home consisted of giving it a coat of paint now and then, repairing the roof when necessary, and keeping the house tight against wind and weather. There was no complex plumbing system to get out of order,

no central heating that required cleaning and maintenance. No one had to have a working knowledge of electricity to light an oil lamp, and the worst thing that could happen to a wash tub was for it to spring a leak.

As the home became full of more complicated equipment, it was often possible to call in the local handyman who seemed to have a smattering of talents in every field and came at regular intervals to do all the various fixing jobs. Unfortunately, the handyman, along with his low pay scale, has vanished in this day of highly specialized mechanics.

When something goes wrong about the house today, the owner has two alternatives: he can do the job himself or call in a specialist in a particular field and let him do the work. The specialist's time, whether he be a plumber, painter, or electrician, is valuable. It must be remembered that it takes considerable knowledge and training to install a modern house plumbing or electrical system, and when you call in such a man to clean out a fixture trap or replace a switch it is much the same as calling a surgeon to remove a splinter from your finger. The master plumber, like the surgeon, is going to charge you on the basis of how much his time is worth to him and not upon the simplicity or the difficulty of the job to be done.

Looking at home repair work from a strictly dollars and cents point of view, it costs the homeowner nothing to replace a loose wallplug on an extension cord. Take the cord to an electrical shop to have it fixed and the charge may be twenty-five cents or more, but call in an electrician to do the work and it may cost two dollars or more—depending on how busy the electrician happens to be and how much time he spends going to and coming from your house. The same holds true for practically every minor repair job that comes up about the house.

Many homeowners complain bitterly over the size of a bill they receive from a workman for fixing a simple home device. They forget that the workman's charge per hour is the same for repointing the masonry on a house as it is for laying bricks on a million-dollar housing project.

Most of the repair jobs, as you will see from this book, that come up in the home are rather simple to fix, provided you know how to go about the job. The number of tools required for most jobs can be found in a home tool kit or in the automobile tool kit. It takes neither great skill nor special equipment to replace the washer on a leaky faucet or clear a stopped-up plumbing trap. Certainly, the average person can do a more than passable paint job if he knows how to prepare the surface, what type of paint to use, and how the paint should be mixed and applied. It is the intention of this book to give to the reader as many valuable tips and suggestions as possible on how to go about repairing and maintaining the various items about the house that usually get out of order or require attention. In some cases it has been necessary to give a little discussion on the workings of a complete system so that the reader will have a better understanding of the system and therefore how to maintain and repair it. When the plumbing gets out of order, it is suggested that the entire section of plumbing be read through first and reference then made to the particular section that covers the specific job to be done. In this way the reader will be better able to do a good job because of his more complete understanding of the problem.

Another point which must be kept in mind is that no two houses are alike, and, consequently, specialized jobs will come up that may not be covered fully in this volume. In a case of this sort, the homeowner can often discover for himself how to deal with the situation if he has some knowledge of how the system works.

So far, we have only mentioned the financial gains that are to be had by doing home repair work yourself. There is another gain, perhaps even more important to some, and this the satisfaction gained from doing a job yourself—and doing it well.

This feeling of accomplishment can be magnified many times over when one branches out into property improvements such as laying garden walks or building a garage.

A few suggestions: It should be kept in mind that so far as the upkeep of a house is concerned, the exterior is more important than the interior, unless, of course, the trouble is with some vital system like the plumbing or heating. A leak in the roof or an outside wall can cause severe damage to the house, while a section of cracked interior plaster is really only an eyesore. Make it a habit, therefore, to do exterior repairs first, for if the weather is allowed to get past the outside walls considerable damage will occur.

Do not let those little repair jobs go unfixed on the assumption that you will take care of them all together one day. Little jobs have a bad habit of growing until they are out of the realm of the home handyman and require the services of a specialist. And lastly, do not try fixing something unless you are certain that what you are doing is correct. The home handyman has many sources of reliable information in hardware, electrical and plumbing shops, and he should not hesitate to take advantage of them.

THE PUBLISHERS

CONTENTS

TOOLS AND MATERIALS

This section contains advice on the selection of a useful tool kit. A number of tools are described, but it would be wrong to give the impression that such a kit is too expensive for the average home mechanic. The tools need not be purchased all at once. It is, in fact, suggested that the particular tools needed for each job be bought when the occasion arises; in this way, a complete kit will gradually be built up.

HAMMERS

The claw hammer is the backbone of any tool kit. Select one on the basis of its weight and balance. For small work, such as driving in tacks and brads, use an upholsterer's, or tack hammer. The striking face of the hammer should be kept free of dirt and rust. This will prevent the face from slipping off the head of the nail and damaging the wood surface. A loose hammer head can be tightened by driving small metal wedges into the top of the handle. Soaking the hammer head in water to tighten it is only a temporary cure and not satisfactory. Do not use a claw hammer for prying up heavy planks, or for pulling out heavy spikes, as the claws will break.

The knack of driving a nail straight is to have the face of the hammer head at the same angle as the head of the nail. By doing this you will avoid the natural tendency to strike the nail head unevenly. Use sharp taps rather than heavy blows. This will give you more control over the hammer, and you will hit the nail-head squarely.

CLAW HAMMER

Fig. 1.

HANDSAWS

There are two kinds of handsaws: the crosscut, used for cutting across the grain of the wood, and the ripsaw for cutting with the grain. The teeth of a crosscut saw are triangular, the front of each tooth being filed to a 15-degree angle and the back to a 45-degree angle. The teeth

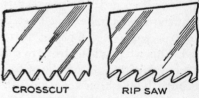

CROSSCUT   RIP SAW

Fig. 2. It is a simple matter to tell a crosscut saw from a ripsaw by looking at the shape of the teeth.

are "set," i.e. bent alternately to one side or to the other. The teeth of a ripsaw are chisel shaped, the front of each tooth filed to an 8-degree angle, and the rear to a 52-degree angle. The teeth of a ripsaw are "set" in the same fashion as those in a crosscut saw. The size of a saw is measured by the number of points to the inch. The number of teeth to an inch is always one less than the number of points to the inch. A crosscut saw of average size is 8 points, while a ripsaw should be about 7 points.

Fig. 3. A safe position for a saw when not in use.

Saws should be kept free of rust by wiping them with light oil after they have been used. Be very careful in sawing used lumber not to strike a nail or some metal object in the wood. This will dull the teeth to such a degree that the saw will be of little use until it has been sharpened. Do not try to work with a dull saw. This is too much of a handicap for even a skilled workman. Sharpening a saw properly requires skill and experience, and unless you are willing to devote considerable time to this job, it is advisable to have your saws sharpened by a professional.

Sawing a straight line can be accomplished by observing a few simple rules. First, the line to be cut should be marked, using a square or rule, so that the line will be straight.

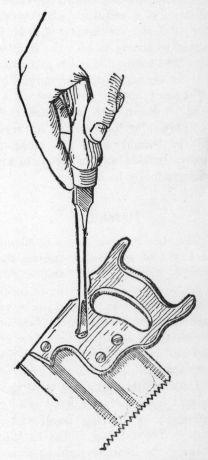

Fig. 4. Tightening the handle of the saw.

Do not trust your eye alone as a guide when sawing. By marking two or more sides of the wood before starting, you provide additional assurance that the cut will be right.

Hold the saw at a 45-degree angle to the wood for cross cutting and at a 60-degree angle when ripping. Use the knuckle of the thumb as a guide.

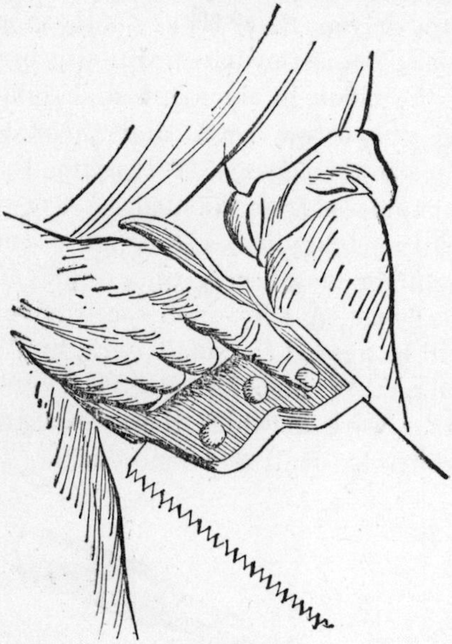

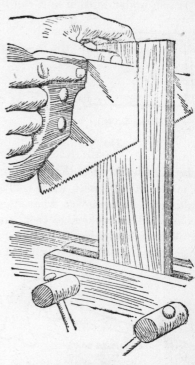

A small nail driven in the opening of the cut will prevent the wood from closing in on the saw and causing it to bind. Do not force down on the saw in an effort to make it cut.

Fig. 5. The correct method of holding the handsaw. Note the position taken by the index finger to control and direct the blade of the saw.

A piece of wood can be used instead of the thumb, and this will prevent injury in case the saw jumps. The

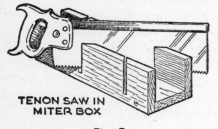

TENON SAW IN MITER BOX

Fig. 7.

first few strokes of the saw will indicate whether you are going to get a square cut or not. Saw with slow, deliberate strokes and do not hurry.

Fig. 6. Sawing with the grain. Allow the saw to cut without applying any downward pressure on the blade.

The weight of the saw is sufficient, provided that the saw is sharp.

Tenon Saw. This saw is also called a backsaw or a miter saw. It is a crosscut saw with 12 to 16 points to the inch, a thin blade, and a reinforced back. This saw is used to make the very fine cuts required in cabinetwork and other fine woodwork. To make the cuts accurate, the tenon saw should be used in conjunction with a miter box. To build a miter box (or block) yourself, see Section Twelve.

Coping Saw. The coping saw is used for fine work and for cutting curves in wood. The blade is held in the frame under tension and can be

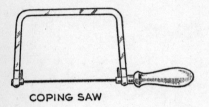

COPING SAW

Fig. 8.

turned in the frame so that cuts may be made at different angles. The blades can be removed when they become dull or broken. Keep a supply of extra blades in the tool kit because thin blades are easily broken.

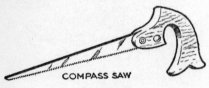

COMPASS SAW

Fig. 9.

Compass Saw. The blade of this saw is pointed, and is used primarily for cutting curves where it would be impossible to use a coping saw because of the frame. The general practice in working with the compass saw is to drill a hole with a brace and bit large enough for the blade of the saw. After this has been done, the saw is inserted in the hole and the remainder of the wood is cut out with the saw. A keyhole saw is similar to the compass saw; the handle is shaped differently and it is smaller.

SCREWDRIVERS

A good tool kit should contain screwdrivers of various sizes. Do not try to remove heavy screws with a screwdriver that is obviously too small. The screwdriver will slip out of the notch in the screw and damage the screw head, and there is considerable chance of twisting the handle loose from the blade. A screwdriver eight inches long is about right for most heavy work found in the home. A three-inch screwdriver will be needed for small work, and a long, thin one for electrical and other work in which the screws are relatively small and inaccessible.

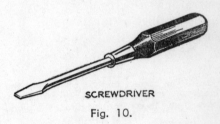

SCREWDRIVER

Fig. 10.

Do not use a screwdriver for any purpose other than turning screws. Screwdrivers used as cold chisels, pry bars, and the like, cannot be expected to last long. Keep the blade of a screwdriver sharp. Use a file for this purpose rather than a grindstone. Grinding the blade of a screwdriver may overheat the metal and cause it to lose temper.

A ratchet screwdriver with interchangeable blades, is an excellent timesaver on jobs that require a great many screws. This screwdriver does away with lifting the blade from the screw after every half-turn.

Change the blades according to the size of screws to be turned. A ratchet screwdriver requires a little light oil now and then on all moving parts.

Special Screwdrivers. Occasionally, you will run up against a screw which calls for a special screwdriver. These screws are mostly automobile and machine screws. Do not attempt to use a common screwdriver on them. A special screwdriver, made to fit the heads of these screws, should be used.

CHISELS

There are many different kinds of wood chisels and gouges; but for general purposes the firmer chisel is the best suited, as it can be used for both light and heavy work. There

are two classes of chisels, the tang chisel and the socket chisel. The names refer to the manner in which the blade is attached to the handle.

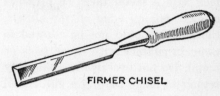

FIRMER CHISEL

Fig. 11.

The tang chisel has a sharply-pointed tang driven into the wood handle, while the handle of the socket chisel is driven into a socket at the end of the blade. Wood chisels are from ⅛ to 2 inches wide, but a ¼-inch, ½-inch,

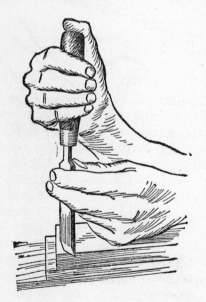

Fig. 12. Showing the method of holding a wood chisel when making a vertical cut. Pressure is applied by the right hand, the blade guided by the left.

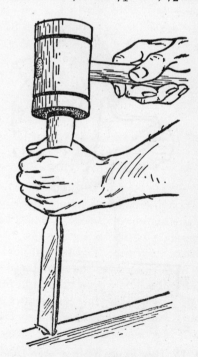

Fig. 13. Correct method of holding a chisel. On narrow section wood, the chisel must be driven in carefully to avoid splitting the wood.

and a ¾-inch chisel will be sufficient for most home repair jobs.

Use a wood- or leather-head mallet for striking a chisel; never a hammer with a metal face. To preserve a good cutting edge on the chisels, the blades should not be allowed to come in contact with other tools or metal. Do not overstrain a chisel by trying to make too big a cut. Small cuts will give you more accuracy in your work, and the job will be done just as quickly in the long run.

BRACE AND BIT

A ratchet brace is a device to hold wood-boring tools. The ratchet as-sembly allows this tool to be operated in a limited space where it would be impossible for the handle of the brace to make a complete revolution.

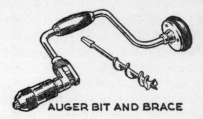

AUGER BIT AND BRACE

Fig. 14.

Auger bits come in many sizes and are measured by sixteenths of an inch, beginning with $\frac{3}{16}$ in. The number stamped on the tang of the bit indicates the size of the hole the bit will make, measured in sixteenths of an inch. A bit stamped $\frac{8}{16}$ would be a ½-inch bit.

Fig. 15. How to use a brace when boring a hole vertically. Pressure is applied by the left hand. The position of the head, as shown, helps to hold the brace in a vertical position.

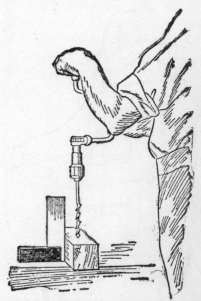

Fig. 15a. Sighting the brace for vertical position, using a square. Align square carefully.

The two main parts of a bit are the twist and the shank. The twist can be either single or double, and terminates in two points. The points score the circle to be cut, while the two sharp edges do the actual cutting. The screw at the center pulls the bit into the wood as it is turned. It is not necessary to get a complete set of bits at the start. One-fourth, ½-, and ¾-inch bits will be sufficient for many jobs.

When boring a vertical hole into a piece of wood, use a square to align the brace and bit with the wood. Once a bit is in the wood, it can be bent or broken if the position of the brace is suddenly changed. When boring deep holes, it is a good idea to remove the bit from time to time and prevent any possibility of choking the hole with waste wood. Bits are self cleaning, in that the waste wood will move up along the twist of the bit and come out at the top; but very often enough waste wood is left in the hole to cause difficulty.

Do not attempt to make a hole right through a piece of wood. Bore through one side until the screw of the bit appears on the bottom side. Remove the bit, turn the wood over, and place the screw of the bit in the opening made from the opposite side. By doing this you will avoid splintering the wood surface, which often occurs when the bit breaks through.

A device known as a bit gauge is used to prevent making a hole too deep. This tool is very handy, when using a bit, to remove excess wood, as is often necessary when making certain kinds of wood joints. The bit gauge fits over the bit and is then screwed on tightly at the proper depth for the hole. The same results can be obtained by drilling a hole in

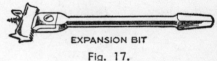

EXPANSION BIT
Fig. 17.

a block of wood and leaving the block on the bit. On the width of the block will depend the depth of the hole. The thicker the block, the shorter will be the portion of bit exposed for drilling.

An expansion bit is used for drilling holes larger than can be made with ordinary size bits.

A rose countersink that can be fitted into the brace

ROSE COUNTERSINK BIT

Fig. 18.

is used for boring conical holes to receive the heads of screws, so that the head will be flush with the surface of the wood.

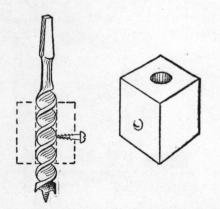

Fig. 16. Illustrating the use of a block of wood and a screw fitted to a bit, providing a useful depth gauge.

Forstner bits are used in boring holes in thin wood or in end-grain wood. They have no twist and make a very accurate cut.

FORSTNER BIT

Fig. 19.

To avoid any possibility of the wood's splitting, it is a good practice to start the hole with an auger bit and finish with a forstner bit.

Twist drills of the type used for drilling metal are made with a square shank to fit a wood brace. They are very useful for making small holes in wood, such as are required for wood screws.

Screwdriver bits are also made to fit the brace. When used in a ratchet

brace the same advantages are gained as with a ratchet screwdriver. However, driving down a screw so that it is straight is somewhat more difficult with a brace than with a ratchet screwdriver.

Keep all bits that have cutting edges free of contact with other tools. The moving parts of the brace should be oiled from time to time to keep them operating properly.

Hand Drill. This tool can be used for making holes in either wood or metal, depending upon the kind of

HAND DRILL

Fig. 20.

drill used. The tool made to fit a hand drill has a round shank instead of the square one used with a brace. The hand drill is excellent for making small and numerous holes in wood, as it can be operated a great deal faster than a wood brace. Both the wood and metal drills are of relatively small diameter, and they

TWIST DRILL

Fig. 21.

can be bent or broken easily by running the drill too fast or moving the drill once it has penetrated the wood or metal. A hand drill and complete set of metal drills are a necessity for

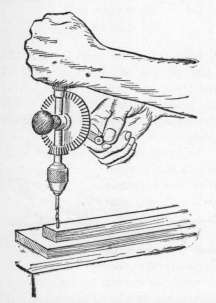

Fig. 22. When drilling vertically through thin or soft material hold the drill as shown to keep the drill steady.

anyone wishing to do any extensive work with metals.

Brad Awl. This small, wood-boring tool can be had in several sizes. It is used for drilling holes for screws and nails. In making a hole, the edge of the blade should be placed across

BRAD AWL
Fig. 23.

the grain and then pressed into the wood and rotated slightly. As the efficiency of this tool depends upon a good cutting edge, it should receive the same care as the chisels and the wood bits.

rough work but cannot produce a very smooth surface because its length will cause the blade to slip over the low spots.

When a greater degree of smoothness is required, a smoothing plane, somewhat shorter than the jack, is

JACK PLANE
Fig. 25.

used. For small work and for end-grain planing, the block plane is needed.

The blade, or plane iron, can be adjusted for depth by moving the knurled knob located at the back of the blade. The lateral adjustment of the blade is made with a lever that fits into a slot on the upper portion of the blade.

The blade has a cap which fits over it to provide additional strength.

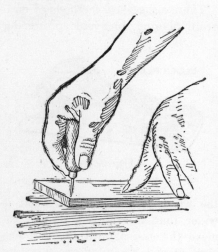

Fig. 24. When boring with a brad awl, apply the edge of the blade to run with the wood grain to avoid splitting.

PLANES

Planes are obtainable in many sizes and shapes, depending on the type of work to be done. For general purposes the jack plane is adequate. This plane is about 14 inches long and 2 inches wide. It is suitable for

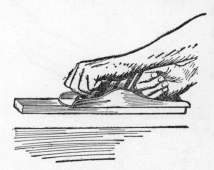

Fig. 26. Using a smoothing or jack plane. Note the position of the hands for planing. The left hand guides the plane, the right supplies the thrust.

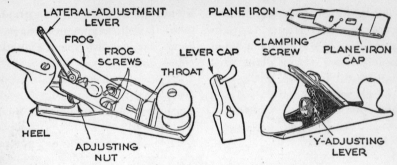

Fig. 27. Parts of a jack or smoothing plane.

On hard-grain wood, or for cross-planing, this cap should be set as close to the edge of the blade as possible. This will prevent the wood from splintering. A block plane does not have this cap, as it is designed for end-grain planing.

The first rule in planing is to work in the direction of the grain. This direction can be determined with the first stroke. If the blade tears the wood and makes a rough surface, reverse the direction and work from the other end. Do not try to take off too much wood at one time. Set the blade so that a thin shaving will be taken off rather than large chunks of wood. If you do this, you will get greater accuracy and a smooth surface.

There are several methods of end-grain planing, to avoid splintering

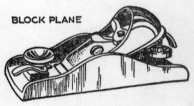

Fig. 29.

the wood. If the piece of wood is wider than is required, do not remove the excess until the end has been planed. Chamfer one edge by cutting the corner off at an angle, and plane toward this chamfered edge. The same result can be obtained by placing a piece of scrap wood against the far edge of the wood to be planed and holding both in a vise. The scrap piece of wood should be level with the piece to be planed. Any splintering that occurs will be on the edge of the scrap wood and not on the piece to be finished.

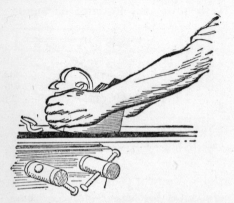

Fig. 28. Using a wooden smoothing plane. Note the position of the left hand which is used to guide the plane.

Do not let waste accumulate in the plane, as this will reduce the efficiency. Always keep the plane blade sharp and never set a plane flat. This will dull the blade. Get in the habit of placing a plane on its side each time you have finished using it.

FILES

A wood file is used in smoothing wood difficult or impossible to work with other tools. Files are classified according to their length, shape, and the spacing of the teeth. A file used for rough work is called a rasp. A

HALF-ROUND FILE
Fig. 30.

metal file is very useful for sharpening screwdrivers, garden tools, and other odd jobs. Both wood and metal files should be fitted with handles to avoid injury to the hands.

MEASURING TOOLS

It is quite impossible to do any sort of building without the aid of proper measuring tools. Always measure before you start work; never depend upon the eye alone.

Rules. A good rule is the first item on any list of measuring tools. Wooden folding rules or flexible steel rules are suitable for large jobs, and a 12-inch straight rule is convenient for shop work. Cloth rules

should not be used when a great degree of accuracy is needed, as the cloth can be stretched enough to cause considerable error.

Squares. A large 24 x 16 in. steel framing-square can be used on any number of jobs. Besides the scale of inches and a right angle, it contains information on laying out numerous other angles. Do not allow the steel square to become rusty, as this will make accurate reading impossible.

STEEL FRAMING SQUARE

Fig. 31.

A try-square is somewhat smaller with a wood or metal handle. It has many uses in the home workshop, such as making angles and squaring off small pieces of wood.

The combination square can be used to lay out 90- and 45-degree

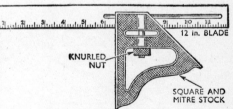

Fig. 32. Combination or try square.

angles. Many of these squares have a level built into the handle. A combination square can be used on almost any construction job.

Marking Gauge. This is a very important tool in making lines parallel. The head is adjustable and fits against the edge of the work, while the metal point on the end of the gauge marks off the line as the gauge is moved. This metal scriber should be kept sharp.

Fig. 33.

Levels. To check any piece of work to be sure that it is either horizontal or vertical, a level is needed. A level has a small glass tube filled with water in which there floats a small bubble of air. The glass tube is marked off so that the level is either vertical or horizontal when the bubble of air is centered between the lines on the tube. There are many uses for a level other than carpentry work. It is useful for checking a table to be sure that it stands evenly and for making certain that pictures hang straight on the wall.

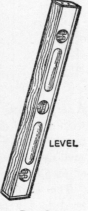

Fig. 34.

PINCERS

A pair of pincers are extremely useful in pulling nails out of wood and for other odd jobs. When pulling nails, insert a piece of wood between the lower jaw of the pincers and the wood to prevent damaging the latter.

Fig. 35. Using a pair of pincers. A wooden block placed under the pincers assists in the removal of the nail and will prevent damaging the wood surface.

NAIL SET

This small tool is used to drive the heads of nails below the surface of the wood. A tool kit should contain

NAIL SET

Fig. 37.

at least two nail sets, one for large nails and the other for small. Keep the end of the nail set flat to prevent its slipping off the nail head.

DRAWKNIFE

For rough cutting on curved or straight wood surfaces a drawknife can be used instead of a plane. The

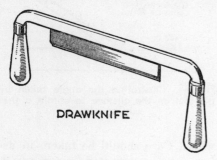

DRAWKNIFE

Fig. 38.

knife is drawn towards the operator, and must be used carefully to avoid taking off too much wood.

CABINET SCRAPER

As its name implies, this scraper is used primarily for cabinetwork.

CABINET SCRAPER

Fig. 39.

This tool should be employed for all heavy cutting work, as it is made especially for hard use. Do not use a screwdriver as a substitute.

SMALL TOOL KIT

For doing odd jobs about the house it is very convenient to have a small kit containing the following items: Hammer, screwdriver, pliers,

jackknife, coil of thin copper wire, can of plastic wood, rubber and friction tape, assorted faucet washers, assorted nails and wood screws, a can of machine oil, a can of putty, and a putty knife.

PUTTY KNIFE

The wide, thin blade of the putty knife is necessary for glazing and

PUTTY KNIFE

Fig. 40.

other work to be considered in later sections. Keep the blade clean and free of rust.

PLIERS

A pair of adjustable pliers is possibly the most used tool in the kit.

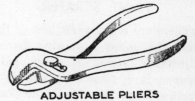

ADJUSTABLE PLIERS

Fig. 41.

It can be used for tightening small machine nuts, bending wire, and many other odd jobs.

WRENCHES

Most home-plumbing jobs require a wrench of one sort or another. A monkey wrench of the type found in most automobile kits can be used on nuts, but pipes require a stilson wrench made to take a firm grip on the smooth, round surface. Do not

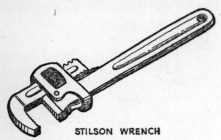

STILSON WRENCH

Fig. 42.

overstrain a wrench by using it on a job that is obviously too big, and do not try to loosen a tight nut by pounding on the handle of the wrench with a heavy hammer.

MONKEY WRENCH

Fig. 43.

PAINT SCRAPER

There are many variations of this tool, the more expensive having adjustable blades. A sharp paint scraper is a timesaver, and it is worthwhile to keep the blade sharp and free of nicks and dents.

SHARPENING TOOLS

All tools with cutting edges must be kept sharp if they are to be of any real use. The method of sharpening will depend upon the kind of tool and its special requirements.

If a tool is very dull and the cutting edge has been nicked, grinding

is necessary before the blade can be sharpened. Grinding can be done either on a grindstone or on an emery

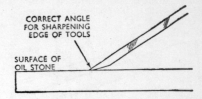

Fig. 44. Illustrating the angle taken by the tool on the oilstone to obtain a true cutting edge.

wheel. Care should be taken, in using a power-operated emery wheel, to avoid overheating the blade. Overheating due to grinding will destroy the temper in the metal, and the blade will never be able to hold a good edge. A grindstone is better for this operation, as it cuts more slowly and the water applied to the stone will keep the metal sufficiently cool.

To grind and sharpen straight-edge tools, such as chisels and planes, hold the bevel side of the blade against the wheel so that the wheel rotates towards the cutting edge. The bevel should be ground to an approximate 25-degree angle. To be sure of getting an even bevel along the blade, move the blade back and forth as the wheel turns. A guide can be attached to the grindstone on which to rest the blade, and this will help keep the right angle. Stop as soon as this angle is obtained.

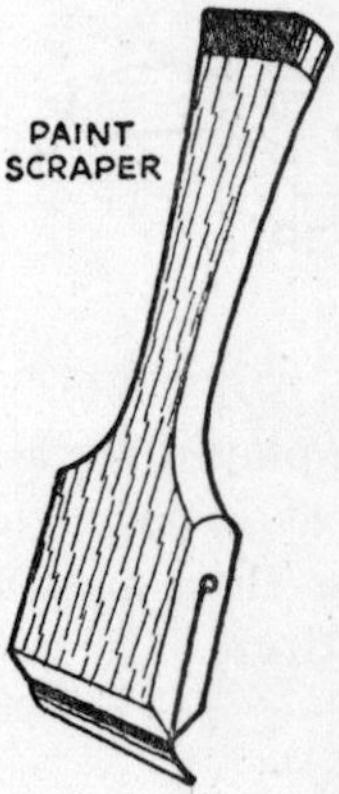

Fig. 45.

The actual sharpening of the blade is done on an oilstone. A light film of oil should first be applied to the stone. Place the blade so that the

Fig. 46. Sharpening a narrow cutting tool. Be careful to retain the correct angle in relation to the oilstone.

bevel rests flat on the stone, then slightly raise the back of the blade. Move the blade back and forth, using the entire surface of the stone

Fig. 47. Correct method of holding a broad cutting tool when sharpening on the oilstone. Apply even pressure on the forward stroke.

to avoid hollowing the stone in the center. A tiny wire edge will form on the back of the blade as the edge appears, and this can be removed by placing the blade flat on the stone and moving it back and forth a few times.

If an especially keen edge is desired, strop the edge of the tool on a leather strop.

NAILS

There are many kinds of nails, but for home repair work and small building projects, the home mechanic will find that wire nails are best suited to his needs.

The wire nail, as its name implies, is made from steel wire. It is inexpensive, comes in a wide assortment of sizes and shapes,

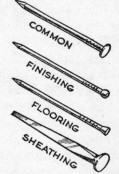

Fig. 49. A few of the more common kinds of nails.

and has good holding power. The other kind of nail that the home mechanic may have occasion to use

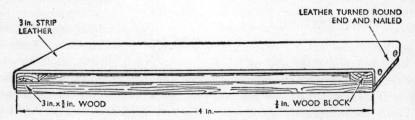

Fig. 48. A simple leather strop for "finishing" the edge of cutting tools and knives.

is the cut nail. This nail is stamped out of sheet steel and is used for such purposes as flooring. It is somewhat more expensive than the wire nail.

The size of nails is designated by the term "penny," expressed as d. This term has come down through the years, and doubt remains as to its origin.

The smallest nail-size measured by the "penny" system is the $2d$, which is one inch long. Nails under $2d$ are classified as brads or tacks, and are measured by the inch.

There are many kinds of wire nails. The common wire nail can be used for most rough work where a finished appearance is not required. The clinch wire nail is made of softer steel, which makes it easier to bend over at the end. The finishing nail has a very small head so that it may be set below the surface of the wood and be as inconspicuous as possible. Finishing nails should be used on furniture and for interior work.

There is a wide assortment of galvanized, rustproof nails for use with wood or composition shingles on roofs.

Nails are sold by the pound or by the barrel.

Nailing. Nailing two pieces of wood together is one of the most common tasks in carpentry and the simplest. If the joint does not hold, or the wood splits, it is generally because the beginner did not observe the few simple rules for nailing.

First of all, if the joint is to hold properly, the nail must be long enough. A good rule to follow here is to select a nail three times the

length of the thickness of the wood to be nailed. If the nail is too short it cannot hold properly, and if it is too long the increased diameter may split the wood.

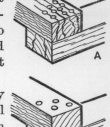
Fig. 50.

A few properly spaced nails will hold better than many nails put in at one point. Improper spacing, or too many nails, will split the wood and add no strength to the joint; see illustration, Fig. 50–A and B.

A nail driven in at an angle, called "toe nailing," will provide a stronger joint than if the nail is driven straight down.

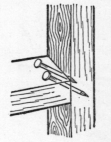
Fig. 51. Toe nailing.

When the end of the nail extends through the second piece of wood, it should be clinched or bent over. While clinching the nail with the grain will give a smoother surface, clinching across the grain will give more strength.

The head of a finishing nail should be set below the surface of the wood with a nail set, and the resulting hole filled with putty or plastic wood. Whenever a finished appearance is desired, drive the nail almost to the surface with the hammer and finish the job with a nail set. This will prevent your striking the wood with the face of the hammer and denting it. See Fig. 52.

When using a claw hammer to pull out nails, a block of wood should be in-serted under the hammer to pro-vide more lever-age and to pre-vent the hammer from damaging the wood. If the nail has been clinched, it should be straightened before any attempt is made to remove it.

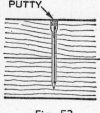

PUTTY

Fig. 52.

Considering how inexpensive are nails, it is a waste of time and ma-terials to try to straighten used nails for re-use. Once a nail has been used, and bent back and forth, it has lost much of its holding power. Moreover, it is almost impossible to straighten a nail perfectly, and the usual result is the bending of the nail as it is driven in. This entails the removal of the nail and possible damage to the wood.

Keep an ample supply of nails and store them according to size.

WOOD SCREWS

Screws have several advantages over nails. First of all, they provide a stronger joint and can be removed easily without danger of splitting the wood, as sometimes occurs when trying to remove nails. On the other hand, screws are more expensive than nails and require considerably more time to install. There is no specific rule as to when to use a nail and when a screw, but where there is a definite pull on the joint, as on door hinges, a screw must be used. Screws should also be used on fur-niture, for they provide greater strength and will not split the wood if properly installed.

Screws are made of several dif-ferent metals, steel and brass being the most common. As a general rule, the brass screw is used for light in-terior work while the stronger, steel screw is used for heavy work. The kind of wood screw used for any particular job will depend on whether or not the head of the screw is to be set above the surface of the

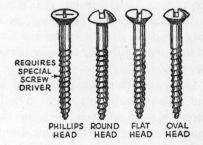

REQUIRES SPECIAL SCREW DRIVER

PHILLIPS HEAD   ROUND HEAD   FLAT HEAD   OVAL HEAD

Fig. 53. Wood screws.

wood or countersunk so that it is flush with the surface. Roundhead screws will protrude above the wood surface. Oval-head screws are coun-tersunk so that half the head pro-trudes, while flathead screws can be countersunk so that the head is flush with the wood or metal. When select-ing a screw for a job, you must de-cide how long it is to be, how thick in diameter, what type head it is to have, and of what metal it should be made.

To join two pieces of wood with a screw, it is necessary first to drill a hole in the wood to avoid any possibility of splitting or the head of the screw being twisted off. The hole in the first piece of wood should be of the same diameter as the shank. The hole in the second piece should be smaller, so that the threads of the screw will gouge

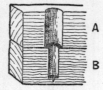

Fig. 54.

into the wood and take a firm grip. See Fig. 54–A and B.

Be sure that the screw is started straight down and that the screwdriver is the right size. Do not put too much pressure on the screw until it is well into the wood, as it may bend. A little soap on the end of the screw will help to make it run down easily.

If you want to hide the head of the screw completely, drill a hole about ¾₆ of an inch deep, of the same diameter as the screw head. Drive the screw down into this hole, then glue in a wood plug. The top of the plug should be cut off level with the surface of the wood and can be stained or painted to match the rest of the wood.

Do not use a hammer and drive screws down by force. They must be run down with a screwdriver to be most effective.

CORRUGATED FASTENERS

These are strips of corrugated steel with one edge sharpened so that they can be driven into wood. They will prove useful for making joints in light work, such as window and door screen frames, and for repair work on inexpensive furni-

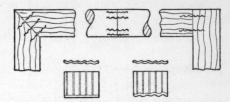

Fig. 55. Two types of corrugated fasteners and a few examples of how they can be used for small wood joints.

ture. They come in several sizes. Drive the fastener into the wood with a hammer and distribute the blows evenly along the entire width. These fasteners should not be used on hard wood, as they will not be satisfactory.

MENDING PLATES

Mending plates are obtainable in many shapes and sizes. They are made of steel with holes counter-

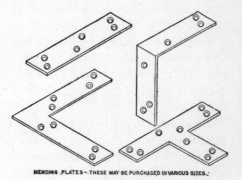

MENDING PLATES—THESE MAY BE PURCHASED IN VARIOUS SIZES.

Fig. 56.

sunk, so that when a flathead screw is used, the head will be flush with the surface of the plate. These plates are ideal for reinforcing almost any kind of wood joint. They are especially good for screen-frame repair work. Mending plates should always be attached with wood screws, never nails.

BOLTS

The advantage of using a nut and bolt to make a wool joint, rather than a nail or wood screw, is that the joint can be taken apart easily and as often as necessary without damage to the wood. The sections of any portable structure should be bolted rather than screwed or nailed together. On many heavy woodworking jobs the home mechanic will find that bolts are easier to install and give better results than wood screws or nails. Drill a hole

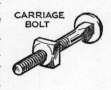

CARRIAGE BOLT

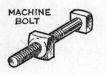

MACHINE BOLT

Fig. 57.

first which corresponds to the size of the bolt to be used. Place a washer over the end of the bolt and run down the nut. The washer will prevent the nut from coming loose and keep the wood from being damaged as the nut is tightened. Turning in the bolt too much will damage the threads.

Machine bolts have a square head that can be held with a wrench. Carriage bolts have an oval head, but the shank is square for a short distance below the head, preventing the head from turning in the wood as the nut is tightened. Use a monkey wrench or a spanner to tighten.

ABRASIVES

Sandpaper. The term sandpaper is used throughout this book to describe the type of abrasive paper commonly used for smoothing down a wood surface. Actually, no abrasive paper is made out of sand because it is not very effective. The very coarse grades of abrasive paper are made with flint, while the finer grades are made out of garnet.

There are two systems for grading abrasive papers, but the one most commonly used starts at 3½. This is very coarse paper, good for little except very rough work. The scale runs to 9/0, which is very fine. In between are the medium papers, such as Nos. 1, ½, 0, 00, and these are suitable for most jobs in the home workshop.

Steel Wool. Steel wool is an excellent abrasive for the workshop be-

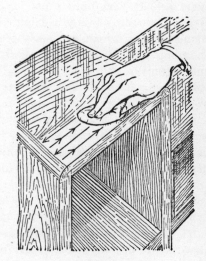

Fig. 58. Always sand in the direction of the wood grain.

cause it is pliable and can be worked around curves in furniture and in other places difficult to work with sandpaper. Steel wool is also less likely to scratch a finish and may, therefore, be used on enamel. Steel wool is graded by the same system used for sandpaper, but it is somewhat finer throughout.

Very fine abrasives, such as pumice stone, are used for polishing.

Sanding should always be done *with* the wood grain, to avoid damaging the wood. You will find that in most cases you can begin with one of the rather coarse grades and work down to the finer grades as the wood surface becomes smoother.

After the sanding has been completed, the wood should be dusted carefully. This is very important if the surface is to be varnished.

GLUE FOR WOODWORK

There are several types of glue that are excellent for joining two or more pieces of wood. A well-glued joint is extremely strong, as you can easily discover in trying to take down a piece of well-built furniture.

Hot Glue. This kind of glue has been used for many years by cabinetmakers and carpenters. It makes a very strong joint. This disadvantage of its use in the home workshop is that the glue must be heated before it can be used. This not only requires additional equipment, but considerable time must be allowed for bringing the glue to the right temperature. In shops where the glue is used throughout the day, the heater for the glue is controlled by a thermostat, so that the temperature of the glue is kept

constant. Another disadvantage of hot glue is that it cannot be applied to a cold joint, nor can it become chilled before it is

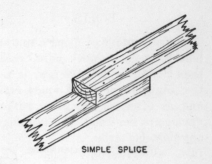

SIMPLE SPLICE

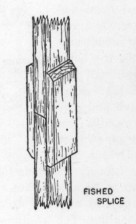

FISHED
SPLICE

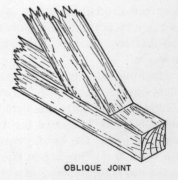

OBLIQUE JOINT

Fig. 59. Some simple wood splices.

hard. In both cases, the glue will not dry satisfactorily.

Casein Glues. For the small workshop these are the best, and

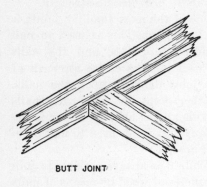

BUTT JOINT

LAP JOINT

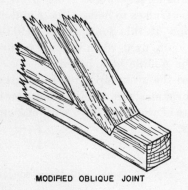

MODIFIED OBLIQUE JOINT

while many of them are made with a casein base, there are some made with different materials which are equally good. These glues are obtained in pow-der form and require only the addition of water. They make a very strong joint, and the powder, as long as it is kept dry, will last indefinitely.

Liquid Glue. This is the most simple glue to use because it comes ready for use. The fact remains, however, that it is not as strong as the others and should not be used where a very strong joint is desired.

There are many brands of all-purpose glues—or so advertised—on the market today. Many of these are quite satisfac-tory in a wide variety of uses. For wood-work, however, use a glue made for this purpose alone. These special glues have been tried over a period of many years, with proven results.

SPLICES AND JOINTS

When two pieces of wood are joined in order to achieve greater length, the joint is called a "splice." When two pieces of wood are joined at different angles, it is called a "joint."

There are many types of splices and joints. The home mechanic should be familiar with a few of the more simple ones likely to be used in home-building projects.

Probably the easiest kind of splice is the simple splice shown in Fig. 59. It is easy to see that this splice depends upon the nails or screws in the wood for all its strength, and accordingly should not be used where there is any stress.

A somewhat stronger splice is the halved splice. Here, the pieces have been cut out so that they will fit together. This splice can withstand considerable compression, that is, pressure upon it from above.

To make the halved splice even stronger, plates are nailed or bolted to each side. This is called a fished splice because the plates used are known as fish plates. The strength of the splice will depend on the length of the plates.

There are probably hundreds of joints used in one form or another.

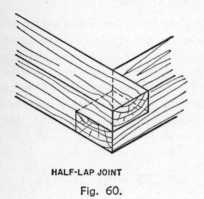

HALF-LAP JOINT

Fig. 60.

Making a perfect wood joint requires the highest kind of skill, and it is becoming something of a lost art, except for a few skilled cabinetmakers who carry on the traditions. Very few of the more complicated joints are ever used in modern construction work because of the time and labor involved in cutting and fitting the wood, and because of the smaller-sized timbers now used.

If you want to see how effective good joinery can be, look at the framework of an old barn or house.

You will see that each piece of timber has been carefully cut out and fitted to the other member, and only the wooden peg through the joint holds the two pieces together. The peg itself provides no strength.

One of the most familiar joints is the butt joint. This is used to nail studding to plates, and the nails are toed in. The entire strength of this joint depends upon the nails. Another joint in which the nails provide all the holding power is the oblique butt joint, used to nail diagonal braces.

While it is always possible to join two pieces of wood by means of nails or screws, the resulting joint is not always as strong as desired. To provide greater strength, each piece of wood is cut out so that it may be fitted to the other in a special fashion. In a well-made joint the wood itself provides the strength, and the nails merely hold the joint together.

Consider the modified butt joint as opposed to the oblique butt joint. It can easily be seen that the modified version is a great deal stronger and requires few nails.

The half lap joint can be used for almost any work, from window screen frames to house sills. Another version of this joint is the middle lap joint, used when a joint occurs in the middle of a board.

Use the cross lap joint in making a Christmas tree stand, where both pieces of wood are flush with one another.

THE WORKSHOP

Light, warmth, and dryness are the principal requirements of the amateur's workshop. Warmth, it should be remembered, does not necessarily ensure dryness, and if the workshop is too warm it will probably become damp. The best way to secure dryness is by providing for ample ventilation under the floor boards if it is a wooden building, or by opening the top window in other cases. With regard to light, if there is a window along one side of the workshop, the long side of the workbench should go against that wall. If there are any electric outlets, rig a long, heavy, insulated cord to a bracket over the bench and suspend the lamp from that. Keep the light well up, where it will be out of the way when handling long pieces of timber on the bench. If you plan a rather elaborate shop, complete with power saws, have an electrician wire the workshop for this additional load. The circuit should be sufficient to carry any electrical power equipment as well as the required lighting and outlets for soldering irons and small electric devices.

Warming the Shop. This is not merely a question of warming the workman but also of providing the warm atmosphere that will be needed if woodwork joints are to be glued together. Glue chills quickly and no satisfactory joint can be made on a cold day, unless the timber is warm to the touch before applying the glue. An oil or electric heater will do quite well for a small workshop, and it should stand on a sheet of iron.

Fire Precautions. Keep paints, cleaning fluids, and other inflammable liquids outside the shop. Oily rags should not be left about, and a good fire precaution is to keep the floor of the shop free of sawdust, wood shavings, and other inflammable matter.

The Workbench. A strong kitchen table can be used for light work, but it is not always firm enough for planing and other woodworking operations. This is because the legs are open and not connected near the bottom with braces. If you can obtain a strong table with square legs, connect the legs with four sections of a 1 x 4 inch board, screwed in about three inches from the base of each leg. A flooring of tongued and grooved boards can be nailed to the top edges of the bracing sections, strengthening the entire structure and furnishing a useful shelf for large tools and other equipment. Another way to strengthen the table is to nail two widths of 1 x 6 inch board from end to end, so that they span the widths of the short ends of the table, midway between the top of the table and the floor, and form a brace.

It is not difficult to construct a strong workbench, and Fig. 1 gives the required information about the joints. The length may vary from 4 to 6 feet, according to the accommodations available. The width should not be less than 2 feet 3 inches, and a comfortable height for the average man is 2 feet 6 inches. Construct the two end frames first. The legs are of 4 x 4 in. stock and are connected at the top by a length of 1 x 4 in. They are also joined near the bottom by a similar piece, the lower edge of which may be about 2 inches from the bottom.

Any difficulty in joining is avoided by screwing the 1 x 4's to the top and bottom of the legs with No. 12 screws, 2½ inches long.

To assemble the end-frames, place the legs in their proper relative positions on the floor with a 1 x 4 inch bearer across them, and check the angles with a square. Mark the position for a hole in one leg by passing a brad awl through the hole made previously in the bearer. Remove the bearer and start the hole at the awl mark. Put the bearer on again and screw it at the one hole only, testing

with the square before tightening. Now square the bearer with the opposite leg, bore one hole there, and turn in the screw tightly. Bore for the remaining two screws and insert them.

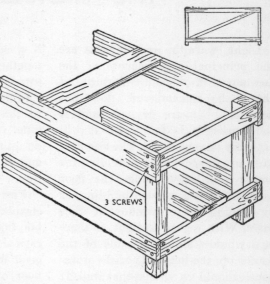

Fig. 1. The general arrangement of a workbench frame, showing the joints and diagonal side bracing, the latter being used to stiffen the frame.

Screwing on the rail near the bottom of the table is easy because the legs are now held in position at the top. Check with the square to be sure, and measure from the bottom to make certain that the rail is equidistant up each leg.

Make the second end-frame in the same way. The two end-frames are connected by top rails, also cut from 1 x 4's, which extend to cover the ends of the frames. Two lower rails, somewhat narrower in width, parallel the top rails and are at right angles to the lower rails of the frame. Use a 12-gauge, 2-in. screw for both sets of long rails and bore holes for two screws at the end of each rail. Place the end-frames on the floor in proper position and the right distance apart. While an assistant holds the frames upright, fit one top rail to one end of a frame, square it with the legs of the frame, and tighten the screw to prevent the rail from slipping. Square the other end of the rail with the legs of the opposite frame and drive a nail a short way through one of the holes to fix the rail in proper position.

Insert one screw into this frame, carefully pull out the temporary nail without altering the location of the rail, and replace it with a second screw. Insert the second screw in the opposite frame. Gently turn the partly assembled bench over and secure the other top rail in a similar manner. Put on the lower rails one by one, following the same procedure.

Cut the boards for the top and nail them on so that they are even with the edges of the top bearer rails at front, back, and sides. Tongued and grooved flooring makes a good top. Saw down one board, if necessary, to maintain the proper width for the top, or plane off the tongue on one outside board and the groove on the board on the opposite end. Countersink the screw heads in the boards so that they are flush, or below the wood surface. A diagonal brace can be fixed to the framework for added strength.

If you wish to floor the bottom, place the lower bearer rails on the inside of the frame. The tongued and grooved flooring can then be finished inside the legs, the ends resting on the top edge of the lower rails and cut off flush.

The diagram shows only one end of the framework, to indicate how the bearer rails and lower rails are put on. If the bench is made longer than 4 feet, one or two boards, 4 inches wide, should be screwed to the underside of the bench top to strengthen it. Fit these boards into notches cut in the top of the upper rails.

The bench should be fixed to the floor and to the wall against which it stands. On wood floors, angle brackets can be used to secure the legs. On a concrete floor, attach the bracket to the floor by means of an expansion shield.

Bench Stop. The bench stop is an invaluable aid in the preparation of wood surfaces by planing, and provides a firm stop for work of similar

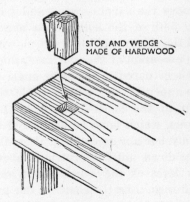

BENCH STOP TAPPED INTO MORTISE CUT IN BENCH TOP

STOP AND WEDGE MADE OF HARDWOOD

Fig. 2. General details of an adjustable bench stop for the workbench.

nature. The stop is located at the top end of the working side of the bench.

The customary type of bench stop is shown in Fig. 2. It consists of a 1¾ inch-square section block of hardwood, 6 inches long, and a hardwood wedge 5½ inches long, 1¾ inches wide, ¾ inch thick at the top, tapering to ⅜ inch at the base. These components are fitted in a hole cut in the bench top, the rear face of the hole being cut to the same angle as the taper of the wedge. The location of the bench stop hole is a matter of choice. So long as the top of the vise is not above the level of the bench, no difficulty should be encountered. The hole should be marked off so as to be approximately 3 inches in from the side face of the bench and at least 7 inches from the top end of the bench. Having scribed the shape of the hole, which should be exactly 1¾ in. wide and 2⅝ in. long, drill out a ⅜ in. hole at each corner and well inside the scribed lines.

Using a keyhole or compass saw, remove the surplus wood and trim the sides of the hole with a chisel. All the sides should be vertical, with the exception of the rear face which must be pared to the same angle as the taper of the wedge. Slide the stop in the hole, followed by the wedge, which must be hammered in firmly but not excessively. Press the stop down until it protrudes above the level of the bench about one-half inch. Lightly chamfer the top edges of the wedge and stop. To alter the height of the stop, tap its base

to loosen the wedge, move the stop to the required level, and secure it by driving the wedge home.

Saw Bucks. When sawing lumber, some form of stool or stand is necessary on which to rest the board to be cut. A short piece of board to be crosscut or ripped, can be held with the knee on any solid stand. Longer boards, however, must be supported at both ends, and a pair of stands are needed. The best support for longer boards—a door, for example —is provided by a pair of strong trestles. These trestles are often called saw bucks or saw horses. Plan to build a pair of them.

The saw buck, as made by a carpenter, is arranged so that the legs slope backward and out. This is to provide a firm stand while keeping the legs out of the way of the saw. Tops of the legs are notched to receive the top beam, which is cut from a piece of 2 x 4, wide face up. The leg tops, owing to the two-way slope, have to be cut with a slant or bevel, that is, a compound of the two slopes, and this is apt to be difficult for the beginner. The same problem arises when making a wheelbarrow, where the legs are joined in a similar two-way slope.

There is a simpler method which will give ample strength and stability. Slope the legs *outward only,* as shown in the drawing. On examining this saw buck, the reader will see that the leg is straight instead of sloping backward. The two legs on each side will thus be parallel with each other, and with the opposite pair. Measure 4 inches from the end of the top beam, square a line down the side of the beam, and ft the top of the leg square to this line.

Fig. 3. How to mark the legs of the saw buck for cutting.

In other words, the distance from the end of the beam to the outside edge of the leg will be 4 inches. Screw the legs to the beam on both sides. The end braces should be screwed on after the legs have been fixed to the beam.

The bottoms of the legs will have to be squared off while the saw buck stands level on the floor. Rest a level on top of the beam and pack up the legs with thin slices of wood until the bubble in the level is centered. Use a straight piece of wood, about ¾ in. by ¼ in., as a straightedge. Place it alongside the legs at one end, narrow edge on the floor, close to the legs. The worker will be viewing the saw buck as seen in the end elevation. Run a pencil along the top

edge of the straightedge, so that it marks a horizontal line across the legs of the saw buck. This indicates the true line at which the ends of the legs should be cut to give a level stance.

Make the legs of the buck out of 2 x 3 inch stock, and the top out of 2 x 4 inch. The end braces ought not to be less than 1¼ inches thick, and may be up to 8 inches wide. They are secured with No. 12 screws, the length being suited to the thickness of the braces. A V-shaped notch may be cut in one end of the top beam for use when ripping boards; it helps to prevent the saw from damaging the end of the saw buck.

Tool Rack. A rack for chisels, screwdrivers, files, and other such tools is convenient and easily made, though it is not wise to leave edge tools continually in such a rack; they ought to be collected and put in a tool box when a job has been finished.

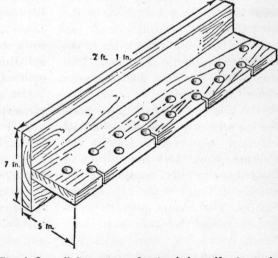

2 ft. 1 in.

7 in.

5 in.

Fig. 4. Overall dimensions of a simple but effective tool rack.

The rack shown in Fig. 4 is intended to be screwed to the wall of the workshop at the back of the bench. Holes for rawl plugs should be made in the masonry, if any, and the rack held by about four screws (for the length shown in the diagram). Some people fix the rack to the bench, but in this case the vertical piece must be made higher to give clearance. An objection is that hammering or planing on the bench will jolt tools in the rack, dulling sharp cutting edges.

The rack shown is 5 inches wide with a back piece 7 inches high; the length illustrated is just over 2 feet but the rack can be made any length that is desired.

Three-quarter inch stock is suitable for all parts, but a strip of hardwood is preferable for the horizontal ledge because of the number of holes which are bored in it. Plane the wood to the chosen dimension. The ledge can simply be attached by screwing it, from the back, to the back piece, but a stronger rack can be made by housing the ledge in the backing to a depth of ¼ inch. This necessitates cutting a shallow groove along the back piece. In either case, fit the ledge to the back, bore holes for the screws and put in about half of them, temporarily leaving out alternate ones. Mark the position of the ledge carefully, apply glue and quickly fit together again and screw tightly. The screws previously inserted should be turned in first. Then, insert the remaining screws and put the rack in a warm place until the glue hardens.

The screws should be countersunk deeply so that the heads are well below the face of the wood.

Holes for Tools. The proper way to space and bore the holes for the tools is as follows. Measure at each end of the ledge to find the center point in the width and connect these points by a penciled line. The width shown in the diagram is 5 inches, so that the lines are 2½ inches from the front edge. Measure and mark two parallel lines, ½ inch on either side of the center line. Use the new lines as guides for the front and back rows of holes. Starting on the back row, place a point for the center of the first hole two inches from the end of the ledge. Set a pair of compasses or dividers to span 3 inches and place the rest of the holes in the back row at 3-inch intervals. Start the first row of holes 3½ inches from the end of the ledge, with a 3-inch interval thereafter, so that the holes of the first row are intermediate between those of the back row. Leave enough wood between the rows so that there is no chance of splitting. The front row can be omitted, if desired.

Get a piece of waste board and place it on the bench. Put the ledge over it and clamp both firmly to the bench. Put a ¾-inch center bit in a brace and bore the first hole, going through the ledge and into the waste piece far enough to leave a clean hole in the ledge itself. Proceed with the rest of the holes, boring slowly and carefully. If the brace has a ratchet action, use it for more gradual boring.

It can be seen from the diagram that some of the front row holes are slotted to the front; this is to allow chisels with wide blades to be inserted from the front and turned with the blade broadside. The slots are cut after the holes have been bored. A center bit is best.

Another useful rack can be made to hold other tools, or to hold metal boxes in which screws and nails are kept. The ledge in this case would be without holes, and would have a shallow guard screwed to the front to prevent articles from falling off. It need not be more than 1 inch high.

HOME CONSTRUCTION

Nearly every piece of material that goes into the construction of a house has a name. While it would be unnecessary for the home mechanic to be familiar with every board, nail, and stone in his house, an understanding of the more important items will aid him in doing various repair jobs, and in deciding whether he can do the work himself or will need the services of a skilled workman.

Footing. The footing is located at the base of the foundation. It is made of concrete and considerably wider than the actual foundation. This is done so that the weight of the house will be distributed over a greater area. If the footing is not the right size for the weight of the house and the soil conditions, it will sink, and the house will tend to settle.

Foundation. The foundation is the masonry on top of the footing and supports the weight of the house. It also provides the walls for the basement. The foundation can be made of stone, cement, cinder blocks, poured concrete, or any other material that can sustain a considerable load.

Sills. Sills are the heavy wood or steel beams around the top of the foundation. These beams are attached and the house is built up from them.

Girders. Girders are large beams running between opposite sills. They are used to provide additional support for the frame of the house as well as carry the flooring.

Floor Joists. The floor joists are the beams that run across the sills and provide a base for the flooring. Floor joists are generally made of 2 x 10 inch lumber, or 2 x 8 inch lumber, depending upon the distance they must run. They are placed broadside upright for greater strength, and in well-constructed homes they are spaced sixteen inches from center to center.

Bridging. The bridging consists of small strips of 1 x 3 inch lumber, or a size near this, which are nailed diagonally between the floor joists along the center of the span. The purpose of the bridging is to keep the joists perpendicular so that they will provide the maximum amount of support, and to distribute the weight on the floor between several joists rather than one or two. Bridging can also be made out of strips of metal.

Subfloor. The subfloor is the under-flooring to which the finish floor is nailed. The subfloor is nailed directly to the floor joists and runs either at a forty-five or a ninety-degree angle to them. The subfloor, or rough floor, not only furnishes a base for the finish floor but also adds a degree of strength to the frame of the house.

Studding. Studding are the 2 x 4 inch upright timbers which form the walls. Studding is placed either 16 or 24 inches from center to center and is braced with diagonals, a protection against fire, as the diagonals prevent the interior of the wall from becoming a flue. Horizontal pieces of studding are also nailed between the vertical studding at floor levels. These are called solid bridging.

At each of the four corners of a house a 4 x 4 inch or a double 2 x 4 inch timber is used to provide additional support. Studding around window and door frames is also doubled.

Rafters. The rafters that form the roof are made of either 2 x 4's or 2 x 6's, depending upon the size of the roof. If the roof has a composition shingle roofing, the entire roof is boarded over with sheathing. If the roofing is made of wood shingles, shingle laths are nailed to the rafters to provide a base for the shingles.

Sheathing. Sheathing is generally made of tongue and groove lumber, and is nailed to the studding to form a portion of the exterior wall. After the sheathing has been put on, building paper is placed over it and the outside wall of wood, brick, or stucco is raised. Sheathing provides additional strength for the frame of

the house and is added protection against the wind and rain. In recent years a type of composition board has been used extensively in place of the regular tongue and groove lumber for sheathing.

Roof Saddle. The roof saddle is made of two boards nailed together to form a V and placed over the top of the roof to cover the joint between the shingles.

Flashing. Flashing is a sheet of metal used for all joints on the exterior of the house formed by two different materials coming together, or by angles in the roof.

BUILDING MATERIALS

Just as it is important to select the right tool for a job, so is it equally important to use the right kind of materials. A simple illustration of the wrong selection of material is the use of a nail rather than a screw to fasten a door hinge. The nail can be driven in quicker, but it will soon become loose and the entire job will have to be done over again and the damage repaired.

If you are not sure of what materials to use, go to your hardware or paint store, or to a lumber yard. Here you will generally get sound and valuable advice, for any business interested in preserving its good name will recommend only the best. This advice should always be sought when planning a major project, such as building a garage, where the cost of the materials required is considerable. Far too many home-construction jobs have failed because the wrong size of lumber was used or the nails were too short.

It is wise to be skeptical of any "cure-all" products unless recommended by a reliable person who has reason to know their value. There are a great many products on the market which are far superior to the older types, but there are just as many worthless ones which cost the home mechanic much in time and money. The old way is not always the quickest, but very often it is the best.

Do not cheat yourself by buying poor quality materials. If you are going to do the job yourself, you will save considerable money in labor cost, and a portion of this saving should be used in buying the best materials.

LUMBER

Lumber yards stock wood in two forms, rough and surfaced. Rough lumber is in the form in which it comes from the sawmill. The edges may not be square, and the surface is rough and shows saw marks. Surfaced lumber is planed on two or more sides and has square edges. Lumber is measured in the rough state, and surfaced lumber, therefore, will measure slightly less, due to the planing. In most cases, the surfaced lumber will be about one quarter of an inch under the rough. Thus, a piece of 2 x 4 inch stock will be about 1⅝ by 3⅝ inches when surfaced on all sides.

The home mechanic will find surfaced lumber best for practically every purpose. It is much easier to work with, particularly when all sides are square. The planing required to make surfaced lumber out of rough takes only a short time with the machine used in a lumber yard, but it would entail hours of hard work with a hand plane, with results always imperfect. The difference in cost between rough and surfaced lumber is not enough to warrant the extra work.

Secondhand Lumber. Secondhand lumber can be purchased at many yards and has many uses, but it should be remembered that used lumber is not as strong as new wood and consequently should be limited to those jobs in which there is no great strain. Be very careful when working with used lumber not to strike a nail with the saw or plane. Examine the lumber carefully before working with it, watching for nails that have lost their heads and are difficult to find.

Measuring Lumber. Lumber comes in many different standard lengths, running to about eighteen feet. The widths vary from two inches to twelve, and the thickness from one inch to eight. Most lumber yards always have a few odd-size pieces of board, and these can be used for small household jobs where it would be impractical to get a full-length board and saw it up into various dimensions and shapes.

The board-foot is the standard measurement for lumber. This unit of measurement is equal to a board one inch thick by twelve inches wide by twelve inches long. To find the number of board feet in a piece of lumber, multiply the length in feet by the width and thickness in inches and divide by twelve.

Green Lumber. When lumber is first cut it contains a considerable amount of moisture. Under normal circumstances, lumber is stacked in piles after it has been sawed, and left to dry. During this period most of the moisture will evaporate, but a small portion will remain, and this may require several months or more to disappear. Still-moist lumber is called "green." After most of the moisture has evaporated, the lumber is called "seasoned." Green lumber is not suited to most building needs because it shrinks as it dries, and to build a house of green lumber is to court much future trouble.

To hasten the drying of the wood, green lumber is often put in an oven called a kiln. This is an artificial method of seasoning the wood and, consequently, makes the wood more expensive.

To test a piece of wood to see if it is still green, weigh it, and then place it in an oven and dry it completely. Remove it from the oven and weigh again. If the weight is considerably less, the wood was green. If one piece of lumber in a load is green, it can be assumed that the rest is also.

Hardwood cannot be artificially seasoned, and only well-seasoned wood should be used for furniture and other precise work.

Boards. One of the most familiar boards is the common board with four flat sides. This can be used for a variety of jobs. Shiplap boards have their edges cut out so that they will fit together. Tongued and grooved boards have a tongue on one side and a groove on the other so they can be fitted together tightly.

MOLDING

Molding is a thin strip of wood that has been machined into a special design. There are many different designs stocked by most lumber yards. Molding is used for interior trim around doors and windows, etc. One of the most familiar types of molding is the quarter-round, used for rounding off square corners, such as the top of a baseboard. Molding is sold by the linear foot.

WOODS

A knowledge of the important characteristics of some of the more popular kinds of wood is advisable. The home mechanic should know what woods are easy to work and which are brittle and difficult to saw and plane. For painting and refinishing furniture he should know what woods are open grained and require a filler before varnishing and which are close grained, in which a filler may not be necessary.

Spruce. A close-grain wood that is used chiefly for framing houses. It is light in color and easy to work. While strong enough for framing purposes, spruce does not stand up very well when exposed to the weather and should not be used for exterior work. It does not absorb paint very easily, and the paint should, therefore, be thinned down before application.

Fir. There are two types of fir, the Eastern and the Douglas. Fir is used extensively for framing and for floors and trim. It is light in weight and easy to work, and is used a great deal in the manufacture of plywood. A close-grained wood, fir takes both stain and paint well.

White Pine. Years ago, white pine was used for almost all home construction. Now that the supply has greatly diminished, this wood is only used for trim and paneling. Light in weight, white pine is easy to work and has a close grain.

Yellow Pine. This wood is also known as hard pine, as well as by other names. It is strong enough to be used for framing, and can still be had in sufficiently wide boards to be used for paneling. It is easy to work but rather difficult to paint.

Hemlock. This wood is not very suitable for the home workshop as it shrinks and splits easily. Hemlock is brown in color, holds nails very well, and can be used for framing, sheathing, and other rough construction work. Handle this wood carefully as it contains innumerable splinters. An open-grain wood, it takes paint poorly.

Cypress. Known chiefly for the pleasant effect obtained when used for paneling, cypress can be used for interior trim. It is very resistant to the weather and, consequently, is suitable for outside fittings such as gutters. The wood has a close grain and will take stain well. It absorbs

paint slowly, so ample time should be allowed between coats.

Chestnut. This wood was once used extensively for building purposes, but it is very difficult to obtain today, owing to the blight which killed off most of the trees in the country. Chestnut has a natural resistance to decay, and is ideal for fence posts and in other places where the wood comes into direct contact with the ground. It is lightweight and easy to work. Chestnut is still used for interior trim and for furniture. An open-grain wood, it requires a filler before varnishing.

Oak. A heavy and a difficult wood to work, oak is used for trim, furniture, and shipbuilding. The home mechanic will encounter it often in flooring. Oak is open grained and needs a filler. It can be painted, but absorbs the paint slowly.

Birch. Frequently used for interior trim and furniture, this wood is hard and strong but does not stand outside exposure very well. Birch is easy to work and is close grained.

Walnut. Due to its high cost, walnut is used primarily for furniture and gun stocks. American walnut is easy to work and has an open grain.

Red Cedar. This wood is used for wood shingles. It has a close grain and withstands exposure very well. It cannot be painted until well seasoned.

Ash. A tough, elastic, and very hard wood, ash is sometimes used for trim but is most often found in handles for tools. It is open grained, requires a filler, and takes paint well.

Redwood. This wood can be used for all types of building work. It is a light wood and easy to work. Close-grained, it takes paint readily and can be stained and polished.

Elm. Elm is tough, hard, and damp resistant, and is used mostly for heavy timbers and framework. It is difficult to work and has an open grain.

Maple. A very hard and strong wood used for flooring and for trim. It is difficult to nail. Maple is close grained and takes paint very well.

Mahogany. Used chiefly for furniture, this wood is very strong and easy to work. It has an open grain.

Poplar. Light in weight and fairly strong, poplar is used for interior trim. It can be stained and polished to resemble more expensive kinds of wood. Poplar does not stand exposure well but is easy to paint.

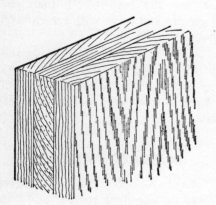

Fig. 1. Plywood.

Plywood. This product, because of the many uses to which it can be put, has often been called the home mechanic's best friend. Plywood is made by gluing thin slices of wood together, with the grain of one layer running at right angles to the other. This method of construction makes plywood extremely strong for its comparatively thin size. Plywood is an excellent material to use for chair seats, paneling for rooms, and even for flooring. Plywood is made from many kinds of wood, and the top layer is often a rare and extremely beautiful wood. Because only the top layer is made with the more expensive woods, the price of plywood is considerably less than a solid piece of expensive wood. Plywood can be sawed, nailed, and glued, exactly like any other wood. It can be had in sheets, and in many thicknesses, from ⅛ in. (veneer) to 1¹⁄₁₆ in. (rough lumber core).

Wallboard. There is a tendency to lump all kinds of composition boards under the general heading of "wallboard." This often leads to disappointment on the part of the user because some of these composition boards are not much more than heavy cardboard, while others are extremely tough and durable and can be used in place of wood sheathing for the exterior walls of a house. Siding is nailed over them.

Do not confuse wallboard with insulating board, because there is a wide difference between them. Insulating board can be used as a wallboard and will provide insulation as well, but most types of wallboard have little or no insulating value. Most kinds of wallboard are fire resistant; they will burn but not rapidly. When a fireproof board is desired, it must be made of asbestos or some other substance which is absolutely resistant to fire.

When purchasing wallboard, find out whether it can be painted. Paint can be applied directly to the surface of some wallboard, but on others a size coat is necessary.

board and work the cement into the opening. Next, force the strip of canvas or netting into the cement as a reinforcement and smooth the edges to make the surface as even as possible. Only an open-mesh cloth or netting will provide sufficient

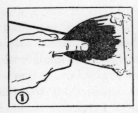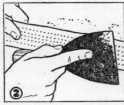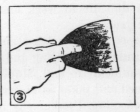

Fig. 2. Method of concealing joints between sections of wallboard. (1) Applying the special cement to the joint. (2) Placing the perforated tape over the cement. (3) Smoothing the edges of the cement.

The wallboard used in bathrooms or kitchens should be tough and damp resistant.

Most wallboard comes in sections four feet wide and eight to twelve feet in length.

Covering Joints. There are several methods used to cover the joints between sections of wallboard and other kinds of composition board, so that the surface can be papered or painted and the seams will not show. Of course, the sections of wallboard must be put up correctly, and must not sag at the seams or in the middle. The studding and furring to which they are nailed must also be secure and solid.

The most effective method of covering the seams is with a special cement and strips of open-mesh canvas or wire netting. Place the sections of wallboard so that there is about a ⅛ inch gap between all seams. Size the edges of the wall-

strength to prevent the cement from cracking out.

In case the sections of wallboard have been put up with no space left between them, it may be possible to cut out the required ⅛ inch and then size and cover with cement and mesh.

Another way to cover the seams is with strips of lath. These break up the wall surface into panels of the same size as the sections of wallboard.

ROOFING MATERIALS

Wood Shingles. Wood shingles make an excellent roofing and can be used as siding over sheathing. Most shingles measure about 16 inches in length, and five thick ends, piled atop one another, should measure 2 inches.

Asphalt Shingles. Asphalt shingles can be purchased individually or in strips containing three or four shingles attached at the butt end. Asphalt shingles are purchased by the bundle, each of which covers 25 square feet.

ASPHALT SHINGLE

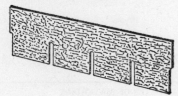

Fig. 3.

Roll Roofing. Roll roofing is made out of materials similar to those used in asphalt shingles. The roll is 36 inches wide, and each roll covers 100 square feet. Roll roofing is graded by weight, the heavier giving considerably longer service.

Asbestos Shingles. Asbestos shingles are fireproof and will last indefinitely. They are more expensive than other types of roofing. At the factory, holes are punched in the shingles for nailing. These shingles can also be used for siding.

Aluminum Shingles. Aluminum shingles have recently come on the market. They, like asbestos, are fireproof and will last indefinitely.

CONCRETE

The home mechanic should master a few principles of mixing and working with concrete. Not only will this knowledge be necessary in doing many kinds of repairs about the house, such as pointing up masonry and repairing concrete walks, but with a little practice and patience the amateur will soon find himself building many useful contributions to his home and garden out of concrete. Outdoor fireplaces, garage floors, and garden pools are all within the range of the amateur concrete worker.

Concrete is one of the least expensive building materials, and the beginner can experiment without fear of wasting a great deal of money. Experience is necessary before a highgrade job can be done, and the beginner should not feel discouraged if his first attempts do not turn out as expected.

Portland Cement. Portland cement is the basic ingredient for all concrete and mortar. Cement is the portion of the mixture that binds the other materials together into a strong, watertight composition. "Portland" is not a trade name. It refers to the type of cement in general use throughout the world. Cement is sold in bags weighing 94 pounds and filling 1 cubic foot. Cement may be purchased in different colors, and this should be remembered when a job requires several bags. Use the same color cement for the entire project to avoid differences in color in the final result.

Cement should be stored in a dry place, particularly after the bag has been opened and moisture can reach the cement inside.

Fine Aggregate. The next ingredient used in making concrete is sand, called "fine aggregate." The sand must be sharp, and free of dirt, clay, or vegetable matter. Sand from ocean beaches is not satisfactory because it contains salt. Test the sand for purity by placing a small amount of it in a glass of water and stirring it. Let the sand settle to the bottom of the glass, and if the water is only slightly discolored, the sand is clean enough to use. Do not expect to obtain good results from concrete if the sand is dirty.

Coarse Aggregate. The third ingredient for concrete is crushed stone or pebbles. This material is called the "coarse aggregate," and ranges

Table 1.

HOW TO FIGURE QUANTITIES

MIXTURES			QUANTITIES OF MATERIALS				
Cement	Fine Aggregate (sand)	Coarse Aggregate (gravel or stone)	Cement in sacks ·	Fine Aggregate		Coarse Aggregate	
				cu.ft.	cu.yd.	cu.ft.	cu.yd.
1	2	..	12	24	0.9	..	....
1	3	....	9	27	1.0	..	....
1	1	1¾	10	10	0.37	17	0.63
1	1¾	2	8	14	0.52	16	0.59
1	2¼	3	6¼	14	0.52	19	0.70
1	2¾	4	5	14	0.52	20	0.74

1 sack cement = 1 cu.ft.; 4 sacks = 1 bbl. If concrete aggregates are sold in your locality by weight, you may assume for estimating purposes that a ton contains approximately 22 cu.ft. of sand or crushed stone; or about 20 cu.ft. of gravel. For information on local aggregates consult your building material dealer.

Table 2.

RECOMMENDED MIXTURES FOR VARIOUS KINDS OF CONSTRUCTION

Quantities of cement, fine and coarse aggregate, required for 1 cu. yd. of compact mortar or concrete.

Kind of Work	U.S. gallons of water to add to each 1-sack batch			Trial mixture for first batch			Maximum aggregate size
	Damp sand and pebbles	Wet sand and pebbles	Very wet sand and pebbles	Cement	Sand	Pebbles	
Foundation walls which need not be water-tight, mass concrete for footings, retaining walls, garden walls, etc.	6¼	Average sand 5½	4¾	sacks 1	cu.ft. 2¾	cu.ft. 4	in. 1½
Watertight basement walls, walls above ground, lawn rollers, hotbeds, cold frames, etc. Well curbs and platforms, cisterns, septic tanks, watertight floors, sidewalks, stepping-stone and flagstone walks, driveways, play courts, outdoor fireplace base and walls, refuse burners, ash receptacles, porch floors, basement floors, garden and lawn pools, steps, corner posts, gate posts, piers, columns, etc.	5½	Average sand 5	4¼	1	2¼	3	1½
Fence posts, grape arbor posts, mailbox posts, etc., flower boxes and pots, benches, bird baths, sun dials, pedestals and other garden furniture, work of very thin sections.	4½	Average sand 4	3¾	1	1¾	2	¾

in size from ½ inch to 2 inches, depending upon the job for which it is to be used. When working on a thin wall, the size of the coarse aggregate should not be more than one-third the thickness of the thinnest section of the wall. The coarse aggregate must be as clean and free of any impurities as the sand.

Water. Pure water completes the list of materials needed for making concrete. A good rule to follow is to use only water fit for drinking to mix with cement. Dirt or other matter in the water will produce inferior concrete just as readily as dirt in the fine or coarse aggregate. Salt water should never be used.

Cement, fine and coarse aggregate, can all be purchased at lumber yards or from masons' supply houses. While it is possible for the home mechanic to screen his own sand and gravel, this task requires considerable time if it is to be done thoroughly. Clean sand and gravel can be purchased either by the square yard or by the pound, and the cost is comparatively slight.

Mixing Concrete. The proportion of cement, sand, gravel, and water used for mixing concrete depends on the class of work to be done and on the condition of the sand and gravel. These two materials are seldom completely free of moisture, and this must be taken into account when adding water. The amount of moisture in the aggregates will vary from a damp condition to very wet. The water required for very wet aggregate is considerably less than that required for damp aggregate.

The strength of concrete depends upon the union of the water and cement to form a paste which, when hard, will bind the particles of sand and gravel together. Accordingly, it is very important that the proper portions of water and cement be maintained. The table gives recommended quantities of water for various jobs. Make up a trial batch of concrete, using this table as a guide. If the mixture is too stiff to work, use less sand and gravel in the next batch. If the mixture is too wet, add more sand and gravel. Do not change the amount of water, as this will affect the bonding properties of the mixture. In other words, keep the ratio of cement to water as set down in the table. Control the workability of the mixture through the use of more or less aggregate. Always make up a trial mixture of concrete, and get it right, before mixing up a large batch for the job.

Concrete that has been properly mixed can be poured into a form with ease and packed down until it forms a dense mass. The concrete should be plastic enough so that the pebbles or gravel will not fall out when the mixture is handled. There should be no space between the elements of the coarse aggregate. The stiffness of the mixture varies with the job, so that the mixture used for a garage floor can be stiffer than that used for small forms.

Mixing the various ingredients together should be done with care. To make certain that the right amount of each material is used, have a pail marked in quarts and gallons for measuring the water and a bottomless box for the sand and coarse aggregate. The box should be built to hold exactly one cubic foot. A bag of cement contains one cubic foot. There is no measurement problem except when mixing up a small mass of concrete. All ingredients must be

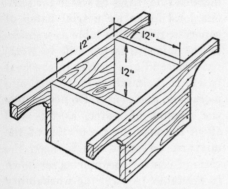

Fig. 4. A bottomless box, holding one cubic foot, for measuring the aggregate in concrete work.

measured out carefully. Do not try to judge the quantity by eye.

Almost any flat, clean, waterproof surface can be used for mixing concrete. While machine mixing is always preferred, the home mechanic will seldom find this very practical unless he is doing a job big enough to warrant the renting of a mixer. Excellent concrete can be mixed by hand, providing it is done thoroughly. Thorough mixing is essential to good concrete; it is the thoroughness of the machine mixer that makes it so efficient.

A garage floor, or a platform built of tongued and grooved lumber, is excellent for mixing concrete. Measure out the quantity of sand in accordance with the type of mixture

and spread it on the surface of the mixing platform.

Measure out the cement and spread it over the sand. These two materials should be mixed together until they form a mass with a uniform color. There should be no streaks, an indication that the work has not been done thoroughly. After the sand and cement have been mixed, measure out the coarse aggregate and spread it over the mixture. Continue mixing until the pebbles or gravel are well distributed throughout the sand and cement. Measure out the correct amount of water and pour it into a depression formed in the middle of the pile of dry concrete. Start mixing again and continue until there is no question that all the materials have been combined and the water distributed throughout the mixture.

The concrete should be placed in the forms, or wherever it is to be used, at least thirty minutes after mixing. This means thirty minutes after the sand and cement are mixed. Remember that sand contains some moisture, and this acts upon the cement when the two are combined.

Spade the concrete, when it is put in the forms, to make it dense.

Too many home concrete jobs have been ruined by not giving the concrete time to dry before stripping off the forms. Concrete does not dry by the evaporation of the water but by a chemical change. It takes approximately ten days for concrete to dry enough so that the forms can be removed. During this period of curing, the concrete should be kept moist and in shade. Cloth, paper, or straw should be placed over it and occasionally sprinkled with water. Concrete should not be mixed in freezing weather.

Coloring Concrete. Concrete may be colored by mixing coloring powders into it while still dry. Paint and hardware stores sell these powders. Outside concrete jobs such as driveways and terraces can be colored best this way, better than by paint because they will not be damaged by moisture and the color will not fade as the surface is worn down. You can buy concrete stains which will give nearly the same result.

Dusty Concrete. It is very important, when making a concrete floor, that enough cement is used so that the concrete is not dusty. A floor in this condition can be remedied by using one of the prepared concrete hardeners.

CEMENT MORTAR

Mortar is used for laying bricks and concrete blocks. It is also used to repair cracks in concrete and for similar work. Mortar is made by mixing 1 part cement to 2 or 3 parts sand, depending upon how rich the mixture is to be. For average masonry work, 1 part cement to 3 parts sand will give a very satisfactory mortar.

The same general rules apply to mixing mortar as were set down for mixing concrete. As mortar cannot be applied as rapidly as concrete, only small amounts should be mixed at a time. A clean iron wheelbarrow or a solidly-built wooden box can be used for mixing, instead of a floor or platform.

After the sand and cement have been well mixed, add water slowly, stirring the mixture as it is added. The finished mortar should be soft enough to work but by no means watery. Do not let the mortar stand after it has been mixed or it will lose its strength.

CONCRETE FORMS

Concrete weighs about 125 pounds per cubic foot, and the forms used for it must be solidly built if they are to stand this strain.

Green lumber is the best lumber from which to make the forms because it will not absorb moisture from the concrete and, consequently, is not liable to warp. If well-seasoned lumber is used, it should be coated with oil or tar paper to prevent the wood from soaking up moisture.

Plan the form so that very little cutting of the wood is necessary. In this way you will be able to use the same wood for many jobs. Construct the forms so that they can be taken apart easily and without damage to the wood or concrete. In this respect, it is better to use bolts, screws, and clamps, rather than nails. If nails are used, do not drive them in all the way. Leave enough of the head above the surface so it can be pulled out easily and quickly.

Tongued and grooved lumber does very well for the sides of the form, and 2 x 4 inch stock is suitable for the studding.

Take time to make certain that the form is as nearly perfect as possible before pouring the concrete. After the concrete has been poured, leave the forms in place until you are certain that the concrete is hard. Do not

CONCRETE BLOCKS

Concrete and cinder blocks have become extremely popular in recent years as a building material. They can be used not only for foundations

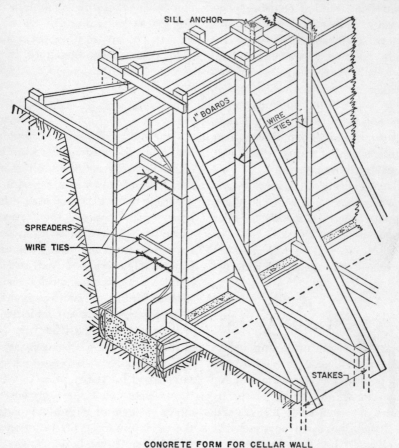

SILL ANCHOR

1" BOARDS

WIRE TIES

SPREADERS

WIRE TIES

STAKES

CONCRETE FORM FOR CELLAR WALL

Fig. 5. Forms for concrete must be strong. Above is a good example of how the forms should be constructed.

make the mistake of ruining a good concrete job by stripping off the forms too soon.

The length of time that is necessary to cure concrete varies, but it is wise to wait at least ten days before removing the forms.

but for the exterior walls of the house; and there is the advantage that they do not require the upkeep that wood siding does.

The home mechanic, looking for materials with which to build a garage, garden wall, or some other project would do well to consider these blocks. They are relatively inexpensive, not difficult to handle or to lay, and a wall made out of a single thickness of blocks will be extremely solid. Concrete blocks may be purchased at most lumber yards.

Cinder Blocks. While concrete blocks are made of Portland cement, sand, and gravel, cinder blocks contain cinders in place of the other aggregate and are consequently lighter in weight than concrete blocks and have greater insulating qualities. They contain 1 part cement to either 6 or 8 parts cinders—both proportions are used.

Concrete and cinder blocks come in many different sizes and shapes, but a size usually available is 12 x 5 x 7¾ inches.

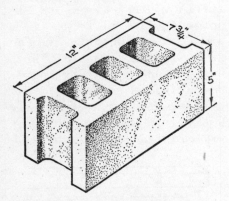

Fig. 5a. A concrete or cinder block.

The blocks must be laid on a solid footing of concrete extending below the frost line. If this is not done there is great danger of the wall buckling and heaving because of frost. The mortar joints between each block should be about ½ inch thick and should be packed tight to prevent the wall from leaking. The mortar is made with 1 part cement to 3 parts sand.

The blocks should be laid in such a fashion that the vertical mortar joints are staggered. To fasten woodwork to a wall of blocks, bolts should be cemented into the blocks with the end extending far enough above the block so that the wood can be secured by means of a nut.

Making Blocks. The home mechanic can realize a very substantial saving in the cost of building materials by making his own concrete blocks. There are special one-block forms to be had for this work and they are so constructed that a block can be made in a matter of minutes. The form does not have to be left on the block until the concrete is hard but can be removed and used to make additional blocks. In this way with a few well-spent winter weekends in a warm basement, the home mechanic can make up a sufficient number of these blocks to build a garage or other small structure when the spring comes.

A good concrete mixture for blocks is composed of 1 part cement, 2.5 parts sand and 5 parts gravel. It is important not to allow the mixture to become overwet. Use 5 gallons of water to each bag or cubic foot of cement.

BRICKLAYING

The home mechanic will probably wish to try his hand at building with bricks and certainly there are few materials so well suited to numerous building projects, whether they be inside the house or outside. Attractive and durable garden walks can be made by laying bricks dry in a bed of sand (See Section 11) and the home mechanic might well try his hand at one of these first to get the general feel of brickwork. Once the principles of bricklaying have been mastered, solid as well as attractive walls, chimneys and fireplaces can be constructed that will add to the appearance and comfort of the home.

Common brick, which can be purchased at the lumber yard in nearly every town and city, measures 2¼ x 3¾ x 8 inches.

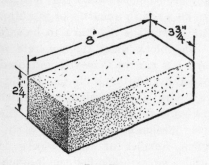

Fig. 5b.

Each row of bricks is called a "course." There are several courses such as the "stretcher course" where the bricks are set down flat and end to end. In the "header course" the bricks are laid with the width facing out. Bricks laid in this manner will make a wall 8 inches thick as the bricks are 8 inches long. This figure, 8 inches, by the way, is the minimum thickness that any brick wall should be.

A brick wall is made by laying several courses, one over another, and the arrangement of the courses is called the bond. Actually it is the pattern of the wall.

Fig. 5d. Common Bond.

In the common bond you will notice that there are five layers of stretcher courses topped with a header course. If the wall is to continue up, another five rows of stretcher courses should be set down and then another header course. This process continues to the top of the wall. As the width of the bricks on the stretcher course is only four inches, another stretcher course must be laid alongside the first to make the total eight inches. The header course will then tie in these two courses and make the wall solid.

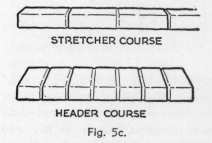

STRETCHER COURSE

HEADER COURSE

Fig. 5c.

Another type of bond is called the "English" bond. In this type there are alternative courses of headers and stretchers. A header is laid first and as this is eight inches deep, two stretcher courses, running alongside each other, go on top. On top of

Fig. 5e. English Bond.

this goes a header course, then a stretcher, and so forth. In laying two stretcher courses, one alongside the other, it is important to stagger the vertical joints. This rule, in fact, applies to all vertical joints. The joints must be staggered so that one will not come directly on top of the other.

Fig. 5f. Flemish Bond.

The "Flemish" bond is so constructed that each course is a combination of headers and stretchers.

Professional bricklayers use a wide assortment of tools to speed up the work of laying bricks and to

form different kinds of joints. As far as the home mechanic is concerned, he will need a trowel, a spirit level, a hammer (do not use a good claw hammer) and a cold chisel. The level should be about two feet long and of the type that can be used to check both vertical and horizontal lines. Do not try to judge whether the wall is plumb just by looking at it. Use the level often to make certain. A good way to keep each course horizontal is to stretch a line along the face of the wall and use this as a guide.

The mortar used for laying bricks is made with 1 part Portland cement to 3 parts clean sand. This mixture works easier if 10 per cent of lime is added. All mortar joints should be about ½ inch thick and the mortar should be packed in to fill the joint solidly. Many damp walls are caused by not completely packing the joints with mortar.

The brickwork should be laid on a solid footing and this must be at least equal in width to the wall that is to be built upon it. The footing should extend below the frost line. The top of the footing must be horizontal.

Before starting to lay the bricks it is a good idea to lay out the first course on the footing, making allowance between each brick for the mortar, to determine whether or not any bricks will have to be cut. Cutting the bricks can be done with the hammer and cold chisel. The bricks should be wet before they are set in with the mortar. Either keep the bricks soaking in a large tub filled with water or have a garden hose handy and spray them down from time to time.

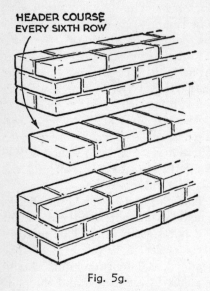

HEADER COURSE EVERY SIXTH ROW

Fig. 5g.

When you are ready to start laying the bricks, spread a bed of mortar on the foundation and work it level with the trowel. The horizontal mortar joint must be level throughout the construction. Take the first brick, cover one end with mortar and set it in place with the mortared end facing in the direction that the course is to be laid. Take up the second brick, spread the mortar on one end and set it down, with the dry end up, against the mortared face of the first brick. Continue this process along the entire course. Be sure to get each joint packed with mortar.

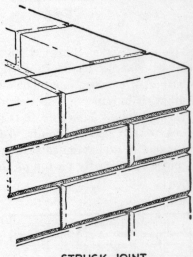

STRUCK JOINT

WEATHER JOINT

Fig. 5h. Types of mortar joint. Note slope of mortar in Struck and Weather joints.

Avoid the necessity of having to move a brick, once it has been set in the mortar. The reason for this is that, if a brick is moved once the mortar has begun to set, the bond will not be perfect, and the slight crack that results will allow water to get into the wall.

The surplus mortar squeezed out of the horizontal joints should be picked up with the trowel and used for the bed of the next course.

There are several kinds of joints used for the face of a brick wall. The flush joint which is the easiest to make should not be used on exterior work as it is inclined to absorb moisture.

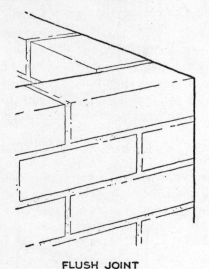

FLUSH JOINT

If the top of a brick wall is exposed to the weather, it should be capped or topped with a rich cement mortar rounded slightly so that the water will drain off. If the top of a brick wall is not so protected, rain is sure to find openings in the joints and flow down into the wall.

FIELD STONE

In some sections of the country, the home builder has an ever-present building material at hand in the form of field stones. Stones are excellent for many building jobs about the house; they are not too difficult to work with, have a pleasing appearance and, of course, if picked up on the premises, cost nothing.

Before you start any extensive building project with stones, take a few days to pile up a good assortment of them at the building site. Do not make the mistake of having to go off searching for the right size stone after your mortar is all mixed. A good rule is to have all the stones you need for the job at hand before you start building. Select only good solid stones. Do not use those filled with cracks. Water will enter these cracks and freeze during the winter and perhaps damage the wall. Stones can be shaped to the proper size with a mason's or sledge hammer, and a cold chisel. Do not bother with very heavy stones except for the foundation of the wall. Large stones are difficult to work with and if they are too heavy to lift will require a derrick of some sort to get them in place. Do not try rolling a heavy stone into position with the aid of a plank as you may ruin the work that you have already done. The best policy is to use only stones that you can lift easily.

In laying a stone wall, keep both faces of the wall flush. Do not let stones protrude beyond the natural wall face, as ledges may be formed that will allow moisture to seep in and thus damage the construction. Use bond stones at frequent intervals to tie the wall together; if used in every 10 square feet or so, these will make strong walls. Bond stones run the full thickness of the wall and are the strengthening factors in a wall, binding it together.

The stones should be washed clean before they are used. If the stones are encrusted with dirt the mortar will not make a bond with the stone.

Mortar for the stones is made with 1 part cement to 3 parts sand. Add enough water to make a workable plastic and pack the mortar joints tight.

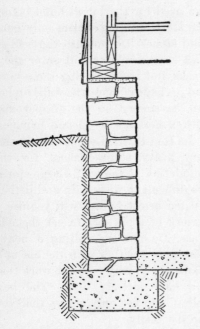

Fig. 5i. Properly constructed wall of stone with both faces flush. Note bond stone running entire width of wall.

ANCHORING IN MASONRY

There are several different devices that can be used to attach objects to concrete, brick, and other masonry. One of the most common for small jobs, such as bathroom fixtures, is the rawl plug.

Rawl Plug. The rawl plug can be used on any material that can be drilled. It is a simple arrangement

consisting of a wood screw and a fiber jacket, specially treated for strength and durability. Drill a hole in the masonry, insert the jacket in the hole, and turn the screw in the jacket. The action of the threads of the screw causes the sides of the fiber

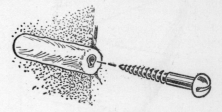

Fig. 6. Rawl plug.

jacket to expand against the sides of the hole.

To fasten a fixture to a wall, using a rawl plug, it is first necessary to drill the holes. Mark the location of the holes on the wall and be very careful that the measurements are correct. Use a rawl twist drill. The size of the drill must correspond to the size of the rawl plug. If the drill is too large, the plug will not work effectively. Place the point of the drill on the mark and strike the drill lightly with a hammer. Rotate the drill by hand after each blow of the hammer; this will make the cutting action more effective. When the drill has penetrated the wall slightly, it can be held loosely, so that it jumps a little after each blow of the hammer. Remove the drill from time to time and blow any loose material from the hole.

After the hole has been drilled to the required depth, the plug should be inserted. The plug must go deep enough so that the screw can be run in tightly after it has passed through the hole in the fixture to be attached. Put the screw through the hole in the fixture, insert the tip in the plug, and turn the screw with a screwdriver until the fixture is tight against the wall.

Expansion Shield. Expansion shields are used on masonry, and are made to take either a machine or wood screw. They can be used on heavy objects when a rawl plug would not provide enough strength. Though different brands of expansion shields vary in design, the basic principle of operation has two shields, internally threaded and hinged, which expand and take a firm grip on the sides of the hole as the screw is twisted down into them. The hole for these shields is made with a concrete, or star drill. This

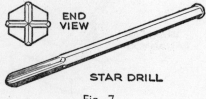

Fig. 7.

tool is not expensive and is well worth having in a tool kit. The drill is operated in the same manner as the rawl twist drill, striking it with a hammer and rotating it after each blow.

Toggle Bolt. Attaching a fixture to a hollow tile wall or cement block wall can be a difficult matter unless the right type of bolt is used. For this task a rawl plug or expansion shield cannot be used, because the material is hollow and has relatively thin sides. Use a toggle bolt. The toggle bolt consists of a bolt, the nut of which contains a hinged wing.

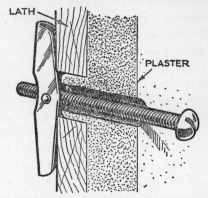

Fig. 8. Heavy fixtures can be attached to a plaster wall by means of toggle bolts.

Drill a hole through the tile and pivot the wing so that it is parallel with the bolt. Insert the end of the bolt in the hole and allow the wing to swing down so that it is at a right angle to the bolt. Tighten the bolt and the wing will be pulled against the inside of the wall.

Bolts in Concrete. A simple method of attaching bolts to a concrete floor is to drill holes in the concrete and insert bolts head down into the hole. After the bolt is in and centered, hot lead is poured in to anchor the bolt to the concrete. This method should only be used when there is no trace of moisture in the concrete and the operator takes the necessary precautions. Should there be the slightest trace of moisture in the concrete, the hot lead will turn the moisture into steam, and this will blow the hot lead out of the hole. When pouring the lead into the hole, stand well back so as not to be burned.

SOLDERING

The procedure and materials necessary for efficient soldering vary according to the type of work, but there are general rules which should be observed at all times. The surfaces to be united must be chemically clean, free from grease and dirt, and sufficient heat must be applied not only to melt and flow the solder but to warm the parts of the joint. The soldering iron must be clean and free from oxide. A flux is used to seal off the surfaces from the air and prevent oxidation, and to assist

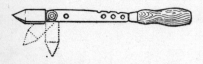

Fig. 9. A soldering iron or copper.

the flow of melted solder. On electrical work, a non-acid flux should be used to avoid corrosion and damage to the adjacent parts. For ordinary work in which functional safety is not involved, acid flux may be used, provided that the excess is removed when the work is finished.

Solder. Solder, an alloy of tin and lead, can be used with a resin flux applied directly to tin-plated objects, but for other materials the joining surfaces must first be coated with a thin film of solder.

Solder can be obtained in bar or tubular form. Tubular solder with an internal core of resin is very useful, but it will be found that soldering is improved by a little acid flux. Paste fluxes are excellent, but the liquid acid is preferable because it

cleans the surfaces, besides preventing oxidation.

Tinning the Iron. No successful soldering job can be done until the soldering iron has been tinned. The first step in this job is to clean the copper of the iron with a file or an abrasive cloth. Heat the iron until it is hot enough to melt the solder (solder melts at 372 degrees F.), but do not let the iron become too hot or it will not hold the tin. Rub the copper of the iron on a brick of sal ammoniac until the copper becomes

BLOCK OF
SAL AMMONIAC

Fig. 10. Rubbing the point of the iron on a block of sal ammoniac.

bright. Cover the surface of the copper with solder and wipe off the excess with a piece of cloth or some steel wool. The iron is now ready for use.

Heating the Iron. A soldering iron can be heated in several ways. Electrical irons are most common in the home workshop, as they take up a minimum amount of space and require no additional equipment. Other kinds of irons can be heated by a blowtorch or by a gas furnace. Regardless of what method is used to heat the iron, do not allow the iron to become red hot or it will require retinning.

"Sweating" a Patch. The technique employed here is to apply a thin film of solder to the patch and to the area surrounding the hole where the patch is to be applied. After both pieces of metal have been treated, place the patch so that the two sides covered with solder are face to face. Hold the patch securely in place and apply heat to it. Keep heat on the patch until the solder under the patch is melted. Remove the source of heat but keep pressure on the patch until the solder hardens.

This method of "sweating" a patch can be used on kitchen utensils made of brass and copper and will prove satisfactory unless the utensil is placed over a flame without water inside.

Aluminum cannot be soldered very effectively, and stainless steel requires a special solder and flux.

FURNITURE

UPHOLSTERED FURNITURE

Renovating the upholstery of chairs, sofas, and settees, is a task which can be undertaken very satisfactorily by the home mechanic. It should be noted, however, that this section does not deal with the extensive repairs to the frame and upholstery, which are best left to a skilled craftsman.

Equipment. A hammer, screwdriver or old chisel, pincers, an upholsterer's needle, and an appliance for stretching the new webbing tightly, are all the tools required. The necessary materials are burlap and springs, if replacement is necessary, webbing, a ball of good twine, and a package of ½-inch tacks. If a regular upholsterer's needle cannot be procured, a packing needle, as shown in Fig. 1, will do. Buy the

PACKING NEEDLE

Fig. 1.

very best quality webbing you can get, as the success of the work will largely depend upon its strength and durability. The twine should be real upholsterer's twine, and its life is lengthened if drawn across a lump of beeswax before use. The beeswax not only protects the twine from deterioration but discourages rust where the knots secure the springs.

For purposes of instruction, it is assumed that the article to be repaired is an ordinary settee, but the method of repair is applicable as well to easy chairs and other upholstered furniture.

Repairs. The first operation is the removal of the canvas or burlap cover on the underside. Turn the settee upside down, supporting the center of the seat on a chair (see Fig. 2). Pull out the tacks holding the burlap in place, and remove it completely. If it is still strong and undamaged, lay it aside to be used again; but if it is faulty, measure it carefully for replacement.

To remove tacks from burlap and webbing, hold an old screwdriver or old chisel against the head of the tack and give it one or two sharp blows with the hammer. Be careful to sweep up all the tacks later, as they are dangerous to the worker when kneeling at the settee during later stages of the work.

The webbing, with the springs attached, is now exposed. Unless only one or two springs are to be repaired or replaced, it is advisable to replace the whole of the webbing. Release

52

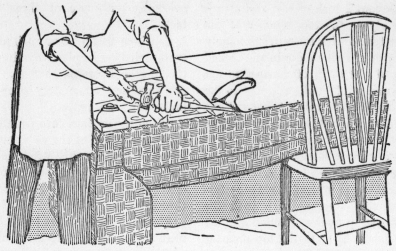

Fig. 2. Method of removing the canvas or burlap undercover from the bottom of a settee. Use an old screwdriver or similar tool to loosen the tacks.

the tacks holding the webbing to the frame of the settee and cut loose the twine securing the springs. Take careful note of the method used by the upholsterer to tie the springs in place. A typical method is illustrated in Fig. 3.

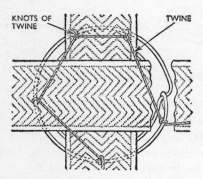

KNOTS OF TWINE   TWINE

Fig. 3. A typical method of tying the springs to the webbing. Note knots.

Next, turn the settee back to its normal position, release the top cover along the front of the settee and turn it back, complete with the stuffing. It will be necessary, of course, to first remove the covered

studs, brass head nails, or other ornamental fixing, together with any binding employed. Lay aside specimens of all these for use when selecting replacement patterns.

The released springs should now be examined for wear and distortion. Take an old spring to the upholsterer's supply house when ordering new ones. It may be necessary to buy a size of spring different from the original to allow for the results of long compression of the remaining springs.

At this stage, it is best to examine the joints of the frame for any looseness or weakness. Ordinarily, the joints may be repaired with glue and screws. A point to remember here is that when regluing any joint, the old glue must first be completely removed or failure will result.

When the frame is satisfactory, cut a strip of new burlap or canvas about 5 or 6 inches wide and as long as the front of the frame. Double back about 1 inch of this and attach it firmly to the top member of the front frame with tacks. Tack loosely a length of twine close to the tacked edge of the strip of canvas, to act both as a guide and a support to the stuffing for the rolled edge (of the canvas). Take the old stuffing, if you are going to reuse it, and beat it with a stick to loosen it and give an even texture; then form it into a roll by tucking it around the twine fastened at the edge. Turn back the canvas strip over the rolled stuffing and firmly fix it to the top member of the front frame.

Turn the settee bottom up to facilitate putting in new springs. Remember, also, to strengthen the old springs where necessary. The new springs should be secured exactly on the site of the old ones which they replace, and securely stitched. Note that in all good work the springs are not only strongly secured to the canvas underside of the top cover but are also tied to each other to prevent any chance of slipping. Examine all springs which are to remain and restich firmly wherever necessary.

The new webbing may now be fixed in place. Double back 1 to 2 inches of the webbing, and secure it by three or four tacks to the site of the old cross strip. Attach the webbing first with two tacks through a single thickness, cut off about 2 inches beyond the width of the settee, and turn back and fasten the overhang with two or three more tacks.

Continue this process until all the cross strips are in place. Fix in place the lengthwise strips. Note that they are threaded alternately over and under the cross strips.

Stitch the springs into position at the intersections of the webbing (see Fig. 4). During this stitching, the string is joined in one continuous length from spring to spring throughout.

Place the settee on its legs for the next stage—the replacement of the cover over the boxed frame. First,

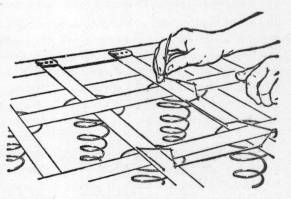

Fig. 4. Sewing the webbing to the springs.

stretch the canvas lining down and secure it to the frame. Arrange the stuffing carefully and spread it evenly over the rolled edge. Draw down the top cover and fix it in position tightly. The edge of the cover is hidden by binding, depending upon the kind of cover used.

Use ornamental nails to secure the edge of the cover. When the canvas or burlap is fastened over the springs and webbing on the underside, the work is complete.

When repairing the springs in upholstered chairs, stitch them as shown in Fig. 4. You will usually find that an odd number of springs, most often five or seven, have been used originally. If you need extra furniture, it is worthwhile to buy the pieces secondhand and spend a few leisure hours putting them into good repair.

FURNITURE UPKEEP

The preservation of furniture depends chiefly on regular dusting and polishing. A good furniture polish applied with vigorous rubbing and a clean, napless cloth will not only make a piece of furniture look attractive but will preserve the wood. Apply the polish sparingly and rub the surfaces well with the cloth.

Cleaning. A table or other piece of furniture which has become grimed cannot be expected to respond to ordinary polishing. Grease and dirt must first be removed by washing with a little warm water containing a small amount of vinegar. The correct proportion is one pint of warm water to a tablespoonful of vinegar. Several washings may be needed, a chamois leather being used for the final removal of the water. When no trace of dampness remains, apply one of the commercial furniture creams and polish the surface. Subsequent polishing should be a weekly routine.

Remember to dust the room before polishing. Pay equal attention to the legs and lower parts of furniture as to the top, front, and sides.

The best piece of furniture cannot be expected to remain in perfect condition, no matter how much regular attention is given to it, if exposed to harmful conditions. These include heat and damp. No piece of furniture should be left too close to a fire or radiator, as this will tend to warp and split the soundest wood. A consistently damp room can prove equally damaging to furniture.

Water Stains. It sometimes happens that a tabletop, too close to an open window, becomes splashed by rain. In this case, moisture should first be mopped up with a clean cloth or chamois, and as soon as the surface is thoroughly dry, furniture cream should be liberally applied, rubbed in, and the surplus wiped off.

If water stains occur, they can be erased, when dry, by vigorous rubbing with the polishing cloth. Stains which are not removed by this treatment will generally respond to lighter fluid or benzine applied with a clean cloth. When all signs of the marks have vanished, polishing in

Fig. 5. White spots on a finish can be removed with alcohol, while a shellac stick is used to fill deep scratches.

the ordinary way should leave the area spotless. If the stains (not ink stains) are deep seated, the following method, used with discretion, may be employed. Wrap a small wad of cotton wool in a square of clean, napless cloth, two inches square. Apply a little denatured alcohol to the pad and lightly rub over the stain, using a regular circular motion. Do not apply an excessive quantity of the alcohol, and if the pad shows signs of sticking, add one drop of linseed oil to the pad. See also the part of this section dealing with polishes and polishing for detailed description of types of polish, ways of preparing them, and the method of application.

Table mats should always be used on polished dining room tables to prevent heat from plates and dishes penetrating to the wood and causing unsightly marks. Vigorous rubbing with a soft cloth, after the application of cream, is needed to remove them.

Removing Dents. Dents in furniture are caused by the wood fibers being compressed out of their natural shape. The best way to bring these fibers back is to remove the polish or finish and apply a few drops of water directly to the damaged wood. This will cause the fibers to swell back to their natural shape. After this has been done, the wood can be touched up and polished. If the dents do not respond to this treatment, wet the wood again and place a damp piece of cloth over the area. Now take a warm—not hot—iron and hold it as close to the cloth

as possible without inflicting additional damage to the wood. The heat thus applied should draw out the base of the dent. This treatment may have to be repeated several times before all traces of the dent disappear.

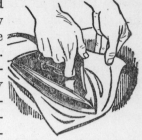

Fig. 6. Removing dents in the wood with a warm iron and a damp cloth.

Preventing Dents. The lower parts of furniture, such as table legs, bookcases, and sideboards, are often damaged from the careless use of a broom or carpet sweeper. If the corners of these objects are not padded, this omission should be rectified. A piece of soft leather or rubber, nailed or screwed to the corners and edges of the broom or carpet sweeper, will prevent many a knock and scratch. A piece of heavy furniture standing close to a door can be safeguarded from injury with a doorstop screwed to the floor a few inches from the possible point of contact. The doorstop should be faced with rubber or leather.

Cane Seats. Chairs with cane seats can maintain their appearance if the cane is kept free of dirt and dust. An occasional scrubbing of the cane may be necessary, using hot water in which has been dissolved a little salt, a tablespoonful of the latter to each quart of water. The scrubbed cane should then be dried with a clean cloth and the chair placed in the open air to complete the drying.

Leather Upholstery. This furniture soon becomes dusty in corners and tucked-in areas. Remove the dust with a stiff brush and wash the leather occasionally with a mixture consisting of a tablespoonful of vinegar to a pint of hot water. The leather must not be made too wet, and should be dried off promptly with a clean cloth. Polish the leather with a cream intended for use on leather upholstery.

FURNITURE REPAIRS

Never keep a piece of furniture in service after a portion of it has broken or a joint has become loose. Good furniture is made of relatively thin pieces of wood fitted together to provide the necessary over-all strength. When one part is broken, the entire structure will deteriorate very quickly. Trying to repair a piece of furniture which is in pieces is a job that may well require the services of a cabinetmaker.

Loose Joints. Probably the most common repair job on furniture is gluing joints that have worked loose over a period of time. Excessive heat and moisture will weaken most wood glues to the point where they will not hold properly, and this is another reason to keep furniture well away from radiators and registers during the heating season.

When it is necessary to reglue a joint, first remove all traces of the old glue from both surfaces to be joined. This is very important. If any of the old glue remains, the joint will not hold properly. The glue can be sanded away with a lightgrade sandpaper. When both surfaces are clean, put a thin film of glue on each. It is not necessary to use more than a very light coat of glue, as too much will weaken rather than strengthen the joint. Remember, also, to use a glue made for wood. Fit the two glued surfaces together and apply pressure to the joint until the glue is dry. This pressure can be applied with adjustable clamps, but if these are not available, wrap several layers of string around the joint and insert a piece of wood under the string. Twist the wood several times so that the strings are pulled tightly over the joint. It is a good idea to put a piece of cloth under the strings to prevent damage to the finish on the furniture. On joints where it is impossible to use either strings or clamps, the necessary amount of pressure can be achieved by placing bricks or books on the joint.

Do not remove any parts of the furniture except those already loose. If one end of a chair rung is loose, it can be reglued without breaking the opposite joint. In this case, remove the glue with a little vinegar and wipe the two surfaces with a damp cloth before applying new glue.

It is very often found, when regluing chair rungs, that the rung has shrunk so that it fits loosely in the chair leg despite the glue. Do not expect such a joint to hold after it has been glued, for glue cannot possibly function unless the two pieces of wood fit snugly together. The only remedy is to make the end of the rung larger so that it will fit tightly in the hole. There are several ways of doing this. One way is to make a thin cut across the diameter of the rung with a fine saw. This cut should be about ½ inch deep, and should be located in the center of the rung.

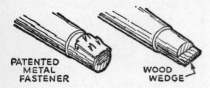

PATENTED METAL FASTENER

WOOD WEDGE

Fig. 7. Two methods of repairing a loose chair rung.

After the cut has been made, drive a small wood wedge into it so that the sides of the rung are spread slightly. The wedge should be very thin, and great care must be taken when driving it in not to split the wood. Now apply the glue and force the rung into the hole. It may be necessary to tap the rung in by means of a hammer. If so, place a piece of wood between the hammer and the part of the furniture tapped, in order that the hammer will not damage the finish.

Another way of making the rung fit tightly is to give the end a coat of glue and wrap silk thread around it until you have built up the surface to fit tightly in the hole. Apply another coat of glue over the silk and then force the rung in. Hardware and five-and-ten-cent stores sell patented metal fasteners that slip over the end of the rung. These fasteners are equipped with metal barbs that catch and hold the two pieces of wood together.

Chair legs and rails cannot be expected always to remain firm, and if any looseness in the joint is neglected, the strain is likely to be

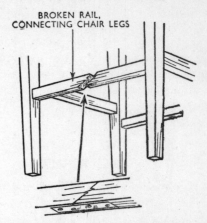

BROKEN RAIL, CONNECTING CHAIR LEGS

Fig. 8. Mending plate used to repair a chair rail.

thrown on the piece as a whole, necessitating major repairs. A great deal can be done with a little glue,

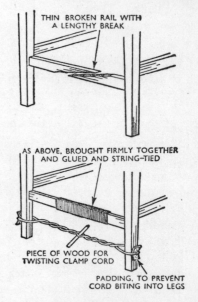

THIN BROKEN RAIL WITH A LENGTHY BREAK

AS ABOVE, BROUGHT FIRMLY TOGETHER AND GLUED AND STRING-TIED

PIECE OF WOOD FOR TWISTING CLAMP CORD

PADDING, TO PREVENT CORD BITING INTO LEGS

Fig. 9. How to repair a broken chair rail with glue.

and with anglepieces, or flat metal plates, in effecting repairs.

Breaks. A chair rail that has cracked or snapped can be secured by means of a flat mending plate screwed to grip securely along both surfaces of the break. It may be possible to sink the flat plate into the wood (see Fig. 8).

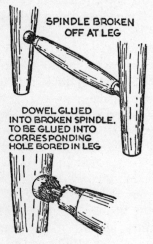

SPINDLE BROKEN OFF AT LEG

DOWEL GLUED INTO BROKEN SPINDLE. TO BE GLUED INTO CORRESPONDING HOLE BORED IN LEG

Fig. 10.

If the broken rung or rail is too thin, or its shape unsuitable for the flat plate attachment, the broken surfaces should be glued, brought close together, and secured with a thin screw, or with two screws if there is space enough. Where only gluing is practicable, maintain pressure by means of some cord or a clamp (see Fig. 9).

A spindle that has broken off may be refixed by means of simple dowels and glue (Fig. 10), or it may be possible to use long screws instead. The head of the screw should be countersunk in the part through which it passes. Where surfaces are

flat, strong joints can be made with angle plates or brackets (Fig. 11). If possible, these metal plates should be placed where they are not visible.

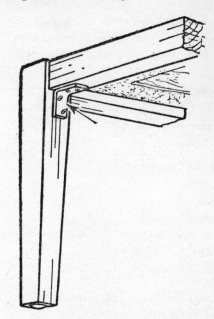

Fig. 11. Table or chair leg reinforced with a mending plate.

Bore screw holes to reduce strain while screws are being worked home and to lessen the possibility of splitting wood at the joints.

A long break in a rung or leg can be repaired with glue, followed by fine screws put in when the glue is dry to reinforce the joint.

Repairing Veneer. Much of the furniture in the home is made of veneered wood, that is, solid but inexpensive stock that has been covered with a thin slice of wood (veneer) that was selected for the beauty of its grain and coloring. The thin slice of wood serving as the veneer is attached to the solid but inexpensive wood with glue, and made fast and dried under heavy pressure. Sometimes due to heat or cold, dryness or moisture, the glue will fail to hold, causing the veneer to crack around the edges, or form blisters on the surface of the wood.

When the veneer becomes loose along the edges of a piece of furniture, it should be repaired at once, for aside from the chance of moisture getting into the opening to loosen up more glue, the slightest knock, under such conditions, may chip off, split or otherwise damage the thin veneer.

Fig. 11a. Two failures of veneer. Top, veneer pulling loose at the edges and corners. Below, blisters.

The first step in regluing the veneer is to slip the thin blade of a knife between the veneer and the base wood and scrape out as much of the old glue as possible along with any dirt or dust that may have collected there. The glue that remains can be roughened up a little with the knife so that it will make a good bond with the new glue. Now a thin coat of glue should be spread under the veneer and worked as far back into the opening as possible. A thin

knife blade will do for this job. After the glue has been spread on, press the veneer down gently and use adjustable clamps to hold it in place until the glue has set. Protect the veneer from being damaged by the clamp, by covering it with a piece of cardboard and a block of wood. If the veneer is brittle, and there is a chance of its splitting or breaking as it is forced back into place, steam it to make it pliable.

Levelling Furniture. A mistake that is often made in the home is to saw off the ends of table legs in an attempt to make a piece rest level. This is done with the idea that the legs are not all the same length. The effected change may have disastrous results. In the first place, it is very possible that the legs are all the same length but the floor is uneven and hence the tilting. Should a fraction of an inch be cut off one leg, the piece might rest solidly on one particular section of the floor but would tilt or wobble if moved to a level surface. Another reason against shortening a leg is that it is difficult to know how much to take off.

A simple and inexpensive method of getting a table to rest level is to glue or nail thin strips of wood to the bottom of a leg. Glue is better than a nail for this job because it eliminates any possibility of splitting the leg. After the glue has had time to set and harden, the piece of wood can be sanded down and stained to match the finish of the leg.

It is also possible to purchase special castors for furniture that can be adjusted, within reason, to make the piece rest level.

REMODELING FURNITURE

In practically every attic or basement you can find pieces of furniture in good condition but which are never used because of their design. This heavy, over-elaborate furniture that was made half a century or so ago does not fit in with modern home decorating. Much of it, however, is well constructed, and made of good materials. It is often possible to remodel furniture of this sort, strip off much of the machine carving, and give it a light finish, with the result that it may be used in good taste. Often, the basic design is good; altering the shape of legs or decoration will do much.

When dismanteling a piece of old furniture first remove as much of the old finish as you can. By doing this you make it easier to find screws or nails that hold the joints together. With most of the old finish out of the way you can go to work on the portions of the piece you want to eliminate. Joints which are held together with glue can be opened by steaming or soaking the glue with water. Screws and nails holding two pieces of wood together are sometimes hard to find because the heads have been sunk below the surface of the wood, and the holes then filled with putty or even wood plugs. Where a nail is set below the surface the two pieces of wood should be pried apart gently so that the wood will not be split.

One type of fastening that is very hard to find is the blind dowel. Here a hole is drilled part way through each of the two pieces of wood that are to be joined. A length of dowel is glued and set in one of the holes;

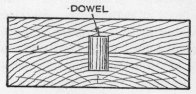

Fig. 11b. Blind dowel joint often used on furniture.

glue is applied to the portion of the dowel above the surface and the second piece of wood is set down so that the dowel goes into the hole drilled for it. The dowel, naturally, cannot be seen and the two pieces of wood cannot be taken apart unless the glue is softened with steam or water.

Any of the machine carving which cannot be removed in sections can be dealt with by planing or with a chisel.

When you have removed all the woodwork necessary, check the rest of the joints to see if any need regluing. Attend to these and then give the entire piece a good sanding to remove the remainder of the finish and to smooth out areas that might have been damaged during dismantling.

POLISHES AND POLISHING

Polishing produces varying degrees of gloss, according to the type of polish employed and the method used. All methods rely to some extent upon friction for the final leveling and smoothing of the surface treated, but perfect uniformity of gloss also depends upon checking excessive absorption by the surface.

Polishing Methods. The three methods of polishing in general use are wax polishing, french polishing, and oil polishing, the last being capable of withstanding long exposure to weather. All can be applied to new wood, or over a stain. If required, they can also be colored and made to combine the duties of stain and polish. Wax gives a rather dull gloss, french polish is a high gloss, and linseed oil produces a semi-gloss finish.

Wax Polish. This term originally referred to the application of a simple mixture of beeswax and turpentine, but is now applied to different brands of wax-base polishes which include varying quantities of other waxes, gums, and resinous substances. These additions undoubtedly help to produce a fine polished surface, but the simple beeswax base possesses a characteristic handsome gloss. Although it is often more convenient to purchase a readymade compound, the preparation of wax polish is simple. Take precautions to prevent the ingredients from catching fire, however. A good method is to shred the beeswax into an earthenware jar, using just enough to fill the jar halfway. Place the jar in a pan of water and heat over a low flame until the wax melts. Any tendency to boil over can be controlled by removing the pan from the fire.

Take the jar of melted wax out of doors, or at least well away from any open flame, before adding the turpentine. This should be added in the proportion of one part of turpentine to two of wax. Stir the mixture and cover the jar to prevent loss by evaporation.

Wax polish imparts a smooth, hard-wearing finish to new hardwood floors or furniture, but several coats, rubbed well into the woodwork at daily intervals, are required before the best results are obtained. When the more porous softwoods are treated, it is advisable to apply a preliminary coat of raw linseed oil (mixed with driers), or a coat of oil stain, in order to reduce the excessive porosity of the wood. Remember that surfaces finished with wax polish cannot be varnished or french polished unless every trace of the wax is completely removed.

Oil Polish. Although the process is not widely known and has the disadvantage of being rather tedious and slow, oil polishing produces an extremely tough and durable finish, particularly suitable for new hardwoods. Preparation consists of filling holes with plastic wood, sandpapering the entire surface, and removing all dust.

The oil is prepared by mixing half a pint of refined linseed oil with one tablespoonful of liquid drier. Apply this mixture sparingly with a piece of clean rag, making about four applications at weekly intervals. Rubbing the final coat briskly produces a gloss which, when hard, is capable of withstanding hot dinner plates.

French Polish. While absolute perfection in this skill demands considerable experience, there are many amateurs quite capable of producing a good finish. Given the right working conditions and materials, any beginner should make good progress in a few hours.

Conditions of dryness and warmth are of great importance. A cold draft or damp atmosphere is almost sure to cause french polish to dry with a permanent, whitish bloom, or with considerable loss of brilliance.

Brown french polish should be prepared from the very best quality orange shellac. White french polish should be made from the best white shellac. Both can be bought prepared.

A stock mixture for brown french polish contains 4 to 5 oz. of shellac dissolved in one pint of denatured alcohol. The standard mixture for white french polish contains approximately 6 oz. of shellac dissolved in one pint of denatured alcohol.

FRENCH POLISHING

New Woodwork. Preparing the surface of new woodwork and polishing it are generally carried out in clearly defined stages, in the following sequence: (a) sanding down the wood and filling holes, (b) staining, (c) grain filling (essential with open-grained and soft woods), (d) oiling in, (e) bodying up, (f) spiriting off. Both new and old work should, as far as possible, be dismantled, handles and other obstructions removed (see Fig. 12).

Sanding. Cracks and nail holes may be stopped or filled with plastic wood (see Fig. 13), which hardens

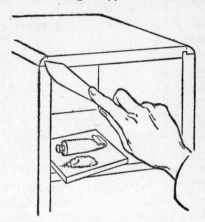

Fig. 13. Filling cracks and holes with plastic wood.

so rapidly that the surface may be sanded within a few hours. Always rub in the direction of the grain, using a flat block of cork inside the sandpaper. Any rust or ink stains have to be bleached out by one or more applications of an oxalic acid bleach or a commercial wood bleach (see BLEACHING).

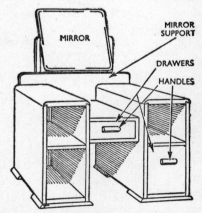

Fig. 12. Remove all hardware before polishing a piece of furniture.

Staining. Staining and filling the grain should be carried out according to the directions given in the section on Painting.

Oiling In. This operation entails a sparing application of linseed oil to check excessive porosity of the dry filler. Use a clean rubber, made with flannel and calico, for the purpose.

Bodying Up. Bodying up is mainly concerned with building up the body or thickness of the shellac and with producing a smooth, level surface. The first few coats of polish may be applied with a brush (see Fig. 14), the stock polish being

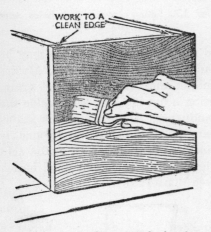

Fig. 14. Apply the first coats by brush and work to a neat, clean edge.

thinned with an equal amount of denatured alcohol. Always allow time for the hardening of each coat and sandpaper, whenever necessary, between coats. Use No. 00 sandpaper.

The rubber, a piece of flannel, wrapped in two layers of calico, is employed for all later coats. Apply half-strength polish at intervals to the unused side of the flannel, un-

wrapping the outer layers to do so. The polish can thus penetrate slowly and evenly to the face of the rubber, keeping it in a semi-dry condition. Move the rubber in a series of overlapping circles across the surface. Prevent any tendency to "stick" by adding a very small quantity of linseed oil to the face of the rubber. The best method of doing this is to allow one drop of oil to fall on the tip of the face of the pad so as to make an even distribution. This procedure should not be resorted to if it can be avoided, as an oily sheen will soften the brilliance of the finished surface.

Spiriting Off. A separate rubber, charged with quarter-strength polish and applied in long strokes following the direction of the grain, should remove any rubber marks and produce a uniform gloss.

Finish the work with a clean rubber barely moistened with alcohol.

Old Surfaces. Old surfaces are prepared by washing with a warm solution of washing soda and rinsing with clean water. Repair small defects with plastic wood and touch up with colored polish. Body up the surface with a rubber, using slightly colored polish to restore the richness of hue.

PAINTING FURNITURE

Furniture can be painted with an oil paint, enamel, or a brush-applied lacquer. The process is the same as for any other woodwork.

To make painting easier, remove all metal hardware from the piece of furniture. Paint the difficult portions first and leave the top, exposed surfaces until last. Use a small brush for this work to achieve a thin, even coat over the entire surface.

STICKING DRAWERS

Most drawers stick because the wood used for the sides has swollen due to the damp atmosphere. If the sticking is not too serious, it can be remedied by rubbing some wax, made for this purpose, along the top edges. If this fails, pull the drawer out and sand down the edges a little

Fig. 15. Soap or wax rubbed along the edges of a drawer will help prevent sticking.

so that the drawer can be worked back and forth easily. Do not take off too much, for interior heating during the winter dries out the wood and causes it to shrink.

Sometimes a sticking drawer is due to a loose bottom. The bottom of an expensive drawer is generally made of plywood and fits into recesses cut along the back, front, and sides of the drawer. When the plywood warps, it pulls out of the front recess and obstructs the movement of the drawers. In most cases it can be fitted back into the recess, with small brads to keep it in place. Take care not to use large nails for this work as you are likely to split the wood.

If the drawer cannot be removed, it is generally possible to take off the back of the piece of furniture. The back is usually made of plywood and only held by a few small nails. Once the back is off, you can discover whether a portion of the drawer has pulled loose and is sticking, or whether the trouble is due to expansion of the drawer. If a piece of wood is loose, it can often be pushed back into place and the drawer pulled out and repaired. If expanded wood is causing the difficulty, put some sort of a heating device—a bright electric light will do—into the drawer or near the sides so that the wood will dry.

METAL FURNITURE

Metal furniture, such as lawn furniture, exposed to the rain during the summer months, should be kept well painted. Treat the metal as you would any other exposed ironwork. It should be cleaned of rust and washed with benzine. After this has been done, give it a priming coat of red lead and follow with several coats of good exterior paint.

When chromium-plated furniture becomes worn, the best thing to do is take it to a metal shop and have it replated.

PAINTING

The subject of painting is a large one, and different situations are constantly encountered by the home mechanic which are not covered in books. When such a situation arises, the best practice is to consult an experienced painter or paint dealer before going ahead with the job. Never apply paint to a surface until you are certain of the results. The application of paint takes only a short time, but removing it is a tedious job at best. Avoid mistakes of this sort by consultation beforehand.

Good results in painting are dependent on the selection and care of the brushes, the selecting and mixing of the paint, and the proper preparation of the surface to be painted. Unless these three factors are properly observed, the hours and money spent will probably be wasted.

PAINT BRUSHES

The importance of buying only the best grade of paint brush cannot be overstressed. A poor quality brush will not only deteriorate quickly and have to be replaced, but

practically precludes any good work while the brush is still in usable condition. A good brush and one that is properly cared for is like any other good tool. It will last through many jobs and always give excellent results.

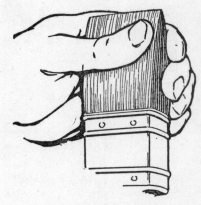

Fig. 1. Testing bristles for shape.

An experienced painter can tell a good brush by the feel of the bristles, their length, the manner in which the bristles are set into the brush, and by numerous other methods that are only acquired by years of experience.

A good brush is made of hog bristles set in vulcanized rubber. The bristles come from hogs found in

China and in other foreign countries where the bristles grow particularly long. Bristles from hogs raised in this country are not satisfactory for paint brushes.

The inexperienced painter is generally forced to rely on the integrity of his dealer when purchasing paint brushes. In most cases, the dealer will see to it that you are sold a good quality brush; but if you should get a poor quality brush after paying for a good one, take your business to another concern. In many other fields besides painting, the home mechanic will have to depend upon the honesty of his local dealer.

but it is not necessary to have a full collection to get good results from your work. A good brush, neither too large nor too small, can be used for many jobs. A painter uses many different brushes to save himself time and work. He uses a wide brush on large surfaces rather than a small brush which would require many more strokes to cover the same area. Have at least one small brush for getting into corners and avoid using a wide brush for this kind of work. Forcing the edge of the brush into cracks and corners bends the bristles and tends to make them lose their shape.

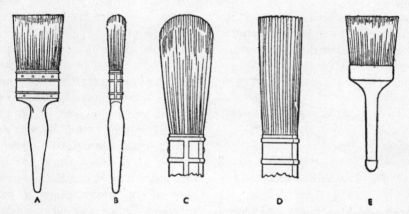

Fig. 2. A, flat wall brush. B, end view of same brush. C, a section of same brush showing contour of bristles. D, end view of inferior brush showing flat, coarse contour of bristles. E, seamless ferrule varnish brush.

Find one that you can trust always to give you the best quality merchandise. Remember, however, that even the best quality brush will have a few loose bristles when new; do not assume from this that the brush is poor.

Types of Brushes. There is a paint brush for almost every kind of job,

A paint brush should never be used for varnish, although a brush that has been used for varnish can be used for paint. The reason is that it is almost impossible to remove every trace of paint from a brush. If a brush containing a small amount of paint is dipped into varnish, the paint will discolor the clear varnish enough to spoil the effect. It is a good plan to keep one brush for varnish only. There are special brushes for varnishing which have a tapered end, permitting the varnish to flow easily.

For house painting or for other large surfaces, a flat wall brush is the best. These come in several sizes, but a brush 4 inches wide with bristles 4 or more inches long is excellent for most jobs.

Small woodwork, such as interior trim and exterior work, requires a flat trim or sash brush. These vary from 1 to 3 inches in width and are similar in shape to the flat wall brush.

An oval sash brush with a chisel end is excellent for working around windows and other difficult places.

Fig. 3. A varnish brush.

For varnishing floors and trim, a 3- or 4-inch varnish brush should be used.

A small, good quality brush is very important for painting furniture. These brushes range in width from ½ inch.

Calcimine is applied with either a flat calcimine brush or a Dutch calcimine brush. These come in widths up to 8 inches.

Whitewash should be applied with a special whitewash brush. Do not use a good calcimine brush for whitewash, as it will be ruined by the lime in this finish.

Fig. 4. Calcimine and Dutch calcimine brush.

A dust brush is extremely useful in removing dirt from the surface before painting.

Do not throw away old brushes that can no longer be used for painting. They are useful in many ways, such as brushing on a bleaching solution or putting a coat of oil rust-preventive over metal. Keep a serviceable brush for painting metal.

Care of Brushes. Once you have purchased a good brush, take proper care of it. Never place a brush in water under any circumstances. Some experienced painters do this, but water is deleterious to the wood portion of the brush and to the bristles. Always make sure that the bristles of the brush are straight and never bent except when painting. A brush should always be laid flat or suspended by the handle so that the tips of the bristles are clear of any object.

Storing Brushes. The best and safest way of storing a brush for any period of time is first to clean it thoroughly. Wipe the excess paint on a board and soak the brush in the proper cleaning liquid. Remove the brush from the liquid and slap out

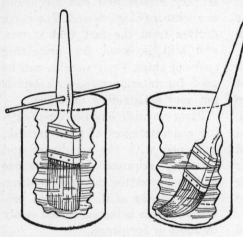

Fig. 4a. Shows, left, a simple method of suspending a brush in solvent. Right hand view illustrates the wrong method, which distorts the bristles.

the fluid and the paint, repeating this operation until most of the paint has been removed. Clean the metal ferrule with a small, stiff brush. Flush out the brush by pouring liquid through the bristles, shake it to remove the excess liquid, and hang it up to dry.

A brush used in oil paint can be stored overnight by rinsing it with a little turpentine and wrapping it in newspapers. Make certain that the bristles are straight and place the brush flat after it has been wrapped. A somewhat easier method for temporarily storing a brush is to drill a small hole in the handle and put a piece of wire through the hole. Now the brush can be suspended in a

can of linseed oil or some equally good solvent with the wire resting on the edges of the container. Have the brush high enough so that the tips of the bristles do not touch the bottom of the container.

Solvents. Brushes used in oil paints can be cleaned with linseed oil, non-leaded gasoline, kerosene, or turpentine. Varnish brushes should be cleaned with benzine or turpentine. Shellac brushes can only be cleaned in denatured alcohol. Enamel brushes should be cleaned with the same solvents used for varnish brushes. Brushes used for lacquer can only be cleaned with a special lacquer thinner, and nothing else should be used. Water-paint brushes can be cleaned by washing them in warm water.

TYPES OF PAINT

There are two general kinds of paint which the home mechanic will most often use. One is oil paint, composed of a pigment such as white lead, with linseed oil used as the vehicle. The other is water paint, in which a whiting and glue are mixed with a water vehicle. There are many classifications of each kind, but we shall list only a few of the more familiar ones.

Oil Paints. Exterior, or house paint, as it is often called, is made for all surfaces exposed to the weather and to extreme changes in temperature. It can be applied to wood or metal—provided that the metal has been properly treated before the paint is applied. A good quality exterior paint is tough, water resistant, and dries with a gloss. Any wood surface that is exposed to the weather should receive three coats of exterior paint for maximum protection.

Interior oil paint is similar to that used for outside work, except that it is not as resistant to moisture and temperature changes. It should, however, be sufficiently tough and durable to withstand washings and to keep moisture from penetrating to the woodwork. A considerable amount of moisture will collect around window sashes during the winter, and if the finish on the wood is not of a good quality, water will damage the wood.

Paints for use on floors must be especially tough and elastic. An ordinary outside paint should not be used as a finish for the floor because it will not long withstand the scraping and grinding of footsteps and furniture moved about the floor.

Varnish. Varnish resembles oil paint in many ways, but it has no color pigment and, consequently, produces a more or less transparent film when dry. Another characteristic of varnish is that it will "flow out" after it has been applied, and the brush marks will disappear. Varnish is made of linseed oil and a fossil gum. It is ideal for furniture, floors, and for exterior and interior woodwork. There are many different kinds of varnish, developed for specific jobs, but only a few of the more important ones will be covered in this section.

Spar varnish is used for exterior work. It is very tough, resists weather, and dries rather quickly. It is very elastic and can withstand temperature changes well. The name derives from the fact that it was, and still is, used for protecting spars of ships. Spar varnish can be used for interior woodwork but is not very satisfactory on floors.

Floor varnish has the quick-drying characteristics of spar varnish, combined with the toughness and elasticity required for endurance and for protecting the wood flooring. This elasticity of floor varnish prevents it from being scratched easily by shoes or furniture.

Interior varnish is similar to spar varnish except that it is lighter in color and is not as hardy. It is, however, sufficiently strong and resilient to withstand the dampness and normal temperature changes that take place inside the house. Interior varnish should not be used for exterior work or for floors.

Furniture varnish includes many kinds used by cabinetmakers. Some of these will produce a high-gloss finish without rubbing.

Enamel. Enamel resembles varnish except that a pigment is added to give coloring. Enamel must be applied with the same care that is used for varnish. Enamels come in either dull or glossy finish and can be used for both interior and exterior work, and for furniture. It has the advantage of drying without brush marks.

Enamel undercoater is used as the base paint for enamel. This undercoater penetrates into the wood pores and provides a smooth surface for the enamel. A flat wall paint can be used for this purpose, too.

Lacquer. Lacquer is a very quick-drying finish, usually made from nitrocellulose. Lacquer should not be applied over oil paints and varnishes because it acts as a remover and softens the undercoat. Lacquer is an excellent finish for metal work, such as brass, that will tarnish if left exposed. There are some kinds of lacquer that can be put on with a brush, but the others should be applied with a spray gun because they dry so quickly.

Shellac. Shellac is made by dissolving a gum obtained from insects in denatured alcohol. The common mixture is four pounds of shellac to one gallon of denatured alcohol. This is called a "four pound cut" and is generally too heavy for most jobs. It can be thinned by adding more denatured alcohol. Shellac is a quick-drying finish but it is brittle and does not wear particularly well. Moisture will turn shellac white. Shellac can be bought in either white or orange.

Water Paint. Calcimine is a type of water paint. It is composed of whiting, glue, and coloring. The water is added by the painter. Calcimine is used extensively for interior walls and ceilings. It is considerably cheaper than oil paints and has the added advantage of being quickly applied and of drying in a very short time. Another advantage is

that calcimine does not have the unpleasant odor of oil paints. A good grade of calcimine does not rub off after it is dry, but it will not withstand water and should not be used in bathrooms and kitchens, where there is a considerable amount of moisture present. Calcimine cannot be washed, and when a new coat is to be applied, the old coating should be removed. This finish can be had in many attractive colors.

There are many different kinds of cold water paints besides calcimine. Some of these are very like calcimine, while others are almost the same as oil paints and can be washed and overpainted. Casein and resin emulsion paints are two examples of this type of finish. As each brand differs somewhat from the others, the painter should read the directions on the package carefully and be sure that he fully understands the limitations of a particular paint before he applies it. These paints can be put on with brush, spray gun, or with a roller.

Plastic Paint. This paint is used to give a rough or textured effect to wall surfaces, or as a finish for plaster walls in such poor condition that a regular oil paint would not prove satisfactory. Plastic paint is stiffened by the addition of whiting, plaster of Paris, or some other material, so that it has sufficient body to prevent flowing once it has been applied.

The composition and, therefore, the characteristics of plastic paints differ according to the brand. For example, some are made with a white lead and oil base, while others are in a powder form and thinned with water before use. In general, the water-thinned paints have more body than the white lead type and produce a rougher texture. Several brands of plastic paint have coloring added, while others can be colored during mixing or painted over when they are dry.

Surface preparation is important when working with plastic paints, and the manufacturer's directions should be followed carefully. The better brands will list the necessary preparations for different wall surfaces, such as plaster, concrete, wood, and wallboard.

When a textured effect is desired, apply the paint with a brush to a small area at a time; and then, before the paint has set, texture it, either by using a stiff brush, special tools designed for this work, or even the fingers. Often, the texture produced by applying the paint with a stiff brush is sufficient.

PAINT THINNERS

The purpose of a paint thinner is to thin down the texture of the paint without destroying any of its qualities as a preservative. Naturally, a paint can be thinned just so much without losing some of its effectiveness. The amount of thinner required for each coat is generally specified by the manufacturer of ready-mixed paints and printed on the label.

It is just as important to select a good grade of thinner as it is to buy a good grade of paint. The best oil paint can be rendered worthless by mixing in a poor quality thinner. Remember that some kinds of finish require a special thinner and read over the directions printed on the container before adding anything to the paint.

Linseed Oil. A good quality linseed oil is an excellent thinner for oil paints. It is obtained by crushing flax seeds and allowing the oil to age before it is put in containers for sale. There are two kinds of linseed oil, boiled and raw. Boiled linseed oil has either been boiled or had a drier added, and thus will dry faster than raw linseed oil. Raw linseed oil, as the name implies, is free of any other ingredients and is commonly used as a thinner for most oil paints.

There has been a considerable shortage of pure linseed oil since the war, and there are many poor substitutes on the market. Be sure that you get the real linseed oil when you order.

Turpentine. Turpentine is another excellent thinner for oil paints. It is made from pine trees and it dries slowly, allowing the paint time to sink into the pores of the wood. Turpentine evaporates, however, and adds nothing to the general quality of the paint, as does linseed oil.

Benzine. Benzine is a light, volatile liquid that is sometimes used as a thinner for oil paints, but it is very inferior to both linseed oil and turpentine.

Alcohol. Denatured alcohol is used primarily for thinning shellac. It is also used for removing old shellac and for cleaning shellac brushes.

MIXING PAINTS

Although the home mechanic can purchase white lead, linseed oil, turpentine, and Japan drier, and mix his own paints, he will find that it is more convenient to buy ready-mixed paints, provided they are of good quality. Mixing paint is not difficult, but it requires time which the week-end painter does not always have, and all the ingredients used must be of good quality or the mixture will be poor.

Ready-Mixed Paint. When purchasing a ready-mixed paint, do not try to save money on a cheap product, particularly if it is to be used on exterior surfaces. A good brand of paint, properly applied, will give many years of service, while an inferior paint quickly disintegrates. If a poor quality paint is used, it will have to be removed before a new finish can be applied. This will require many hours if you do the work yourself, or considerable expense if a painter does it for you. Good paint, on the other hand, when it finally shows signs of wear, can be painted over with only a few minor surface preparations.

Be wary of the all-purpose paints that, according to the advertisements, can be used on practically any material. It is wise to get the opinion of a professional painter before trying any paints other than those which have proven their worth over many years.

Before applying a ready-mixed paint, read over the manufacturer's directions printed on the label of the container. These directions are provided so that the best possible results can be obtained. The manufacturer is just as anxious as you for the paint job to be a success, and these directions have been carefully prepared to make it possible for you to get the most out of the paint. Make it a practice to use each brand of paint according to the instructions furnished with it.

It is necessary to stir a can of ready-mixed paint before it can be used, because the white lead and oil tend to separate in the container. The lead sinks to the bottom of the can and the oil floats above it. The lead and oil must be thoroughly mixed before the paint can be used. Pour off the oil from the top of the can into a clean container. Stir the lead at the bottom with a clean stick into a smooth paste free of lumps. Pour the oil back into the paste, stirring as you do so. When all the oil is mixed with the lead, pour the entire contents into a second container and repeat this operation several times. Should there be any lumps in the paint at this stage, pour the paint through two thicknesses of clean cheesecloth.

When mixing several cans of paint for one job, it is best to mix them all together in one large container. There is sometimes a slight variation in color or shade between the several paints, and by putting them together you insure a uniform color for the entire job.

Replace the top on a can of paint as soon as you are finished. This will prevent evaporation, and the paint will be ready for some future use.

SURFACE PREPARATION

Paint can only be applied to a clean surface. Grease and dirt should be completely removed by washing the surface with water and a non-soapy cleaner, as soap leaves a thin film on the surface to interfere with the action of the paint. A cloth soaked in turpentine can be used to wipe off a surface before painting. If the surface has been previously painted, and the paint is still in good condition, cleaning is all that is necessary before applying the new coat. If the old paint has cracked or blistered, scrape or sand it off.

Moisture will spoil any painted surface. The surface must be absolutely dry, with no possibility of moisture seeping through from the opposite side and penetrating beneath the paint. After a rain, no outside painting should be done for several days, so that the wood will dry completely. It is equally important not to do any outside painting in the early morning when there is dew on the surface or late in the afternoon or early evening when the dew is gathering. Temperature must be considered as well. Do not attempt to paint if the temperature is less than 50 degrees F., as the cold will cause the paint to thicken and not flow properly. It is a waste of time and money to paint when conditions are not favorable.

FLAWS IN PAINTING

Paint failures can generally be attributed to the fact that the painting was done on a damp surface, the quality of the paint was not good, or the paint was not applied properly. Here are a few common types of paint failures and their chief causes.

Fig. 5a. Checking.

Checking. These small, hairline cracks on the surface of the paint indicate that the first coat was too soft to support the finish coat. As these cracks are only in the finish coat, they can be sanded and a new coat applied.

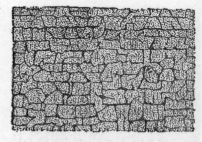

Fig. 5b. Alligatoring.

Alligatoring. This condition resembles checking except that the cracks are bigger and run deeper. This state of affairs is due to the application of the final coat before the previous coat is completely dry, or to an error in mixing, causing the undercoat not to dry hard. Do not attempt to repaint a surface in this condition. The old paint must be removed and a completely new job done.

Fig. 5c. Cracking and scaling.

Scaling. Scaling is the result of moisture penetrating cracks in the paint. It can be caused by poor quality paint or by improper mixing, so that the paint is not elastic enough to withstand the constant expansion and contraction of the wood with temperature changes. Paint in this condition should be removed.

Fig. 5d. Blistering and peeling.

Peeling. Peeling starts with blisters and occurs when paint is applied to a damp surface, or when moisture penetrates beneath the paint from the opposite side of a surface, such as an outside wall. This paint should be removed.

REMOVING PAINT

Old paint can be removed from wood by several methods. For small jobs, a hand scraper and sandpaper can be used. The blade of the scraper should be sharp, and care should be taken not to let a corner of it gouge into the wood.

Liquid Removers. A liquid paint remover is one that will soften the paint or varnish so that it may be

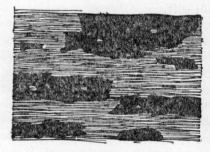
Fig. 5e. Peeling.

scraped and wiped off the surface with moderate ease. Lye can be used as a remover, but it is an extremely strong chemical and may damage the wood surface. Commercial removers for paint and varnish can be purchased at hardware and paint stores, and these are more desirable removers. Brush the liquid over the surface and allow it to remain until the paint begins to soften. The paint can now be removed with the scraper. Where there are a great many coats of paint, apply the remover several times. After the paint has been removed, the surface should be wiped with alcohol to remove all traces of the remover. Do not use a liquid paint and varnish remover in a room where there is an open flame.

Blowtorch. To remove all the paint from a large surface, such as the exterior wall of a house, would be a considerable task with a scraper and sandpaper and an expensive one with liquid remover. For removing large quantities of old paint, professional painters use a gasoline blowtorch, together with a broad putty knife. The flame of the torch softens the paint, and it can easily be removed with the scraper while still soft.

There are a few simple precautions to be observed when using a blowtorch. It should be pointed down, never up. This is done to keep the flame from the underside of the boards where there might be inflammable material. Do not allow the flame of the torch to become too hot, or it may char the wood. When working on the outside of the house, be sure that there are no birds' nests or other inflammable matter under the eaves.

Some communities forbid the use of a blowtorch for this purpose, so it is well to consult the local authorities before beginning work. Likewise, consult your insurance agent to find out whether there is any clause in your home fire insurance policy that forbids work of this nature.

If these precautions are observed, and the operator has familiarized himself with the use of the blow-torch, removing paint by this method is both safe and efficient.

EXTERIOR PAINTING

The outside of a house, garage, or any other exposed woodwork, is painted mainly to protect the wood from the weather. Protection is the first consideration and should be kept in mind when selecting the paint, preparing the surface, and applying the paint. A poor quality paint will not give the necessary protection, no matter how carefully applied, and good paint will be equally unsatisfactory if carelessly or improperly applied. An outside surface not adequately covered will soon rot and be attacked by insects. A good paint job with good materials will pay for itself by preserving the wood for many years.

The homeowner will often select spring as the time of year best suited for outside painting. This does not happen to be the best time of year from a standpoint of good painting, because the wood has been exposed to the snow and ice of winter and is generally damp on the inside. While it is all very well to have the house freshly painted for the summer, the prime consideration must be to put a good, lasting coat of paint on the wood. The best time for outside painting is in the summer or early fall when the wood surfaces are dry and the temperature is neither too low nor subject to violent changes. Painting, as previously mentioned, should not be done when the weather is damp.

Rigging a Ladder. Time spent in rigging a ladder properly is not wasted. Too many accidents happen each year involving people on ladders. First of all, see that the ladder is strong and in one piece. Be wary of any ladder that is patched together in several places. The legs of the ladder should rest evenly on the

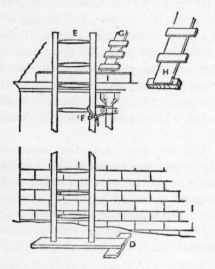

Fig. 6. Shows ladder E standing on boards arranged at D, on soft, uneven ground and secured at F for safety. G is held in position by board I, set between ladder and lower end of H. The top of G is shown inverted at H.

ground, and the top should rest firmly against the wall. A good rule to remember when rigging a ladder is to see that the distance from the legs to the wall is one-fourth the height of the ladder. For added security, tie one end of a rope to the bottom rung and the other end to the wall opposite. Ladders used by professional painters are equipped with various kinds of hooks to preclude any chance of the ladder's

slipping. You can rent a ladder from a hardware or paint store.

Amount. The amount of paint needed for one coat will depend upon the wood to be covered and the extent of the painter's plans. Another point to be considered is whether the coat is the first or the finish coat. One gallon of paint for every 500 square feet is an approximate figure to use in determining the amount for a particular job.

NEW WOOD

A few years ago, green lumber was so seldom used in building that the home mechanic was never confronted with the problem of how to paint it. Today, however, a great deal of green lumber is being used, and the sap found on the surface of this wood presents a serious prob-

Fig. 7. How to rig a ladder placed against a window.

lem. The best method, if possible, is to allow the wood to go unpainted until it has aged and most of the sap and moisture evaporated out of it. Green wood can be given a coat of shellac which will keep the sap from bleeding through the paint, but the shellac will seal off the pores of the wood and prevent the paint

Fig. 8. Bleeding knots and sappy areas should be coated with orange shellac before the first coat of paint is applied.

from making a strong bond with the wood.

Surface Preparation. Before paint is applied to unpainted wood, the surface should be free of dirt and dust. Paint penetrates the tiny pores in the wood, and if they are filled with dirt and grease, the work will not be successful. Turpentine can be used to remove the grease. All rough spots in the wood should be sanded smooth, and knots and sappy spots should be coated with orange shellac to prevent the sap from discoloring the paint.

The First Coat. The first coat of paint should be thinned with a good grade of turpentine. The amount of thinner used will depend somewhat on the condition of the wood. If the wood is well seasoned and extremely dry, the thinner can be linseed oil. The purpose of the first coat is to fill the pores and form a strong base for the following coats. By adding more turpentine, the drying of the paint is retarded, allowing it to permeate the pores. If the wood is dry and the pores are open, however, linseed oil can be used instead. Turpentine will dull the gloss of paint, while linseed oil will increase it.

Dip the brush into the paint so that about two inches of the bristles are covered. Remove the brush and wipe off the excess paint by drawing the brush across the edge of the container. By repeating this process several times, the end of the brush

Fig. 9. Draw brush over rim of container to remove excess paint.

will be well filled with paint, with no surplus to run down the handle. A paint brush can carry only so much paint. If you dip the entire length of the bristles into the paint and try to move the brush to the surface, you are almost sure to lose a quantity of paint in the process.

Brush the first coat of paint into the wood vigorously, so that not only is the entire surface covered with an even coat but the paint is forced down into the wood pores by the brushing action. Do not brush the paint too much after it has set, as this constant rebrushing will give a rough surface.

Start painting at the highest point and, if possible, work across the surface rather than up and down. This will prevent any vertical joints in the painted surface if you are unable to finish the job in one day.

Use a wide brush wherever possible, but keep a small trim brush for corners where the wide brush cannot be used without bending the bristles.

After the first coat is dry, fill all cracks and nail holes in the wood with putty. This work is done after the first coat is on because unpainted wood will absorb the oils in the putty and cause it to dry out and crack. Use a good grade of putty, work it into the holes with a putty knife, and smooth off the surface.

The number of days required for paint to dry varies, but allow at least a week and longer if necessary.

Second Coat. The thinning requirements for the second coat of paint differ somewhat from those of the first, or priming coat. While the purpose of the first coat was to penetrate the wood, the second coat must make a tight bond with the first and present a hard and non-gloss surface for the final coat. The second coat should completely cover the first and must, therefore, be somewhat thicker.

Third Coat. The final coat can generally be applied without thinning. It should contain plenty of oil and no turpentine, and it will dry to a glossy finish.

Three coats of paint should always be used on unpainted wood to provide maximum protection.

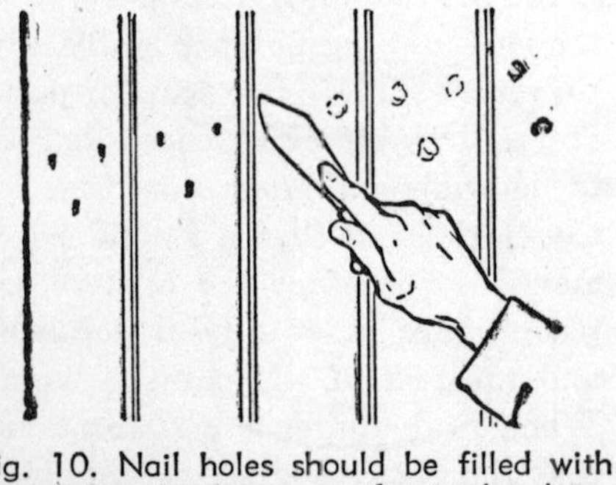

Fig. 10. Nail holes should be filled with putty after the first coat of paint has been applied and is dry.

PAINTING OVER PAINT

The requirements for painting over a painted surface vary according to the condition of the old paint. Paint that is discolored but otherwise sound can be given two coats of new paint, unless a change in color is desired. In this case, three coats will be necessary. The old paint should be washed, and any rough spots sanded smooth before painting.

Fig. 11. When painting the outside of the window frame, paint the upper portion of the top frame A and the lower frame B in the position shown. Next, lift the frame A to expose the unpainted portion of B and complete the painting of the outside of the window frame and sashes.

It is often found, on examining an old painted surface, that there are spots where the paint has blistered but the finish otherwise unimpaired. It is not necessary to remove all the paint in this case. Remove the cracked and blistered paint with a putty knife or paint scraper. sand down the paint surrounding the area and give the wood three coats of paint, allowing each coat ample time to dry before brushing on the next. In this way, you will build up the surface of the unpainted area until it is level with the surrounding paint. Finally, give the entire surface two coats of paint. It requires an experienced painter to determine whether a surface has so deteriorated that it should be removed, or whether the blisters and peeling are only a local condition and the rest of the paint is sound. When in doubt, it is best to assume that the entire surface is impaired; do not risk painting over it.

Exterior Woodwork. In painting the exterior of a building, take care that all woodwork around the windows is fully covered. This is a difficult and tiresome job, and the amateur is likely to skip over it as quickly as possible. The woodwork in a window sash is as exposed to the weather as any other portion of the building and should receive equal attention. Use a small sash brush for this delicate work, and if paint should get on the glass, wipe it off with turpentine before it dries.

Fig. 12. How to hold the brush to work into corners.

Thin metal plates can be purchased at hardware and paint stores, and by holding these against the glass, you can do neat work. Tape can also be used to keep the glass free of paint.

Exterior woodwork close to, or in direct contact with, the ground should be given special consideration. Wash off all dirt before painting and be sure that all four sides

are painted—not merely the side exposed.

Porches. Porch floors and steps should not be painted with the same type of paint used for other exterior work. If the floor and steps are protected from the weather by an enclosed porch, cover them with a good grade of floor paint. If the porch is open, use a paint made for exposed surfaces that both withstands weather and resists wear and tear by shoes.

METAL

Any metal exposed to the weather should be painted as often as is necessary to prevent it from rusting. Remove the old paint and rust from the surface with steel wool and emery cloth. When the metal is clean, wipe it off with benzine to remove any grease that is present. If this is not done, the grease and oil will prevent the paint from sticking, and it will chip off easily and quickly once it is dry.

After the metal is clean, apply a coat of metal primer. Ordinary exterior paint is not suitable for priming. Red lead is one of the best metal primers, and the entire metal surface should be given a full coat of it. Do not use a good paintbrush for metal work, but have a special brush for this purpose alone. After the priming coat is dry, put on the finishing coat. This can be any good exterior paint.

Check painted metal work often, and when it begins to crack and chip off, scrape or sand and repaint.

Galvanized Iron. When a piece of metal is galvanized, it is given a thin coat of zinc to prevent the metal from rusting. As long as the zinc coating remains undamaged the ing completely, can be made by mixing 2 oz. of copper chloride, 2 oz. of copper nitrate, 2 oz. sal ammoniac, 2 oz. of crude hydrochloric acid, and 1 gallon of soft water. Brush this

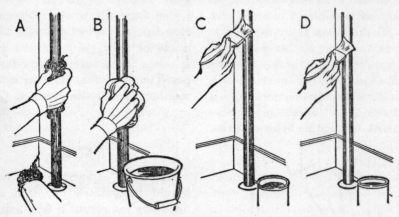

Fig. 13. Four steps in painting metal. A, remove rust and dirt; B, wipe metal with turpentine or benzine to remove grease; C, apply metal primer; D, apply finish coat.

metal will not rust, but the first scratch in the zinc surface will allow moisture to reach the metal. When galvanized iron is new, the zinc will prevent paint from adhering to it properly, but after the metal has been exposed to the weather for a few months, the zinc surface will be rough enough to receive paint successfully. The only preparation required is to remove any grease from the metal with benzine.

Before new galvanized iron can be painted, the surface must be chemically treated in order that the paint will hold. Do not use strong acid solution for this purpose, as it will completely remove the zinc coating. A solution that will roughen the zinc surface enough so that paint will adhere, without destroying the coat-

solution on the metal surface and allow it to dry; then rinse with fresh water.

Metal Toys. Good quality toys are expensive items and when a bicycle or coaster wagon begins to show signs of wear it should be taken in hand at once. A few hours spent in fixing a toy will make it as good as new in most instances.

Metal coaster wagons and other toys of this type when dented can usually be straightened by the home mechanic with the aid of a ball peen hammer and some blocks of wood. An alternative measure is to take the dented part down to a local garage. Here, a mechanic possessing the proper tools and skill can knock out the dents in a matter of minutes and give the cart its original shape.

The charge is usually slight. Broken metal parts should be welded back together—solder will not hold on a joint subject to stress.

Before you attempt to paint any complicated toy it is a wise plan to strip it down as far as possible. Remove all the parts and while doing this look to see if any nuts or bolts are worn or badly rusted. If they are, use new ones of the same size when you reassemble the parts. Once you have the cart or bicycle disassembled, give all the parts a good cleaning in gasoline or benzine. Do this job outdoors so as to avoid any fire hazard. With the grease and dirt out of the way, inspect each part to see what sort of condition the finish is in. If the paint is chipped in a few spots, it will not be necessary to scrape all the rest of the paint off. To fix up the chipped spots, take some steel wool, emery cloth, or sandpaper, and remove any sign of rust. Sand the edges of the paint around the exposed metal until you get a tapered edge. Rub a piece of sandpaper over the entire painted surface to cut the finish enough so that the new paint will adhere properly. Now go back to the chipped spots, wipe them off with gasoline, and apply one coat of metal primer. When this is dry, apply a coat of finish paint over the primer. After this is dry, brush on another coat or coats until the surface has been built up level with the rest of the painted metal. After this, give the spot a light sanding, wipe all the painted surface clean, and apply enamel for a finish coat.

If whole paint job is in bad shape, it is best to scrape and sand all the paint off and start anew. Pitted or tarnished chrome or nickel-plated parts should be replated at a metal shop or garage.

Painting Aluminum. Aluminum must be treated differently from other metals as there is a chemical reaction between it and the lead in base paints. First scrub the surface with a non-alkaline cleanser. Then apply a prime coat of zinc chromate. When that is dry, any good exterior paint can be applied.

INTERIOR PAINTING

Painting the interior of a house is done in two general stages. First, paint the walls and ceiling, using either an oil or a water paint. Next, paint or varnish the woodwork, according to personal taste and the nature of the wood.

Plaster. Before any type of finish can be applied to plaster walls and ceilings, the surface must be made ready.

Fill all cracks and holes in the plaster with patching plaster, or

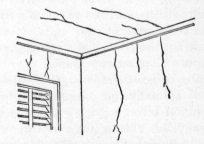

Fig. 14. Cracks in plaster walls and ceilings must be filled before paint or wallpaper can go on.

linseed oil mixed with turpentine (see PLASTER WALLS). If the walls have been previously painted, wash them down to remove grease and dirt. After the holes have been patched, touch up the patches with several coats of paint to prevent uneven absorption of the final finish.

Neutralizing. The active lime contained in new plaster will have a bad effect on oil paint, so do not cover fresh plaster with an oil paint. Either leave the walls unpainted or apply a coat of water paint, which is not affected by lime, until the lime in the plaster has neutralized. If waiting for the lime to set is an inconvenience, you can neutralize it by brushing on a solution made by dissolving 3 pounds of zinc sulphate crystals in 1 gallon of water. Apply this solution to walls and ceiling and allow it to dry. Every inch of plaster must be covered with this liquid, or the paint will be damaged by the lime. In the long run, it is best to use a paint like calcimine on new walls until they have set. By doing so, you eliminate any possibility of the lime attacking the paint.

Stains on old plaster caused by water or smoke should be covered with either shellac or aluminum paint to prevent the stain from showing through the new finish, giving it a blotched appearance.

Removing Calcimine. Old calcimine on walls and ceilings must be removed before any new finish can be applied. This includes both water paint finish and oil paint. Remove the calcimine with warm water, an old brush, and a sponge.

As this is messy work, it is a good idea to move all the furniture out of the room or cover it so that it will not be harmed by the water. The floors should be covered as well.

Brush a small section of the wall or ceiling with the water and wipe over the area with the sponge. Repeat this process until all the old calcimine has been removed. It is important that none remain on the plaster to interfere with the new finish. Change the water in the pail at frequent intervals.

Applying Calcimine. Before applying calcimine, cover the surface of the plaster with sizing, so that the paint will dry to a uniform color. Glue sizing is commonly used for calcimine and can be purchased with the paint. Mix the glue size with water and brush it over the entire wall and ceiling. Take care to cover the whole surface, because any spot missed will be apparent when the calcimine dries. If the plaster is very porous, seal it with a sealing varnish.

Calcimine can be purchased, ready-mixed, in powder form and only requires the addition of water before it is ready for use. Follow the directions on the package carefully, as there are some brands of calcimine which are mixed in hot water while others require cold water.

Be sure to mix the calcimine in a metal container, not one that is made of wood. Wood absorbs the glue that is the binder for calcimine, and the mixture remaining would be worthless. Make certain that the pail is clean and the brush free of dirt and dust. Before using, strain the mixed calcimine through a piece of wet cheesecloth to remove any lumps or other bits of undissolved matter.

Once you start to apply calcimine, finish the job as quickly as possible. Have everything ready so there will be no unnecessary interruptions, such as moving furniture or covering a portion of the floor. These matters should be accomplished before you begin painting. When doing an entire room, start with the ceiling. This will require some kind of a scaffold. An old table of sufficient height, or two stepladders with a plank between them, will serve. As it will be necessary to move the scaffold several times, do not use one that is too heavy or complicated.

Calcimine should be rather thick for brushing. A second coat cannot, as a rule, be applied; accordingly, the first coat must fully cover the plaster. If the paint is too thin, or the coat brushed out too thin, the cover will not be adequate; this usually means removing the first coat and repainting the entire surface.

Work with a full brush and work away from the light, in order that you can see whether the surface has been properly covered. Do small sections at a time, seeing that each section is joined with the previous one before beginning another. All sections must be joined before the edges dry. In this respect, it is wise to keep all doors and windows closed while painting. The draft through open doors and windows will dry certain areas of the finish, such as the edges, before the painter can

join them, and this will mar the final effect. To avoid a seam between areas, make the strips narrow. In this way, you will be able to join them before they dry.

Fig. 15. Applying calcimine to a wall in vertical strips.

When calcimining the walls, start in a top corner and work across and downward. After the calcimine has been applied, open the doors and windows to speed the drying. Do not apply a second coat. It is occasionally done but it is not a good practice, and the amateur painter ought not to attempt it.

Calcimine on Paint. Calcimine can be applied to a surface that has previously been covered with an oil paint. Wash the paint with water and a little washing soda to remove the dirt and cut the gloss of the paint a little. After doing this, apply a coat of glue size and then the calcimine. When using washing soda on the walls, be careful to keep it off painted trim or it will injure the finish.

Other Water Paints. The preparations required before other kinds of water paints can be applied to plaster are about the same as those for calcimine. As before, take care to read the directions carefully and be sure that the paint is all you think it to be. Also, remember that water paints, as a rule, are not suitable for the bathroom or kitchen.

Oil Paint. Prepare the plaster surface for oil paint in a similar fashion. Fill the holes and cracks and give the new patches a coat of shellac to prevent the absorption of too much paint.

A better method is to apply several coats of paint over the patches; this will preclude any shiny areas.

Plaster that has never been painted will be porous and absorb the paint unevenly. One of the best methods of filling the pores is to apply a coat of paint, which acts as a size coat and provides the aftercoats with a good adherent surface. Give this priming coat ample time to dry, for the final result will depend on the foundation it has provided. If a time element is involved, use a varnish sealer. Thin a good grade of varnish with turpentine so that the varnish does not have a gloss. Oil paint will not stick well to a glossy surface. You may add a small quantity of paint to the varnish to give it color. The varnish sizing can be applied as the priming coat, and it will dry in a few days. When using a varnish size, only two coats of paint are required; but it is better to use three.

Old plaster that has been painted will not need a size coat before the new finish is applied. If the old paint still has a high gloss, sand it down until the surface is rough. After this is done, clean the surface to remove all traces of dust and dirt.

Smoothing Walls. Walls that have a rough finish can be smoothed considerably by first sanding down the surface and then applying a coat of plastic paint to fill around the remaining high points.

The sanding operation can be done by hand, but a small electric sander is a great timesaver. After the wall has been sanded, it must be washed to remove all dust, as well as any dirt or grease. Then apply the plastic paint and smooth it to give as even a surface as possible.

The effectiveness of this operation depends, of course, on the roughness of the wall surface. In most cases, the surface will be smooth enough to hang wallpaper.

Wall Fabrics. In some cases a wall, plaster or wallboard, will be in such poor condition that it cannot be painted or papered satisfactorily. For cases of this nature, special wall fabrics can be put over the wall surface first and then finished with either paint or wallpaper. There are many kinds of these fabrics and as a general rule the preparation of the wall for them is the same as for wallpaper. The wall should be made as smooth and level as possible. Holes in the plaster should be patched and seams between sections of wallboard with patching plaster. The wall fabric is fastened to the wall with glue that is either applied to the fabric in the same manner as you would for wallpaper, or applied to the wall and the fabric then placed over it. The sections of the fabric are joined with a close fitting butt joint.

WOODWORK

After painting the walls and ceiling of the room, do the woodwork. Use a good quality interior trim paint. Enamel is very popular for this work because it dries with a high gloss finish and without brush marks.

The interior wood trim does not necessarily have to be painted. It can be stained and varnished if it is good enough to warrant this extra attention.

Fig. 15a. Numbers indicate door parts, to be painted in that order.

The Surface. Woodwork that has never been painted should first be sanded down until the surface is smooth. Use No. 1 or ½ sandpaper, dust the surface, and give any knots a coat of orange shellac. Green wood contains considerable sap and such wood should go unpainted until seasoned. If that is not possible, give the entire surface a coat of orange shellac.

First Coat. When these steps have been taken, prepare the first coat of paint. Thin the first coat with raw linseed oil or turpentine, depending upon the condition of the wood. If the wood is dry and absorbs paints quickly, use more linseed oil and less turpentine for thinning. If, on the other hand, it is green and only moderately porous, use turpentine and little if any linseed oil.

Fig. 16. Illustration shows which parts of the casing should be painted the same color as the door.

Second Coat. After the first coat is dry, fill cracks and nail holes with putty. Do as neat work as possible, to make subsequent work easier. Allow the putty to dry for about twenty-four hours, then sand the entire surface of the wood with No. 1 sandpaper. Dust the wood carefully and be sure to remove all traces of putty and dirt. Apply the second coat of paint and when it is dry, sand with No. 0 sandpaper. Add a third, and even a fourth, coat for best results. Each coat should be sanded before brushing on the following coat.

an open fire in the room. After the wood has been cleaned and all holes filled with putty, sand the surface with No. 0 sandpaper. After dusting,

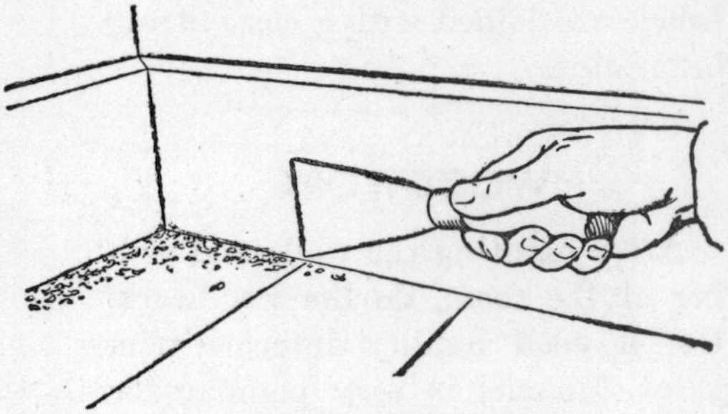

Fig. 16a. Before painting baseboards, all dirt and loose material must be scraped away from corners and angles of baseboard and flooring, etc.

OLD WOOD TRIM

Old wood trim that requires freshening and a change of color should first be washed with warm water or a small amount of benzine on a clean cloth. Do not use benzine if there is

apply the first coat and allow it to dry. Sand this coat with No. 0 sandpaper and apply the second coat. Trim which has been previously

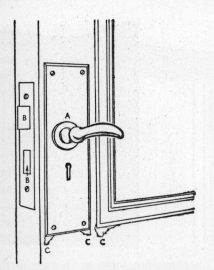

Fig. 17. Do not paint the handle at A or the lock, B. Remove any runs at C.

Fig. 18. Filling small holes with putty and a broad putty knife.

painted will require only two additional coats.

Enamel can be applied directly over an old finish if the finish is still in good condition. Clean the old paint with a cloth and some benzine, and sand with No. 00 sandpaper. This must be done in order to remove any rough spots in the paint

stains change the color of the wood by a chemical reaction and are seldom found in the home, as they are very difficult to use. Spirit stains have denatured alcohol as their chief

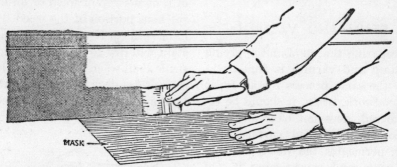

MASK

Fig. 19. A good method of obtaining a clean finish around baseboards is with a mask made of stiff cardboard.

which would appear through the enamel. Next, apply a coat of enamel undercoater, and when this is dry add two coats of enamel. You can improve the surface by sanding the first coat of enamel with No. 00 sandpaper. An enamel brush, with soft bristles and a beveled tip, is best suited for applying enamel.

STAINS

Use a stain to color the wood without hiding the grain. This is a particularly desirable finish to use on floors, furniture, and other woodwork about the house where it is important not to cover the natural wood grain with layers of paint. After the stain has been applied, the general practice is to give the surface of the wood a transparent coat of varnish, shellac, or wax, to protect it.

Types of Stain. Stains can be divided into several types. Chemical

solvent, and this makes them a quick-drying and difficult medium to handle without experience. Water stains are made of coloring that is soluble in water. They were once used extensively, but they require considerable skill if good results are to be obtained.

Oil Stain. The most popular and widely used stain today is the oil stain. Some kinds of oil stain are used only for protective measures against the weather—such as shingle stains—while others are for decorative effect and are called oil pigment stains. These are the ones with which the home mechanic will most likely deal when staining furniture, floors, and other woodwork about the house.

Stains can be purchased ready mixed or they can be mixed at home. If you plan to mix your own, be sure to use only the best materials.

Varnish Stains. Varnish stains are a combination of varnish and a stain.

This kind of finish will usually not be as fine as that produced by the regular process of stain followed by varnish, but it provides an excellent finish for minor pieces of wood.

STAIN AND VARNISH

Preparing the wood and applying oil stain and varnish is fundamentally the same process for all types of woodwork. Stain, it should be remembered, does not offer any protection to the wood surface. The stain permeates the wood, coloring the grain and emphasizing it. On practically every job where stain is used, the surface should be given a coat of varnish, shellac, or wax for protection and added lustre.

The Surface. The first step in staining is to smooth the wood surface. This can be done with sandpaper or steel wool, and the grade used will depend upon the type of work involved. Start sanding with No. 1 sandpaper and use finer grades as the surface is worked down. Always sand with the grain. If the surface was previously painted or varnished, remove the old finish with a scraper, sandpaper, and steel wool, or with a liquid paint remover (see REMOVING PAINT).

Bleaching. If the wood has been previously stained and the stain is too deep to be removed by sanding, it can be bleached with oxalic acid or with a prepared commercial wood bleach (see BLEACHING). After bleaching, give the wood another fine sanding, as the bleaching tends to raise the grain of the wood a little.

Applying Stain. After the wood has been sanded and all the dust removed, apply the stain with a brush or cloth. Mix the stain thoroughly, then check the color by putting some of it on a scrap of wood or an inconspicuous portion of the wood that is to be stained. Keep in mind that the stain will dry to a somewhat lighter shade than when first applied. If the stain is too dark, it can be lightened by the addition of a little linseed oil.

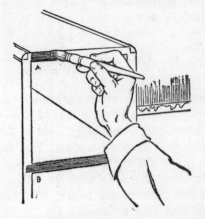

Fig. 20. Applying stain to narrow edges, at A and B. Do not overload the brush or the stain will dribble, as at C.

Take special care with edges that contain end grain. The open pores of this part of the wood will absorb more stain than the other surfaces and, consequently, will dry to a darker color. One way to avoid this condition is to apply a small amount of stain to the end-grain edges. This will keep their coloring light and uniform with other surfaces. Another method of achieving the same result is to give the end grain a light coat of linseed oil and turpentine, in equal proportions. A light coat of shellac, applied as a filler, will also prevent the absorption of the stain.

Stain is generally applied with a brush and left on the surface for a few minutes in order that it may soak into the wood. Use a clean cloth to wipe off what remains on the surface. The longer the stain is left on the wood, the deeper it will penetrate into the grain of the wood. Wipe evenly so that the surface will be a uniform shade. It is much better to have the surface too light than too dark. If the surface is too light, you can apply another coat of stain, but if it is too dark, the only alternative is to bleach the surface and resand it.

Most stains will require at least twenty-four hours to dry.

FILLERS

The surface of a piece of wood contains innumerable small openings which are the cells of the wood. On open-grain woods, such as chestnut

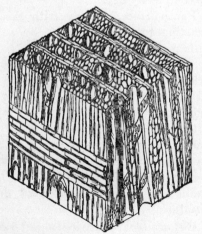

Fig. 21. Section of a piece of wood many times enlarged. The wood cells or pores must be filled before a smooth varnish finish can be achieved.

and walnut, the openings are very pronounced. If varnish were to be applied directly to the surface of the wood, a portion of the varnish would flow into these small openings and fill them. The result would be that the varnish, when dry, would have an uneven and pitted surface. To avoid this condition, use a wood filler, after the stain is dry, to fill up the cells so that the varnish can be applied to an even surface. It is possible to apply varnish directly to the wood and sand out any irregularities after it is dry. This entails considerable sanding, as it may be necessary to sand not only the first coat of varnish but the second as well, before obtaining a really smooth surface. Using a filler, however, produces good results with less work.

Wood fillers are obtainable in paste or liquid form. Use the paste filler on all open-grain woods and the liquid filler on close-grain woods (see WOODS).

Paste Fillers. Paste fillers can be had in several different colors to blend with the commonly used wood finishes. There are also natural fillers which are transparent, and these are used either with a natural finish or with some of the blonde finishes. It is sometimes impossible to get a filler of the right color for a particular surface, and a natural filler can then be tinted with stain to produce the desired effect. White fillers are used on many blonde finishes instead of a natural filler.

Fillers can produce the necessary amount of color alone, but they are, in most cases, used over a stain.

Do not use a filler that is darker than the stained wood.

Before using, the paste must first be thinned with turpentine or benzine until it is of a thick brushing consistency. Do not make up more filler than can be used within a few minutes, for it sets very quickly and cannot then be used.

Apply the filler with a brush, working with the grain and across it, so that the filler is forced down into the wood cells. Pay special attention to any portion of the woodwork that has been milled out, as these places are easily overlooked.

A filler requires about fifteen minutes to set, but the exact time will vary according to its consistency. A filler will become light in spots after a few minutes. This is the time to wipe off the excess.

Wipe the filler off the surface with a piece of burlap or some excelsior. Wipe across the grain and then make a few light strokes with the grain to finish off the job.

The purpose of wiping is to remove the excess filler on the surface of the wood, leaving only the portion that has penetrated to the pores. Do not wipe off the filler too soon or an insufficient amount will enter the pores, and do not leave it on too long or it will become hard, making removal extremely difficult. If a filler is too thick in the beginning it will not penetrate the wood, no matter how hard it is brushed.

Liquid Filler. Use a liquid filler on the close-grain woods and brush it on with the grain. When dry, sand the surface with No. 00 sandpaper.

Shellac can be, and often is, used as a filler for close-grain woods. After the shellac is dry, sand the surface until only the shellac absorbed by the wood remains.

VARNISHING

Varnishes are numerous and as varied in character as paints. Each is designed for a definite purpose and should not be expected to prove equally efficient when used for other purposes.

But regardless of the type of varnish, whether it is spar varnish for exterior work, floor varnish, or varnish suitable for furniture, certain conditions must be observed if the work is to be completely satisfactory.

Surface Preparation. The surface to which the varnish is to be applied must be hard and firm. It should be thoroughly free of dirt and grease and it must be smooth and nonporous. Above all, the surface must be completely dry.

Few surfaces comply with these exacting conditions but they can be achieved by a little extra work.

Cracks and holes should be filled with putty and

Fig. 22. Large cracks or holes can be filled with plastic wood or putty.

stained to match the color of the wood.

Cleanliness is of major importance in varnishing. The floor of the room should be swept or washed and the dust allowed to settle before varnishing. This applies not only when woodwork in a room is being varnished but even when a piece of furniture is to be refinished.

Certain weather conditions must also be considered if the varnish is to dry properly. No outdoor work can be done immediately after a rain, or when the air is particularly humid. Do outside work late in the morning, after the dew has had ample time to evaporate. In like manner, do not try to varnish in the late afternoon when the dew has begun to collect.

Seventy degrees Fahrenheit is a good temperature for both outside and inside work. If the temperature is too high, the varnish will dry too quickly and the quality of the finish will be poor; if too low, the varnish will not dry well. Sudden changes in temperature also affect varnish adversely.

Applying Varnish. Varnishing requires a technique different from that used for painting. Paint is applied sparingly and is finished off with light brush strokes. Varnish, on the other hand, must be flowed on with a full brush and enough force applied to spread the coat evenly. Brush varnish just enough to make a uniformly thin coat. If brushed too much, it will not spread and will leave brush marks on the surface.

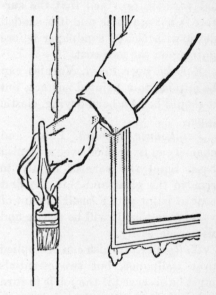

Fig. 24. Clean off any surplus varnish at edges of doors, corners of moldings, etc., particularly at horizontal edges.

Apply the varnish across the grain and finish with light, lengthwise strokes. Runs and sags in varnish must be caught before the varnish sets. Complete each door or window frame one section at a time, joining the new section before the previous section begins to set. Pay particular attention to molding, for it is here that excessive coating may occur and cause a run if not removed with the brush.

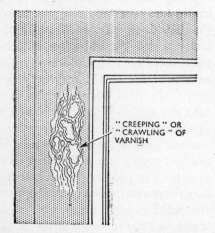

"CREEPING" OR "CRAWLING" OF VARNISH

Fig. 23. If varnish is laid on too thickly it will tend to form wrinkled patches.

Additional coats of varnish can be applied after the previous coat has dried and the surface sanded down with No. 00 sandpaper to remove the gloss. It is not a good plan to put one kind of varnish over a different kind, as the variation in elasticity may cause cracking. Use at least two coats of spar varnish on exterior work. New varnish can be applied to old varnish, provided that the surface is not too thick and it is sanded down with No. 00 sandpaper before putting on the new coat.

Varnish over Paint. Varnish can be applied to a painted surface, but it should be of a hard-drying, elastic type.

Paint over Varnish. Paint and enamel can be applied over a varnish base. Sand the varnish lightly to remove the gloss and thin the first coat of paint with a small amount of varnish so that it will be elastic and not crack easily.

Wallpaper. Varnish can be applied over wallpaper, but two essentials must be observed if the job is to turn out well. In the first place, it is necessary to see that all joints of the wallpaper are firmly attached to the wall. All cracks between the walls, in the baseboard and window frames, must be filled, or varnish may get behind the paper and cause discoloration. Second, apply two coats of weak glue size as a protection against the staining action of the varnish.

BLEACHING

Wood is usually bleached to remove old stains or to make the wood lighter so that one of the blonde finishes may be used. Floors, if left too long unfinished, will require bleaching to remove the stains in the wood. If the surface to be bleached has been painted or varnished, this finish must be removed in order that the bleaching agent can act upon the exposed wood and bleach out the stain that is in the grain.

Kinds of Bleach. A bleaching chemical can be purchased ready-made, or a very effective one can be made by dissolving ½ lb. of oxalic acid crystals in ½ gal. of warm water. Oxalic acid may be purchased at hardware stores and is not expensive. This is an excellent bleach to use on large surfaces, such as floors, but on furniture it is generally easier to use a prepared brand of wood bleach. Needless to say, any chemical strong enough to bleach wood should be used with care, and steps should be taken to prevent its getting on hands, face, or in the eyes

Using Oxalic Acid. In using an oxalic acid bleaching solution, brush the liquid on the wood while the water is still hot and allow it to remain there until dry. Several applications of the bleach may be necessary if the stain has penetrated deep into the grain. When the bleach is dry, a white powder will appear on the surface. If more bleaching is needed, apply an additional coat over the dry powder. When satisfactory results have been obtained, rinse the wood several times with fresh water to remove every trace of the acid. Add a small amount of vinegar to the final rinse to neutralize any remaining acid. It is very important that the wood be free of acid before any sanding is done. Oxalic acid is poisonous, and the fine dust of sanding which contains this acid can readily be inhaled. Sanding is necessary after bleaching, because the action of the water tends to raise the grain of the wood.

Other Bleaches. Hydrogen peroxide can be used as a bleach for small spots, as can some of the chlorine solutions used for bleaching clothes.

ENAMELING

There are many kinds of enamel available, and their composition varies greatly according to the brand. Although the formula may vary, enamel can be described roughly as a varnish with pigment added. Enamel can be used for floors, toys, exterior and interior trim, and has many other uses. When you buy enamel, buy the right type for the job to be done, for there is just as much difference between certain kinds of enamel as between paints and varnishes. You can obtain enamels that dry with either a dull finish or a high gloss, and, in general, they will produce a surface smoother and harder than that produced by oil paints. Most enamels will hide a surface almost as well as oil paints, and enamel flows so freely as to leave no brush marks on the finished surface.

Application. Do not apply enamel with an ordinary paint brush. For best results in your work, use a brush made for enameling purposes. This brush has softer bristles than an ordinary brush, and the bristles are beveled on each side to flow on the enamel more smoothly and to help eliminate brush marks. A good enamel brush should be used only with enamel, never for oil paints.

Test the enamel on a small area in order to find the brushing technique required. Apply a brushful to about a square foot and completely finish the area before dipping the brush again and proceeding. In this way, the brush marks will flow out. Join the adjacent section to the first and continue in this manner. Do not attempt to go back over the work, as later brush marks are not likely to flow out and will spoil the finished appearance of the work.

Undercoater. In order to fill minute indentations, level off, and hide surfaces upon which enamel is to be applied, use enamel undercoaters. These dry to a dull finish and, with a little sanding, form an excellent surface for the enamel. They should be brushed on in the manner previously described, since brush marks made in the undercoater will show through the enamel unless they are completely sanded out. Undercoaters are usually white, but, if desired, they may be colored by adding a small amount of enamel.

Although undercoaters are not required when enameling new wood or unfinished old wood, the finish will last longer and look better if an undercoat is applied. Make sure that the wood is clean and dry, as it should be for any finish. Apply two coats of enamel, but allow the first to dry and sand it down with No. 0

sandpaper before you put on the second coat.

Enameling Old Wood. To enamel old, finished wood, the procedure is a little different. If the old finish is in good condition, remove any wax or polish with benzine, or sand it down with No. ½ sandpaper until the surface is smooth to the touch. Apply the undercoater, sand it down, and brush on the enamel. If the old finish is in bad condition, it should be removed either by scraping or with a liquid remover. Sand the surface and finish with undercoater and enamel. Always remember to sand *with* the grain and never against it.

Stained Surface. If you wish to enamel a piece of woodwork that has previously been finished with a stain, you will be faced with a problem of preventing the stain from bleeding through the enamel and discoloring it. Several coats of enamel will not prevent this action from taking place. The remedy is to remove the old finish down to the bare wood with a varnish or paint remover, sand the surface, and give it a coat of aluminum paint. This will seal off the stain from the wood. After the aluminum paint is dry the undercoater can be applied, followed by the enamel.

As with any other finish, poor quality enamel or improper application will cause the finish to crack and scale. If the cracks run down to the bare wood, the entire finish should be removed. If the cracks run only as deep as the top coating, the surface should be sanded, washed, and a new enamel coat applied after the surface has dried.

Metal. When painting metal with enamel, apply a priming coat to the metal, as is done when using an oil paint on metal.

RADIATORS

Special pains should be taken when painting a radiator to avoid having the paint crack and peel off within a few months. With the proper procedure, you can usually avoid this condition.

Do not paint a radiator when it is hot. If you paint it during the summer, you avoid turning it off when it is needed to heat a room and you allow yourself sufficient time to do lasting work. If this is inconvenient, you can paint a radiator when it is *warm.*

If the old paint has chipped and is cracked, it should be removed before a new finish is applied. Use a stiff wire brush, coarse sandpaper, and steel wool for this task. It may be necessary to chip off some of the paint with a cold chisel or an old screwdriver. Remove all traces of rust and wipe off the grease with benzine. Apply a coat of red lead or some equally good metal primer.

Use a special radiator brush for this work. These brushes are long and thin so that they can be worked into difficult places with a minimum amount of effort to coat with paint places otherwise inaccessible.

After the priming coat is dry, use a flat wall paint for the finish coat. Add a small amount of linseed oil to the paint to prevent it from cracking.

CONCRETE

Cement, and Portland cement stucco, can be painted with nearly any kind of paint, provided that certain conditions are observed.

Cement Paints. Cement paints are special water paints intended for use on concrete. They are mixed with water and are obtainable in several colors. No special preparation of the surface is necessary when these paints are used, but do not put them over another finish. They must be applied directly to the concrete.

Water Paints. Water paints, such as calcimine, can also be applied directly to a new concrete surface; as these are water soluble paints, however, they can only be used for interior work. Apply the paint with a brush or a spray gun.

Oil Paint. Oil paint can be used on cement if the cement does not contain any moisture. Do not paint cement for several days after a rain, as its porous texture holds a good deal of moisture.

Do not put oil paint on new concrete until a solution is applied to neutralize the lime. Lime has the same destructive effect on oil paints as on new plaster.

You can make a solution for neutralizing lime by dissolving 3 lbs. of zinc sulphate crystals in 1 gal. of water. Apply this solution freely to the surface and allow about a week to soak into the concrete and dry. After this has been done, you may apply the oil paint. Any white crust on the concrete must be removed before painting (see EFFLORESCENCE).

Concrete that has been standing a year or more can be painted with oil paints, and it is not necessary to use a neutralizing solution. Brush the concrete to remove any dirt or loose bits of cement. Use any good exterior paint for the finish, but use a varnish base paint for the first coat, because of the rough, porous nature of concrete. This will seal off the pores so that the following coats of paint can be easily applied and produce an even finish.

Cement Floors. Cement floors can be painted only if there is no moisture present. A good test is to put a strip of waterproof paper on the floor and leave it there for several days. If at the end of this time there is no moisture under the paper, the floor can be painted. Use a tough floor enamel on cement floors, as other kinds of paint will not stand up very long.

WOOD SHINGLES

Wood shingles used on roofs and as siding can be painted or stained to prevent rotting. Shingle stains may be purchased ready for use in various colors. A somewhat less expensive method is to finish shingles with creosote, which can be colored or applied as it is bought.

The best time to stain shingles is before they are nailed on. This is done by dipping them into a bucket of stain and putting them aside until dry. If this is not done during the construction of the house, you can stain the shingles by applying the stain with a brush or, better, a spray gun. This is not as effective as the first method because only the top of the shingle is covered. It does, however, offer some protection to the most exposed portion of the shingle.

If the stain is applied with a brush, use a large, old brush, as the uneven surface will damage a new one. After a rain, allow plenty of time for the shingles to dry before staining.

When singles are to be painted, thin the first coat with linseed oil so that it can be brushed into the wood pores.

Once shingles have been painted they cannot be stained unless all the paint is removed—and this would be a large undertaking. Stained shingles, in turn, should not be painted for several months, as the stain is likely to bleed through the paint.

STOVES AND STOVE PIPES

Stoves, stove pipes, and other metal objects about the house that are subject to excessive heat can be refinished with a special, heat-resist-ant enamel. These enamels are designed to withstand rather high temperatures, but they will not last long on surfaces which become red hot.

Before the finish is applied, the surface must be free of rust and dirt. Use sandpaper or emery cloth to remove the rust, and wipe the surface with benzine to get rid of all grease. *Do not apply the finish if the surface is hot.*

WHITEWASH

Whitewash is the cheapest kind of finish available, but it has many valuable characteristics which make it ideal for use on unfinished basement walls where some covering is desirable but where the use of an expensive paint would be a waste of money.

Whitewash should be applied only to a clean surface. Brush off all dirt and loose bits of concrete with a stiff wire brush.

Old whitewash can be removed with warm water and a stiff fiber brush.

HEATING

HOME HEATING SYSTEMS

There are three types of heating systems for homes, steam, hot water, and warm air, and the basic requirements of each are the same—that they heat the house properly at a minimum cost and with a minimum amount of effort on the part of the homeowner. No matter how well a house is heated, if the fuel bills are exceptionally high the system cannot be considered efficient. Likewise, a furnace that requires constant attention is equally unsatisfactory.

With the advent of modern, automatic, oil-burning furnaces, automatic coal stokers and gas furnaces, all equipped with various devices to regulate the amount of heat produced, the care required to keep the heating plant operating has markedly decreased. But even the most modern and automatic plant can, and often does, run up excessive fuel bills, or fails to deliver the required amount of heat throughout the house, if certain factors are overlooked.

Regardless of the type of system used, hot water, steam, or warm air, or what kind of fuel is burned, the heating system must be big enough for the house. Do not try to coax an undersized furnace to heat a house for which it was never designed. The final result of this practice will be the deterioration of the plant from being forced to remain overheated for long periods.

Many a warm air system in an old house was installed with the intention of heating only a few downstairs rooms. A system such as this cannot be expected to keep the entire house comfortable.

In the event that the heating plant is too small for the house, the homeowner can either close off various parts of the house during the cold months or have a larger heating system installed. An alternative to both of these remedies is to install additional equipment in the part of the house not heated by the main system. There are many excellent portable heating plants that operate with oil, gas, or electricity. Any one of these will keep a room comfortable and is inexpensive to operate. Remember that in the long run it is cheaper to keep a room moderately warm throughout the day than to let it become thoroughly chilled and try to heat it for only a few hours.

Before taking any of these steps, however, determine whether all the heat provided by the system is being fully utilized or a large portion allowed to escape through the walls, roof, and small cracks around windows and doors. If this is the case, insulation throughout, in addition to weatherstripping, may well be the answer.

CHIMNEYS

Every unit using fuel that produces gases during combustion must have a chimney connected to allow these gases to escape. If the chimney does not function properly, the gases will smother the fire or keep it from burning properly. A great many heating problems are due to the faulty construction of the chimney. Modern heating equipment is scientifically designed to operate efficiently, provided it is properly installed and the chimney meets the necessary requirements. All too frequently, the furnace is blamed when the real cause

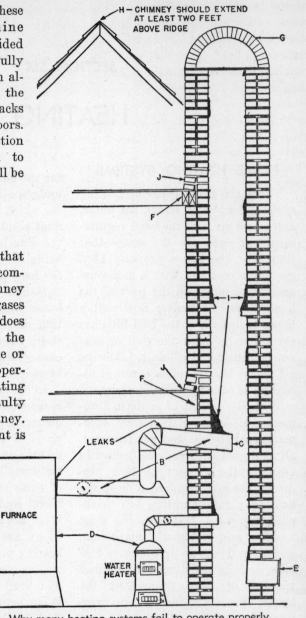

Fig. 1. Why many heating systems fail to operate properly. (a) Fire pot and clean-out doors fail to shut tight. (b) Leaks in stove pipe. (c) Stove pipe extends too far into chimney. (d) Both furnace and water heater connected to the same chimney flue. (e) Chimney clean-out door does not shut tight. (f) Movement of house girders has damaged chimney. (g) Chimney has cap. (h) Chimney not high enough. (i) Heavy deposits of soot and dirt in chimney flue. (j) Numerous leaks in chimney.

of the trouble is the chimney. This seems rather strange when you consider that chimneys have been built for hundreds of years, and the basic requirements for chimney construction are listed in practically every book on the subject of heating. The fact remains that chimneys are being built today that will not operate because these basic needs are ignored. The annoyance and expense connected with a poorly constructed chimney will eventually have to be borne by the homeowner.

Construction. The best location for the chimney is in the center of the house, to minimize heat loss through the walls of the chimney. A chimney placed on the outside of the house will lose considerable heat. A well-constructed outside chimney will have to be several inches thicker than an inside one to compensate for this loss.

A chimney should run straight up with no angles or bends. Angles will cause resistance to the passage of air and gas through the chimney and thus cut down the draft. They also afford an excellent stop for the accumulation of heavy deposits of soot.

The interior of the chimney should be lined with fire-clay flue lining. This provides not only a smoother surface than can be obtained with either bricks or stones but also a measure of safety. The heat and oils in smoke will eventually cause ordinary mortar to disintegrate, with resulting leakage in the chimney.

There should be a separate flue for each piece of heating equipment. When two or more heating devices

are connected to the same flue, they nullify each other's draft. This is often the reason why coal-burning hot water heaters do not operate as they should. They are connected to the same flue as the main heating system and thus have little or no draft.

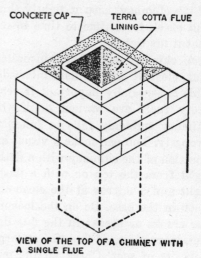

CONCRETE CAP — TERRA COTTA FLUE LINING —

VIEW OF THE TOP OF A CHIMNEY WITH A SINGLE FLUE

Fig. 2.

The top of the chimney should rise at least three feet above the top of the roof. Branches of trees should not be allowed to extend over the chimney top. Covering the top of the chimney will impair the draft, although it is quite common to see chimneys with caps of one kind or another.

No beams or girders employed in the construction of the house should protrude inside the flue of the chimney. This will have a serious effect on the draft, and is a fire hazard as well.

Stove pipes from other heating equipment should not protrude into the chimney. The end of the stove pipe should be flush with the inside of the flue.

Regular Inspection. See that all connections with the chimney, such as stove pipes, are airtight, so that the draft will not be impaired. If there is a clean-out door at the base of the chimney, keep it tightly shut and check from time to time to see that it fits tightly.

A chimney should be inspected and cleaned at regular intervals. This is especially important if very sooty fuels are burned or if the chimney suddenly fails to function properly. You can make a visual inspection of the chimney with a flashlight from the top or with a flashlight and a mirror at the clean-out door in the base. Be on the lookout for cracks or breaks in the flue lining, loose pieces of flue tile, or large deposits of soot. Check all the masonry around the openings in the chimney where stove pipes enter.

Leaks. To test the chimney for any possible leaks, start a fire in the stove, furnace, or fireplace, and when it is burning well throw on some material that will cause smoke. When the smoke begins pouring from the top of the chimney, cover it with a piece of heavy, wet cloth. This will force the smoke to find some other exit from the chimney, if one exists. In this way, any leaks in the chimney can be easily and quickly located and their location marked with a piece of chalk.

Once the leaks have been located, their size and number will govern what should be done about them. If

there are a few small ones, they can be refilled with cement mortar made of 1 part cement to 3 parts fine sand. If, on the other hand, the chimney appears to be in generally poor condition, a chimney expert should be called in to examine the structure carefully and determine whether it can be repaired safely or must be completely rebuilt.

A chimney that leaks is a fire hazard, for a small piece of burning soot could pass through the opening and set fire to the roof or some other inflammable building material.

Cleaning. A straight chimney with a clean-out door at the bottom is relatively easy to clean. To do this, weight a burlap bag with old rags, sawdust, or some other waste material, and lower it into the chimney from the top. Raise and lower the bag several times, and the soot will fall to the bottom of the chimney where it can be removed with a shovel and hoe. If the chimney serves a fireplace, cover the fireplace opening with a piece of cloth, hung from the mantle, to prevent soot and ashes from entering the room.

The Draft. The amount of draft a chimney can provide depends on the size of the flue. When a chimney is too small to provide the required draft, it can be improved by having a blower installed. This blower compensates for the lack of flue area by increasing the volume of air passing through the chimney. The size of the chimney, the size of the blower, and the draft required by the piece of heating equipment, must all be taken into consideration; consequently, the installation of a blower in a chimney is best left to a heating expert.

Very often, the flue area is too large for a particular piece of heating equipment, or the draft fluctuates widely with the prevailing wind.

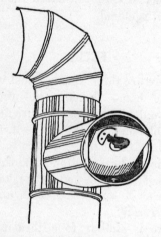

Fig. 3. Automatic chimney draft regulator.

This condition makes it very difficult to regulate the fire, because the draft is small at one minute and very great the next. An excellent remedy for this condition is to have an automatic draft regulator installed in the stove pipe. This regulator is a type of damper which is opened and closed by the suction in the chimney. The regulator is first set to provide the required amount of draft. When the draft starts to increase, the disk of the damper closes far enough to reduce the draft. When the chimney draft decreases, the disk opens wider to compensate for this reduction.

Condensation. In combustion, gas produces a considerable amount of water vapor. As this moisture is in a gaseous state it will flow out of the flue or chimney opening, provided it does not become chilled and thus condense into a liquid. If the chimney is well constructed and holds the heat, the vapor should have no difficulty in escaping, but if the chimney is poorly built or a large section of it is exposed to the wind and weather, the vapor will condense into a liquid. This liquid contains certain acids which are capable, in time, of soaking through mortar joints and eventually working out of the chimney to damage wall and ceiling decorations. Homes heated with gas where such a condition exists should consult a chimney expert or the local gas company. There are several methods used to eliminate this trouble, but it takes firsthand knowledge to know which one to select. Be sure you get someone who really understands this field, as many homeowners have paid out large sums to have their chimney rebuilt only to find that the condition still exists.

Gas-fired hot water heaters are often connected into the house chimney with several lengths of metal flue pipe. In some cases this pipe runs right up through an opening in the roof, and provides the necessary escape for the fumes from the burning gas. As a general rule, a long run of metal pipe will not hold the heat very well and in this event there will be condensation of vapors inside the pipe. This moisture may drip back down the pipe and find an exit at the pipe joints. One simple remedy is to cover the pipe with asbestos paper so that it will hold the heat longer. There is a special type of flue pipe made of materials that are poor heat conductors and this can be used instead of the metal pipe.

COAL FURNACES

One of the oldest and still most common kind of heating plant for the home is the coal furnace. A good coal furnace fired with high-grade fuel will give very satisfactory service with minimum effort on the part of the owner. When people complain about the work required to coax heat from their coal furnaces, the fault is generally with the fuel, the chimney, or the manner in which the furnace is operated.

Efficient operation of any coal-burning furnace is largely dependent upon the chimney. Any leaks about the chimney will interfere with the draft and prevent the furnace from working properly. The stove pipe from the furnace to the chimney should slant upward and be sealed tightly into both furnace and chimney.

There are many minor points connected with operating a coal furnace that should not be overloked, especially if you are having difficulty in keeping the furnace operating properly.

First of all, put only coal on the fire—never rubbish of any sort. Ashes should not be used, as they sometimes are, to bank the fire for the night. Never poke a fire, as this will mix the hot coals with the ashes and form clinkers.

If the basement is tightly shut, air will not circulate properly, the draft will be feeble, and the fire will burn poorly.

Check to see that all the furnace doors shut tightly and that there are no leaks around the check damper when it is closed.

FUELS

There are three kinds of coal used in the home furnace, anthracite, coke, and bituminous. Anthracite is probably the most widely used. It is very hard, and because it is low in volatiles it burns without smoke. It does not tend to swell and cake together as do some other coals, and it ignites easily.

Coke is similar to anthracite in that it burns without smoke, and it can be fired in much the same manner.

Bituminous is a soft coal, high in volatiles, and produces more smoke and soot than anthracite or coke. It is used mostly for industrial work.

In the United States, coal is graded according to size by passing it through screens or sieves of different sized mesh to separate the pieces. Each size is known by a specific name.

The following table shows the diameter of the mesh through which the largest piece of a given size of coal will pass. Thus, egg size coal will pass through a mesh which is $3\frac{7}{16}$ inches in diameter but not through one which is $2\frac{1}{2}$ inches in diameter. Stove coal will pass through a $2\frac{1}{2}$ inch but not a $1\frac{9}{16}$ inch mesh, etc.

ANTHRACITE

Name of size	Diameter of mesh (in inches)
Broken	4½
Egg	3⁷⁄₁₆
Stove	2½
Chestnut	1⁹⁄₁₆
Pea	1¹⁄₁₆
Buckwheat (1)	½
Buckwheat (2)	¼

BITUMINOUS

Lump	more than 4
Egg	4
Nut	1½
Slack	¾

Sizes of Anthracite. The first consideration in burning anthracite is to get the proper size for the furnace. Anthracite is obtainable in several sizes, and each size is best suited for a particular firebox.

Egg size is intended for fire pots not less than 24 inches wide and at least 16 inches in depth.

Stove coal is suited for fire pots 16 inches wide and 12 inches deep. Most home furnaces are designed to burn stove coal.

Chestnut is made for kitchen stoves and hot water boilers, where the fire pot is 10 to 16 inches deep and approximately 20 inches in diameter, and for furnaces with this size firebox.

Pea coal is used for kitchen ranges and water heaters, and can be used in the furnace, provided there is an excellent natural draft and special care is taken, when shaking the grates, not to allow the hot coals to fall.

The very small sizes, No. 1 buckwheat and No. 2 buckwheat, are intended for use in heating equipment with mechanical stoking devices and forced-draft blowers.

What Size to Burn. Coal, or any fuel for that matter, must have air if it is to burn. Large-sized coal, when put in the firebox, will not pack very close together, and there will be ample space between each piece of coal for the circulation of air. Air enters from the bottom of the fire and must work its way through the entire fire bed. Small-sized coal, put into a fire pot, packs together so that

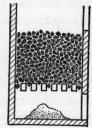

Fig. 4.

only a small amount of air can penetrate. If only a little air circulates, the fire will burn poorly and go out.

Small-sized coal can be used for kitchen ranges or hot water heaters because the fire bed is not very deep.

While each furnace is best suited for one size of coal, it is possible to use a smaller size. This is generally done for the purpose of economy, as the smaller anthracite coals are somewhat cheaper per ton than the larger sizes. Using smaller coal is also a very good means of retarding the fire during warm weather. Lastly, it is sometimes impossible to get the larger coal, and then the small sizes must do. When burning chestnut and pea coal, a somewhat thinner bed is required. These small coals pack quite densely, and if you try to build up a full fire pot with them, the fire will not burn very well. Probably the best method of burning small coal is to mix it with the regular size. This is done by putting on a layer of stove coal and then adding a layer of the smaller. Start the fire with stove coal, and when this is burning well, add the first layer of small coal. In a furnace, the fire bed is many inches thick, and if small-sized coal is used exclusively, a blower should be provided to force the air up through the fire bed.

BURNING WOOD

Wood is still used as a fuel in rural areas for cooking and heating purposes. A familiar sight in rural kitchens is the coal and wood stove that does the cooking as well as keep the kitchen warm and comfortable.

As wood is usually sold by the cord rather than by weight it is best to get such wood as hickory, oak, and maple, rather than pine, elm, and birch. The hardwoods will produce considerably more heat than the others.

You will frequently find with wood burning stoves that a brown liquid oozes out of the seams between lengths of stove pipe. This is creosote which has condensed in the chimney. One way to avoid this trouble is to see that only small hot fires are burned in the stove. A hot fire will warm up the stove pipe and chimney so that the creosote is carried out of the chimney as a gas. If there is a smoldering fire in the stove, the chimney will never get warm and the creosote will condense into a liquid.

Sawing Firewood. Any homeowner who likes to keep a fire going in the fireplace can save himself a considerable amount of money each year by buying his firewood by the cord length and cutting it himself rather than purchasing the more expensive fireplace length wood. Saw-

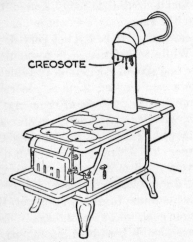

CREOSOTE

Fig. 4a. Creosote in the chimney of wood burning stoves can be kept at a minimum by burning small, hot fires.

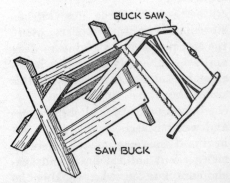

BUCK SAW

SAW BUCK

Fig. 4b. With a good saw buck and saw the home handyman can keep the fireplace supplied with wood.

ing large size wood is not difficult provided you have the right equipment, and it also provides a mild form of exercise which is beneficial to a great many of us.

For working alone, a buck or swedish saw is an excellent tool for cutting wood up to four or five inches in diameter. The tension of the blade can be adjusted with a turnbuckle or some other device.

Wood over five inches in diameter is best cut with a one-man crosscut saw, which has a blade about 4 feet long. Some of these saws can easily be converted into two-man saws by changing handles. The trick of using a two-man saw is never to push the blade back towards the other fellow. Let him pull it back. As soon as you try to push the saw it will buckle and the work will go slowly. Saws used for cutting firewood should be cared for like any good handsaw. Have them sharpened from time to time and hang them up when not in use so the teeth will not get damaged.

For easy sawing you should have a good saw buck. This should be solidly constructed out of 2 x 4 in. or 2 x 6 in. lumber (see SECTION Two). The legs should be wide enough apart so that the buck will not tilt easily and it should be high enough to suit the person using it.

As far as axes go, the home mechanic does best with a single blade ax, and the head should not be too heavy. A three-pound head is about right, for if the head is too heavy, chopping and splitting wood will be an exhausting business. Double-bitted axes are very heavy and should be used only by those with considerable strength, not to mention experience.

Keep the edge of the ax blade sharp and free of nicks by not allowing it to strike metal objects or rocks. Be sure that the head is secure on the handle. If it begins to pull loose, use wedges driven into the handle to tighten it. Do not tighten the head by soaking the ax in water. This will cause the wood handle to expand, and while the head may seem secure the wood in time will dry out and shrink away from the head.

FURNACE DAMPERS

The modern furnace is equipped with four dampers. Their purpose is to regulate the amount of air reaching the fire and thus control the rate at which the fire burns. It is essential that these dampers operate properly if the furnace is to give good service.

Ash Pit Damper. This damper is located at the base of the furnace. It controls the flow of air to the fire. When the damper is closed, the fire burns slowly, and when wide open, it produces the maximum heat.

Check Damper. This damper checks the flow of air through the fire by opening the chimney, so that air flows directly through it rather than passing through the fire. This damper works in conjunction with the ash pit damper. When one is open the other is closed, and vice versa. Keep the check damper closed when a great deal of heat is required.

Smoke Pipe Damper. This damper is located somewhere in the length of stove pipe that runs from the furnace to the chimney. It is operated by a small handle attached to a disk in the pipe. The purpose of the damper is to prevent heat from escaping through the chimney and, at fraction of an inch more each day, and continue this practice as long as the fire burns properly and there is no sign of coal gas in the basement. The amount of heat lost through the chimney is very great, and keeping this damper sufficiently closed is a great fuel saver. During very cold

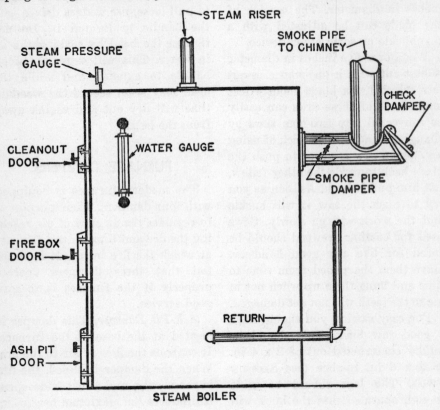

STEAM RISER

STEAM PRESSURE GAUGE

SMOKE PIPE TO CHIMNEY

CHECK DAMPER

CLEANOUT DOOR

WATER GAUGE

SMOKE PIPE DAMPER

FIRE BOX DOOR

ASH PIT DOOR

RETURN

STEAM BOILER

Fig. 5.

the same time, to provide enough draft for the fire. This damper should be kept as nearly closed as possible without putting out the fire. The best method of finding the right setting for this damper is through trial and error. Close the damper a weather, of course, the damper will have to be opened enough to provide the additional draft. Use this damper for seasonal rather than day to day settings. In other words, set the damper either for mild weather or cold weather.

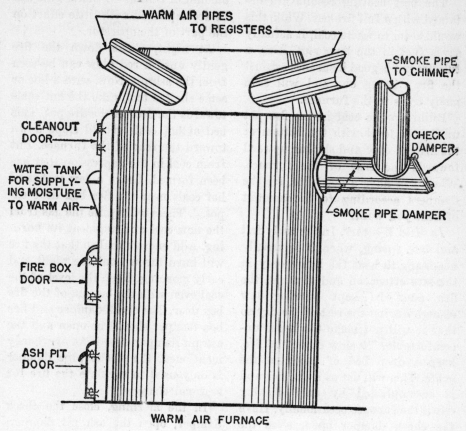

WARM AIR PIPES TO REGISTERS

SMOKE PIPE TO CHIMNEY

CLEANOUT DOOR

CHECK DAMPER

WATER TANK FOR SUPPLYING MOISTURE TO WARM AIR

SMOKE PIPE DAMPER

FIRE BOX DOOR

ASH PIT DOOR

WARM AIR FURNACE

Fig. 6.

Fire Door Damper. The purpose of the fire door damper, which is located in the door of the fire box, is to allow a small amount of air to flow over the surface of the fire and thus aid combustion. When open, it also checks the draft through the fire.

STARTING THE FIRE

When starting a fire at the beginning of the season, have about two inches of ashes on the fire grates. On top of this place the paper and a good supply of kindling or charcoal. The ash pit damper should be wide open, the smoke pipe damper open, and the check damper closed. It is very important to get the best possible draft when starting the fire.

As soon as the kindling is burning well, put on a light covering of coal. Add more coal as soon as the first layer begins to burn. Do not try to add coal until the previous layer has ignited, as too much coal added too soon will smother the fire.

The best heating results are obtained with a full fire pot. While this would seem to waste coal, it actually saves fuel in the long run. Also, a full fire pot is good insurance against the fire's going out and will save many trips to the furnace.

Build up the coal in the fire pot until it is level with the bottom of the fire pot door and sloping upward towards the rear of the furnace. When you have a good fire, set the dampers according to the amount of heat you want.

In Mild Weather. In the early fall and late spring, when it is usually necessary to heat the house only in the late afternoon and at night, the fire must be kept burning low enough during the rest of the day so that it will not make the house uncomfortable. To slow down the fire, keep a deep bed of ashes on the grate. This will act as a damper and is accomplished by only shaking down the furnace occasionally. Have the check damper open, close the smoke pipe damper as far as possible without shutting off the draft completely, and close the ash pit damper. The fire door damper should be open. If the weather turns suddenly cold, and you want more heat, shake down some of the ashes on the grate, add more fuel, close the check damper and open the ash pit damper. A smaller size coal is also useful in retarding the burning rate. Keep a supply of chestnut or pea size on hand for this purpose.

In Cold Weather. During very cold weather, it is important that the furnace deliver the maximum amount of heat at all times. This can be accomplished with little effort on the part of the operator.

At night, shake down the fire gently until a red glow can be seen from the ash pit. Now, with a hoe or some similar tool, rake the hot coals towards the door of the fire pot. This bed of hot coals should slope down toward the rear of the furnace. Put fresh coal in the depression that has been formed. Leave a few inches of hot coals near the fire box door exposed. These will ignite the gas from the new coal and augment its burning. Add enough coal so that the fire will burn throughout the night and early morning. Keep the level of the coal even with the bottom of the fire box door. The check damper and fire box damper should be open and the ash pit damper closed. As previously mentioned, the smoke pipe damper is only used to regulate the fire for seasonal changes.

In the morning, close the check damper, open the ash pit damper, and close the fire box damper. Allow the fire a few minutes to come up and then add coal to the level of the fire box door. Do not shake the fire down unless it is necessary to make room for more coal. Rake the hot coals in the same manner as was done for night firing. To control the fire during the day, set the check and ash pit dampers. When full heat is required, close the check damper and open the ash pit damper.

The exact setting of the dampers is largely a matter of practice, of trial and error. You will soon learn just how far to open or close them.

REMOVAL OF ASHES

If ashes are left to accumulate in the ash pit, they will not only cut down the flow of air to the fire but will also cause the fire grates to burn out. Taking the fine ashes out of the pit is an unpleasant task unless they are sprinkled with water to keep down the dust. A short length of garden hose can be attached to a nearby faucet and kept on hand for this purpose. Ashes should always be placed in a metal container and never in cardboard or wood.

Make it a practice to keep the basement as free of ashes as possible. They collect very rapidly and you will soon have a collection that requires several hours to remove.

It is a good plan to remove ashes daily, or at least every other day.

COAL STOKERS

In recent years, several manufacturers have produced automatic coal stokers designed for the home furnace. These stokers bring fuel to the fire and remove the ashes by dumping them in containers. The only attention required is to remove the ash cans from the basement when they become full and to see that there is a proper supply of coal on hand. Some stokers have a small hopper that must be filled every day or so, while others are attached to a large bin and therefore do not require frequent refilling. Automatic stokers are equipped with blowers, and a special grate is used in the furnace so that the small coal can be burned.

The design, and consequently the maintenance, of these stokers varies with the make, and the homeowner buying a coal stoker should get full operating and maintenance instructions from the manufacturer or dealer.

Each stoker is equipped with either a sheer pin or a similar device, such as a clutch, so that the machine will not become badly damaged if the mechanism is jammed by too large a piece of coal. Be sure that you are familiar with the procedure for removing any obstruction in the stoker, and how to reset the clutch or replace the sheer pin.

Use the size of coal specified by the manufacturer, and it is wise to equip the hopper or bin with a wire-mesh screen to keep out any oversize coal, as well as any other material that might cause a malfunction in the stoker.

OIL BURNERS

Oil is very efficient fuel for heating the home. A modern oil burner is fully automatic and capable of delivering the required amount of heat in a very short time. It works equally well in hot air, hot water, and steam furnaces.

Like any other type of heating equipment, an oil burner is made to deliver a definite amount of heat. If the burner is too small for the house, it will not prove satisfactory, especially in very cold weather. Another point to remember is that a modern oil burner will work better in a furnace designed for it.

Inspecting. Because it is automatic, the oil burner is often neglected until the day when it suddenly fails to deliver any heat. Failure of the burner can often be prevented by having it checked at the beginning of the heating season by an oil burner expert. Arrange to have him come and examine your equipment before it is turned on. The best time is late in the summer, before everyone else is trying to do the same thing. If you are in doubt as to qualified experts in your community, write to the company that manufactures your oil burner and ask them to name someone in your locality who is familiar with the equipment and can do a satisfactory job.

If the oil burner is put in proper condition by an experienced and well-trained man at the beginning of the season, you should have satisfactory service throughout the entire winter.

Repairs. A modern oil burner is a very complex piece of machinery and it is not recommended that the home mechanic try to make any repairs unless he is very familiar with the equipment. A good plan is to have a serviceman explain how to make any adjustments that might be needed, and what steps to take at the end of the season for turning off the burner and preparing it for the summer.

Fuel. The type of fuel used in the burner will have much to do with how efficiently it operates. Find out what type of fuel the burner requires, either from the manufacturer or from the serviceman, and use it rather than a cheaper and inferior grade.

A properly adjusted oil burner should not smoke at all, except when it first starts, and then for only a short period. This is because the fire box is cold and complete combustion is not taking place. If smoking continues, it is probably due to the fact that the burner is out of adjustment or that a low-grade fuel is being burned. Smoking means that fuel is being wasted.

KEROSENE OIL HEATERS

One of the most widely used small oil heaters is the vaporizing kind known as the blue flame heater. The main portion of the burner consists of a wick at the base of two or more perforated cylinders. This type oil heater is used extensively for hot water systems, kitchen ranges, and space heaters. It produces a considerable amount of heat for its size and requires little maintenance besides cleaning and keeping the fuel tank full.

Most of these heaters are equipped with small fuel tanks, but they can be connected with larger tanks on the outside of the house, thus limiting the need for daily filling. Adjustment of the flame is done manually.

When one of these heaters is used constantly, it is wise to shut it down every few months and give it a good cleaning. Remove all the carbon from around the burner with a brush, clean out any foreign matter and inspect the condition of the wick. In all probability it will need replacing and you will do well to take the old wick down to your heating or hardware store when you purchase new ones so as to be absolutely certain of getting the right size and shape.

Oil burning space heaters of the blue flame kind can be had in many sizes, from small portable ones that require no chimney or flue to large units which require a flue and are capable of keeping many rooms comfortable. If a chimney or flue is required, it is important that it meet with the manufacturer's specifications.

As all these heaters are of the gravity feed type, they must sit levelly if they are to operate properly.

The kind and grade of fuel used is important from the standpoint of efficient operation. Most manufacturers recommend kerosene, a good grade range oil, or No. 1 distillate.

The heater should have a separate flue if other heating mechanisms use the chimney. This flue should be free of sharp angles.

AUTOMATIC REGULATORS

In order to save frequent trips to the basement to set the drafts on the furnace in accordance with the temperature desired for the house, various kinds of automatic draft regulators can be installed to do this work. They are operated either by

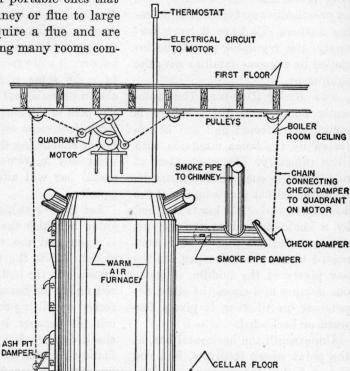

Fig. 7. How the output of a hand-fired warm air furnace can be regulated by a thermostat.

means of a thermostat or by the pressure in the furnace boiler.

Thermostat. On hot air furnaces where there is no boiler, a thermostat, placed in a convenient location in the house, is wired to an electric motor near the furnace. This motor is connected to the ash pit damper and the check damper by means of chains or rods. The thermostat is set at a certain temperature, and when the house temperature falls below this point, the thermostat starts the motor which opens the ash pit damper and closes the check damper. When less heat is desired, the action is reversed. This device can be used on practically any type of coal-burning furnace. To have it work correctly, the regulator should be installed by someone familiar with the equipment.

The Boiler Damper. The automatic damper used on boilers is somewhat different and can be adjusted by the home mechanic with little difficulty. The mechanism of this device is comparatively simple. A horizontal bar pivots on top of the boiler. One end of the bar is attached by a chain or rod to the ash pit damper, and the other end is connected to the check damper. As the bar pivots at the middle, it opens one damper and closes the other, depending on whether it pivots forward or backward.

Underneath the horizontal bar, at the point where it pivots, is a rod operated by the pressure in the boiler. When there is no pressure the rod drops, allowing the horizontal bar to tilt backward, opening the ash pit damper and closing the check damper.

On the horizontal bar will be found one or more adjustable weights that can be moved back and forth. These serve to control the pivoting of the horizontal bar.

Adjusting. To make the first adjustment on this damper regulator, see that there is no pressure in the boiler. Move the weights so that the horizontal bar tilts to open the ash pit damper and close the check damper. Adjust the weights so that the bar can be tilted in the other direction with only a slight pressure of the finger. Move the bar in the other direction, to be sure that the ash pit damper is fully closed and the check damper wide open. If this does not happen, it will probably be necessary to make some adjustment on the chains or rods that connect the two dampers to the horizontal bar. Make the adjustments either by lengthening or shortening the chains or rods until any movement of the horizontal bar will affect each damper equally.

Let the bar swing back to the position in which the ash pit damper is open and the check damper is closed. Allow the fire to build up pressure in the boiler, and the small rod under the horizontal bar will be forced up, tilting the bar so that the ash pit damper is closed and the check damper is open. This immediately retards the fire and, consequently, causes a drop in the boiler pressure. As the boiler pressure drops, the rod descends, permitting the horizontal bar to tilt back again, opening the ash pit damper and closing the check damper. This operation will continue indefinitely.

The amount of boiler pressure required to move the horizontal bar can be regulated by moving weight *A.* When more heat is desired and, accordingly, greater boiler pressure, move weight A away from the pivot point toward the end of the bar. A greater amount of pressure will now be necessary before the horizontal bar will pivot back to check the fire.

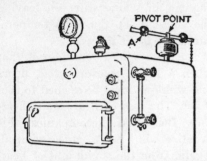

Fig. 8. By moving weight A away from the pivot point, greater heat will be produced by the furnace.

The normal position for the weight, or weights, will depend upon the amount of heat required to make the house comfortable in average, seasonal weather. Mark these positions on the horizontal bar so that the weights can be adjusted easily. It will be necessary to move the weights when taking out the ashes, or to bank the fire for the night.

THERMOSTATS

A thermostat is a device used to control the amount of heat developed in a furnace. Thermostats can be used with hand-fired heating equipment as well as automatic types, such as coal stokers, oil burners, and gas.

As has been pointed out, a thermostat controls the amount of heat developed in a hand-fired furnace by regulating the position of the damp-

ers. On automatic coal stokers, the thermostat controls the position of the drafts as well as the amount of fuel fed into the furnace by the stoker. On oil and gas burning equipment, it controls the flow of fuel into the burner.

Basically, a thermostat is an electric switch actuated by a change in temperature. The thermostat is set for any temperature desired, and when the house temperature falls below this setting, the thermostat automatically makes the changes necessary in the heating unit to produce more heat. When the house temperature rises to that set on the thermostat, the heat is automatically reduced.

There are many kinds of thermostats. The simple ones are set by hand, while the more complex have built-in clock mechanisms and can increase or decrease the heat at the hours for which they are set. This is particularly welcome on cold winter mornings, for the house can be comfortably warm by the time the household arises.

Location. Because the action of the thermostat depends upon the temperature of the air around it, some thought must be given to its location. If the thermostat is placed near a radiator or hot air register, it will naturally heat very quickly and reduce the fire in the furnace before the air in the rest of the house has reached the desired temperature. Likewise, if it is too near the floor, where air is cooler, or near an outside door where it will be constantly chilled by drafts, the thermostat will keep the heating unit burning high even though the rest of the house is too warm. In some cases, where the thermostat has been set on the wall directly over an electric light fixture, the heat produced by the light bulb is sufficient to cause the thermostat to lower the fire.

Fig. 9. A furnace thermostat installed near a radiator or exterior door will not prove satisfactory. It should be located where the temperature around it will be uniform.

When a thermostat is so located that it does not give a true indication of the temperature in the house, it must be moved, or continually set at a different temperature to compensate for the inaccuracy.

FUEL ECONOMY

One of the chief advantages of a thermostat is that it maintains an even temperature in the house throughout the day.

Avoid heating the house to a high temperature during the winter months. It is generally agreed that an overheated house is detrimental to health, particularly when the system is exposed to sudden, sharp changes in temperature on leaving the house. Keep the room temperature at 68 to 70 degrees.

Another point to consider is that when a house is overheated, doors and windows must be opened to cool it off. The loss of heat—and therefore fuel—that accompanies this practice is most uneconomical. Again, from the standpoint of heating economy, it should be remembered that when the house temperature rises above 70 degrees, fuel consumption will go up sharply. A house heated to 80 degrees will require about 15 per cent more fuel than is needed at 70 degrees.

The first step in saving fuel is to avoid letting the fire burn so rapidly that it must be allowed to die down to reduce the heat. For hand-fired furnaces, keep a full bed of coal and regulate burning by means of the drafts.

Keep the temperature of the house as near 70 degrees as possible during the day. There is a general practice of letting the fire burn very low at night and forcing it in the morning. A better plan is to reduce the fire slightly during the night, so that the house does not become chilled. When a room is thoroughly chilled, it requires a great deal of heat to make it comfortable again. Heat must be absorbed by the walls and ceiling before the air is warmed.

Most people like to sleep with a window open, and this can be a source of considerable loss of heat unless the radiators in that room are turned off and the door shut, to prevent chilling the rest of the house.

WARM AIR SYSTEM

The warm air heating system is one of the oldest in use today, and, in recent years, its compactness and efficiency have been markedly increased. Many revolutionary types of warm air systems are being put on the market, and some of them differ as greatly from the older systems as the automobile of today differs from early models. Since these new systems are not in general use, however, this section will be concerned with the conventional hot air system found in the majority of homes.

Operation of this system depends upon the principle that warm air, being lighter than cold air, will rise; and, if pipes or openings are provided, the warm air will flow through these and into the rooms of the house.

Some types of warm air systems have numerous ducts, blowers, and registers, so that the warm air from the furnace will be forced through the entire house. Additional registers and ducts are provided so that the cold air will be brought back to the furnace to be heated. Other types of warm air systems draw the cold air directly from outdoors by means of a large duct, heat it by circulation through the furnace, and thus provide a continuous supply of warm, fresh air.

The kind of warm air system installed will depend upon the heating requirements of the house. A pipeless furnace, for example, sends a blast of hot air through one central register. The inefficiency of this kind of system in a large house is that the warm air will escape through the first available opening upstairs and leave the rooms on the lower floor unheated. Also, if the rooms have high ceilings, there will be a concentration of heat in the upper portion of the room, while the lower part remains relatively cold. A pipeless furnace is best suited for small, compact homes where ample opportunity is provided, by means of doors and other openings, for the warm air to circulate about the house.

INCREASING EFFICIENCY

The effectiveness of a warm air system with ducts to bring the air to various portions of the house will depend on how well the system is installed.

Ducts. In the first place, the ducts should be as free of sharp angles and turns as is possible. Sharp bends in the ducts will increase the resistance to the flow of warm air from the furnace. If a warm air system is not giving satisfactory service, check to see if there are any sharp bends that can be eliminated. Another cause of resistance to the passage of air is that the ducts slant downward from the furnace rather than up to the registers.

Preheating Cold Air. A warm air system can be made considerably more efficient if you connect a duct from air intake at bottom of the furnace to a register on first floor. Thus air need be heated less and fuel is saved. Ducts should not be run inside an exterior wall or heat will be lost. Registers should be low on a wall as warm air rises.

Eliminating Dust and Dirt. Newer warm air heating systems usually have a filter to remove dust and dirt from the warm air. Since older systems lack such filters, remove the registers and place a piece of cheesecloth in back of them. The register, when replaced, holds the cheesecloth in place, but it must be removed now and then to be washed or replaced by new cheesecloth.

One new filter works on an electrical basis. As air and dust pass through filter, the dust gets an electrical charge. Then a metal plate containing an opposite electrical charge attracts it.

Humidifiers. The air in a house will often become very dry when the house is heated with a warm air system. This dry air is not only uncomfortable but unhealthy as well. Warm air furnaces are equipped with water pans that help maintain a comfortable humidity, providing they are kept full of water. If, in spite of a full water pan, the air in the house is still too dry, a humidifier can be purchased to remedy the situation. Before you increase the moisture content of the air too much, remember that this increase will cause condensation on the walls and windows of the house during the heating season (see CONDENSATION).

STEAM SYSTEM

In steam heating systems, the furnace heats water in a boiler until steam is formed. This steam flows through pipes into radiators which are located throughout the house. When the steam in the radiators condenses into water, it returns to the boiler to be reheated.

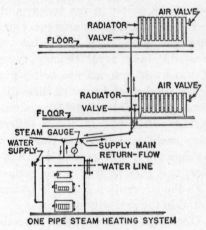

ONE PIPE STEAM HEATING SYSTEM

Fig. 10.

Basic Types. There are two basic kinds of steam systems, the one-pipe system, and the two-pipe system. In the one-pipe system, the same pipe brings the steam to the radiators and returns the water to the boiler. In the two-pipe system, one pipe brings steam to the radiators while the other pipe carries the water back to the boiler. The two-pipe system is considerably more expensive to install and is not very often found in the home. The one-pipe system gives excellent service if it is properly installed.

Radiator Valves. Each radiator in a steam system is equipped with a special valve. The purpose of this valve is to allow the air in the system to be driven out by the pressure

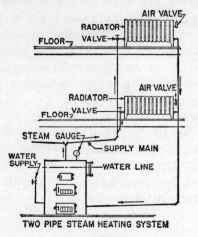

TWO PIPE STEAM HEATING SYSTEM

Fig. 11.

of the steam coming through the pipes. This valve is so designed that when the steam comes in contact

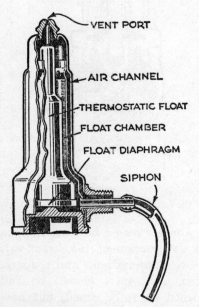

Fig. 12. A radiator air valve.

with the inner mechanism, the valve closes and prevents any steam from escaping from the radiator.

If one radiator in a steam system fails to heat, it is probably because the valve is clogged with dirt or otherwise out of adjustment. This prevents the air inside the radiator from escaping and, consequently, the steam cannot enter the radiator. The valve should be removed and cleaned, or replaced if it still fails to function. Close the shut-off valve to the radiator before removing the small valve for cleaning or replacing.

Vacuum System. A variation of the one-pipe steam system is the vacuum system. Here, a special valve prevents air, forced out by the steam, from returning to the radiator when the steam condenses. The result of this action is the creation of a partial vacuum in the system. When the steam condenses, the air pressure in the system is lowered; this means that the water in the boiler will turn to steam at a lower temperature, with a consequent saving of fuel. The boiling point of water decreases as the air pressure decreases. Another advantage of the steam vacuum system is that with less air in the pipes, the steam will reach the radiators more quickly.

The efficiency of this vacuum system depends on there being no leaks throughout the entire system of pipes and radiators. A normal one-pipe system may have several air leaks which will not necessarily cause trouble, but if it is converted to a vacuum system, the leaks will seriously impair its operation.

Faulty Pipes. Many difficulties in a one-pipe steam system are caused by improper installation of pipes. The pipes should be as free from sharp angles as possible. Sharp angles offer resistance to steam just as sharp angles in warm-air ducts offer resistance to the air. Bends make the system sluggish as well. The pipes must be large enough to allow steam to rise while the water is coming down. If the pipes are too small, there will be a certain amount of friction between the water and the steam, and this will cause the system to work poorly.

pression and become a serious obstacle in the path of the oncoming steam. The meeting of the steam and the trapped water results in pounding. When it occurs near a radiator, it can generally be eliminated by putting small blocks of wood under the legs of the radiator. This will increase the pitch of the radiator, and the pipe connected with it, so that the water will find an easy path back to the boiler. When hammering occurs in some other part of the system, try to find a section of pipe that has sagged, causing a hollow where water can collect.

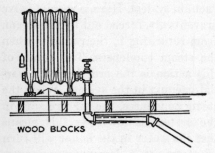

WOOD BLOCKS

Fig. 13. Raising a radiator with wood blocks under the legs will prevent it from knocking.

Noise in a System. There are a number of conditions which will make a steam system noisy. Dirty water in the boiler is one of these, and causes the familiar rumbling noise (see BOILERS). A knocking sound is often due to the improper pitch of the pipes. All pipes must have a downward slope, in order that the water may flow without difficulty from the radiator to the boiler. If, for some reason, a piece of pipe has sagged, water will collect in this de-

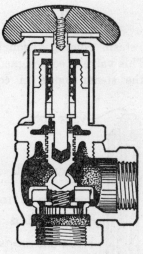

Fig. 14. A cutaway view of a radiator shut-off valve.

Another reason for pounding may be the position of the steam valve between the radiator and the steam pipe. This valve should be fully opened or fully closed, but never halfway.

HOT WATER SYSTEM

Here, we find two kinds of systems, both of them operating on the principle that water, when heated, expands, and in expanding becomes lighter and rises.

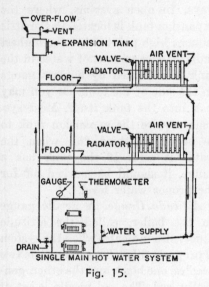

SINGLE MAIN HOT WATER SYSTEM

Fig. 15.

sion tank has no overflow pipe but is completely airtight. When the water in the system expands, it compresses the air in the tank and puts the water in the entire system under pressure, making possible the maintenance of a higher water temperature. In the "closed," or pressure.

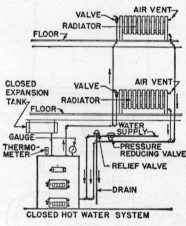

CLOSED HOT WATER SYSTEM

Fig. 16.

The "Open" System. The simplest kind of hot water system is called the "open" system. In this arrangement, the increase in volume due to the expansion of the heated water is taken up by an expansion tank located above the highest point in the system, usually in the attic. This tank is open, with an overflow pipe at the top, so that if the tank becomes too full of water, it will flow out through the pipe and not over the side of the tank to the attic floor.

The "Closed" System. The other kind of system is called the "closed" system, and here the expansion tank is located at the base of the system, together with the boiler. The expan-

hot water system, the purpose is to force the temperature of the water as high as possible without forming steam. Needless to say, there is a limit to the amount of pressure that the system can stand, and a relief valve must be installed somewhere in the line to relieve excess pressure, should it be necessary.

While the normal water temperature in an open system will be approximately 180 degrees, in a closed system it may be well over 200 degrees.

Another advantage of the closed system is that smaller pipes can be used than are required for the open system.

Hot water systems have two sets of pipes to each radiator. One carries hot water from the boiler, and the other returns the cool water from the radiator to the boiler.

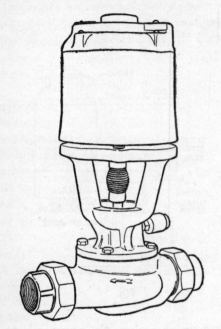

Fig. 17. Pressure reducing valve for a hot water heating system.

INEFFICIENT OPERATION

Difficulties in hot water heating can usually be attributed to air in the lines and radiators, the water level too low in the system, or pipes and fittings that are too small or have been incorrectly installed.

Radiator Air Valve. Each radiator is equipped with an air valve that can be opened to allow air inside the radiator to escape and water to fill the radiator. This valve should be kept open until water begins to flow out, indicating that all the air has been displaced by water. If air is left inside the radiator, it will not heat properly.

The Water Level. A hot water system will work well only when the entire system is full of water. The water level can be checked in several ways. In open systems, where the expansion tank is located in the attic or some high point above the highest radiator, the amount of water in the tank is indicated by a glass gauge on the side of the tank. Or you may look into the tank itself. Most systems require the expansion tank to be about one-third full when the water is cold. If the tank has a gauge, it should be marked off for the proper water level.

Altitude Gauge. A needle gauge on the boiler, called the altitude gauge, also indicates when the system is properly filled. This gauge has two needles, one black and the other, generally, red. The red needle is set at the proper water level for the system. The black needle indicates the true water level and varies with the water level changes. When the red needle is over the black, the system is properly filled with water.

In pressure systems, the amount of water is automatically controlled by a valve. When the water level drops, and with it the pressure, the valve opens and allows water to enter. Reading the altitude gauge is a check, to see that the valve is operating properly. If, for some reason, the altitude gauge reads higher than it should, have the valve examined and the malfunction corrected before turning on the furnace.

Pipes and Fittings. Like other heating systems, much of the difficulty encountered in a hot water mechanism is due to poorly installed pipes and fittings. A steam fitter or plumber should make the necessary changes, as the home mechanic usually does not possess the tools required for the work. The pipes used must be large enough to allow the passage of sufficient water. Resistance caused by small pipes will prevent the system from operating efficiently. To avoid replacing the pipes, pumps may be installed at various points, and these will increase the volume of water flowing through the pipes. These pumps are electric, and will increase the circulation as well as the volume of water through the pipes, forcing water to any part of the house which is not well heated.

Ninety degree angles in the pipes will also cause resistance in the system. These should be replaced, where possible. with forty-five degree fittings.

Radiators. Many hot water systems have been installed which do not give satisfactory heating because the lower radiators do not function as well as those on the upper floors. This condition can be remedied by installing larger main lines, removing excess branch lines, and other rearrangements. The cost of having a hot water system redesigned is high, but so long as it is faultily installed, the system will not function well. The homeowner must decide whether to continue to put up with a troublesome heating system which wastes fuel, or pay for a redesigned system which will, in time, pay for itself in reduced fuel bills.

FILLING THE SYSTEM

The important fact to remember in filling a hot water system is that air in the pipes and radiators will prevent the circulation of hot water through the system, and the radiators will not heat.

The first step in filling the system is to open all the radiator shut-off valves and close the air valves. After this has been done, open the shut-off valve to the water supply. As water enters, open the air valve on the radiator nearest the boiler to allow the air inside to be replaced by the incoming water. Keep the air valve open until water comes out of it, then close it. Repeat this operation on each radiator, working from the lowest to the highest, until the air in each has been replaced by water. After this has been done, check to see that the water level in the expansion tank is correct.

In a closed pressure system, leave the water supply shut-off valve to the boiler open, as the pressure valve will allow the passage of water when necessary. When the air valves on the radiators are opened, the air will escape and the pressure will drop. This decrease in pressure opens the intake valve and allows the proper amount of water to enter.

Fresh water always contains a certain amount of air, and this becomes trapped in radiators when the system first goes into operation. The air should be expelled by opening the air valve, in the manner employed for filling. After the air is out and the valve closed, more water will have to be added. Should it be necessary to add water at frequent intervals, continue to clear the radiators.

Altitude Gauge. In some instances, the position of the colored needle on the altitude gauge of an open system will not give the correct reading when the system is full. This needle can be reset to conform with the water level in the expansion tank by removing the glass cover plate on the gauge and positioning the needle manually.

RADIATORS

The radiator is one of the most familiar mediums used to transfer heat to a room. A radiator transfers heat by two methods, radiation and convection. In radiation, the heat waves from the radiator strike other objects and warm them; in convection, the radiator warms the air around it, which rises and circulates through the room.

Size and Design. Many home heating problems are due, not to the method itself, but to the size and location of the individual radiators. The amount of heat that a single radiator can produce is dependent primarily on the size of the unit. Obviously, a large radiator with a greater heating surface will provide more heat than a smaller unit. Also, the components of the radiator and its construction have a great deal to do with the amount of heat it can transfer. The modern tubular radi-

ators are made to emit a great deal more heat than an old-fashioned radiator of the same size. Thus, it is quite possible to increase the efficiency of a heating system by installing larger or more modern radiators.

Location. The location of the radiator in the room is important to its effective operation. As stated above, a radiator gives off heat both by radiation and convection. To allow a maximum amount of air to come in contact with the radiator, it must be exposed so that the air can circulate around it. The best location for a radiator is away from the wall, but a radiator is not a thing of beauty and is often recessed in the wall, where it will be out of sight. If this is done, the heat from the rear side must somehow be utilized; otherwise, it will be lost by absorption in the wall.

Scientifically constructed radiator enclosures are made to reflect heat

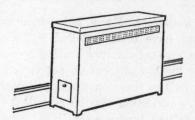

Fig. 18. An improperly designed radiator enclosure will reduce the heat produced by the radiator.

back into the room by means of a piece of metal at the rear of the enclosure. Old-fashioned enclosures can be improved by painting them with a metallic paint, such as aluminum, or placing a rectangle of shiny metal in the rear. If openings are provided at the top and bottom of the enclosure, cold air will flow in at the bottom, and flow out of the opening at the top after it has been warmed.

A good location for a radiator is near an outside wall, under a window. This location permits better circulation of air and prevents drafts across the floor. Needless to say, the window should not be opened while the radiator is on or considerable heat will be lost.

Painting. The type of paint used on a radiator is important, too, from the standpoint of efficiency. Gold and bronze paint will cut down the amount of heat produced. Paint the radiator with a good quality flat oil paint of the same color used for the walls of the room. If the old paint is in good condition, the fresh coat can be applied over it.

Leaky Valve. The shut-off valve of a radiator will often leak a little. Repair this as soon as possible, or the water will damage the floor finish.

Sometimes a valve will leak because the packing nut is not tight. It can be turned down with a wrench. If this fails to correct the leak or prevents the handle of the valve from turning easily, then the valve should be repacked.

To repack a leaky valve, be sure that the fire is low, then draw out enough water to bring the level below the radiator on which you are going to work. Draw off the water by opening a valve located at a low point in the system. Check to see if the water is low enough by loosening the packing nut around the valve. If water starts to drip, the water level is too high. In a steam system, allow the fire to burn low so that there will be no steam.

The packing used for these valves can be purchased at any heating, plumbing, or hardware store. It is a metallic compound and is very easy to use. With the packing nut unscrewed from the valve body, pack the compound in the nut around the valve stem. You may find this easier to do by removing the valve handle and slipping the packing nut off the valve stem. After the valve has been packed, screw it down and check to see whether it can be turned on and off with ease. After this is done, refill the system.

BOILERS

For the sake of economy and efficiency, the interior of a steam or hot water boiler should be kept free of dirt and oil. A certain amount of oil is present inside a new boiler, and this will mix with the water and cause rumbling when the water is heated. The presence of oil will also necessitate more heat to change the water into steam. Oil in a boiler can sometimes be eliminated by using one of the commercial brands of boiler cleaning compound, or by having a plumber blow out the boiler.

Cleaning. The amount of dirt that gets into the boiler will depend upon the water supply. Dirt can be removed, in most cases, by opening the drain cock at the bottom of the boiler and allowing the dirty water and sediment to drain out. The boiler can then be flushed with clean water and refilled.

It is not a good practice, however, to clean out boilers too frequently, as there is an advantage in keeping the old water in the boiler as long as possible. When water has been heated, it loses most of its air content and is less apt to rust the interior of the boiler than fresh water. If your boiler contains a great deal of sediment, however, it must be cleaned, as the sediment will cause more damage than the rust.

Water Level. It is very important to keep enough water in the boiler. A hot water boiler has an altitude gauge which registers the amount of water in the entire system. A steam boiler has a glass gauge attached to the outside of the boiler.

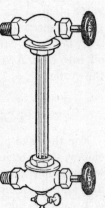

Fig. 19. Glass gauge indicating water level in a boiler.

In most cases, the correct water level will be indicated on the glass gauge, but if there is no mark, keep the water halfway up the gauge. If there is too much water in the boiler, more fuel will be required to produce steam, so keep the water at the proper level.

When it is necessary to add water to a boiler, see that the fire is low

and add the water very slowly. A sudden rush of cold water into a hot boiler may do serious damage.

Clean Glass Gauge. The glass gauge on the boiler will often become so dirty inside that it is impossible to make an accurate reading. Removing the glass tube and cleaning it by hand is a tiresome job, and there is always danger of breaking the tube. A clever method is employed in cleaning these gauges without removing them. The only equipment needed is a cup of hot water, to which has been added a tablespoonful of muriatic acid. There should be a few pounds of steam in the boiler, and the valves at each end of the water gauge should be closed. Open the bottom petcock and, at the same time, the top valve. Steam will be blown out through the petcock; as soon as this takes place, close the top valve and place the cup so that the opening in the petcock is below the surface of the liquid. The vacuum formed in the gauge will draw the solution into the gauge. Keep the petcock submerged and open the top valve again, so that the solution is forced out of the gauge and into the cup. Close the valve and draw the liquid back into the gauge. Repeat this operation until the inside of the gauge is clean. Close the petcock and open the two valves.

MAINTENANCE

The Furnace. During the heating season, soot and fine ashes collect inside a furnace. These have excellent insulating qualities and will effectively reduce the amount of heat delivered by the furnace per ton of coal. If they are left to accumulate too long, they can easily cause a great heat loss which, translated into fuel bills for an entire season, is an expense that few can afford.

As soon as the heating system is shut off in the spring, it should be given a complete cleaning. This is not a pleasant task, but it will provide you with a more efficient heating plant for the coming season.

The best way to clean a furnace is to do a complete job—including the taking down and cleaning of the stove pipes. Use a long, stiff wire brush to scrub the interiors of the pipes. If your basement is damp during the summer, it is well to store the pipe sections in a dry place where they will not rust. After thoroughly cleaning the pipes—inside and out—give the outsides a coat of stove pipe paint or rub them with kerosene. Replace any that are in poor condition due to rust, for a leaky pipe interferes with the draft and is a fire hazard as well. If you do not disconnect the pipes, be sure that all connections to the chimney are tight and the pipe is flush with the wall of the flue. See that all joints are tight, particularly where the pipe enters the chimney. If the pipe is shaky and tends to sway, reinforce it with wire or metal bands attached to the ceiling rafters.

Each furnace has one or more clean-out doors, making possible the removal of soot and fly ash from any of the heating surfaces. Work from the top opening down, so that any

soot and ash not removed will fall into the ash pit. Remove all the ashes from the ash pit.

Brush the outside of the furnace to remove soot, dirt, and rust particles. It is a good plan to give both the inside and outside of the furnace a thin coat of oil or grease. A spray gun can be used for this purpose, and old crankcase oil makes an inexpensive rust preventative.

Oil door hinges and see that they are tight and that the door shuts firmly. A poorly fitting ash pit or fire box door will impair the performance of the furnace.

Examine the fire grates. If they are warped or in poor condition, replace them.

Remember that if soot is left on any metal portions of the furnace, it will absorb moisture and form sulphuric acid. This will corrode the metal.

The furnace doors should be left open during the summer to allow free circulation of air through the furnace and prevent moisture from collecting.

Check all automatic dampers for any sign of wear, or maladjustment in chains or rods. Apply oil where necessary.

Oil Storage Tank. The storage tank for oil burning furnaces should be filled at the end of the season. This will prevent the inside of the tank from rusting.

The Boiler. When preparing a boiler for the summer, remember to keep it full of water to prevent the inside from rusting. In a steam boiler, add water until the glass gauge indicates that the boiler is completely full. In a hot water system, leave the same amount of water in the system as is required during the heating season. Do not completely drain and refill until fall, or just before turning on the furnace.

Loosen the tie rods that hold the sections of the boiler together, to allow for contraction. This is done by loosening the nut at the end of the rods.

Some automatic steam boilers are provided with an aquastat, and continue to operate during the summer to heat hot water for the plumbing system. The aquastat regulates the amount of steam so that enough is generated to heat the water but not enter the radiators. Obtain the right setting for the aquastat from the dealer, along with the necessary operating instructions for the boiler.

Oil Burners. Oil burners and coal stokers should be cleaned and prepared for summer in accordance with directions supplied by the manufacturer. If you do not possess the necessary information, have the work done by a serviceman.

Warm Air Furnace. To clean a warm air furnace completely, first remove the outer casing from around the fire pot. The casing is in several sections held together with bolts. The sections are comparatively light, and the only difficulty encountered will probably be rusty bolts which need a few drops of oil before they turn easily. Clean the inside of the casing as well as the outside, and clean the fire pot by the same method used for the boiler furnace. Apply a

coat of oil or grease to all metal surfaces and check the condition of doors, hinges, and dampers.

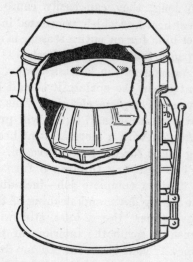

Fig. 20. Due to the method of construction, the outer casing of a warm air furnace must be removed to clean the furnace thoroughly.

While the casing is off, inspect the cemented seams between the sections that make up the fire pot. The cement used to make these seams airtight will not last indefinitely, and when it finally breaks down, coal gas or oil fumes will enter the heating system. The fire pot is made up of several sections, and if the cement appears to be in poor condition, you will do well to remove the sections of fire pot and recement them. This work will require assistance, as the individual sections of the fire pot will probably be too heavy to handle alone. Remove all the old cement with a cold chisel and scrub down the surfaces of the joint with a wire brush. Put furnace cement on the joint and replace the sections.

Smooth off the cement forced out of the seam by the weight of the section.

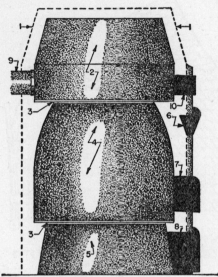

1. OUTER CASING   2. RADIATOR
3. SECTION JOINTS   4. FIRE POT
5. ASH PIT   6. WATER POT
7. FIRE DOOR   8. ASH PIT DOOR
9. SMOKE PIPE   10. CLEAN-OUT DOOR

HOT-AIR FURNACE

Fig. 21. Warm air furnace with casing removed to show the joints between sections that require filling with furnace cement.

While the furnace is apart, give the entire system a good cleaning. Remove dirt and dust from the fresh air intake line, ducts, and registers. A vacuum cleaner is very useful for much of this work.

INSULATION

The Heating System. No heating system will give best results unless it is well insulated. Tests have shown that the loss of heat from uninsulated pipes and boilers may run as high as 25 per cent of the boiler capacity. There is no insulating material that will not conduct some heat, but a good grade of insulation will reduce this loss to a fraction. The insulating material used must not only be a poor conductor of heat, but it should also be fireproof.

When ordering insulating material, get the highest quality. The initial expense will be high, but the cost will be payed back several times over, during the course of years, in reduced fuel bills.

There are many excellent insulating materials, made in block form and in various shapes, to be used on boilers. Magnesia makes an excellent block for boiler insulation. These blocks are cemented to the boiler and covered with an asbestos cement. While this type of insulation is somewhat more expensive than others, it is also more efficient.

Asbestos Cement. One kind of boiler insulation which the home mechanic can apply with relative ease, and at a reasonably low cost, is asbestos cement. Asbestos cement is not the best kind of insulation, but will provide a good measure of protection.

Asbestos cement is obtainable in 100 pound bags and in smaller quantities. You can figure that 100 pounds will cover from 20 to 25 square feet of surface, at a thickness of one inch. Mix the cement with water until it becomes a workable paste. The only other requirement is some one-inch mesh wire, commonly known as chicken wire, which is used as a reinforcement for the cement.

Before applying the insulation, remove any dirt or rust scales from the outside of the boiler. Check all gauges and pipe connections at the boiler for signs of leaks. The boiler should be warm when the cement is applied; a cold boiler will expand, when heated, and crack the cement.

Mix the asbestos cement with the water and apply it to the boiler with a trowel. The first coat

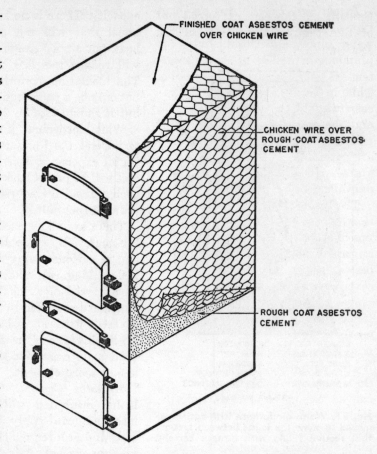

FINISHED COAT ASBESTOS CEMENT OVER CHICKEN WIRE

CHICKEN WIRE OVER ROUGH COAT ASBESTOS CEMENT

ROUGH COAT ASBESTOS CEMENT

Fig. 22. How chicken wire is placed over a boiler after the first coat of asbestos cement has set.

should be about one inch thick and should be worked into all joints and cracks so that the surface is even. Allow enough room around the ash pit and fire doors, and other openings, so that they may be opened without chipping the edges of the insulation. Scratch this first coat until it presents a rough surface to which the second coat can cling.

Allow enough time for the first coat to become moderately dry, then carefully stretch the chicken wire over the boiler surface. Flatten the wire along the entire surface and cut the necessary holes in the wire for gauges and other fittings. Cover as much of the surface as possible with the wire and do not be concerned if some of the first coat cracks during this process. After the wire has been secured, apply the second coat of asbestos cement.

The second and final coat should be about one-half inch thick, and the surface smoothed off with a trowel.

Insulating Pipes. An excellent type of insulation for steam and hot water pipes—and this includes the plumbing as well as the heating system—is asbestos air cell insulation. This is very easy to apply, and the only tools required are a sharp knife and a pair of pliers.

The insulation is composed of corrugated asbestos paper covered with a canvas jacket. It is in tubular form, and

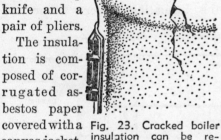

Fig. 23. Cracked boiler insulation can be repaired with asbestos cement.

is split lengthwise on one side so that it can be slipped over the pipe. After the insulation is on, a flap of the canvas jacket is pasted over the joint to seal it. For additional support, metal bands are provided to put around the insulation at regular intervals.

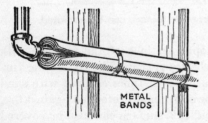

METAL BANDS

Fig. 24. Insulation for hot water pipes.

Air cell insulation can be had in several thicknesses, the thickest having the best insulating qualities. The sections are about three feet long, and the insulation is ordered according to the size of pipe to be covered.

To estimate the amount needed, measure the length of all pipes to be covered—minus fittings and valves, which cannot be covered with this material. Apply later a coat of asbestos cement to fittings and valves.

Inspect the pipes, before covering them, for leaks. Clean the pipes thoroughly. Open a section of the insulation and apply paste to the flap. This paste is usually provided with the insulation, but it can be made by mixing one part powdered alum with 50 parts sifted white flour. Add sufficient cold water to make a smooth paste. Pour in boiling water until the paste is thick.

Slip a section of insulation over the pipe, with the opening up, and press the canvas flap down tightly so that the joint is sealed. One end of each section of insulation has a canvas overlap in order that a tight seal can be made between two sections of insulation. Push the two sections together so that they fit tightly against each other and paste the canvas overlap around the joint. Cover the entire length of pipe, with the exception of fittings and valves. When short lengths of insulation are needed, they can be cut with a knife.

The metal bands should be put around the sections of insulation at eighteen-inch intervals, and should be spaced to cover the joints between sections as well as provide support in the middle of each section. The bands can be fastened tightly by using a pair of pliers.

After the tubular insulation is on, cover the fittings and valves with asbestos cement. Put on two coats of cement, the first coat one-half inch thick and the second coat applied until this insulation is as thick as that on the pipes. Leave the valves free of insulation. The return line on a two-pipe heating system is usually not insulated, because if the steam fails to condense the moisture in the radiator, leaving the line uninsulated will let the steam condense before it reaches the boiler.

Storage Tank. The hot water storage tank can be covered with insulation in much the same manner as the boiler. More efficient is ready-made insulation which comes in sections and is attached to the tank by means of metal bands or other devices. Holes can be cut in this insulation for the pipes. Cover the top and bottom of tank with asbestos cement. Ready-made insulation is made for both vertical and horizontal tanks and is ordered to the capacity of the tank.

Make it a practice to check the condition of the insulation on boilers and pipes to see if there are any cracks and breaks. These can be quickly filled with a little asbestos cement.

Warm Air Furnace. Warm air furnaces and ducts are usually insulated with three layers of corrugated asbestos paper. This paper is purchased in rolls containing about 250 square feet of paper. The paper is held to the pipes and furnace by means of metal bands or wire.

Measure the circumference of the furnace and pipes before cutting the paper, and add several inches to this figure to allow for the thickness of the insulating paper. Cover the

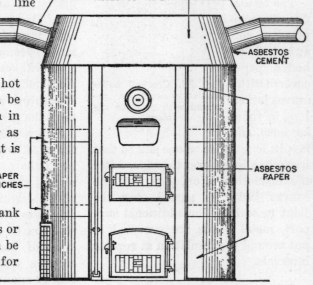

Fig. 25. How a warm air furnace can be insulated.

sloped sections of the furnace with asbestos cement. The top of the furnace is sometimes covered with sand for additional protection against fire, and this surface can also be covered with two or three thicknesses of asbestos paper.

In most cases the outside of the furnace casing will not require insulation because the air between it and the firepot will act as insulation. The

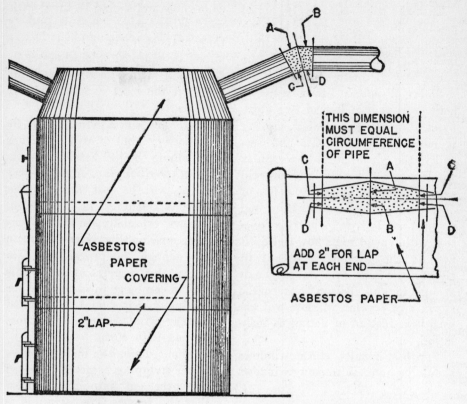

Fig. 26. Detail of insulating a warm air furnace and pipe elbows.

greatest heat loss in a warm air system takes place in the ducts.

PREVENTING HEAT LOSS

Even the most efficient and up-to-date heating equipment will fail to keep a house comfortable during the winter if a large portion of the heat is allowed to escape. Heat can be transferred from point to point in three ways, by conduction, convection, and radiation. Secondly, heat will always flow from a warm surface to a cold surface.

The amount of heat loss in a house through conduction is considerable. Heat will flow through a pane of glass in a window, for example, and be absorbed by outside air in much the same manner that heat will flow up the handle of a spoon placed in a cup of hot coffee.

A great deal of heat also moves out of the house with the air. No house is completely airtight and even those which appear to be tight and wellbuilt may contain innumerable openings too small for water but ample for the passage of air.

To make a house as heatproof as possible, it is necessary to stop up as many openings as you can, and to make all exposed surfaces of the house poor conductors of heat.

Storm Windows. Storm windows help prevent heat loss in two ways. First, they seal the window, making it more nearly airtight, and secondly, the air between the regular window and the storm window will act as insulation and prevent loss of heat through conduction. How well a storm window performs this function will depend upon how tightly it fits. If the window does not fit tightly, air will find an easy exit around it, and the air between the storm and regular window will absorb heat instead of acting as insulation.

For best results, storm windows should be hung on as many windows

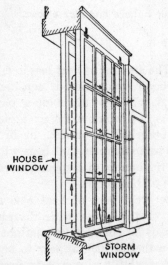

HOUSE → WINDOW

STORM WINDOW

Fig. 27. Poorly fitted storm windows or those that are not weatherstripped have little insulating value.

as possible and should be fitted with weather stripping, particularly if they are not tight. If you cannot afford to equip all the windows in the house with storm sashes, put them on the most exposed side of the house.

There are storm windows to fit nearly every kind of window, from double-hung to steel casement.

Weather Stripping. A great deal of heat will be lost through the numerous openings in the house. Windows, especially, provide openings because no window can be made tight enough to prevent all air leakage. But a great deal of this heat loss can be stopped by weather stripping, and it should be installed on every window, including those equipped with storm sashes.

Without doubt the most effective weather stripping is metal, installed in grooves cut into the window sashes and frames. The stripping is usually put on by a professional, as special tools are required to cut the grooves, and unless the job is done precisely, the weather stripping will do no good and more openings may be exposed.

There are many good brands of weather stripping that can be nailed directly to the sash or frame. Some of these are flexible, while others are in rigid strips.

One of the cheapest kinds of stripping is felt, available in a roll. Attached to the sash and frame by means of tacks or small brads, it will give fairly satisfactory service for a season or so. In time, it will shrink and have to be replaced.

A somewhat more effective stripping is made of metal, with a felt interior that protrudes far enough to form a tight seal between the sash and frame. A small cardboard gauge is sometimes provided to make the proper location for the stripping along the frame and sash before nailing it. This will insure tight stripping without causing the sash to bind and damage the stripping when the window is opened or closed.

sash, affix a piece of stripping to each side and a piece to the bottom of the sash, so that it fits snugly against the sill. Nail the last piece of stripping to the top of the lower sash to cover the crack between the upper and lower sash. Its exact location on the sash will depend on the space between the lower and upper sash when the window is closed.

When using rigid weather stripping, make sure that your measure-

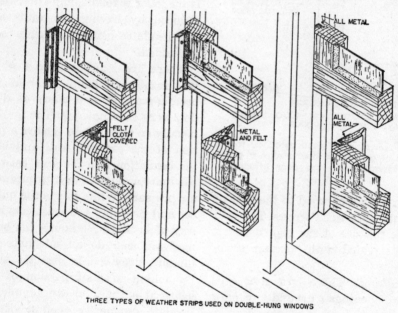

THREE TYPES OF WEATHER STRIPS USED ON DOUBLE-HUNG WINDOWS

Fig. 28.

For double-hung windows, nail the weather stripping for the upper, or outside sash to the outside of the frame. For the inside sash, nail the stripping on the inside of the stop beads. The window should be closed when the weather stripping is attached. For the upper sash, use one long, flexible piece of stripping for both sides and top. On the lower

ments are correct before you cut off a piece to nail. The corners should be mitered to make a tight joint.

On steel casement windows, attach the weather stripping by means of a special clamp or with a prepared adhesive. If the adhesive is used, clean the metal, if you intend to have a strong joint, with benzine. Be sure the metal is dry.

Put weather stripping around doors as well. If the distance between the bottom of the door and the floor is too great to be covered effectively with weather stripping,

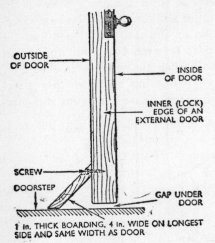

OUTSIDE OF DOOR

INSIDE OF DOOR

INNER (LOCK) EDGE OF AN EXTERNAL DOOR

SCREW

DOORSTEP

GAP UNDER DOOR

1 in. THICK BOARDING. 4 in. WIDE ON LONGEST SIDE AND SAME WIDTH AS DOOR

Fig. 29. A strip of wood attached to the bottom of an outside door makes it possible to weatherstrip the door effectively.

fasten a strip of wood to the base of the door with wood screws. This will reduce the size of the gap so that it can be sealed with weather stripping.

Caulking. There are numerous small openings around window frames and at other points on outer walls which should be filled. Use caulking compound for this work.

INSULATING THE HOME

Walls and Roof. The most practical and effective means of preventing the passage of heat through the walls and roof of a house is by insulation. The value of insulation as a means of keeping the house warmer

in winter and cooler in summer has been so well established that today insulation is built into the house along with the heating and plumbing systems. A well insulated house will be considerably cheaper to maintain than one in which insulation was omitted because of the additional cost.

The best time to add insulation is during the construction of the house. A large part of the cost of insulation is the labor involved, and this can be reduced by having the walls and roof insulated before the inside walls are added.

There are many concerns which will insulate a house after it has been completed, and many of them do a very thorough job. The method usually employed is to remove a portion of the exterior wall and blow the insulation into the area between the inner and outer wall by means of air pressure. While this is the quickest and probably the most complete way of insulating a house, the home mechanic can do an adequate job himself, provided he has the time. By taking a small portion of the house at a time, he can completely insulate during the course of the summer and save himself a great deal of money.

Types of Insulation. There are several kinds of insulation. Some come in rigid sheets and can be used like wallboard. Do not, however, expect the inexpensive grades of wallboard to provide good insulation. They are not made for this purpose and should not be used for it. Another form of insulation is the blanket type, and a third type is the dry fill. The choice will depend upon what is to be insulated. In the case of an unfinished attic, for example, it would be impossible to use a dry fill between the roof rafters, and the choice would be either rigid or a blanket type. Likewise, in filling the space between an inner and outer wall, blanket or rigid insulation would be of little value, and dry fill would be selected.

A good insulating material, aside from being a poor conductor of heat, must be fireproof, or at least fire-resistant. Using any inflammable material between the walls of a house is a very dangerous practice.

Tested Insulation. Many materials have been tested by the Government laboratories for their insulating qualities. The findings of these tests can be had by writing to the Superintendent of Documents, Government Printing Office, Washington, D. C., and requesting the leaflet entitled "Thermal Insulation of Buildings," Circular No. 376, price five cents.

The Attic. The best place to start insulating a home is the attic. The greatest heat loss occurs through the roof of a house, and this can be easily verified by noting the length of time required for snow on the roof to melt. If the snow melts rapidly, an excessive amount of heat is being lost. If the snow remains for a long period, it can be assumed that the heat loss is slight.

If the attic is semifinished, and is a sloped type, a very good insulation to use is the blanket variety.

Blanket Insulation. Various kinds of insulating material are to be had in this form. While the initial expense of such materials as asbestos and spun glass is greater than that of cotton, wood fiber, and other cellulose compositions, the former materials offer the advantage of being fireproof while the latter are usually only fire-resistant.

Whatever the insulating material, it comes in rolls, with waterproof paper glued to one or both sides, and in standard widths. In order to be effective it must be wide enough to completely cover the space between the studs or rafters.

To install, place strips of insulation against the sheathing and nail the edges of the paper tightly to the sides of rafters or studs.

If this cannot be done, the insulation can be held in place by means of strips of wood nailed along the rafters, or with wires run between

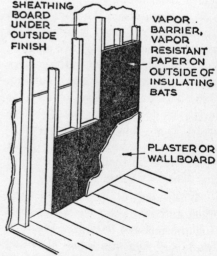

SHEATHING BOARD UNDER OUTSIDE FINISH

VAPOR BARRIER, VAPOR RESISTANT PAPER ON OUTSIDE OF INSULATING BATS

PLASTER OR WALLBOARD

Fig. 30. Insulating a wall with insulation backed with vapor resistant paper.

the rafters. Cut the insulation to the desired length with shears.

If asbestos or spun glass is used, the mouth and nose should be covered with a damp cloth and the hands and arms protected from coming in contact with the fibers. This is most important as the fibers are usually very irritating to the skin and to the nasal passages.

When only one side of the blanket insulation is covered by waterproof paper, be sure to place the paper on the roomside and the insulating material directly against the sheathing. This will prevent most of the moisture in the air of the room from reaching and damaging the insulating material. The small amount which penetrates the paper and reaches the insulation will pass through it to the roof and do no damage.

Do not apply insulation until you are certain that the area to be covered is free from leaks.

Rigid Insulation. Another way to insulate the attic roof is to use rigid insulation boards, which are made so that they can be nailed to the rafters and studding without much cutting. These boards can also be used as partitions to provide one or more rooms. To do this, put up some additional 2 x 4 studding at the point where the attic roof and floor are at least four feet apart. Cover this studding with insulation board to form walls. Insulate the roof with sheets of the insulation nailed to the rafters. Put in any additional studding required so that the insulating board is properly supported, particularly

where the board sections are joined.

Most rigid insulation boards in the home are of cellulose. These are usually made by crushing the fibers of southern pine or sugar cane and molding them into flat sheets. Gypsum boards, which are often used as wallboards or to cover a ceiling, are not true insulation, possessing no heat insulating qualities.

Cellulose boards have good insulating qualities and are lightweight and easy to handle. They come in sizes from 4 x 4 to 4 x 12 feet.

Another method of providing a vapor barrier is to give a plaster wall two coats of aluminum paint. Then put wall paint or wallpaper over it.

Aluminum foil is sometimes used on insulation. It serves to reflect summer heat and keep the house cool.

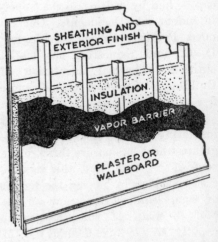

Fig. 31. The vapor barrier of waterproof paper must be placed on the roomside of the insulation and not between the insulation and sheathing.

Unfinished Attic. An easy attic to insulate is one without finished floor and with the rafters exposed. Here, it is necessary only to insulate the attic floor. This will prevent heat from entering the attic and additional insulation on the attic roof, in most cases, will not be required. Be sure to keep the door tightly shut, as an open door provides an excellent means for warm air to escape into the attic and out through the roof.

Almost any kind of insulation can be used for this job. For dry fill insulation, put down a sheet of waterproof paper and pour the insulation over it to the desired thickness. When using blanket insulation, place it so that the paper side is on the bottom. Nail rigid insulation sheets over the roof rafters.

Exterior Walls. A great deal of heat may be lost through the exterior walls, and a brief description of their construction may help toward a clearer understanding of the insulating problem involved.

The exterior walls are composed of two separate parts, the outside and the inside wall. In between them is a dead air space cut into vertical sections by the studding. This space is about three inches wide. In a well-constructed house, this area is closed at the top and bottom to prevent circulation of air between the walls. As a precaution against fire and to strengthen the frame of the house, horizontal pieces of two by four studding are placed between the vertical studding at each floor level. These

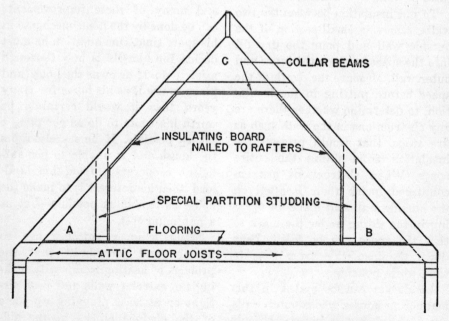

Fig. 32. Rigid insulating sheets will make the attic more heatproof and also provide the beginning of an additional room for the house.

fire-stops, as they are called, may have several bricks on top of them as added protection against fire in the basement rising through the walls.

If the inside walls are cold, go to the basement and see whether the space between the walls has been left open, allowing cold air to flow up between the walls. You can correct this condition by nailing strips of wood over the openings at the bottom and at the top, where the walls open into the attic.

Insulation between the walls helps greatly to increase the comfortableness of the house and the efficiency of the heating unit. The work is best done by a concern with the necessary blower equipment, but it can in some cases be done by the home mechanic.

To put insulation between the two walls, remove a small section of the outside wall and pour the dry fill into the space between the inner and outer wall. Measure the depth of the space before putting in the insulation, to determine whether there are any obstructions in the wall, such as fire stops, that would prevent the insulation from filling the entire space. When obstructions are encountered, mark their location on the outside wall and make an opening in the siding under the mark so that the space can be filled. Pack down the insulation from time to time while pouring.

Insulation can be added in this manner to houses whose outer walls are of wood, but it is very difficult with brick and stucco walls. Here, the best thing to do is to line the in-terior walls with insulating board nailed to furring strips attached to the wall. This provides a dead air space between the insulating board and the old interior wall.

WINTERPROOFING COTTAGE

Housing shortages, in many cases, force a great number of families to purchase homes which were never built or intended for winter occupancy. As a general rule, these houses are rather flimsily built, lacking insulation, central heating and other major items which are normally found in a house built for year-around living. There are several things that can be done to such a house to make it considerably more comfortable during the cold weather, and many of these improvements can be done by the home mechanic in his spare time. One question he must decide for himself is how thorough a job to do. If he owns the house and plans to use it as his home for many years, then it would certainly be worth his while to do as complete a job as possible. If he merely rents the house and is unable to get sufficient cooperation from his landlord, then his interest is to make the house as livable as possible—but at a minimum cost.

Many summer cottages are so flimsily and jerry-built that the problem of heating begins with making the exterior walls and roof airtight or at least plugging up some of the obvious cracks in the siding. One quick and rather inexpensive way of doing this is by tacking sheets of heavy waterproof paper on the outside and covering these with composition siding, such as asphalt designed to resemble red bricks. This comes in rolls and is easily nailed on. A somewhat more expensive, but certainly more attractive method, is to use wood shingles over the waterproof paper. This work can be done during spare time over the course of a summer and will insure the outside walls being air tight.

More heat escapes through the roof of a house than at any other point, so steps must be taken to reduce this loss as much as is possible. If it is possible to get at the under side of the roof or the floor of the attic, then insulation applied here will give the best results (see INSULATION). Many cottages, however, have no attic or even sufficient space under the roof to allow this work to be done. One alternative measure would be to cover the ceiling with insulation board. The other would be to put down another layer of roofing which would serve in some degree as insulation as well as make the poorly constructed roof watertight.

Many summer cottages do not have basements and, in fact, do not even have complete foundations, the structure being supported on blocks or posts at the corners. In a case like this cold winds will blow under the house and if there are any openings or cracks in the flooring, and there usually are, cold air will be constantly displacing the warm air in the house. There are practicable ways to deal with a situation of this sort. One is to build foundation walls of stone, brick or cement blocks around the house. Wood should not be used for this purpose as the lower portion would rot from contact with the damp ground. By building foundations around the entire house, cold winds would not be able to blow up through the floor, and the task of insulating the plumbing would be easier because the still air would not drop to the same temperature as the outside air. When putting in such foundations, a concrete footing should be put down first and this must be below the frost line. After this has set hard, the wall is built on top of it. Allow space in the wall for windows, because during the summer months you'll want some ventilation under the flooring to prevent excessive moisture collecting here and possibly rotting the under portion of the floor boards.

Before the foundations are laid, a thought should be given to a heating plant. There are several brands of gas and oil floor furnaces that require no basement. These are secured to the underside of the floor with strong fasteners, and a register forming the top of the furnace set in a mortise cut the full depth of the flooring. These are comparatively inexpensive plants, producing considerable heat and equipped with automatic controls. Should the homeowner contemplate having such a furnace installed, the installation should be done before the foundation walls are put in. It may be necessary to dig out under the house for the furnace, and if the sides are enclosed, this is all the more difficult. Also some sort of flue or chimney will be required and this will be connected to the furnace and run under the floor to the outside air. The flue can run up the side of the house or into a chimney.

If building up around the bottom of the house is not practical, or under existing circumstances, impossible, the under portion of the floor can be covered with insulation and this in turn covered with waterproof paper to protect it from dampness. This insulation will do a lot towards keeping the floors free of drafts.

Water pipes set in the ground below the frost line will not freeze but those exposed to the weather will, unless insulated.

As a precaution against severe cold weather freezing the pipes in spite of the insulation, it is a good idea to have a plumber install some conveniently located valves at low points in the system so that the plumbing can be quickly drained.

FIREPLACES

There is nothing quite like a fire burning in a fireplace to make a room comfortable during the winter. Unfortunately, there are many fireplaces that cannot be used because they either fail to burn or they smoke to such a degree as to be unserviceable.

Improvement. The primary reason for most fireplaces not operating well is poor construction. Either the chimney is too short, or the dimen-

sions of the smoke chamber and fireplace opening are not correct. It is sometimes possible for the home mechanic to correct the latter error by building up each side of the fireplace opening with bricks, but he should first have an expert on fireplaces make an examination and recommend the steps necessary to correct the faults.

The Draft. If the fireplace smokes only when first lit, a lighted piece of paper thrust into the fireplace throat will warm the air and start the draft working.

Wood. The kind of wood used in the fireplace will also have an effect on how well the fire burns and how

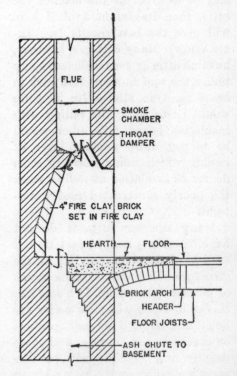

FLUE

SMOKE CHAMBER

THROAT DAMPER

4" FIRE CLAY BRICK SET IN FIRE CLAY

HEARTH   FLOOR

BRICK ARCH

HEADER

FLOOR JOISTS

ASH CHUTE TO BASEMENT

Fig. 34. Section view of properly constructed fireplace.

much heat it produces. Soft woods, such as pine, will ignite quickly and burn fast, without supplying much heat. These are best for starting the fire. Hardwoods burn slowly and will give considerable heat.

CONDENSATION

Virtually all air contains a certain amount of water vapor. This vapor is a gas and can pass through many solids. The amount of water vapor that the air contains is de-

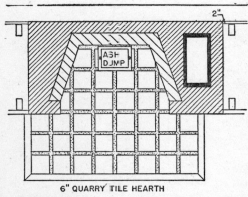

MANTEL SHOULD CLEAR OPENING

FLUE LINING 1'-"x1'-6"

FLUE FROM HEATER IN BASEMENT

SMOKE CHAMBER

12"

8"

FIREPLACE OPENING SEE PLAN

2"

ASH DUMP

6" QUARRY TILE HEARTH

Fig. 33. A well-constructed fireplace with correct proportions will not smoke.

pendent upon the temperature of the air. Warm air contains a great deal while cold air absorbs very little. When warm air comes in contact with a cold surface, the temperature of the air is immediately reduced and, consequently, it drops some of this water vapor in the form of moisture.

In old houses, with many openings, moisture can easily pass out with the air. In well-constructed houses, there are few openings and the moisture cannot escape; accordingly, it remains as sweat on the walls and on the storm windows. Warm moist air, passing around the inside window, condenses on the cold surface of the storm window. Excessive condensation of moisture can cause considerable damage to woodwork and decorations.

Reducing. It is almost impossible to eliminate all the moisture from the air, and unhealthy to reduce the moisture content of the air too much. Reduce condensation by keeping the temperature of all surfaces, such as walls and windows, as close to that of the room as possible, and avoid saturating the air in the house with moisture.

The temperature of the inside walls can be made to coincide more closely with that of the room by insulating between the inner and outer wall. Another method is to have a warm air circulating between the inner and outer wall, but this would cause loss of heat through the exterior wall. Good circulation throughout the house will reduce condensation, and this can be improved by installing flues over gas stoves and leaving the chimney throat open.

WARM INSIDE

CONDENSATION

COLD OUTSIDE

Fig. 35. Condensation or "sweat" on a window is caused by the warm inside air striking the cold window pane and dropping water vapor in the form of moisture.

To prevent excessive moisture in the air, avoid hanging wet wash in the house and remove steam from kitchen or bathroom by forced draft.

Humidity. While many homeowners suffer with the problem of excessive moisture in the house during the winter, many others have just the opposite trouble—the air is too dry. Dry air is harmful in several respects. First of all, as far as the health of the family is concerned, medical authorities say that dry air in the home is the cause of many head colds. Dry air will also tend to cause wood joints in the furniture to loosen. If the air is dry, it will require more heat to make persons comfortable than if the air contained the right amount of water.

Warm air furnaces are usually provided with a water pan and if this is kept full of water the air coming up through the registers will contain some water vapor. Radiators may be equipped with special water pans which will help somewhat to increase the moisture content of the air. For other cases there are many different brands of humidifying devices made for the home. These are regulated so that they will keep the moisture content of the air just right for comfort and health.

PLUMBING

In most cases, the home mechanic will be concerned with the repair and maintenance of the present plumbing system in his home, rather than with new installations. In the first place, the tools required to cut and fit pipes together are expensive and so limited in their use that it would not be worthwhile to buy a complete set for the few tasks in the home. Secondly, most communities have building codes which specify that plumbing installation in homes, or in other buildings, must be done by licensed plumbers. You may, however, be able to do certain jobs.

If you want to do a small job, such as running a cold water line to the garage or placing hydrants about the lawn and garden, you should first consult the building authorities in your community and obtain permission, provided such permission is required. After this, you may be able to borrow or rent the necessary tools to do the work. Running a cold line to a garage is not difficult, once you have the necessary tools, fittings, and a basic understanding of the plumbing system.

THE PLUMBING SYSTEM

The plumbing system in the average home is a rather complicated arrangement of pipes and valves that often causes the homeowner great trouble. In general terms, the plumbing system may be divided into three separate systems. First, there is the cold water system, composed of the pipes necessary to bring fresh water from the well or water main and deliver it to the various fixtures. Second, there is the hot water system, consisting of a means of heating the water, a tank in which to store it after it has been heated, and the pipes to convey it to the fixtures. The third branch of the plumbing is the sewage, or drainage system, and this must remove all waste water from the house fixtures quickly and efficiently.

Learning the System. Each member of the household should have some understanding of the plumbing system and know the location of the main shut-off valve and the various branch valves. Should a leak occur in any part of the system, anyone in

145

the house can shut off the branch in which the leak occurs from the water supply. In the case of a leaking pipe, the minutes wasted in trying to locate the shut-off valve may mean the difference between slight or extensive damage to decorations, flooring, and furniture.

Fig. 1. Plumbing valves should be tagged for quick identification.

All shut-off valves should be tagged to indicate clearly what part of the system each valve controls. This will also save a plumber much time, as he will not have to trace out the entire system before working on it.

To determine what branch of the system a particular valve controls, close the valve and open the faucets throughout the house. List all faucets that are dry when the valve is turned off as part of that branch of the plumbing. The main shut-off valve, controlling the water supply for the entire house, is generally located in the basement. Keep it clear —not covered with coal or other matter. If the basement is finished with wallboard or other material,

indicate the position of the valve clearly and make it easily accessible. This may necessitate cutting out a small square of the wallboard and nailing it back into place with a few short nails that can be quickly pulled out by hand.

Many failures in the sewage system are due to the fact that the system is forced to carry away not only liquids and water soluble waste but all types of rubbish as well. Caution every member of your family against throwing solid matter of any kind into flush toilets or down sink and fixture drains. A sewage system that is properly installed can dispose of liquid matter, but it cannot cope with such items as dishcloths, metal bottle tops, and similar objects. Cleaning out a sewer pipe is expensive and messy, and the blockage is usually due to carelessness on someone's part.

FRESH WATER SUPPLY

The fresh water supply for homes in large communities is generally furnished by a municipal water system that delivers pure water to the home at small cost. The pipe running from the house to the water main is connected to a meter which measures the amount of water consumed. The meter is maintained by the municipality or by a water company.

The Pumping System. In rural areas, the water supply is obtained from a well or a lake. Either of these sources can become contaminated, and it is a good idea to have a sample of the water tested each year to be sure that it is pure. The water is brought into the house and forced through the system by means of a pressure pump and a pressure tank. Electrically operated pumps are so designed that a pressure switch inside the tank automatically turns on the pump when the air pressure inside the tank falls below a certain level. The pump forces water into the

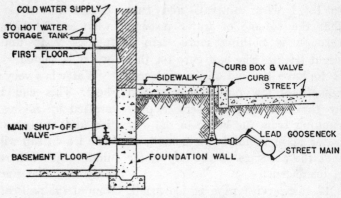

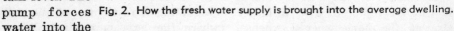

Fig. 2. How the fresh water supply is brought into the average dwelling.

tank until the air pressure has been built up again. As water cannot be compressed, the air inside the tank is compressed instead, and this pressure forces the water through the pipes in the house.

Relief Valve. Other than general maintenance of the electric motor, there are few repairs that the home mechanic can make on the pumping system. Occasionally, the pressure switch will stick and keep the pump operating indefinitely. A relief valve should be installed, either in the pump or between the pump and the pressure tank, to ease this condition. Excessive pressure in the tank will force open the relief valve, and the water will flow out through the valve. When a pump continues to operate after sufficient pressure has been built up in the tank, it should be turned off by hand as quickly as

possible to prevent flooding the basement and to stop unnecessary wear of the electric motor and pump. In most cases, there will be a hand-operated electric switch between the motor and the fuse box. In the event that there is no switch, the pump can be turned off by removing the fuse of the circuit to which the pump motor is wired.

A pump will operate but fail to deliver water to the tank if the water level in the well drops below the pipe leading to the pump. The pump will also fail to deliver water when the foot valve at the end of the pipe in the well is out of order.

In time, the washers in the pump, or in other parts, will become so worn that the pump will fail to deliver water, and this will require extensive overhauling.

Low Water Pressure. It sometimes happens that the water pressure in a house is so low that no water can be drawn from an upstairs bathroom faucet when a lower faucet, such as one in the kitchen, is open.

This condition is most annoying as it limits the use of the bath or shower to those periods when the kitchen sink is not in use.

In some cases this lack of pressure is caused by the pipes being so lined with minerals and rust that the volume of water passing through is nothing more than a slight trickle. The best cure for this is to have the old pipes replaced. Sometimes low pressure is caused by the fact that the service pipe running from the house to the city water main is not large enough, or that the pressure of the city water is insufficient.

If the service pipe is too small, it can be replaced with a larger size at the homeowner's expense. Very often by the time the cost of the labor for digging up the pipe, buying a larger size and having it installed is added up, it will be found to be cheaper to install a small electric pump and pressure tank in the house. The pump will fill the tank with water under enough pressure to maintain a good flow of water at all faucets throughout the house. The same combination of pump and tank can be used when the city pressure is not great enough, a condition that may occur in homes at the outskirts of the city.

HOT WATER SYSTEM

The hot water heating system in the home is often a mystery as well as a source of annoyance to the home mechanic. Either it fails to deliver the needed amount of hot water, or the system constantly rumbles and makes other strange noises. Often, the water is either too hot or not hot enough.

Before taking up the various causes for these deficiencies and what can be done about them, it is necessary to understand how the water is heated.

Water is a very poor conductor of heat. This can be easily demonstrated by taking a bucket full of ice and applying heat to the top. The ice on top will melt, while that underneath will remain frozen. The only way that the water at the bottom of the pail can be warmed is by circulating it to the top of the pail where the heat is applied. When water is heated it expands and becomes lighter. Consequently, warm water will rise to the top, while the cold will remain at the bottom.

If you were to join a U-shaped piece of pipe to a tank full of cold water and apply heat to the pipe, the heated water would rise to the top of the tank and the cold water would sink to the bottom, flow through the pipe and be heated. At first, circulation of water would be slow, but as steam began to form, the circulation would become more rapid.

The Water Back. To demonstrate how this principle operates in a home hot water system, let us select what is probably the simplest kind of mechanism—the water back. This consists of a cast iron box containing either a baffle plate or a U-shaped section of pipe. The box is fitted into the kitchen range and is connected to the hot water storage tank. Cold water flows from the bottom of the tank into the water back, is heated, and flows back into the tank. As warm water is lighter than cold, it rises to the top of the tank. In rising, it displaces the cold water, forcing it to the bottom of the tank and through the pipe into the water

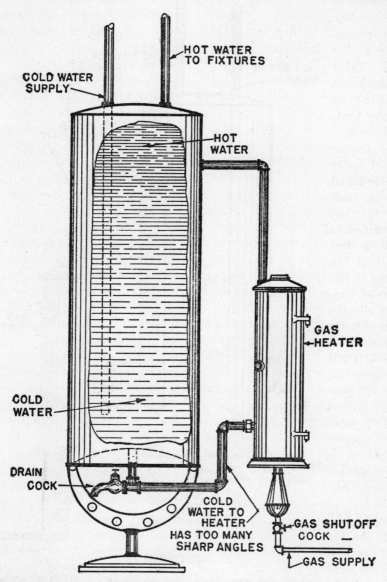

COLD WATER SUPPLY

HOT WATER TO FIXTURES

HOT WATER

COLD WATER

DRAIN COCK

COLD WATER TO HEATER HAS TOO MANY SHARP ANGLES

GAS HEATER

GAS SHUTOFF COCK

GAS SUPPLY

Fig. 3. Most home hot water troubles are due to the fact that the tank and heater were not connected properly. Above is a typical example.

back; this process continues indefinitely.

Faulty Connections. While the principle of operation is simple enough, poor performance is often caused by improper connection of the water tank with the house plumbing or with the heating element.

The incoming cold water should be piped into the tank from the top and carried to within a few inches of the bottom. If the cold water supply is allowed to flow directly into the top of the tank, it will mix with hot water and produce a constant supply of lukewarm water. The hot water line from the tank to the outlets should, of course, be connected at the top of the tank.

Many hot water failures are due to the

manner in which the tank is connected with the heating element. For example, a common case is that in which the water in the upper por-

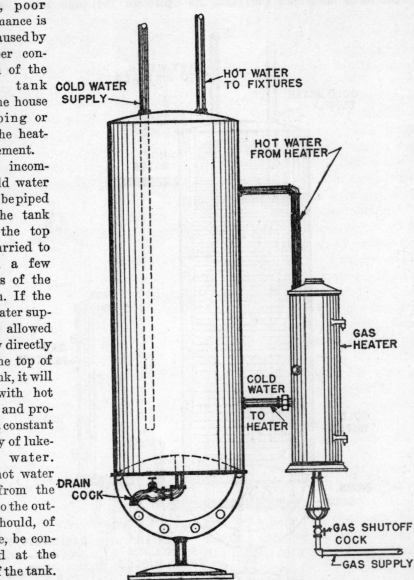

Fig. 4. Hot water heater and storage tank properly connected. The area in the tank between the drain cock and cold water line allows sediment to collect so that it can be drained off from time to time.

tion of the tank becomes too hot, while the water at the lower portion remains cold. This occurs when the cold pipe between tank and heater is placed too high on the side of the tank. The water in the tank below the level of the cold pipe is not affected by the circulation inside the tank, and, as water is a poor conductor of heat, the water below remains at a low temperature. This condition can be corrected by lowering the cold pipe on the tank. When this is done, nearly all the water in the tank will flow through the heating element and provide an adequate supply of evenly heated water.

Another reason for an inadequate hot water supply is the kind of pipe connecting the heating element to the supply tank. Sharp angles in a pipe will give marked resistance to the free circulation of water. To have free and rapid circulation of water between heater and tank, be sure that the cold pipe is as nearly horizontal as possible, and the hot pipe slants up from the heater to the tank. For any of these pipe connections, use 45-degree angles at the bends instead of the sharp, 90-degree elbows.

Horizontal Tank. While most hot water supply tanks found in the home are the vertical kind, the horizontal tank is frequently used, particularly in large houses. In this tank, the cold water supply must be brought to the bottom where it can flow through the heating element. If the cold and hot pipes are too close together, the circulation of water will be limited to a small portion of the total capacity of the tank.

HOT WATER HEATERS

There are a great many methods of heating water for the home. The water back, previously described, is one of the simplest, but it is now largely replaced by more efficient equipment designed to provide a greater quantity of hot water.

Gas and Electric. Modern gas and electric hot water heaters are usually built into an insulated hot water storage tank. They are completely automatic and maintain the water at a fairly constant temperature, depending upon how large a quantity

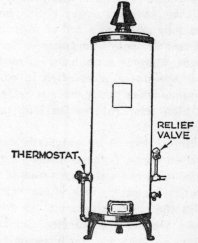

RELIEF VALVE

THERMOSTAT

Fig. 5. A modern hot water heater equipped with a thermostat to regulate the temperature of the water and a relief valve to prevent excessive pressure from building up in the tank.

of hot water is drawn off at a time. These heaters are provided with a thermostat, and a safety valve in case the thermostat should fail to shut off the heat. A specialist must be called when automatic heaters are inoperative. There are also gas and electric hot water heaters which are turned on and off by hand.

Coal Stove. A common type of independent hot water heater is the coal burning stove. The heating equipment is built into the stove and connected with the hot water storage tank. The chief drawback in this kind of heating device is that the water often becomes too hot. Another source of difficulty is the flue, which is either connected with the furnace or with the chimney by pipe sections with sharp elbows. In either case, there is not sufficient draft for the water heater to operate properly.

Furnace Heaters. Many homes with a hot air furnace obtain hot water by means of a coil of pipe inside the fire pot of the furnace. Here again, there is a tendency to overheat the water, most often in cold weather when the furnace is heated to high temperatures for long periods.

Homes heated by automatic coal and oil steam furnaces can be supplied with hot water by means of a heating element which is connected with the steam pipe from the furnace. During the summer months, when no heat for the house is required, the temperature of the hot water is maintained by an aquastat which regulates the furnace so as to heat the necessary amount of water without circulating steam through the radiators. This process is automatic, but the aquastat must be set to maintain the hot water at the desired temperature. When this device is not used, an auxiliary heater can be attached to supply hot water after

the furnace has been turned off for the season.

Kerosene Heaters. Kerosene heaters are still used extensively in rural areas, and aside from replacing the wicking from time to time, they require little maintenance.

HOT WATER TANKS

Range boilers or hot water storage tanks are made of either galvanized steel or copper. Galvanized steel is

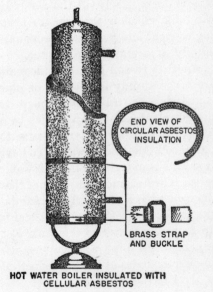

END VIEW OF CIRCULAR ASBESTOS INSULATION

BRASS STRAP AND BUCKLE

HOT WATER BOILER INSULATED WITH CELLULAR ASBESTOS

Fig. 6.

subject to internal rusting in time and must be replaced when the condition becomes serious. Copper, on the other hand, while more expensive than galvanized steel, will last almost indefinitely. The tank must be large enough to hold an adequate hot water supply. If the tank is too large for the amount of hot water required, move the cold water pipe from the tank to heater higher on the tank to reduce the quantity of water heated and prevent excessive consumption of fuel.

Safety Valves. The storage tanks used for automatic gas and electric heaters are provided with a safety valve in addition to the mechanism controlling the heating element. Other types of heaters may or may not have a safety valve, but it is a good idea to have one installed, regardless of the type of heater. These valves are placed at the top of the tank and connected to a length of pipe running to the floor. If the tank overheats and steam is blown off, it will run down the pipe into a pail or onto the floor of the basement and not splash over walls and ceiling, or possibly a person. In a home where the hot water system has not been installed correctly, the hot water, on reaching a certain temperature, will occasionally back up into the cold water line. This condition can be remedied by having a valve installed on the tank.

Dirty Hot Water. Nearly all water, regardless of the source and treatment by purification plants, will contain some sediment which will eventually settle at the bottom of the hot water tank. Combined with this sendiment will be rust from the pipes and tank—should they be made of galvanized steel. Note that on a well-designed hot water system, the cold pipe from the tank to the heater is connected several inches above the bottom of the tank. This positioning of the pipe allows the sediment in the water to

settle at the bottom of the tank, where it is only slightly disturbed by the circulation of the water. The sediment will accumulate in the tank until it flows through the cold pipe into the heater and thence into the hot water pipes throughout the house. Most tanks are equipped with a drain valve at the bottom of the tank, and opening this will remove a large part of the sediment. Do not use any hot water for several hours, to allow the sediment to settle at the bottom of the tank. Open the drain valve and allow the water containing

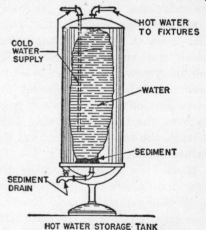

HOT WATER STORAGE TANK

Fig. 7. If no hot water is used for several hours, the sediment will settle at the bottom of the tank and can be drained off.

the sediment to flow out of the tank into a pail or some other container. It is not necessary to drain all the water in the tank—drain until the water runs clear. If the water in your community contains much sediment, drain the tank at regular intervals to ensure clean hot water.

If the cold pipe is connected to the bottom of the tank, there will always be some sediment circulating through the hot water system, as there is no place in the tank for it to settle. Placing the cold pipe higher on the tank will correct this situation.

The coils of a heater will collect sediment, and this can be flushed out by disconnecting the pipes and attaching a garden hose to the coils. The sediment will be forced out by the pressure of the water.

THE SEWAGE SYSTEM

The house drainage system serves two purposes. First, it must safely carry away all waste matter from the house to some disposal point, which may be either a community sewage system or a cesspool or septic tank. Second, it must prevent the gases formed by the sewage from entering the house by flowing back through the sewer pipes and out the fixture drains.

It is very important, from the standpoint of health, that this system be properly installed and function correctly. A faulty hot water system is an inconvenience and a leaky pipe may cause damage, but sewer gases are poisonous and sewage carries many harmful germs.

Unfortunately for the home mechanic, most minor repair jobs involving the house plumbing system will deal with the sewage system. As no work of this type is considered pleasant, the home mechanic should see to it that the system is not abused.

Vent Stack. To provide a safe means of disposing of sewer gas, an extension of the sewer pipe runs through the roof of the house. This is called a vent stack, and it allows the gases in the system to pass harmlessly into the outside air. A fresh air intake for this venting system is provided in the lower portion of the sewer pipe. This must be done so that the gases may flow freely out of the system. If this fresh air intake becomes blocked, the ventilating system will not operate properly. In a correctly installed system, however, the intake will be so located and designed that no foreign matter can enter it, under normal conditions.

The tops of the vent stacks above the roof must not become choked with ice, leaves, or any other substance. If this should happen, the pressure generated by the sewer gas in the system will cause the water to rumble as it flows down the drain. If the pressure of the gas is great enough, it can force its way through a fixture drain, bringing sewage along with it.

Any cracks in sewer pipes should be immediately repaired, for these provide an easy escape for sewer gas.

SEWAGE DISPOSAL

There are several methods of disposing of sewage. In cities, or in any densely populated areas, the drain pipes from the house run into a community sewer pipe which brings the sewage to a disposal plant for treatment to render it harmless. In this case, the homeowner is only concerned with the pipe from the house to the city sewer line.

Cesspools. In rural areas where houses are not close together, a leaching cesspool or septic tank is used to dispose of all waste from the house. A cesspool is nothing more than a large hole in the ground lined with stone or concrete blocks placed in such fashion that the water can pass through the walls into the surrounding soil.

The disadvantage of this system is obvious. The soil around the cesspool will become contaminated in time, and this may lead to the pollution of the water supply, should it be drawn from a nearby well. Even if the well is located a considerable distance from the cesspool, there is no assurance that the water will not become contaminated. It is quite possible, due to rock formations, for the sewage to reach the water supply even though the cesspool is lower than the well. When a well and a cesspool are in the same vicinity, it is wise to have the water in the well tested occasionally to be certain that it is pure.

Another disadvantage of the cesspool is that unless the top is tight and secure, insects and vermin will get into the sewage and possibly spread diseases. The top of a cesspool should be of concrete, with a small opening left in the center for inspecting the cesspool and pumping it out. This opening should be covered with a heavy block of concrete not easily moved. Do not cover a cesspool with wood planks; they are not airtight and will soon rot.

After a while, a cesspool will fill up and cause sewage to collect in the sewer pipes, often resulting in a flooded basement. The chief cause for a cesspool's filling up, aside from abnormally heavy use, is grease. Grease from the kitchen sink will penetrate between the rocks and bricks that line the walls of the cesspool and make a watertight coating.

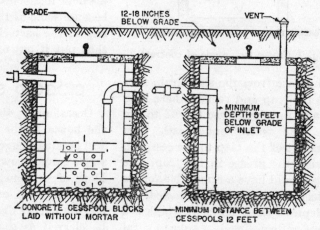

Fig. 8. When a cesspool fills up, the only effective remedy is to build another alongside and connect the two.

As grease floats on water, it will rise with the water level, sealing the walls of the cesspool as it rises, until the entire wall surface is coated and the water cannot flow out into the soil. The cesspool may be pumped out, but the walls will remain sealed and the cesspool will soon be full again. The only alternative, under these conditions, is to dig a new cesspool alongside the old one and connect the two with a few sections of soil pipe. The overflow from the first cesspool will pass into the second.

Grease Trap. A grease trap will prevent most of the grease from entering the cesspool. This trap is installed between the kitchen sink drain and the cesspool. The water

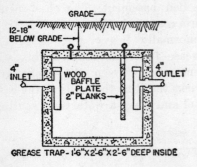

Fig. 9. Grease trap made of concrete.

and grease from the sink drain flow into the trap and remain there long enough for the grease to rise to the top. The water underneath then flows out of the trap to the cesspool, leaving the grease in the trap. The trap should have a removable top, so collected grease can be removed.

Septic Tanks. The septic tank is a means of disposing of sewage in rural areas. It is a watertight, airtight container which holds the waste matter until natural bacteria in it, act on it and change most of the solids to liquid which then flows out of the tank into a disposal field. Some solids are never reduced to liquid but remain in the tank, and it must be cleaned out every few years. Hire a reliable firm to do that job.

The size of the septic tank will depend on the amount of waste from the home. A tank which is too large for amount of waste delivered will not operate properly. If the tank is too small for the volume of waste, the bacteria will not have sufficient time to work on the solid matter and the tank will fail to perform its function.

As a septic tank is a complicated piece of equipment, a specialist should be consulted if it becomes inoperative. It is necessary to have a complete understanding of the system before making any repairs.

The use of chemical drain cleaners should be restricted as much as possible in homes with septic tank, because some of these chemicals will kill off the bacteria in the tank and thus put it out of operation.

CLOGGED SEWER PIPES

Occasionally, the sewer pipe from the house to the cesspool or sewer will become clogged so that the waste water cannot flow out of the system. More often than not, this stoppage is due to some bulky object forced down a fixture drain. The pipe must be cleared as soon as possible, because a stopped-up sewer pipe will put the entire drainage system out of order. Do not allow any water to go down a drain until the pipe is cleared, or the waste will very likely back up in the pipes and come through the drains at low points in the system.

Most home sewer systems are equipped with a special clean-out plug for just such stoppages. The clean-out plug is usually located in the basement at a point where the sewer line runs through the wall. A brass clean-out plug can be removed with a stilson or a monkey wrench. If the plug is made of iron, it may be necessary to use a cold chisel to start it. If the plug is damaged in this process, you can replace it with a special tapered plug.

Cleaning Pipe. Once the plug is out, a "snake" is inserted into the pipe to remove the obstruction. The sewer line, a plugged-up pipe is not uncommon, and it would be well to purchase a snake to keep handy.

Needless to say, cleaning a sewer pipe is an unpleasant task at best, and if the system continues to clog for no apparent reason, it should be dug up and put down properly.

Underground sewer pipes are subject to attack by tree roots. The small roots work their way through the pipe connections and, if given sufficient time, they will effectively clog the system.

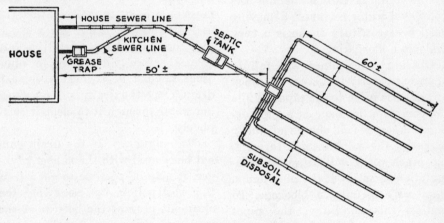

Fig. 10. A properly constructed septic tank system.

"snake" is a long, thin, steel band with a heavy point at one end. The steel band is very flexible and can be worked around bends until the point comes in contact with the obstruction in the pipe. By working the snake back and forth, the object in the pipe is either pushed through the pipe or is broken up into pieces small enough to be carried away by the water. A plumber's snake can be rented from hardware and plumbing stores. In a poorly installed

Copper sulphate, poured down the fixture drains, will kill the roots but not necessarily remove them completely. A plumber's snake can be used to clear the roots out of the pipe, but this requires considerable effort, especially when the roots are large and densely packed in the pipe. Plumbers use a powered rotor with a flexible shaft inserted into the pipe, and this will clear the pipe effectively. These are temporary measures, however, for the roots will come back into the pipe. Special sewer pipes are available, which are so constructed that roots cannot penetrate the pipe joints. When a sewer line is repeatedly attacked by tree roots, the only lasting remedy is to dig it up and have this type of pipe installed.

Caustic soda is often used to clean fixture drains. This is not a good practice, for the chemical will cause the grease inside the pipes to harden. After a period of years, the sewer line will be so coated with this hard grease that it cannot handle the volume of water required. Removing hard grease with a snake is a very difficult undertaking.

Outside sewer pipes will fail to operate properly if there is too much or too little pitch to the pipes. While the complete drainage of a pipe depends upon a full charge of water to carry the solid matter through, too much pitch will cause an accumulation of solids at the pipe joints, eventually forming a blockage. To rectify this condition, the pipes should be removed and put down at the right pitch.

CLOGGED DRAINS

In attempting to clear a stopped-up line, use a device called the "plumber's friend." This is a piece of equipment that no home mechanic should be without. It consists of a rubber, bell-shaped cup on the end of a long wood handle. To use this plunger, partially fill the fixture with water and place the rubber cup over the drain opening. Work the

plunger up and down, and the resulting alternate compression and suction will generally dislodge any object caught in the drain. If there

PLUMBER'S FRIEND

Fig. 11.

is no water in the fixture, the plunger will not work, because water must be present to make an airtight seal around the drain. Be sure to give the "plumber's friend" a fair chance before you resort to some other method of trying to clear a drain. Once the drain is clean, flush hot water through it to clear it completely.

Cleaning Trap. If the drain cannot be cleared with the rubber plunger, it may be possible to get rid of the obstruction by removing the clean-out plug at the bottom of the trap and using a piece of wire to push the obstruction out or pull it back through the opening. Place a

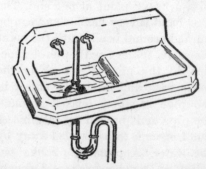

Fig. 12. How to clear a stopped-up fixture drain with a "plumber's friend."

pail under the trap to prevent the water that is in the trap from splashing the floor. Remove the plug carefully so that the water will pour into the bucket. You will need an adjustable wrench to loosen the plug. If the plug is plated, put a piece of cloth around it to prevent the wrench from damaging the plating. Once the plug is out, try to dislodge the obstruction in the pipe with a piece of stiff wire. If this method fails to do any good, you can remove the entire trap by unscrewing the slip nuts located at the top and bottom connections of the trap. When these two nuts have been loosened and moved out of the way, take off the trap and push out the obstructions. While the trap is off, clean it thoroughly inside with a stiff brush and hot water.

Clearing Beyond Trap. If the object blocking the pipe is beyond the trap, use a steel spring auger. This resembles a snake in that it is flexible and can be inserted in the pipe.

SPRING STEEL AUGER

Fig. 13.

The auger can be rotated, and this action will either break up whatever is clogging the pipes, or the auger bit will pierce the obstacle so that it can be pulled out of the pipe.

Before replacing the clean-out plug of the trap, examine the washer to be sure it has not been damaged. Any leakage around this plug will cause the trap to run dry.

Chemical Cleaners. Chemical drain cleaners can be used to clear a pipe when it is impossible to get at the obstruction with a plunger or a steel spring auger. The best chemical for this work is caustic potash, but it is very strong and should be used with a great deal of caution.

Remove as much water as possible from the fixture and the drain so that the chemical will not be diluted. Mix the caustic potash, according to the directions on the container, with hot water. Be very careful not to let any of this solution touch any part of the body, particularly the eyes. To avoid damaging metal fixtures, pour the solution into the drain through a funnel. Do not expect any immediate effect from a chemical drain cleaner. The chemical must burn through whatever has clogged up the pipe, and this action may require several hours at least. Do not pour any water down the drain until the chemical has had ample time to work. After sufficient time has elapsed, say overnight, flush the drain with boiling water.

When caustic potash comes in contact with grease, it converts the grease into a substance soluble in water. Some types of drain cleaners contain caustic soda, but this chemical turns grease into hard matter that cannot be easily removed. Chemical cleaners should be used only in the drainage system—never in any fresh water supply lines. Gasoline and coffee grounds should not be used as drain cleaners. They will not do any good, and gasoline in a drain may cause an explosion if the fumes are accidently ignited.

Clogged Toilet Traps. The construction of the modern toilet bowl makes it very difficult to remove any object caught in the trap, particularly since the object is usually large or made of metal.

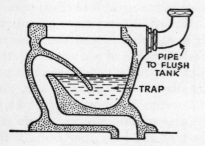

Fig. 14. Cross section of a toilet flush bowl.

To clean the trap, try first the "plumber's friend." If this fails, work a piece of stiff wire into the trap and attempt to dislodge the obstruction so that it can be pulled or pushed through. A steel spring auger is a very effective means of clearing toilet traps, particularly when there are two persons present, one to turn the auger while the other guides it down into the trap.

Floor Drains. Floor drains such as are used in basements and garages to drain off water very often become clogged up with various refuse which is almost bound to get past the strainer over the pipe opening. These drains should be kept as clean as possible because once they are blocked up and the water floods the floor, cleaning them out is a messy proposition.

In most cases the strainer over the drain opening is attached to the drain flange with screws, but in many cases these screws or the edge of the strainer may be covered with cement from the surrounding floor. This cement will have to be chipped away with a cold chisel or an old screwdriver before the strainer can be taken off.

Once the strainer is out of the way, the drain can usually be partially cleaned with the aid of a long handled ladle or large cooking spoon. Dig out as much of the dirt and refuse as possible with the spoon and then use a steel auger or a piece of heavy wire to clear any obstructions in the pipe. Floor drains connected into the house sewer system will be provided with some sort of trap. Once the drain is open, use hot water to flush it

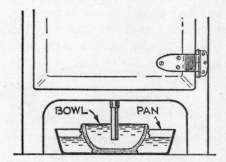

Fig. 14a. Ice box drain. This method keeps warm air from entering box. Pipe end extends below water surface in bowl. Overflow enters pan. You can connect pan to plumbing with length of pipe. Include a trap in the connection also.

clean, probing with the wire to loosen up any dirt that might be sticking to the sides of the pipe. Soften grease with caustic potash.

If the strainer over the drain has rather large openings, it might be worth while to cover it with a piece of wire netting before it is replaced in order to prevent large particles of dirt and other matter getting through.

PLUMBING TRAPS

Every plumbing fixture is provided with a trap to prevent sewer gas from coming through the drain pipes. A trap is a very simple device that allows drainage but effectively keeps out gas. Most often, these traps consist of an S-shaped piece of pipe connected to the drain directly under the fixture. A small

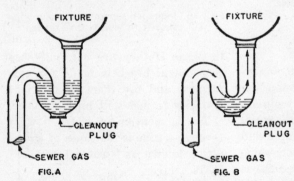

Fig. 15. The water in trap A makes an effective barrier to the passage of sewer gas. In trap B the water level is not high enough and sewer gas can flow up through the fixture drain.

amount of water remains in the low portion of the S, and this water forms a barrier to the passage of sewer gas.

So long as there is sufficient water in the trap, no gas can enter; but water in the trap of a fixture seldom used will evaporate, breaking the seal and allowing gas to escape through the fixture drain. Pour water occasionally down the drain of fixtures not in constant use, so that the trap will always be effective.

A trap can go dry for other reasons besides evaporation. An improperly installed plumbing system can cause water to be siphoned out of the trap. If a trap goes dry for no apparent reason, a plumber should be consulted immediately. Examine the washer around the clean-out plug of the trap, however. If it is worn, it can cause the trap to go dry, and replacing it is a task for the home mechanic.

There are many kinds of traps, some more effective than others. The less complicated ones are satisfactory until the sewer gas behind them builds up so much pressure that it can force its way out in spite of the seal of water. This condition can be due to the vent stacks of the sewer lines not working correctly.

Other than the traps located under each fixture, there is generally a main trap located in the sewer line in the basement.

Drum Traps. Bathtubs, showers and other plumbing fixtures located close to or at floor level are usually provided with a drum type trap. This trap is located a short distance from the fixture and the trap body is below floor level. A removable lid is exposed, flush with the bathroom floor, and can be unscrewed with a monkey wrench. When the lid is replaced, after the trap has been cleaned or a stoppage in the pipe removed, it is a good idea to put some grease on the threads of the lid to make a tight seal and prevent gas from working up around the fitting.

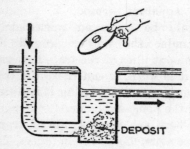

Fig. 15a. Drum trap often used for bathtubs and shower fixtures.

is opened, water flows through the entire branch of the system of which the faucet is a part. When the faucet is closed, the momentum of the water will cause a loose section of pipe to vibrate. This vibration soon can cause joints to leak. Make certain that all pipes are held securely

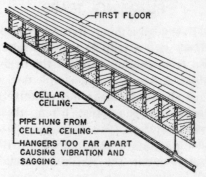

Fig. 16. Improper support for water pipe will cause it to vibrate and rattle.

NOISY PLUMBING

There is nothing quite so annoying as the rumbling and pounding that is characteristic of many plumbing systems. In most cases, the cause of the noise is relatively simple and can be repaired by the home mechanic. In a few cases, the noise is due to faulty installation of the system and will have to be corrected by a plumber.

Causes. A faucet that pounds when it is opened usually does so because of a loose part inside. This can be easily repaired by replacing the washer with a new one (see FAUCETS), or by tightening the loose screw or nut inside the faucet.

Chattering in the pipes can be caused by overhead pipes not secured to the ceiling. When a faucet

in place. If they are not, purchase some metal brackets made for this purpose and use them in sufficient quantity to make all piping secure.

The momentum of water flowing through a pipe is the cause of a condition known as "water hammer." This will cause a chattering and pounding in the system when a faucet is closed. It can be corrected by having a plumber insert a short

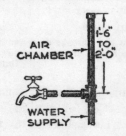

Fig. 17. "Water hammer" can be eliminated by a length of pipe which acts as a shock absorber.

section of pipe in the system which will act as a shock absorber.

Hot Water System. Noises in the hot water system are more frequent than in the cold water lines, and they can be due to several factors. A rumble in the hot water tank is generally caused by the water's having been overheated so that it forms steam in the tank. The remedy for this condition is not to let the water get too hot. For household purposes, the temperature should be somewhere between 130 and 140 degrees F.; never so high that the water will boil.

Another common cause of noise in the hot water supply tank is faulty installation of the pipes between the heater and the tank. The water passing through the heating coil gives off steam, which tries to force its way through the coil and into the tank. If the hot line from the coil to the heater slopes upward, the steam has a free passage into the tank. If, however, the pipe is horizontal, or on a downward slope, the water in the line will impede the progress of the steam, causing noise in the line. To remedy this condition, it is necessary to change the position of the hot pipe so that it slopes upward from the heating coil to the tank.

LEAKY HOT WATER TANK

There are several methods of stopping a leak in a hot water tank, the one used depending on the size of the opening. It should be remembered, however, that a tank that has rusted through in many spots or has opened up at the seams cannot be readily patched by the home mechanic. In most cases, it is cheaper to purchase a new tank than to repair an old one in such poor condition that it will require constant attention. Large leaks and open seams require welding, or other methods of repair, that the home mechanic does not have the equipment to undertake.

Repairs. Small, pin point leaks in a tank can often be stopped by pointing a thin piece of wood, such as a toothpick, and driving it into the opening. The water inside the tank will cause the wood to expand, and it will form a tight but not permanent plug.

A more efficient means of stopping a leak is to use a toggle bolt. This bolt can be obtained at hardware stores, and the size and exact type will depend on the leak to be filled. Drain the water in the tank below the level of the leak. Close the inlet valve so that the tank will not fill up while you are working. If the leak is at the bottom of the tank, turn off the heater. Use a hand drill to drill the hole in which the toggle bolt is inserted.

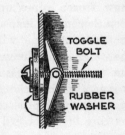

Fig. 18. Toggle bolt and washer used to repair a leak in hot water storage tank.

Make the hole large enough for the toggle bolt to slip through. After the hole has been made, insert the toggle bolt so that the wings attached to the end of the bolt will open on the inside of the tank. Have the washer on the outside of the tank. Tighten the bolt carefully, so that the washer is pulled tight against the side of the tank and covers the hole. Do not try to tighten the bolt too much or it may break. The washer used with the toggle bolt must be the type made to withstand hot water. Any other type will not last very long. After the toggle bolt is in place, fill the tank with water and see whether there is any leakage around the washer.

There are several patented devices on the market which may be used for stopping up leaks in tanks. In principle, they are all more or less similar to the toggle bolt and washer and, in most cases, will give good results.

FROZEN PIPES

No attempt should be made to thaw frozen pipes until they have been thoroughly inspected for cracks or splits. A pipe will crack when the water inside freezes—not during the thawing process. If there are any cracks, they should be repaired or a section of pipe replaced before thawing begins. Until the necessary repairs have been made on a cracked pipe, keep it shut off from the water supply and no great amount of damage will be done if it thaws unaided.

The fact that the water inside a pipe is frozen does not necessarily mean that the pipe has split, but it is best to assume that the pipe is defective until proven otherwise by a close inspection.

If the pipe appears to be sound, open all faucets connected to it. This is done to decrease the pressure in the line, should there be an opening undetected. Thawing should begin at the point nearest a faucet, to allow the water to run out.

Heating. There are various ways of applying heat to the frozen pipe. Bath towels, dipped in hot water and applied to the pipe, are an efficient and safe means of thawing, if there are no decorations or painted woodwork that might be damaged.

A blowtorch can also be used, provided there are no inflammable objects about. Play the blow torch back and forth along the length of pipe, and avoid concentrating too much heat at one point.

It is possible to use electric heating pads, but this is not recommended because all the conditions for a dangerous electric shock are present. If electric pads are employed, they should be insulated from the pipe with insulation material, and care should be taken not to touch either the heater or the pipe while the current is on.

Frozen drain pipes can be thawed by pouring hot water down the drain or by using chemicals which generate heat inside the pipe. Pour the chemicals down a drain in the same manner as chemical drain cleaners. A very good method of thawing drain lines is to insert a length of small-diameter rubber tubing into the pipe until the end comes in contact with the ice. Attach the other end of the tubing to the spout of a tea kettle containing boiling water. The steam from the kettle will flow through the tubing and soon melt the ice.

CLOGGED WATER PIPES

Water pipes will become clogged by the accumulation of minerals found in most water. Given sufficient time, this mineral deposit will reduce the flow of water to such a degree as to impair the efficiency of the entire plumbing system.

Galvanized steel pipe is especially vulnerable to this condition because the rough interior of the pipe provides a surface to which the minerals cling; see

Fig. 19.

Fig. 19. A galvanized pipe that is lined with minerals must be replaced, for there is no effective way to remove the deposit. Brass pipe is less affected by these minerals, due to its smooth interior. When brass pipe does become lined, the sections of pipe can be taken apart and the minerals reamed out, if the lining is not too thick.

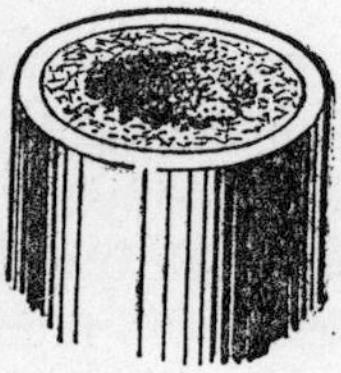

Minerals often collect on the coils of the hot water heater and in the space between the heater and tank. Some of these minerals are impossible to remove effectively, but limestone, which is the most common, can be taken out of the pipes without much trouble.

To do this, remove the coil or water back from the fire box of the furnace or stove. This will require a stilson wrench. Some of the mineral deposit can be removed by tapping along the surface of the heating element with a hammer and flushing with water. After this has been done, pour a solution of 1 part muriatic acid to 8 parts water into the water back or through the coil, and use a funnel to avoid spilling the liquid. Plug the bottom of the coil before pouring in this solution. Take care not to splash the hands, face, or clothes with it. Muriatic acid is strong as well as poisonous. If possible, heat the element with the acid solution inside, as this will quicken the action of the acid on the mineral deposits. If this cannot be done, let the solution remain in the coil or water back for an hour or more, then pour it out. Several treatments may be necessary if the deposit is very heavy.

After removing as much of the deposit as is possible, flush the inside of the heating element with fresh water several times, to remove all traces of the acid. Brass pipe can be cleaned in a similar manner, or the deposits can be reamed out. Galvanized pipe, due to its rough interior, does not clean readily and can be replaced at moderate cost.

HARD WATER

The amount of minerals in the water will vary according to the source. Some water is extremely hard, and soap will not lather in it.

Special equipment, called water softeners, can be installed in the home plumbing system to soften the water for domestic use. Briefly, this equipment consists of a storage tank, containing various chemicals, attached to the fresh water supply line. After the water has passed through the tank, it is soft and safe, as well, for drinking and cooking purposes. In some tanks the chemicals must be replaced from time to time, while others require no refilling. Another type of filter removes the iron content from drinking water.

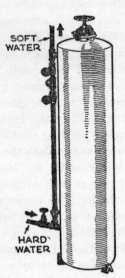

Fig. 20. Type of water softener used in the home.

FAUCETS

There are two kinds of faucets commonly found in the home plumbing system, the compression faucet and the Fuller faucet. The compression faucet is the more widely used, as it stands up better under the high-pressure water system in use today.

Compression Faucet. The compression faucet controls the flow of water by compressing a fiber washer down onto a valve seat when a threaded spindle is turned. This arrangement enables the compression faucet to control the flow of water easily, even though the pressure of the water is considerable.

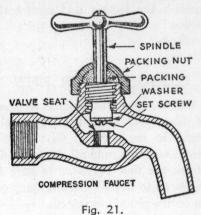

Fig. 21.

Replacing Washer. The most common reason for a compression faucet's dripping water, after it has been tightly closed, is that the washer inside the faucet has become worn, and no longer fits tightly on top of the valve seat. A package of assorted washers should be kept in the tool

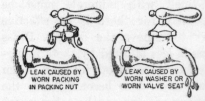

Fig. 22. Two common causes of leaking faucets.

kit for just such repairs. In selecting washers, be sure to obtain the kind that can be used on both hot and cold water faucets. These are made of fiber, for a leather washer will not long endure hot water.

To replace the washer, close the nearest shut-off valve to the fixture.

If the shut-off valve controlling this particular faucet cannot be located, close the main shut-off valve. Using an adjustable wrench, remove the large packing nut on top of the faucet body under the handle. Place a piece of cloth between the jaws of the wrench and the nut to avoid scarring the finish. After the nut is off the body of the faucet, remove the entire spindle from the faucet by turning the handle counterclockwise. The threaded spindle will unscrew from the faucet and can be lifted out. The washer is located on the far end of the spindle. Take out the set screw holding the washer with a screwdriver. Often, this set screw is so rusted that it cannot be easily removed. In this case, put a drop of light oil around the screw head and allow a short time for the oil to penetrate. If the screw is badly rusted, replace it with a new one before putting the faucet together.

Select a new washer of the right size and secure it to the spindle with the set screw. Be sure that the set screw is tight. Put the spindle back into the body of the faucet and turn the handle clockwise, as if to close the faucet. Run down the packing nut and tighten it sufficiently to prevent water from coming through the packing inside the cap.

Worn Valve Seats. Sometimes the cause of a leaky compression faucet is the valve seat inside the faucet. If this valve seat has been nicked by a worn washer or by the careless dropping of a tool upon it, the washer will not sit tightly and a leak will result. Check valve seats for signs of roughness each time you put on a new washer. A special valve seat dressing tool can be purchased for filing down the valve seat until it is smooth. After the seat has been

VALVE SEAT
DRESSING TOOL

Fig. 23.

smoothed, flush all loose bits of metal out of the faucet before replacing the spindle. If, after dressing down the valve seat and replacing the washer the faucet continues to leak, it can be assumed that the faucet must be replaced.

The Packing Nut. Another point of leakage is around the stem, when the faucet is open. Such leakage will occur when the packing nut is not tight enough or when the packing or packing washer inside the cap becomes worn. Tighten the nut first, giving it a slight turn and checking to see whether the faucet still turns easily. If this fails to do any good, the packing washer should be replaced. Unscrew the set screw that holds the handle to the spindle and slip the handle off. The packing nut can then be taken off the spindle for repacking.

Fuller Faucets. The Fuller faucet is designed for quick opening and closing and is so constructed that only a small movement of the handle is necessary. The washer used in this faucet is a small ball made of hard rubber or a type of composition. It is attached to the handle of the faucet by means of an eccentric spindle or cam that pulls the rubber ball against the valve seat when the faucet is closed and pushes it away from the valve seat when the handle is in the open position.

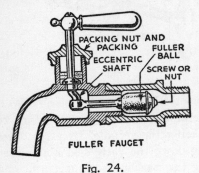

Fig. 24.

Replacing The Ball. To repair a leak in a Fuller faucet, you must remove the entire faucet from the pipe so that the ball washer can be taken out. Turn off the water line to the faucet and remove the faucet with a stilson wrench. Once the faucet is off, you can remove the ball valve in the back of the faucet. This ball is held in place by a screw or nut. Move the handle of the faucet to the open position and the ball will be forced to the rear, where it can be easily detached from the rod connecting it to the eccentric spindle. Obtain a new Fuller ball valve from a hardware or plumbing store, and it is important to get one of good quality and the same size as the old ball valve. After the new ball has been attached to the rod, make sure that the ball is brought against the valve seat when the handle is

turned to the closed position. If there is any clearance, it can be taken up by tightening the screw or nut holding the ball to the rod.

A Fuller faucet will leak if the eccentric shaft has become worn and no longer brings the ball valve into the correct position. If this condition exists, the eccentric will have to be replaced.

Shower Mixing Valves. In many homes equipped with shower baths, separate compression faucets are provided in the shower fixture to control the hot and cold water to the spray. This arrangement is not satisfactory for several reasons. First of all, if the pressure in the cold water line should suddenly drop, the person taking the shower might get scalded. A bad scald can also be due to accidentally turning a faucet in the wrong direction.

Fig. 24a. A special shower mixing valve will eliminate any danger of scalding by overheated hot water.

There are special shower mixing valves designed to prevent any possibility of scalding hot water coming out of the shower spray. If a shower is not equipped with a safety mixing valve of this type, then special effort should be made to keep the temperature of the hot water in the plumbing system under 140 degrees F.

LEAKY FLUSH TANKS

Before attempting to repair a toilet tank which leaks, it is necessary to understand how the water enters the tank and how it is regulated so that the tank will not overflow.

Operation. Water enters the tank of the water inside the tank. As the water rises in the tank, the float rises with it until, at a predetermined point, the inlet valve is closed by the action of the rod attached to the float. The flow of water into the tank is thus stopped.

The handle on the outside of the tank is connected by wire rods to a rubber flush valve which fits over the opening at the bottom of the tank. This opening is connected to the toilet bowl by a section of pipe. When the flush valve is lifted from the valve seat by turning the handle, water rushes out of the tank into

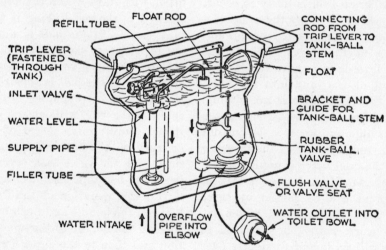

Fig. 25. Toilet flush tank.

through an opening fitted with a valve. This valve has a washer, so that it will completely stop the flow of water when the valve is closed. The opening and closing of this inlet valve is governed by the copper or glass float which is connected to the valve by means of a rod. The float is airtight and rests on the surface the toilet bowl. As the water level in the tank drops, the float drops with it, and this action opens the inlet valve so that water can flow back into the tank. As soon as the handle on the outside of the tank is returned to its normal position, the flush valve drops over the valve seat to prevent any more water from flowing from the tank into the bowl. The tank then fills with water until the inlet valve is closed by the float's reaching a set height.

An overflow pipe inside the tank allows water to flow into the bowl, should the inlet valve fail to close at the proper time.

Keep in mind that all the mechanism inside the tank is delicate and can be thrown out of adjustment rather easily. Make sure that all the rods are working correctly before you begin replacing valves and washers.

There are several places inside the tank where a leak is likely to occur. It is possible to locate the cause of a leaky tank by removing the top and looking at the water level. If the water level is low and water is flowing out of the tank into the toilet bowl, the flush valve is not closing. If the level of the water inside the tank is high and water is flowing out of the tank by way of the overflow pipe, the inlet valve is not closing.

Leak At Flush Valve. A leak at this point can be caused by three conditions. A flush ball which becomes worn, rotten, or distorted in shape will no longer fit tightly over the valve seat. Rust or dirt on the valve seat will also prevent the ball from fitting evenly. The third condition occurs when the thin metal rods which connect the flush ball with the tank handle become bent or bind, and the ball cannot drop back over the valve seat.

To find which part of the system is at fault and to make the necessary repairs, you will have to shut off the water supply. Most tanks have a small valve located on the pipe running from the bottom of the tank through the floor. This is the supply line to the tank, and when this valve is closed no water will be able to enter the tank. If the tank does not have this valve, shut off the water by closing the right branch valve in the house plumbing system or by lifting the copper float inside the tank, and propping it to hold the inlet valve in a closed position.

Once the water has been shut off, you can remove the flush ball and examine it for wear. This ball is fitted with threads at the top and screwed to the rod linking it to the tank handle. If the ball is worn or out of shape, it should be replaced.

Check the flush valve seat for dirt or rust after the ball is removed. If it appears to be rough, smooth it by rubbing the rim with emery cloth. Remove any sizable pieces of scale or rust with an old knife. After smoothing the valve seat, screw the new flush ball to the connecting rod.

Test the operation of the linkage between the handle and flush ball by turning the handle to the open position and then to the close. The ball should drop on the valve seat when the handle swings closed. If it fails to do this, examine the rods to see if they are bent. The lower rod attached to the flush ball is held in place by a metal guide arm connected to the overflow pipe. This guide arm is adjustable and should be positioned so that it is directly over the valve seat. If it is out of adjustment, the flush ball will not line up properly on the valve seat. If any metal rod is badly rusted it should be replaced, for a corroded rod will not long maintain its shape.

Leak At Inlet Valve. A leak due to failure of the inlet valve to close can also be caused by several factors.

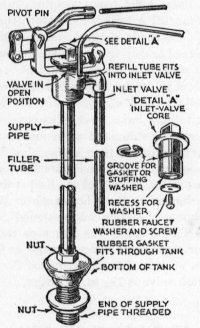

PIVOT PIN

SEE DETAIL "A"

REFILL TUBE FITS INTO INLET VALVE

VALVE IN OPEN POSITION

INLET VALVE

DETAIL "A" INLET-VALVE CORE

SUPPLY PIPE

FILLER TUBE

GROOVE FOR GASKET OR STUFFING WASHER

RECESS FOR WASHER

RUBBER FAUCET WASHER AND SCREW

NUT

RUBBER GASKET FITS THROUGH TANK

BOTTOM OF TANK

NUT

END OF SUPPLY PIPE THREADED

Fig. 26. Detail of inlet valve.

It may be due to a worn valve washer or a rough valve seat. If the rod connecting the float to the inlet valve were bent out of shape, it would cause the valve to remain open, as would a leak in the copper float.

To replace a worn inlet washer, shut off the water from the tank before disassembling the inlet valve. In some tanks this valve is located near the top of the tank, while in others it will be found at the bottom.

If the latter, you will have to flush all the water out of the tank to get at the valve. The plunger of the valve is held in place by thumb screws which will probably have to be started with the aid of pliers. The washer is held in place by a nut and a brass ring cap. The ring cap may be so rusted that it will break while it is being removed. If this occurs, you will need a new cap as well as a new washer. While the valve is disassambled, check the valve seat to be sure that it is not rough or nicked.

A copper float which contains water will not rise high enough to shut off the inlet valve. You can solder a small leak in the float after draining the water out of it, but replace a float which has a bad leak.

The rod connecting the float to the valve has a great deal to do with how much water flows into the tank before the valve is closed. If the rod is bent upward, the level of water in the tank will be higher. If the rod is bent down, the water level will be lower. When a tank that is otherwise working correctly fails to deliver enough water to the toilet bowl, it is likely that the rod is bent out of shape. This takes only a moment to repair. The water level in the tank should be almost to the top of the overflow pipe. If it is too far under this point, the toilet bowl will not be flushed properly.

Condensation on Tanks. A source of constant annoyance in many homes is moisture dripping off the sides of the toilet flush tank and onto the bathroom floor. This is usually a year around affair and can, in time, ruin the flooring and damage the ceiling below. A common cause of the trouble is due to the fact that the sides of the flush tank are kept at a low temperature by the fresh water entering the tank each time the toilet is flushed. This is especially the case if the fresh water supply comes from a deep well. As the air in every bathroom has a high moisture content, there is bound to be considerable condensation on the sides of the tank.

One remedy is to cover the tank with cold-water pipe insulation and to cover this, in turn, with linoleum, sheet plastic, or other material for the sake of appearance.

One homeowner solved the problem by running a hot-water line to the tank and connecting this to the inlet line. A gate valve was installed on the cold-water line and this was adjusted so that the temperature of the water in the tank remained between 70 and 90 degrees F. A check valve was also installed on the hot-water line to prevent cold water from backing into it. While the cost in materials and labor for such a job might be somewhat high, many housekeepers would gladly pay the price to get rid of this problem.

Another method is to install a small enameled pan under the tank and connect it to bowl by a short rubber hose. Water from tank drips onto pan and runs into bowl. Such drip pans are sold in plumbing shops.

Cracks in Toilet Bowls and Flush Tanks. There is no sure way to seal a crack in a toilet bowl. Cracks in flush tanks can be mended by draining out all the water, letting entire inside get perfectly dry, and then coating it with roofing compound.

FLUSH VALVES

Some toilet bowls are flushed by means of a flush valve rather than a flush tank. A flush valve is designed to deliver a measured amount of water into the toilet bowl at very short intervals. This makes it an excellent piece of equipment for institutions, but a flush valve requires a greater volume of water and more water pressure than is furnished by most home plumbing systems. Consequently, the use of the flush valve is limited to those homes where the plumbing system was designed for this equipment. The size pipe used for most home water systems is $\frac{3}{4}$ in. or 1 in. The size required for a flush valve is $1\frac{1}{4}$ in. or larger.

REMOVING TOILET BOWL

This work is not often necessary, but sometimes it must be done to put in a new bathroom floor or clear a stoppage in the bowl.

The first step is to pump and sponge all the water out of the bowl and trap. It is best to shut off the water supply into the tank and have the flush tank empty, so that there will be no leakage of water to the floor. Next, disconnect the pipe from the tank to the bowl. Inspect the packing at the connections to bowl and tank and replace it if it is worn.

The bowl is fastened to the floor with bolts which pierce the closet floor flange. This flange is attached to the sewer pipe. The nuts for these bolts may be covered with porcelain caps held in place with plaster of Paris or putty. Insert a sharp knife under the cap and gently tap or pry up the cap very carefully until it is loose. Once the caps are off, remove the putty or plaster of Paris and unscrew the nuts. To free the bowl from the floor flange, jar it slightly with the hands. This will break the putty seal between the bowl and the flange. Now the bowl can be lifted up and put where it will be out of the way. Clean all the old putty from the flange and around the base of the bowl. In some cases, the joint between bowl and floor flange is sealed with a gasket. Cover the opening in the floor so that nothing can fall into the sewer pipe.

About three pounds of a special putty will be required to seal the joint when the bowl is replaced. If the joint was sealed with a gasket, it is better to use a new one than to take a chance with the old one. Gaskets will make tighter seals.

Tighten the nuts, making sure that the bowl sits level. After the nuts have been tightened, remove the excess putty from along the edge of the bowl and connect the pipe to the tank. If there is any sign of a leak at the joint between the bowl and floor flange, you should remove the bowl and reseal the joint with a new application of putty.

Handle the bowl with care, as it cracks or chips easily.

LEAKY PIPES

The best method of dealing with a leaky piece of pipe is to replace it with a new section. The fact remains, however, that pipes always seem to spring a leak when it is virtually impossible to locate a plumber or the necessary pipe and tools to do the job yourself. A situation like this calls for some sort of temporary measure; otherwise, the entire plumbing system, or at least a portion of it, will have to be closed down until the leak can be repaired.

A small leak in a section of pipe can sometimes be repaired by using a nail punch and hammer to force the metal around the leak to cover the opening. This will work very well on lead because it is an extremely soft metal.

To stop a leak in a section of galvanized or brass pipe, split a section of garden hose along one side so

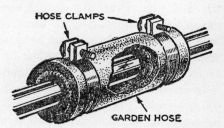

Fig. 27. A section of garden hose and two hose clamps make an efficient patch for a leak in a water pipe.

that is can be fitted over the pipe where the leak occurs. Hold the piece securely in place with adjustable hose clamps, such as are used for the radiator connections on automobiles, or by a piece of wire wrapped around each end of the hose and pulled tight before the ends are entwined.

If the break is too large to be repaired with a patch or even several patches, a length of garden hose can be sometimes used. This entails removing the damaged sections of pipe and substituting the garden hose until a new length of iron pipe can be installed.

DRAINING PLUMBING

One of the most important steps in closing a house during the winter, if only for a short period, is draining the plumbing system. The entire system must be drained and prepared to preclude any possibility of a pipe's freezing and breaking, with consequent damage to decorations and furniture. Many owners of summer homes have returned after the winter months to find extensive damage caused by water from a cracked pipe. Plumbing should also be drained immediately if there is any breakdown of the home heating system during freezing weather.

Drain the plumbing system thoroughly. If one pipe is left undrained, it can cause great damage; consequently, it is recommended that a check list be used when draining the system. This list should include each branch line and plumbing fixture of the system. By checking off each portion of the system as it is drained, the home mechanic can be sure that he has completely emptied the system. Use the list, as well, for reference when putting the system back into service.

Close Water Supply. The first step in draining the system is to shut off the water supply to the house. If this supply is furnished by a city water main, there is a valve located on the service line between the house and the water main. This valve is underground, below the frost line. A concrete curb box, fitted with a removable top, covers the valve. Remove the top of the curb box and use a long rod with a key at the end to turn off the valve. This key can be obtained from a plumber or from the local water authorities. After the curb valve has been closed, close the main shut-off valve inside the house. This valve should be fitted with a small drain cock to drain the valve and connecting pipe. Do not open this drain cock until the rest of the system has been emptied, or all the water remaining in the system will flow through the opening.

Hot Water System. Open all faucets after you have shut off the water supply at the curb valve and main shut-off valve. This will drain the water out of the pipes to the level of the lowest fixture. With the faucets open, drain the hot water tank. Be sure that the hot water heater is out. Faucets must be kept open when draining the tank, or a partial vacuum will form inside the tank and prevent complete drainage. Drain the hot water tank by means of the valve located at the bottom of the tank. You will have to dispose of the water issuing from the tank, and you can do so by connecting a length of garden hose to the valve so that the water flows out of the basement or by having a few pails on hand. Remove all the water from the coils of the water heater. It may be necessary to remove a section of pipe and use air pressure to blow the water completely out of the coils.

Cold Water Supply. With the hot water system completely drained, move on to the cold water supply. If the shut-off valve inside the house is provided with a drain cock, the system is easily drained. With all faucets opened, open the drain cock and allow the water to flow into buckets. If there is no drain cock, it will be necessary to disconnect a section of pipe at the lowest point in the system. You will need a stilson wrench for this. Have the faucets on the line closed while the pipes are being disconnected, to prevent a minor flood. After the pipes are apart, place a bucket under the break and open the faucets.

Make a careful check of any horizontal sections of pipe to be sure that there is sufficient pitch to the pipe for drainage. If water remains in a horizontal section, you will have to disconnect a section of pipe and force the water out of the line with air pressure.

It is not necessary to drain the plumbing system when closing a house for the summer, but the main shut-off valve should be closed to

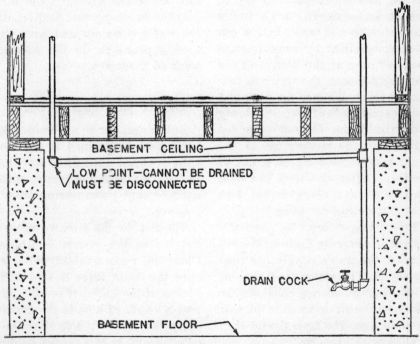

BASEMENT CEILING

LOW POINT—CANNOT BE DRAINED
MUST BE DISCONNECTED

DRAIN COCK

BASEMENT FLOOR

Fig. 28. When draining the plumbing system, watch out for low points in a horizontal run of pipe. The pipe must be disconnected so that the water can be completely drained.

prevent any loss of water through leaky faucets.

Pumping System. If the house is supplied with water by means of a pump and pressure tank, great care should be taken to remove all the water from pump, tank, and connecting lines. There is a special valve at the end of the pipe running from the pump to the well or spring. This valve prevents water from draining out of the pipe into the well and must be forced open to empty this section of pipe.

PREPARING TRAPS

The traps for all fixtures should be drained and filled with some nonfreezing and nonevaporating liquid, such as kerosene. The traps under kitchen sinks and wash basins can be easily drained by removing the clean-out plug at the bottom of the trap and allowing the water to flow into a bucket. Replace the plug and pour several pints of kerozene slowly down the drain. Do not pour too rapidly, or the momentum of the liquid may force some of it out of the trap. After the trap has been filled, see that there is no leak around the clean-out plug.

Toilet traps can be partially cleared of water by flushing the toilet after the water supply has been turned off. The water that remains at the bottom of the bowl can be bailed out with a small container and a sponge. The trap should then be filled with kerosene.

Bathtub traps are difficult to get at unless there is an opening at the floor level. A good way to fill any bathtub trap is to slowly pour kerosene a few inches from the drain in the tub; the kerosene will flow into the trap and replace any water there. The main trap in the basement can be filled with kerosene by pouring a considerable quantity down a fixture located near the main trap. The kerosene will flow into the trap and replace the water as it did in the bathtub trap.

It is very important to fill a trap with kerosene after it has been drained. If this is not done, sewer gas can enter the house.

Water meters are sealed by the water company to prevent tampering with them. If there is no provision made for draining the meter without breaking this seal, contact the water company and have them send someone to do the necessary work on the meter.

DRAIN HEATING SYSTEM

Steam and hot water heating systems must be drained if the house is to be closed during the winter, or if, for any reason, the heating system must be shut down during freezing weather.

The fire in the furnace must be out before the system is drained. Close the main shut-off valve and open the drain valve located at the bottom of the boiler. If possible, connect a length of hose to the drain to carry the water to a floor drain or out-of-doors. If this cannot be done, have buckets on hand. Open the water supply valve to drain this line to the boiler. Open all the valves on the radiators in order to drain them and their connecting lines. This must also be done on a steam system, as there will be some moisture in the radiators from the condensed steam.

TURNING ON WATER

When the time comes to turn on the water, refer to the check list made when draining the system.

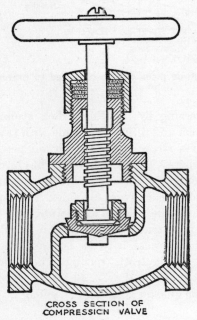

CROSS SECTION OF
COMPRESSION VALVE

Fig. 29.

Check the entire plumbing carefully to be sure that everything has been connected and that all the pipes are sound. Close all the branch valves and open the main valve and curb valve. If the system appears to be in good condition, open one branch valve at a time. Make certain that each branch line is in good working order before opening another valve. Do this carefully and there should be no difficulty. Do not open valves until you are sure that the system is performing satisfactory.

TYPES OF PIPE

Probably the most common kind of piping used in the home is galvanized steel. This pipe is rust and acid resistant and it is inexpensive, but it will eventually rust and have to be replaced. Also the inside of the pipe is extremely rough and provides an excellent surface to which minerals can cling. As there is no practical method of removing these minerals, new pipe will have to be installed.

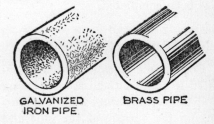

GALVANIZED
IRON PIPE

BRASS PIPE

Fig. 30. One of the advantages of brass or copper pipe is that the smooth interior discourages minerals from collecting on the inside and reducing the flow of water. Note the rough interior of the galvanized iron pipe.

Brass pipe has several advantages over galvanized steel. A brass plumbing system should last as long as the house, since brass will not rust and effectively resists corrosion by acid. The inside of brass pipe is smooth, and this smooth surface reduces the friction of water flowing through the pipe. Thus, a greater volume of water can flow through a brass pipe than through a galvanized pipe of the same diameter. This advantage should be taken into consideration when replacing galvanized pipe, for while the brass pipe is more expensive, a smaller size can be used.

Copper tubing is well suited to interior plumbing when it would be difficult or too expensive to install rigid piping. Copper tubing can be bent enough to run through partitions and around beams. It is often used as a replacement for galvanized pipe or for installing a plumbing system in a house after the house has been completed.

INSULATE COLD PIPES

Cold water lines should be insulated to protect them from freezing and to keep moisture from condensing on the outside of the pipe and dripping on the floors. The type of insulation used for this work is made of hair felt and asphalt.

contractor, plumber, or gardener, can give you this information.

Pipes that are exposed to the weather but cannot be put underground, may be protected from

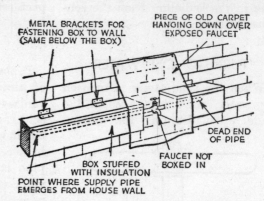

METAL BRACKETS FOR FASTENING BOX TO WALL (SAME BELOW THE BOX)

PIECE OF OLD CARPET HANGING DOWN OVER EXPOSED FAUCET

DEAD END OF PIPE

FAUCET NOT BOXED IN

BOX STUFFED WITH INSULATION

POINT WHERE SUPPLY PIPE EMERGES FROM HOUSE WALL

Fig. 32. How outside pipes can be insulated to prevent freezing.

freezing by building a box around them and filling the inside with sawdust, straw, hay, or even old newspapers. The box should be large enough so that the pipe is at least four inches from all sides. The box should be tight at the joints, and if it is fastened to a wall, there should be no cracks between box and wall to admit frost. Insulate the pipes from the wall with strips of wood. One quarter inch is thick enough.

Fig. 31. A cold water pipe can be insulated with hair felt and asphalt insulation to prevent freezing and sweating.

All pipes laid underground should be well below the frost line to keep them from freezing. The depth of the frost line will vary according to the section of the country, but any

CORROSION BY WATER

The water in some communities contains various chemicals and minerals which, though harmless to humans, will eat through pipes and water tanks. Many homeowners have installed new pipes and tanks, only to find that in a short time these too have been damaged beyond repair. Where the water is extremely corrosive, have it analyzed by a laboratory. After the contents of the water have been analyzed, you will be able to select the pipe which can best withstand the water's action.

CLEANING FIXTURES

Stains on sinks, wash basins, bathtubs, and other fixtures can generally be removed by rubbing with kerosene, a scratchless cleaning powder, or a paste made of kerosene and powder. Do not use a chemical to remove a stain, as most fixtures are cast iron coated with enamel, and the chemical will remove the enamel.

SECTION EIGHT

ELECTRICITY

Most of us are apt to forget the important part that electricity plays in making our homes more comfortable and efficient, until the current is cut off for one reason or another. How often this occurs depends somewhat upon how well the electrical system is maintained by the home mechanic. Electric appliances, switches, and cords, are rather delicate pieces of equipment which cannot, for the most part, endure rough treatment. The home mechanic should inspect all the electrical equipment from time to time and either replace or repair any parts that appear to be worn or damaged.

There is enough current flowing through a home electrical system to be dangerous. If this current were any less, it would not provide enough power to cook meals, afford entertainment through the means of radio and television, or supply various kinds of heating equipment. But the current necessary to perform these functions is potentially as dangerous as a loaded shotgun and should be used and maintained with the same caution and care.

Electrical work in this country is governed by a code set down by the National Board of Fire Underwriters. This code is called the National Electrical Code and it provides minimum standards of safety for all electrical installation. One of the provisions of the code is that no electrical equipment will be used that has not been approved by the National Board of Fire Underwriters Laboratory. This laboratory tests all kinds of electrical equipment and gives its seal of approval to those which meet its safety requirements. This seal means that the equipment is safe to use. Always look for the Underwriter's seal of approval before purchasing any kind of electrical equipment, whether it be an extension cord or a new lamp switch.

The National Electrical Code sets only minimum standards, and each community may have other regulations over and above those set down in the code. For example, many communities forbid electrical installation work to be done by anyone other than a licensed electrician. This would prevent the home mechanic from adding extra circuits or doing work involving the installation of additional electrical equipment of a fixed nature. This would not forbid the use of extension cords plugged into existing sockets, as these are considered temporary hookups. Other communities have codes which demand that all electrical repair work be done by a licensed electrician. This would mean that if a lamp socket had to be replaced or a wall outlet repaired, the work could not be done by the home mechanic unless he had a license.

Fig. 1. Never use any electrical equipment that does not carry this seal of approval.

Many small communities have no code at all governing electrical installation or repair and in this case one should comply with the National Electrical Code to do the work properly and safely. Before attempting any electrical work, the home mechanic should check with his local authorities and find out what the local building code requires. In most cases, minor repairs can be made, but extensive wiring may not be allowed.

Keep in mind, when doing any electrical work, that fire may be caused by improper installation or poor quality materials.

Definition. Electricity is a form of energy found in all matter. It cannot be created or destroyed. Although we speak of the generation of electricity by one means or another, all that is actually done is to force the electrons, which are components of atoms, to move along a desired path. This movement is called electrical current.

Volts. In electricity, the volt is a unit of measurement in determining the electrical pressure in the line. This would be the same as measuring the pressure of water in a pipe as so many pounds per square inch. The fact that there is pressure in the line does not mean that the water is flowing.

Amps. The ampere is the unit used to measure the rate of flow of electrical current. It can be compared to the term "gallons per second," used for measuring the amount of water passing through a pipe line. Voltage (electrical pressure) is not capable of doing any work until there is amperage.

Resistance. Resistance is the opposition to the flow of electrical current offered by the conductor, or the line through which the current flows. This resistance is measured by a unit called the Ohm. The length, thickness, and composition of the conductor will determine the amount of resistance to the flow of current. The greater the resistance offered by the conductor, the smaller will be the flow of current. Likewise, a conductor that offers slight resistance will allow a greater flow of current.

Ohm's Law. The relationship between the volt, amp., and ohm, is called Ohm's Law and is expressed in the equation, I (amperes) $=$ $\dfrac{\text{E (volts)}}{\text{R (ohms)}}$. You can also express the relationship as $R = \dfrac{E}{I}$ or $E = I \times R$.

Short Circuit. This equation explains why a short circuit between two wires in the home can be dangerous. A short circuit is nothing more than the lowering of the resistance between the lines. When the resistance is lowered, a great flow of current takes place. The fuse installed in each circuit prevents this high flow of current from lasting more than a fraction of a second by breaking the circuit when overheated. But the fact remains that for a short interval a large amount of current is flowing through the line, and if a person is the cause of a reduction of resistance, the flow of current can be fatal.

Insulation. It is very important, therefore, that wires carrying electrical current be covered with some protective coating to prevent short circuiting when the wires are placed beside one another. This covering is called the insulation. There is no perfect insulation, just as there is no perfect conductor, but some materials reduce the flow of current through them to a negligible degree. Among others, asbestos, cotton, rubber, and silk are poor conductors.

Conductors. Electrical current generates heat in overcoming the resistance of a conductor. This heat leaves the conductor by convection and by radiation. Energy used by the current to heat the conductor is lost; consequently, avoid having excessive resistance in the circuit.

Heat produced by electrical current causes an electric light bulb to incandesce. The filament in a bulb is not much more than a thin piece of wire which becomes white hot when current flows through it. A heating appliance, such as a toaster or an iron, contains special wiring which becomes very hot without melting.

Copper is used as an electrical conductor because it offers less resistance to the flow of current than any other practicable material. There is, however, some resistance even in copper, and this cannot be eliminated. The amount of resistance offered by a conductor depends upon the material, the length, and the diameter. There is less resistance in a short conductor of large diameter than in a long one with a small diameter. Since all the resistance cannot be eliminated from copper, and changing the length of the wiring is impractical, the only way to reduce resistance and carry the required load is to increase the size of the wire.

It is a waste of money to use large size wire when a smaller size is adequately safe, and the National Electrical Code contains a table of minimum wiring sizes, stating the size of wire required for various jobs. The wiring for the usual circuit in a house is No. 14, but sometimes it is necessary to use a larger size because of an additional load placed on the circuit. If the wires are not heavy enough for the load, the insulation may burn off and start a fire.

The Watt. As the primary function of electrical energy is to do work, there must be a means of measuring the amount of work a given amount of current can do in a given time. The unit used for measuring the amount of work done by electrical current is the watt. It is derived by multiplying the volts times the amperes by the time in hours (EI x t). Thus, a piece of equipment demanding 110 volts and 1 amp. will use 110 watts each hour.

CURRENT

There are two kinds of electrical current, alternating and direct. In A. C., the direction of the flow is reversed at regular intervals in much the same fashion as a pump which forces water through one line on one stroke and through the other line on the following stroke. In D. C., the direction of the flow never changes.

Most homes today are furnished with A. C., but there are still a few communities served with D. C. only. A. C. is more adaptable because it can be carried over lines at very high voltage, and then reduced by means of a transformer. Most appliances manufactured today are made for either A. C. or D. C., or for A. C. only. The type of current required by the appliance is stamped on the

name plate. Serious damage to the appliance will result if it is plugged into a circuit that does not carry the designated current. Always see what kind of current is listed on the name plate of the appliance. This is espe-

Fig. 2. Manufacturer's plate on electrical appliances giving type current, number of volts and watts.

cially important with old appliances, as many of them were made for D. C. only.

SOURCES

Dry Cell Battery. Nearly everyone is familiar with the dry cell battery, which is a chemical method of forcing electric current to flow. While the contents of a dry cell vary according to the make, the basic ingredients are a zinc casing and a carbon rod suspended in the center of the casing. The negative terminal is connected to the carbon rod. The zinc casing is lined with blotting paper which has been soaked in various chemicals, and the space between the rod and casing is filled with granulated chemicals. The top of the cell is covered with a waterproof composition to prevent the moisture inside the cell from evaporating. A dry cell can be placed in any position without injury. A dry cell does not produce a flow of current until the negative and positive terminals are connected, either directly with one another or with some type of appliance, such as a door bell, between them. When this circuit is closed, current will flow from the positive to the negative terminal. A dry cell will eventually become dead, even though it may not have been used. Sometimes, it is possible to bring life into a dry cell for a short time by punching a hole in the top and pouring a little water into the cell.

A standard-sized dry cell will deliver approximately 1½ volts when it is new. Greater voltage can be had by connecting two dry cells in series. This is done by connecting the positive terminal of the first battery to the negative terminal of the second. If both batteries are rated at 1½ volts, the total voltage between the negative terminal on the first and the positive terminal on the second will be 3 volts. If three dry cells are linked in this fashion, the combined voltage will be 4½ volts. This type of hookup is very useful with signaling systems which require more than 1½ volts. Electric current obtained from batteries is D. C.

Storage Battery. The storage battery used on cars has the advantage over the dry cell in that it can be recharged and kept in service for many years.

Generators. Home generators are used in various parts of the country where it is impossible to get current from power companies. These generators are operated either by a gasoline motor or by small windmills. Home generators can be had for both A. C. and D. C. The advantage of

D. C. is that the current can be kept in storage batteries until needed. As A. C. cannot be stored, the generator must run whenever electric current is desired. The more expensive types of A. C. generators are provided with a self-starter actuated by a switch inside the house. Full operating and maintenance instructions for these generators should be obtained from the dealer or manufacturer. Generators are useful as auxiliary power plants, particularly in areas where power lines are subject to frequent breakdowns, and the home is equipped with refrigeration equipment that must be kept in operation.

Commercial Power. Most homes, however, are provided with electric power supplied by a power company that charges the consumer for all current used. This current is about 110 volts, except in a home containing a piece of electrical equipment, such as an electric range, which requires 220 volts. In this case, the power company will bring in an additional 110 volt line to supply the appliance with the added voltage. The rest of the circuits in the house will carry 110 volts.

Every piece of electrical equipment is designed to operate on a given number of volts. This figure is stamped on the name plate or etched on the glass, as on electric light bulbs. If a light bulb designed to operate on 110 volts is put into a line carrying only 50 volts, the bulb will not burn well. If, on the other hand, a bulb designed for 50 volts is placed in a line carrying 110 volts, excessive pressure of the current will cause the bulb to burn out. There will be some fluctuation of voltage in the circuit, but the variance will be between 10 and 120 volts.

ELECTRICAL SYSTEM

Current is brought into the house by means of two or three heavy-duty wires. These run to the main fuse box which is generally located in the basement, together with the electric meter, main switch, and house fuse box. The main fuse box is maintained by the power company and may be sealed with wire to prevent anyone but an employee of the company from tampering with it. The function of this fuse box is to act as a safety valve for the power lines in the event that a serious short circuit occurs in the house. Inside are heavy-duty fuses which can withstand a heavy flow of current before burning out.

From the main fuse box, the current runs to the meter which is also sealed. This meter measures the amount of current used in the house, and on the basis of this reading the power company charges the home-owner.

After passing through the meter, the current is brought to the main switch. This is a knife switch and is so constructed that it cannot be closed accidentally. The knife must be pushed up to the closed position. When this switch is open, no current passes through the circuits in the house. From the main switch the wires run to the house fuse box, and

this is the point from which the home mechanic can work.

House Circuits. The electric wiring in a house is divided up into a number of circuits. Each circuit has a given number of outlets and fixtures and is provided with a fuse. The reason for dividing up the electric wiring into several circuits is twofold. By breaking down the electric system into small subsystems, the amount of current required is reduced and a smaller size wire can be used. In the second place, each circuit has an individual fuse, and a defective circuit will not put the entire house system out of order. Only the defective circuit will go out.

Fuses. There is a fuse in the house fuse box for each circuit. The capacity of

TYPICAL HOUSE
ELECTRIC LIGHT FUSE

Fig. 4.

the fuse is expressed in amps., and we find fuses of 10, 15 and 20 amps. The number of amps on the fuse indicates how much electrical current can flow through that particular fuse. The size of the wiring

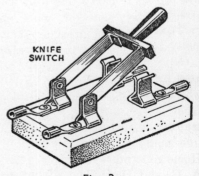

KNIFE
SWITCH

Fig. 3.

in the circuit will determine the size fuse to be used, and this is important to remember when changing fuses.

A fuse is actually nothing more than an extension of the wiring. It contains a thin strip of metal which will melt if the wires of the circuit reach a certain temperature. When this metal strip inside the fuse melts, the electrical circuit is broken and no current can pass through the fuse until it has been replaced.

There are two reasons for the wires in a circuit to overheat and burn out a fuse. One is a short circuit, which is nothing more than a sudden lowering of the resistance between two wires. A short circuit can be due to improper insulation on the wires or a piece of metal accidentally falling across them. The other reason for wires to overheat is overloading the circuit with too many appliances.

Overloading. The wiring in most homes was installed when electric appliances were not very common and the primary purpose of electricity was to supply light. Electric lights require a relatively small amount of current, and the circuits were put in to carry this load with safety. Today, however, more and more electric appliances are being used in the home and, in many cases, the circuit is greatly overloaded. This overload will manifest itself in two ways. Either the electric wiring will become overheated and a fuse will blow out, or the appliances will not receive the amount of current necessary for them to operate properly. The appliance is often thought to be faulty, and the homeowner expends much time and money in having it checked to find the nonexistent defect.

To find out how much current a circuit can carry safely and efficiently, multiply the voltage, which is usually about 110, by the number of amps stamped on the fuse. Assuming that the voltage is 110 and the amperage of the fuse is 10, the circuit can carry 1,100 watts. Each piece of electrical equipment requires so many watts, and this amount is stamped on the name plate of the appliance. A light bulb is classified by the number of watts, and this will vary according to the size of the bulb. Appliances like toasters and electric heaters demand many hundreds of watts. Some electric heaters need over 1,300 watts. When the sum of the watts required by various fixtures and appliances in one circuit is more than the number of watts the circuit can carry, the circuit is overloaded. If all the appliances are turned on, the fuse will blow or the appliances will not operate properly.

One of the first calculations the home mechanic should make is the maximum load that can be placed on each circuit in the system.

Blown Fuses. When a fuse blows, the first thing to do is to determine the cause. If a faulty extension cord or a fixture plugged into the wall socket causes the short circuit, it should be removed and repaired. After you have done this, insert a new fuse in the fuse box, and the circuit will be back in working order.

If the short circuit or overload on the lines is not removed, the new fuse will also blow out.

A great mistake is to try to relieve an overloaded circuit by putting in a larger size fuse. This will allow the circuit to come alive, but what you have done is equivalent to holding down the safety valve on a steam boiler. The wires in the circuit will overheat, just as they did with the smaller size fuse, but now there is danger that this heat will burn through the insulation around the wires.

If the wiring in a circuit is inadequate for the number of appliances required, either have heavier wire installed or another circuit added. The wiring in a kitchen is often deficient because of the number of electric appliances being used at the same time. Do not change the size of the fuse unless the wiring is designed to withstand this additional current flow.

Many people still use a penny as a substitute for a fuse. This is very foolish, and there is no excuse for doing it. It is commonly believed that the main fuse will compensate for any serious short circuits or overloads until the penny can be replaced with a fuse. The main fuses are heavy duty, intended for use on large, main lines. Smaller wiring in the house can become very hot before these fuses blow out, and this is a principal cause of electrical fires in the home. Substituting a penny for a fuse can easily cause such a fire, particularly when the circuit is overloaded with appliances.

Always replace a fuse with one the same size. Keep a box of extra fuses on hand and in a convenient place.

Before changing a fuse, it is a good idea to pull the main switch to the "off" position. This stops the flow of electricity into the fuse box and prevents any possibility of a shock while making the change.

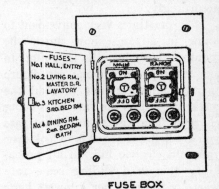

FUSE BOX

Fig. 5. The information contained on the inside of the fuse box door makes it easy to know which fuse has blown out.

Much time can be wasted trying to find the blown fuse. Make a chart showing the location of each fuse in the fuse box and the rooms and fixtures each fuse controls. To do this, turn on all the lights in the house. Turn off the main switch and unscrew one fuse. Turn the main switch on and note which lights fail to respond. Write this information in the chart alongside the fuse and repeat this test until every fuse is accounted for.

READING A METER

Electric power is sold by the electric companies to the householder at so much for each kilowatt hour. One kilowatt is equal to 1000 watts. The amount of current consumed by the household is measured by an electric meter usually located in the basement along with the main switch and fuse box. A representative of the power company comes each month to make a reading of this meter and the homeowner is billed accordingly.

It is sometimes very convenient to know in advance how much the month's electric bill is going to amount to, and anyone can figure this by knowing how to read the meter as well as the rate he is being charged. The way to find what rate you are being charged is to look over your old electric bill. In all probability this is a sliding scale rate whereby the cost per kilowatt hour is decreased in relation to the amount of current consumed.

The average home electric meter has four dials. As you face the meter the dial at your right indicates 10 kilowatt hours when the needle hand makes one complete revolution in a clockwise direction. The second dial registers one hundred kilowatt hours and this rotates in a counterclockwise direction. The third dial turns clockwise and registers up to a thousand kilowatt hours. The fourth dial on the extreme left rotates counterclockwise and measures up to ten thousand kilowatt hours.

The meter is so constructed that the needle on the right hand dial must make one complete revolution before the needle on the dial to the left moves one point. For example,

the needle on the ten kilowatt dial must go from zero to zero before the needle on the hundred kilowatt dial moves from zero to one. Because of this, when reading the meter and the needle is found to be between two numbers, take the smaller of the numbers. When the needle is directly on top of a number, check with the dial at the right. If the needle here has not passed zero, then use the low number.

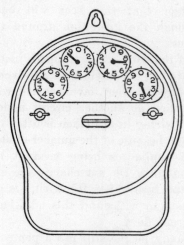

Fig. 5a. Meter used for measuring the amount of electric current used in a home.

The correct reading on the meter shown in Fig. 5a would be 1874.

To calculate the amount of electric power consumed since the last reading, subtract the present reading from the one taken previously. The difference between these two sets of figures is the amount of power for which you will be billed. When you multiply this figure by the rate you are being charged, the result will be the amount of your bill to that reading.

PRECAUTIONS

The best way to prevent shocking yourself while doing electrical work is to pull the main switch in the basement. As this cuts off the supply of current for the entire house, it is sometimes more convenient to unscrew the fuse of the circuit on which you are working. It is foolish to do any electrical work while there is any chance of coming in contact with a live wire. Your hand is never completely dry, and the small amount of moisture present will turn it into a very good conductor. Never work around electricity with wet feet or when the floor is damp. Never do electrical work when you are liable to come in contact with plumbing and heating pipes. These furnish the current with an excellent path to the ground. Special attention should be given to the elec-

METAL
FIXTURE
AND
CHAIN

Fig. 6. An electric fixture of this kind located near a plumbing fixture can give a dangerous electric shock.

tric fixtures in the bathroom, for here are combined all the elements that can cause a severe shock, the moisture present in baths and the iron plumbing and fixtures. *Anyone standing in a bathtub and pulling an electric light chain is in a position to receive a serious shock.*

Light fixtures in the bathroom should be made of porcelain rather than metal and equipped with a cord which is a nonconductor. Fixtures should be placed in such a manner that no one can touch them who is also in contact with plumbing fixtures. Electric appliances, such as electric razors and curling irons, should not be used in the bathrooom.

The same precautions with regard to light fixtures should be followed in the kitchen, where the plumbing in the sink makes an excellent ground.

Fixtures with metal chains should have an insulating link inserted in the chain in order that the chain will not be affected in the event of a short circuit.

Washing machines often operate in rooms where the floor is damp or wet. If the insulation on the machine is worn, the operator is in danger of receiving a bad shock. For this reason, you should ground the frame of the machine to a nearby pipe.

The basement is another danger spot, so far as electricity is concerned. If the basement is very damp, all light fixtures should be of a waterproof type.

Static Electricity. An electric shock received when touching a door knob, or some other metal object about the house, is due to static electricity, not to house current. This annoying shock generally occurs when the atmosphere is dry and cold and the building or home is heated.

CORDS

Just as the wiring in the house differs according to the load it is intended to carry, so various cords differ according to the functions they are designed to fulfill. Appliances that require only a small amount of current do not need the same type of cord that a heavy-duty appliance must have.

The first thing to look for when buying a new appliance cord is the Underwriter's seal of approval. This indicates that this type of cord has been tested and found satisfactory when used with the appliances for which it was designed.

For electric lamps, where the load is not very heavy and the wire must be thin and pliable enough to enter the fixture, use a thin, rubber-coated cord.

Electrical appliances of the nonheating type, like vacuum cleaners, sewing machines, and kitchen mixers, require a somewhat heavier cord to carry more current and resist the wear and tear to which they are subjected. This kind of cord should have a tough, rubber cover to protect the interior insulation from being damaged.

Heating appliances, such as toasters, irons, and heaters, require a very heavy and well-insulated cord. This cord should have an asbestos

insulation to prevent the rest of the insulation from burning, should the wires become too hot.

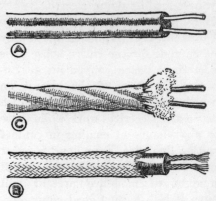

Fig. 7. Three common kinds of appliance or extension cords. Type A should be used only for lamps. Type B is designed for nonheating appliances, such as vacuum cleaners and sewing machines. Type C with a layer of asbestos is designed for heating appliances like toasters, irons, and room heaters.

Never nail extension and appliance cord. to the woodwork with staples or tacks. If the insulation around the staple should weaken and break, there is a possibility that

Fig. 8. Tacking appliance cords to woodwork is a bad practice. They should not be used as permanent wiring.

the woodwork may be set afire. Likewise, never place cords under rugs or carpets. A break in the insulation will go undetected, and a spark can easily ignite the rug. Always keep any kind of electric cord in the open where it can be seen and inspected frequently for signs of wear.

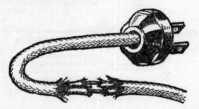

Fig. 9. An appliance cord in this condition may set fire to the house. It should either be replaced or repaired.

Plug a heating appliance directly into a wall outlet, never into the socket of an extension lamp. The lightweight cord used for an extension lamp is not made to withstand

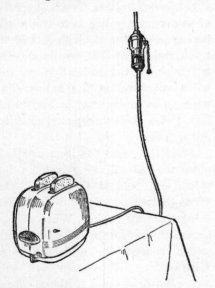

Fig. 10. Heating appliances should not be connected to fixture wired with a light lamp cord.

the load it will have to carry when a heating appliance is added. When a heating appliance is plugged into an extension lamp, the function of the heavy-duty cord of the appliance is negated. Similarly, never try to lengthen an appliance cord by adding a lighter cord to it.

SPLICING

Splicing is a method of joining two pieces of electric wire together. Splices are used as little as possible in electrical work, for they offer increased resistance to the passage of the current. If a splice must be made, however, it is important that it be done correctly.

The National Electrical Code specifies that a splice should be "mechanically and electrically secure." This means, first of all, that the two wires should be joined so that they will not become loose and pull apart; and, secondly, that they should be cleaned thoroughly to offer as little resistance to the current as possible. After the splice has been made, use some material to insulate the splice. This insulation should be at least equal to the insulation around the rest of the wire.

Remove insulation with a knife from the ends of the wires to be spliced and scrape the wires clean of any bits of insulation with a knife, sandpaper, or emery cloth.

Western Union Splice. The Western Union Splice is used to lengthen a piece of wire. Remove 3 inches of insulation from both pieces of wire and clean the bare wire until it is bright. Cross the wires about ¾ of an inch from the end of the insulation. Make five short turns with each end of the wire and squeeze the ends together with pliers so that there are no sharp angles.

WESTERN UNION SPLICE

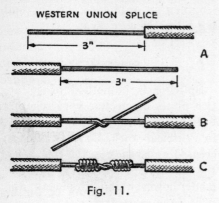

Fig. 11.

Tap or Branch Splice. This splice is used to connect a wire with a main conductor. To make it, remove about 1 inch of the insulation from the main conductor and from 3 to 5

TOP OR BRANCH SPLICE

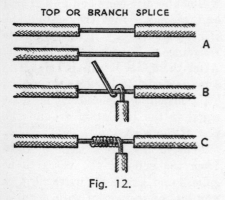

Fig. 12.

inches of the insulation from the branch wire. Place the branch wire across the main conductor so that the insulation of the two wires almost touches and make about seven turns on the branch wire.

Pigtail Splice. The pigtail splice is often used in connecting the fixtures in the house system and for wiring multiple lamp fixtures. To make this splice, remove from 2 to 3 inches of insulation from each wire

PIGTAIL SPLICE

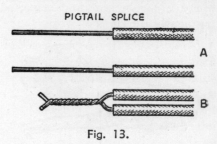

Fig. 13.

and scrape the wire clean. With the wires parallel and the insulation even, twist the wires together, using pliers, until the twist is approximately 1 inch long. Do not cut off the excess wire, and the splice is ready for soldering and insulating.

Soldering Splices. The best means of soldering a splice is to use a soldering iron, but a small alcohol blowtorch can be used if one is careful not to burn the insulation on the wires surrounding the splice. The wires to be soldered must be free of dirt and a soldering paste, or flux, put on them.

After the paste has been applied, place the hot soldering iron on the splice and hold it there until the wires become hot. Feed wire solder along the entire splice. When all the turns of the splice are filled with solder, remove the soldering iron. Wire solder, with a rosin core, will not require any additional flux. Learning to solder wire properly requires a little patience and skill. If the job has been done properly, the solder will fill up all the spaces between the turns and there will be no excess solder on the wires.

It is worthwhile to use a few odd pieces of wire for practice until you have attained sufficient skill to do quick, neat work.

Insulating. After a splice has been made and soldered, it should be insulated carefully. A poorly insulated splice can cause much trouble. The insulation around the splice should afford the same degree of protection as the rest of the insulation. Cover the splice first with rubber tape and then with friction tape. Do this as neatly and uniformly as possible. If the tape is carelessly wound around the splice, it will be impossible to determine whether the splice has been fully covered or not.

Splicing Cords. When an appliance cord becomes broken, or the insulation wears off in spots, the cord should be thrown away. Faulty

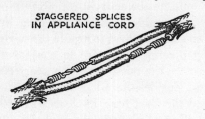

STAGGERED SPLICES IN APPLIANCE CORD

Fig. 14.

appliance cords are fire hazards. If it is necessary to patch a cord for temporary use, keep in mind that it is only a temporary arrangement and replace the cord as soon as possible.

A broken cord can be spliced by removing enough of the insulation

to stagger the splice, i.e., the splice on one wire beginning where the splice on the second wire ends.

The reason for doing this is to avoid a short circuit, should the insulation around the two splices be insufficient or become worn. The splices should be soldered and well insulated with rubber or friction tape. It is practically impossible to make a secure splice in stranded wire unless the splice is soldered.

PLUGS AND SWITCHES

Wallplugs. There is a tendency on the part of many of us to remove a wallplug from the outlet by pulling on the wires rather than taking hold of the plug itself. This treatment will eventually pull the wires out of the plug, probably resulting in a short circuit. Check the connections inside wallplugs from time to time,

UNDERWRITER'S KNOT

B   A

Fig. 15. How wires should be connected to a wallplug. A, tying an Underwriter's knot. B, ends of the wires firmly secured under terminal screws.

and tighten the wires if necessary. Plastic wallplugs can be broken rather easily, and have to be replaced.

In replacing wallplugs, first trim off the end of the wire and slip it through the opening in the base of the plug. Remove about 1 inch or more of the outer insulation, taking care not to cut the inner insulation. Make a knot in the two wires and fit it into the recess at the base of the plug. This is called an Underwriter's knot, and it takes up the strain on the connection caused by pulling out the plug by the wires.

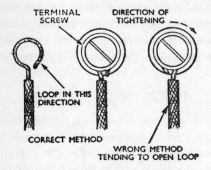

Fig. 16. There is a right and a wrong way to connect a wire to a terminal screw.

As an added precaution, wrap the knot with friction tape. Wrap each wire around one of the prongs of the plug and remove enough insulation to securely twist the wires around the terminal screws. Twist the wires around these screws in the direction in which you turn the screws to tighten them. Turn the terminal screws down with a screwdriver until they are firm. Trim off any loose strands of wires which slip out from under the head of the screw.

Appliance Plugs. Appliance cords are equipped with a plug at each end. One is the wallplug, and the other is a special type of plug for attachment to the appliance. Before detaching the plug from the appliance, shut off the current. By stopping the flow of current, you avoid the sparking that sometimes results

when the plug is removed from the appliance. This sparking can burn and pit the prongs of the appliance so that a good electrical contact cannot be made.

To replace an appliance plug, it is necessary to remove the screws or metal clamp that hold the two halves of the plug together. When the plug is apart, examine its construction carefully. The first thing to note is

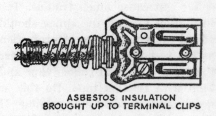

Fig. 17. Proper method of wiring appliance plug.

the wire spring over the wires which fits into a recess at the base of the plug. This wire spring prevents the wires from bending at the point where they enter the plug, and it should not be omitted when the plug is reassembled. Inside the plug are two small grooves to cradle the wires. By placing each wire in a separate groove, the possibility of a short circuit inside the plug is minimized and the need for a knot, as was used in the wallplug, is eliminated.

Remove a portion of the outer insulation to separate the wires and put them in their respective grooves. Do not take off any of the asbestos insulation, however. Attach the wires to the small metal clips at the end of the plug by means of screws. The insulation on the wires should run up to this connection. Twist the wires around the screws in a clock-wise direction, or in the same direction that the screws turn when tightened. Be sure that there are no loose strands of wire to cause a short circuit. Finally, fit the spring at the base of the plug into the recess provided for it and assemble the plug.

Feed-Through Switch. It is inconvenient to have to pull out a wall-plug each time you want to disconnect a toaster or a flat iron, and some type of switch should be installed in the cord so that the current can be shut off without having to remove either end of the cord. Appliance plugs are made with a switch built into them, and this is a great convenience. If your plug has no switch, you can add a "feed-through" switch. This can be installed at any convenient point along the cord.

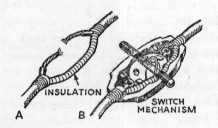

Fig. 18. How to install a feed-through switch.

Examine a feed-through switch and you will see that it is designed to stop the flow of current through only one wire, the other wire by-passing the switching mechanism To install the switch, select a location for it on the cord and remove just enough of the outer insulation of the cord to separate the two wires

as they enter the switch. Be sure that they are brought together by the outer insulation on the other side of the switch. Cut one of the wires and remove sufficient insulation to enable you to twist the ends around the terminal screws of the switch. Do not cut the inner insulation on the second wire. Tighten the terminal screws upon the ends of the cut wire and place the uncut wire in the channel provided for it. Trim off any loose strands of wire and reassemble the switch.

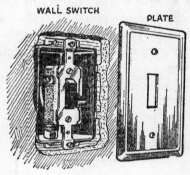

Fig. 19.

Electric Switches. An electric switch is a mechanical means of opening and closing an electric circuit. There are many different kinds of switches in the home, but in principle they are alike.

If a slight electric shock is received on touching the metal portion

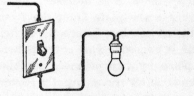

Fig. 20. Single-pole switch for controlling lights from one point.

of a switch, it is an indication that the insulation inside the switch is faulty, and the switch should be replaced at once. Most switches are attached to only two wires, but there are some connected by three or four wires. Such a connection is used on 3-way switches, designed to control one fixture from two different locations in the house. A hall light that can be turned off and on at the head of the stairs and at the bottom is an example of the operation of this switch. With more complicated wiring, a light can be controlled from three different points. To replace an ordinary two-way switch with a 3-way type involves much extra wiring.

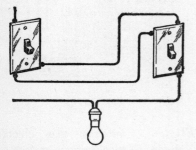

Fig. 21. Three-way switches used to control lights from two different points.

To replace a switch, first cut off the power, either by pulling the main switch or by unscrewing the fuse controlling the circuit. On most wall switches, it is necessary to remove a cover plate from the front of the switch box before the switch itself is exposed. This cover is held in place by two or more machine screws. After removing the cover, take out the screws holding the switch in place and pull the switch

out far enough to detach the wires. When attaching the wires to the new switch, be sure that the wire is turned around the binding post in the same direction that the screw is turned when tightened.

Fixture Sockets. The home handyman, at some time, will have to replace a defective lamp socket. The switch inside these sockets is operated by a chain, a push bar, or a key, and this mechanism eventually wears out. Be sure to cut off the current to the fixture before you begin work. You will have to disassemble the socket before disconnecting the wires from the switch and removing the switch. Remove the outer shell of the socket by pushing down on the metal where it fits into the socket cap. On most sockets, this spot is indicated by the word "push." By

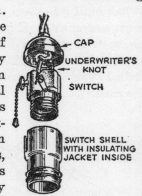

Fig. 22. Lamp socket.

pressing down at this point with a screwdriver, you can detach the shell and fiber insulation jacket inside it from the main body of the switch. Remove the wires connected to the switch mechanism by loosening the terminal screws. Take out the defective switch and attach a new one to the wires. Make a knot in the wires, to fit inside the socket cap and ease the strain on the connection. This is especially important for ceiling lamps, where the entire weight of the lamp fixture is often held by the wires. It is best to replace such a fixture with a type having a chain or other device to hold the socket to the ceiling. After the knot has been made and pulled into the socket cap, attach the two wires to the terminal screws. Tighten the screws and trim any loose strands of wire; then replace the fiber insulating shell and the metal shell. Be certain that the metal shell fits tightly into the socket cap.

HOME LIGHTING

The lighting facilities, such as the type, location and number of fixtures in many homes is very inadequate. This is especially true in homes that were wired many years ago when relatively little was known about proper lighting. Improper lighting can be the cause of headaches, eye strain and fatigue, and the lighting industry has done a tremendous amount of research to find what is the best kind of light for certain specific jobs. These findings are used to good advantage in the office, factory, and school. They can apply as well at home.

If you plan on having additional electrical work done around the house, such as having more circuits installed or new type fixtures put in, it would be well to get the advice of your local power company before the work is begun or before you buy the new fixtures. In most cases the power company will send a trained representative around and he is well qualified to help you plan not only efficient but economical lighting. It should be remembered that good lighting is not the result of guesswork but is something that can only be achieved through proper and careful planning.

While there are many types of lighting used for many purposes, they can be broken down into three groups; direct, semi-indirect, and indirect.

Direct Lighting. Here the ultimate amount of light is produced because there is no covering over the lamp bulb. This type light can

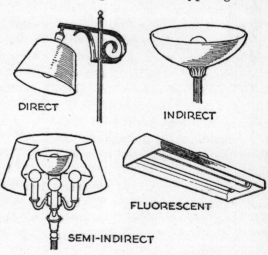

DIRECT

INDIRECT

FLUORESCENT

SEMI-INDIRECT

Fig. 22a. Common types of home lighting.

be used in halls and other places where there is no need of anything more than light for light's sake. Direct lighting is not, however, satisfactory for reading, sewing, or writing due to the glare and shadows.

Semi-Indirect Lighting. With semi-indirect lighting the fixture is so arranged that some of the light comes directly from the bulb but a large percentage is reflected back from the ceiling and walls. Much of the glare present in direct lighting is eliminated by this method but not all the light which is emitted by the bulb will be reflected back from the ceiling and wall; accordingly, there is bound to be some loss.

Indirect Lighting. In this kind of lighting practically all the light output is reflected back down from the ceiling. Its efficiency, therefore, will depend a great deal on what color the ceiling has been painted. White or other light colors are more satisfactory than the dark shades which tend to absorb too much of the light. Because it has no glare, indirect lighting is ideal for reading, sewing and other close work of this nature.

Fluorescent Lamps. The fluorescent lamp consists of a long tube filled with gas, taking the place of the filament in an incandescent bulb. Electric current passing through the tube heats the gas and causes it to emit light.

Light from a fluorescent lamp more nearly approaches daylight. The light produced has less glare than an incandescent bulb of comparable wattage. A fluorescent lamp will also effectively light a greater area than will an incandescent bulb. Fluorescent lighting is still more expensive to install, however, and requires special equipment. But it is probably less expensive in the long run, with good light on less wattage.

Repair of Electrical Appliances. A broken heating element is the usual reason why appliances such as an iron, curling iron, toaster, etc., stop working. Dropping the appliance often causes the break. Soldering broken wires of a heating element is of no use for the heat generated by the element will melt the solder.

Sometimes you can make temporary repairs by removing the element and twisting the broken wires together or by clamping them together with a tiny machine screw and nut. But that is only a temporary measure and a new element should be purchased from an electrical shop and installed as soon as possible. In fact, many of the most modern type appliances have elements sealed in special material and when such an element breaks, the only solution is replacement. Before removing an element check to be sure that the source of current and all cords and switches are functioning properly.

ELECTRIC MOTORS

The average home has a number of fractional horsepower electric motors that provide the necessary power for running refrigerators, vacuum cleaners, washing machines, and other pieces of equipment.

Some types of electric motors are equipped with removable brushes. These carbon brushes are under spring tension and provide current for the commutator of the motor. The spring is held in a small opening by means of a plastic cap. Occasionally, these brushes become worn to such a degree that the spring cannot supply sufficient pressure to make a good electrical contact between brush and commutator, and the motor will fail to operate. A new brush can be easily installed by removing the cap and pulling out the spring and old brush. It may be possible to stretch the spring enough to obtain the proper amount of tension. If the contact between the brushes and the commutator is not good, there will be a great deal of sparking and an unpleasant odor while the motor is running. A brush that is partially broken or worn unevenly can cause this condition. Replace the brush with a new one. If a new brush is not procurable, the old one can be resurfaced by sanding with fine sandpaper. (Do not use emery because the particles may burn out the bearings.) As the commutator is curved, the face of the brush should be curved out slightly to fit tightly against the commutator.

Oiling. Almost every type of electric motor requires an occasional oiling, although some new motors are equipped with sealed bearings which do not require oiling for several years. If the motor has oil cups, it will require oiling to prevent the bearings from burning out. Large electric motors, such as are used for pumps and washing machines, should be filled with No. 20 oil, used in automobiles. Do not use a light grade of oil on these motors or the oil will evaporate quickly and leave the bearings unprotected. Fill the cup to the top and allow about five minutes for the oil to soak down into

the wicking. The wicking is located near the bearing and absorbs the oil to release it to the bearing when needed. Refill the oil cup to the top. The oil cups are the only points on a motor which receive oil. Keep oil out of the motor and off the rubber insulated cord. Oil will rot rubber and cause extensive damage if allowed to enter the motor. As oiling instructions differ with various sizes and types of motors, get full maintenance instructions from your dealer when a new motor is installed.

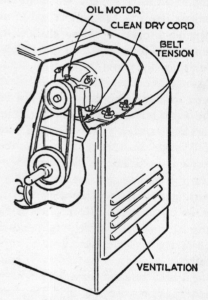

Fig. 23. Fractional electric motors in the house should be inspected at frequent intervals.

Motors should be kept clean and dry. Never wash an electric motor with water or any other liquid. You can wipe the exterior of a motor with a dry cloth to remove dirt and grease. Keep as much dust and dirt away from the motor as possible.

Dirt inside the motor will cause an undue amount of wear of the moving parts. Electric motors will heat while running, but they should not become too hot. If they overheat, shut off the motor, for this is a sure indication that something is amiss. Motors are self cooling, but they must be installed where there is ample circulation of air. They should never be covered up or confined in a small, unventilated area.

Belts. Motors that operate appliances by means of a belt should be inspected at frequent intervals to make sure that the belt is not slipping or broken. A loose or broken belt will allow a motor to run indefinitely, if it is provided with an automatic start and stop switch. Most belts used on electric motors are of the V type and can be purchased at hardware and electrical stores. These belts come in several sizes, so take along the old belt to make sure you buy the right size. It is very important that the belt fit correctly. If it is too loose, it will slip and be of no use. If it is too tight, it may cause a bearing to burn out. You can repair temporarily a worn belt by taping it with friction tape. This is only a stopgap, however, and the belt should be replaced with a new one as soon as possible.

SIGNALING SYSTEM

The home signaling system provides the amateur electrician with an excellent proving ground to test his knowledge and skill in electrical work, without any of the hazards or restricting codes associated with the regular house electrical system. Door bells, chimes, and buzzers, are made to operate on a very low and harmless voltage. The signaling system should, however, be treated with the same respect given to the regular electric system. Do all installation work as neatly as possible, for not only is this good training for future electrical jobs, but locating a short or open circuit in a signaling system is a long and onerous task. Install the system correctly and spare yourself much difficulty.

Sources of Power. As door bells and buzzers are made to operate on lower voltage than the 110 volts used for other electrical equipment, the power for these systems is furnished either by dry cell batteries or by the house current run through a transformer. The number of dry cells required depends upon the voltage required by each piece of equipment, with some allowance made for the voltage drop in the lines. A simple door bell may need only 1½ volts, while a set of door chimes may demand 3 volts or more. When more than 1½ volts are necessary, the batteries should be connected in series. A transformer will reduce the house voltage to the required level.

Transformer. A transformer has a high voltage side and a low voltage side. Connect the high voltage side to the house circuit, using wire of same size as that used throughout the 110 volt system. Some codes require that a transformer for signaling equipment have a special fuse between it and the house circuit.

On the low voltage side of the transformer are two or more terminal screws. If there are more than two terminals, each will have a different rating to supply power for several pieces of equipment requiring different voltages. The voltage rating at each terminal is clearly indicated by the maker. When connecting equipment with the transformer, be sure that the correct voltage is furnished each piece. If

the voltage is too low, the equipment will not operate correctly; if it is too high, the equipment may burn out or the insulation on the wires may catch fire.

A transformer only draws current from the house supply when the circuit of the signaling system is closed. Pressing the button switch

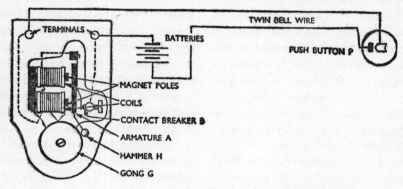

Fig. 25. Typical wiring circuit, showing the arrangement of the bell components. Note the adjusting screw at the contact breaker.

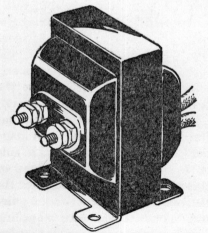

Fig. 24. Small transformer of the type used for home signaling systems.

will close the circuit, but a short circuit in the wiring will also cause the transformer to draw current. If properly installed and maintained, a transformer will last indefinitely.

Once the transformer has been installed, there should be no reason to test the high voltage side. All tests should be made on the low voltage side.

Vibrating Bells. One of the most familiar pieces of home signaling equipment is the vibrating bell. It will ring as long as the circuit is closed.

The arrangement consists of a bell, an electromagnet, and an armature, at the end of which is a hammer. When the circuit is closed, the current flowing through the windings of an electromagnet actuates it, causing an attraction between the magnet and the armature. As the armature is drawn to the magnet, the hammer strikes the bell and, at the same time, the armature breaks the circuit on contact with the electromagnet. This causes the armature to return to its original position, being under slight spring tension. As the armature returns, the circuit is restored, and the concatenation continues until the circuit is broken by releasing the switch in the push button. A buzzer works on the same principle, except that there is no hammer and the sound is not as loud.

There are many kinds of bells, buzzers, and chimes. Choose signals with regard to intensity of sound and location. A single, loud bell which can be heard throughout the house is, for example, sometimes more desirable than several softtoned chimes placed at scattered points in the house.

The size of wire used on low voltage signaling systems is No. 18, known also as bell wire or annunciator wire.

Select push buttons and other switches to harmonize with the surrounding decorations and household hardware.

Bell Systems. Fig. 25 shows the wiring diagram for a simple, onebell system. It consists of a source of power (dry cell batteries or a transformer), a switch to control the flow of current, a bell or buzzer, and the necessary wire to complete the

circuit. A system of this type can be used at the front door or between the dining room and the kitchen. Install the push button in a suitable location, and attach two wires to it. One of these wires runs from the button to the source of power, and the other runs directly to the bell. Connect a wire between the other terminal of the bell and the second terminal of the battery or transformer. You may attach the wires to the woodwork by means of insulated staples. Avoid using one staple for both wires. If you can keep the wires a fraction of an inch apart, there will be less chance of a short circuit occurring in the system.

Splices in bell wire do not have to be soldered, but you will make a better system by doing so. Tape splices with friction tape.

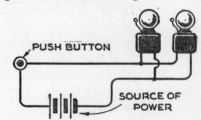

Fig. 26. Wiring diagram with one push button ringing two bells.

Fig. 26 indicates wiring for a twobell system with one push button. This arrangement permits multiple installation of signals, such as a buzzer or a set of chimes at the front of the house and a bell in the kitchen.

Annunciator. An annunciator is a device to register the source of a call, using only one bell. An annunciator is so constructed that when the bell rings, a number or letter, indicating the source of the call, comes into view. Annunciators are made to register any number of calls. Fig. 28

cannot be cut, use a simple arrangement like that shown in Fig. 29.

The master switch shown next to

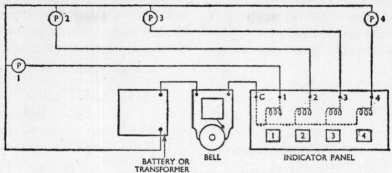

Fig. 28. A diagrammatic wiring circuit for an annunciator. Four push buttons, P, are wired in the circuit to the indicator panel.

shows a wiring diagram used in a four-call system.

Burglar Alarms. A simple bell circuit may be installed as a burglar alarm. You can obtain special, concealed switches to fit to door frames and window sashes. If you can lay the wiring in such manner that it

the battery is a single pole switch like that used for ordinary electric lighting, and it puts the alarm system in or out of operation. The drawback of this switch is that,

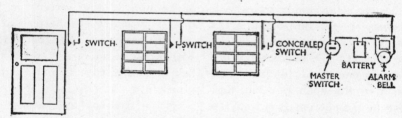

Fig. 29. A battery-operated open circuit burglar alarm.

cealed switches to fit to door frames and window sashes. If you can lay the wiring in such manner that it

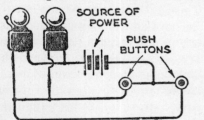

Fig. 27. In this system, both bells will ring when either button is pushed.

should someone forget to close it at night, the alarm system will not function. To avoid this, use a time switch, which can be set to turn on and off at predetermined times. In shops or offices, a time switch with a seven-day dial, which makes allowance for different closing times on weekends, can be used.

If the wire is placed so that any part of it can be cut, use the system shown in Fig. 30. In this system,

the main circuit is normally energized, and the alarm bell is on a
secondary circuit which operates
only when a break occurs in the
main circuit. All the points to be
protected are provided with switches
of the normally closed type, in con-

REPAIRING SYSTEM

A signaling system becomes out
of order for a number of reasons,
and there is a special procedure to
be used in checking the equipment
which saves much time.

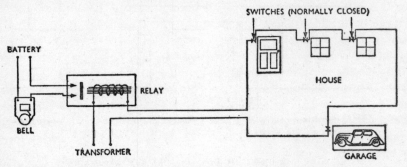

Fig. 30. Wiring circuit for a burglar alarm. Note that the switches are closed.
Opening of door or window also opens switch and sets off alarm bell.

trast with the normally open type
shown in the first system. These
switches are connected in series with
a magnetic relay. In principle, the
relay is a switch actuated by an
electromagnet. The current flowing
in the electromagnet holds the switch
contacts in the open position, and
as soon as the current is cut off the
contacts close under spring tension.
These contacts are wired in the secondary circuit and operate the alarm
bell.

The current consumption of the
relay is very low, but since it must
be continuously energized for long
periods, it is advisable to use house
current reduced by a transformer.
Connect the bell with a battery and
not with the house circuit, or the
whole alarm system can be defeated
by deliberate interference with the
house current.

Power Supply. When a signaling
system fails, check first the source
of supply. If the current is furnished by a dry cell battery or by
several batteries, test the voltage
with a voltmeter or by means of a
bell or buzzer with two short wires
attached to the terminals. Place the
wires on each of the battery terminals. If there is life in the battery,
the bell will ring. Another method of
testing dry cells is to connect one
wire to a terminal, then touch the
wire lightly on the other terminal.
If a slight spark can be seen between
the wire and the terminal, the battery is good. Some electricians test
dry cells with their tongue. Place
the tongue across both terminals. If
the battery is alive, you will have a
salty taste on the tip of your tongue.
Never test a transformer by this
method. Use a voltmeter or a bell

to test a transformer and be sure that this equipment is placed on the low voltage terminals, not on the high voltage side of the transformer.

The Bell. If the source of current is satisfactory, check next the ringing mechanism. The best method of doing this is to connect a good dry cell directly to the bell or buzzer. It may be that the armature of the bell is stuck or the adjusting screw on the contact breaker has been moved. If this is unscrewed far enough to leave a gap between the contact points, no current can flow and the bell will not ring. If, on the other hand, it is screwed in too far, the contacts will not part when the armature is drawn to the magnet. Adjust the screw while the push button is depressed, to give the most satisfactory ring. There is usually a locking screw to keep the contact screw in adjustment.

Push Button. If the bell works correctly when supplied with current from a dry cell, examine the push button.

To test the push button, it is usually necessary to remove it from the mounting and place a piece of metal between the two wires connected to the rear of the button. If the button causes the system to fail, shorting out with the metal will make the bell ring. A push button will not operate after long, hard use because the contact points are worn or bent.

Wiring. Assuming that the bell did not ring when the push button was shorted out, check the wiring for a possible break which would cause an open circuit. In most cases, a break in the wires can be detected by a close visual inspection. If you cannot see the break, however, test out the circuit, by means of a bell with two wires attached to its terminals, at a point near the source of supply and remove a small portion of the insulation from both wires. Touch the testing bell wires to the exposed parts of the circuit wires. Work back over the entire circuit, testing at intervals. As long as the testing bell rings, the circuit is complete. By this process of elimination, you can narrow the potential location of the break until you easily find it.

Short circuits occur in bell wiring circuits when two uninsulated wires come in contact with each other. A short circuit will cause a transformer to become overheated and dry cell batteries to go dead. In some instances, it will cause the bell to ring continuously. Disconnect one of the wires from the source of power immediately and do not connect it again until the short circuit has been found and eliminated. Check the push button as a possible cause of continuous ringing. Dirt inside the button will often cause it to stick in a closed position.

EXTERIOR REPAIRS

The materials used for the construction of the outer walls and roof of a house are selected on the basis of how well they stand up under weather and temperature changes. Some types of materials are considerably better than others, but each requires some maintenance and repair if it is to give the best service. Do not put off doing exterior repair jobs any longer than is necessary. A small leak in the roof can damage the plaster in an entire room, as will a leak in the wall. Keep the exterior of your house in good repair, even if it means neglecting the interior. Do not paint the interior walls until you are sure that the exterior walls are well protected. Be less concerned with cracks in the inside plaster than with cracks in the exterior stucco or masonry. The exterior walls and roof keep out the weather and if they fail, the entire house may fail with them.

DAMP BASEMENT

A damp basement is not only uncomfortable but unhealthy as well, and it invites rot to attack the wood sills and other important parts of the house frame.

If a basement is constructed with poured concrete, properly mixed, and there are no open seams between the walls and the floor, it will be completely watertight. Unfortunately, there are often seams between the floor and walls, and if the basement is built of concrete blocks, there are literally hundreds of seams. Unless care is taken to make each one of these watertight, the basement cannot be kept dry when the water in the soil is above the lowest point in the basement.

When concrete is properly mixed and cured, it will be waterproof. In hasty construction, however, sufficient care and time are not often taken with the foundation, causing the concrete to dry porous and allow water to seep through.

Drying Basement. There are many ways of preventing moisture from permeating a basement. In some cases, it will be found on close examination that the walls and floor of the basement are watertight, and the moisture is the result of condensation. The best preventive for this is a plentiful supply of fresh air. Have the basement windows open as much as possible during the summer. Use an electric fan, if necessary, to produce the necessary circulation of air throughout the entire basement. You can place containers of calcium chloride in the basement, and this chemical will absorb the moisture from the air and keep the basement dry. It is not expensive but will have to be replaced when it becomes saturated.

Fig. 1. Grading the soil down and away from the house is one way to prevent water from entering the basement.

The proper grading of the soil around the basement can do much to prevent water from soaking into the ground along the wall and entering the basement through a crack in the foundation. Slope the ground down and away from the wall, so that the water will tend to flow away from the house. Keep this earth well seeded with grass and free of any depressions where water can collect. To grade the soil around the basement in this manner, it may be nec-

essary to have boxes built around the basement windows in order that they will not be covered with earth. These boxes, or frames, should be made of concrete or brick and provided with tops so that they can be opened in good weather to allow fresh air and sunlight to penetrate the basement.

Water discharged from downspouts must not be allowed to soak into the soil adjoining the foundation. Pipe this water to a dry well some distance from the house, so located that the water cannot drain toward the basement.

In many cases, a few simple corrections, such as those mentioned above, will be all that is necessary to keep the basement dry.

Drainage Trench. For more serious conditions, you may have to dig a trench around the entire house to the level of the footing, located under the foundation wall. Lay drain tile in the trench with a slight gap between each section of tile to permit water to enter the tile pipe. Cover the top of these openings with a piece of metal or tar paper to prevent as much dirt as possible from falling into the pipes. Put down the drain tile with enough pitch so that the water will drain through the tile and lay additional pipes to connect this system with a dry well some distance from the house. The pitch in the system should be about one inch to every foot, and this can readily be checked with a level. Test the system by introducing water at various points. In this way, you make sure that the pitch of the pipes is correct and the water drains away from the house rather than settling at some low point in the system. After the system has been checked, fill in around the drain pipe with gravel, being careful not to disturb the position of the pipes. Put in about two feet of gravel and crushed stone. Over this place some old wire screening or other material which will allow water to pass but prevent dirt from mixing with the gravel. On top of this put earth and, finally, the sod.

WATERPROOFING A WALL

While the trench around the foundation is open, it is a good idea to coat the exterior side of the basement walls with some kind of waterproofing material. The waterproofing to be used is dependent on the seriousness of the leakage through the wall. If the condition is rather bad, use one of the special waterproofing materials made of asphalt or tar. These are obtainable in liquid form or in sheets which can be cemented to the wall by means of asphalt. Sheets of waterproof paper, overlapped and well cemented at the seams, form a completely watertight covering for the wall.

The effectiveness of these and other waterproofing materials de-

pends upon their being exactly applied. For this reason, it is not recommended that the home mechanic do this work unless he has the time and the skill to do it precisely.

If the wall is not in serious condition but merely becomes damp during wet weather, a coating of rich cement, applied to the outside, may suffice.

Clean the walls with a stiff wire brush to remove dirt and any loose particles of concrete. Poured concrete generally has a smooth surface which prevents the coat or mortar from sticking to it. To overcome this difficulty, you can rough the foundation wall with a cold chisel and a hammer. Chip the surface just enough so that the mortar will adhere. Be sure to brush off any

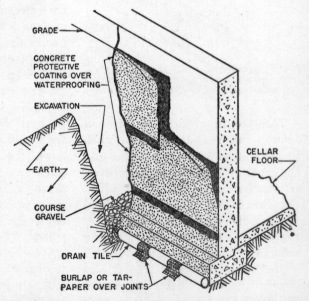

GRADE

CONCRETE
PROTECTIVE
COATING OVER
WATERPROOFING

EXCAVATION

EARTH

COURSE
GRAVEL

DRAIN TILE

BURLAP OR TAR-
PAPER OVER JOINTS

CELLAR
FLOOR

Fig. 2. Waterproofing a basement wall through the use of drain tile, waterproof paper, asphalt, and cement.

loose bits of concrete after you have finished.

Mix a thin paste of cement and water. Wet down the wall surface and apply this grout with an old, clean paintbrush or with a trowel.

It is well worth the additional cost to apply some kind of waterproofing to the walls when drain tile is being put down, as the greater part of the expense connected with waterproofing the walls is in digging the trench.

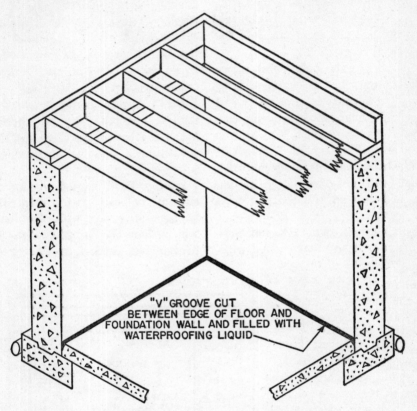

"V" GROOVE CUT BETWEEN EDGE OF FLOOR AND FOUNDATION WALL AND FILLED WITH WATERPROOFING LIQUID

Fig. 3. Making a watertight seam between basement wall and floor.

Next, mix a mortar of 1 part cement to 3 parts sand and cover the entire wall to a thickness of about ½ inch. Keep this moist and out of the sun until it is set. This coat should be left rough so that the second will bond to it. Mix the second coat and apply in the same fashion, to about the same thickness.

When waterproofing material is put over the inside walls and floors of the basement, the pressure of water from outside is likely to force it away from the concrete and masonry. When used on the outside, the water pressure forces waterproofing against the walls, and it is not necessary to use any reinforcement. Take care to ensure that all seams are tight when applying waterproofing to interior walls and floor. As a reinforcement, add a layer of cement to the waterproofing material. This work is generally done by professionals because if the smallest opening is left, water will find its way through the seam and into the basement.

Sometimes, the only point where a leak occurs in the basement is at the seam formed by the walls and floor. This can sometimes be corrected by cutting out a V along this seam and filling it with hot asphalt or a similar waterproofing material, which will not completely harden and will expand and contract with the seam.

Sump Pump. Some types of basements cannot be waterproofed without rebuilding them completely. In such cases a sump pump (see Fig. 4) is the best solution.

Porous Concrete. There are many different kinds of masonry waterproofing compound which can be applied to the inside of the wall and will often take care of moisture when it is due to the concrete being very porous. These compounds come in dry form and are mixed with water before use. The vital point in using these compounds is to be sure the masonry is absolutely free of paint, dirt, grease, or any other matter that might prevent compound from filling pores of the masonry.

CRACKS IN FOUNDATION

Cracks appear in foundations when there is any settling, or if the foundations are not well constructed. Small cracks can be filled by the home mechanic, but large, structural cracks which run the entire height of the foundation and continue to increase in size should be examined by an expert, for they may indicate serious trouble.

Small cracks should be filled as soon as possible. They will become larger if frost strikes them and they constitute a possible entrance for water into the basement.

Filling. To fill a crack in concrete, cut out the crack with a cold chisel to form a wedge with the inside wider than the outside. This will prevent the patch from falling out

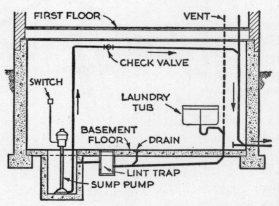

Fig. 4. Basements with drains below the sewer level can be kept dry with a sump pump.

after it dries. Use a stiff wire brush to remove any dirt or loose concrete from inside the crack. Wet down the sides of the crack and mix mortar of 1 part cement and 3 parts fine sand, adding enough water so that the mortar can be worked into the opening. Force the mortar in, making certain that it completely fills the opening, and smooth off the outside surface. Keep the patch moist and covered until it sets.

CRACK

CUT OUT WITH A COLD CHISEL

Fig. 6. Proper method of cutting out a crack in concrete before patching.

Exterior Walls. Exterior walls must be waterproof, or serious damage to the house will result. Inspect the outside walls at frequent intervals and try to locate any opening which might allow leakage.

WOOD SIDING

One of the most common materials used for exterior walls is wood siding. Wood siding is rather thin, and while it is usually backed with waterproof paper and sheathing, any flaw in the siding is bound to develop into a leak sooner or later.

There are several kinds of siding to be had. Some are thin, flat boards nailed so that they overlap, while others have edges machined to fit and lock together. To keep wood siding waterproof, keep it properly painted. No other portion of the house needs good paint as much as the siding.

COLD CHISEL

Fig. 5.

When a piece of siding cracks, pulls loose, or is broken, make repairs at once. If the board is damaged, it should be removed or replaced. Take care, when removing a piece of siding, not to split the edge of the board above. It may be possible to remove the nails from the broken board by prying up gently the board above, thus providing enough room to pull out the nails on the top portion of the lower board.

Notice the size of the nails and use this size when adding a new piece. Large nails will easily split thin siding.

Wood Shingles. Wood shingles are another kind of wood siding commonly used. To remove a cracked or rotting shingle, split it length-

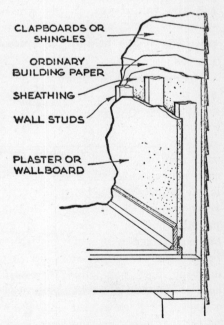

CLAPBOARDS OR SHINGLES

ORDINARY BUILDING PAPER

SHEATHING

WALL STUDS

PLASTER OR WALLBOARD

Fig. 7. Detail of outside wall construction.

wise with a knife or wood chisel and remove the pieces. If the nails under the upper shingles cannot be pulled out, use a hacksaw blade to cut off the top portion of the nails so that the new shingle can be slipped into place. Select a shingle of the same width as the one removed, put it into place, and nail with shingle nails.

STUCCO WALLS

Stucco exterior walls are usually made with several coats of Portland cement stucco, built up from wood or metal laths. Small hairline cracks may appear on the surface and these should be examined to determine their depth. If just the surface coat has cracked, they can be disregarded. Deep cracks or large openings that run the full depth of the stucco should be filled, as they will allow moisture to get behind the stucco

and cause much damage, not only to the laths but to the interior walls as well. If large sections of stucco drop out, and large cracks appear, you may be sure that something is radically wrong with the stucco, the laths, or the construction of the house as a whole.

Fig. 8. Cracks in stucco, particularly around window and door frames, should be patched immediately.

Cracks in stucco can be repaired with a mortar made of 1 part cement and 3 parts sand, or with a special stucco patching mixture, sold at hardware stores, which requires

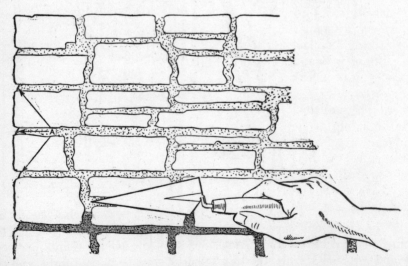

Fig. 9. Pointing irregular mortar courses. Note the pointing angle of mortar at A.

only the addition of water. These patching powders can be had in various colors, so that one can fill the

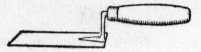

Fig. 11. Small trowel suitable for pointing up mortar joints and patching concrete.

crack with the same color stucco as the rest of the wall and avoid having an obtrusive patch.

Cut back the edges of the crack in the same manner employed in filling can be filled by brushing in a mixture of cement and water. After this is dry, the surface can be painted (see PAINTING CONCRETE).

BRICK WALLS

Brick walls come in for their share of leakage, as do walls of wood or stucco. A brick wall, if properly built, should be waterproof under all normal conditions. When leaks do occur, it is usually due to the fact that the joints between the bricks were not properly filled with mortar or

Fig. 10. Clean out loose mortar between bricks before patching.

a crack in concrete. Wet down the sides of the crack and force in the patching mortar. Keep the patch damp and protected from the sun until it is dry. Small hairline cracks the low grade mortar used has shrunk, leaving a space between the bricks. All mortar joints between bricks must be packed tight, and the mortar brought out flush with the surface of the brick. On horizontal joints, the mortar is brought out at the bottom, so that the joint slopes and resembles a shingle in its ability to shed water. If there are any depressions in the joints, water can collect in them and penetrate the smallest crack in the wall. Once moisture has made its way into a brick wall, more cracks are sure to

damage any of the sound mortar or the bricks. After cleaning the mortar brush out the cavity and wet it down. Mix some cement mortar, 1 part cement to 3 parts fine sand, and pack this into the joint. Trowel it smooth and build out the lower portion slightly.

If all mortar joints appear to be sound, but water continues to seep

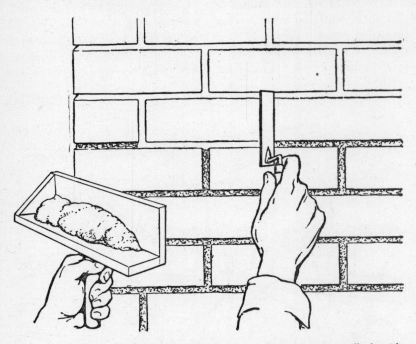

Fig. 12. Pointing regular brickwork mortar courses. Apply mortar flush with brickwork, then point mortar to slope down and out.

occur when the moisture freezes during the winter and expands.

Examine the brick wall carefully and mark any bricks around which the mortar is cracked or falling out. Remove all loose and cracked mortar before filling the joint. Use a cold chisel or small pick to clean out the loose mortar, but be careful not to

through the wall, coat the entire wall surface with a waterproofing composition designed for use on bricks.

Occasionally, an entire brick will become loose or break. Remove all the mortar around the brick with a cold chisel or pick, taking care not to damage the other joints or bricks.

Clean out the cavity in the wall and wet down the sides. Select a brick of the proper size and soak it in water for a short time. Spread cement mortar generously around the sides of the opening and over the brick. Force the brick back into place and pack the joints tightly with mortar.

stone, washing out through the joints. The efflorescence in a new wall is due to the moisture from the mortar, but in an old wall it is an indication that moisture is penetrating the masonry. The principal concern here is not the removal of these deposits but the location of the leak.

When efflorescence appears under

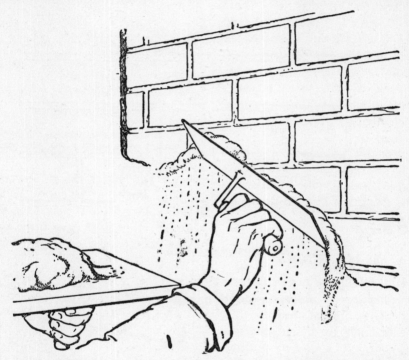

Fig. 13. A leaky brick wall can be waterproofed by giving it a coat of cement mortar.

EFFLORESCENCE

Efflorescence is the name given to a whitish substance found on masonry. It is most noticeable on brickwork, where it contrasts sharply with the red-colored bricks. It is caused by the soluble salts in the bricks, cement, lime, sand, and even

the window sills of a brick exterior wall, it is an indication that water is entering the brickwork at that point. A brick wall, uncapped, will show considerable efflorescence because the water does not drain off, but seeps down through the wall. Moisture can also enter the masonry from the ground and even draw the soluble salts from the surrounding earth.

In short, efflorescence is a good indication that the wall is not watertight, and steps should be taken to eliminate this condition. As for removing the efflorescence, this can sometimes be done with a wire brush and water. On more stubborn spots, scrub with a solution of 1 part muriatic acid and 5 parts water, and a fiber brush. Keep this solution away from the mortar joints as much as possible, and when the spot has been removed, flush the masonry with water, to which has been added some ammonia, to remove all traces of the acid.

This is by no means a certain method of removing efflorescence, and great care should be taken to avoid getting the acid on the hands or in the eyes.

LEAKY ROOFS

Even a small leak in the roof can cause considerable damage, and it should be repaired at once.

The first step in patching a leak in the roof is to locate its position. This can be done from the attic, provided the ceiling is unfinished. The best time to find a small leak, of course, is during a rain. If the work must be done in fair weather, have someone pour water on the roof in the general vicinity of the assumed leak. Once the opening has been located from the inside, push a thin piece of wire through it to locate the position from the outside. Do not take for granted, however,

that the leak is where the water drips from the attic ceiling. It may be that the water is penetrating at a higher point on the roof and flowing along rafters before dripping. Trace

Fig. 14. Streaks of efflorescence on a brick wall usually indicate that the wall leaks.

the wet portions of the rafter until you find the point of entry. If the leak is a large one, it may be possible to locate it by a close inspection of the underside of the roof, noting

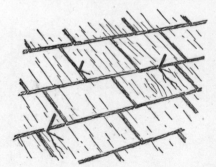

Fig. 15. Wires pushed through leaks to locate them from above.

where light appears. If the attic ceiling has been covered with wallboard or other finish, you will have to remove it before the leak can be located.

Working on Roofs. Take all precautions, when on the roof, to avoid a bad fall. A strong rope, thrown over the roof and attached to some object on the side opposite to where you plan to work, is a simple and effective safety measure.

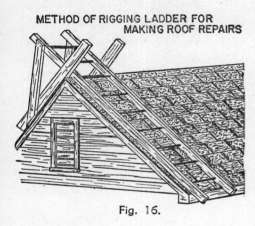

METHOD OF RIGGING LADDER FOR MAKING ROOF REPAIRS

Fig. 16.

If you plan extensive work on the roof, obtain a ladder with hooks that can be fastened over the ridge of the

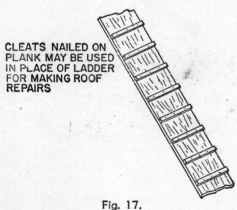

CLEATS NAILED ON PLANK MAY BE USED IN PLACE OF LADDER FOR MAKING ROOF REPAIRS

Fig. 17.

roof to provide you with a solid footing. If a ladder is not available, nail cleats to a long, wide board and

hang it over the ridge of the roof by means of hooks or boards. Wear shoes with rubber soles, if possible, and be very careful of wet and slippery wood shingles. If you have not had much experience in working on roofs, you had better work on hands and knees rather than upright.

Remember also, that walking on a roof can be harmful to it. By walking about, you are liable to open additional leaks; consequently, limit yourself to the area which is to be repaired. Do as much work as possible from a ladder against the side of the house, to avoid walking on the roof. Be sure that the ladder is secure and that there is a solid object at the top for you to seize, should you lose your balance.

Wood Shingles. If the roof is covered with wood shingles, it is likely that the leak is caused by a shingle's having split or warped out of shape, or because a shingle nail has rusted and the shingle has slipped out of place.

Do as little tinkering with the shingles as possible, for you may do

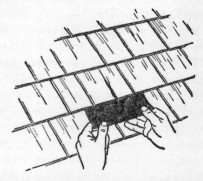

Fig. 18. Leak in a roof repaired by slipping a piece of metal or tar paper under the damaged shingle.

more harm than good. If the shingle has split but is still held securely, slip a piece of copper or tar paper under it. This will seal off the shingle from the under portion of the roof and stop the leak. A piece of copper is best for this work because it is noncorrosive. Tin can be used, but it is a temporary measure and will have to be replaced sooner or later. It should not be necessary to nail the copper, as the shingle will hold it in place.

If the shingle is loose, push it back into position and nail it with a shingle nail driven into the exposed portion of the shingle; then coat the top of the nail with roofing compound.

If the shingle is badly split, or is rotting, it will have to be replaced. Remove the old shingle by splitting it lengthwise and removing the pieces. Slip a new shingle, the same width as the old, into place and nail. If possible, use a shingle that has been weathered, for it will not be as sharply apparent as a new one.

When an entire wood-shingled roof is in poor condition, you can give the surface a coat of special composition which will prolong the life of the roof for a few more years.

Composition. Leaks in composition shingles should be repaired in the same manner described for wood shingles. Composition shingles usually come in sections consisting of three, or even four, shingles linked together at the end. To remove one of these sections without disturbing the other sections is ticklish work. Tar paper or copper, slipped under

the shingle where the leak occurs, will give satisfactory service for a long period. A compound can also be used on these shingles. Some composition shingles are so light in weight that a strong wind can force them up enough to drive water underneath. If such shingles are causing the roof to leak, lift them enough to apply a coat of roofing cement to the under portion.

Slate and Asbestos. Both these types of shingles are very brittle and must be handled with care or they will break. Most leaks in roofs covered with these materials occur when one or more of the shingles breaks loose. To make repairs, you must first remove the defective shingle.

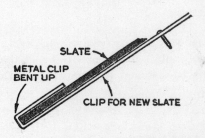

SLATE
METAL CLIP BENT UP
CLIP FOR NEW SLATE

Fig. 19. Metal clip used to attach slate shingle in place.

This is rather difficult, as the nail holding the shingle to the roof is covered by the shingle above. Cut the nail by inserting a hacksaw blade under the shingle and working it back and forth until the nail is severed. When you have removed the old shingle, attach a strip of noncorrosive metal, such as copper, to the wood portion of the roof. This strip should be several inches wide and long enough so that it extends at least an inch below the end of the shingle. Insert the new shingle into position and bend the end of the metal strip to form a hook which will hold the shingle in place.

REROOFING

Putting on the original roof is a job usually left to professional roofers, but reroofing is not too difficult a task for the home mechanic, since the old roof can be left to serve as a base for the new. The old roofing also provides a limited degree of protection until the new one is completed. After the new roof is on, the old will afford additional protection against any leakage, as well as provide an appreciable amount of insulation.

It is not suggested, however, that the home mechanic attempt to reroof the main dwelling, for he is likely to encounter varying roof angles which will necessitate valleys and flashings. Work of this type requires knowledge and experience

and is best done by professionals. But the home mechanic should not have very much difficulty in reroofing a simple structure like a garage or workshop.

Nearly any type of roofing material can be used over wood shingles. Cost is a primary factor in determining what materials to use, but remember, if you plan to do the work yourself, that the saving in

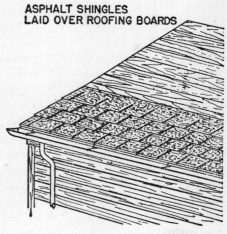

ASPHALT SHINGLES LAID OVER ROOFING BOARDS

Fig. 21.

labor should allow you to use the very best grade of materials.

Under normal conditions, the roof rafters will support the added weight of a new roof, but if the structure is very old or poorly constructed, it is wise to check the condition of the rafters and shingle laths.

Recondition the old roof before adding the new. Nail down any loose shingles, replace any that are missing or rotten, and be sure that there are no protruding nail heads.

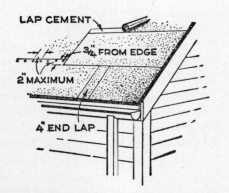

Fig. 20. Roll roofing is durable and very easy to put down. One roll will cover approximately 100 square feet.

To put on another roof of wood shingles, cut back the old shingles along the edges of the roof for several inches (see Fig. 22-A, C, and E) and fill the space with board of the same thickness as the old roofing (B, D, and F). This is done to provide a solid base on which to nail the first course of shingles and to preserve a neat, even appearance along the edges of the roof.

Begin shingling at the edge of the roof and double the first course of shingles, with the top layer spaced so that the seams between the shingles on the bottom

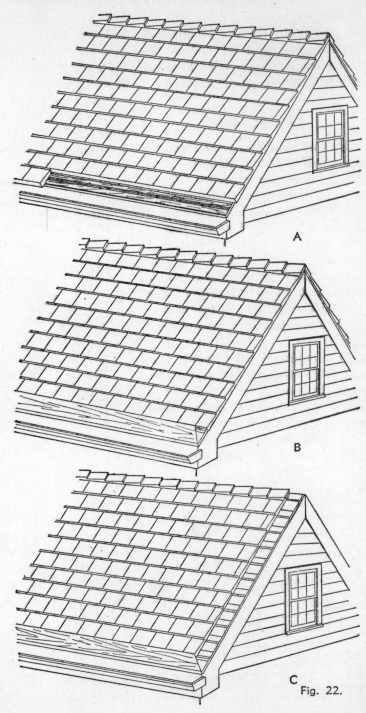

Fig. 22.

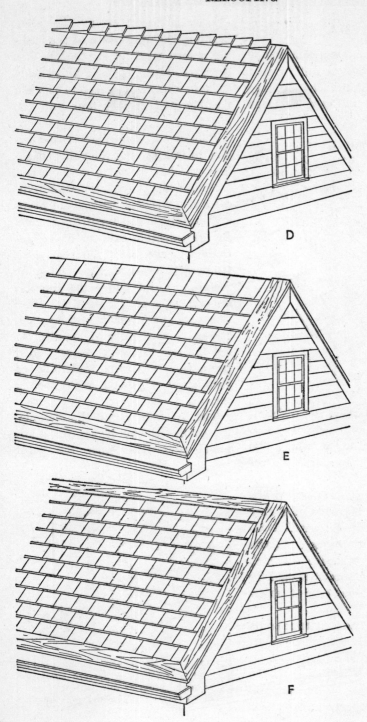

D

E

F

course are all covered. Thereafter, lay the shingles in a single course. The amount of shingle exposed may be from 4 to 5 inches, in most cases, but very long shingles, such as those 2 feet long, can be exposed as much as 10 inches. If the shingles are to be stained, do so beforehand.

Be sure that you use rustproof shingle nails, as any other kind will not last long. The nails must be long enough to penetrate the thickness of the roofing. Use a 3d nail for shingles, but if you are reroofing with shingles over shingles you will need a 5d nail.

LEAKS AT FLASHING

One of the most common points for leaks to occur in a wall or roof is around the flashing. The flashings are strips of metal used to make

DETAIL OF CHIMNEY FLASHING

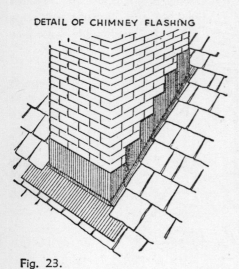

Fig. 23.

watertight joints where two different structures, such as the chimney and roof, come together, or where two roof angles join to form a roof valley.

Because flashing is exposed to the weather it must be made of a noncorrosive metal like copper. Galvanized steel is sometimes used as flashing, and this and other metals which are not fully rustproof should be kept coated with some type of waterproofing.

Put on flashing so that it presents no opening which water can penetrate. When two sheets of flashing are used, the top will overlap the bottom in the same fashion as shingles that are properly laid.

Leaks will occur around the valley flashing when the width of the flashing is insufficient or the flashing has corroded. If the flashing is not wide enough, water will penetrate between flashing and roofing and into the house.

Patching Leaks. When a roof begins to leak around the valley flashings, the best thing to do is to call a roofing expert. This situation indicates that the flashing was not properly installed, and repairing it calls for considerable skill in order not to damage the rest of the roof. As a temporary measure, slip triangular pieces of metal under the shingles on each side of the flashing. Start this work at the bottom of the valley, and make each piece of metal overlap the one below it. As an added precaution, coat the underside of each sheet of metal with roofing cement.

The flashing around the chimney is usually in two layers for additional protection, since the point

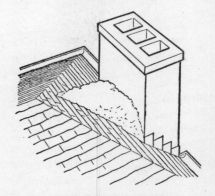

Fig. 24. Special flashing is required in back of a chimney to prevent snow and ice from collecting at this point and eventually melting and leaking through the roof.

where the chimney and roof join is vulnerable. Flashing is laid along the side of the chimney and turned into the masonry. The cement mortar in the masonry holds the flashing in place and prevents water from getting under it. The bottom of the flashing is turned under the roofing, precluding the penetration of water apply roofing compound wherever necessary.

Frames. Place the flashing around window and door frames under the siding and then over the frame, so that water cannot enter this joint. Never nail down the exposed portions of the flashing, for this will provide a possible entrance

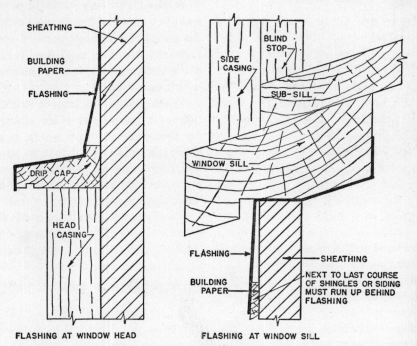

FLASHING AT WINDOW HEAD   FLASHING AT WINDOW SILL

Fig. 25. Metal flashing provides a waterproof joint between window frames and exterior walls.

under the roofing. A leak in the flashing at the chimney or the roof can easily be stopped. If the flashing has pulled out of the masonry because of high winds or poor mortar, secure it again by cleaning out the joint, reinserting the edge of the flashing, and filling the joint with cement mortar. For other leaks where the flashing enters the roof, for water. Pay particular attention to the flashing around window and door frames of brick and stucco houses; it is possible to make a tight fit between the siding and the frame when both are of wood, but almost impossible to do so when the side is of one material and the frame another. The frames should be flashed, not only at the top and sides, but also at the bottom, to prevent water from flowing along the underside of the sill and into the masonry. If there is no flashing at the bottom, a groove, cut along the underside of the sill, helps in keeping water from flowing into the masonry.

CAULKING

There are many small seams on the outside wall of a house which cannot be very effectively covered with flashing, yet they provide openings for both wind and rain. One of the best fillings used for these small openings is a good quality caulking compound. This resembles putty, except that it never dries completely. Its advantage lies in the fact that it will expand and contract with the crack, rather than split and fall out as a hard material would do. While caulking compound never becomes hard, a film will form on the surface and the compound can be painted to match the surrounding surface. Caulking compounds can be obtained in several colors and can be used on both wood and masonry.

Caulking Gun. You can apply the compound with a putty knife, but this is slow work and requires considerable practice before the right technique is developed. A more practical method of application is with a caulking gun. This device is some-

CAULKING GUN

Fig. 26.

what like a grease gun in that it shoots the compound into the opening under pressure, filling the entire depth of the crack. Caulking with a gun can also be done much faster than with a putty knife. The gun can be purchased with several sizes of nozzles, used according to the size of the crack to be filled.

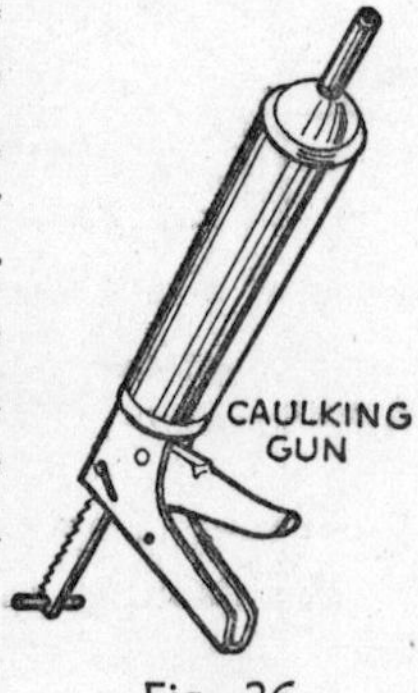

Oakum. Fill large openings with oakum, employed for filling seams in boats. After packing the oakum well into the opening, coat the surface with caulking compound to make the joint watertight.

When doing a complete caulking job on a house, pay close attention to the seams around window and door frames, the joint formed by the chimney against the side of the house, and the places where front and back steps meet the exterior wall.

Use Indoors. Caulking compound is also effective for indoor use, where sink or bathtub joins the wall.

GUTTERS AND DOWNSPOUTS

When gutters are installed along the eaves of a house, they have sufficient pitch to carry water to the downspouts. If the pitch of the gutter is reduced because one of the brackets holding it to the roof is loose, water will collect in the depression and flow over the sides of the gutter. This overflow can wash out a section of the lawn, or it may be the cause of a damp basement. If the pitch of the gutter is incorrect, it can generally be remedied by tightening the bracket holding the gutter to the roof.

Clogged Gutters. Gutters should be kept as free of leaves and other rubbish as possible. If the gutter is made neither of a rustproof material nor of wood, a collection of damp leaves will cause rust and rotting.

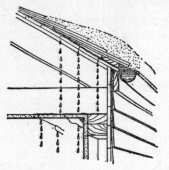

Fig. 27. Improperly installed gutters will allow water from melting snow and ice to back up under roofing and cause leaks.

Leaves are similar to a sponge in that they absorb a great amount of water. This added weight may be too great for the brackets holding the gutters and may tear them loose from the roof. Keeping the gutters clean during the winter is particularly important. An accumulation of ice can cause a great deal of damage to the gutters, and there is always the possibility that snow and ice may back up along the edge of the roof. During a thaw, or if the roof is not insulated, the snow and ice will melt, and when there is a sufficient accumulation, water will run under the roofing and into the house.

Clean the gutters thoroughly in the fall, after the leaves are off the trees, and again in the spring. While cleaning, inspect the entire gutter for rust. Patch any rusted spots on the bottom of the gutter with a heavy piece of canvas and some white lead. Paint the white lead over the rust, coat the canvas with white lead on both sides, and place it over the rusted area.

Paint metal gutters that are liable to rust with a good exterior paint (see PAINTING METAL). Paint wood

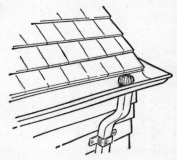

Fig. 28. A wire cage over the top of a downspout will prevent leaves and other refuse from clogging it up.

gutters on the outside with exterior paint and on the inside with a waterproofing coat; this will do much to increase their length of service.

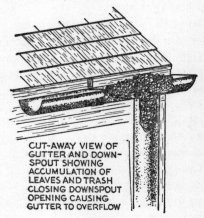

CUT-AWAY VIEW OF GUTTER AND DOWN-SPOUT SHOWING ACCUMULATION OF LEAVES AND TRASH CLOSING DOWNSPOUT OPENING CAUSING GUTTER TO OVERFLOW

Fig. 29.

Downspouts. Keep downspouts, or leaders, free of any object that might clog them. The best method of doing this is to place a piece of wire mesh over the opening of the downspout where it connects with the gutter. Small wire baskets are available for this purpose. If a downspout becomes clogged, it will not only fail to carry the water away from the gutters, but in winter the water inside the metal spout may freeze and split the sides.

CARE OF SKYLIGHTS

As a skylight might be considered to be a cross between a window and a roof it is subject to deficiencies of both and should be given considerable care and frequent inspections.

The putty around the glass must be kept in first class condition. If it appears to be cracked and loose, then it should be removed and new putty put in.

You will notice that the joint between the roof and the skylight frame is made watertight through the use of metal flashing. If this flashing is not made of some non-rusting metal, it should be examined for any small pin point rust holes. If the metal is in good condition, it can be kept so by painting. (See PAINTING METAL.) Check to see that the flashing is secured to the frame and that there are no exposed nail-heads or nail holes. If there are small holes, these can be covered with roofing cement, but be careful not to use too much cement as an excess may act as a dam, causing water to back up under the roofing. Small seams can be filled with roof-

ing cement, observing the same cautions.

Check the woodwork of the frame and sash for any signs of rot. If the wood is kept properly painted, you will not have much to worry about on this score. If the old paint is cracked or peeling, it should be removed, the wood given a chance to dry and then covered with at least three coats of exterior paint.

Do not let leaves or any other rubbish collect around the skylight. Leaves are spongelike and will hold rain water for a considerable length of time, thus keeping the woodwork damp.

DRY WELLS

The purpose of a dry well is to allow the water discharged from the downspouts to be absorbed by the earth without damage to lawns, and to eliminate the possibility of water seeping along the foundation walls and entering the basement.

It is wrong to allow water which flows off the roof to be carried to cesspools or septic tanks. These containers are designed to dispose of a limited amount of water per day, and if they are filled to capacity with water they cannot take care of the sewage from the house. Some communities allow the drainage from roofs to be carried away in the same pipes used for the sewage system, and this is a simple solution to the problem. For homes where this is illegal, or for those with cesspools and septic tanks, a dry well is best. See drawing in Fig. 30.

Making a Dry Well. A simple dry well can be made by removing the top and bottom of a barrel and sinking it in the ground so that the top of the barrel is about a foot below the surface. The location of the barrel in relation to the house must depend on local drainage conditions. On level ground, the well must be a considerable distance from the house, but when the ground slopes away from the foundation, the well may be as close as six feet. Fill the barrel with rocks and place a piece of wire netting over the top to prevent dirt from falling into the rocks. Connect the downspout to the barrel with sections of 3-inch soil pipe.

When a larger dry well is required, it can be made out of concrete blocks or stone. This well should be located some distance from the house, and the pipe running between it and the downspouts must have a slight pitch to carry the water into the well. The well should have a removable concrete top.

SNOW REMOVAL

Many homeowners have worked out ingenious ways to avoid the task of shoveling snow from their walks and driveways. A favorite method is to install pipes inside the concrete walk so that when snow falls, hot water can be pumped through the lines to warm the concrete and melt

the snow. While these home-constructed snow melting systems work out very well, most of us are content to tackle the problem of snow removal with the old fashioned snow shovel. There are several little points, which if observed will lessen the chore.

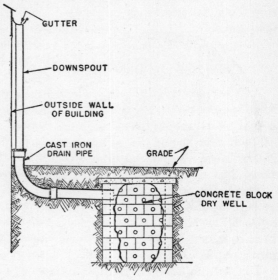

GUTTER

DOWNSPOUT

OUTSIDE WALL OF BUILDING

CAST IRON DRAIN PIPE

GRADE

CONCRETE BLOCK DRY WELL

Fig. 30. A large dry well built of concrete blocks.

Try to remove the snow as soon as possible after it has ceased to fall— before it has been packed down by footsteps and car wheels. In any event, get at the job before there is a thaw followed by freezing weather. Once there is a layer of ice under the snow, the job of removal becomes increasingly difficult. A coat of paraffin rubbed on the shovel will keep the snow from sticking. With a metal shovel, the paraffin can be rubbed directly on; if you have a wooden one it is easier to melt the paraffin and brush it on. Do not use the shovel for breaking ice as you will spoil the edge and perhaps ruin the entire shovel. Use a broad-bladed cutter for this purpose.

Calcium chloride and rock salt will melt snow and ice when sprinkled over the surface. Care should be taken, however, to keep them off the lawn or garden.

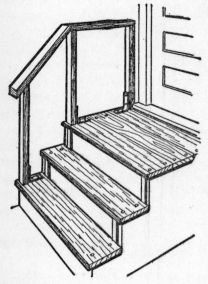

Fig. 30a. Concrete steps are sometimes dangerously slippery in the winter unless covered with a wood frame, as shown above.

If snow and ice from the roof collect in the gutters it is usually a sign that the gutters have not been hung properly. The weight of the snow may easily tear out the gutter brackets. The best remedy is to re-hang the gutters properly. (See GUTTERS AND DOWNSPOUTS.)

Concrete and masonry steps often become covered with ice and are the cause of nasty falls. This condition can be partially eliminated by building removable wood frames that are fitted over the steps during the winter months.

TERMITES

Termites are insects, and although they are sometimes called "white ants," they belong to a different species than the ant. Termites obtain their food from the cellulose in wood and can do extensive damage to homes and furniture. Termites are to be found in almost every section of this country.

To get rid of termites it is necessary to know something of their habits. There are many types of termites but they have similar characteristics.

Classes. There are roughly, three classes of termites. First, are the reproductives. These have wings which enable them to move about and start new colonies. When the reproductives reach a new nest, they shed their wings and disappear underground to lay eggs. They do not damage

WORKER

REPRODUCTIVE (NOTE WINGS)

Fig. 31. Termites.

wood, but their presence indicates that destructive termites are also near.

The second member of the termite colony is the soldier who remains near the colony to guard it from other insects and is often mistaken for a white ant.

Finally, there is the termite worker who causes all the damage.

The worker provides food for the other members of the colony. The worker is white, and about ¼ inch in length. He has no wings and is blind. He always remains in darkness, and the only way you can find

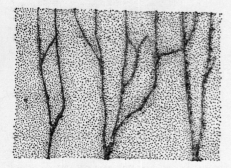

Fig. 32. An indication of termites. Earthen tunnels built up the side of concrete foundations.

him is to break in on him. Because he cannot stand the light, he eats wood from the inside, leaving only the outer shell. In many cases, this outer wall is so thin that it can be broken with a fingernail.

Not only is the termite worker unable to endure exposure to light, but he must return to the moist earth at intervals if he is to live.

In order to remain in the dark and still have access to the woodwork, the termite workers build earthen passageways. If these passageways are broken, the termites in the wood will die, and unless the passageways are rebuilt, the termites on the outside will have to look elsewhere for their food.

Eliminating. The best method of eliminating termites is to prevent them from reaching the woodwork of a building. This is done by plac-

ing a piece of copper between the masonry of the foundation and the wood sill. The copper should extend beyond the masonry on each side about 3 or 4 inches. Bend this projection down to an approximate 45-degree angle. The smooth surface and the sharp edges of the metal will prevent the termites from building their earthen tunnels from the masonry to the wood.

Few buildings are provided with this safeguard, however, and the home mechanic must determine whether his home is being attacked by termites and, if so, destroy the clay tunnels. The most likely place to look for termites is in the basement, where the woodwork is either in direct contact with the ground or separated from it by only a few inches of masonry. Remember that termites work from the inside, and the exterior of wood attacked by

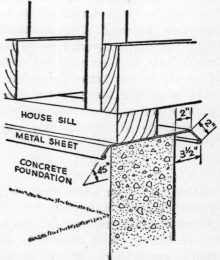

Fig. 33. How sheet metal is used to protect the woodwork of a house from attack by termites.

them will look perfectly sound. Stick a penknife or an ice pick into the wood. If it goes in easily, you can feel reasonably sure that termites are at work. Earthen tunnels on masonry also indicate termites. By destroying these tunnels you effectively stop any further action by termites. While this method is sound in theory it is difficult to execute, as you must maintain a constant search for new tunnels. The home mechanic can do much to keep his home free of termites, nevertheless, by making sure that all the masonry work is in good condition. Termites can build their tunnels through cracks in masonry and cement blocks. Fill all cracks and smooth all joints to make as even a surface as possible. Replace any woodwork in direct contact with the ground with concrete.

There are certain chemicals which, when forced into the wood and into the ground surrounding the house, are poisonous to termites. To be effective, however, these chemicals must literally be forced through the wood fibres, and the home mechanic does not possess the equipment for this work. In nearly every community are concerns that will rid your house of termites this way.

DRY ROT

Dry rot is the name given to a fungus that attacks woodwork if it is alternately wet and dry and poorly ventilated. If it is allowed to remain, the strength of the timber will be destroyed and must be replaced. When woodwork is likely to

be subject to dry rot, it should be treated with a wood preservative. Many of these now on the market can be applied with spray gun or brush. Or you can buy wood impreg-

Fig. 34. A piece of timber attacked by dry rot.

nated with the preservative. Ordinary painting may not preserve wood from dry rot as any small crack in the paint will let moisture in.

WASHING A HOUSE

The exterior of a house can be freshened considerably by washing, provided that the paint is in good condition.

If the surface is not too dirty, this job can be done with plain soap and warm water. In some communities, however, where there is a good deal of soot in the air, it will be necessary to use a commercial paint-cleaning powder in the water. Test this cleaning agent on a small portion of the wall to make sure that it is not so strong as to soften the paint.

Start washing at the bottom and work up, so that the dirty water will not run over dry portions of the wall and leave streaks. If these streaks occur on a dry and dirty surface, they are very difficult to remove, but if the surface has been washed, they can be rinsed off easily.

You will need a scrubbing brush and a ladder, and it is very important to get the entire wall clean. Any dirty spot will be sharply conspicuous. After the wall has been scrubbed, it can be rinsed with a garden hose.

Drip Stains. These stains, found under window sills and door frames, can be removed by scrubbing the area with a cleaning solution made of 1 cup of trisodiumphosphate in a pail of hot water. The solution should be rinsed off with plenty of water.

INTERIOR REPAIRS

FLOORS

The floors in most homes are composed of two separate layers. The bottom layer is called the subflooring and is made of rough, tongued and grooved lumber nailed directly to the floor joists. In some cases the subflooring will run diagonally to the joists, while in others it will run at right angles to them. A layer of building paper covers the subfloor to keep out dust and dirt, and the finish, or hardwood, floor is laid over this. The finish floor runs at right angles to the subfloor and is nailed to it. The finish floor can be either of planks or of hardwood.

Creaking Floors. In most cases, a creaking floor is caused by a loosening of the nails holding the subfloor to the joists. These may either pull loose or be loosened by shrinkage in the wood. Creaking is usually in the subfloor but it will sometimes occur in the finish floor, particularly if the floor was put down before the wood was completely seasoned. If the creak is in the subflooring and the underside is exposed, as when the flooring functions as the ceiling for an unfinished basement, drive a

small wedge between the joist and the loose board. This will take up the play in the board and the noise will stop. If several boards are loose, nail a piece of wood to the joist, high enough to prevent these boards from

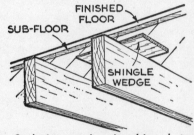

Fig. 1. A thin wood wedge driven between the joist and the flooring will often stop floor boards from creaking.

moving down. The nail heads will keep the boards from moving up, effectively ending the noise.

In many cases, it is impossible to reach the subflooring without tear-

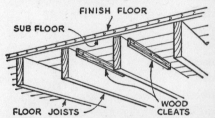

Fig. 2. A wood cleat nailed to the floor joist will stop a squeak in the floor caused by a loose subfloor board.

ing up the finish floor or moving a ceiling. As neither of these is feasible, the only alternative is to try to locate the floor joist by tapping on the floor. If a floor joist near the

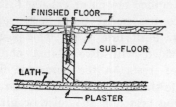

Fig. 3. Squeaky floors repaired by driving finishing nails through flooring into one of the joists.

creak can be located, then 2- or 3-inch finishing nails can be driven through the finish floor and subfloor into the joist. Drive the nail at an angle and when it is near the surface of the floor, use a nail set to drive it below the surface of the wood. This will prevent hitting the finish floor with the hammer and marring the finish. Make the nail inconspicuous by filling the hole with putty and applying a little paint or stain to match the rest of the floor.

Occasionally a creaking floor will be caused by a loose board in the finish floor. The board can be located by its movement when weight is placed upon it. Use 2-inch finishing nails for this and drive them in at an angle, using the nail set in the manner described above. It is often possible to take the creak out of a finish floor by putting a little wood glue on a putty knife and running the blade between the boards.

When boards in the finish floor warp to such an extent that they pull away from the subfloor and bulge, they can sometimes be driven back into place by putting a piece of heavy paper and a block of wood over them, and tapping the wood sharply with a hammer. The piece of wood prevents the hammer from damaging the flooring. Take care in doing this, however, for the thin edges of tongued and grooved boards can easily be split.

Sagging Floors. When this condition is found in a very old house, it is generally because the floor joists and girders have been weakened by rot or by insects. In a new house, a weak floor can, in most cases, be blamed directly on the builder. A flooring built of undersized materials and tacked together will be neither substantial nor capable of bearing much weight.

In dealing with a weak and sagging floor, you will first have to raise it to its proper level. If it is the first floor, with a basement underneath, the work is in the range of the home mechanic. Use heavy lumber and a screw jack to accomplish the work. The size of the lumber should be about 4 x 4 inches. Place one of the 4 x 4 timbers on the basement floor directly under the sag and put the screw jack on top of it. This beam will distribute the weight of the flooring over a relatively large portion of the basement flooring. If the basement flooring is of heavy concrete, this step will not be required. Nail a piece of 4 x 4 along the sagging joists. Use a third piece of timber as a vertical beam from the top of the jack to the under portion of the 4 x 4 nailed to the joists. Turn up the jack until the floor is level. Do not attempt to bring the floor to a level position all at once. If this is done, you are almost sure to crack the plaster walls and ceiling in the room above. Raise the jack only a fraction each week and you will avoid doing extensive damage to the rooms above. Check the position of the floor with a level and when it is correct, measure the distance from the bottom of the horizontal 4 x 4 to the floor of the basement. Cut a piece of 4 x 4 to this length. Turn the jack up enough to allow this beam to stand on end under the horizontal 4 x 4. Make sure that it is perfectly vertical and that it rests firmly on the floor. Remove the jack, along with the other timbers, leaving only one vertical and one horizontal 4 x 4. If one entire floor is

sagging, it will probably be necessary to use more than one vertical support. In this case, place a vertical 4 x 4 under each end of the horizontal beam.

Another means of raising a floor is to use metal posts with screw jacks built into them. The post is provided with two plates, one of which rests on the basement floor while the other fits between the top of the post and the joist or girder to be raised. These posts are made so that they can be adjusted to different heights. Once the floor has been brought to the right level, the post can be left as a permanent support. As before, turn the jack only a small amount each week, so that the floor will be raised slowly.

Footing. When part of the total weight of a floor and the objects on

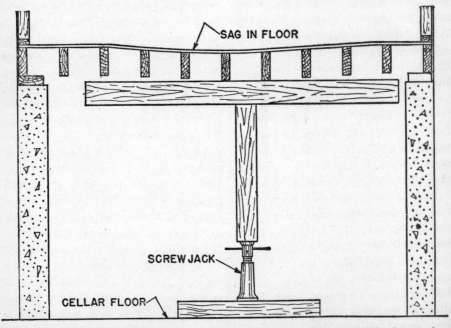

Fig. 4. Lifting up a sagging floor with a screw jack and several lengths of 4 x 4 in. timber.

It is supported by posts, it is important that each post have the proper footing. Most concrete floors in the basement are rather thin and it is often necessary to prepare the floor before installing the posts.

To make a substantial footing for the posts in the basement floor, break up about two square feet of the concrete floor at the point where the post is to stand. Do this work with a heavy hammer (don't ruin a good claw hammer on it), or with a piece of pipe. Once the surface is broken, dig a hole about 12 inches deep and fill it with concrete made with 1 part cement, 2 parts sand, and 3 parts coarse aggregate. Level this with the floor, making a smooth surface, and allow about a week for the footing to dry before placing the posts upon it. Cover the concrete during this period and keep it moist.

Fortunately, most defects are associated with the first floor, and the basement underneath allows one to put in posts and other kinds of reinforcements. Sagging floors above the first floor level cannot practicably

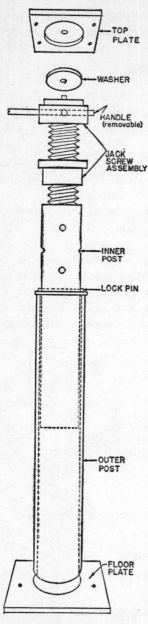

Fig. 5. Sagging and weak floors can be reinforced and made level with this combination jack and steel post.

TOP PLATE

WASHER

HANDLE (removable)

JACK SCREW ASSEMBLY

INNER POST

LOCK PIN

OUTER POST

FLOOR PLATE

be remedied, short of taking up the flooring and making extensive repairs. The services of a good carpenter are recommended for this job.

Cracks in Floors. If the wood in a matched hardwood floor is properly seasoned, there should be very few cracks appearing between the boards. Many houses, however, are equipped with plank floors in which cracks of varying size are almost sure to appear between each board. In very old houses these cracks can be quite large. There are several kinds of plastic fillers, but many of these tend to shrink and crack as they dry. A good filler can be made of sawdust and wood glue mixed into a paste. If possible, the sawdust should be of the same wood as the flooring.

Before attempting to fill a crack, clean it out, for any dirt in it will prevent the filler from adhering to the wood. Pack the filler in tightly, so that it stands slightly higher than the surface of the floor. After it is dry, sand the top to the floor level and apply a little stain to match the finish on the rest of the floor. Over very wide cracks glue a thin strip of wood and sand or plane it to match the floor surface.

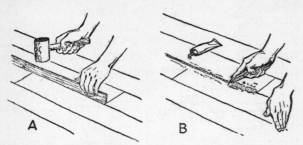

Fig. 6. Two ways to fill cracks in flooring. A, shows strip of wood set into large crack. B, filling a crack with plastic crack filler.

Defects and Repairs. Wooden floors become uneven through much wear, and leave high places, particularly where knots and heads of nails occur, since these possess a greater

If the underlying joists warp and twist, or if there is some settlement of the foundation walls on which these joists rest, the level of the floor may be disturbed.

Replacing Worn Boards. First study the diagram of a single wooden plank floor given in Fig. 7a. The joists, as will be seen, are usually two inches wide. The boards, which cross the joists at right angles, are nailed at the center line of the joist. If the ends of two boards meet in the form of a heading joint on one joist, both boards must be nailed to the joist. To remove the boards without damage is not easy, but on the

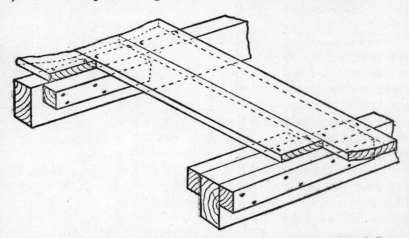

Fig. 7a. Shows how short lengths of wood secured to the sides of floor joists may be used to repair an area of defective floorboards.

resistance to wear. Unevenness from another cause occasionally takes place along the edges of the floorboards, which become raised due to the boards curling up as they warp.

assumption that one board is to be discarded, in any case, we can bore a round hole as near as convenient to the side of the joist, and use a keyhole saw and compass saw to cut one board close up to the joists. If the other end of the board runs to a heading joint on another joist, work back along the board, prying it up at the intervening joists and taking it off the joist where it ends.

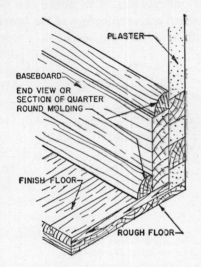

PLASTER

BASEBOARD
END VIEW OR
SECTION OF QUARTER
ROUND MOLDING

FINISH FLOOR

ROUGH FLOOR

Fig. 7. Quarter round molding is ideal for covering cracks between the floor and baseboard or the wall and baseboard.

Perhaps only part of the lifted board is defective, in which event we can cut it across to end on a suitable joist, ready for replacement later. In prying up the board, the nails will most likely be pulled up out of the joist; rest the board, bottom side up, on a stool or saw horse, and tap the nails back sufficiently for the heads to be gripped by pincers, or by the claws of the hammer. Obstinate boards may have to have the nails punched fully down into the joist to free the board. If a heading joint is not conveniently near, the board may have to be cut through at two places to remove the

defective. Electricians and carpenters often use a special floorboard saw, with a curved cutting edge; it is possible to saw straight across one board without damaging the boards at either side. The handyman, however, will generally bore a half-inch hole and cut across the board using a keyhole saw, as previously mentioned.

Find the run of the joists. The position of the nail heads will indicate this, and on the assumption that they mark approximately the middle line of the joist, measure an inch to either side of the nail, and square a line across with a square. Mark a pencilled line. Put a fine bradawl through the board about a quarter of an inch away from the pencil line, on the free side, then bore a hole with a brace and bit or with a twist drill. If these dimensions have been correctly established the joist will be visible and the saw can be put through to cut alongside the joist, across the board.

As soon as the cut is long enough, take out the keyhole saw and enter a compass saw, or a small crosscut saw, and complete the cut.

Beware of water pipes, gas line and electric cables, when cutting the boards; they run usually in the space between joists. When there is a room below the floor where work is in progress, some guide to pipes and cables, etc., can be secured from the position of lighting and plumbing fixtures in the room below.

Having cut the board, the ends of the fixed parts can be trimmed with a sharp chisel to a square edge. If several boards have to be cut away, take them back to joists one or two away to right or left from the one originally selected for the patch. In other words, break the joints, so that a board extending over a given joist is next to one at which a board ends, and so on. Thus we shall not get a weak line of joints running along jointed over a single joist. In this instance it is assumed that both boards can be taken to the bench and cut by a tenon saw to a suitable angle. This makes a neat and sound job, the nails being driven through the oblique portion. The angle can be marked across the edges of the board with an adjustable bevel.

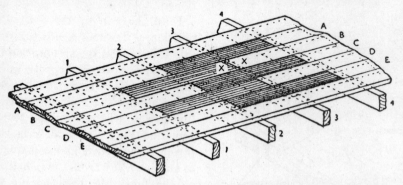

Fig. 7b. Showing an area of defective floorboards between joists 2 and 3. The boards in the shaded area should be removed and replaced.

the same joist. A typical job is shown in Fig. 7b; the joists are numbered and the floorboards lettered. A heading joint is shown at X, X, on board B. It is not always practical to make heading joints when replacing the boards, and the best thing to do is to support the ends of the replacement boards by nailing or screwing a strong cleat to the side of the joist where the end of the new board will rest. The cleat should be at least 1½ inches thick and about 3 inches wide; take it halfway along and under the boards adjoining the one that it will support. This arrangement is illustrated in Fig. 7a.

Two boards can be cut through obliquely, when they have to be

Leveling a Worn Floor. Sweep the floor, and brush out the cracks with a stiff brush. (A wire brush is excellent for the purpose.) Scrub down the floor and let it dry well before beginning operations. Then go along the boards with a hammer and nail punch, driving down the nails well below the surface, so that they will not damage the sharp cutting edge of the plane. Set the smoothing plane to make a medium cut and work over the high places. Follow the grain and if the wood tears, change the direction of the planing. In bad cases a broad chisel may be convenient for removing the worst part. Next, reset the plane to make a finer cut; trim the edges of the boards and take off irregularities.

After new flooring has been laid, it may be found that the ends stand up higher than the old floor; punch down the nails, and taper off the end part of the new board so as to make a gradual change. Of course, in order to make a really good job, the replacement boards ought to be reduced in thickness to match the older flooring, though this may not often be practicable.

Parquet and Wood Block Floors. Loose blocks in a floor, if there are not many, should be removed. It will then be possible to scrape off the old mastic underneath. Put in fresh mastic, which you can get at hardware stores, and bed in the block. If the defect is extensive, the repairs may be more than an amateur can successfully undertake.

Parquet floors are glued and, invariably, pinned; dampness may cause the parts of the design to come loose, and in such cases the cause of the dampness should be found before attempting a remedy. Wood glue can be used to hold the different parts of a pattern together if a whole unit is defective. These diamonds, etc., are bedded upon a piece of low quality material with an open weave, which helps to hold them together. It will probably be best to unite the various parts of an element first, and let the glue harden, before relaying, so as to ensure that all joints are firmly set and safe to handle.

Opening a Floor. Quite often the home mechanic is faced with the task of opening a floor to repair a water line or heating main running under the floor. If the floor is made out of planks this job can be done with the same directions as those given for replacing worn floor boards. If the flooring is made with tongued and grooved boards the job is somewhat more complicated because the tongue of one board is fitted into the groove of the next and any attempt to pry up a board would result in damage to either the tongue or the groove. It is quite true that in some cases the boards are so badly shrunk that there are large spaces between each board, allowing one to be lifted out without damage to the others, but this is the exception more than the general rule. The most practical way to lift one or two boards and not damage any of the flooring is to cut off the tongue of one board and then make crosscuts along the joists. After these three cuts have been made the board can be lifted out and additional boards removed by cutting them crosswise at the joists.

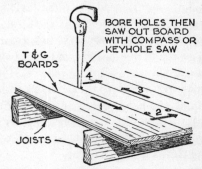

Fig. 7c. Method employed to open a hole in a floor made of tongued and grooved lumber.

The first thing to do is to make a hole through the board at the tongue side so that a sharp pointed compass or keyhole saw can be inserted to saw away the tongue. This hole can be made with a brace and bit or with a sharp chisel. Make the hole as close to one of the floor joists as possible as you will need some method of nailing the board back in place. This can be done by spiking a cleat to the side of the joist as was done when replacing a worn floor board. Once the hole has been made take the keyhole saw and start cutting up the length of the board. After you have cut a few inches you can use a compass or a handsaw to make the work go quicker. Be sure to saw straight and only remove the tongue of the board. When you have sawed from one joist to another, take out the saw and cut across the board at each end as close to the joist as you can. Slip a chisel into any one of the cuts and the board can be lifted out.

When one board has been removed, as many as needed can be lifted out by cutting them along the joists. When you are ready to put the flooring back, nail wood cleats to the side of each joist and use these to support the ends of the boards and as a base on which to nail the boards. Use finishing nails for this work and punch the heads below the wood surface, filling the resulting hole with plastic wood and staining to match the finish on the floor.

FINISHING FLOORS

A floor requires a very hard, elastic, and durable finish to protect the wood and maintain a handsome appearance. Floors are subject to heavier wear than any other woodwork in the house, and a poor quality floor finish will become so badly damaged in a short time that the floor will have to be refinished—a job that entails considerable work and expense.

Hardwood floors are divided into two classes, open and close grain. Open-grain hardwood flooring, such as oak or mahogany, requires a filler before the finish is applied. Close-grain woods, such as maple, do not require a filler; but if the wood is very porous, a priming coat is necessary to seal off the pores and provide a smooth surface for the finish coat.

Varnishing. Varnish is one of the most popular finishes for a hardwood floor. This finish affords the necessary protection for the wood without covering the natural grain and coloring.

After sanding down the wood, the next step in varnishing an open-grain floor is applying a filler (see FILLERS). When the filler is dry, sand the surface lightly to remove any trace of filler remaining. Remove all dust and dirt from the floor and be certain that the floor is dry before applying the varnish. The room temperature should be about 70 degrees and the air as dry as possible.

Fillers are obtainable in different shades and colors, and one can often buy a filler that matches the color of the wood. If a stain is used, the filler should be mixed with stain before it is applied. For this you will need a light filler. Do not try to stain a dark filler, for the results will be unsatisfactory. Allow the stain in the wood ample time to dry before applying the filler.

Use a good grade of floor varnish and a good varnish brush about three inches wide. Apply the varnish with a full brush, spreading it first across the grain and then brushing lightly with the grain. Work over one small area at a time and try to make a thin, even coat. Take care to avoid runs and wrinkles. Do not attempt to brush out bad spots after the varnish has set, as this will leave brush marks on the surface which will not flow out. Give the first coat of varnish sufficient time to dry before applying the second. For best results, put on two or, better, three coats.

Staining. To change the color of the floor, you will have to apply an oil floor stain before the filler. Put on the stain with a wide brush and allow a few minutes for it to sink into the wood; then wipe off the stain remaining on the surface with a clean cloth. Always remember that if the stained wood is too light, it can be darkened with another application of stain; but if the stain is too dark, the wood can only be made lighter by bleaching. Stain will only darken wood, it cannot make it lighter. It is always wise to make a few tests with the stain on some inconspicuous part of the floor before staining the entire surface. Allow these tested spots to dry, in order that you will know what color the stained wood is going to be.

Wax Finish. Shellac alone does not make a very good finish for floors because it is not tough enough. It can, however, be used as a base for a wax finish. Some kinds of wax finishes have no undercoat but consist of several layers of wax on the bare floor. This kind of finish is not very durable and requires constant attention. The best foundation for wax is one or two coats of varnish. Use a filler, if needed, and then apply the varnish. After the last coat of varnish is dry, put on the wax. Wax can be had in either paste or liquid form. Apply it to the floor with a soft cloth and when it is dry, polish with a clean, soft, wool rag or an electric waxer. Wax provides an excellent protection for the finish as long as it remains; accordingly, you should add coats often enough to prevent the varnish or shellac underneath from being exposed and damaged.

Paint. Softwood floors are generally given several coats of floor paint as a finish. Exterior paint is not very satisfactory for this purpose because it is not elastic and tough enough to withstand constant scuffing.

One of the best kinds of paint for use on floors is a floor enamel. This paint contains a sufficient amount of varnish to produce the tough, elastic film so desirable for floors.

In painting over a previously painted floor, the wood must first be washed clean and the cracks filled before applying the paint (see FLOORS). If there are any spots where the old paint has been worn away, they should be sanded down and given a coat of floor paint thinned slightly with turpentine. Allow this paint to dry before painting the entire floor. If this is not done, the bare spots will dry to a different color after the final finish is applied. Give the entire floor two coats of paint and allow ample time between the coats When painting an unfinished floor, or one with the finish com-

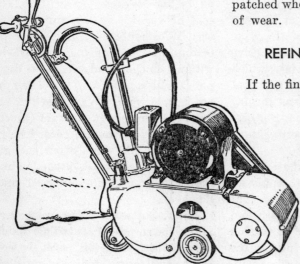

Fig. 8. An electric floor sander. These can be rented by the day.

pletely removed, thin the first coat with turpentine.

Oil Finish. Oil makes an excellent finish for soft-wood floors, maple in particular. You can buy oil ready-mixed or add a little turpentine to a high-grade boiled linseed oil. Be sure that the floor is clean and dry before brushing on the oil. Apply it while hot and let it soak into the wood. Wipe off the excess. Put on several coats, allowing one coat to dry overnight before apply-

ing the next. Wax the oiled floor and apply another oil coat when the finish shows signs of wear. Oil will darken the wood slightly.

Floor Seals. Floor seals are a good way to finish wood flooring. Other finishes just cover the surface but these seals are brushed into the actual wood grain. This makes a durable finish, and can be easily patched when it begins to show signs of wear.

REFINISHING FLOORS

If the finish on a floor is left long enough unprotected, it will get into such poor condition that it must be completely removed before a new finish can be applied. If the finish is neglected so long that the wood becomes scarred and damaged it must be resurfaced before it can be refinished.

Resurfacing an entire floor calls for a great deal of sanding, and the best means of doing this is with an electric sander. These can be rented by the day from many hardware and paint stores. The machine is not difficult to operate, and the dealer will supply all the necessary instructions. If you can't get one, do the work with a scraper and sandpaper.

Revarnishing. Do not let a varnish finish on a floor become so scuffed it has to be wholly removed and a new coat applied. When varnish begins to show signs of wear, add an additional coat. Wash the old varnish first with a damp cloth and soap. When the floor is dry, put on one or more coats of varnish. If there are patches from which the varnish has completely worn away, give them a coat of shellac so that they will match the new surface. Dark spots in the wood can only be removed by sanding and bleaching.

If the entire finish is in poor condition, you will have to remove the varnish completely. This can be done with an electric sander or with a liquid varnish remover. When you have taken off the old varnish, wipe with denatured alcohol to remove any remaining wax. In some cases, the wood will be so badly soiled and stained that nothing short of bleaching will be effective.

Treat the surface as though it had never been varnished. Apply a filler if necessary, then the varnish.

SCREENS

The frames for window and door screens are made of relatively light pieces of wood in order that the screens can be put up and taken down with a minimum amount of effort. Moreover, the wire screening is easily torn and great care should be taken, when working with screens, to prevent any damage to frames and screening. The effectiveness of the screens depends upon their being tight and unbroken, for the smallest opening will provide an entrance for insects.

Storage. When the screens are taken down in the fall, they should be stored in a dry place where they will be out of the way and where no heavy object will be placed on them.

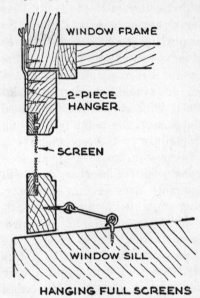

HANGING FULL SCREENS

Fig. 9. How full window screens should be hung and attached.

A rack can be built in the attic for them, or an overhead rack in the basement, hung from the ceiling rafters. This will suffice, provided that the basement is not damp.

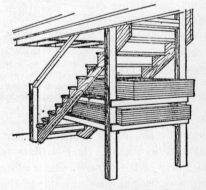

Fig. 10. A rack built under the basement stairs is a good place for storing window and door screens.

Clean screens and repair them before storing them for the winter. Brush the wire netting to remove any dirt collected in the mesh. Give rusty screening a coat of paint before putting it away. Brush off the rust before you apply the paint. Use a special screen paint for this purpose, or a regular exterior paint thinned with turpentine or linseed oil to prevent the paint from filling the openings in the screening. It is a wise precaution to keep all iron screens painted, because rust will irreparably damage thin screening. Giving unpainted iron screens a coating of kerosene will also help prolong their life. If the screens are put away in good condition, it is likely that they will require very little attention when the time comes to put them over the windows.

Marking. One can avoid much inconvenience by marking each screen and its corresponding window. The sizes of the windows in a house vary somewhat, and fitting screens to their proper windows

NUMERAL NAILS

Fig. 11. Numeral nails used to mark screens, storm windows, and the corresponding window frame.

is a long and arduous task. One of the best ways of marking the screens is to use little metal plates with numbers stamped on them. Attach a plate to the frame of the window and a plate with a corresponding number to the screen frame. Numbers can also be painted or chiseled on the window

frames and screens, but this requires considerable time.

Repairing. Repair a small hole in the wire screening with thin wire woven into the screening, or with a patch of screening having the end wires bent at ninety degree angles. The end wires pierce the mesh around the hole and are bent down to make a strong joint. If screening is badly damaged or rusted beyond the need for paint, you will have to remove it and replace it with new. Use either copper or iron screening.

EMERGENCY SCREEN PATCH

Fig. 12. Holes in wire screening are easily patched with a small piece of screening. A patch of this kind can be purchased at hardware and ten-cent stores.

Copper screening is more expensive but it does not rust and with proper care will outlast iron screening. Rain will wash through it, however, and stain painted surfaces around the screen, but you can prevent this by giving the copper a coat of thin exterior varnish. Paint can also be used, but it will change the color of the copper—varnish will not.

To remove the old screening, take off the strips of molding nailed around the edges of the screen which cover the tacks holding the screen in place. Pry these strips off with an old screwdriver or a chisel, being careful not to break them, for they are very thin. When you have removed the molding, pull out the tacks. If the screen frame is well built, you can remove a few of the tacks from one corner and pull the screening hard. This will remove the screening and most of the tacks with it. Pull out any remaining tacks with a claw hammer or a pair of pincers.

Screening can be purchased at hardware stores. It comes in several widths, so it is necessary to measure the frames to determine what size, or sizes, are needed.

Be very careful when taking off this molding, as it is extremely thin. Do not try to pry it off, for you are almost sure to split it. Remove each brad individually with pincers.

The best screening will not last very long on the bottom of doors which are continually kicked open. To save the thin screening, use a piece of heavy mesh wire over the screening on the lower part of the door. This will help a great deal in keeping the screening from being torn or pushed out.

Loose Frames. Screen frames are most likely to become loose at the corners. You can repair and rein-

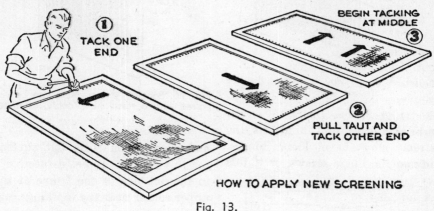

HOW TO APPLY NEW SCREENING

Fig. 13.

To attach the screening to the frame, tack down the top edge. Pull the screening down evenly and tightly to the bottom and check to see that the sides are even with the frame. Nail down the bottom and then the sides. Tack the molding with wire brads.

Doors are somewhat more difficult to rescreen because they are often made up of several panels, necessitating the removal of much molding.

force them with mending plates. One method of doing this is to place a right-angle plate on the surface of the joint. Mark around the plate, then cut out the wood to a depth equal to the thickness of the metal plate. Set the plate in this mortice and secure it with wood screws. An angle plate inside the joint can also be used.

Door and window screens are exposed to the weather and should be treated like any other exposed woodwork about the house. See that they are given a coat of exterior paint whenever necessary.

When the entire frame of the door sags, due to poor construction, you can bring it true by using a turnbuckle. It is best to remove the door

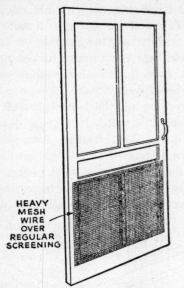

Fig. 14. A simple way to extend the life of door screening.

Sagging Screen Doors. A screen door that sags and binds at the bottom may have loose hinges. Tighten the hinge screws, or if this

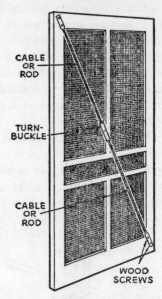

Fig. 16. Sagging screen doors can be repaired with a turnbuckle, cable, or metal rod.

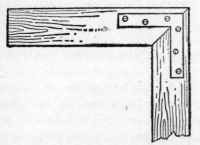

Fig. 15. Mending plate used to repair joint of window screen frame.

is impossible due to the condition of the wood, move the hinges to other locations on the door and frame where they can be secured tightly.

and place it on some flat surface for this repair. Insert a screw eye in the flat side of the frame at the upper corner near the top hinge and another screw eye at the corner diagonally opposite. Attach a piece of wire to each screw eye and the turnbuckle to the other ends of these wires, so that it is located about halfway between the two screw eyes. Tighten the turnbuckle, and check the frame by placing a square along the lower corner where the screw eye is located. Tighten the turnbuckle until the corner of the door is an exact right angle. Replace the door in the frame and make additional adjustments with the turn-buckle so that the door works easily.

Most screen doors are equipped with some sort of device to keep them closed. This may be either a long spring attached to the wall and to the door or a spring loaded hinge. To prevent a door from slamming, and eventually tearing itself loose, install some kind of door check.

AWNINGS

Awnings should be taken down at the end of the summer. An accumulation of snow or high winds may tear the awnings beyond repair. When the awnings are removed, inspect the metal frame work, cords and pulleys for signs of rust and wear. Attend to these matters now so that the awnings will be ready to go back up as soon as the mild weather sets in. The awnings should not be stored away until they are absolutely dry and then care should be taken to put them away only in a dry place where they will not get damp and possibly mildew. It is a wise plan before storing the awnings to coat them with some type of mildew preventive. A fungicide designed for use on awnings should also be brushed on during the summer as many awnings are attacked by mildew even when they are up and exposed to the fresh air and sunlight.

Dirty awnings can be washed with soap and warm water and this will freshen them up considerably, provided the colors are not too faded.

If the colors need restoring, the material can be painted with a special paint made for this purpose. Awnings can also be painted with regular exterior paint thinned down so that it will not make the awnings so stiff that they cannot roll back easily. In the long run, however, the homeowner will do better to use a special paint for this job rather than take the risk with regular exterior paint.

Repainting awnings with stripes or designs may prove difficult unless one is extremely adept with the brush, hence it might be wiser to paint the awning a solid color.

WINDOWS

There are two kinds of windows to be found in most homes, casement and double hung windows. The casement window consists of one window sash attached to the frame by means of hinges. This is a simply constructed window and should require few repairs save an occasional loose hinge. The double hung window consists of two sashes, one above the other, and this window can fail to operate for several reasons.

The smooth opening and closing of the two sashes of the double hung window are controlled by sash weights attached to the cords which, in turn, are attached to the sides of the sash. These cords run over pulleys in the top of the window frame, and the weight at the end of each cord rises and falls in a space provided in the interior of the frame.

When a sash cord breaks, the weight on the end of it ceases to be of use in raising and lowering the sash until the broken cord has been replaced.

Replacing Sash Cord. Due to the construction of the window, it is necessary to remove the sash from the frame before attaching a new cord. If the lower sash cord is broken, only the lower sash need be removed, but if the upper sash cord is broken it is necessary to take out the lower sash before the upper sash can be removed.

The first step in removing the sash is to take off the length of beading which extends from the top to the bottom of the frame. This is called the "stop bead," and it is necessary to remove it only on the side with the broken cord.

Work from the inside of the window rather than from the outside. This is not only more convenient, but on most windows the outside stop bead is built into the window frame and cannot be removed. Pulling off the stop bead is rather delicate work and should be done carefully to avoid breaking or damaging the wood. Use an old screwdriver or a wood chisel to pry off the beading and work from

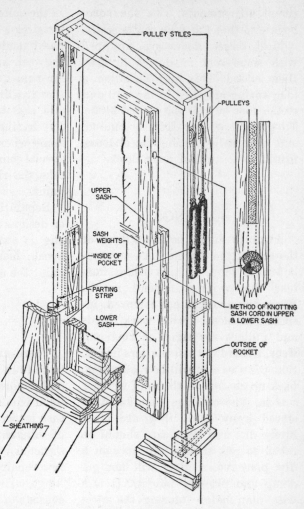

Fig. 17. Detail of the construction of a double hung window. At right, note how sash cord is attached to the sash.

the bottom upward. Pull out as many nails as possible, and save the painted finish of the beading and frame by putting a piece of cloth around the blade of the tool. Some stop beads are held to the frame with wood screws and these can be easily removed and the bead pulled from the frame, with only a light tap needed here and there to loosen any paint that might be acting as a seal. Too often small bits of paint will chip off, but these can be touched up easily.

When the stop bead is off, you can pull out the lower sash of the frame. To reach the sash weight, it is necessary to remove the pocket cover in the frame. You can locate it by looking for horizontal cracks marking the top and bottom of the cover on the inside of the frame. If it is not to be found because of a heavy coat of paint, tap lightly with a hammer and crack the paint along the joint. The pocket cover is attached to the frame with wood screws or nails. Once the cover is removed, you can pull out the weight with the broken end of the cord attached to it.

Remove the piece of broken cord from the weight and the other end from the sash. The latter is attached by means of a knot fitted into a hole in the side of the sash.

Pass one end of the new sash cord over the pulley. This can easily be done by tying a piece of string to the cord and attaching a small weight to the other end of the string. Push the weighted end of the string over the top of the pulley and allow it to drop inside the frame to the pocket opening. Draw the string through the opening until the end of the cord appears. Detach the string, taking care not to pull the other end of the cord through the pulley. Draw the cord gently through the pocket until the weight can be attached to it. Unite the top of the cord to the sash by means of a knot. Lift the sash close to the frame and pull the cord until the weight is close to the pulley. Measure the cord to the sash, leaving a few extra inches so that the knot may be tied. Make the knot in the cord and insert it into the mortice on the side of the sash. It may require a few light taps to force the knot to be flush with the surface of the sash. Replace the pocket cover and put the window back in the frame. It is a good idea to check the operation of the window at this stage to be sure that the cord is long enough. If the cord is too short, the weight coming against the pulley will prevent the sash from completely closing. When the sash opens and closes fully and easily, nail or screw the stop bead back into place. Use a little putty in the nail holes and touch up with paint where necessary.

In dealing with a broken cord on an upper sash, it will be necessary to remove the lower sash, as described, and then remove the parting strip, which is a thin piece of wood between the upper and the lower sash. This parting strip is generally only tacked into place, or not tacked at all. After removing this strip, you can pull out the upper sash in the same fashion as the lower one.

When a cord must be replaced, examine the other cords for any sign of wear and renew them both if necessary. Cords will often stretch and should be shortened when the sash is out.

Window Panes. To replace a broken pane of glass, you will need a new piece of glass, some putty, a putty knife or an old stiff-bladed knife, an old wood chisel or screwdriver, a hammer, and some glazier's points. If the glass is to be cut at home, a glass cutter is necessary. Glass can be purchased at hardware stores, and the clerk will cut it to your specifications. The exact measurements of the new glass are important, and should be ⅛ inch less in both length and width than the space the glass is to fill. This reduction is made in order to allow for any irregularities in the edges of the glass, sure to occur when it is cut. Before you can measure the space accurately, you must remove all old putty and broken glass. Pull out what glass you can, and the remainder will come out as the putty is removed. You may have to chip out the putty with an old screwdriver or chisel, so take care not to damage the wood. As you remove the putty, you will encounter glazier's points, and these can be pulled out with a pair of pliers or forced out with a knife or screwdriver. Scrape away all traces of putty and give the wood surface a thin coat of paint or a coat of linseed oil. This must be done in order to prevent the wood from absorbing the oils from the putty, causing it to dry out and crack.

GLAZIER'S POINT

Fig. 18.

Bed the new glass in a thin layer of putty which is pressed into the groove in the sash. Place the glass on the putty and press down gently until all edges of the glass are enclosed. This will make the seal watertight. The glass is held in place with glazier's points, small, triangular pieces of metal, and you should use about four to each side. Force the points into the wood with a screwdriver. The outside of the joint between the glass and wood is now ready to be sealed with putty. Roll some putty with the hands into a long roll and place it along the edge of the glass. Smooth it to an even slope with the blade of the putty knife. It takes a good deal of practice to smooth putty properly. Study the manner in which the putty has been applied to the other sashes and follow this example.

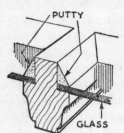

Fig. 19. How putty should be applied around a pane of glass.

Some of the putty used as the bed for the glass will be forced out on the inside of the sash, and this should be removed before it dries. Allow the putty on the outside to dry for a day or more; then give it a coat of paint. Painting is important in preventing the putty from drying out completely.

The sash does not have to be removed from the frame when a pane of glass is replaced, but the home mechanic will find it much easier in the beginning, to do so. Put the sash on the work bench, where it can be repaired with comparative ease.

Cutting Glass. Cutting glass is not difficult, and a few large pieces of glass and an inexpensive glass cutter in the workshop guarantee that windows can be replaced without delay.

The piece of glass to be cut should be placed on a clean, flat surface, and the glass wiped with turpentine or kerosene. A glass cutter will not work well on a dirty surface. Place a straightedge on the glass where the cut is to be made and hold it securely with one hand. Draw the glass cutter along the line so that the small steel wheel of the cutter makes a slight scratch in the glass. Do not try to go over the line again or turn the glass over and cut the other side. Only one cut should be necessary, and additional cuts will impair the result. Once the glass has been scored, there are several ways of breaking it along the line. One method is to place the handle of the cutter under the scored line and press down gently on each side. If the glass has been cut properly, it will break along the line. Another method is to tap on the underside of the line with the handle of the cutter, then break the glass by placing it on the edge of the table and pressing down on the overhanging edge.

Be very careful when cutting glass not to injure the hands or eyes. It is best to wear gloves and some kind of goggles.

Frosted Glass. Regular window glass can be given the effect of frosted glass by the use of special paints and treated paper on sale at hardware and paint stores.

GLASS
CUTTER

CUTTING
WHEEL

Fig. 20.

Tight Windows. There are several reasons for sashes in a double hung window to stick. The most common is that paint between the sash and the beading has hardened. A sash sometimes absorbs moisture and expands, causing it to bind against the side of the frame. It occasionally

Fig. 21. One way to break glass after the line has been scored with the glass cutter.

happens, when a house is settling, that an entire window frame is thrown out of alignment, and this often necessitates removing the entire frame to set it correctly.

A sash that is stuck because of paint can usually be set free by cutting through the paint around the sash with a pointed knife. If this, coupled with a few taps around the side of the sash, fails to do any good, then remove the stop bead, pull out the sash, and remove any paint on the edge of the sash or beading which appears to be the cause of sticking. Remove excess paint with sandpaper.

If the sash is binding because it has expanded, you will have to take it out of the frame before attempting to eliminate the binding. In all probability, it will require sanding or planing to reduce the sides of the sash sufficiently to move easily up and down in the frame. Remove as little wood from the sash as possible; it too much is taken off, the sash will be loose and rattle in the frame when it becomes dry.

A little soap or a special window wax applied to the edge of the sash will allow it to slide up and down more easily.

Leaky Windows. One point where windows often leak water is at the small seam under the window sill where the sill joins the outside wall of the house. What actually happens is that water, instead of dropping off the window sill, is blown along the underside of the sill and forced through the small seam by the force of the wind.

One easy remedy for this is to take a wood gouge and make a semicircular cut along the underside of the sill a few inches from the front. This cutout portion is called a drip gap and water will not be able to cross it and consequently will drop to the ground.

Another means of achieving the same result is to tack a strip of quarter round molding along the bottom of the sill.

Storm Windows. Storm windows are hung with special hinges which enable one to put them up or take them down with ease. This hinge is in two sections, one attached to the window frame and the other to the storm window. The proper method of removing a storm window hung

on this kind of hinge is to pull the window out from the vertical position and lift up. If the hinges are installed correctly, the two sections will separate and the storm window is free. When taking down the windows at the end of the winter, check the hinges to be sure that they are held securely enough with wood screws. It may be necessary to

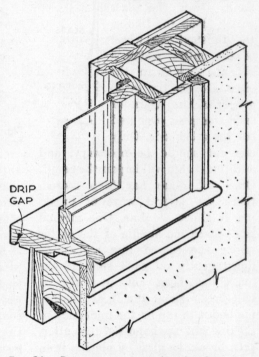

DRIP GAP

Fig. 21a. Drip gap cut in underside of window sill will prevent the wind from forcing water along bottom edge of sill, into outside wall.

tighten these screws.

Storm windows should not be put away until they have been repaired and repainted. If the putty around the glass is loose and cracking, it should be removed with a putty knife and replaced with fresh putty. Follow the instructions given for replacing glass in windows. Keep the woodwork of storm windows well painted, both inside and out, for the moisture from condensation along the inside of a storm window can damage an unpainted wood surface as much as the rain and snow on an unprotected outside surface. Store the storm windows where they will be dry and protected from breakage.

Fig. 22. Screens and storm windows hung with this type of fastener are easily put up or taken down.

Steel Casement Windows. Many homes are today equipped throughout with steel casement windows. In other homes they are often encountered in the basement and while they have several advantages over the wood frame window, especially insofar as installation goes, certain disadvantages will be encountered and they do require their share of maintenance just like any other window and window frame.

The metal portion of the frame and sash must be kept well painted. This does not only apply to the outside of the frame and sash but to

the inside as well, because during cold weather the inside of the steel frame is bound to be cold and there will be considerable moisture from condensation about. This moisture will rust unpainted metal on the inside just as surely as rain will rust any exposed surfaces on the outside.

Fig. 22a. A steel casement window.

As soon as any rust spots are observed, the rust should be sanded off and the metal painted like any other metal surface (see PAINTING METAL).

Do not allow the sash to strike violently against the frame such as might occur with a high wind. This may bend the sash or frame out of alignment so that the window could never be closed tight until the bent portion of the window had been straightened out. This job will usually require the services of an expert. The hinges should be oiled from time to time, and if the window is opened by some mechanical method, this too should be kept oiled.

When it is necessary to replace a broken pane of glass in a steel sash, the new pane is usually fixed to the sash by means of clips, or with a special putty made for glazing steel windows. Do not use wood putty as it will not hold up.

The joint where the window frame meets the exterior wall of the house is very vulnerable and must be kept well caulked. If water should get into this joint it might very well cause rusting on some unexposed portion of the frame which if left undetected might eat through the metal and ruin the window.

WINDOW SHADES

Renewing Shades. Old window shades may be renewed either by washing, painting or turning, depending upon the condition of the material. Even when the shade itself is beyond hope, a saving can be effected by removing the old shade from the rollers and buying new shade material to be tacked on the old roller. While this saving may only amount to a few cents for each window, its total may reach several dollars by the time every window shade in the house has been replaced.

Washing. Washable window shades are easily cleaned with a clean cloth dipped into warm soapy water. Do not let the cloth become overly wet. The shade must be taken down and spread out on a clean table or bench. Wash the shade first with the soapy water and then rinse it with a clean cloth dampened in fresh water.

Painting. Most washable window shades may be painted with good results with a special window shade paint made for this purpose. Ordinary paint does not work very well on shades, because it is not sufficiently elastic and will crack. Window shade paints are on sale at paint and hardware stores. Be sure that the shade is clean before the paint is applied.

Turning. When a shade becomes discolored and torn at the bottom, it can be taken off the roller and its position reversed so that the damaged portion is on the roller and the unused section is at the bottom. Take the shade down and unroll it. To prevent damaging the shade material it is a good idea to spread it out on a table rather than let the material fall to the floor. The shade is attached to the roller by means of small staples or tacks. Pull these out with pincers or pry them out with a screwdriver. Now take the bottom edge of the shade and cut off the hem which contains a strip of wood. Fold the edge over to get a double thickness of material and tack this to the roller. Use the same size tacks or staples as were originally used. The next step is to take the strip of wood that was inside the old hem and place it on the bottom edge of the shade. Fold the material over and sew a new hem. Replace the roller and rewind the shade tightly.

LINOLEUM

Linoleum is deservedly one of the most popular of inexpensive flooring materials. It can be used in rooms throughout the house, and particularly in rooms where frequent cleaning of the floor is necessary.

New linoleum should be placed over a layer of felt cemented to the floor. The linoleum, in turn, is cemented to the felt. Use a special type of waterproof cement made for this purpose. Do not nail linoleum under any circumstances and do not try to put linoleum on a rough or uneven surface, for this will cause the material to crack.

In most cases, the felt underlay will compensate for the roughness in the floor, but if it is highly uneven, it should be sanded or planed to make it as smooth as possible. Since many houses are built today with only one layer of flooring, linoleum is laid mainly to prevent dampness from coming through the flooring. This should not be done, because the dampness will soon rot the linoleum. What can be done is to put down a layer of building paper or some heavy plywood. This will provide a smooth and moderately dampproof base for the linoleum. Linoleum should never be laid over a floor that is constantly damp, such as a concrete basement floor. There are special composition floorings which are damp resistant, and these should be used to cover damp floors.

Fitting. Cementing the felt does not require great skill, but putting down the linoleum calls for both skill and patience.

Cutting and fitting the linoleum into corners and around fixtures will present the greatest difficulty to the home mechanic, but there are two methods which will simplify this task. The first is the same method used by dressmakers when cutting out a dress. Take a large sheet of

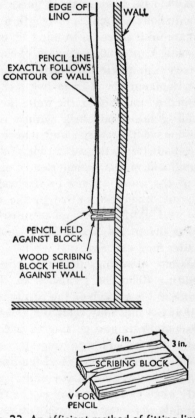

Fig. 23. An efficient method of fitting linoleum to an uneven wall contour.

paper and cut it to fit the corner exactly. Transfer this pattern to the linoleum and mark around the edge with a pencil; then cut accurately to the line. Use a special knife called a linoleum knife, which has a curved blade, for cutting. It is not expensive and is a faster and more efficient tool than an ordinary straight-bladed knife.

Another method of cutting the linoleum, and one particularly useful when fitting linoleum to a curved or crooked wall, is called "scribing," represented in Fig. 23.

You will need a short piece of wood about six inches in length and square on both ends. In one end, cut a small V just large enough to hold steady the point of a pencil. Lay the linoleum about from five inches from, and parallel to, the wall; then, holding the wood block against the wall, move it steadily along, marking the linoleum at the same time. Take care to keep the pencil steady and keep the block square to the wall. Having lined the entire profile of the wall, cut the linoleum accurately along the pencil mark, for it must fit the wall exactly.

When applying patterned linoleum, match the patterns at the joints in the middle of the room and make sure that they remain matched while marking and cutting to fit the walls and corners.

At doorways, the edge of the linoleum should come halfway under the door when shut. You may encounter difficulty in fitting accurately around molding and trim. The easiest solution is carefully to cut, with a thin saw, enough linoleum from the bottoms of these pieces of trim to allow them to slip underneath.

After being laid, new linoleum will always expand to some extent,

according to its thickness and quality, and provision must be made for this before finally securing it or it will buckle into folds and wrinkles. A patterned linoleum must be matched and fixed at the center joints and a gap of about a quarter of an inch left around the edges of the room until spreading is completed. For plain linoleum, the procedure is just the reverse. It is fitted and cemented around the edge and allowed to overlap in the center until spreading has ceased. It is then cut and cemented in place.

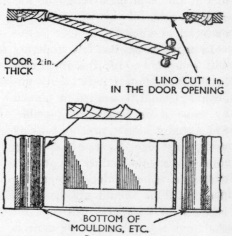

DOOR 2 in. THICK

LINO CUT 1 in. IN THE DOOR OPENING

BOTTOM OF MOULDING, ETC.

Fig. 24. Fitting linoleum to a door opening. Cut away the base of molding or stop to the thickness of the linoleum.

When laying linoleum, try to make as few cuts in the material as possible, for the resulting holes and slits will allow moisture to penetrate beneath the material and rot it.

Since it is as difficult to fit and lay poor linoleum as good, it is worthwhile to buy the best you can afford. In living rooms and kitchens, where the floors receive hard use, it is important to purchase inlaid linoleum, as the pattern is solid throughout, and there is no danger of the "bald spot" one so often sees in printed linoleum after a year or two of heavy wear around the kitchen sink or living room door.

Patching. After laying linoleum, save the larger scraps as a useful reserve for patching later, especially if the linoleum is patterned and difficult to match. To insert a patch, lay a new matching piece of linoleum large enough to fit easily over the worn spot. Cut around it with a linoleum knife and tear out the old piece. Cement the new piece into place and weight it down until the cement has hardened. If the cut is made along the line of the pattern, it will not be conspicuous.

Sometimes, the repair is a small one necessitated, perhaps, by the wear from a chair castor. In this case, cut out a patch of an irregular shape, rather than rectangular. It will be much less conspicuous, particularly if the linoleum is plain.

Having prepared the new patch, lay it over the worn spot in such a way that the pattern, if any, matches, and secure it with two or three brads. Cut around the edges and into the worn piece, lift out the old piece, and cement the patch into place.

Bulges. Linoleum bulges usually when an insufficient amount of cement is used on the felt or when the linoleum is not forced down upon the cement. The only way to remedy this condition is to put cement under the linoleum where it has bulged

and press the linoleum down until it clings to the felt. This can easily be done if the bulge is near a seam, but if there is not a natural opening the linoleum will have to be split at the bulge to insert the cement. After the cement is under the linoleum, place a weight on the surface to press the linoleum flat until the cement is dry.

Cleaning. Frequent washing is injurious to linoleum, and there is always the possibility of water penetrating between the joints and causing rot or mildew. Clean linoleum with a damp rag and mild soap and wipe the surface dry as soon as it has been cleaned. A good wax polish is much more preferable. It is easy to use and will protect the linoleum from wear by grit and dirt.

Painting. Old linoleum which has become faded and worn can be satisfactorily painted. As a preliminary, clean the surface thoroughly with benzine to remove all traces of wax and grease. A noninflammable cleaner is somewhat better than benzine because it eliminates the fire hazard. Do not use benzine near an open flame, such as a pilot light on a gas stove, and open all windows and doors to provide full ventilation. After cleaning, give the linoleum two coats of any good floor enamel or a special linoleum lacquer.

Sink or Counter Tops. A rather difficult way of laying linoleum is required when the top of a kitchen sink counter rots or becomes so worn that it has to be replaced.

The metal trim around the fixture first has to be taken off. This is done by removing the screws which are usually located on the underside of the trim. Be careful when removing the trim not to bend it out of shape, as it may be difficult to replace. Once the trim is off, you can remove the old linoleum with water and a putty knife. When you have done this, inspect the surface of the sink or counter for any rotten wood. A slight crack in the linoleum will allow water to penetrate to the wood and damage it. Any part of the woodwork that has rotted should be removed and replaced with a sound piece of wood before putting on the new linoleum.

The new top should fit tightly at all seams, and it is suggested that a pattern first be cut out of heavy paper. This pattern should fit exactly, and it may be necessary to cut several patterns before a perfect one is obtained. Do not try to cut the linoleum until you are sure that the fit is correct or you may spoil a good piece of material. With the exact pattern as the guide, carefully trace the outline on the linoleum and cut it with a linoleum knife. Apply linoleum cement to the surface, place the linoleum on it, and press the linoleum flat. Place weights on the linoleum to hold it down until the cement is dry. Replace the trim and inspect the work carefully to be sure there are no openings for water to get under the linoleum.

Asphalt and Linoleum Floor Tiles. Many a home mechanic has let a poor looking floor go uncovered because he did not feel that he had the skill to lay linoleum suc-

cessfully, and could not afford the cost of having an expert do the job. There is little doubt that laying linoleum, say in the bathroom where there are numerous fixtures and fittings attached to the floor, is tricky work and takes considerable skill, and is best done by an expert. Asphalt and linoleum floor tiles, on the other hand, do not require the same degree of skill because these tiles come in separate squares and are laid individually. When the flooring must be fitted around a pipe, it is

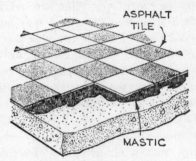

Fig. 24a. Asphalt or linoleum tile makes a good floor finish for either concrete or wood floor.

generally only necessary to cut one piece of tile, which is an easy matter. If the fitting is not done correctly the first time, the tile can always be put aside and another used. These tiles are not expensive and therefore, even if several are ruined in the interest of a well-fitted job, the cost will be negligible.

Floor tiles are attached with a special cement that should be purchased along with the tile, as it is always best to use tile and cement made by the same manufacturer.

Once the tiles are on the floor they should be given a coat of water wax for a finish. This will improve the appearance of the floor and also save the tiles from wear. Varnish should not be used as a finish for either linoleum or asphalt tiles.

PLASTER WALLS

Plaster, as used by the builder, is a mixture of lime or some other binder, water, sand, and, sometimes, a fiber. The lime combines with the water to form a hard mass, and the fiber gives the plaster additional strength. Plaster is applied in three coats, the scratch coat which is put on the laths, brown coat, and, finally, the finish coat. Plaster can be applied over brick, stucco, or concrete walls—after making sure that no moisture can penetrate the wall and come in contact with the plaster. You can keep moisture out by applying a waterproofing compound to the wall. The ordinary method of applying plaster, however, is to nail laths to the wall and apply the plaster to the laths. The laths provide a dead air space between the outer wall and coat of plaster, thus preventing moisture from attacking and destroying the plaster. The laths are spaced so that the first coat of plaster can be forced between them, and the plaster acts as a binder to hold the following coats to the lath. There are several types of laths, made from either wood or metal. Plaster board that comes in sections is also used as a base for plaster.

Improper mixing of the plaster results in the presence of many unslaked particles which may later spoil the work. For this reason, the home mechanic is well advised to use one of the prepared brands of patching plaster which lack only water. These patching plasters can be obtained in small packages from hardware stores. Plaster of Paris makes a good filler for small cracks, but it hardens quickly and consequently is not very suitable for extensive plastering.

Since lathing and large plastering jobs are usually done by professionals, this section will concern itself only with cracks and holes which can generally be repaired by the home mechanic.

Cracks. Once plaster has dried, it is a solid mass which can be easily cracked if there is any movement of the base to which it is attached. Consequently, plaster will crack for many reasons. If the house should settle to any great degree, large cracks are almost sure to appear in the walls and ceilings. If the wood used in construction of the house was green when the plaster was applied, the shrinking of the wood will, in time, crack the plaster. Poorly constructed houses, in which the floors sag, will have their share of cracked plaster. Small, hairline cracks will appear if the plaster is improperly mixed or the materials used are of an inferior quality.

There is no certainty that a patched crack will remain unimpaired. If the crack was caused by settling of the house and this process has ended, the patch should last indefinitely, assuming that it was properly made. But if the house continues to settle, the patch will probably crack just as the original plaster did. Moisture is very injurious to plaster, and a leaky water pipe inside a wall will cause the plaster to weaken and pull away from the lath.

Filling Cracks. Small, hairline cracks in plaster can usually be filled by rubbing into the plaster some linseed oil thinned with turpentine. White lead thinned with turpentine can also be used for this purpose.

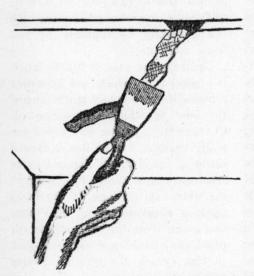

Fig. 25. Filling the cavity with patching plaster or plaster of Paris.

To fill larger cracks, cut around the crack and down to the lath. The bottom of this opening should be wider than the top so that when the patch is inserted into the crack, the wide base will prevent it from falling out when it shrinks after drying. Use an old knife or a cold chisel for cutting the plaster. Wet the plaster around the cracks with water to pre-

vent the old plaster from absorbing all the water from the patch, causing it to dry too quickly and crack. Force the patching plaster into the crack with a putty knife or small trowel but do not build it out flush with the surface of the old plaster. Leave it a fraction of an inch below. When the first application is dry, apply the second and finish coat over it. Do not forget to wet down the surrounding plaster again before putting on the last coat.

Replacing Laths. Inserting a plaster patch is a more difficult task than filling a crack, but after filling a few cracks the handyman will probably be experienced enough to attempt it. Chip off all the loose and broken plaster around the hole down to the laths. Make a close examination of the laths for any evident defects. The laths may be loose, decayed, or broken, or the woodwork supporting them may have warped or twisted. In bad cases, enough plaster must be cut away to expose the laths where they are nailed to the nearest stud, in order to replace the faulty laths. Laths can be bought at a lumber yard and should be matched for thickness with those of the partition. If the laths are broken, remove them with a hammer and chisel as shown in Fig. 27, midway across a wall stud, leaving enough room to nail the end of the new lath and also the remaining end of the old lath. See illustration in Fig. 27.

Old Plaster. In dealing with old walls, it may be found that any attempt at making extensive repairs will bring down adjoining areas of plaster. If this happens, it is evident that the entire plastered surface has

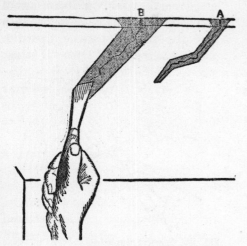

Fig. 26. Cutting out plaster to repair a crack. Follow main line of crack, as at A or B, and cut a wedge as shown.

deteriorated to such a point that the wall must be completely replastered. This job should be done by a professional plasterer, but if this entails too great an expense, the home mechanic might finish the room with wall board, which is easier to work

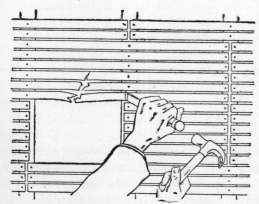

Fig. 27. Removing lengths of defective laths.

with and can be put up more quickly.

Plaster Patch. When repairs on the laths are completed, brush all dust and fragments of plaster from the area to be plastered. Apply the plaster in two layers if the patch is fairly small, a coarse layer which adheres to and protrudes behind the laths, and a fine coat over it to make a smooth surface.

Before plastering, cut back the lower layer at the edge of the patch (see Fig. 28) so that the new plaster gets behind the old top coat and binds the surrounding plaster. This is done with an old knife in the same manner as for a crack. See that the spaces between the laths are free of plaster, providing an opening through which the new plaster can be forced so that it will spread out in back of the laths and hold the plaster securely.

Dampen the surface of the lathing and the edges of the hole with water. Mix the patching plaster in accordance with the directions, adding water sparingly until you are sure of the correct amount to use. A small trowel will do for small jobs, and a flat plasterer's trowel is more convenient for larger areas. Lay on the plaster and press it well into the lathing until a fairly level surface is produced, as thick as the surrounding underlayer. Score the finish work as shown in Fig. 29, making crisscross lines to increase the adherence of the next coat. To complete the job, dampen the surface and edges with water after the first coat has set and apply the final coat. This coat should be level with the old plas-

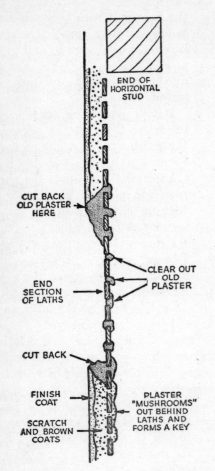

Fig. 28. An end view, cross section of a lath and plaster wall, showing old plaster removed and areas to be cut back to form a key for new plaster.

ter. On large patches, where it is difficult to make a smooth surface with a trowel, a flat board can be used, moving it edgewise to smooth the plaster.

Bulging Plaster. A bulging plaster ceiling indicates that a portion of the plaster has fallen loose from the laths, or the laths have pulled loose from the studding. Laths rarely pull away from the studding, so it is generally safe to assume that the plaster has separated from the laths.

Fig. 29. Scoring the undercoat to increase adherence of the next coat of plaster.

In any event, the bulged section should be taken down as soon as possible to prevent it from pulling the rest of the plaster with it. Test the bulge by pushing it with your hand. If it does not move, the plaster has pulled away from the laths and should be removed.

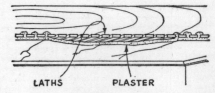

Fig. 30. Bulging plaster is often caused by the plaster's having pulled loose from the laths.

When an entire plaster ceiling has to be removed, the home mechanic is not advised to do the replastering himself. Either call in a plasterer or cover the ceiling with wallboard.

Lath Marks on Ceiling. Very often the outline of laths will appear on a plaster ceiling. This is generally due to the condensation of moisture on the back of the plaster which along with the accumulated dust, usually found in such places, soaks down through the plaster. As

Fig. 30a. Lath marks on the ceiling caused by moisture and dirt.

a general rule the best way to cover these marks is with paint as it is not surface dirt and therefore difficult if not impossible to remove by washing. Insulation above the ceiling will prevent these lath marks and more important, it will keep the plaster from becoming damp and in time perhaps falling.

TILES

The tiles used for the walls and floors of bathrooms and kitchens are laid in a concrete base and attached to it by means of a thin cement mortar. When individual tiles become loose and fall out, it is usually due to the fact that they were not installed correctly.

Tiles can be cemented into place by means of a special plastic cement made for this purpose, which can be purchased at most hardware stores. This cement is very strong and only a thin film should be applied to the tile, so that it will not

rise above the surrounding when it is replaced. Scrape off the old cement mortar from the tile and apply the plastic cement. Replace the tile and see that it is not moved until the cement is dry.

Tile Board. Covering a wall or a floor with tile is difficult work, and the home mechanic should not attempt it unless he has the necessary information and experience. Special tools are needed to cut the tile, which are not found in most home tool kits. A very good substitute for tile is tile board, a composition board painted to resemble a solid piece of tile work. It is attached to the walls by means of plastic cement and screws. Tile board is moistureproof, making it excellent for bathrooms and kitchens. The manufacturers provide full and detailed instructions on how to apply it, and these lucid directions should be followed to the letter for best results.

CARE OF CARPETS

Every carpet should have a felt underlay, not only to give the carpet a softer tread but also to improve its wearing qualities and prolong its life. Before laying the felt, examine the floorboards carefully for any protruding nails or tacks and for uneven boards. These should be smoothed down with a plane or chisel after the nails have been punched well below the surface with a nail set. The greatest enemy of carpets is damp. It causes mildew and rot, and any sign of dampness in the floorboards must be investigated and the condition corrected if a new carpet is to have a long life.

Cleaning. The best means of cleaning carpets is by the use of a good vacuum cleaner. If used regularly, there will be no need for the annual beating over a clothesline. This is well, for many carpets are damaged by over-vigorous beating with a stick. If heavy, gritty dirt does get into the carpet, beat it out but do not use too much force. It is preferable to go over the whole carpet two or three times, beating rather lightly, than to make a determined attack on a small area and so damage the fibers. If a vacuum cleaner is not available, use a stiff carpet brush regularly and always brush with the nap of the carpet; otherwise, the dirt and grit will be pushed deeper into the nap.

To brighten the colors, you may use a good carpet soap occasionally, in accordance with the manufacturer's directions. If possible, avoid washing the carpet in the room in which it lies and, in any case, avoid using too much water.

Castors. Carpets are often damaged by the castors on the legs of furniture, such as heavy armchairs, which are rarely moved. The comparatively small surface of the castor wheel is forced deep into the nap and soon damages the fibers, leaving a permanent mark (Fig. 30b).

The best way to avoid this is to remove the castor altogether, replacing it with one or more metal domes. These, as seen in Fig. 31, are small, plated, circular studs fixed in the legs of the furniture by a tap or

two of a hammer. If the legs are large—the legs of a settee are often more than five inches square—use two or three domes on each leg.

Fig. 30b.

Domes allow the heaviest piece of furniture to slide about easily and silently on almost any surface, and as they protrude only a fraction of an inch, leave no mark in the carpet. Alternatively, where it is not necessary to move a particular piece of furniture, such as a piano, it will be sufficient to house the castor in a bowl shaped foot (see Fig. 32). These are made of glass, wood, or plastic.

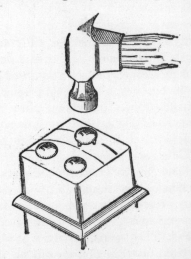

Fig. 31. Fitting metal domes to a table leg.

Stains. An acid stain is a real emergency and the utmost speed is essential. Take up the carpet and turn it upside down over a chair or a bench. Drench the area affected by the acid with a weak solution of ordinary washing soda, bicarbonate of soda and water, or ammonia.

Fig. 32. A castor in an insulator.

When a carpet is attacked by moths, the best thing to do is to take it up and send it to a firm specializing in cleaning carpets. They will see to it that the moth eggs deep in the carpet are destroyed.

Inkstains will usually yield to skim milk rubbed well into the nap with a cloth.

Scatter coarse salt or sawdust over a place dirtied by soot and brush it vigorously into a dustpan. Repeat several times and finally wash carefully with carpet soap. Do not, however, allow water near the spot until all the loose soot has been removed.

Tar is best dealt with by applying a paste of Fuller's earth and turpentine. Allow the paste to dry and then go over the area with a stiff carpet brush.

Fiber Rugs. After a few years service fiber rugs lose much of their coloring and become so soiled and stained that they are anything but attractive additions to the house. It is a very simple matter to refinish these rugs to make them once more pleasing to look at.

There are several ways of doing this job. Regular paint can be used, but it tends to chip even when thinned down with turpentine or benzine so that it acts more like a stain than a paint. Dye can be used on the rugs with good results and there are special paints formulated for this work.

The rug should be given a good washing and allowed to dry before any attempt is made at painting it. If possible, take the rug outside for the painting. If this cannot be done, put several layers of newspaper under the rug to prevent the stain soaking through the rug to the floor.

WALLPAPER

While the choice of color and pattern of wallpaper depends largely on the taste of the individual, there are other factors to be considered which may help to avert disappointment. With regard to color, many people, in choosing a wallpaper, stand in the brightest part of the room, near a window, and later wonder why the papered walls appear so much darker than originally expected. Even in well-lighted rooms, dark colors will appear darker and light colors paler than the sample chosen. Give more thought, as well, to the sensible use of both warm and cool colors. Yellows, pinks, and yellow green, for example, give an im-

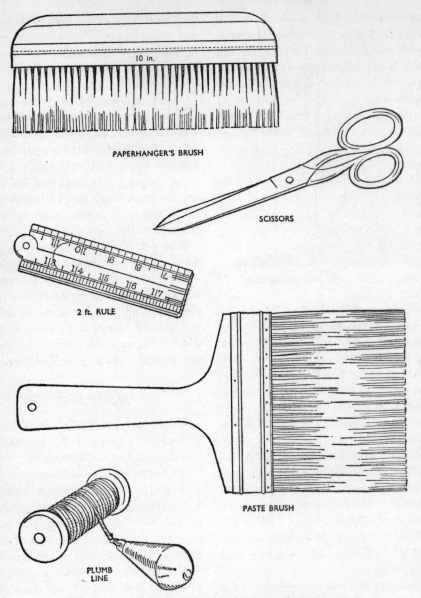

10 in.

PAPERHANGER'S BRUSH

SCISSORS

2 ft. RULE

PASTE BRUSH

PLUMB
LINE

Fig. 33. Equipment required for paperhanging.

pression of warmth and light to sunless northern rooms, while cooler tints of mauve, blue, and blue-green, may be used to advantage in toning down the glare in sunny rooms.

Pattern. The effect of a large pattern—except in very large rooms—is to make a room appear smaller and more amply furnished; small patterns have the opposite effect. Vertical lines, whether in the form of striped pattern or by the use of upright panel borders, impart an impression of increased height; horizontal lines seem to reduce height and accentuate space. Thus defects in the proportion of a room may be rendered less obvious.

It is a great advantage, wherever possible, to see a roll instead of a small, pattern book sample. This will often bring to light any unsuspected spottiness or other undesirable features of color or pattern. Lastly, do not be unduly influenced by the amount of gold in a pattern. Choose a wallpaper with sufficient color interest to retain its decorative quality when, after two or three years, the material has become discolored.

Plain and Semiplain. Both papers form an ideal background for the display of furniture, choice pictures, etc., and when moderately light in color give a pleasing effect of cleanliness and spaciousness to bedrooms and sitting rooms. A touch of bright color can always be introduced by a suitable border or panel arrangement.

The value of semiplain or mottled papers, especially when several nicely blended colors are used, should not be overlooked. It is often possible to find in them several of the colors present in the furnishings, thus helping to bring about a harmonious relationship.

Old Wallpaper. It is possible to put new wallpaper directly over the old paper, but this is not a very sound practice. The water used in the paste for the new paper may easily soften the paste holding the old paper to the wall and spoil the entire papered surface. It is much better to remove the old wallpaper and start with a clean surface.

The best and safest way to remove old wallpaper is with warm water and a wide putty knife. Apply the water to the paper with a sponge or a wide brush, begin working at one end of the wall and work in vertical strips, from top to bottom, until the entire wall surface has been moistened. It may require several applications of water to soften the paste sufficiently to remove the paper. Do not use too much force when working with the putty knife or you may damage the plaster. If you encounter stubborn spots, apply more water to soften the paste. When there is more than one layer of paper, it is generally necessary to take one off at a time, for the greater thickness will prevent water from penetrating to the paste on the plaster.

A small quantity of washing soda can be added to the water to help soften the paste, but great care must be taken to avoid getting this solution on any painted woodwork. By far the safest way is to use nothing but warm water. Some wallpaper is given a coat of varnish and this presents a problem when it comes to removing the paper, for the varnish will keep water from soaking through the paper to the paste. The best means of cutting through this varnish is with sandpaper, but you must be careful to sand away only the varnish and not cut through the paper to the plaster. When the varnish is removed, brush water on the paper and remove it with a putty knife.

After you have taken all the old paper off the wall, go over the surface again with clean water and a clean sponge to catch any paste or bits of paper that still remain.

It goes without saying that if the wall has been painted with calcimine or a water soluble paint, this finish must be removed before the wallpaper can be hung (see INTERIOR PAINTING). If the wall has been painted with an oil paint, this finish can remain on the wall.

Prepare the wall surface in the same fashion as for oil painting or calcimining, by filling cracks and holes in the plaster (see PLASTER WALLS).

Glue Size. After the old wallpaper or calcimine has been completely removed and the plaster repaired or patched, apply a thin coat of glue size over the entire surface that is to be papered. Size for this purpose can be purchased in package form and requires only the addition of water. Be sure that you follow the directions for mixing the size correctly. If the wall has been painted, sand lightly before applying size.

Measuring. Wallpaper usually comes in rolls 8 yards long and 18 inches wide, giving an area of 36 square feet. There may, however, be some variation in these figures, particularly in the width, and it is suggested that you check the size of the rolls before ordering.

To determine how many rolls of paper will be required for a room, multiply the length of the room by the height and double this figure. Do the same for the width and add this figure to the one above. This will give you the total number of square feet of paper required for all four walls. Divide 36—the number of square feet in a roll of paper 8 yards long and 18 inches wide—into the total number of square feet for the entire room and the result will be the number of rolls required. This makes no allowance for openings, such as doors and windows, but it is always a good idea to have paper left over to compensate for any error and for patching.

The wallpaper requirements for the ceiling are easily found. Multiply the width by the length and divide this sum by 36.

Making Paste. Good surface preparation and good paste will do more than anything else to ease the work of paperhanging. A good paste will not only hold the paper instantly but will allow you to slide the paper enough to match patterns.

The best and cheapest adhesive is made from common (not self-rising) flour, and is prepared as follows:

Mix 2 pounds of flour with enough cold water to form a stiff batter; stir briskly until the mixture is quite smooth; add one large pinch of borax and pour in about a gallon of boiling water, again stirring briskly until the paste thickens. When cool, dilute to a brushing consistency with cold water. Wallpaper paste may also be purchased in powder form.

Hanging Paper. If both walls and ceiling are to be papered, do the ceiling first. You will need some sort of scaffold in order to reach the ceiling and the top of the wall. A large table will suffice, or two step-ladders with a wide plank between them. Be sure that the scaffold is strong enough and can be moved without difficulty.

Stretch out the paper on an improvised paste bench, such as a large kitchen table. The table should be wider than the paper and about six feet in length. It is important that the table or bench be kept clean and dry; otherwise, the paste will soil the pattern side of the paper.

Fig. 34. Removing the trim.

Unroll the paper, with the pattern side up, on the table and measure off a section to be cut. Allow a few extra inches of length for waste. Cut several sections, being careful to see that the patterns on each section will match the pattern on the section to be pasted beside it. Most brands of wallpaper have some type of marking system along the edges to indicate the exact point where the patterns will match.

The sections are now ready to be trimmed. This is the cutting or trimming of the self-edges of wallpaper and may be done either with scissors or with a sharp knife and a straight-edge. Those papers which are thin enough to permit a lap joint when hanging should have one edge trimmed clean and the other edge left with the trim untouched. Very thick papers have to be hung with a butt joint, which necessitates the clean and accurate removal of both edges. When the first method is adopted, the left-hand edge can be trimmed clean and the paper hung from left to right until the room is completed. A better method is to begin at, and work away from, the window, thus papering from left to right on some walls and in the reverse direction on others. Trim the paper according to the method you adopt.

When the paper has been trimmed, it is ready for pasting. Place the first section on the table with the pattern side down. Apply the paste with a wide brush, starting at the center of the paper and working out to within a few inches of the edges. To paste the edges, either move the paper so that the edge is slightly over the side of the table or lift up the edge with one hand and carefully brush on the paste. This must be done in order to avoid getting face and pull the rest of the section onto the table. After this area has been pasted, make another fold. The number of folds in the paper will

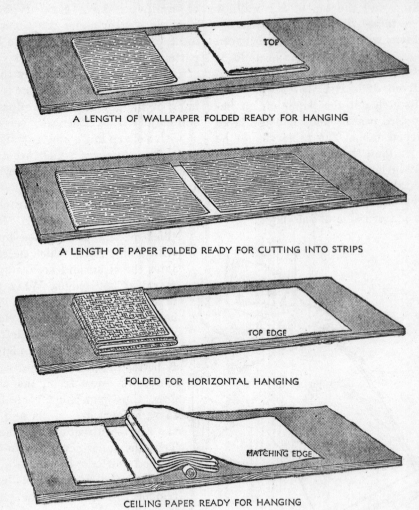

A LENGTH OF WALLPAPER FOLDED READY FOR HANGING

A LENGTH OF PAPER FOLDED READY FOR CUTTING INTO STRIPS

FOLDED FOR HORIZONTAL HANGING

CEILING PAPER READY FOR HANGING

Fig. 35. Four examples of wallpaper pasted and prepared for hanging. In each instance the folds are arranged so as to facilitate handling.

paste on the table and staining the pattern side of the paper. When one portion of the paper has been pasted, fold it with the pasted sides face to depend upon the length. Any number can be made for convenience in handling. Avoid creasing the paper. Pasted sides must face each other.

When papering the walls, if you begin at one side of the window, it is good workmanship to find out whether the window is plumb, as in Fig. 37. If it is, a plumb window be trimmed off afterward. An alternative is to make a vertical line the width of the paper from the window and use this as a starting point.

To handle the first length for the

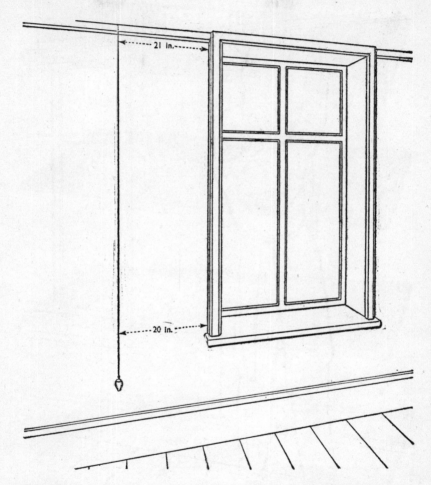

Fig. 37. Using the plumb line to check the window frame. Note that in this case the window is not vertical and the adjacent strip of wallpaper must be cut accordingly.

makes the best guide in establishing a vertical edge for the paper; if not, the paper can be plumbed while lightly attached to the wall and any surplus along the window edge can wall, place the right edge of paper against the ruled line, meanwhile holding the left edge a few inches away from the wall. By raising or lowering the left hand the whole length can be controlled until about three feet of the right edge are properly place and attached. Use the smoothing brush to hang the remainder and brush out any wrinkles.

the edges of the paper. Paste on the second length after the first is in place and be sure that the edges overlap correctly. After the second length is on, smooth the seam with a

Fig. 38. Hanging the first strip of wallpaper. Allow surplus at top and bottom and trim as required. Hold left edge away from wall until paper is vertical.

You will find that when it is first applied, the paper can be moved about. Have a clean cloth on hand for removing any excess paste from

brush or a seam roller made for this purpose.

The Ceiling. Before pasting the paper to the ceiling, it is a good plan to make some sort of mark to ensure your putting the first section of paper on straight. Measure out from the wall at each end of the ceiling a

It is best to work from left to right when hanging paper, as you can easily support the paper upon an odd roll held in the left hand,

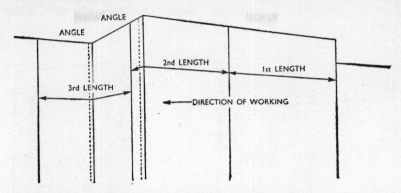

Fig. 39. Shows the direction of working and how to negotiate a series of wall angles.

distance of 2 inches less than the width of the paper. If the paper is 18 inches wide, this mark will be 16 inches from the wall. Connect these points with a string and mark along it with a pencil or a piece of chalk.

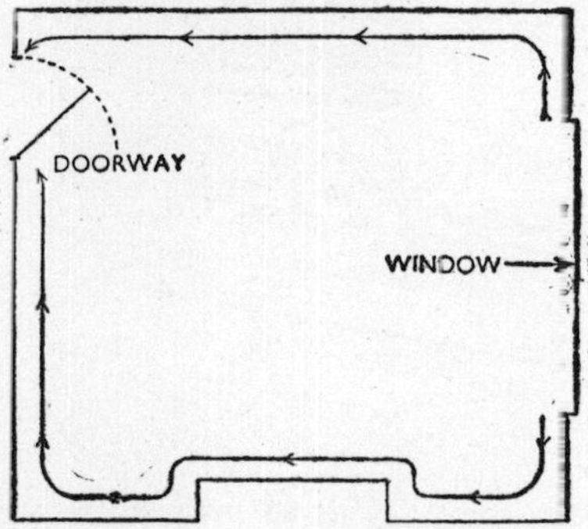

with the thumb gripping the folds. By employing this method, it is possible to release one fold at a time

Fig. 36. The directions in which paper hanging should progress.

This can also be done by coating the string with chalk and snapping it against the ceiling. The extra two inches allow the paper to be turned down at the side, along the wall.

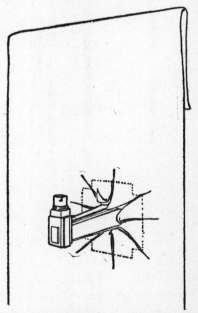

Fig. 41. How wallpaper can be fitted around fixtures which cannot be removed from the wall.

(see Fig. 42). The right hand remains free to unfold and attach the
first few feet of paper to the ceiling
and secure the rest by brushing.
Waste ends should be systematically
tective coatings which allow them to
be washed by sponging with clean
water. Nonwashable wallpaper can
be cleaned with a special wallpaper
cleaner, resembling dough, which can

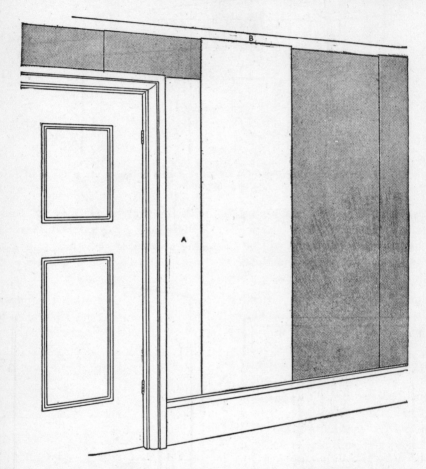

Fig. 40. Shows method of fitting paper around door. Dark portions indicate
wallpaper already hung. Cut A and B in that order.

trimmed, as shown in Fig. 43, to
insure a clean and accurate finish.
   Cleaning. Before attempting to
clean wallpaper, be sure that it is
the type of paper which can be
washed. Some wallpapers have pro-
be purchased at hardware, grocery,
and department stores. When it is
rubbed on the surface of the paper,
the dirt is picked up. The cleaner
exposes a new surface, when kneaded
like dough, and can be used until

Fig. 42. Applying ceiling paper. Note folds held in left hand together with a stiff roll to support paper. After first stretch, open and apply one fold at a time.

it has become completely saturated with dirt. It is always wise, before trying out any patented wallpaper cleaner, to test it on some inconspicuous part of the wall to make certain that it will not affect the coloring of the paper.

Grease spots on paper can be removed by mixing a paste of Fuller's earth and carbon tetrachloride, or some noninflammable cleaning fluid.

Apply this paste to the grease spot and allow it to dry; then brush off gently. Several applications may be required if the grease has been on the paper for a long time.

Varnish can be applied over wallpaper to preserve its appear-ance. Varnish may stain the paper, however, and steps must be taken to prevent this (see VARNISHING).

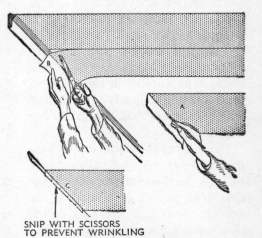

SNIP WITH SCISSORS
TO PREVENT WRINKLING

Fig. 43. Mark the end of paper, as at A, and trim with a pair of scissors, as indicated at B and C.

MENDING UTENSILS

The repair of broken china depends, of course, on the extent of the damage. A teapot, cup, or saucer, broken into small pieces is hardly worth mending unless it has great or intrinsic value. Vases and antique pottery may well be repaired if the damage is not so great as to make assembling the pieces an almost impossible task.

Pottery. Simple breaks involving large fractures, without irrevocable small chippings and fragments, may be mended by the use of a liquid cement glue. A good, cellulose-based, cement glue is very efficient. Apply the cement thinly to the broken faces and allow it to harden a little. Smear another thin layer on the faces and join quickly all the broken pieces. If practicable, supplement the glue by some temporary means until it is dry. Tall vases and circular pots, having high walls, may be carefully bound with cord to hold the broken pieces in position until the glue has set hard. Then, trim off the surplus cement with a sharp knife or razor blade. A piece of adhesive tape applied to the crack on the underside or inside of the article will help strengthen the joint. See Fig. 44.

China. Teapot handles or cup handles will not respond satisfactorily to this method of repair. These should be pinned or riveted in the manner described below. Saucers, plates, and cups, which are not badly broken, may be mended with cement, the broken part—of the plate and

saucer only—being held in position as shown in Fig. 45. A clean joint is important. Rubber bands may be employed on small utensils to keep the broken parts in place until the cement hardens.

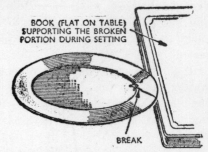

BOOK (FLAT ON TABLE) SUPPORTING THE BROKEN PORTION DURING SETTING

BREAK

Fig. 45. How a broken piece of china can be held in place until the glue has set.

Riveting. Riveting is a more difficult method of mending pottery. The home handyman, if he is interested in trying this sort of repair, should practice drilling on scrap pieces of pottery to acquire a better sense of the delicate nature of this work than is possible to describe.

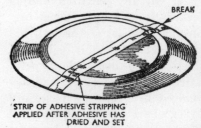

BREAK

STRIP OF ADHESIVE STRIPPING APPLIED AFTER ADHESIVE HAS DRIED AND SET

Fig. 44. A strip of adhesive tape applied to straight fracture after glue has set.

A small hand drill is requisite, and the size of the drill will vary according to the thickness of the material. Heavy pottery will require thick gauge wire to rivet the joints together. Ordinary metal drills will do the job fairly well.

Gauge the position of the holes to be bored with the eye and bore, if possible, with the article filled with water, the broken parts having first been secured, where necessary, by cement. Do not apply heavy pressure on the drill when operating it and allow the speed of the drill to carry away the material. If the object is fairly thin, it is advisable to drill the holes with it submerged in water; and as the drill penetrates the other side of the object, the drilling should be slower and more controlled to avoid chipping. Drill holes about 3/16 inch or more in diameter on each side of the fracture and bind together by inserting soft brass or copper wire of the same gauge as the hole. Turn in the edges of the wire, as shown in Fig. 46. The length

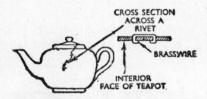

Fig. 46. Showing type of riveting for china.

of the wire used to make the joint should equal the distance between the two holes, plus twice the thickness of the pottery, plus at least half the distance between the two holes.

Metal Utensils. Pots and pans and metal utensils, such as kettles, enamel or plain, may be mended, if the leak occurs in the base or walls, by fitting one of the sealing washers (Fig. 47). Leaking seams may be repaired by soldering, if the metal is

not aluminum, and dents may be removed by hammering with a blunt, round, metal tool or ball peen hammer. This method of removing dents can also be used with silverware, pewter, etc., but excessive force should not be applied.

Kettles, and all kitchen utensils, should be regularly and thoroughly cleaned and washed on the inside, outside, and bottom.

Deposits. Kettles are very often subject to the formation of a white deposit containing lime. This deposit is difficult to remove, but it can be softened by putting a tablespoon of vinegar in the kettle with some water and allowing this solution to remain overnight. This will loosen the deposits so that the kettle may be rinsed out. The harder particles may be pried away with a knife, and if this is not satisfactory, a further soaking in vinegar and water may help. When the kettle is once more thoroughly clean inside, make a

Fig. 47. Hole in kettle repaired with bolt and washers.

practice of rinsing and cleaning the interior every day so that the white deposits do not have an opportunity to form. A small pebble, marble, or oyster shell, placed in the kettle will discourage the formation of the deposits.

THE REFRIGERATOR

When an electric or gas refrigerator breaks down it is best to call in an expert at once as this machinery is very delicate and should not be worked on by one who does not possess complete knowledge on the subject.

The home mechanic can, however, do much towards keeping the refrigerator in good working order by giving it a little attention now and then.

If the refrigerator is electric with the motor accessible, it should be given the care as outlined in the section on Electricity. When cleaning and oiling the motor inspect the tubes of the condenser for dirt. These coils are usually located in back of the motor. Air is forced over the coils by a fan attached to the motor and in time the coils will become covered with a heavy coat of dust. This dust will act like an insulation and keep the refrigerator working overtime. It can be removed with a cloth or soft brush but better still with a vacuum cleaner.

Gas refrigerators have an opening at the back of the top and this will collect dust in time. The best method of cleaning is with a vacuum cleaner with a nozzle attachment.

Many refrigerators run almost constantly and thus cut down their life expectancy, because the strip of rubber around the door has become worn. This rubber strip acts as an airtight gasket and unless it is in good condition, cold air is allowed to escape through the opening between the door and the refrigerator. Therefore, as soon as this gasket shows signs of wear, it should be replaced. Your dealer can either supply you with a new strip of the proper size or order one for you from the manufacturer.

HINGES

Of all types of hinges, the butt hinge, used for room doors, cabinets, and furniture, is perhaps the best known. Butt hinges used for room doors have to support much weight, plus the leverage exerted when the door is opened and closed. This type of hinge consists of two plates held

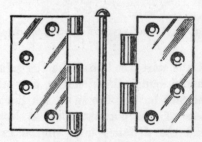

Fig. 48. The butt hinge disassembled.

together by means of a pin. In most cases, this pin can be removed so that the two plates will come apart, and some pins are threaded and must be unscrewed before they can be removed. The plates are sunk in the edge of the door and into the frame of the door so as to be flush with the surface, or slightly below, with the knuckle of the hinge, through which the pin passes, centered on the crevice between the door

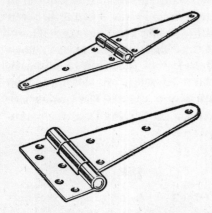

Fig. 49. A strap hinge (upper) or T-hinge (lower) is used for heavy doors, such as those on the garage.

and the frame. Examine a door which has been correctly hung and verify these points. It will be seen that the door does not fit closely to the frame, but that there is a regular clearance of about $\frac{1}{16}$ of an inch at the top and the sides. Hinges on room doors are commonly placed about 6 inches below the top and 12 inches above the bottom of the door, unless there are joints to be cleared.

Fitting Hinges. Two hinges are customary for light doors, with three for heavier ones such as the front door of a house. In fitting a new door, the worker will need two marking gauges and two thin wedges. Prop the door against a bench or table with the hinge side up. Mark the top edge of the first hinge 6

inches below the top of the door. Lay the hinge in position and carefully scribe around the hinge with a sharp knife, keeping the point close to the edge of the hinge. Gauge for both hinges in this manner. Set the marking gauge to the thickness of the hinge plate. This gives the depth of the recess to be cut, and this depth should be scribed by the gauge along the inside face of the door, for both hinges. With a square, connect the depth line and the end lines.

Attaching Hinges. Using a fine-toothed tenon saw, cut down along the squared lines until the depth line is reached. Use the point of the saw. It will not be possible to go full depth the entire length of the line. Make two other similar cuts in between, to facilitate removal of the surplus wood with a chisel. Use a sharp chisel and outline the back margin by accurate cuts, taking care not to go too deep; also, complete the cuts where the saw cannot penetrate full depth. Use the chisel on the inside face of the door to incise the line here and eventually cut out the waste wood and form the recess. Be very careful at this point not to take out too much wood. When the recess is correctly cut, fit the hinge and, using a brad awl, bore the holes for the screws. Insert the screws and turn them until they are tight and the hinge is secure.

Door Frame. With the first marking gauge, outline the width of the hinge on the inside edge of the door frame at the approximate position (top of hinge 6 inches from top of frame plus top clearance $\frac{1}{16}$ inch).

You will need someone to hold the door in position against the frame, with the hinges opened out and the plates close against the door jamb. Use wedges under the bottom of the door to raise it for accurate top clearance. The butts must align with the scribed lines made by the first marking gauge. Use a fine awl or a steel scribe to mark the position for the top and bottom of each wing, or flange, and to confirm the marks scribed by the first gauge.

be replaced until the rest of the screws are inserted and turned down tightly. A mistake can then easily be corrected. A misplaced hole can be plugged with a small piece of hardwood driven in tight and cut off level with a chisel.

Sticking Doors. When a door fails to open and close easily, look first at the hinges. It very often happens that some of the screws holding the hinge become loose, causing the entire door to sag and stick against the

Fig. 50. When removing or fitting a hinge, the door should be wedged at its outer edge to maintain the correct position. Wedge up full width of door and obtain assistance to hold door steady.

Remove the door and, with the second marking gauge, scribe the line for the depth of the recess. Cut out the recess, replace the door with wedges beneath, and bore a hole for one screw in one hinge. Insert the screw and repeat the process for the second hinge. Slip out the wedge and test the door gently. It will probably be satisfactory, and the wedges can

frame. Try to tighten the screws with a screwdriver. If this fails because the screws will not hold properly in the wood, it may be possible to use longer screws. Another method is to remove all the loose screws and insert wood plugs, which should be glued into the wood frame. These plugs will provide a firm anchorage for the old screws. As a last resort, the position of the hinges can be changed so that the screws will go into sound wood.

The position of the door in the frame can be altered considerably by placing small wedges of cardboard or wood behind the hinge plate

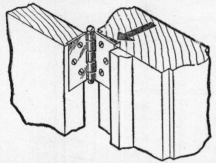

Fig. 51. Cardboard and wood shims and wedges can often be used to fix a door that sticks.

attached to the frame. Cutting out the hinge recess in the door frame so that the front is slightly deeper than the rear will tend to pull the entire door toward the frame jamb.

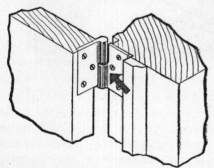

Fig. 52. A washer inserted between the plates of a hinge to correct a door that sticks at the bottom.

Not all sticking can be corrected by repositioning the hinges. Sometimes, it is necessary to plane off a portion of the door.

Whether or not it is necessary to remove the door from the frame to do this work will depend on how much wood is to be removed and whence it is to come. If the bottom or outer edge is the cause, the door should be taken down. If the top is to be cut down a little, this can often be done with the door in the frame.

The plates that make up the hinges on most doors are held together by means of a pin, and this can be taken out and the door removed without having to remove the hinges entirely. Free the bottom hinge first, and then the top. When removing the hinges, raise the door with a block or have someone hold it so that the entire weight of the door is not thrown on one hinge.

Before you remove the door, mark carefully the place from which wood is to be removed and plane off only enough to make the door fit easily. When it is necessary to plane an entire side, it is easier to do this on the hinge side rather than remove the lock and latch and then reset them again after the wood has been removed.

Be sure to set the blade of the plane to take off only a small shaving at a time and be very careful not to split the end grain of the door.

Sagging Garage Doors. One of the most frequent troubles encountered in the garage is sagging doors. If not given proper attention, a heavy garage door will sag so much that the bottom edge will strike the ground and the door can only be opened and closed with great effort.

The condition can be due to several factors, but the first step in repairing it is to take a block of wood or a wood wedge of some sort and drive it under the edge of the door until the door hangs properly. Now take a large screwdriver and check the screws in the hinges to see if they are loose. Use a heavy duty screwdriver for this because you will not be able to get sufficient leverage with a small tool to do much good. If the screws can be tightened and appear to be holding, then the chances are that the trouble is over. Should the screws go into place too easily they will not get a tight hold and will soon pull loose again. Either replace them with longer screws or move the hinges so that the screws can be set in solid wood.

If the screws and the hinges appear to be holding well then the sag is probably in the door itself. This can be fixed without the need of taking the door down. Jack the door up with a wood wedge until it is hanging plumb. Then attach a diagonal brace or a rod and turnbuckle between the upper inside corner and the lower outside corner.

LOCKS AND LATCHES

There are many different lock designs, but the type most commonly

Fig. 52a. Heavy garage door can be brought into proper position by the use of a large wood wedge.

found on interior doors is the mortice lock, recessed into the front edge of the door.

Adjusting Latch. When a door is first installed, the latch and the striking plate on the frame are aligned so that the spring latch will slip into the hole in the striking plate when the door is closed. Any subsequent movement of the door will throw the latch out of line with the striking plate and it will strike the metal instead of entering the hole.

In most cases, the latch will leave a mark on the striking plate, and this can be used as a guide in determining how much to move the striking plate so that the latch will slip easily into the hole. If there is only a slight variation between the latch and the plate, it may be possible to move the plate enough by

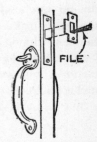

Fig. 52b. Sagging garage door repaired by the use of a wood diagonal brace.

BRACE

placing a screwdriver against it and tapping it with a hammer. If there is a greater discrepancy between the location of the striking plate and the latch, remove the striking plate and enlarge the hole enough so that the latch will fit. This can be done with a metal file. Replace the plate on the frame to see whether any wood will have to be removed from under the enlarged striking plate hole. In some cases, it may be necessary to reposition the striking plate before the

latch will catch properly. Remove the striking plate and, using a wood chisel, enlarge the mortice in the frame so that the striking plate can be positioned properly. Fill old screw holes with plastic wood or wood pegs to provide a firm base for the new screws.

Removing Lock. Occasionally, mortice locks require oiling, or a key will break off inside the lock. It is necessary to remove the lock from the door before any oil can be applied or the broken half of the key removed.

Unscrew the set screw holding one of the door knobs to the shaft. The shaft and knob may be threaded. If so, you will have to unscrew the knob from the shaft after the set screw has been removed. Pull the shaft out of the lock by means of the other knob and remove the two screws at the face of the lock. With these removed, you can easily pry the lock out of the door with a screwdriver. A set screw on the side of the lock will have to be taken out to remove the plate. The working parts of the lock are now exposed.

FILE

Fig. 53. Enlarging the hole in the striking plate with a metal file so that the door latch will hold.

If some of the parts inside the lock fall out of position, they can easily be put back in their proper place. Remove the broken portion of the key or apply the oil. Replace the plate and check the operation of the lock to be sure that it works correctly.

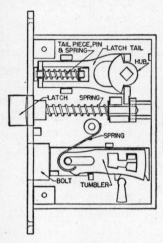

Fig. 54. Mortice lock with cover plate removed exposing the working parts.

Padlocks. Padlocks used on doors of garages and other outbuildings should be regularly oiled inside, as they are exposed to rain and damp weather. The moisture inside a lock during the winter will freeze, and this may make the lock impossible to open. Thaw the lock with a small flame rather than hot water, for the water which leaks inside the lock will soon freeze again.

BRASS HARDWARE

The brass hardware and other fittings of this nature about the house are usually brought to a high polish during the process of manufacturing and then coated with a clear lacquer to keep them from tarnishing. In time this coat of lacquer will wear off and subsequently the brass will tarnish and become unsightly.

Before the metal can be polished all the remaining lacquer must be removed from the metal surface. This can be done with a clean cloth and some lacquer thinner—nail polish remover can be used as well as a regular thinner. Go over the metal several times to be sure that all the old lacquer has been removed. After this has been done, the metal should be polished with a cloth and a good brand of metal polish. The next step is to wipe off any oil or grease that may have been left by the polish or from soiled hands. This job should be done with a clean cloth dampened in benzine. Once the article has been wiped down, take great care not to touch it as this will leave grease spots and will spoil the finish. Be careful also that dust is not allowed to collect on the surface as this too will spoil the finish. Immediately after wiping, apply a coat of clear lacquer and be sure to cover all the metal surface. Brass hardware such as that used on front doors receives considerable wear, hence it should be given at least two coats of lacquer.

Copper articles about the house can be given the same treatment as used for brass to prevent the need of constant polishing.

Brass Plated Hardware. Many homes are furnished with brass plated hardware instead of the more expensive solid brass kind. When the brass plating wears off, the metal underneath may rust unless given a coat of paint. There is no home method of replating the metal with brass. The remaining brass plate should be removed with emery cloth and steel wool. After this the surface should be treated and painted like any other metal surface (see PAINTING METAL).

SCISSORS

One of the most common reasons why scissors do not cut properly is not that they are dull but because the two blades do not come anywhere near meeting. This can be caused either by the pivot bolt or rivet that holds the two blades together being loose, or the blades having been bent out of shape through misuse.

Examine the cutting edge of a scissor blade and you will find that it does not have the same edge as a knife. While a knife has a blade that tapers down on each side to a sharp edge, the scissor blade has a beveled edge such as is found on chisels and plane blades. The cutting action of scissors depends upon a shearing action when the two blades come together, rather than a cutting action as is the case with a knife.

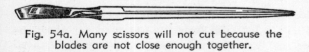

Fig. 54a. Many scissors will not cut because the blades are not close enough together.

Thus, if the blades are not properly adjusted to one another they will not cut, no matter how sharp the edges may be.

In some cases the two blades are held together by means of a screw and a nut, and if the blades appear loose, it is a simple matter to tighten the screw and then strike the end of the screw that protrudes through the nut with a ball peen hammer. This will peen the end of the screw and prevent it from becoming loose. Be careful not to get the screw too tight as this will cause the blades to bind and make cutting difficult, if not impossible. If the two blades are held together by means of a screw alone or a rivet, they can be tightened by peening the end of the screw or rivet with a ball peen hammer. If the blades are bent out of shape, it is best to have the work of straightening them done by an expert, as it is quite possible to break the blades while hammering them.

After the two blades have been properly adjusted, try the scissors and see if they still need sharpening. If they do, this job can be done on an oilstone such as is used for knives and tools. There are two methods of sharpening scissors but they have to do only with ways of holding the blade or the stone and not with the actual sharpening. If there is a vise available, you may find it easier to place the blade in it and work the stone back and forth, rather than to put the stone down on a flat surface and work the blade across the face of the stone. The choice depends on which method you find more convenient. Place the bevel edge of the blade on the fine side of the stone and move the blade back and forth. Be sure you keep the blade at the correct angle during the sharpening. Work the entire length of the bevel across the stone and when a thin wire burr appears, turn the blade over, lay the flat side down on the stone and grind off the burr. This will only require a few strokes. *Sharpening Knives.* One of the most important assets of a well-equipped kitchen is a selection of well sharpened knives. Unfortunately, most knives used in the kitchen are dull and this not only makes working with them more difficult, but is dangerous because added pressure is required to cut with a dull knife and should it slip the result might be a bad cut. Many homeowners make it a practice to take all the household knives down to the local hardware store or a shop specializing in knife grinding at regular intervals. In some communities, experts make regular trips from house to house and for a slight charge keep the knives in good cutting condition.

Sharpening a knife is not difficult and does not require much time, especially if the knives are hung in some type rack where there is no chance of the blade being dulled and nicked by striking metal objects. If a knife blade becomes nicked, it must be ground down and this requires considerable work.

The best kind of stone to use for grinding is a grindstone, which will not overheat the metal causing it to lose its temper. If another type of stone is used, take extreme care not

to allow the metal to become overheated. This is something you have to watch out for, particularly on power-driven stones rotating at high speeds. It takes only a few seconds on a stone of this kind to overheat the knife blade and perhaps ruin it.

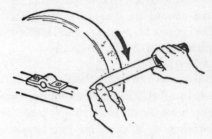

Fig. 54b. Correct method of grinding a blade on a grindstone.

The blade should be held flat on the wheel so that the wheel turns towards the cutting edge. Hold the blade against the stone at an angle that will produce a long tapered edge rather than a short one which will soon become dull. Begin grinding at one end and move the blade slowly across the stone so that the edge is ground evenly. Should the blade become hot, dip it at once in water. After grinding one side, turn the blade over and grind the other side. When a small burr of metal appears along the edge of the blade, the grinding should stop.

The next operation is done with an oilstone or wetstone. These are the same type as used for sharpening chisels and other cutting tools. The stone usually has two sides, one coarse and the other fine. Use the coarse side and put a few drops of oil on the surface. Place the blade flat on the stone and then raise the back slightly to get the proper taper to the edge. Work from the point of the knife back to the handle and when one side has been completed, turn the blade over and do the other side. If you desire an extremely sharp edge, turn the stone over and use the fine side of the stone after you have finished grinding on the coarse side. A razor-sharp edge can be had by stropping the blade on a piece of leather.

Fig. 54c. Sharpening a knife on an oilstone.

FIRE IN THE HOME

Each year many lives are lost and homes destroyed by fires. The home mechanic should take all steps to make his home as fireproof as possible and to see that the proper equipment is on hand for fighting a fire. There is nothing about the house more important than fire prevention.

Precautions. Frequent inspection trips should be made throughout the house, from attic to basement, looking for anything that could cause a fire or provide fuel for one that has started. Be on the lookout for faulty electrical equipment, such as appliance cords and heating devices placed near inflammable material.

Do not allow combustible trash to collect in the attic, basement, or closets. Inflammable cleaning fluids should never be used indoors. Paint,

paint removers, kerosene, and gasoline, should never be stored in the house, and never use kerosene or gasoline to start a fire. Burn or throw out oily rags and keep oil mops in the open and away from an open flame. The fire hazards found in the average home number in the hundreds, and every one should be eliminated.

When a fire breaks out in a home, the first thing to do is to get everyone out of the house. If there are any rooms in the house isolated from the stairways or other exits, these should be equipped with some type of rope ladder or even a rope tied to a radiator or some other object in the room. Turn in an alarm after everyone is out of the house. You can then turn your attention to bringing the fire under control. It is true that the first few minutes of a fire are the most important, but it is even more important to clear the house of all persons.

Fig. 55. In case of fire, never open a door suddenly. Check first to be sure that there is no superheated air, gas, smoke, or flame on the other side.

Each member of the household should be warned never to open a door when there is a fire in the house without first checking around the bottom of the door for heat or smoke. Any indication of overheated air on the other side of a door should be sufficient warning not to open the door.

Extinguishers. The type of fire fighting equipment used depends entirely on the cause of the fire and what materials are burning. Water can be used effectively on burning wood and trash. A large quantity of water will be needed, and needed in a hurry, so it is wise to keep a garden hose connected in the basement or at a nearby outside faucet. A garden hose can deliver enough water to deal with most small fires.

Water should never be used on burning gasoline, cleaning fluid, or kerosene, for it will cause the fire to spread. The best way to combat a fire of this sort is with sand, a heavy cloth, or by using a foam type fire extinguisher. Any of these will cut off the supply of oxygen to the fire and so kill it.

An electrical fire resulting from failure of a cord or appliance must only be treated with a nonconductor type of extinguisher, such as one containing carbon dioxide or carbon tetrachloride. Water is an excellent conductor of electricity and if used on an electrical fire, may cause the individual applying water to receive a fatal shock.

Fire extinguishers should be placed where they can be reached quickly, and each member of the household should know their location and how they operate. Inspect or refill extinguishers according to the type and the manufacturer's specifications.

Fireproofing. Most homes are far from fireproof, but there are certain steps that the home mechanic can take to prevent a fire from spreading and getting out of control too quickly.

The average frame house is well suited to provide a fire with its prime necessity—a good draft. A fire which starts in the basement draws air from the outside and rushes up through the basement door and between the walls into the upper portion of the house, as though it were a giant fireplace.

The first step in fireproofing a house is to line the ceiling of the basement with some type of fireproof composition board. This can be done easily and at no great expense. Once the woodwork in the basement has been covered, the source of fuel for a fire has been removed.

The second step is to provide a heavy, tight-fitting door between the first floor and the basement. This will not only act as a fire stop and delay the fire's progress to the first floor but will prevent the draft necessary for the fire to burn vigorously.

The door from the basement to the outside should also be made tight fitting, as this will reduce the amount of air reaching the fire. Remember that a fire must have plenty of fresh air if it is to burn at all.

After you have taken these steps, do not neglect to remove all combustible materials, or place them in fireproof containers.

IMPROVED BASEMENT

Until a few years ago, a basement in a house was considered more or less wasted space. It contained the coal bin and furnace but little else. It was damp, poorly lighted, and was far from being a comfortable living place. Recently, however, a great deal has been done to make the basement as pleasant and livable as any other room in the house. The basements of new homes are planned and decorated as carefully as the rest of the house. Attractive game rooms, childrens' play rooms, and the equivalent of a second living room, can occupy the space that once was almost completely wasted.

While improving a basement requires considerable work and some expense, it is far from being beyond the scope of most amateur carpenters, and the time and money spent will be repaid many times over by the addition of pleasant rooms to the house.

Nothing can be done to a basement until it is completely dry. If the basement is flooded each time there is a heavy rain, or if water seeps into it at any time, one or more of the waterproofing methods outlined in Section Nine should be employed.

Walls. The concrete walls of the basement can be left as they are, after giving them a coat of paint for decorative purposes, but the objection to this is that some moisture is bound to condense on the cold masonry and keep the basement damp and uncomfortable. It is easy to get around this problem by lining the walls with wallboard, plaster board, or some other composition board.

Before any sort of wallboard is put up, the walls of the basement should be lined with 2 x 2 inch furring as a base to which the wallboard can be nailed. Place one piece of furring along the bottom of the wall and attach it to the basement floor with expansion bolts. Secure another strip of furring along the top of the wall. You can generally nail it to the ceiling rafters. When the furring is securely in place, nail the uprights, or studding, between them. Place the studding either 16 or 24 inches from center to center to obtain the maximum amount of support and avoid having to make unnecessary cuts in the wallboard. The studding should be fastened to the top and bottom horizontal furring with nails toed in.

When working with any kind of wallboard, make the measurements carefully before you cut. If you are doing the job yourself, you will find that it is easier and, in the long run, quicker to use the six-foot lengths of wallboard rather than the twelve-foot sections. These latter are very difficult to work with unless two people are present.

Paint the back of the wallboard before nailing it to the studding, to protect it from dampness. This is particularly important when any type of wood paneling is used for the walls.

Partitions. A basement can be divided into two or more rooms by building partitions. To do this, you must first mark on the floor, walls, and along the ceiling, the location of the partition. This can be done accurately with a chalk line, a level, and a square. Mark the line across the floor and check with a square the angles that it forms, at each wall. They should each be 90 degrees. Now, with the level held against the wall in a vertical position, make a line the height of each wall. When these two lines are made, they can be connected at the top, along the ceiling rafters, with a length of cord.

Place a piece of 2 x 4 inch lumber along the line marked on the floor. This is called the shoe and should be attached to the floor with expansion bolts. Put another piece of 2 x 4 along the line on the ceiling and nail it to the rafters. If there is to be a door in the partition, cut the width of the door out of the shoe. By doing this, you eliminate a step at the door and make it easier to sweep and clean the rooms.

The studding used for the partition should be of 2 x 4's placed either 16 or 24 inches center to center. The studding must be cut to fit exactly between the shoe and upper 2 x 4; consequently, be sure that your measuring is right before sawing.

The studding should be placed on the shoe and at right angles to it. Check to see that each piece of studding is exactly vertical by means of

a level or a square. Nail the studding to the horizontal 2 x 4's so that the 2-inch side faces out. Double the studding around the door. Cut two pieces of studding long enough to run to the floor, where the shoe has a section removed for the door. On the inside of each of these put an-

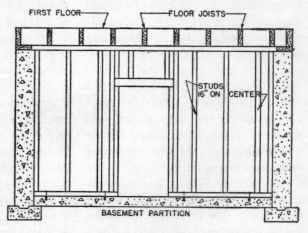

Fig. 56. Detail of partition in basement. Note double studding on each side of doorway.

other piece of studding and nail it on top of the shoe. As the door will not come to the ceiling, you will have to nail a piece of 2 x 4 between the door studding. This is called the header and should be located slightly above the top of the door. Use several short lengths of studding to connect the header to the top piece of 2 x 4.

The frame of the partition is now completed, and the wallboard can be nailed to each side. If one of the rooms formed by the partition is to remain unheated, put insulation in the partition before walling up the second side or use insulation board instead of ordinary wallboard.

Covering Ceiling. Before adding the ceiling covering, be sure that there are a sufficient number of electric fixtures. There must be enough lights and light fixtures to make the basement a pleasant, cozy place.

You can cover the ceiling with the same material used for the walls. It is suggested that two persons do this work, for it is very difficult to put wallboard on the ceiling alone and do it properly.

CREAKY STAIRS

A noise in the staircase usually occurs when the tread, or board on which one steps, pulls loose from the riser, the upright board on which the tread rests. There are two ways of attaching the tread to the riser, nailing them together or fitting them together by means of a tongue and groove.

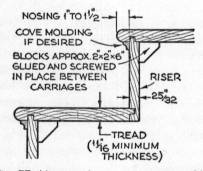

NOSING 1" TO 1½

COVE MOLDING IF DESIRED

BLOCKS APPROX. 2"×2"×6" GLUED AND SCREWED IN PLACE BETWEEN CARRIAGES

RISER

25/32

TREAD (11/16" MINIMUM THICKNESS)

Fig. 57. Most creaking stairs are caused by treads not firmly attached to the risers.

To eliminate the noise in a flight of stairs where the tread and riser are nailed together, force the tread down until it fits tightly on the riser. Fasten it securely with finishing nails driven through the tread and into the riser. These nails should be about two inches long and driven down in pairs and at an angle, in such a way that if they were long enough the points would eventually meet. This will provide greater strength than if they were driven straight down. Be sure that the nails are placed far enough from the edge of the tread so that they will enter the riser and not pass in front or behind it. Set the head of the nail below the wood with a nail set and fill the hole with plastic wood.

On stairs where the tongue and groove method of construction is used, the procedure is somewhat different. There is a tongue on the top edge of the riser that fits into a groove along the bottom of the tread. To tighten this joint, it is necessary to remove the molding at the point where the tread and riser meet and drive thin wedges between the tongue and groove to take up any play.

BASEMENT STAIRS

Rickety or poorly proportioned basement stairs constitute one of the chief danger spots in the home so far as bad falls go. While in some cases it is possible to repair the stairs satisfactorily with a few well-placed braces, more often than not the entire structure is in such poor condition that it is easier and better to tear it down and start off fresh, using new and sound lumber.

Unless you possess considerable skill at carpentry, it will pay you in the long run to make the stairs along as simple designs as possible. A flight of basement stairs does not have to be beautiful, but it must be rugged and safe to use.

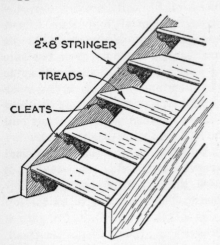

Fig. 57a. A flight of stairs of this type is easily constructed.

Fig. 57a shows a flight of stairs which is not only good and solid but requires only a medium amount of skill to build. The stringers or sides are made of 2 x 8 in. or better still, 2 x 10 in. lumber. The treads, the part you step on, are made of the same size material. In the interest of simplicity, risers are not used. The treads are attached to the stringers by means of wood cleats made out of 2 x 2 in. lumber. These cleats allow the treads to be nailed at two points. Nails are driven down through the edge of the treads into the cleats and other nails are driven through the stringer into the end of the tread.

The distance between each tread should be about seven inches or so,

for this makes an easy step for the average person. Measure up from the floor seven inches and mark the spot on the stringer. Now measure up another seven inches from this point. Do not measure along the side of the stringer but measure the vertical distance from the location marked for the first tread. Continue to measure and mark the approximate location of each tread until you reach the top of the stringer. In all probability you will find that the distance between the top tread and the first floor of the house will not come out an even seven inches by any means. A slight discrepancy at this top step can be overlooked, but if you are off several inches, work back down changing the location of each tread just enough until they all are spaced the same distance apart. This may seem like a great deal of trouble just to get the top step to equal the others, but there is nothing more annoying, or in fact dangerous, than to put out your foot for the top step and not find it where you expected it to be. So take the time to get equal distance between all the treads. Once you have these points marked on one stringer, use it as a guide to mark off the remaining stringer. Put them together and square the lines across both.

The stringers can be nailed at the top or you can attach them by means of a metal hanger. An easy way to figure out the angle to cut the stringers at the floor is to set them in place and then lay a thin board on the floor alongside of the stringer. Draw a pencil line across the width of the stringer where it meets the board, and by cutting along this line the stringer will fit properly at the floor. Some basement stairs are not attached to the floor, but to be on the safe side, cut a piece of lumber, the same size as used for the treads, so that it just fits between the stringers. Bolt this to the floor between the bottom ends of the stringers and spike the stringers to the board from each side.

Once the stringers are in place, take a level and draw a horizontal line across each stringer where the cleat is to be nailed. Spike on the cleats and then set and nail the treads.

Be sure you put up some sort of handrail when the stairs have been completed. This can be made out of 2 x 4's, one at top and one at bottom to serve as posts and a long one running between them for the rail. The top edges of the rail should be planed off so that the surface is rounded and easily gripped by the hand. Give the wood a good sanding so that there will be no chance of splinters.

HARDWOOD FLOORS

It is not difficult to put down a hardwood floor, provided that necessary preparations are made, the new flooring is well seasoned, and the worker does not hurry and plans the work carefully before beginning.

Hardwood floor boards have a tongue on one edge and a groove on the other and are laid so that the tongue fits into the groove. They present a much neater appearance than do ordinary planks, and if the flooring is put down properly and the wood has been seasoned, there will be no cracks between the boards to collect dust and dirt.

Before laying the hardwood flooring, punch all nail heads below the surface of the subflooring. The subflooring should be nailed tightly to the floor joists, for when the finish floor is put over it, any squeaks caused by loose subfloor boards will be difficult to eliminate. If there are any rough edges on the subflooring, these should be planed. It is not essential that the floor be perfectly smooth, but it should be level.

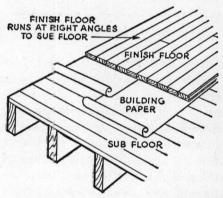

Fig. 58. Proper method of laying a hardwood floor over subfloor.

Remove the baseboard around the walls, as well as the threshold of the doorway. You will probably have to take down the door also, and remove some wood from the bottom to allow for the added height of the new flooring.

Laying Floor. Put a layer of heavy building paper over the subfloor and nail the finish floor at right angles to the old floor, rather than in the same direction. Lay the first board about ¼ inch from the wall to prevent any possibility of the floor's buckling, which might happen if the boards were nailed flush against the wall. Be sure that the first board is parallel to the wall. This can best be done by means of a cord running from wall to wall. Check the work with this cord from time to time to be sure that the boards are put down parallel with the walls of the room.

Fig. 59. How to nail flooring.

The first row of the new floor boards may be held in place, making certain that ¼ inch is left for expansion, by first driving in finishing nails and then using floor nails. Put down the first row with the tongue towards the center of the room and the groove facing the wall. Drive the flooring nails in at a 45-degree angle and begin nailing at the top of the tongue. In this way, the nails are covered by the upper lip of the groove of the following board. Do not attempt to drive the nail all the way in with the hammer, as you are almost sure to strike the tongue and damage it. Use a nail set to finish driving the nails and force the heads down to the surface of the tongue so that the groove of the next board will slip over it easily. Nails should

not be more than nine inches apart, and all end joints between boards should be staggered and more than a foot apart.

To obtain a tight fit between each board and yet not damage the wood, keep a small piece of flooring to use as a buffer between the hammer and the floor. Put the groove of this short piece over the tongue of the board about to be nailed. Drive this board tight against the one already nailed by striking the small piece of wood with a hammer. While nailing each piece of flooring, apply pressure to it by kneeling or standing on it.

GAS RANGES

The enamel portion of a gas range should not be washed with cold water when the surface is hot. Clean the enamel daily with a cloth and soapy water but do not use a gritty cleaning powder. If this is done, there should not be any thick accumulation of grease requiring scraping or other harsh treatment. Stains that will not respond to soap and water can generally be removed with kerosene. The pilot light should be cleaned from time to time by running a thin piece of wire through the opening.

Burners must be clean if they are to function satisfactorily. The burner can be lifted out of the stove and given a brushing with a stiff brush. It should then be boiled in a solution of 1 tablespoon of sal soda to 2 quarts of water. After boiling, the burner should be washed with clean water and placed in a warm oven to dry. If the burner is put back in the stove with moisture inside, it will not function properly.

Adjusting Burner. The operating efficiency of a gas range depends on the proper mixture of air and gas.

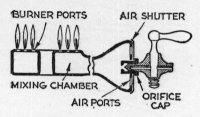

Fig. 59a. Gas cock of the type used on many kitchen ranges.

The amount of gas reaching a burner is controlled by a six-sided nut located on the gas cock. The volume of air is controlled by the air shutter on the gas cock. This shutter is held secure with a set screw. The burner should be lighted when adjustments are being made.

The best flame from a standpoint of heat and gas economy is one with a green cone and darker blue edges. It should be 1½ inches high. If the flame is too short, the size can be increased by turning the six-sided nut. If the flame has a yellow tip, the air shutter should be moved to allow more air to mix with the gas. A flame that sputters and jumps indicates too much air. This is corrected by closing the air shutter enough to make the flame burn steadily with proper height and color.

As soon as the proper flame has been obtained, the set screw on the air shutter should be tightened to prevent the shutter from being thrown out of adjustment.

HANGING OBJECTS

Small pictures and other not-too-heavy objects can be hung on a plaster wall with one of the patented wall hangers made for this purpose, which are obtainable at hardware and five-and-ten-cent stores. The nail enters the plaster at an angle and does not pull out easily. Ordinary nails driven into a plaster wall will not hold well unless they are spaced to strike a piece of wall studding behind the plaster. You can find the position

Fig. 60. Patented fasteners for hanging light articles on plaster walls.

of the studding by tapping on the wall or by examining the baseboard for nail heads. The baseboard is nailed directly to the studding, and if you draw a line straight up from the nail heads in the baseboard, you are fairly certain to have a solid wood base behind the plaster there.

When an object is too heavy for a hanger and it is impossible to locate a piece of studding in the proper position, a toggle bolt can be used. Drill a hole for the bolt through the plaster. In all probability, there will be a lath behind the plaster and the hole should be drilled through this.

Do not hang a very heavy object, such as a wall cabinet, with toggle bolts through the plaster and laths, or the weight may pull out one of the laths and damage a large section of wall.

AIR CONDITIONING

There has been a great deal of progress made in the field of home air conditioning, but as yet the equipment necessary is priced somewhat beyond the average homeowner's means. It seems very probable, however, that within a few years air conditioning equipment will be priced low enough so that it can be incorporated into a new home just as the heating system is today.

The homeowner can do a great deal, nevertheless, to make his home more comfortable in the summer, without installing equipment and without great expense.

The prime factor in making a house comfortable during the hot months is the free circulation of air. This can be accomplished by leaving the attic windows open and allowing the air to move up from the lower parts of the house and leave by means of these windows. If there is no window in the attic, the home mechanic can install a louver without much difficulty. This consists of an opening cut at the gable ends up near the top. It should be at least 8 x 12 inches or larger and equipped with slats pitched at about a 45-degree angle to keep rain from entering. Screens should be added to prevent insects from entering the house. Metal louvers can be purchased at some hardware stores.

This opening will allow the overheated air in the attic to flow out, thereby drawing the air from the room below. This small amount of air circulating will do a great deal

toward keeping the house comfortable. To increase the flow of air, you can install a fan at the louvre or window.

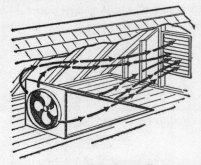

Fig. 61. One method of installing an exhaust fan in the attic to cool the house in summer.

Remember, however, that a forced circulation of air through the house is dangerous if a fire breaks out. For this reason, it is a good idea to close the ventilating system before retiring at night or have some type of device installed that will close it in case of fire.

A well-insulated attic roof will do much to keep the air in this space from becoming overheated.

Exhaust Fans. There are several rooms in a house which should be equipped with some kind of ventilating system during the summer. The kitchen especially tends to become very uncomfortable, and this can be remedied by installing a small exhaust fan to draw out the air. These fans can be had in many different sizes. A small one can be installed in a window sash after a pane of glass has been removed to make an opening for it. The larger and more expensive ones are installed in a hole made in the exterior wall or in the ceiling, and the air then piped out of the house by a duct.

A good exhaust fan in the kitchen will not only keep it cooler in the summer but it will also prevent cooking odors from permeating the rest of the house.

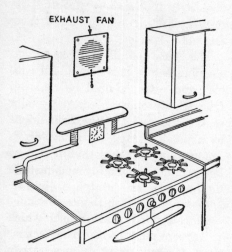

Fig. 62. An exhaust fan installed over the range will make the kitchen more comfortable in both summer and winter.

DAMPNESS IN THE HOUSE

During the summer months when the air is excessively humid, many homes become extremely damp. The walls, furniture and clothing all have a musty odor and sometimes even mold and fungi will be found. As this condition is caused by the high moisture content of the outside air, there is no sure cure short of complete air conditioning.

To prevent various articles about the house from being damaged by mildew, they should be coated with one of the many brands of fungicides on sale at hardware and de-partment stores. Some brands of fungicides will not only kill the mildew and prevent its regrowth for a considerable period but will also eliminate the unpleasant odor.

One of the best remedies for a damp house is to give it frequent airings whenever the weather outside is warm and dry. Take advantage of such days, especially in the fall of the year, to open all doors and windows from attic to basement, letting the fresh air circulate throughout the entire building. Remove clothes from closets and hang them up in the sun. Getting rid of the excess moisture at this time will not only make the house more comfortable for the remainder of the warm weather, but will help reduce the condensation on walls and windows that occurs when the heating plant goes on and the weather outside is cold.

A cause of considerable dampness in the house is the basement. If the basement is continually damp, then this moisture is sure to be carried by the air into the rest of the house. Leaky basement walls should be treated as suggested in Section Nine. Good ventilation in the basement will help to take care of the moisture.

Many homeowners find that paint or paper on the plaster walls around the fireplace and chimney does not last very long but peels or chips off easily. This is usually because the plaster has been applied directly to the masonry of the chimney. The warmth of the plaster is absorbed by the cold masonry and thus you have condensation of moisture on this surface during the summer months. The surest cure for this difficulty is to insulate the plaster from the chimney, either by setting laths away from the chimney or with insulating board between the masonry and the plaster.

Damp Closets. The ventilation facilities in most closets are poor, and so they usually become damp during a wet summer or in the winter from condensation. Having a window installed will allow the closets to be aired out with the rest of the house. Another way to improve the circulation of air at this point is by the use of electric fans.

CLOSING THE HOUSE

Whenever a house is to be vacated for any length of time, at any season of the year, precautions should be taken so as to be sure that it will be in good condition when the family returns. Many a summer camp or cottage has been seriously damaged during the winter months because windows were left unlocked to invite house breakers, or chimneys were uncovered, inviting squirrels and other rodents inside the premises. The same holds equally true of winter homes where the family has gone away leaving the plumbing or heating systems undrained or a back door unlocked. Taking the necessary time to close a house properly will save both grief and money.

Any home that is to be closed during the winter months, for any time whatsoever, should have the plumb-

ing system drained and prepared for freezing weather (see DRAINING PLUMBING). If the house has a water or steam heating system, this too must be drained of all water. These may seem like very obvious precautions but many homeowners neglect to follow them and find the results of their neglect upon their return.

The house should be given a good cleaning before it is closed. All rubbish and refuse should be removed from the premises, especially oily rags, mops, and the like, that might be a possible cause of spontaneous combustion. Matches should not be left around and highly combustible liquids such as paint, gasoline, or kerosene should be disposed of.

Bottles filled with liquids which will freeze must be removed because the bottle will probably break when the liquid freezes.

Articles of clothing, linen, blankets, and other materials that are to be left in the house should be cleaned or washed, allowed time to dry completely, and then packed away in trunks or closets with moth balls or some equally effective moth preventive.

Naturally, all food stuff should be either taken away or thrown out, and the kitchen, pantry and ice box given a good scrubbing to rid them of any small particles of food matter that might attract rats and mice.

Inspect the outside of the house to see if there are any loose shingles on the roof, cracks in the siding, or other such flaws in the exterior walls. Re-putty any loose window panes and replace any that might be cracked. Cover the top of the chimney and any other such opening with fine mesh wire netting to keep birds and squirrels out of the house.

A few days before you leave the house, call up the telephone company and arrange to have them disconnect the telephone. It is a wise idea to have the gas turned off too, and if you do not know how to do this yourself, call the gas company and give them a few days notice so they can send a serviceman over after you have cooked your last meal. Turn off the electricity by pulling the main switch. This will prevent the possibility of a fire caused by a short circuit in the house wiring.

It is a good idea to inform the local officials or state police that you are going to be away. If they know the house is empty, they can make a point of keeping an eye on it.

The last thing before you leave, lock and close all windows. If there are shutters these should be closed and locked too. Make sure that all outside doors are locked and that you have the keys. Do not make the usual mistake of forgetting the outside basement door or the garage.

REGULAR INSPECTION

Most of the trouble caused in the average house by faulty and worn locks, hinges, electric lamp fittings, etc., is due to lack of regular inspection and proper lubrication. It is a good plan to go through the house

every six months with a screwdriver and oil can and inspect and repair every fitting, from the padlock on the garage door to hinges on the skylight.

In general, inspect screws to see that they are secure. All moving parts, such as hinges, window catches, etc., should be lightly oiled or greased and any metal parts, in places where corrosion is likely to occur, should be regularly examined for rust. This is particularly important with chromium fittings, and an occasional drop of oil rubbed into angle corners of the fitting will prevent the deterioration of the chromium plating.

Tighten the hinges on the door and check the lock and latch to be sure they operate easily.

Windowshade and curtain rod fixtures are too often attached to the woodwork by means of small brads, which will not hold for very long. It is worthwhile to replace these brads with wood screws, for a neater and a more permanent fixture.

Check each window to see that both sashes operate easily but are not loose in the frame. Inspect the cords for signs of wear and put a drop of oil on each pulley.

See that all doors are equipped with some kind of door stop to prevent damage to the door and adjoining wall. Door stops are available to fit into the baseboard or the floor. They should have rubber pads at the point where contact is made with the door.

Check all the electric light fixtures to be sure that they work properly and do not flicker when turned on. See that each fixture is attached securely to the wall and ceiling, and that the electric cord is not carrying the entire weight of the fixture.

Examine the attic and basement stairs to be sure that they are solid. Many accidents occur each year when people fall down poorly built basement stairs. It is wise to have some kind of banister or, if there is none, a strong rope will help. It is better to build a banister out of wood smoothed down until there are no splinters. It can be attached to the wall by means of brackets, or supported by 2 x 4 studding based on the floor if there is no wall near the stairs.

Slippery treads are another cause of accidents, and these can be corrected easily by nailing rubber mats to the treads. Mats are obtainable in different widths and provide sure footing.

There should be a light near attic and basement stairs, and they should be kept clear of any trash or other objects over which someone might trip.

Look for signs of rot, not only in woodwork near the ground but any place where the air is damp. Inspect the wood flooring under each plumbing fixture. This is particularly important in the case of a cabinet type kitchen sink, where a leak at the trap can go undetected for a long time. While checking the floor, look for rat holes in corners and around the baseboard. These should be covered with metal.

PROPERTY IMPROVEMENTS

Attractive garden paths can be made of flagstone, concrete, or brick. Choosing which to use is largely dependent upon the nature of the house and garden, for the material chosen must fit in with the surroundings.

FLAGSTONE PATHS

Stone slabs of irregular shape but uniform thickness are employed to lay a flagstone path. Such material can be bought from lumber yards and stone yards. A thickness of 2 inches is usual.

First, set out the paths, if they do not already exist. Cut a few boards, the exact width of the path to be prepared, to use as gauges. Drive in several stakes at each side of the proposed pathway, spacing them about 6 feet apart. Indicate the turn line of the path by two strings stretched between end stakes at each side of the site. Dig out the turn and put the earth aside for use elsewhere in the garden. Dig to an even depth of 6 inches along the pathway, leaving the sides vertical.

As a temporary guide, tack thin, narrow boards to the side stakes; the boards may be ½ inch thick by 4 to 6 inches wide. You will need cinders or crushed stone for the foundation of the path and similar material of a finer grade for the top layer of the foundation (see Fig. 1).

Fill in the path with a layer of foundation material about 2 inches deep. Roll it with the garden roller a few times to make it firm, or tamp it solid with a tamper. Follow with a thinner layer of finer grade material and roll that also. Drainage will be improved if the surface is given a slight camber, i.e., higher at the middle than at the sides. Mark a board with a pencil to a suitable curve and cut out with a saw. When laying the fine stuff, stroke it lengthwise with the cambered board to shape the surface before rolling.

Paving on Sand. Spread a bed of sand about a yard long at one end of the site. Try one or two pieces of paving on it to judge the depth of sand to be added, then proceed with the rest. Dump piles of sand at suitable positions beside the pathway.

Also, sort out the stones roughly and pile them at convenient intervals along the edge of the path. Much time may be lost unless this part of the job is systematized. It is best to begin laying the stone at the margins and work toward the center line of the path. Fill in the path with large pieces of stone as much as possible, particularly when laying in sand. If a large piece has to be cut or broken, use a sledge hammer and a cold chisel. Strike along a determined line on top of the slab; then turn the stone over and work from the other side.

joints may be left a little wider. When you cease work for the day, leave the slabs irregular at the finishing point. If the joints are to be filled with concrete, this can be done with a bricklayer's trowel as the stones are laid. Assuming the joints are to be pointed, perhaps in a colored or a white cement, rake out the joints an hour or two after laying, and do not use the path for a day. The next day, fill the joints with pointing material and level off flush.

General Hints. A sledge hammer can be used to level the stones and

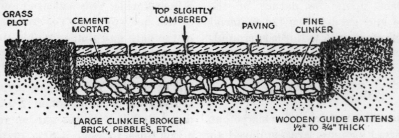

Fig. 1. Cross section of garden path, showing the foundations, intermediate layers and top layer of paving.

Laying in Mortar. Another method is to lay the paving in mortar. A mixture of 1 part cement, 2 parts sand, and 4 parts gravel, is suitable for this mortar. After digging out the pathway, add the two layers of fill described above. Roll and tamp the top layer after giving it the proper camber. Mix a quantity of cement and sprinkle the pathway with water at the place where you begin working.

Lay a thin bed of mortar and proceed with the setting of the stone. A distance of ½ inch between the edges of the slabs is usual, but the

bed them into the sand or cement immediately after laying. Often, a light blow with the end of the handle will suffice. After laying, the stones must not rock; should they do so, lift the stone and remove a little of the bedding material, or add a little, as the condition requires. When paving has been laid on sand, sweep over the section of work completed with a stiff broom, to fill the cracks with surplus sand, but do not brush too heavily. Similarly, after laying paving in mortar and filling the joints with ordinary mortar, brush with an old broom, sprinkling a little water from the can if necessary. This will grout the slabs.

Mortar should be filled in at the sides of the path and packed down well with the edge of the trowel. Later, the boards can be removed, if desired. They were put down as guides and form no integral part of the path. It is essential, however, to form a good side edge with cement mortar, independently of the guide boards. After removing the boards and stakes, fill the remaining holes with ordinary soil.

CONCRETE WALK

It is possible to make an attractive stone walk without the expense involved in purchasing the stone slabs. In this type of walk the slabs are made of concrete, and there is nothing very difficult about making the slabs or putting down the walk.

The forms used for the flagstones can be made of 2 x 4's, with a bottom of 1-inch planks. The 2 x 4's are set on edge so that the slabs will be approximately 4 inches thick. Fig. 2 shows one method of constructing the forms to make several sizes of flagstones, but the home mechanic can use any design he chooses. The form should be constructed so that it

is solid yet easily taken apart, in order that several batches of flagstone can be made from the same form. Do not nail the bottom planks, and removing the flagstones after they have hardened will be greatly facilitated. Green lumber is best for the forms. Give the inside of the form a coat of oil.

The proper mixture for making the flagstone is 1 part cement, 2.5 parts sand, and 3 parts coarse aggregate. After the concrete is mixed, pour it into the form and smooth with a float when it has set sufficiently. Allow the concrete several days in which to dry.

It is not necessary to set the flagstones in a foundation, and a very pleasing effect can be obtained by digging holes in the lawn slightly deeper than the flagstones and setting them therein.

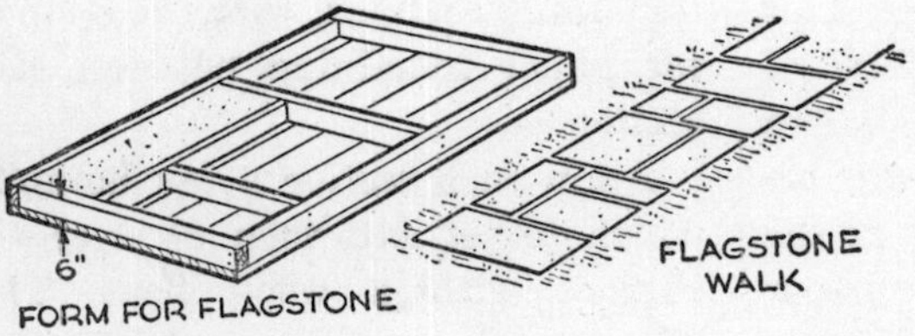

CONCRETE SIDEWALK

Concrete sidewalks are usually from 4 to 5 feet in width, with subsidiary walks leading to the basement or kitchen about 3 feet or less in width.

A foundation will be necessary, unless there is such good natural drainage that water will not collect under the walk. Sand or very loose soil will drain quickly, but if you are in any doubt as to how good the drainage is, it is best to put in a good foundation and avoid having the walk crack during the winter.

FORM FOR FLAGSTONE

FLAGSTONE WALK

6"

Fig. 2. Forms for concrete flagstones can be made of either 2 x 4 or 2 x 6 lumber.

The concrete portion of the walk should be about 4 inches thick, and there should be about 6 inches of gravel or cinders under it to serve as the foundation. Dig out the soil to a depth of about 8 inches, and this will place the walk 2 inches above ground level. To improve the drainage, pitch the walk to one side, about ½ inch.

the two sections of concrete separated after removing the spacer.

When the form is ready, mix the concrete. Make up a trial batch in accordance with the table given in Section Three. Make any corrections necessary to get a workable but plastic mass. Wet down the cinders or gravel of the foundation and pour the concrete into the first section.

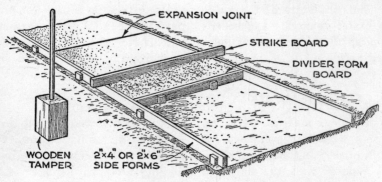

Fig. 3. A concrete sidewalk under construction.

After digging the trench, tamp the bottom or roll it with a garden roller and add 6 inches of cinders or gravel. Level this fill and roll it. Make the forms of 2 x 4 inch stock and level the tops so that a board can be worked across them to smooth the top of the concrete. Drive stakes into the ground along the outside of the forms to hold them in place.

The walk should be divided into sections to allow for the expansion and contraction of the concrete. This can be done easily by means of boards cut the width of the walk and inserted at 4- to 6-foot intervals between the outside forms and at the same level. Place a strip of tar paper the width and depth of the concrete on one side of these spacers to keep

After the section is full, set a board on edge across the two outside forms and work it back and forth like a saw. This will both level the concrete and remove the excess. After the first section has been poured, move to the third section rather than to the second. In other words, do alternate sections, and follow this plan throughout the entire job. After these sections have had time to set, remove the spacer boards and fill the remaining sections, with the strip of tar paper remaining between each section.

Allow each section a few hours in which to set and then go over the surface with a wood float. This roughens the surface enough so that the walk will not be slippery.

Fresh concrete should be covered and kept damp until it is hard. This may require as long as ten days, depending upon the climate.

BRICK WALK

A brick walk is not only easy to build, but attractive and interesting designs can be worked out with the bricks to make the walk a handsome addition to any home or garden. Brick walks have an advantage in

the bottom of the path and make it as even as possible by adding or removing soil. After this has been done, add the sand and level it.

Place the bricks as close together as possible and use a board or line to get each course straight. After the bricks are in place, pour sand over the walk and sweep it into the joints between the bricks. At this time, it is a good plan to spray the walk with a garden hose, using the fine spray to pack the sand down in the joints.

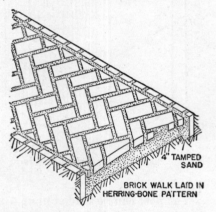
BRICK WALK LAID IN HERRING-BONE PATTERN
4" TAMPED SAND

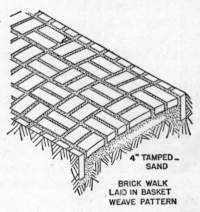
4" TAMPED SAND
BRICK WALK LAID IN BASKET WEAVE PATTERN

Fig. 4. Attractive brick walks can be built with bricks laid in a bed of sand.

that the bricks can be put down on a bed of sand without the preparation necessary when using cement mortar.

The pathway should be carefully marked to the desired width and the sides cut down vertically. The average size brick is about $2\frac{1}{4}$ inches thick; consequently, the path should be dug at least $3\frac{1}{2}$ inches deep. This will allow $1\frac{1}{2}$ inches for a sand foundation, and the bricks will rest only a fraction of an inch above ground level. When you have made the excavation, roll or tamp earth at

CONCRETE STEPS

Concrete is an excellent material with which to build steps and stoops for either the front or back door. The concrete is not subject to rot or termites and it will last indefinitely. Another advantage is that the stoop can be made any size you wish.

The base for the steps should be dug out below the frost line so that the steps will not heave up and crack during winter. The area of the excavation should correspond with the area of the steps at the base.

While the steps and the base can be poured in one operation, keeping the form for the steps in the right position may prove difficult. It is easier to pour the base first and then, after a day or two, set the form for the steps around it and pour the concrete into it.

The form for the stoop and steps must be solid and tight. Use 1-inch thick lumber for the form and 2 x 4 inch stock as studding. The vertical distance between each tread should be around 7 inches and the treads ought to be about 10 inches wide. Use braces where necessary so that there will be no chance of the concrete pushing the sides of the form out of position.

The concrete should be poured into the form in one operation. Spade it in as you pour to get it solid. When the entire form is filled and the concrete has had a few hours to set, work over the surface with a wood float.

The concrete should then be covered with burlap or straw and kept damp for about 10 days. Allow about this same amount of time before removing the wood form.

CLOTHES LINE POST

The post may be fixed permanently in the ground or set in a socket for removal whenever desired. In the second arrangement a wooden socket is commonly used, but a concrete one is better. Dig a hole in the ground, 2 feet deep and about 15 to 18 inches square. It is important to have enough room to use the shovel;

accordingly, allow a little extra space. At the bottom of the hole lay a piece of paving stone about 2 inches thick.

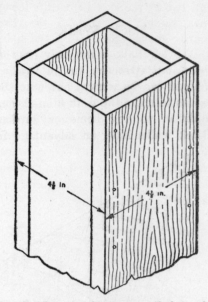

Fig. 5. Outside dimensions of form for concrete base.

The post can be made out of 4 x 4 inch stock, and its length should be 2 feet more than the desired height above the ground. A form can be made out of four pieces of 1-inch board nailed together so that the outside dimension is that of the post, plus a little more for clearance. The form should be at least 2 feet 2 inches long. Do not nail the form together too tightly, for it may have to be broken out to remove it after the concrete has set hard.

When the hole has been dug and cleared of any loose earth, lay in the piece of paving stone described above and set the form on it, centered in the hole and resting plumb.

Secure it in place with four pieces of board tapped down edgewise between the sides of the form and the side of the hole, two near the bottom and two at the top. Leave the lower ones intact but remove the two boards above when filling the hole. Shovel in the concrete around the form and tap it down from time to time. Stop about an inch from ground level, so that the top of the form is about two or three inches above. Do not try to smooth off the surface at present. The concrete will have to be left for a day or more. Cover the hole to prevent soil from falling into it.

cut a piece of lead or copper to make a cap for the post, as in Fig. 6. Nail on the metal cap with galvanized nails. About 8 inches down from the top of the post, bore a hole through the wood. The hole should be large enough so that a section of a broom handle inserted will fit tightly. At a point 2 inches lower, bore a similar hole at right angles

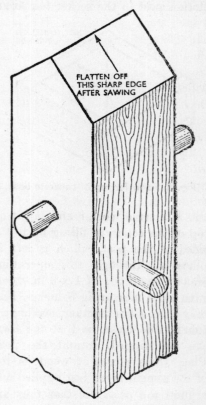

FLATTEN OFF THIS SHARP EDGE AFTER SAWING

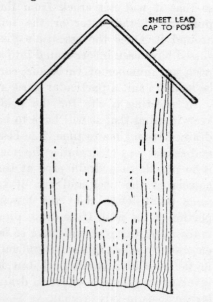

SHEET LEAD CAP TO POST

Fig. 6. Cap the post with sheet metal to prevent the wood from rotting.

Fig. 7. How to shape the top of a clothes line post. Bore holes and insert two pegs, as shown, to support lines.

Shaping. Saw off the top of the post to an inverted V shape, thus providing a surface that will shed water. Saw or chisel away the sharp edge at the top. For finished work,

to the first and drive in another piece of round wood, as in Fig. 7. Some housewives prefer a pulley arrangement in order that the line can be raised and lowered; in this case, you will need a strong brass or galvanized pulley screwed to the front face and a metal cleat below to secure the loose end of the clothes line.

The Socket. When the concrete is hard, pull out the form, if necessary driving in two of the side boards with a hammer and a cold chisel and bringing it out in pieces. Set the clothes post in the socket temporar-

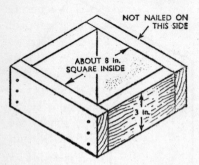

Fig. 8. Form for top of concrete base.

ily. Mix some mortar and lay it on top of the concrete, filling up to the sides of the post, which is left in place all through this operation. Make a small box of 1 x 3 in. wood, with sides measuring 8 inches. Nail only three sides together, leaving the fourth side loose, so that the form can be slipped around the post. Place these pieces of wood on top of the cement layer just applied and around the post. See that they are square and level.

Fill in the mortar until it is flush with the top of the box; let the box remain until the concrete sets hard, and do not move the post for several days.

Permanent Post. The disadvantage of this type of post is that the wood will rot, particularly if it is sunk in concrete. As the wood shrinks away from the concrete, water will get down into the form and remain there. When putting a post into soil or concrete, give the lower part a good coat of some wood preservative, such as creosote.

GARDEN POOLS

A garden pool is not difficult to build, and an attractive one will do credit to any garden. The pools outlined in this section contain only the essentials. They are made of watertight concrete which is reinforced so that it will not crack from the pressure of the water or the soil around it. Once the essentials discussed have been incorporated into a pool, any number of variations can be made to suit a particular garden.

In selecting a site for the pool, keep in mind that it will have to be drained from time to time. The best and easiest way of draining the pool is to put down a drain pipe at the bottom of the pool and run it to some point lower than the lowest portion of the pool. If no drain pipe is installed, the pool will have to be emptied by hand; this is not difficult in the case of a small pool, but it involves considerable effort to drain larger pools in this fashion.

Dig out the necessary amount of earth and then set the drain pipe in place. The opening of the drain pipe should be at the lowest point in the pool. A very effective way of combining an overflow pipe with a drain pipe is to attach a coupling to the drain pipe so that the coupling is almost covered by the concrete bottom of the pool. Screw a length of pipe into the coupling, and this pipe will act as an overflow. When draining the pool, unscrew the overflow

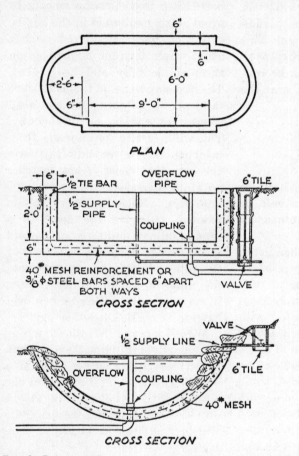

PLAN

CROSS SECTION

CROSS SECTION

Fig. 9. Either of these two concrete pools can be easily built by the home handyman.

pipe, and the water will flow out through the coupling.

Forms. The forms for the curved portions of the pool can be made out of No. 20 galvanized iron. If the soil is solid, only a top form will be re-

quired; if it is loose, both a top and bottom form should be used. To reinforce the concrete, use 40 lb. mesh wire, placed between the forms. Space the forms 6 inches apart, with the reinforcement running midway between them. The faces of the forms should be covered with oil so that they can be removed easily.

Concrete. The concrete used on an average pool should be about 6 inches thick, and it should be placed over a cinder bed about 6 inches deep.

Mix the concrete in accordance with the table listed in Section Three for watertight concrete and take great care that the proportions are right. To prevent seams in the concrete, do all the pouring in one operation. Shovel in about 8 inches of concrete and spade it so that it becomes a well-packed mass. Shovel in another batch and continue until the entire pool has been completed. Keep the fresh concrete moist and covered for a week or ten days until it has set. Do not try to remove the forms for several days.

The alkaline that is present in new concrete will kill fish. It is possible to check the amount of alkaline in the water with pink litmus paper, obtainable at a drug store. If the paper turns blue when placed in the water, it is not safe for fish. Change the water at weekly intervals until the paper remains pink.

Filling. Small pools can be filled with a garden hose, but a half-inch line connected to the house plumbing system is more convenient. This line should be fitted with a valve so that the flow of water can be controlled easily from a point near the pool.

GARDEN TOOLS

While garden tools are built to withstand hard use, they should be given the same care as any other tool in the shop.

The wood used for tool handles is a special kind that is very resistant to moisture; nevertheless, no tool should be left where it will get wet. Keep the wood well covered with paint to give the handle a longer life. Keep the metal portion of a tool that does not come in direct contact with the ground painted too. Use a red lead priming coat for this work and follow with two coats of good exterior paint. Keep the cutting edges of shovels and hoes even and free of nicks and dents. Use steel wool to keep the blade clean and a metal file for removing nicks.

When the handle of a tool breaks, it can often be repaired or even replaced more cheaply than buying a new tool. Hardware and garden stores supply wood handles with the necessary rivets for attachment.

Long diagonal splits in wood handles can, in many cases, be repaired by winding wire or strong cord around the handle along the length of the break. Use enough wire or cord to give the wood plenty of support. Keep wood handles smooth to avoid getting splinters in the hands.

Garden tools should not be left about where someone might step on them accidentally and be injured. The best way to avoid this is to store the tools in the garage or tool shed where they will be out of the way. This will not only keep persons from injuring themselves but will also prevent the tools from getting broken or damaged.

Rollers. Keep garden rollers painted and give the bearings a drop of oil now and then. At the end of the season, drain the water out of the roller. If this is not done and the water inside the roller freezes, it may split the casing, which will have to be welded together again.

Wheelbarrows. Oil wheelbarrows occasionally and paint them as well. When carrying a heavy load in a wheelbarrow, do not dump it on one side. This throws the entire weight on a single leg, and in time the joints will become loose or break off completely.

LAWN MOWERS

Whatever the type or make of lawn mower, there are general directions which must be observed. The most obvious precaution and perhaps the most often neglected is clearing the lawn of stones and other small rubbish before mowing. The blades of the machine rotate rapidly, and it needs only the introduction of a small stone or nail between the blades to damage the mower.

The best plan, therefore, is to see that the lawn has been properly cleared of all foreign matter before starting to cut the grass.

The bearings should be oiled between mowings. This ensures easy operation of the machine and, consequently, better mowed grass. The holes for the oil are easily located. If any have become clogged with dirt, use a piece of stiff wire to clear them. Thick oil is a hindrance to free movement and is apt to collect dirt and bits of grass. No. 20 oil is a good substitute if the oil recommended by the makers cannot be obtained.

It is not possible for any machine to cut wet grass satisfactorily, and this includes motor powered machines. Moderately dry grass is best for mowing, and the cool of the evening is a comfortable time in which to mow. Short strokes, then a pause, another stroke, and so on, constitutes a common and bad method of mowing. Push the machine briskly and without pause to the end of the strip.

Bearing down on the handle, or handles, is another common error. The front roller should always be in contact with the ground.

Regulating the Cut. The closeness of cut can be regulated in some types of machines by adjusting the bottom blade to the rotating knives. On other types, the bottom blade is fixed and the cutting knives have to be adjusted to the blade. The method in either case is simple, tightening or slackening of screws being all that is required. These screws fix the position of bearings located immediately above and at either end of the cutting cylinder.

The importance of this adjustment must not be disregarded. If the cutting blade and the rotating knives make too close contact, the machine will be very hard to operate. If the bottom blade rubs on the ground, the mower will be difficult to push, the grass will be pressed down and not properly cut, turf will be sliced off, and the knives may be damaged.

Remember, also, that young grass should not be cut too short nor any grass cut close in midsummer.

Hints. After using the mower, wipe the cutting blades and working parts dry. Store the machine in the tool shed, the garage, or some other shelter. Dampness and moisture can quickly cause deterioration of both the appearance and working efficiency of the machine.

When the machine is to be stored for the winter, clean all the parts with a rag and a stiff brush. Remove the two large wheels and scrape out all the grass and dirt collected inside them. After all metal parts have been cleaned, they can be coated with some petroleum jelly diluted with light oil. Examine the painted parts and touch up any spots that need repainting before storing the machine.

GARDEN HOSE

A good, long, garden hose is an important asset, not only for the garden, but for the entire house. Almost any hose on the market will give several years of good service, provided it receives proper care.

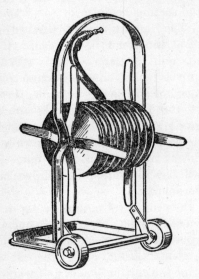

Fig. 10. The garden hose should be drained and coiled when not in use.

The first thing to remember in regard to a hose is never to leave it about when not in use. When you have finished using the hose, drain out the water, coil the hose, and store it in a dry place. If a hose is hung up when not in use, it is important to use a hanger that will not allow the hose to bend sharply at any point. These sharp bends will crack the rubber in time, and the hose will start to leak.

When working with a hose, take care not to treat it like a length of heavy rope. Do not pull it around corners or trees, as this can wear away the rubber or badly scrape it.

Leaks. Eventually, even the best hose will leak, generally at the ends where the fittings are attached. The remedy is to cut off the worn end of hose at a place where the rubber is firm and reset the fitting. One can purchase replacement attachments which fit into the hose and are equipped with clamps to hold them on tightly. When a leak occurs along the length of the hose, cut the hose in two at the leak and install a coupling, attached in the same fashion as the fittings. These couplings are screwed together so that the two halves of the hose can be reunited.

Fig. 11. Metal coupling used to repair leaks in a garden hose.

Hose Reel. The best way of preserving a hose is to keep it on a hose reel. The cheapest form of reel is a skeleton drum on which the hose is coiled. It is rotated by rolling along the ground. The first measure to take, after purchasing such a reel, is to give it an extra coat of paint as protection. Usually, such articles when purchased have a pleasing but not very durable coat of paint. If you put off painting until after the reel has been in use for several weeks, spots of rust may appear, and no amount of painting afterwards will restore the surface to its original condition. Rust that has penetrated under the edges of the corroded area will continue to eat away the metal.

POWER EQUIPMENT

Gasoline-powered lawn mowers, plows, and other equipment designed for home use must be maintained properly. Give these engines the same care that you give to an automobile. If you do not have a complete set of operating and maintenance instructions, you can get a copy from your dealer. Probably the most important thing to watch is the oil. If a gasoline engine is allowed to operate without a sufficient supply of oil, a bearing is almost sure to burn out, and this will call for major overhauling.

Store equipment of this type in a dry place. Needless to say, when adding gasoline to the fuel tank, be sure to do it out of doors where there is no chance of the fumes from the gas tank being ignited.

COLD FRAMES

The simplest form of cold frame is a wooden box without a lid, a sheet of glass covering the top. This is useful for raising seedlings and for covering plants that need winter protection. Owing to its small size,

its uses are limited. For ordinary purposes, involving the use of more ground space, the orthodox cold frame is to be recommended. This can be made of either concrete or wood. It should consist of a solid frame with one or more movable sashes.

As the object of a frame is to afford protection against cold weather and to trap the warmth of the sun, it should be both watertight and airtight. Also, the sash should slope down to the front, so that the rainwater runs off the sash and frame.

The best site for a frame is one sheltered by a wall or a fence from the north wind. The back of the frame should be against the shelter, with the glass sloping to the south. The sashes of the frame can either be installed so that they can be pushed back when it is necessary to open the frame, or attached by hinges so that they can be raised. The latter is the simpler arrangement, but some device must be made to hold the sashes up. This can be done either with a hook or by a pulley and weight arrangement.

Window sashes do not serve very well as coverings on frames because they are so constructed that the water does not drain off properly when they are laid flat. In time, this moisture will rot the wood and the frame will admit both water and cold air. Regulation cold frame sashes are the best. They are built so that the water can drain off quickly and easily, and they can withstand the strain of raising and lowering. The usual size for a cold frame sash is 3 feet wide by 6 feet long. It is a good plan to obtain the sashes and build the frame to fit them. In this way you will avoid mistakes. There is a kind of wire netting covered with transparent plastic that is very suitable for cold frame sashes. It comes in rather large sizes, and as it is light in weight it requires only a moderately strong frame to support it.

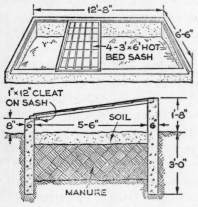

Fig. 13. Hot bed frame made of concrete.

In order to make the whole firm and tight, the sashes must rest on the frame solidly, with the edges flush. For a standard 3 x 6 sash, you should deduct 3 inches at both top and bottom and about 1 inch on each side. Thus, a frame for one sash should be about 5 feet 6 inches long on the inside and about 2 feet 10 inches wide. This will allow enough support for the sash. When using two or more sashes, make some provision for support along the seam where the sashes come together. Make the back of the frame about 6 inches higher than the front, in order

that more sunlight will enter the frame and water will drain off.

If the frame is to be of concrete, make the sides about 6 inches thick and take care, when erecting the forms, to be sure that all the dimensions are correct. If the frame is to be made of wood, a good size to use is 1 x 6 in. tongued and grooved.

HOT BED

Hot beds are much the same as cold frames except that other provisions are made for heating them beside the warmth of the sun. The most familiar kind of hot bed is one heated by manure under the top soil. In building this bed, sink the walls deep enough to put down a layer of about 15 inches of manure with 6 inches of top soil over it. Another means of heating the bed is by placing it near a basement window which can be opened to allow the warmth from the basement to enter the frame.

SCREENS AND ARCHES

Sound timber is essential for rustic screens and arches. Stack the poles in an airy, dry place for several weeks before using. It is best to strip off the bark, as timber will rot much more quickly if the bark is left on.

The main timbers should be stiff and solid. Sink the poles about 18 to 24 inches into the ground, and it is important to treat this end of the wood with a preparation like creosote, to preserve it. Small, slender posts can be driven into the ground with a mallet after the ends have been pointed, but heavier posts will require holes to be dug for them. Use a shovel or, even better, a post-hole digger for this work.

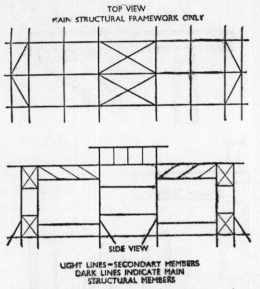

TOP VIEW
MAIN STRUCTURAL FRAMEWORK ONLY

SIDE VIEW
LIGHT LINES = SECONDARY MEMBERS
DARK LINES INDICATE MAIN
STRUCTURAL MEMBERS

Fig. 14. Plan and side elevation of a strong garden trellis. Intervening creas between the main timbers may be filled in with designs in light rustic wood to suit individual requirements.

In erecting a screen, first mark out the line on the ground with stakes and cord. Dig the holes all on the same side of the line or centered on it. Erect the two terminal posts of any main bay or portion of the screen or trellis; then, at a suitable height, stretch a line across horizontally. A simple plumb bob suspended on a string from the top line will give the true vertical and indicate where to place the intervening uprights. To get the horizontals level, use a line and a small level, for, due to the irregular surface of the timber, an ordinary level is almost useless on this job.

After setting the main posts in the lengthwise run of the screen or trellis, insert any opposite posts to pair with them, using a square to get the angles correct. Next, tie the pairs of posts together by top bars joined as shown in Fig. 16 (2 and 3), and by crossbars below, shown in (4) and (5). Insert one or two diagonals (1), for they stiffen the structure considerably.

It is advisable to bore holes for the nails in the outside members of all rustic work. A gimlet or brace with the right size bit can be used. Bore carefully, or the timber will split. Previous boring avoids heavy hammer blows which weaken the whole structure.

GARDEN GATES

Defects in gates usually occur in the posts and hinges. Posts rot or become loose in time, and deteriorate much sooner than they should if poor work or bad materials are present.

Loose Post. An easy way to repair a loose post is through the use of a piece of angle iron about 30 inches long, with a point at one end and three holes drilled in it large enough to take a ¼-inch lag screw. Force the post into an upright position and drive the iron into the ground against the post. When the iron is about 18 inches into the ground, secure the post with three lag screws.

Decayed Post. If the top portion, above the ground, is sound, it is ment, a new post must be installed.

Sticking Gates. When the posts are not at fault, hinges may cause the gate to stick. Screws may have

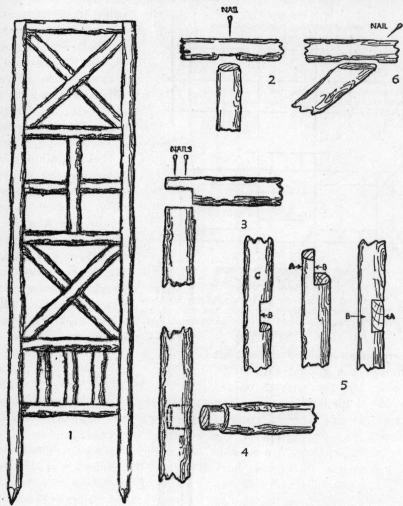

Fig. 16. Detail of joints for rustic screens and arches.

best to put another post beside it and bolt the two together with carriage bolts. This will obviate removing the gate and rehanging it. If the old post is too decayed for this treatment rusted or the hinges themselves may have become eroded by rust. In either case, it is a simple matter to tighten the screws, move the hinges, or replace them.

OUTDOOR FIREPLACES

Nearly anyone can build a serviceable outdoor fireplace, and the only difference between the one made by the expert and the one constructed by the beginner will be in appearance. The reason is that in the ordinary outdoor fireplace there is no

RUSTIC SCREEN

Fig. 15.

necessity for a complicated smoke chamber and damper such as are required for an indoor fireplace. An outdoor fireplace can have a good draft by locating it so that the opening of the firebox faces towards the prevailing winds. These winds will provide enough natural draft to keep even the poorest of fireplaces from smoking.

The first consideration, then, is to select the site for the fireplace in relation to the prevailing winds. The next point to remember is to have the firebox high enough so that the cook will not have to bend or stoop. An outside fireplace is designed for pleasure cooking, so make cooking on it as pleasant as you can. If there is a natural rock foundation nearby, this makes an excellent place on which to set the fireplace, as height and a foundation are combined here. If there is no such formation, it is better to build up the base of the fireplace to the desired height than to build the fireplace at ground level.

Build the fireplace as simply as possible. After you have done so, you can go on and expand with all sorts of additional equipment. Many a fireplace has been left unfinished because the project was too ambitious. It will come as quite a surprise when you learn how many bricks are needed to make even a small fireplace.

There are several manufacturers who make not only the grills and other accessories for a fireplace, but also a complete metal fireplace which can be used alone or with bricks or stones built up around it. The concerns that make this equipment also furnish plans and suggestions for the style of the fireplace.

Materials. A fireplace can be built of bricks, fieldstone, or poured concrete. Bricks are probably the most popular of all these materials because they come in a standard size, are light in weight and easy to work with, and are inexpensive. Stones are excellent—provided there is an ample supply nearby. A rather large number of stones are required to

planned with considerable care to resist extremes of the weather.

While not essential, it is a very good idea to line the firebox with firebrick set in a fire clay mortar. Ordinary bricks and mortar will not stand the heat indefinitely, and you can save future repairs by using

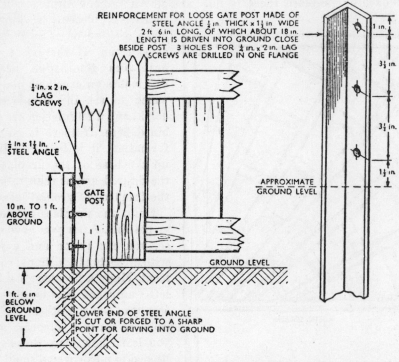

Fig. 17. Broken or loose gate posts can be repaired easily with a steel angle and a few lag screws.

finish a fireplace; consequently, be sure that you will not run out of stones before the work is completed and have to import more. Stones are of irregular size, and many will require splitting before they can be used. You will need a sledge hammer for this work. Poured concrete makes a good fireplace but requires wood forms, and these must be

these materials during the construction. The only other equipment required is a piece of 8 x 8 inch flue tile, a metal grill, some sections of pipe, and a piece of heavy angle iron to serve as a front support for the chimney.

Dimensions. There is no set rule as to what the dimensions of the firebox must be, but a good one is 18 inches wide and 16 inches deep. The walls around it should be at least 8 inches thick, which is the approximate width of two bricks. When figuring the total area of the fireplace, one must not forget the flue tile on the back of the firebox. This adds another 8 in. to the depth, and the total depth should be figured as 16 in. for the firebox, plus 8 in. for the flue tile, plus 8 in. for the rear wall, making a total of 32 in. Calcu-

frost line to prevent its cracking. If you are in doubt as to how deep to dig, check with any local contractor or builder.

For a concrete fireplace, make the necessary excavation and then build the form for the concrete. The proper mixture for this job is given in the table in Section Three. Allow the foundation plenty of time to cure before you begin building the fireplace upon it.

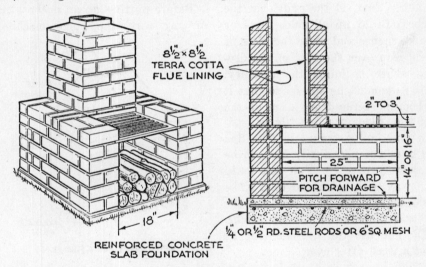

8½" × 8½"
TERRA COTTA
FLUE LINING

2" TO 3"

25"

PITCH FORWARD
FOR DRAINAGE

14 OR 16"

18"

REINFORCED CONCRETE
SLAB FOUNDATION

¼" OR ½" RD. STEEL RODS OR 6"SQ. MESH

Fig. 18. An outdoor fireplace of this general design can be built with bricks or stone.

late the width as 16 in. (two walls 8 in. thick) and the firebox which is 18 in., making a total of 34 in. Thus, the dimensions of the base of this fireplace should be 34 in. by 32 in.

Foundation. In warm climates, it is possible to build the fireplace on a foundation about 4 inches deep, and level, but this is not advisable in any section where the ground freezes in the winter. Here, the foundation should extend below the

The mortar for bricks or stone can be made with 1 part cement to 3 parts sand, and 10 per cent hydrated lime. Add enough water for a workable mixture but do not make it watery.

Wet down bricks and stones before putting them on, as this will help the mortar to make a good bond. Pack each mortar joint tightly.

Completion. Build the fireplace first 14 to 16 inches high, leaving only the 16 x 18 opening at the front. When you have reached this height, place ½-inch iron pipes, or a grill, over the top to act as a grate. The space below is the ash pit, and it will provide the fire with a good draft as well as facilitate removal of ashes. Continue building up, but leave a space slightly less than 8 x 8 inches at the rear for the chimney. Center this space evenly at the back of the firebox. Build up for 14 inches or more, then set the grill over the firebox. Build up all sides for 2 or 3 more inches and place the piece of angle iron over the rear of the firebox where it joints the chimney. This iron must be spaced so that it will support the front edge of the flue tile. Place the flue tile in position and build around it. The flue tile does not necessarily have to be completely covered. You can build part way with brick and then make a sloping mortar joint between the tile and the edge of the top bricks.

Do not use the fireplace for at least a week after completion.

INDOOR FIREPLACES

While outdoor fireplaces are rather simple to build, an indoor fireplace that functions properly is a more complicated affair. If the home mechanic is tempted to build one for his summer camp, it is recommended that he first purchase a metal frame which contains the smoke chamber, throat, and damper. This will take the guesswork out of the fireplace, and the actual construction around this frame is not overdifficult.

SMALL BUILDINGS

Most homeowners can do very well with another building, to be used as a garage, tool shed, summer guest house, or childrens' playhouse. While putting up such a building is a large undertaking, it does not require a great deal of skill, and as for tools, a hammer, saw, level, and square, are actually all the equipment necessary.

Before putting up an outbuilding of any sort, the home mechanic

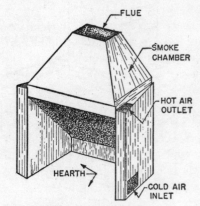

METAL FRAME FOR A FIRE PLACE

Fig. 19.

should find out whether there are any restrictive building codes in his community that must be complied with. This information can be obtained from the city officials. It is important that you look into this matter before you start to work, for in some communities there are codes so strict as to forbid anyone other than a licensed contractor from erecting a building of any sort.

In a case where the property on which the building is to be put up is rented, some agreement should be made with the landlord as to the future of the building in the event that you vacate the property.

Then, you can proceed to plan the approximate size of the building. Unless you are very familiar with the various lengths in which lumber can be obtained, it is better to draw up only approximate dimensions at first. Take these down to the lumber yard and go over them with one of the men. He will be able to tell you what size lumber they have in stock, and by making a few changes here and there you can so arrange things as to have a minimum amount of waste. There is nothing so discouraging as to find that you have to waste a foot or more of each piece of timber because the specifications you drew up were inaccurate.

Explain to the men at the yard just what you are going to build, and it is likely that they will give you helpful advice. At the same time, order enough nails of the right sizes to complete the job.

Foundation. The foundations must be solid and they must be level and square. Corner posts made out of heavy timber, rocks, poured concrete, or cement blocks, are enough foundation for small buildings. If you are building in a cold climate, the bottom of the posts should be below the frost line. If you plan to have foundations on all four sides, make them of poured concrete or cement blocks. If the building is to have a wood floor, build the foundations about 3 feet high to prevent dampness from penetrating the

wood. In the case of a concrete floor, build the foundation high enough so that the wood portion of the building is not in contact with the ground. It is best to make the foundations independent of the floor, so that in the event the floor cracks, the building itself will not be damaged.

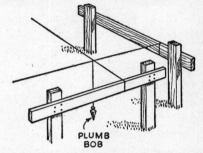

Fig. 20. Using batter boards and a plumb bob to lay out a foundation for a small building.

Lay out the approximate rectangle of the building, driving small stakes into the ground to indicate the four corners. Put up batter boards (see Fig. 20) a few feet from each corner and run cords between them. The

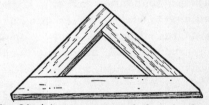

Fig. 21. A large square made from 1 x 3 in. stock is helpful in laying out right angles for the foundation.

batter boards should be solid because they are used to lay out four right angles. To obtain perfect right angles at each corner, it is suggested that you build a large square about five feet long (see Fig. 21) and use this to make and check your right angles. It will be a real help.

Sills and Joists. After the foundation is finished, place sills across it to form the base of the building. The size and method of construction will have much to do with what size sills are used. If a complete foundation is built, use a box sill made with the same size lumber as the floor joists.

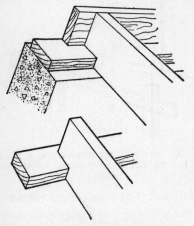

Fig. 22. Detail for constructing box sill.

Bolt this sill to the foundation and set it in mortar to make a tight joint between foundation and sill. If the building merely has four corner posts, the sill must be heavy enough to carry the load, unless additional posts are installed in the middle. You can join the sills at the ends by means of a half lap joint, but this should be cut carefully so that the surface is perfectly flush.

After the sills are in place, run the floor joists across the width of the building and spike them to the sills. There may be some variation in the width of the joists, and this must be taken into account before nailing them. Joists of different widths will make the floor uneven;

accordingly, measure each one and size it if necessary, cutting out a portion at the bottom of each end so that all joists will be level at the top. The floor joists can be set 24 inches on center. When joists are over 8 feet long, it is advisable to put bridging on the center. Bridging is 1 x 3 in. lumber cut so that it will fit diagonally across the joists (see Fig. 23).

Flooring. After attaching the joists to the sills and checking your work, nail down the flooring. It is possible to nail at right angles to the joists, but most builders prefer to run it diagonally. This will require more cutting but it will give better results.

All the end joints in the flooring must rest on a joist. If this is not done and the joints are allowed to go unsupported, they will sag or break when stepped upon. For most outbuildings a rough floor is sufficient, but if you wish to lay a finished floor, do not do so until the walls and roof have been completed.

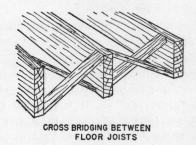

CROSS BRIDGING BETWEEN FLOOR JOISTS

Fig. 23.

When the flooring is on and well nailed at each joist, place a shoe around the edge of the floor on all four sides, flush with the sill and nailed. The shoe will form a base for the vertical studding, and it is important that all four corners be square and the joints flush at the top.

Rafters. Unless you know exactly how to use a steel framing square to measure and cut roof rafters, you

to block up the end of the roof rafter so that it is level with the shoe. The other end of the rafter should run diagonally across to one of the lengthwise shoes. Move this end of the rafter along the shoe until it is

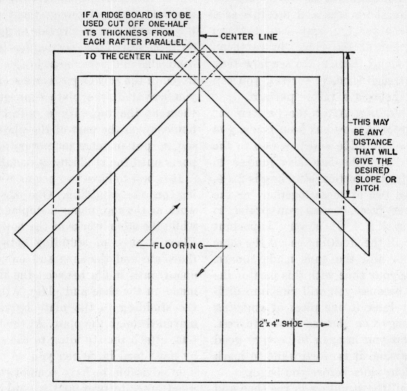

Fig. 24. A simple method of cutting roof rafters for a small building.

can cut the rafters using the shoe as a guide. The first thing to do is measure along one of the end shoes to determine the exact center of the building, where the ridge will be. Make a clear mark on the shoe at its center point. Place one of the 2 x 6 in. boards to be used as a roof rafter against the shoe at this point. You will need a piece of 2-inch stock

at the pitch you want the roof to be. Nail it lightly to the shoe to prevent its moving, go back to the other end that rests next to the center mark on the shoe, and place a square along one edge of the shoe, with the other leg of the square running along the center line and across the rafter. Mark this line, and the angle formed on the rafter will be the one necessary to obtain the roof pitch you want. Return to the other end of the rafter nailed to the shoe. Mark this end for a cut which you will make to allow the rafter to fit on the shoe. Allow an extra inch or more for the wood siding. Cut the rafter according to the marks and use this as a pattern for the next. Nail the two together at the ridge, brace them, and stand them up to see how they fit at each shoe. If correct, you can use them as a rafter pattern.

Studding. After the pattern for the roof rafters has been made, you can set it aside and move on to the studding. The best size lumber to use for the vertical studding is 2 x 4. Spike two of these together for the corner posts, unless you prefer to use a 4 x 4. It is very important that all the studding be cut the same length and the ends made square. Take your time with this part of the job, because you will run into difficulty later if one piece of studding is longer or shorter than the rest. Unless you happen to be very good at sawing, it is worthwhile to mark all four sides before you begin.

Nail the studding to the shoe and hold it at the top by a 2 x 4 inch plate, wide side facing down. You can save a great deal of time by placing the piece of wood to be used for the plate alongside the shoe and marking them both together for the location of the studding. Studding should be set about 24 inches on center, and when marking on the shoe and plate, use two lines to indicate the exact place where the studding is to fit. Mark the plates and

shoes on all four sides of the building before you begin to set up the studding.

Erect the four corner posts first and check them with a line and level to be sure they are perfectly upright. Spike these to the shoe, then nail diagonal braces between them and the sill and shoe to provide support until the rest of the framing has been completed and permanent braces put in. Once the corner posts are secure, you may nail the plate connecting them at the top. There will be a tendency on the part of the plate to sag, so put in some temporary supports until the studding is installed.

It is best to have two people working on the studding. One should work at the top, using a stepladder, while the other works at the bottom. Place a piece of studding between the plate and the shoe and move it about until it fits between the lines made on the shoe and plate. Attach the studding to the plate by nails driven through the plate. At the bottom, attach the studding to the shoe by nails toed in. When you do this, it is advisable to have some sort of wood brace to prevent the studding from moving as you drive in the nail. Check each piece of studding before it is secure to see that it is vertical. Continue in this manner until all the studding is in place. If there are to be openings for doors and windows, double the studding around them. In the case of a door, you will have to cut out the width of the door from the shoe and place studding on either side which reaches to the floor. Attach the studding to the shoe by nailing through the studding into the end of the shoe. Indicate the top and bottom of window openings with a piece of horizontal studding, and a piece of studding under it to provide proper support.

Use all the temporary braces that you need to keep the frame plumb. In most cases, it will not be necessary to cut the timbers used for braces, as they can protrude without causing difficulty. It is important that the frame be well braced, or else there is danger of throwing it

over the plate and the ridge should be at the center of the frame. If this is the case, take down the set of rafters and cut the rest to match. Rafters must be flush at each end of the building, and the intervening ones spaced 24 inches on center. You can hold rafters at the proper intervals, until the roofing is on, with a 2 x 4 nailed to the bottom of the ridge. The rafters should be spiked to the plate and should extend about 12 inches or more beyond it.

Sheathing and Siding. With the

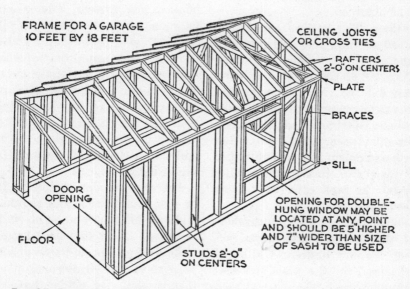

FRAME FOR A GARAGE
10 FEET BY 18 FEET

CEILING JOISTS
OR CROSS TIES

RAFTERS
2'-0" ON CENTERS

PLATE

BRACES

SILL

DOOR
OPENING

OPENING FOR DOUBLE-
HUNG WINDOW MAY BE
LOCATED AT ANY POINT
AND SHOULD BE 5" HIGHER
AND 7" WIDER THAN SIZE
OF SASH TO BE USED

FLOOR

STUDS 2'-0"
ON CENTERS

Fig. 25. Frame for a garage. This method of construction can be used for any small one-story building, such as a tool house, child's play house, etc.

out of plumb when the rafters are put up.

When the frame has been completed, lift the two rafters that were made as a pattern into their proper position. If everything is correct, the "seat cut" at the ends should fit

frame completed, you are ready for the siding. As a general rule, sheathing is put down first and a layer of building paper laid over it, followed by the siding. If this is too much work for the size of the building, you can use a type of composition board instead of the wood sheathing. This has the advantage of coming in large sections which can be quickly nailed to the frame. Some kinds of novelty siding do not require any sheathing at all, and these should be put over building paper nailed to the frame.

Build the walls from the bottom with the tongue up, and take time to see that each joint is tight before you nail the board in place.

Put on the exterior trim around windows, doors, etc. before the siding so that a good weathertight joint may be obtained.

Roofing. The roofing can be of matched sheathing covered with any of the prepared roofing materials. Start work at the eaves and work up toward the ridge, allowing the boards to overhang at the gable ends. These can be trimmed off later when the roof is completed. After the boards are down, put roofing paper over them and, finally, the roofing material. In each case, work from the eaves up.

As soon as the building is weathertight, the interior can be finished off in any manner desired. Wallboard can be used for the walls and ceiling, but for the latter you will need ceiling rafters made of 2 x 4's to support the sections of wallboard. These, of course, should be put on during the framing.

GARAGE FLOORS

A garage having a dirt floor can be kept free of dust by sprinkling calcium chloride over the floor surface. The chemical will absorb moisture from the air and this will keep the dirt damp and eliminate the dust. Calcium chloride can be used on dirt driveways for the same purpose.

A concrete floor is not difficult to lay and will take care of the dust problem once and for all. In a small one-car garage the floor should slope towards the doors so that water will drain out of the garage. If this cannot be done, then a floor drain can be installed in the floor and be connected to a dry well or into the house sewer system. The concrete floor should be given a slight pitch towards the drain so that it will not be necessary to sweep the water with a broom to get it out of the garage. The pipe and drain must, of course, be set in before any concrete is poured. Plug up the opening of the drain with a piece of cloth so there will be no chance of concrete falling in it by accident.

The concrete slab should be four or five inches thick and should be laid over six inches or so of cinders or gravel. If the dirt floor happens to be well packed and well drained, the slab can be set down right over this without the cinder base, but strips of waterproof paper should be put down first or else the concrete will pick up moisture from the ground and be damp a great deal of the time.

The floor of small one-car garages can be poured in one operation but for larger size buildings it is best to cut the floor up into sections between eight and ten feet square. Use 2 x 6 in. boards for forms and coat these with crude oil so they can be removed easily. Pour alternate sections and when the concrete has set hard, remove the forms and pour alternate sections against the concrete. Some allowance must be made for the expansion of the concrete and this can be done where the floor joins the building sill or wall. Line the perimeter of the building with oiled 1-inch boards and when the concrete has set, remove these boards and fill the space between wall and floor with asphalt or tar.

Either a one or two course method of construction can be used. In one course work the entire depth of the floor is poured in one operation

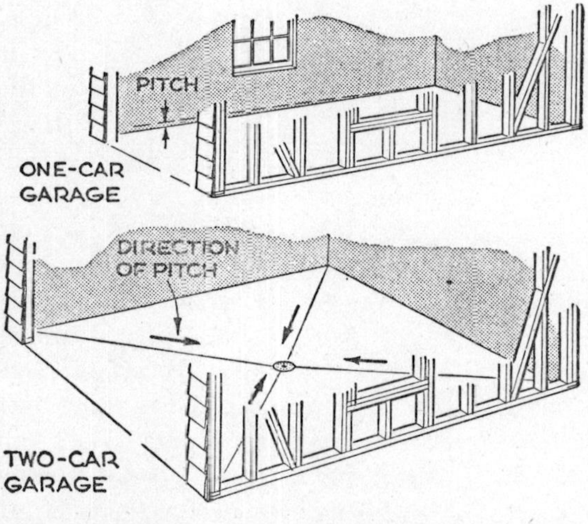

Fig. 25. Concrete floors in the garage should be pitched so that water will drain either out to the door or to a floor drain.

while in two course a thick base is poured first and a ¾ in., or 1-inch, finish coat is put over this after the base is hard. The two course method of construction will give a smoother

surface than the one course but this is not too important as far as garage floors are concerned. In any event, if the floor is going to be poured in two courses, the first course must be left very rough so that the second course will adhere properly. The mortar used for the second course or finish coat is made with 1 part cement to 2 parts sand.

It is very important that the concrete, after it has been poured, be worked into a solid mass. Use a wood float or trowel for this work.

PESTS

Insects which attack and eat flowers and vegetables can now be rather effectively controlled by means of chemical sprays and powders that you can purchase at your hardware or garden store. The insect that causes the most annoyance to humans is, without doubt, the mosquito. There are several ways of controlling this pest. Mosquitos breed in any stagnant water. Inspect the grounds around the house and empty any cans or pails that might be full of water. In the case of a swamp or a small body of water that cannot be drained, pour a little kerosene over the surface to kill off the mosquito larvae in the water. Screening will keep the insects out of the house, but it is important that all screens be tight and solid. When the insects get into the house, they can be eliminated with a spray of a good insecticide.

Garden Snakes. These are harmless reptiles and there is no very effective way to kill them. In fact, harmless snakes are beneficial, as they live on insects and small rodents. Frogs, toads, and bats all live on insects and should be left alone.

Rats and Mice. These rodents will do a great deal of damage if they are allowed to get into a house, and the most effective way to keep them out is to make careful inspections of the house, plugging up their entrance holes with metal or concrete. To eliminate those in the house, use traps and poison.

Squirrels. While these little animals are amusing to watch, they can do a great deal of damage if allowed to run wild in the attic. The best preventive is to locate their entrance into the house and close it.

CARE OF TREES

Few things add more to the appearance of a house than the trees surrounding it, and the homeowner would do well to give these as much consideration as possible. For example, newly planted trees should be braced with guy ropes for a season or two until their roots have taken a firm hold in the ground. If this is not done the trees may blow over during a high wind. Wire is very good for these supports but it should be insulated from the tree by pieces of hose to prevent its cutting into the bark. Some kinds of shrubs

and bushes must be covered during the winter to protect them from cold winds. If your home has been newly

Fig. 26. Steps in removing a dead limb without damaging the tree.

landscaped, check with your nurseryman as to the proper care of shrubs and bushes.

Removing Dead Limb. One job that often comes up in regard to tree care is removing a large dead limb. If this job is undertaken properly, it can be accomplished with no harm to tree or to the individual doing the sawing. If the limb is high off the ground you will need a ladder of some sort and a good crosscut saw.

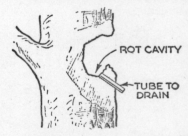

Fig. 27. Drain tube inserted in cavity to allow water to drain out.

Set the ladder so that you will be able to make a cut on the underside of the limb about a foot from the tree trunk. Saw up until the saw begins to bind—a sign that the limb is beginning to drop. Now re-rig your ladder so that you can make another cut on the top side of the limb. Do not make the not uncommon mistake of resting the top of the ladder against the limb that is to be removed. Make this second cut an inch or so beyond the lower one and continue to saw until the limb drops off. Now you will have a stump a foot or so long and this can be cut off flush with the tree trunk. Do not injure the live bark on the tree with the saw, and hold the limb stump with one hand to keep it from dropping and perhaps tearing the wood. After the stump is out of the way, the exposed wood on the trunk should be painted with shellac and then creosote.

Tree Surgery. While the accepted method of filling a cavity in a tree is to cut out the rotten wood and fill the hole with concrete, experts in the field do not recommend this practice for the home mechanic because unless every trace of decay is removed, it will start up again in spite of the concrete patch. It is much safer to remove as much of the decayed matter as possible and then paint the inside of the hole with asphalt paint. To allow for drainage, it is necessary either to put a tube into the bottom of the hole or else to cut it out in such a manner that it will drain without the need of a tube.

Removing Stumps. The homeowner is sometimes faced with the problem of how to remove large stumps without the expense of hiring someone to do the job for him. Digging the stump out is hard work and can go on until it seems like an endless task. One easy method of getting rid of the stump, providing that there are not shrubs or flowers around, is to drill holes into it with a brace and bit and pour in kerosene. Add additional kerosene as the holes become empty until, finally, the stump and roots are saturated. The stump can now be set on fire and burned out. Another method of removal is with a weed killer containing sodium chlorate. This is poured into holes and will in time destroy the stump and roots. There are special products on the market which are advertised as being safe for the surrounding vegetation and will destroy stumps and roots effectively. They are on sale at hardware and garden stores.

Removing Rocks. The usual methods of removing large rocks are with power equipment, blasting, or breaking with a sledge hammer into small pieces. One simple way to break up large rocks that does not require any expense, skill or strength is to build a fire around the rock and when it is good and hot, pour cold water over it. The sudden change of temperature will usually split the rocks into pieces that can be removed with relative ease. An even simpler method is to wait until a cold day in winter and then pour boiling water over the rock.

SIMPLE CARPENTRY

BOOKSHELVES

The first design, as shown in Fig. 1, is a simple tier of bookshelves built into a wall recess. This tier is about 6½ feet high. Shelves in a bookcase should be deep enough for medium-sized books, 7 inches or more. The shelves in the illustration are 13½ inches deep. The recess is assumed to be 4 feet wide and 13½ inches deep. Bring the top of the structure a few inches below the line of the picture molding. This will solve the difficult problem of lining up the cornice with the picture molding, which seldom looks well.

Preliminary Work. Remove the baseboard in the recess. You may have to remove it for some distance back to get the entire board away. Cut to the required length for replacement later. It is best to cut the baseboard flush and form a "return" molding on the edge to make a neat finish.

Cut a piece of ¾ x 1 inch stock so that it will fit easily across the recess from wall to wall near the floor. Test the width of the recess with this rod at, say, 3 feet and 6 feet above the floor. This will disclose whether the walls are reasonably free from bulges. The sides of the shelving will have to be vertical when fixed but must be close against the wall (at the sides of the recess). If the wall bulges a little at about the 3-foot height, insert some packing or wedges at top and bottom in order to bring the woodwork vertical and to give a firm backing. Likewise, if the wall is hollow or concave at a midway point, but is satisfactory at higher and lower levels, insert packing between the woodwork and wall at the concave position. This packing should consist of pieces of thin plywood, or layers split from plywood, cut down to give a firm backing at the required place.

Make a gauge rod by cutting a piece of stock about 7 feet long and squaring the ends. Sweep out the floor of the recess, test the floor with a spirit level, and if necessary nail down a thin strip of wood at one side to bring the two sides level. Test for level also from front to back and make any similar adjustment which may be necessary. These preliminary details may seem tedious, but no satisfactory work can be done if we ignore them. Next, mark on the gauge rod the distance from the top

330

edge of the molding to the floor line. Note that this line is the *levelled* line at which the foot of the bookshelf upright stands, and it denotes, in fact, the lower edge of the bookshelf side.

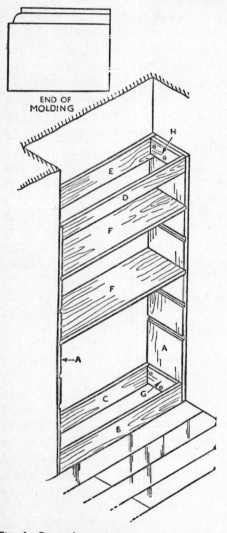

Fig. 1. General arrangement and assembly details of a bookshelf built into a recess. Figure above shows how the end of the molding can be suitably shaped.

Mark the positions of the shelves, indicating the top side of each shelf. Mark off the position of the top edge of the bookshelf sides at 6½ feet, if that is the height selected. All these lines should be squared across the face of the gauge rod and carried around one adjoining face. We will use the rod to mark the lumber.

Lumber. One-inch tongued and grooved boards are as good material as any for the sides and shelves (for a shelf length up to four feet). If the wood for the shelves is too thin, they will sag in the course of time. Fig. 1 shows a recess 13½ inches deep, and the boards must be wide enough to make up this dimension when the tongues are fitted into the grooves and the tongue on the outermost board has been sawed off. Remember that tongued and grooved board of nominal six-inch width will be only about five and a half when fitted, as the tongue is cut out of the six-inch width; in other words, two such boards when fitted together will have a total width of only eleven inches.

The worker may find it convenient to have the lumberyard saw a board for each side, in order to get the desired total width. In assembling the bookshelf sides, put the grooved edge of one board at the back, and the tongues on all the boards will face the front. If a board has to be sawed to obtain the proper width, it will have a plain edge at the front. If a board of ordinary width can be used, the tongue must be sawed off or taken off with a jack plane—perhaps the easiest method for a novice. The same considerations apply when making up the shelves.

Assembling the Sides. Saw the boards for the sides to length. Put one set together and stand it in the recess, close against the wall. Have an assistant hold it while testing for vertical position and note where any packing may be required. This gives an opportunity to see whether the front edge comes in line with the front of the recess. If the edges protrude slightly when the sides are in place, remove the surplus material with a plane. It may be advisable to make the width of the sides a fraction less than the depth of the recess from front to back.

On referring to Fig. 1, it will be seen that C is fitted between the sides at the rear, and that a similar board parallels it at the front. Note also the similar members D and E at the top. Between B and C and between D and E, short pieces of wood G and H should be fixed to the sides by screws after the side boards are assembled and glued. Beside serving as a stop for attaching the members B,C, and D,E, these short strips hold the side boards in place. The sides A should be notched out at the back edge to fit around the members C and E, which extend from one side wall of the recess to the other. The members B and D fit between the sides A and are nailed to the front end of the short strips G and H.

Clean the sides A for assembly. Have some good wood glue ready, and a pair of adjustable wood clamps. Glue the tongues and grooves and put the boards together with a

sliding movement to squeeze out any surplus glue. Lay the side assembly on a level surface and apply clamps near top and bottom to pull the joints together. If the clamps tend to open the joint midway, ease one clamp slightly and move it along a few inches. Tack strips of wood across the side at two places to secure the boards temporarily. Put on the battens G and H (previously prepared, with screw holes bored and countersunk), then screw on firmly. Lay the assembled side on a level floor in a warm room to dry and set. Assemble the other side in the same manner.

Assembling Shelves. Assemble the shelf boards, putting them together with glue and clamps. If you lack sufficient clamps, use those you have to hold the boards until you can attach short strips of wood to hold them together, as suggested above. The net length of the shelves must be decided, of course. Whatever the distance between the inner faces of the sides when standing in place in the recess, add one-half inch for the depth of two grooves (each one-quarter inch deep) ; this will give the extreme length of the shelves. It is safer to make the shelves about two inches longer than necessary and saw them to actual length when the sides have been fixed to the recess walls. These two extra inches allow for final cuts at each end.

Grooves for Shelves. When the sides have set hard, lay them down on edge, face to face, and hold them together with a pair of clamps. If a bench is available, fix the two sides in the vise and support the opposite ends with a stool or bench.

Place the gauge rod on top and transfer the markings for the top faces of the shelves. Make these marks on the front edge of the side assemblies and mark both at the same time. Take off the clamps and square the marks across the inner faces of the sides. Remember that the marks indicate the location of the top face of the shelf. Measure the exact thickness of the shelf boards. If they vary, and they may, take the thickness for each shelf separately and mark them 1, 2, 3, etc., so that you may fit them in their proper grooves. Mark these thicknesses on the side boards by squaring lines across the front edge and inner face, *below* the shelf lines previously drawn. The distance between each pair of lines on the side boards should equal thickness of shelf.

Set a marking gauge to a bare quarter inch and scribe this distance on the edges of the side boards, front and back, where the parallel lines have been pencilled. Use a fine-pointed, hard pencil for marking or, better, a fine scriber. Use a fine-toothed back or tenon saw to outline the grooves. Saw down the quarter-inch depth lines on the edges, then across the face of the boards. Take out the waste wood with a sharp paring chisel of suitable width. Be careful not to make the grooves too deep. At the back of the side boards cut out notches to receive the boards C and E.

Installing the Shelves. Put the board C in place at the back of the

recess; stand the two sides in place, fitted over C. With someone holding the sides, fit the top board E in place and mark its position on the back wall. Ease the notches if necessary. Mark the position of E by a pencil line on the wall at top and bottom edges. Bore two holes through E, about six inches from each end. To secure E to a plaster wall, you will have to use rawl plugs. Mark through the holes the points for drilling. If an assistant holds the sides in place while all this is done, so much the better. Take down the sides, drill holes in the wall, and insert the plugs and screws. Use No. 12 iron screws, flathead, about 1¾ inches long. Fix boards E and C, secured to wall in same way as E.

Try the sides in place again. If correct, remove the righthand one and bore it for three screws, one midway, the others about six inches from floor and top line. Be sure they are clear of the grooves. Mark the wall for rawl plugs; drill; secure the side to the wall. Fasten the other side in the same manner. Fix B and D in place, secured to G and H. Board B will be about one inch lower than the top of the molding attached later to the sides. The depth of the board D will depend on that of the molding used as a cornice. This cornice should be far enough above D so that a dust board made of plywood, seated on top of D, E, and A, can fit behind the cornice and be flush with the top of the cornice.

Put in the shelves one by one. They should fit tight enough so that a gentle tap with a wood mallet will drive them into position. Try a shelf in its groove; ease the ends with a smoothing plane (or a block plane if available), should this be necessary. Hold a smooth piece of wood against the front edge of the shelf and tap against this with a mallet.

Cut the bottom shelf to fit snugly in place and screw it to the top edges of B, C, and G. This shelf should be flush with the front edges of the side boards. Screw on the trim, fix the cornice and dust board in place, sand your work with two grades of sandpaper used in succession, and you are ready for staining and varnishing.

You can achieve a handsome, finished appearance by facing the edges of the side pieces and the shelves with strips of oak, walnut, or mahogany, about 1¼ inches deep, and by using the same wood for trim and cornice. Groove the strips of hardwood so that they fit over the tongue of the lumber used in the construction of the bookshelf.

After the shelving has been completed, fix a strip of molding to align with the baseboard and chamfer the ends of this molding to match the pattern used for the front face. The baseboard and molding are now aligned, but they are marked off from each other by the slight molding of the abutting ends. Details such as these are large factors in the appearance of the work.

SHORT BOOKSHELVES

Fig. 2 shows a set of shelves 3 feet high, 23 inches wide, and 6½ inches deep. The principles here used can be applied to larger con-

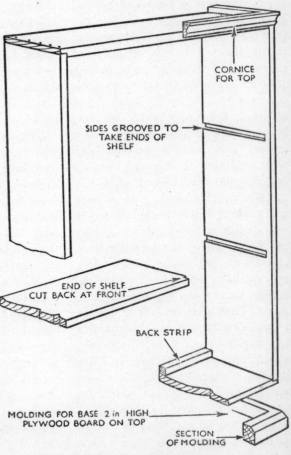

CORNICE FOR TOP

SIDES GROOVED TO TAKE ENDS OF SHELF

END OF SHELF CUT BACK AT FRONT

BACK STRIP

MOLDING FOR BASE 2 in HIGH PLYWOOD BOARD ON TOP

SECTION OF MOLDING

Fig. 2. Detail of small bookshelf showing framework joints and the general construction. The joints for the cornice and trim should be plain mitered, glued and nailed. Trim fits outside front and side.

structions, but the span should not exceed 3 feet between the sides, and the wood in such case should not be less than 1 inch thick for the actual shelves. In the fittings illustrated, the outer members are from 1-inch board, while the shelves are ¾ inch thick. Cut out the sides, 1 inch less in height than the total overall height; but cut the top and bottom boards to full width.

Use a marking gauge to scribe the line for the rabbet at each end of both top and bottom boards, a little less than ½ inch deep and extending back from the end to the width of the side boards. Saw across with a tenon saw to the proper depth and remove the waste wood by chisel or saw it out with a fine saw, cutting entirely in the waste wood. Smooth off the rabbet with a rabbet plane, if one is at hand, or use a broad chisel, and finish with coarse sandpaper wrapped around a block of wood.

Cut and fit all rabbet joints, and carefully square off the ends of the side boards. Do not fix together yet. Cut the two shelves to length, allowing for the depth of the housings, or dados, into which the shelf ends fit. Cut out these dados, of a size to receive the thickness of the shelf boards. It will be seen that the dado ends are about ¾ inch from the front of the bookcase, so that no groove will show from the front.

Make two saw cuts for each groove, working from the back of the side boards and going down as far as the saw will allow; then finish the work with a chisel of the proper width, first deepening the saw cuts at the front end, where the saw has not cut to full depth. Use the chisel to separate the waste into small portions by midway cuts from the face of the board and also to chisel out the waste and gradually form the groove. Avoid making the dado too wide for the board; it is better to have the dado a little tight and to pare off the end of the board that will go into the dado. Fit each board to its intended dado; they are sure to vary slightly, and when once fitted should be marked.

Having made sure the shelves will fit, and can be driven in from the back with light blows of a mallet, we can assemble the outside four members and nail them, through the top and bottom, into the ends of the vertical pieces. Bore holes with a fine brad awl a little smaller than the nails. Two-inch finishing nails are suitable, the heads being invisible after a slight punch with a nail set. Next, tap in the shelves, inserting them from the back. Any defect in fit will force out the sides, so work carefully and pare the shelf if necessary. A little glue can be used on the ends if desired, though nails put in from the side boards will hold them quite firmly.

Screw down at the bottom of the bookcase a strip of wood (Fig. 2, back edge); on this, and on the top edge of the base molding, nail a board cut from plywood. This comes flush at front and back. The base molding is a piece of 1 x 2 in., planed to a bevel at the top edge and mitered. It is nailed to the front and sides. The board at the back must align with the top of the base molding, and the latter, for about half of its thickness, must be square at the top, to provide a seating for the plywood. When nailing the latter, use veneer pins, having bored holes first.

Finish the top of the bookcase with a piece of molding to form a cornice; miter and pin it to the sides and to the edge of the top member of the frame. Cut a sheet of plywood to cover the entire back of the bookcase and attach with veneer pins.

The piece may then be sanded, stained to match the other furniture in the room, and given a finish of either shellac or varnish.

TWO-TIER BOOKCASE

Each tier of this bookcase can be built in such a way that it can be dismantled and re-erected, and each can stand free in a recess—not secured to the wall. In the illustration, the depth of the recess has again been taken as 13½ inches. The bottom shelf is 13½ inches deep; the top shelf is 8¼ inches deep.

The preliminary work and the shelving are much the same as in the bookshelf previously described, but the sides are spaced in from the recess walls by the blocking pieces E. These pieces, plus the thickness of the side boards G, equal the width of the hardwood facing on the sides A. Screw the blocking pieces E to the outside of G, but otherwise follow the procedure previously outlined for assembling and shelving. Screw bottom boards F (Fig. 3) to the

bottom of the uprights of the lower tier to support the bottom shelf H. This shelf is situated behind, and level with the top of, the facing piece

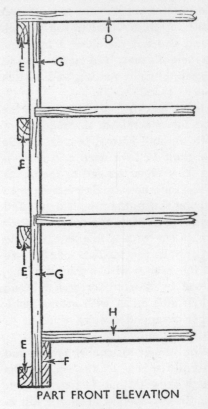

PART FRONT ELEVATION

Fig. 3. A part front elevation showing the constructional details and the use of blocking pieces, E, necessary to the fitting of the bookcase in the recess.

C, shown in Fig. 4. The facing C should be tenoned into A, or halved enough to make a sound and neat joint.

After you have glued and assembled the sides of the lower tier and attached the blocking pieces E, stand the sides in the recess and screw down the top board D. Screw the bottom shelf H to boards F. This lower tier should fit easily into the recess and is not normally secured to the walls; but should it be necessary, you can insert back boards at the top and at the floor line (as C and E in Fig. 1) and attach them to the wall by means of rawl plugs.

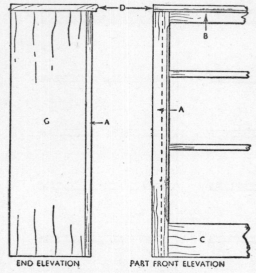

END ELEVATION   PART FRONT ELEVATION

Fig. 4. An end and part front elevation of a simple bookcase for fitting into a recess, showing finished details of facing pieces and molding.

Top Tier. Prepare the top tier (Figs. 5 and 6). Backboards (not shown) may be needed at the bottom and at the top; fit these in the same manner as C and E in Fig. 1. Insert the shelves after the top tier has been placed in position on top of the board D of the lower tier. The entire assembly should stand firmly, but if necessary you can screw two brass mirror plates to the backboards and to the wall with rawl plugs. This will not be necessary, however, if the bookcase stands tightly in the recess.

Hardwood Facing. Use hardwood facing pieces on the front edges A of the sides, as in Figs. 4 and 7; face the rest of the front framing in hardwood to match. The front of D (Figs. 3 and 4) should also be of hardwood.

Join the trim and the rails B and C (Fig. 4) in some simple manner for neatness. You can do this by forming tenons, or projecting tongues made by cutting away the wood, and inserting the tenons into mortises cut from the rails; you may also join them by short halved joints, at the corners. Screw the trim to the sides G with fine screws (No. 6), countersink, and plug the holes with similar plastic wood stained to match the rest. To further improve the appearance of the bookcase, face the edges of the shelves with hardwood strips to show the same grain as the front framework.

Fix a simple cornice at the top of the upper tier, with a rail behind it—like B in Fig. 4. Screw on a dust board. Dusting will be easier if the top of the dust board is made flush with the top edge of the cornice, fitting behind the latter. When the bookcase is fully erected, you may want to put a small molding around the feet of the top tier. Use quarter round molding about 3/8 inch across the flat face for this; miter or bevel it to fit and secure it to D with veneer pins.

Variations. The bookshelves, as illustrated, are each of moderate height, but the number of shelves and the height may be varied to suit individual requirements. Where the depth of the recess is great, it will be found more practicable not to carry the shelves back to the full depth. To eliminate an unsightly gap behind the bookcase, secure a thin sheet of plywood to it. You can carry the topmost shelf to the full depth of

with round rails cut from birch dowel rod, ¾ in. in diameter. This rod can be purchased at lumber yards and at many hardware stores. Cut the uprights—or posts—from wood measuring 1½ x 1¼ inches across adjacent faces. Since ¾-inch holes must be bored for the rods, bore through the wider face.

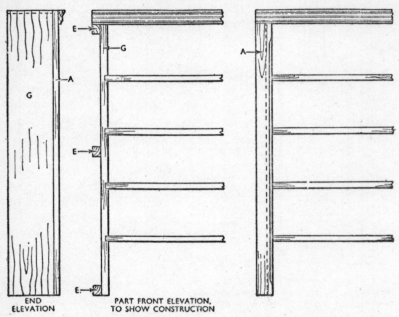

END ELEVATION   PART FRONT ELEVATION, TO SHOW CONSTRUCTION

Figs. 5, 6, and 7. End and part front elevations illustrating the construction of the top tier for the bookcase, similar in design to that shown in Fig. 4.

the recess, but if the top of the bookcase extends beyond the rest, it will be necessary to secure a light wooden batten to each of the side walls of the recess.

CLOTHES HORSE

The clothes horse described below is of convenient size, 4 feet high by 3 feet wide when closed. Fig. 8 shows part of a clothes horse built

Marking Posts. Wood for the posts should be such that, after planing, it will not measure less than 1½ x 1¼ inches across adjacent faces. Choose lumber which is not bent or warped. When cutting the posts make them about 2 inches longer than the finished length. Clamp all four posts together, after planing, with the ends even. Square a line across them, 1 inch from the ends. Mark each of these ends "T" for top before removing them from the clamp. Measure a distance of 4 feet from the top and square a line across all the posts at this point to ensure posts of equal length.

gauge to scribe a center line down the post. Mark this side or face "I" for inside. Gauge and mark the remaining posts in the same manner.

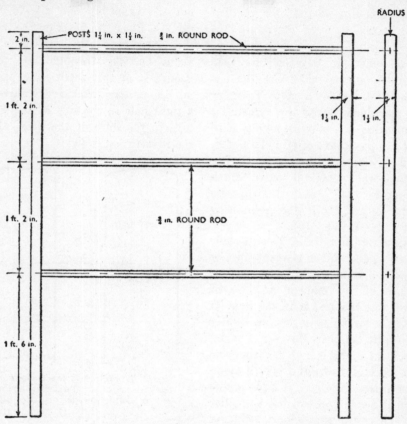

Fig. 8. Dimensions for one side of a clothes horse.

Remove them from the clamp and —singly—square lines across the other faces of each post to connect the lines previously drawn. Do this at the top and at the 4-foot line. Set a marking gauge to half the width of the wider face of the upright (the setting will be approximately ¾ inch, depending upon the exact width of the face), and use the

It is best to keep the lowest rail well above the floor; 18 inches is a satisfactory height. Space the top rail 2 inches from the top of the post. This leaves a distance of 28 inches between. Place the middle rail 16 inches from the top line. Thus, from the top line "T," place the first rail 2 inches, the middle rail, 16 inches, and the lower rail 30 inches below.

Measure the diameter of the rails carefully and with a ruler and fine-pointed pencil mark this distance across the vertical line at the point marked for the location of each rail. Draw this line so that the vertical line passes through its midpoint. This crossing is where the point of the bit must cut. Lay the four posts on the bench or table with the top ends close against a stop. Transfer the markings across the remaining posts with a square, making sure that the posts do not slip. Thus far, we have sides of all posts marked.

Mark the posts for pairs. Mark one post "A-1" and the opposite post "A-2." Mark the remaining pair "B-1" and "B-2."

Inserting the Rails. Bore a hole with a ¾-inch bit in a waste piece of the same wood used for the posts; smooth off an end of a piece of dowel rod and test it in the hole. It must fit tightly, but not so tightly as to split the post. Dowel rod varies somewhat, and it is best to bore a hole in a piece of scrap and take it along when purchasing rod. If a test shows it to fit slack, you can use a smaller bit. This will necessitate reducing the diameter of the ends of the rod, but you can do this with coarse sandpaper. Bits in intermediate sizes are obtainable, and as this tool is useful in many tasks, like making or mending deck chairs or ordinary chairs, it would not be unwise to buy one for the job.

Taper the ends well back, to avoid splitting the post when driving in the rod. When drilling holes for the rods, it is advisable to use a depth gauge, either a commercial or a homemade one. You can make a satisfactory depth gauge from a block of hardwood about 1½ inches high and 1¼ inches thick and bored with the same bit (see Fig. 16, Section 1). Place the block on the bit so that it allows a hole to be bored about halfway through the posts. Secure it at this setting by inserting an ordinary wood screw through a tight hole in the side of the block to grip the flute of the drill, as in the illustration.

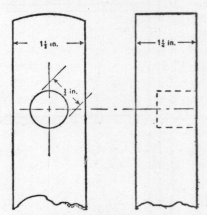

Fig. 9. When boring the sockets in the vertical rails to the depth shown, use a depth gauge on the bit.

Lay one of the posts on the bench and clamp it down. Make a mark with a punch at the point where the gauge line and vertical line cross on the "inside" face, tapping the punch lightly with a hammer. This will guide the point of the bit to the exact point of entry. Bore out the hole (Fig. 9) until the depth gauge touches the surface. Hold the brace square and upright and press lightly if the wood is birch.

When a pair of posts have been bored, lay them with "inside" faces toward each other and spaced so that the distance from outside edge to outside edge is 3 feet. Cut a rod to approximately the proper length, 3 feet less $1\frac{1}{4}$ inches—since each end of the rod penetrates $\frac{5}{8}$ inch into the uprights. Pare off the ends of the rods to make a tight fit, if necessary; otherwise, remove the rough edges with coarse sandpaper.

Insert the rod into the two topmost holes, tap it in with a wood mallet struck against the outside of one post. Measure with a rule across the assembly, after checking to see whether the rail is square with the post. You will probably have to remove a little from one end of the rod to bring the overall length to 3 feet. If so, ease off one post, remove the rail and trim the end. With this rail as a guide, prepare the other two. Lay aside this pair of posts and appurtenant rails; bore and fit the other posts and rails, and make ready for gluing and assembling.

Final Assembly. After heating or mixing the wood glue, apply it thinly to the rail ends and put a little in the holes also. Place one post on the bench, "inside" face uppermost; tap in the three rails; bring the opposite post into position and insert the other ends of the rails, easing them in gently. Have ready a block of clean wood. Place it on top of the topmost post, over a rail, and tap with a mallet or hammer. Do the same for the middle and lower rods.

Do not try to force in the rails; go from one to another, tapping lightly, until all have been driven home. Test the framework with a square at four corners. Correct any irregularity by a light tap on the inside of the framework.

When the assembly is satisfactory, lay it on a level floor. With a fine brad awl, bore a hole for a pin which will secure the rail end to the upright. This pin should be 1 inch long for the size post specified. A fine twist drill, as used for metal, may also be used to drill the holes. This will make a cleaner hole than a brad awl but must not go in too deeply—only through the upright at one end and slightly into the rail end. Drive in the pins, one at each end of the rail. Stand the frame in a warm place until the glue hardens.

Whatever the finished width of the first frame, the other must be the same. It does not matter whether the finished width is slightly more or less than 3 feet, provided that the two frames are identical. Assemble the second frame, glue and pin as before.

Clear out all chips from the bored holes. A gouge is the best tool for this work, but a $\frac{1}{2}$-inch chisel will serve. Often, a bit leaves part of a core at the bottom of the hole, and this must be cut out and smoothed off with the gouge. Test the holes for depth with a ruler. The improvised depth gauge previously described is not a guarantee of exact finished depth. Make the depth accurate before gluing, as it is difficult to make corrections later.

If one rail proves to be too long, it is possible to increase the distance between the frames to compensate. The other rails do not necessarily have to go full depth in the posts, if

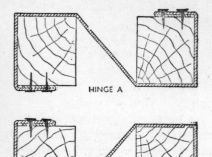

Fig. 10. How to make a hinge from webbing. One strip A to be secured at upper ends of uprights, and B at lower ends. Note: Ends of webbing are folded over for extra strength.

they fit tightly. Any adjustment to one frame, however, must also be made in the other frame.

An alternative method of construction is to drill the holes all the way through the uprights and drive in the rails until they are flush with the outside edge. This makes a stronger unit but is not so attractive. Put a piece of flat board under the post when boring, so that the wood on the underside of the post does not split. Bore through the post and into the waste wood for a clean hole.

When the rail joints have set (24 hours or more after gluing), cut off the ends of the posts to the proper length, as marked earlier.

The tops should be rounded slightly, as viewed from the end. Clean up all surfaces with sandpaper and scrape off any glue that has been forced out.

Simple hinges made of upholsterer's webbing should be secured by tacks or short, broadheaded wire nails. Fig. 10 shows how the webbing is wound around the posts to form two opposed hinges. Fix one each of A and B about 9 inches from the top of the post, and one of each 9 inches from ground level.

Alternate Construction. Fig. 11 illustrates a clothes horse of somewhat more solid construction, having baseboards on which the frames are mounted. Ordinary butt hinges are used, and these, together with the baseboards, make a steadier framework. One wide and two narrow frames are used. This makes for easy storing when folded.

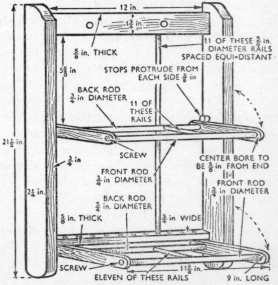

Fig. 12. General dimensions and assembly details of the two-shelf drain rack attached to wall, adjacent to the kitchen sink.

DRAIN RACK AND BOARD

The rack shown in Fig. 12 hangs on the wall above the sink and accommodates twelve plates on the lower shelf, and the same number of smaller plates, or saucers, on the upper shelf. Both shelves swing upward to a vertical position between the side pieces of the framework.

The side pieces are 21½ inches long, 2¼ inches wide, and ¾ inch thick. They are connected at top and bottom by pieces 12 inches long, to which the sides are screwed, but this attachment is not completed until the vertical rails are in position and the back rods of the top and the bottom shelves have been lodged in the side pieces. It is on the back rods

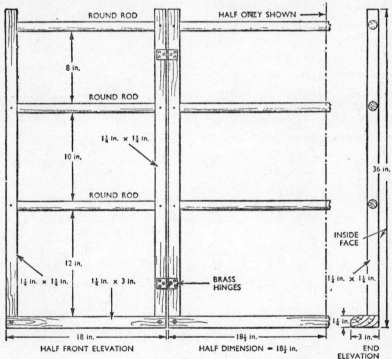

Fig. 11. End and part front elevation of an alternative arrangement of a clothes horse of sturdier construction, showing use of metal hinges and base boards.

The advantage of this arrangement is obvious where space is limited. When the plates or saucers have been drained in the rack, they are removed from their spaces between the bars and put away, and the shelves are swung upward out of the way.

that the shelves swivel upwards when the rack is not in use.

The top piece of the framework is 1¾ inches wide and ⅝ inch thick; the bottom piece is ¾ inch wide by ⅝ inch thick. The members, together with the sides of the shelves, are made of hardwood. The eleven vertical rails, and the corresponding eleven in each shelf, are ⅜ inch in diameter, and ordinary curtain rods will serve admirably. The vertical rails have their ends lodged ¼ inch deep in holes bored, at equal distances apart, in the inner edges of the top and bottom pieces of the framework.

The side pieces of the shelves are 9 inches long, and the ends (front and back) are rounded. They are 1⅛ inches wide and ⅝ inch thick. They are joined (in pairs) by rods ¾ inch in diameter. The front rods (Fig. 13) are positioned ¼ inch in from the ends and fixed by screws passing through the sides. The back rods pass tightly through the sides of the shelves and project ½ inch into the socket holes bored in the side members. The centers of the holes for these back rods are 1¼ inches from the back end. Watch all details for perfect fit. Holes in the framework sides in which the back rods lodge are slightly more than ¾ inch in diameter, so that the movement is free when the shelves are raised or lowered (Fig. 12). The distance between the outer edges of each shelf is 11⅝ inches, and front and back rods are 7⅛ inches apart (inside measurement). The rails are sunk ¼ inch deep in these rods, with a tight fit.

When the bottom shelf is lowered, further downward movement is prevented by the bottom piece of the framework, against the underside of which the inner

ends of the shelf sides rest. In the case of the top shelf, this function is fulfilled by two stops set well back, one in each side member. These are pieces of ⅜-inch diameter rail sunk ⅝ inch deep in the side members and protruding horizontally a distance of ⅝ inch.

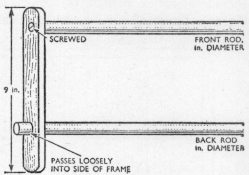

SCREWED

FRONT ROD. in. DIAMETER

9 in.

BACK ROD in. DIAMETER

PASSES LOOSELY INTO SIDE OF FRAME

Fig. 13. Detail assembly view of one shelf in part construction.

Bore holes in the top member, for hanging. To keep the edges of plates well away from the wall, nail or screw a block 1 inch thick to the wall. Insert the nails or screws, on which the rack hangs, in the block. A similar block keeps the bottom member at the same distance. When the rack needs cleaning, it is a simple

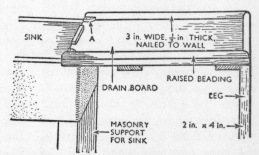

SINK

A

3 in. WIDE. ⅛ in. THICK, NAILED TO WALL

RAISED BEADING

DRAIN BOARD

LEG

MASONRY SUPPORT FOR SINK

2 in. x 4 in.

Fig. 14. Details of a drainboard showing raised beading and, A, wood blocks to divert water drained from dishes into sink.

matter to lift it from the two supporting nails or screws.

It may happen that a water pipe, or similar obstruction, passes down the wall where the rack would most conveniently hang. The pipe can be cleared by positioning a block, of the necessary thickness, on either side of the pipe.

Drainboard. A drainboard (Fig. 14) is essential to a sink and it is most conveniently placed at the side of the sink opposite to the rack. To be a permanent structure it should be of hardwood, preferably beech or sycamore, and the boards should be not less than ¾ inch thick, if possible tongued and grooved to ensure tight and waterproof jointing. Its width should be that of the sink. Length may be dictated by limitations of space, but a useful length is 3 feet. It may, of course, exceed this if the far end can be supported on a piece of board nailed to a wall.

The boards are held together by two pieces of lumber 4 inches wide and as long as the drainboard is wide, secured to the top by screws from the underside. A raised ledge runs along the sides and one end, as a barrier against dishes sliding off; this is a molding ⅜ inch wide, ⅜ inch thick, nailed from the top, thin nails passing vertically through the molding. The corners, where the two pieces meet, should be neatly mitered.

If the surface is given sufficient slope, about 1 inch per foot of length, water will drain freely into the sink without the aid of the shallow channels which disfigure many

drainboards and also make cleaning difficult. And there will be no drip at the outside edge of the sink if the board overlaps the edge about 2 inches. At about 1 inch from the end, of the drainboard cut across the board, on the underside, a ⅜-inch wide groove; this will prevent drainage water from "creeping" back along the underside. To make certain that all water is diverted quickly into the sink, a piece of wood, shaped as in Fig. 14, may be screwed at the two lower corners.

The back of the drainboard is supported on a length of board, 1 inch thick, nailed to the wall. Fix the board to it with brass screws, after cutting recesses in the top edge of the support to hold the ends of the strengthening pieces on the underside of the drainboard. To protect the wall from moisture, nail a piece of wood the length of the drainboard, 3 inches wide and ½ inch thick, to the wall, the lower edge flush with the bottom surface of the drainboard.

Unless the outer end of the board butts against a wall to which it can be fixed, a leg will be needed at the front corner. This may be a vertical piece of 2 x 4 inch lumber. Fix a horizontal piece to the top of it, the other end of the horizontal entering the wall to a depth of a few inches and cemented. Be sure to cut the leg to the right length, or the drainboard will be twisted. Secure the bottom of the leg to the floor with a small angle plate.

Alternate Construction. An alternative to the upright leg is a strut, its lower end cut at an angle so that it fits neatly into the angle formed by the floor and the wall and its top end angled for screwing to the underside of the strengthening piece of the drainboard. If this type of leg is adopted, the strengthening piece should be located at the extreme end of the underside and the top of the strut fastened to this and not to the drainboard itself (Fig. 15).

This must be remedied by filling the crack or cracks neatly with a filler or with putty before water has a chance to soak in and cause the wood to rot.

Shelves. The space beneath the drainboard can be put to good purpose by installing a shelf or shelves or by placing there a small cupboard on castors, easily moved for cleaning the floors. Shelves can be supported on boards 1 inch thick, nailed to the

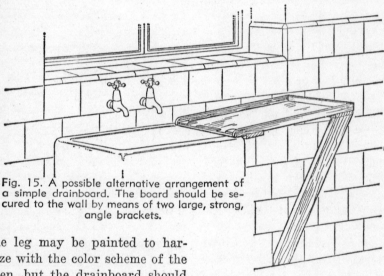

Fig. 15. A possible alternative arrangement of a simple drainboard. The board should be secured to the wall by means of two large, strong, angle brackets.

The leg may be painted to harmonize with the color scheme of the kitchen, but the drainboard should not be painted. Clean the drainboard by scrubbing: apply hot water, then a little scouring powder, and scrub vigorously with a brush and wipe dry. The surface should never be left wet; always wipe it off after use. After a period the board may become stained and this can be removed by bleaching, as outlined in Section Five.

Faulty construction may show later in cracks between the board, where there should be a tight joint.

sink support and to the leg, the inner end of the leg board resting on a block 1 inch thick, secured to the wall.

FIREPLACE FENDER

A fireplace fender, which is nothing more than a removable border of wood or metal around the outside edges of a hearth, will provide extra interest as well as a decorative touch to any fireplace. This added interest is especially welcome during the summer months, when most fireplaces tend to look rather empty and bare. To conform with current fashion the curb should be plain or with restrained ornament. It should be heavy enough to stay in proper position and should have an inner facing of some fire-resistant material. This may be thin sheet iron, attached by screws. Sheet copper is more decorative, however, and may be polished and left to assume its natural color. Give sheet iron two coats of stove polish before attaching.

Dimensions. The length of the fender depends upon the width of the hearth upon which it stands. A depth from front to back of 15 inches is usual, and a height from the floor to the top of the fender of 3 inches. The style of the fender and the material used are governed by the decoration of the room, the furniture, and the nature of the room itself. Oak is a good wood for dining and living rooms, but mahogany or walnut may be preferred. The decorative characteristics of grain and coloring in these hardwoods should be taken into consideration when selecting pieces of timber. Figured grain in oak possesses a fine decorative quality.

Ornamentation. The inside and outside top edges may be molded, as in Fig. 16(1), or merely chamfered, as in Fig. 16(3). If the wood is french polished, such a curb will be quite satisfying in appearance, although somewhat plain. After all, undue

ornamentation is out of place in such an article. Fig. 16(2) shows another simple shape which looks well; here the top edges are slightly rounded off. After this we come to "built up" shapes, in which the base of the curb is made of solid wood 3 inches wide and 2 or 2¼ inches high, and the

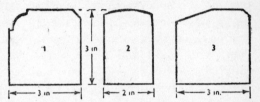

Fig. 16. Three alternative cross sections of wood, shaped with simple ornament.

top (ornamental) member is composed of a flat piece edged by two strips of molding. Such moldings should be rather heavy and substantial, or they will be difficult to nail down firmly and will break off.

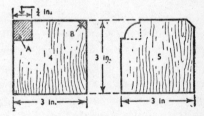

Fig. 17. How to utilize finished "quarter round" as an alternative to Fig. 16 for ornamentation.

A compromise is to rabbet the solid wood, as at A in Fig. 17, and then insert a strip of quarter round molding, as shown completed by Fig. 17. The inner edge of the top is bevelled or chamfered slightly. Undoubtedly a solid curb is the best, and the handyman can produce a pleasing shape by the use of planes and chisels. If some simple molding is to be run in the solid curb, this part of the job should be done while the lumber is in a single length, i.e., before separating it into three component pieces. A good allowance for waste should be made, perhaps an extra foot in the total length. In forming the molding shown in Fig. 16(1), first plane a shallow rabbet, or groove, on the two outside faces; then, with chisel and plane, carefully shape by removing surplus wood. A heavier design, like that shown in Fig. 17, can be carried out in the same way, using a molding.

When the curb is to be covered with sheet copper or brass, inexpensive lumber may be used for the core. Good seasoned wood should be chosen. Ask the lumber yard to find a piece that has stood in stock for a good while, as ordinarily this lumber gets very brief seasoning. It is safer, on the whole, to use oak as the core, though the cost is more and the labor greater than with a soft pine.

Joints. For the sake of good appearance the corners should be mitered. Three inches is rather deep, and the usual miter box found in the home workshop will not accommodate such stock. The only thing to do is to mark off the cuts with a square and saw down carefully with a fine backsaw. It is essential to keep the saw blade upright with the work, while following the mark on the top. Fix the corners with screws and glue. The screws go into end grain in one member, which theoretically will not afford a good "bite" for the threads, but in hardwood it is prac-

ticable. Sink the screws by countersinking, and plug the hole left at the top with a round piece of the same wood to match the run of the grain.

Where a good grip is needed, drill out a hole in the underneath member large enough to take a rawl plug, insert the plug so that it is a trifle below the joint line, and when assembling the fender, guide the point of the screw into the hole of the fiber plug. Two screws at each corner joint will be wanted, and they should be No. 12 iron screws about 2½ inches long. When the miters have been cut and fitted, clamp the front piece of the fender and one end piece to the bench or to a table, in the correct position, with front and end fittings as tightly against each other as possible. Then bore guide holes with a fine gimlet, or a small bit in a brace, boring through the end pieces into the front piece. Bore the two holes before taking the pieces apart for enlarging the holes.

This will give an accurate guide for enlarging the holes to the proper size. The next thing is to counterbore the end piece, and to enlarge the holes farther in, to take the shank of the selected screw. Finally enlarge the holes in the end grain of the front piece to take the rawl plug (if one is to be used), or to accommodate the threads of the screw. Secure the front piece again, with the remaining end piece, in contact at the proper position, and repeat the operation of boring pilot holes, enlarging, countersinking, etc., for that joint.

Gluing and Assembly. Make some simple form of clamp, with stop blocks fixed temporarily to the bench about 2 inches wider than the full width of the fender, and a pair of folding wedges that will be about 3 inches wide when fully closed (see Fig. 18). When the assembly has

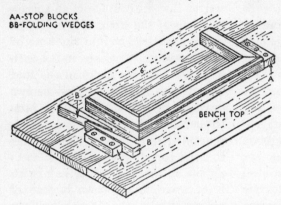

AA-STOP BLOCKS
BB-FOLDING WEDGES

BENCH TOP

Fig. 18. How to assemble fireplace fender, when gluing, applying pressure by stop blocks.

been glued, it will be put in the clamp between the stop blocks (close against one block) and the pair of wedges tapped in to hold the whole assembly closely together. Have the appliances all at hand. When the glue is ready, apply a thin coat to the joint faces. Lay the front piece and one end piece in position and insert two screws, but do not attempt to drive them in fully. The stop block should come to such a height that it clears one screw, at least.

Glue the other joint and assemble it in similar manner. Now put the fender between the blocks on the bench and tap in the wedges on one end until the ends of the fender are forced against the mitered faces of

the front piece. Next, drive in the screws at the opposite end and turn them in quite tight. Take out the wedges, push the fender hard against the other stop block, insert the wedges now at the opposite side and drive them in as tightly as possible. Turn in the screws at the end first wedged. Owing to the countersinking, the screws will be sunk after the first few turns have been made, and will not foul the stop blocks or wedges. It may be found that only the top screw at each side can be worked, owing to the height of the stop block. In such a case, drive home the accessible screw at each end, while the fender is clamped; then, while it is temporarily out of the clamp, turn in the other two screws. Replace in the clamp, and leave until the following day to set. The fender can then be taken out, but should remain flat on some level surface, undisturbed, for another twelve hours.

Bracing. Procure from a hardware store two right-angle metal mending plates. These should be about 4 inches long on each leg, set in flush at each corner joint on the underside of the fender, and screwed on. This job must not be attempted until the glued joints are firm and hard. Even then, be careful in chiselling out the shallow recess needed to take the plates below the surface, and do not strike heavy blows with the mallet. It should be pointed out that the mending plates will add much to the strength of a good glue joint at the miter, but will not compensate for badly fitting miters, or for indifferent gluing and assembly.

Alternative Joint. The miter joint, glued and screwed, needs careful workmanship, but is the only one practicable for the amateur when the job must not show joint lines at the front or sides. An ordinary half lap joint, as used in many jobs, is a substitute, but shows the joint.

The lap and miter joint may be combined, as shown in Fig. 19, and only a small portion of the joint will show at the end faces. The laps on the end of the front pieces are scribed with a square and a steel point (a pencil is not accurate enough for this), the miter is sawed down to the exact depth required. A horizontal cut made from the end of A will separate the triangular piece of waste wood and leave the portion C, which fits into the notch cut in the short member B of the fender, as illustrated in Fig. 19. In preparing the member B, the miter is first sawed and fitted, and the notch is then cut out.

Although this joint needs careful scribing and cutting, it is well within the capacity of the man with some experience of simple woodworking. Fig. 19 above shows a plain section (not molded) for clearness. This type of curb should be assembled dry, put into the clamp (Fig. 18) bottom upwards, and bored for screws. Two at each corner, through C and into B, will be needed. Countersink the holes. Take the assembly

from the clamp, glue the joint faces; replace in the clamp, bottom upwards, drive the edges together and turn in the screws. Leave twelve hours for the glue to set.

Lining. The sheet iron lining should be cut to proper length and height, and punched for small screws that will attach it to the inside face of the curb. If it is left all in one piece, and bent at right angles at the corner, take care it is accurately sized. If too short in the long (front) section, the ends of the fender may be pulled in and the joint wrenched by the action of screwing the lining to the wood. This applies to sheet iron lining; copper is more pliable and yielding, and may be attached with brass tacks instead of screws. Punch the holes along the flanges first.

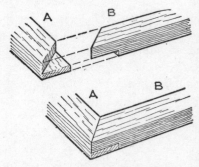

Fig. 19. Assembly details of miter and half-lap joint for fireplace fender. The half-lap gives additional strength to the miter and facilitates assembly.

Metal Covered Fender. Construct the wooden fender as described earlier, except that the ordinary half-lap joint may be used at the corners. It is unnecessary to use small molding for this type of curb, and the shape should be bold and simple, as in Figs. 16(2) and 16(3). No. 20 gauge is suitable for the sheet of copper or brass, which should be ordered in a piece of the desired width and length. It should go over the fender and be turned under about ¾ inch at the bottom. Lay a piece over the front section, long enough to overlap the miter line about ¾ inch (this miter line should be pencilled across each corner before attaching the metal).

It is assumed that the fender is in the position shown by Fig. 18. Bend the sheet over the wood, following the contour of the rounding or chamfering. Use only the hands for most of the bending; a pair of old gloves should be worn. When starting, allow the ¾ inch for the underlap at the bottom inside edge; or bend up this lap first, so that the wooden fender can be placed against the copper and the latter bent back over the top surface.

The fender, standing on the underlap, will hold the sheet tight during the rest of the procedure. Draw the fender close to the edge of the bench and bend down the copper over the outer side. Bend the copper close against the front or outer face and give it one or two gentle taps with a mallet. Then, with the fender standing up, sides in the air, the underlap at the front can be bent over and driven down. Lay the fender face downwards for the final touches, using some soft material underneath to prevent bruising. When the underlaps have been formed, drill a series of holes, 2 inches apart, along the edges of the underlaps about ³⁄₁₆ inch in from the edges. The holes to be drilled should be for No. 6 screws. Make a shallow countersink for each hole and run the screws down flush with the surface. If they do not come flush, file the heads.

VALANCE

The use of the valance in window treatment should be confined to those windows which are greater in height than in width. The wide short window which one meets in some houses is much better treated simply with curtains and without valances.

The designing, making, and fitting of window valances forms one of the most interesting and useful jobs the handyman can undertake to improve the appearance of a room.

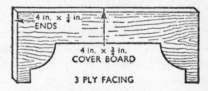

Fig. 20. General dimensions of a simple valance design with a plywood facing and light wood frame.

A valance may be of either fabric or wood, the latter being most useful in effecting the more formal and simple designs.

The making of a wooden valance is very simple. It is a three-sided box with a cover board (Fig. 20). The ends are of ¾-inch material with a facing of three ply, and the formal pattern is made on this facing piece. Hardwood, such as oak, walnut, or mahogany, should be used for the job and then stained and polished, or it may be constructed of soft wood and painted to match the other woodwork in the room.

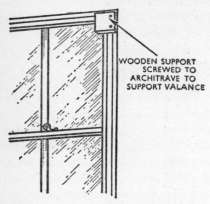

Fig. 21. Shows how to provide support for a wood valance.

The valance should be deep enough to enclose the hanging device from which the curtains are suspended, say three or four inches, and it may be conveniently fixed to metal brackets fixed to the architrave, or frame of the window, or to wooden supports, screwed to the edge of the frame (Fig. 21). A very heavy valance may cause too much strain on the window molding, and an alternative method is to fix it by means of rawl plugs to the wall.

Strictly formal designs are most suitable for use with tall narrow windows and with French casement doors as shown in Fig. 22.

An even simpler form of wood valance may be made by the use of deep section molding, which may be purchased and cut to length with miter joints to suit the angles and

length required. This method of constructing a valance is particularly suited to a bay window, being both effective and unobtrusive in appearance. This type of valance is, of

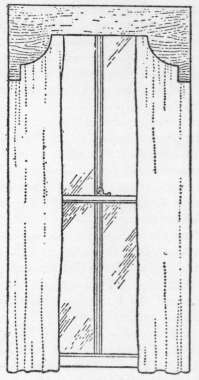

Fig. 22. A simple but effective design for a valance fitted in place on a tall, narrow window frame.

course, very suitable in many cases for use with the ordinary double hung window.

A valance made of fabric to match the curtains and permit less formality in design may be used in a variety of ways. Care should be taken, though, to avoid any suggestion of Victorian fussiness caused through over-elaboration. Whatever fabric is used, it will be necessary to provide a lining or backing. Buckram made especially for this purpose is the most suitable and may be bought in widths up to a yard. Buckram linings are essential for heavy fabrics, such as velvets. For lighter materials such as silks or cottons, heavy calico sheeting is quite good enough. The covering fabric is stitched to the lining after the shape has been cut out of both. In the case of buckram, hand stitching is to be preferred as it is beyond the capabilities of the ordinary sewing machine. The edges of the valance may be finished with a narrow braid.

In order to insure symmetry of design at both ends of the valance, it is advisable to cut a pattern out of stiff paper or cardboard and use the same pattern at both ends.

A point to remember is that, while a calico lining may be washed with the fabric cover complete, these valances mounted on buckram will have to be detached for washing as the buckram is stiffened with a glue solution. On the whole, it is better to make a valance from washable material, so that they may be renovated whenever it is necessary. When fixing such a valance always be sure it can be removed without damage to the valance material.

PICTURE FRAMES

In estimating the length of molding required for making a wooden picture frame, the basis is the length and width of the picture plus the mount (if the picture is to be mounted). The length and width of the mount must agree with the distance between the limits of the rabbet (the recess at the back of the molding) as measured from side to side and from top to bottom. But allowance has to be made for the width of the molding, and also for a certain amount of wastage in cutting the eight miters.

Each piece of the frame is cut, with a tenon saw, at an angle of 45 degrees. In marking for the cuts remember that each of the eight miters must slope inward to the rabbet, the first attempt at making a frame can easily be marred by going wrong, in this respect, with just one miter.

For accurate cutting a miter block or a miter box is desirable (see Figs. 28 and 29).

If a miter box is used, the molding to be cut is placed on the bottom of the box and pressed there and against the back while the saw is worked between the corresponding guide lines and through the molding. Mark off the exact length for each side of the frame and carry the pencil marks vertically up the outer side of the molding in order to permit the molded face to be turned uppermost and at the same time give visible location for the saw cut. Sawing from the face downward avoids the chipping of the molded surface which is apt to result if the wood is cut through from the back to the face of the molding. Having cut the first miter, turn the molding and be sure that the next miter to be cut will agree with the joint angle to be made.

An alternative method, dispensing with the miter box or block, is to mark the lines directly on the molding with a 45-degree square, or with a bevel gauge set at that angle, and do the cutting with the molding in the bench vise, the jaws of the latter gripping the rabbet and the outside edge. But this is practicable only when the molding is plain faced and flat; also, it tends to be inaccurate.

When the four lengths have been cut they should be placed together, flat on the bench, to form the frame. Any inaccuracy in cutting will then be apparent, after testing with a square, and can be remedied with a jack plane or smoothing plane used in conjunction with a shooting board. This, at its simplest, takes the form of a ¾-inch-thick base board to which is nailed or screwed an inch wide strip of wood ½ inch thick, this forming an angle of 45 degrees with the perfectly straight edge of the base board (Fig. 23). The outer edge, against which the jack plane or smoothing plane, used on its side, will run, ensures each miter being trued and smoothed at the same time. Pressure of the left hand, which holds the molding against the inch wide strip, keeps the shooting board steady on the bench.

After the eight miters have been given this final attention, the frame is ready for gluing. Place newspaper below the corners to prevent sticking to the bench. There are several methods of clamping the frame while the glue is setting, one being to run

a stout cord or string around the frame, with corner blocks to prevent the molding from injury. After the tightly pulled string has been tied, wedges can be used to increase the tension, but care must be exercised that the sides are not forced out of square. Another method is to butt strips of wood as tightly as possible to each of the four sides of the frame, screwing the strips to the

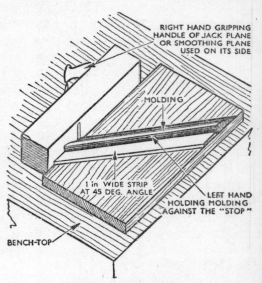

RIGHT HAND GRIPPING HANDLE OF JACK PLANE OR SMOOTHING PLANE USED ON ITS SIDE

MOLDING

1 in WIDE STRIP AT 45 DEG. ANGLE

LEFT HAND HOLDING MOLDING AGAINST THE "STOP"

BENCH-TOP

Fig. 23. Shows how to finish the joint face of a molding after cutting in a miter box or block.

bench, looseness being corrected by the use of folding wedges (Fig. 24).

If the latter method is adopted, further securing of the miters (when the glue has set) by nails or screws is simplified. Before the fine screws or thin nails are driven home, holes should be bored at the corners with a brad awl. If the string method of tension is adopted, and it is thought desirable to strengthen the joint after the glue has set, the nailing or screwing will require caution, to prevent both splitting and weakening of the joints.

The nails or screws should be sunk well into the wood, ample depressions being made for the head at the same time as the holes are bored. These depressions are later levelled up with plastic wood which is stained to match the wood. An alternative method is to fill them with pieces of waste wood from the frame; these are cut and glued into the holes.

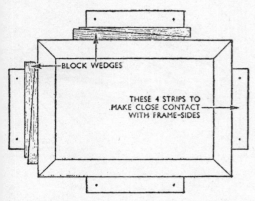

Fig. 24. How to assemble a picture frame, after gluing, by use of wedges and strips secured to bench.

Surplus glue should be cleaned from the jointed frame, and the wood should be rubbed with fine sandpaper, though use of this will be possible only on the back when the front is heavily molded. Then the glass, picture mounting, and backing can go into position, though oil paintings are generally left unglazed. If there is any difficulty with surplus glue on the face and sides of the frame, this can be removed with a wad of cloth dipped in hot water.

The glass should be thoroughly cleaned, particularly on the inner surface. It should be cut to an easy fit for the rabbet, though not too loose, and it should not be fingered on the inside while the picture is being placed on top of it. The mounting (if any) and picture having been put in place, a backing of thin plywood or very stiff cardboard is introduced and secured with glazing brads or other fine nails.

These are driven horizontally into the sides of the rabbet, while the frame is flat on its face. It is advisable to make certain that the bench or table has no loose nails or other small items on its surface to scratch or indent the molding, and a flat iron on edge, or block of wood, should be pressed against the outside edge of the frame (the edge that is being dealt with) as a support during the hammering. The backing must not be pressed down too tightly, or the glass may crack, but the brads must be sufficiently low in the rabbet to hold the back securely in the frame.

Do not drive the brads into the rabbet more than half their length. For a neat finish, and to exclude dust, a sheet of brown paper, in area a shade less on all sides than the over-all dimensions of the frame, may then be pasted or glued over the back. When this has dried, any surplus due to the paper's stretching during the pasting should be cut away. Small screw eyes (preferably the kind with loose rings) may now be inserted in line with each other in the back of the molding, to take the cord or, if the frame is heavy, flexible picture wire will be found more satisfactory.

Hanging. The eyes may be about one third of the distance from the top of the frame, though this depends on the angle at which the picture is required to incline from the wall. If the inclination is to be slight, the rings will be inserted higher up. If the molding is thin, the eyes should be screwed in cautiously, to prevent the screw points from penetrating the front surface of the frame.

Generally speaking, the pictures on one wall should have the same inclination, and there should be some symmetry as to height. The most convenient method of hanging is from picture molding, but patented fasteners or rawl plugs can also be used (see HANGING OBJECTS).

SHELVES

The essentials for strong shelving are (a) boards stiff enough not to sag noticeably over the span required; and (b) good support at the ends and at intermediate points, according to the span. It is assumed, for example, that several shelves are needed in the kitchen for pots and pans. The walls are usually of plaster on laths, or wallboard, so that one end of the shelves can be fixed to wall, with brackets for the other.

Saucepan Shelf. Inch board is suitable, two pieces of 6-inch tongued and grooved board being used to make up a width of slightly less than a foot. For the outer end

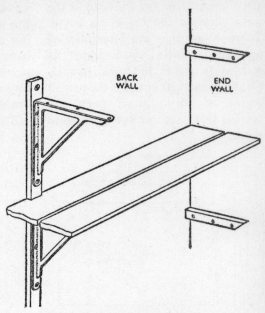

Fig. 25. How to utilize steel braces and wood strips for mounting shelves.

of each shelf a steel bracket, about 12 inches by 10 inches, will be needed. A common length for shelves in such a position—flanking the sink, say—is about 39 inches; the bracket will be set in about 6 inches from the outer end of the shelf, as illustrated in Fig. 25.

Begin by measuring on the wall the position of the bottom face of the shelf or shelves. It is a good plan to measure from the floor to the lowest shelf, then to lay off the distance above, from the first line. Remember that the top of the shelf will come about 1 inch higher than the line.

On the end wall we shall need a bearer for each shelf, cut from 1 x 2 inch stock, neatly planed and cut back to a slope at the outer end. Prepare these bearers first, and bore holes for the screws. Use rawl plugs or toggle bolts to fix them to the wall. If the wall is constructed out of wallboard, the bearers should only be nailed at points where there is studding in back of the wallboard. Countersink the holes in the bearers, so that the screws go in flush. If the bearer is to be nailed to the studding this will not be necessary, as the nail heads may be punched in to provide a flat surface. Square off pencil lines on the wall to show the line for the top of the bearer (bottom face of the shelf). Hold the lowest bearer in position, with a spirit level on top, and verify the level. Use a fine awl to mark, through the screw holes, the location of the plugs. Drill the wall for the latter, fit the appropriate size plug, and screw on the bearer.

Fix the bearers for the remaining shelves. Now put in place the upright to which the steel brackets are screwed. This upright may be made from the same timber as used for the bearers. Cut it to length and chamfer the two front edges. Bore holes for the screws as before. Get someone to hold the upright in position while testing it for vertical. A plumb bob and line will give the true upright, but it may be had approximately by measurement from the end wall, though the wall may not be dead true. Mark the back wall through the upright for rawl plugs, drill the holes, and secure the board.

Cut the inch board to length; plane off the tongue, and let the groove on the other side go against the wall. The shelf can be strengthened by screwing a ledge (made from 1 x 2 inch board) across the two boards underneath, midway in the length. Do this before fixing the shelf. The shelf, at the open end, should be rounded, planed, and sandpapered.

The back edge of the shelf should be notched to fix around the vertical board, close to the back wall. After fitting—but before nailing—the lowest shelf, the latter can be used as a guide for marking those above it, after attaching the ledge. In any case, where several shelves are fixed, do not fasten the lowest, or fix brackets, until the preparatory work above has been completed. If large saucepans are to be accommodated, remember that they often have a loop handle opposite the long handle; when turned upside down, the loop will prevent the vessel from lying flat unless there is an open space at the far side of the shelf. In such cases, do not place the boards close to the wall. Otherwise, to make a neater job, a length of wood, planed and chamfered along the lower front edge, can be fixed to the wall under the back of the shelf. Oval brads can be nailed through the board obliquely into the top of the back strip.

When ready to fix the brackets, lay a shelf in place on the end wall bearer and adjust the height of the other end until a level placed on top shows the shelf to be horizontal.

Mark the position on the upright (for the underside of the shelf). Place the bracket so that its top arm is at the level line and bore for a screw through one of the holes in the vertical arm of the bracket; insert the screw, adjust the brackets for perpendicular, and put in the next screw. Lay the shelf in place and test with a level; if correct, insert remaining screws in the upright. Only short screws are needed to hold the shelf to the bracket. No. 8, ⅜ inch long will do. Two oval brads will hold the other end of the shelf to the bearer on the wall.

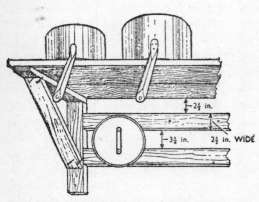

Fig. 26. Method of arranging a single shelf by use of wooden brackets.

Shelves in a Recess. Two types of recessed shelves are described. The first is used when the recess has a baseboard and picture rail which for some reason cannot be cut (see Fig. 27).

Fix two vertical strips at each side of the recess, on the flanking walls. Only one side wall is shown in the diagram, for clearness. Cut the uprights (1 x 2 inch or 1 x 3 inch stock) at the bottom to fit close

to the baseboard and bevel them for that purpose. At the top make a longer bevel to bring them over the picture rail; if this is a thick rail, the uprights can be fitted only part way over the molding. The essential

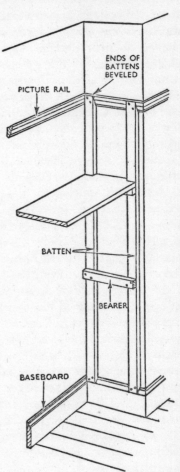

Fig. 27. Construction of shelves showing the method of attachment in a recess.

requirements are that the uprights shall come close to the wall and fit tightly to baseboard and picture rail.

Nail the uprights at top and bottom, after plugging them at two intermediate points to the wall. Next, cut and fit cross bearers where the shelves are to be. The sketch shows these screwed flush to the verticals and of the same thickness, but a better way is to use 2-inch bearers and notch them around the verticals, so that they also fit close to the walls and give double the bearing surface for the shelf ends. When cutting the shelves, cut them long enough to fit tightly against the uprights. Do not attempt to make the projecting narrower portions fit close to the wall. The shelves, wedged tightly to the uprights, will hold everything firm and solid. Put in the lowest shelf first and work upwards; tilt the shelves to insert them, then gently tap with a mallet, or a hammer on a block of wood. Undue force will loosen the assembly.

Second Method. This is used when the baseboard and rail can be removed. Remove them, and fit the uprights straight through to the floor and up to the height required. When the uprights have been fixed solidly, screw on cross pieces as before, to support the shelves. Where the baseboard and picture rail were taken down, glue short end pieces and nail them to make a miter joint with the flanking lengths of baseboard and picture rail.

It has been assumed that the full depth of the recess has been taken up by shelving. If this is not the case, suitable pieces of baseboard and rail will have to be fitted in, to make a neat finish.

MITER BLOCK AND BOX

In order to cut wood or other material at an angle, a miter block (Fig. 28) or a miter box is desirable. Either can be purchased, but the box

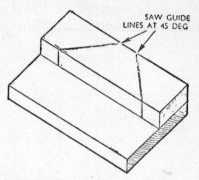

Fig. 28. This miter block is constructed from two pieces of wood glued and screwed together. Guide lines cut in the upper block must be at exactly 45 degrees. These guide lines must be sawn very carefully.

is more accurate because of its paired guide lines. Manufactured miter boxes that can be set to cut at any angle are available. However, as the angle most used is one of 45 degrees, the handyman will find the less expensive single-cut box or block satisfactory for most of his needs, if not for all of them.

Construction. Construction of either presents no great difficulty. For the block, two pieces of wood are used. The bottom piece should be about 6 inches wide and the top or back piece 3 inches wide. Both should be of ¾-inch stock and 18 inches long. These are screwed or glued together and the saw guides (miter lines) marked out as shown. They are then cut through to the top side of the bottom piece with a backsaw. The utmost care should be taken to ensure the cuts being absolutely vertical.

The miter box offers the advantage of paired guide lines which hold the saw securely in place so that it cannot deviate from the correct angle. As shown in Fig. 29, three pieces

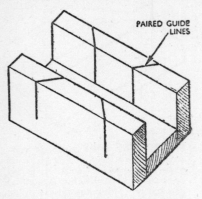

PAIRED GUIDE LINES

Fig. 29. The miter box, constructed from three pieces of wood glued and screwed together, is a good alternative to the miter block shown in Fig. 28. For deep section work, the miter box is more efficient than the miter block.

of wood are required to construct it, the inside measurement of the box being about 4 inches from front to back, and the depth about 3 inches. Use ¾-inch stock of about 18 inches in length. The pieces should be screwed or glued together. Before cutting the guides it is important to mark guide lines on both faces as well as on the top of the side pieces —for the accuracy of the marking and cutting will govern the trueness of the mitering done with the box.

The molding, or other material to be mitered, is placed on the bottom of the block or box and pressed there against the back while the saw is worked between the corresponding guides until the desired cut is made.

45-Degree Angle. If no combination try square is available the 45 degree angle can be determined easily by the following method: Lay an ordinary carpenter's square across the top of the two uprights of the box and mark them. Now measure the distance between the outside edges of the uprights and, starting at the marks you made, measure the same distance along the outside edges of the tops of the uprights. Mark these points and again lay the carpenter's square across the tops of the uprights and mark each one. Where these four marks you have made intersect the outside edges of the uprights you have the four corners of a square. A straight edge laid diagonally across this square from two opposite corners provides an angle 45 degrees. Mark these lines and continue the lines down on the inside surfaces of the sides or uprights of the box, making sure that the latter lines are absolutely vertical. Make your cuts as previously described.

AIRING CUPBOARD

Modern housekeeping has imposed new standards on the design and functional efficiency of household appliance and equipment. One need, however, has not been given sufficient attention by house designers; it is for the provision of proper facilities not only for drying and airing, but storing the family clothes and wash efficiently.

During the summer months when the air in the house is humid, many homeowners complain of musty smelling closets and mildewed clothing. As far as keeping a large storage closet dry, this can best be done by increasing the circulation of air in the closet either by having a window installed or by using an electric

selection of the best, and at the same time, the most convenient location in the house. The cupboard should

DOOR

Fig. 30. Details of airing cupboard.

fan. Chemicals can also be used to absorb the moisture from the air. For airing and storing the family wash an airing cupboard can be made, and this will ensure that these articles get completely dry even in very damp weather and that they remain dry until put to use.

Location. Before proceeding with the preparation of an airing cupboard it is advisable to consider the

Fig. 31. Distances between cross bearers and cross members should be arranged to suit requirements and overall height.

not be located in the bathroom or kitchen as the humidity in these rooms is usually high. Neither should the cupboard be built against an outside wall.

With regard to heating of the cupboard, light bulbs, as shown in Fig. 30, are very satisfactory.

This cupboard will provide constantly dry warm air for the airing of freshly laundered linen, and racks for its storage when aired. An existing cupboard may be found suitable for the purpose, or a plywood cabinet can be made and fitted along the lines described. Dimensions are not given in the illustrations (Figs. 30 and 31) since these must depend on individual requirements, but the general layout should be followed in principle.

Heating. The cabinet is heated by one or more incandescent lamps. These are easily installed, have a long life, and are cheaply replaced. The current consumption is low, and there is little risk of causing a fire. The size of the cupboard or cabinet determines the number of lamps required, and this requirement is best found by trial, starting with one lamp and adding additional lamps if necessary. It is obviously better to use a low power source of heat burning day and night than a higher power switched on intermittently. One 15 watt lamp burning continuously will consume very little current in a week and this should be adequate in a small cabinet.

Construction. The cabinet is made on a light framework of finished stock about 1 inch by 2 inches cross section. It is not necessary to make tongued or halved joints. The frame joints can be secured by screws or nails, but care must be exercised to ensure that all are square and true.

First make the two side frames as a matching pair, and carefully fix the back panel to these with small finishing nails. Strips of wood, 1 inch by 2 inches, are then fitted and screwed across the front, one at the top and one at the bottom. The assembly can then be stood upright and the slats forming the storage rack nailed to the side uprights. The top and bottom and side panels are then fitted and fixed with nails, and the door hung on suitable hinges. If the cabinet is large and wide it is advisable to use double doors, as one large door, unless expertly made, is liable to warp.

A reasonably rigid door can be made quite simply by gluing and nailing plywood panels on both sides of a light wood frame. In this case the frame should be jointed with halved or mortice and tenon joints, so as to present flush surfaces for attaching the panels.

It will be seen in the illustration (Fig. 31) that the cross members at the top of the side frames are positioned a few inches down from the top. These members act as bearers for the removable airing rails and sufficient clearance must be left to allow room for handling and loading the rails.

The lamps are mounted at the bottom of the cabinet and there should be several inches clearance between the top of the bulbs and the bottom of the first shelf. Warm air is carried upwards by convection, passing through the spaces between the slats, up round the piles of stored linen, to the airing space above.

The top part of the cabinet is provided with a number of removable rails over which is hung the newly laundered linen for airing.

Very little ventilation is required. Indeed, too much ventilation is wasteful since cold air freely entering the cabinet not only reduces the temperature but may, on many occasions, carry considerable moisture. Some change of air there must be, in order to carry away the moisture taken out of the linen, but this requirement is likely to be met by opening the door in the course of normal use. Alternatively, the door could be left slightly ajar for half-an-hour during the day.

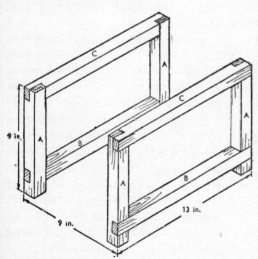

Fig. 32. Shows general details and overall dimensions of the framework for a shoe box.

SHOE BOX

This is 13 inches long, 9 inches high, and 9 inches from back to front (see Figs. 32 and 33). Plywood may be used for the sides and the frame is constructed of 1 inch square stock, see Fig. 32. The uprights (A) are 9 inches high; the crosspieces (B) are notched in at 1 inch from the bottom; the top crosspieces (C) are halved to the uprights level with the top end of the latter. The crosspieces at the narrow ends are inserted after the plywood is screwed in place to join the front and back units. This step is explained later in this article.

For simplicity, the lid (Fig. 33) merely fits into the top of the box, having four cleats of half inch wood about 1½ inches wide nailed on with small nails from the top face of the plywood. The cleats should be thinly coated with glue before being attached. Four or five "spots" of glue will suffice, and the joints also should be glued. As the cleats are nailed down, the glue will spread out over a wider surface. Avoid putting on too much glue, as only a thin film is needed. The wood must be clean where the glue is to be applied.

In order to locate the cleats in their proper position, lay down the lid flat, under side uppermost; square lines across with a pencil where the cleats are to go; glue the cleats, lay them down on the lid and drive in a few nails to fix them for the time being. Then turn the lid over, top side now being uppermost, and drive in ⅝-inch brads so that they go through the plywood and into the cleats underneath. If the brads protrude on the other side, after the heads have been punched down slightly with a nail punch, file off the points below. The cleats should be so fixed that the lid fits easily between the framework of the box at the top opening. If desired, the nail heads can be concealed by nailing around the top a strip of shallow molding, mitered at the corners.

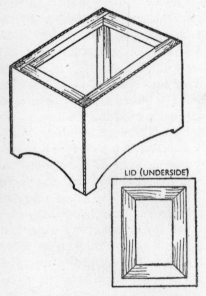

LID (UNDERSIDE)

Fig. 33. Shows the completed shoe box and the construction of lid as viewed from the underside. Four mitered cleats, glued and pinned to lid, brace the lid and allow it to fit snugly.

It will be seen from the sketch (Fig. 33) that the bottom edge on each of the four sides of the box, is cut away to a sweep for the sake of appearance. Put the plywood in a vise and saw the curve with a coping saw; finish with sandpaper rolled around a piece of broom-handle, etc.

Always saw downward away from the face surface, to avoid burring the face side of the work.

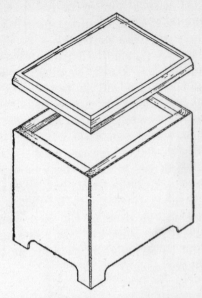

Fig. 34. A bathroom box or cabinet covered with thin sheets of plywood.

The front and back frames, made up of pieces A, B and C, should be cut and jointed, and the plywood attached. Note that the plywood projects at each side just enough to cover the edges of the plywood forming the ends of the box; it is flush at the top, of course. Thus, looked at from the front side, no end grain will be visible. The piece B is better let into notches made in the outer sides of the uprights, where the joints will be covered and reinforced by the plywood facing. Also, the halved joints at the top should be similarly cut and joined. In order to get a finished surface, the plywood should be about $\frac{1}{16}$ inch longer than the finished dimension at each side, to be rubbed down with sandpaper to the exact level last thing, after assembly of the box.

After covering the front and back frames, cut a piece of plywood to fit the bottom of the box and glue it in place on top of the side pieces (B in Fig. 32). It should go in fairly tightly, but not so tightly as to force out the plywood covering. Next, nail on the end pieces of plywood. A spot of glue here and there will make a stronger job. Lastly, lay the box on a table, end uppermost, and cut a piece of 1-inch stock to fit tightly between one pair of end uprights at the top, where the halved joint comes. Before inserting this crosspiece, apply glue to each end and to the side that will touch the plywood. Then force the crosspiece into place. Hold it with a pair of clamps to the plywood until the glue sets. Later, fix a similar piece between the opposite pair of uprights, thus giving a neat and flush finish to the box opening.

As a finish the box can be either painted with enamel or stained and later varnished.

LAUNDRY HAMPER

This (see Figs. 34 and 35) is a similar, but larger edition of the shoe box. A suitable size for the body of the hamper is 20 inches long, 15 inches wide and 18 inches high but these dimensions depend on how much space there is available in the bathroom. However, the dimensions

are easily modified to suit the circumstances. Again a framework is needed (Fig. 35), and this frame should be of 1½-inch stock. Tenoned joints for the two end frames are desirable, and dowelled joints for the long front and back rails that connect the end frames. Again, as in the shoe box, there is a top rail and another lower down on which the floor of the box rests. The long rails also support this floor.

In this case we make up the two end frames as independent units.

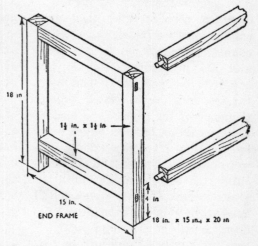

Fig. 35. Part frame and joint construction of cabinet.

Cut and fit the joints; glue, and leave in clamps to set. Next, cut the two long rails for each long side. Square the ends of the wood and bore for two ⅜-inch dowels. A cardboard template can be marked out and applied to the places where the dowels are to enter, to mark the points for boring the posts. The same template will be used to mark the ends of the rails. Notch in a crossbar to the middle of the bottom pair of rails, cutting the notches in the top or uppermost face of the rails. This bar is to support the plywood bottom. If pieces of board from boxes are to be used instead for the floor of the cabinet, the middle crossbar may be omitted.

When the dowelled joints are set hard, and not until this is certain, the plywood sides can be attached to the frame; small screws with countersunk heads are best in this case. Tack the plywood temporarily at two opposite corners, and then proceed to bore for the screws. Slightly countersink the holes with a brace and the proper bit. Put in two screws to each post or rail, and insert the rest in between. Watch for any tendency of the plywood to buckle; this may occur, but can be corrected by working from the middle outward toward the sides, and not tightening the screws finally until all seems correct. If the plywood is first fixed at the outside of the piece, it may buckle at the center portion, and will be difficult to put right without making fresh holes.

The lid is reinforced at the edges by gluing and screwing on some pieces of 2-inch wide and ½-inch thick stock. (Figs. 34 and 36). As with the shoe box, these are mitered, but in the present case they come flush with the edges, on the underside of the lid. Farther inside the lid, some strips of ¾ inch by 1 inch wood should be screwed on from

below, to form a sort of guide so that the lid will fit into its proper position. Glue and miter these, leaving plenty of freedom for an easy fit. Also, at midway in the length, cut and fit a stiffening piece of the same material as used for reinforcing. This fits tightly across the lid under-

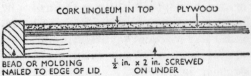

CORK LINOLEUM IN TOP   PLYWOOD

BEAD OR MOLDING   ½ in. x 2 in. SCREWED
NAILED TO EDGE OF LID.   ON UNDER

Fig. 36. Cross section of linoleum-covered lid for bathroom box.

neath, and is glued in.

When all the glue joints are hard, sandpaper the top surface of the lid, and clean off the edges nicely. We now have to consider what is to be done with the top surface. A piece of linoleum will serve very well for this purpose and should be of some neutral shade and have no pronounced pattern. This is glued down to the top of the lid, and finished off by a strip of molding which is mi-

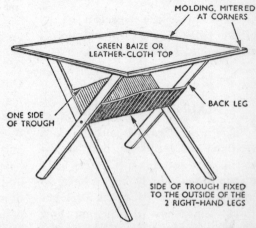

MOLDING, MITERED AT CORNERS

GREEN BAIZE OR LEATHER-CLOTH TOP

BACK LEG

ONE SIDE OF TROUGH

SIDE OF TROUGH FIXED TO THE OUTSIDE OF THE 2 RIGHT-HAND LEGS

Fig. 37. Completed folding table suitable as a card or tea table.

tered and glued and nailed around the edge of the lid, as shown in Fig. 36.

FOLDING TABLES

A folding or collapsible table which can be used for card playing, or a side table for the garden or lawn, can be made with reasonably small expenditure in material and effort. The example shown in Fig. 37 may be constructed from oak or walnut, if it is desired to obtain the best decorative results; but for a table of this kind, likely to have casual handling, the use of less expensive wood, to be either stained or painted, will serve the purpose. If it is constructed from oak it may be left unpolished, although if used much in the garden a protective coat of spar varnish should be applied. The top, overall size is 21 inches square (including the 3/8-inch molding) and may even be made of heavy plywood covered with green baize, or

with artificial leather. The leather has one advantage in that it is easily cleaned with a damp cloth. A strip of plain molding fitted along the

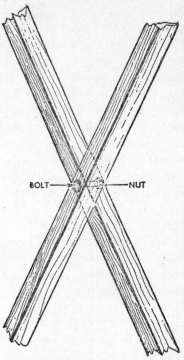

Fig. 39. Shows the midway pivot point for legs of the folding table.

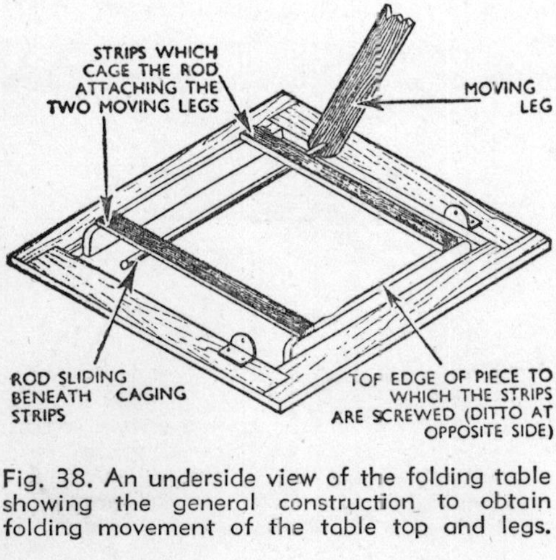

edges of the table top falls flush with the surface, holds the material in position and gives a neat, finished appearance to the table top.

The plywood top is on a frame (Fig. 38) 2¼ inches wide and ½ inch thick; two of the pieces are 18¾ inches long and are jointed to the two longer sides, each 20¼ inches long, and glued. When the glue has set, the top is glued to this frame. Finally the covering is put on, and then the molding.

STRIPS WHICH CAGE THE ROD ATTACHING THE TWO MOVING LEGS

MOVING LEG

ROD SLIDING BENEATH CAGING STRIPS

TOP EDGE OF PIECE TO WHICH THE STRIPS ARE SCREWED (DITTO AT OPPOSITE SIDE)

Fig. 38. An underside view of the folding table showing the general construction to obtain folding movement of the table top and legs.

The four legs are each 30¼ inches long; 1¼ inches wide, ¾ inch thick, and are rounded at top and bottom. At a point 16¼ inches up from the bottom, where touching legs will cross and are attached, holes are bored, to take 2¼ inch bolts. (Fig. 39). A bolt is passed through each pair of legs, from the outside of each of the two fixed legs, and the nut then screwed in place. One leg only, of each pair, is actually fixed to the underside of the table top frame, a

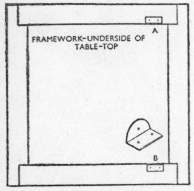

FRAMEWORK—UNDERSIDE OF TABLE-TOP

A

B

Fig. 40. Brackets A and B in position for securing legs. See also Fig. 38.

single screw securing the leg to a metal bracket on the appropriate side. The brackets are fixed, each by two screws, to the inner edge of the frame and are located as shown in Fig. 40.

The two free legs are connected at the top by a rod, ½ inch in diameter; the rod-ends pass through holes of the same diameter bored ⅘ inch down from the top, this measurement being taken to center of hole. There the rod is glued, ends flush with outside edges of the legs. (Fig. 41).

These legs move from one side of the table top to the other when the table is collapsed, and are "caged" by two strips of wood each 15¾ inches long, 1⅜ inches wide, ¼ inch thick, which in turn are screwed to the inner edges of the two longer sides of the frame (Fig. 38).

If the trough shown at Fig. 37 is to be added, the legs should not be caged, or screwed to the brackets, until the pieces of board which form the trough have been fixed in place. This is useful for holding newspapers, magazines or other articles and in no way hinders the folding of the table, provided the precaution is taken of placing the sides as shown. One of the two pieces is screwed to the outside of the two fixed legs, the other to the inside of the movable legs.

The pieces forming the trough run from the extreme edges of the legs, and are 5½ inches wide and ¼ inch thick. Their top edges can be left straight, but a better effect is secured when they are shaped with a plane or drawknife and sandpaper.

When the table has been assembled, the movement of the legs should be tried. If there is any hin-

Fig. 41. A part view of top sliding legs, illustrating the method of housing the rod in the legs. Use wooden rod with good straight grain for extra strength. The rod must fit firmly in the legs.

drance here to complete contact between the leg-tops and the underside of the table top, a shaving or two should be removed from these, until there is no hindrance to free movement. It will be noticed that as the free legs lodge securely in the angle of the framework there is no possibility of an accidental collapse; the only precaution to take is to see that the legs are open to the full extent.

To cover the top, cut the material to an area which allows the edges to come flush with the lowered edges of the framework, and attach it to the surface and to the framework edges with the minimum amount of glue. If too much of the latter is used it may soak through the surface of the cloth; when this is being smoothed down it must not be unduly stretched. A flatiron will assist in eliminating wrinkles.

The glue should be smeared thinly over the wood, and the material attached first to one edge, from which the covering will be smoothed flat inch by inch until top and frame edges are covered. When the glue has dried, and surplus material is removed with scissors, then the 3/4-inch wide molding is screwed to the frame edges, the ends of the beading being mitered to make a neat joint at the corners. The heads of screws used in the construction, should be countersunk below the surface of the wood, and the holes filled with plastic wood; or sawdust from the wood itself can be made into a stiff paste with a little glue and worked in over each countersunk screw head. If the top should ever need re-covering, the molding can be removed for that purpose. If any object is to stand on the table semi-permanently, the baize (which is more likely to be marked, or worn, than the artificial leather) can be protected with a false top of wood to match, in kind and finish, the material used throughout.

A point to observe is that with each of the two bolts which join pairs of legs, a thin metal washer, about 1 inch in diameter, should be placed between the crossing legs so that these do not rub throughout their length when the table is collapsed or opened. Also it saves time and makes for accuracy when dealing with the trough-sides if both pieces of wood are worked together in the vice; the pattern to which the top edges are to be cut first being outlined on a strip of paper, which is then pasted to one of the pieces as pattern for the cutting.

Formal Table. A formal table, for the hall or to hold the radio, can be constructed in oak, walnut or mahogany (Fig. 42). The top, consisting of two or possibly three boards glued together, is 24 inches long, 15½ inches wide and 3/4 inch thick. The edges may be left square or may be "scalloped" with a coping saw. The four legs are 27 inches long and 1¾ inches square. If these can be turned on the lathe, the appearance of the table is improved; or turned legs may be purchased.

The top rails are secured to the legs by mortice and tenon joints; the long sides measure 17½ inches from leg to leg, the short sides 10 inches; the wood is 3 inches wide and ¾ inch thick. The tenons are ½ inch long and ⅜ inch thick.

The bottom rails are 1¾ inches wide and ¾ inch thick, and the jointing is done with dowels, ¼ inch diameter and 1 inch long. These rails are positioned 4 inches up from the bottom of the legs; their lengths correspond, of course, with those of the top rails. Joints of top and bottom rails should be completed and the frame given a trial assembly. Any slight correction indicated can then be made before the frame is finally glued together. One dowel per rail is sufficient, and it should be situated centrally.

When the glue has dried, any which has been squeezed out should be removed carefully with the chisel, and the frame tested for level. If it does not stand perfectly level, a shaving can be removed from the bottom of the leg, or legs at fault. Alternately, if one leg is just a trifle short, a piece of wood of the necessary thickness can be glued to the lower end, and shaped so that this addition is not noticeable, being next to the floor.

The top is then secured, with glue and screws, the latter being inserted at an angle from the inner face of each of the two long pieces of rail so that they bite into the underside of the table top. Four screws are needed, each 2 inches in from the ends of the long rails. This fixing is done by first gluing the top to the frame, taking care that the top is placed centrally. When the glue is

dry, the positions of the four screws should be marked, ¾ inch down from the top edges of the long rails, and a trial hole at each position bored with a brad awl or small twist drill.

The angle at which the holes are bored will determine the length of the screw, from 1 inch to possibly 1½ inches. It is sufficient if the screw passes about ¼ inch into the underside of the table top. When the holes have been made, a larger drill completes the boring and the

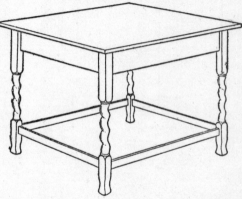

Fig. 42. A general view of a more formal occasional table.

screws are driven all the way in. The heads should be countersunk so that there is no projection on the inner face of the rail.

When the table is not in use do not leave it exposed to rain and damp. Store it in a dry sheltered position, preferably in some convenient place inside the house.

TOWEL RACKS

Roller Towel Rack. The rack can be attached to a plaster or tile wall by the use of toggle bolts or rawl plugs. Often times the most suitable and convenient place is on the inside of a door.

In the example (Fig. 43), the

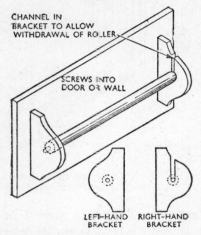

CHANNEL IN BRACKET TO ALLOW WITHDRAWAL OF ROLLER

SCREWS INTO DOOR OR WALL

LEFT-HAND BRACKET   RIGHT-HAND BRACKET

Fig. 43. General details of towel rack and end elevations of the two left-hand and right-hand brackets.

backboard is 19 inches long, ¾ inch thick and 5 inches wide, with the front edges slightly chamfered. Brackets to hold the roller are fixed ½ inch in from each end, by two screws inserted from the back. These brackets (Fig. 43) are cut from a piece of wood to the length of 4¼ inches, width 2¼ inches and thickness 1 inch. The shaping can be done with a coping saw or the combined use of saw, chisel and rasp.

On the inner face of the left-hand bracket is marked the position of a hole in which a spindle of the roller will revolve. The hole is ½ inch diameter, ⅝ inch from the back edge of the bracket and 2⅛ inches down. The hole should be bored with brace and bit taking the necessary precau-

tions not to split the wood when the bit comes through.

To allow the roller to be removed when the towel has to be changed, the right hand bracket (Fig. 43) has, in addition to a similar hole on its inner face, a slope cut from the hole as far as the top edge of the bracket. This vertical piece to be cut away is removed by two cuts with a tenon saw after boring the hole.

The positions of the two prepared brackets are marked on the face of the backboard, their inner faces 16 inches apart. Their bases outlined in pencil on the baseboard, holes to take the screws are bored through the backboard, these holes then being extended into the corresponding brackets, about 1¼ inches from the top and the bottom of each. When the screws have been driven home (from the back), the base can be attached to door or wall; a screw hole first being made a few inches in from either end and along the central line of the board, for fixing to the door, or nail holes bored for attaching to the wall.

If a ready-turned roller cannot be bought, a piece, square in section, can be suitably planed to shape. The finished length is 16¾ inches, and diameter 1⅝ inches. The length includes the two spindles each ⅜ inch long and ⅜ inch in diameter. The roller ends are cut with tenon saw and chisel to form the spindles. Exercise great care when sawing the roller ends not to undercut the diameters of the spindles.

Having carefully cut the shoulders with the tenon saw, at both ends, the roller is held vertically in the vice and the end marked, with compasses, for cutting downwards with the chisel as far as the saw-cuts. The chiselling should be done piecemeal, carefully working inwards from the circumference. The other end is dealt with similarly. The spindles should be perfectly round, and smoothed to run in the bracket holes without friction. The roller must revolve quite freely; if the fit is too tight, the shoulder can be suitably reduced in diameter.

This fixture may be painted, to match the wall or door; or it may be stained, or polished, or stained and polished. If there is likelihood of the brackets making contact with and damaging the wall when the door is opened, a door stop should be screwed to the floor to limit the angle of opening. A similar precaution saves the door from injury if the towel rail is fixed to the wall.

Stationary Rack. Lighter fixtures for ordinary towels take a variety of forms and these may be purchased at most hardware stores. Others, equally simple, can be made at home. For fixing a rail behind a door, perhaps the simplest arrangement of all consists of a length of brass curtain rod coated with white enamel paint, and fastened between two brackets of the type used for holding small window curtains. This does not provide much space between rail and door (or wall) but it serves its purpose.

Greater space is allowed in the fixture at Fig. 45, which is suitable for fixing to the side frame of a

washstand, or to a door or wall. Two semi-circular pieces of hardwood, each 1 inch thick, are cut 3 inches long and 3 inches wide, as brackets.

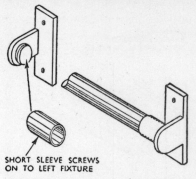

SHORT SLEEVE SCREWS
ON TO LEFT FIXTURE

Fig. 44. A towel rail made from curtain rod and brackets.

These are joined by a strip 1 inch wide and 3/8 inch thick, its length being adapted to the space it is to occupy. If there is nothing to limit the distance between brackets (as on a wall) this should exceed by about

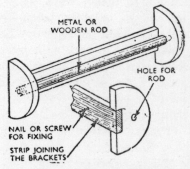

METAL OR
WOODEN ROD

HOLE FOR
ROD

NAIL OR SCREW
FOR FIXING

STRIP JOINING
THE BRACKETS

Fig. 45. A towel rail suitable for attachment to side of door.

2 inches the width of an ordinary towel. The strip is sunk to its own thickness centrally in the straight edge of each bracket and there glued and screwed. In the center of each bracket, a hole is bored to take the

metal or wooden rod. This fixture is polished or stained or painted to match the surface to which it is attached by two screws or nails. Should any difficulty be experienced in cutting the brackets to the semi-circular form shown, these can equally well be oblong: 3 inches wide by about 4 inches long.

Swivelling Rack. A swivelling towel rack is sometimes a great convenience, as in limited space. It is especially adapted for fixing to the wall above a kitchen sink. Before installing, be careful to select a location where the rack cannot swing in the way.

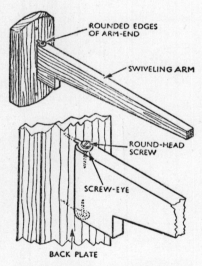

ROUNDED EDGES OF ARM-END

SWIVELING ARM

ROUND-HEAD SCREW

SCREW-EYE

BACK PLATE

Fig. 46. A swivelling towel rail and a part view of the hinge on back piece.

As shown in Fig. 46, it consists of two pieces of wood only, the swivelling arm being attached to the back plate by means of two round-head screws which are lodged in fairly substantial brass screw eyes in the face of the back plate. Both pieces are of hardwood 3 inches wide and ¾ inch thick.

The back plate, or supporting block, is 6 inches long and is rounded off at top and bottom. A slender brass screw is set 1 inch from each end to fix it to the wall surface. The swivelling arm is about 16 inches long. The length may be varied to fit your needs but it should fall short of the front of the sink by about 1 inch. At 3 inches from the inner end it is cut in 1 inch, and from that point it narrows to ¾ inch at the outer end. The edges of the inner end are rounded, to allow free movement against the back plate.

The two brass screw eyes which form part of the hinge are screwed into the face of the back plate a shade in excess of 3 inches apart, in line down the center. When these are in place, the tapered arm is placed between them and pencil marks made on top and bottom edges where the roundhead screws (which will engage in the screw eyes) are to go. Holes for these are then bored, but not to the full depth of the screws, and the latter inserted, one from below, the other from above, as shown in Fig. 46).

STEPLADDER

Strength is an essential factor in the design of a stepladder, but lightness and dimensions which permit easy movement from one part of the house to another are important considerations. The ladder to be described meets these requirements, but the dimensions may be varied according to the particular use to which it is intended.

The lumber used throughout is of 1-inch stock (⅞ inch when finished) and of good, sound quality. The quantities required are as follows:

MEMBERS	NUMBER OF LENGTHS	DIMENSIONS IN INCHES
Legs	2	51 x 2½
Top Brace	1	13 x 2½
Bottom Brace	1	18 x 2½
Treads	1	84 x 5
Top Piece	1	15 x 8
Back Piece	1	13 x 6
Stringers	2	63 x 4

First mark off the bottom of one stringer at an angle of 30 degrees on the width and some 5 degrees on the thickness and cut off the waste. At intervals of 10 inches draw guide lines parallel with, and measured from, the bottom. These guide lines indicate the center line of treads; the marking off for the saw cuts should therefore be $\frac{7}{16}$ inch on either side of these lines. Now mark off a total length of 5 feet and saw off the waste, making the cut parallel with the bottom. Note that no sawcuts for the tread grooves have yet been made. Cut and mark off the second stringer similarly, remembering that the guide lines will face each other when the stringers have been cut as shown in Fig. 47. Measurements must again be made from the bottom so that the stringers will correspond.

Check the marking by placing both lengths of wood together with the pencil marks outwards.

Having confirmed that the tread positions agree, lay the stringers on

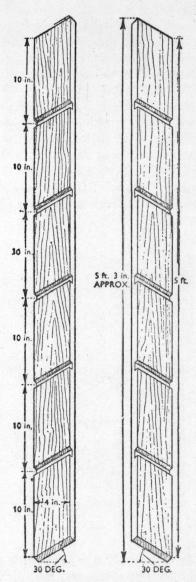

Fig. 47. Dimensions for stringers of stepladder showing inside faces, each cut to house five treads. The angles at tops and bottoms of stringers must match the angles of the tread housings.

edge, guide lines inwards, and position them 12 inches apart at the fifth

tread from the bottom and 18 inches apart (inside measurement) at the bottom tread. Secure the stringers in this position by tacking a piece of scrap board at each end to hold them. By this arrangement the angle of the groove cuts can be marked.

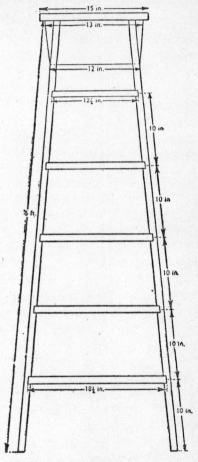

Fig. 48. Showing front view of stepladder and overall dimensions of the assembled treads, stringers, and strengthening pieces at back.

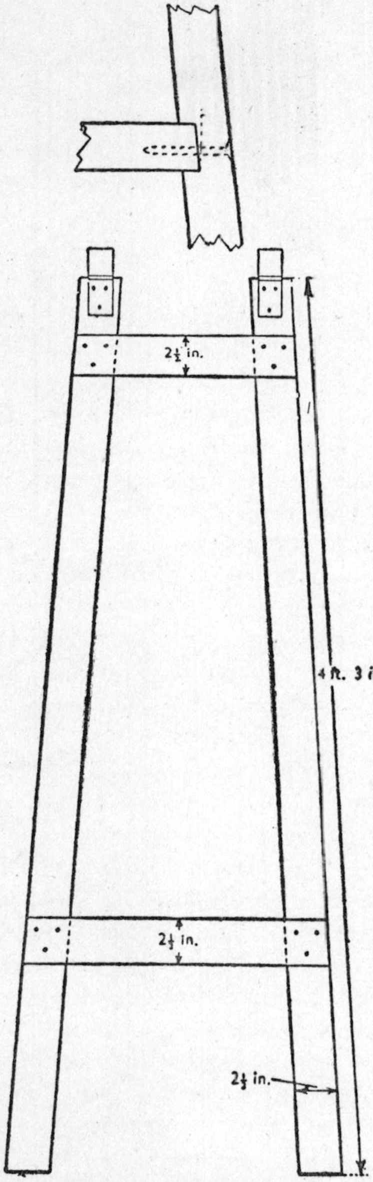

Fig. 49. Shows legs and braces assembled, back flap hinges in position. Top insert: Part view of a tread secured in a groove of a stringer by a nail.

Mark the depth of the grooves using a marking gauge set to ¼ inch.

The tread grooves can now be cut to the required depth with a tenon saw. Chisel out the waste. It is better to chisel out slightly less than the required depth, the final chiselling being done when the treads are fitted.

With all grooves cut, position and temporarily secure the stringers as before. Now mark off the length of the bottom tread, using as a guide the distance between the deepest parts of the tread grooves already cut into the stringers for this tread. If the grooves have been cut accurately, and the stringers properly placed, the length of the tread should measure 18½ inches, including the ¼ inch allowed at each end for fitting into the grooves in the stringers. Trim each end of the tread to match the tapering angle of the stringers, i. e. about 5 degrees. If the tread fails to fit the grooves snugly, adjust the grooves to fit the length of the tread. The front edge of the tread should project about 1 inch and the back edge must be flush. If the back of the tread projects even slightly it will interfere with the closing of the legs.

Mark off, cut, and fit the fifth tread from the bottom in a similar way. While countersunk screws are more stable, three 2-inch nails may be used to secure the ends of each tread in the grooves of the stringers. If nails are used, use a nail punch to drive the heads below the surface. The other three treads may now be marked off, cut and fitted (See Fig. 49).

Take particular care to mark the exact length of each tread. Chamfer the forward corners of treads. With these fitted, the most difficult part of the work is completed.

Before the front section of the steps is complete, a back piece and top piece must be fitted. (See Fig. 48). Cut the top piece first. It is to be 15 inches by 8 inches. Lay it centrally over the head of the stringers with a projection of 1 inch to the front. Nail the top piece firmly into place at the top of the stringers with 8*d* nails.

The cutting of the back piece is a little more difficult. First cut a piece 13 inches by 6 inches and plane one edge to an angle of 30 degrees. Try this under the top piece. It should fit snugly into the angle formed by the back projection of the top piece and the stringers. Center it and mark off the point of intersection of the bottom edge and the outside face of the stringers. Mark off from this point to the top corner and cut. Nail into position. This completes the front section.

Next, cut the legs in the following manner. Take the front section and lay it face downward. Place one of the legs so that one end butts on the bottom edge of the back piece and the outside edge lies flush with the outside face of one of the stringers. Mark the top end of the leg and cut it at an angle so that it will butt flush against the bottom edge of the back piece. Mark off 4 feet 3 inches and make another cut parallel to the cut at the top end of the leg. The other leg is dealt with similarly. It will be noted that the bottom ends of the legs are not at right angles to the edges of the legs.

Place the legs in position again on the front section. Mark off the bottom brace by placing a length 12 inches from the foot of the legs. The top brace is marked off 3 inches from the top of the legs. The braces can now be screwed on to the legs.

All that remains to be done is the fitting of the restraining cords. Drill a ⅜ inch hole in each stringer 18 inches from the foot and one in each leg 17½ from the bottom.

Cut two lengths of sash cord each 4 feet long. Make a "figure eight"

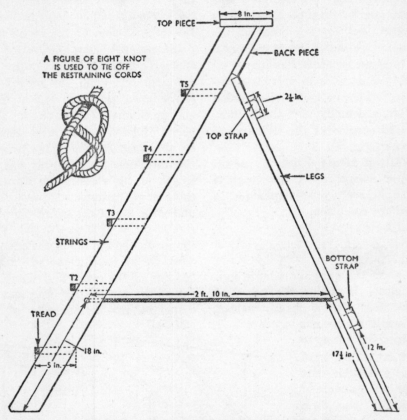

Fig. 50. Side elevation of completed stepladder showing restraining cord and enlarged view of the knot to be tied at the ends of the cords, after fitting to ladder.

Hinges are fitted to the legs as shown in Fig. 49 and then to the back piece. Care should be taken in fitting these hinges otherwise the steps will not stand evenly when open.

knob at one end of each length and thread through the holes in the stringers. (See Fig. 50). Place the steps upright and open the legs until the treads are horizontal. Make sure that this operation is effected on a level floor. Thread the cord through the legs and tie off again with a knot. Make the cord a little less than the actual measurement to allow for stretching. But be certain that each cord takes equal strain when the ladder is subjected to loading.

The steps are now complete and should stand firmly on a level floor although a little trimming of the bottom ends of the legs may be necessary to achieve this. Sandpaper all corners and edges to prevent splinters entering the hands when using the steps. Finally, cut the bottom, forward corners of the stringers as shown in Fig. 50.

While it is not absolutely necessary, a coat of good spar varnish will help keep your stepladder in shipshape condition.

STAIRWAY CLOSET

A good place to build a large storage closet is under the basement stairs. This area is usually wasted, and while it may not be an ideal place to store articles used frequently, it does make an excellent place for long term storage and thus frees closet space throughout the rest of the house for daily needs. Naturally, if the basement is damp, no articles should be stored there until the cause of the dampness has been eliminated or the

articles have been treated to prevent them from rusting or mildewing.

Assuming that the basement floor is made of concrete, the first job is to outline the base of the closet with 2 x 4's. These should be placed with the 4-inch surface up and secured to the concrete by means of expansion bolts. They should extend in length from the bottom of the stairs to a point directly below the top of the stairs. To find this exact point, drop a plumb line from the top of the stairs down alongside one stringer and mark the location on the floor below. Make this same measurement on the floor on the opposite side. Use these two points to lay out the length of the closet, then attach a short length of lumber between them under the top of the stairs. Now uprights, made of 2 x 4's, should be dropped from the top of the stringer down to the base. These will frame one end of the closet and should be cut at the top so that they can be nailed on the bottom edge of the

Fig. 51. Suggested arrangement for building large storage closet under basement stairs.

stringer. To find the right angle to cut the uprights, place the lower end at the proper point and let the top end extend up a few inches along the side of the stringers. Take a pencil and mark along the upright where it meets the stringer. Cut along this line, and the upright should then fit snugly under the bottom edge of the stringer. Do this with the other upright and nail them into place.

You will need a similar set of uprights about half the total length of the closet. If the closet is to have a single door, the opening for it should be framed with additional uprights. If a double door is selected, there should be an upright where the two doors are to meet, in addition to one on each side, on which to hang the doors.

Shelving. When all the uprights are in place, you can put in the shelving, if any is to be used. Some method will be needed to hold the shelving in place and this can be done by nailing 2 x 4 cleats between the two rear uprights and also between the front uprights. One simple way to nail the shelving running to the stairs is to nail cleats to the bottom of the risers. Each riser is about 7 inches high, and if every other riser is used it will give a distance of 14 inches between each shelf. If more space is required, skip another riser. Make sure that all cleats for one layer of shelving are the same distance from the floor.

The shelving should be made out of 1-inch tongued and grooved stock. If short pieces are to be used, make sure that the joint occurs at the rear frame so that the end of each board can be nailed to the cleat. The first piece of shelving will have to be notched out to fit around the uprights.

The last piece of shelving will probably have to be cut down in length to make up the exact width of the closet.

The sides and back of the closet can be made of plywood or composition board. As a final point, it would be wise to have some sort of lighting facilities inside the closet. The best would be a light fixture hung to the underportion of the stairs and controlled by a switch near the closet door.

FLUSH DOOR

It is presumed that a room door fitted with a mortise lock is to be the subject of the operations. First of all, examine the door to make sure it hangs correctly and is not warped. It is impossible to make a success of a door that has bent or warped out of line.

In order to avoid complications, endeavour to work so that the hinges need not be shifted. This means, if both faces of the door are to be covered flush, that the plywood cover on the inside face (the side where the knuckles of the hinges are) will have to be bevelled back and cut around the knuckles. The plywood, of course, adds to the thickness of the door, but if the edge mentioned is bevelled, the fact that the door projects inward here will hardly be noticed. At the locking side, the door stop can be adjusted so that the face of the door, after covering, comes flush with the door casing. The door stops will have to be taken down and replaced to suit the added thickness of the door on the outer side (opposite to the knuckle face).

The lock will not be altered, and the striking plate also should stay as before. Obviously, any defects should be noted and remedied before fitting the flush covering or in the process of that work.

Furthermore, the door hardware will have to be taken off, and it is probable that a longer shaft for the door knobs will be needed to allow for the extra thickness of the altered door.

Take off the door knobs first, unscrewing the set screw in one knob and then drawing the other knob and the shaft out. The escutcheon plates should be removed and marked in accordance with the side of the door to which each belongs. Next, unscrew the hinge from the door jamb, *not* from the door itself. If the hinge plates are held together by means of a removable pin, it will not be necessary to remove the hinge; merely take out the pin. If any molding around the door panels stands out from the general level of the door face, this must be taken off or planed away and sandpapered down level. If the door is painted or varnished, take a cabinet scraper and scrape off the finish all around the door framing, that is, the stiles and rails or upright members. The object is to leave a clean surface to

which glue can properly adhere. If the door is merely stained, rubbing with coarse sandpaper at the places mentioned will suffice. Remember that furniture polish, grease or oil will repel glue and must be removed before gluing is begun.

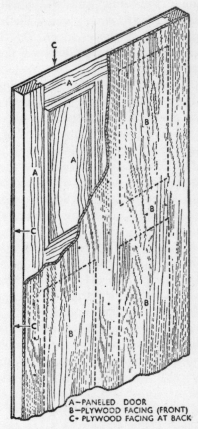

A—PANELED DOOR
B—PLYWOOD FACING (FRONT)
C—PLYWOOD FACING AT BACK

Fig. 52. A flush door. Location of door hardware omitted. If the door is fitted with a mortice lock it should be removed to facilitate the planing of the plywood edges if necessary.

Plywood. Choose two sheets of plywood having a pleasant grain and reasonably matching, for the faces of the door. Cut to size, a piece for each face of the door. Mark the pieces for the respective sides and for top and bottom. See that they are used for the corresponding positions as indicated. The plywood may be left a little wide and long, and planed down after fixing. It should be cut with a fine-toothed saw, while resting solidly on two saw horses or benches. This is a job where some assistance will be required. The saw will leave a burr on the underside, so cut from the top or best side, to leave the burr on the side that will not show.

Flush Facing. The method recommended is to get the main fixing by means of fine screws (No. 4, 5/8 inch long), and to use 1-inch veneer pins where the board shows any tendency to belly out. Hot or cold water wood glue is to be applied to the underside of the board where it will come against the cleaned parts of the frame, and these parts also are to be spread with glue. The worker will need as many small clamps or handscrews as he can provide—up to eight or a dozen. Go around the edges of the plywood, about 1 inch in from the outer edge, and bore holes with a drill to take the shank of the screws. These holes should be placed about a foot apart. Countersink the holes somewhat deeply, but leave enough wood for the screw heads to bite on. After the screws have been inserted, the holes are filled with plastic wood, which on drying, is sanded level and stained to match the plywood. Plastic wood will not adhere in very shallow holes, so countersink as deeply as is safe.

Screws are to be inserted wherever there are crossbars or intermediate rails or uprights in the old door. There is not time to do all this once we have laid the plywood in place on the glued surface.

Use sandpaper to smooth off any burr left by drilling on the underside of the plywood; try the latter in place, while the door is resting ready for the job. Then apply glue to the door frame, fairly liberally; lay the plywood in place and test it at the edges for correct position. Tap four 1-inch veneer pins partly through at the corners, to prevent movement of the sheet; these pins will have to be pulled out later. Now, working from the middle part of the door, bore holes one by one into the door frame for the screws, going in through the holes already made in the plywood. Insert the screws and turn them until they are securely set (avoid overtightening). Work from the center toward the edges of the door, to sides, top and bottom. If these operations proceed satisfactorily, insert the screws in the holes bored along the edges.

Now is the time to use the clamps, inserting slips of waste plywood between the jaws of the clamp and the faces of the door. Take out the temporary pins first inserted. Watch carefully to see that the sheet does not bulge or belly out between the screwed fixings. By taking out a screw here and there such a defect can be at once remedied. Speed is as important as cautious and accurate assembly, if disappointment is to be avoided. Perhaps here and there a veneer pin can be driven in so as to take down any swelling, but if the door face is level there should not be much trouble. Go over the screws to ensure that they are fully set; after which, the door, with clamps on, should be placed approximately upright against the wall in a warm room, with the faced side showing. It will thus rest on the uncovered edge, and there will be no end pressure on the plywood edge at the bottom.

Face the second side of the door after the glue has set hard. But before the second side is put on, mark and bore the holes for the door knobs and keyhole. These are marked with a fine brad awl from the uncovered side of the door, where the existing holes will serve as guide. The knob shaft hole is merely a round one of ample diameter; after marking its center with a fine bradawl from the uncovered side, bore through the exposed or outer face of the plywood sheet with a brace and bit; this will avoid splitting the plywood.

Similarly, mark two holes to show where the bit has to go in at top and bottom of the keyhole; bore these holes through the exposed face of the plywood panel, as before.

A keyhole saw can be used to connect the two holes and form a slot to allow the doorkey to enter. Do not drill and saw out the second piece of plywood until it is finally fixed.

The final job is to glue on and fix the second sheet of plywood. Lay the door on some clean paper to protect the face already covered. Proceed with the attachment of the second sheet of plywood as with the first. Allow this side to rest until the glue has set hard, and then clean off the edges of the plywood sheet all round, using a block plane and a chisel, and finish with sandpaper. Mark and bore the holes for the shaft and key. If the door was painted, the edges will have to be cleaned and stained to match the plywood. The edges of the plywood will have to be stained also but be careful not to use more stain than is necessary to give them the proper color.

When all the rest of the work has been done, the door hardware can be replaced. As mentioned earlier, the shaft, if short in the first place, may need replacement by a longer one, which can be bought at most hardware stores. Usually, however, there is ample length as fitted.

Door Stops. Take off the stops carefully if they have to be used again. Pry them away with a thin chisel; the nails may come out easily, or the stop may pull away over the heads of the nails, leaving the nails to be pulled out with pincers. In some cases the edge of the stops may require planing down to reduce the width, though usually there is plenty of room in the casing to allow the stop to set farther back, and it is merely a question of readjustment in a suitable position to accommodate the extra thickness of the door. Knock out the nails, and use new finishing nails to fix the stops again.

But before putting the stops back we must rehang the door, so as to see where they should go. The door being hung again, cut slips of cardboard, about as thick as a penny, and, the door being fastened by its latch, place one of the long stops against the door face, with two pieces of cardboard inserted, one about 6 inches from the floor and the other at the same distance from the top. The idea is to allow a little clearance between the door and the inner face of the door stop. After the latter has been fixed, there will be the thickness of the cardboard between it and the door face. Tack the stop in place temporarily with two nails driven in only part way. Attach the top stop similarly, and the remaining long side. If all is correct, and the door shuts satisfactorily, without too much play, proceed to nail the stops tightly. The nails are driven in, the heads punched down below the wood surface, and the holes filled with putty or plastic wood.

Since so much trouble has been taken to remodel the door itself, it is worthwhile, when the other decorative finish is in keeping, to fix new door stops made of wood to match the plywood face on the door.

BUILDING A DOORWAY

In an effort to make a house more comfortable and efficient, the home mechanic is often faced with the task of putting a doorway through an inside wall. This is a sizable undertaking and calls for much planning and measuring before the real work begins. On the other hand, the home carpenter possessing the average skill with saw and hammer can do the job and do it well provided he takes his time and utilizes all his skill.

The first point to settle is the exact location of the doorway in the wall. After you have selected the approximate position for the doorway, try and visualize the door in place and see how this fits in with the rest of the room. It may be that a door in the spot you first had in mind would spoil the appearance of the room, or not be as conveniently located as another position. Give this matter of location plenty of time and thought, because once you have cut through the wall the only alternative, besides going ahead with the project, is to try and patch up the damage.

Try to locate one side of the doorway to take advantage of the vertical wall studding. This will make the job easier and also save lumber. You can usually locate the position of the studding by tapping on the wall surface. If the wall is made of wallboard instead of plaster, then the studding can be located by the nail heads in the wallboard.

Once you have the studding located you can set about measuring for the opening in the wall. To find out how wide the opening should be, measure the width of the door and the thickness of the two jambs or casing which go on each side of the door frame. You must also figure in one eighth of an inch between each side of the door and the jambs for clearance, and one half inch between the jambs and the studding or rough door frame. The purpose of this half inch clearance is to allow you to plumb the jamb with blocks of wood or wood wedges. The final figure that enters into the width of the opening is the studding on each side of the frame and this should be made of two 2 x 4 in. If it has been possible to use one of the lengths of wall studding for the door frame, then you will only have to add the widths of three 2 x 4 in. to get the final measurement for the frame width.

As for the height, you first measure the height of the door and add to this the thickness of the threshold (if one is to be used) plus the thickness of the head or top casing and plus the thickness of a head 2 x 4 in. which is nailed horizontally between the vertical studding. Leave a half inch clearance between the head 2 x 4 in. and the top casing so you will be able to bring the casing up level.

At this point you may decide that it would be a great deal easier to purchase a door complete with casing and these can be had at most lumber yards. They naturally are more expensive than just a door with the necessary boards for the casing, because with these complete door assemblies, all the work of cutting and fitting the casing has been done at the lumber mill.

When the width and height of the opening for the doorway have been determined, the next job is to mark out the area on the wall. Use both a level and plumb line to get these lines true, or the door will neither fit nor hang correctly.

Now begins the job of cutting through the wall. If the wall is made of wallboard, there is not much of a problem as this material is easily cut with a handsaw. Cut out one side of the wall first and remove the wallboard. In almost every case it will be necessary to pull some nails holding the board to the studding. If these nails are pulled out carefully you will have sections of wallboard that can be used for some other job, but if you try to rip the wallboard off, you will ruin it for any other possible use. With the wallboard out of the way, the studding and backside of the opposite wall will be exposed. Mark out the doorway on this side, cut and remove the wallboard. Now all that is left in the opening will be some studding, and this can be removed by cutting at the top and then pulling out the nails holding it at the bottom. Studding is usually nailed at the bottom to a piece of 2 x 4 in. resting on the floor. This is called the shoe and a section of it will have to be cut out the same width as the doorway. The usual method of framing a door is to have the inside pieces of studding on each side of the door nailed at the bottom onto the shoe. The shoe is then cut off flush with side of the studding and the outside piece of studding is then nailed directly to the floor and sideways into the shoe.

Plaster walls present more of a problem so far as the cutting out is concerned. One way of doing this job is to cut through the plaster with a cold chisel and then cut through the laths with a saw. Be as careful as possible when you cut the plaster because if large chunks are broken off, they will not be covered by the door trim and you will be in for an extensive patching job. Another point to watch for is to be certain that all the plaster has been cut before you begin sawing. If you try to saw through plaster, the saw will become dulled. Once the plaster has been cut along the marked lines, a compass saw can be inserted and this will quickly and efficiently cut through the wood laths.

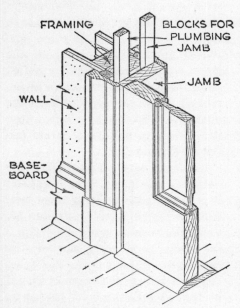

FRAMING

BLOCKS FOR PLUMBING JAMB

JAMB

WALL

BASE-BOARD

Fig. 53. Detail showing how door jambs are attached to rough frame.

The job of cutting and removing plaster will naturally make a considerable mess so it is a good plan before starting to cover the surrounding floor with newspapers, or, better still, a large sheet of canvas.

Once the plaster and laths have been cut, they can be removed and the studding taken out.

The next job is to frame the doorway. If you were lucky enough to arrange the location of the doorway in such a manner that the wall studding forms one or even both sides of the door, this job will not be too difficult because the additional studding can be spiked to the wall studding. If such an arrangement is impossible, then additional plaster must be removed so that the door studding can be nailed securely at the ceiling.

Take the necessary time to get the door frame as plumb as possible, as this will save you time and work when you put in the jambs. When the vertical frame is up and nailed at top and bottom, place a horizontal stud between the sides to frame the top of the doorway. Check this with a level and toe-nail it to the vertical pieces.

When the frame is finished the opening is ready for the jambs. These must be plumb or else the door will never open and close properly. Use wood wedges and blocks placed between the jamb and the frame to hold the jambs plumb in the frame.

STORM PORCHES

Two of the greatest sources of heat loss in a house are the front and back doors which are opened innumerable times each day to let in a blast of icy wind and let out a lot of warm air. One way to combat this difficulty is to build a storm porch around one of the doors and use the remaining door as little as possible. The storm porch will act more or less as an intermediary between the warm interior of the house and the cold outside. Not only will a well-built storm porch help to keep the house comfortable, but if it is built large enough it also will provide a place for members of the household to remove their heavy overshoes, leave their umbrellas, etc., and thus save the house from being tracked up with snow and water.

As to the question of size, the porch should be at least large enough so that the house door can be closed by the person on the porch with sufficient room to turn comfortably to open the porch door. In the long run it is best to build a porch large enough to accommodate several persons.

The porch can be as decorative as you can make it. Some householders have the porch made out of the same material as used for the house. Thus, the porch might have white clapboard siding to match the outside walls of the house and a roof of shingles the same as the main roof. This is purely a question of taste, but it should be remembered that a storm porch is only up for a few months of the year and no great harm is done by letting it look like what it is—a temporary structure.

The average home mechanic would want a porch that he could take down and put up by himself and for this purpose he will find that asbestos board, plywood, or a composition wood is best suited for the sides of the porch. These materials come in large sheets, are light in weight and can be sawed and nailed. They can be purchased in sheets of sufficient size so that one sheet alone will serve as an entire side of the porch.

If there is an open porch or large stoop at the front doorway, this can be used as the floor of the porch and a base upon which to attach the sides. If there is not sufficient space, or no stoop or porch at all, the floor of the porch should be made as a separate unit. Another question that must be decided in advance is whether or not the storm porch is to have a separate roof. If there is a roofed porch at the front of the house and the roof is under 8 feet from the floor, this can serve as the roof of the storm porch. Should the house porch roof be over 8 feet high it is better to build a separate one for the storm porch.

Once you have a base or floor for the porch and have decided what size it is to be, make up your three wall sections accordingly. The frames for these units can be made out of 2 x 2 in. stock, although a smaller size can be used in some cases. The opening for the door of the porch should be framed with 2 x 4 in. lumber as these will have to carry the entire weight of the door. You will find it easier to set all the sections up first and then hang the door when the porch is completed.

The best method of attaching the sections of the porch together is by the use of hooks and screw eyes, using at least two, and better still, three sets for each joint. The porch in turn is fastened to the side of the house by the same method. If the house siding is made of wood you will have no difficulty in attaching the screw eyes, but if the walls are made of brick, stone or stucco you will have to use rawl plugs or some type of expansion bolt.

can go up and this will be supported by the two side pieces.

If a roof is required it can be of the same material used for the sides. Cut the section for the roof so that it overhangs at the front and at the sides. The frame for the roof should be fixed in such a way that it will fit snugly around the inside of the open-

Fig. 54. How a storm porch can be built using floor and roof of open porch.

Mark on the floor or porch base the exact location of each side. Place the section upright on this mark and brace it while you attach it to the floor with wood screws. Put the two side sections up first and attach these to the walls of the house. When these are secure, the door or front section

ing made by the three other sections. In this way it will be possible to attach the roof to the sides with hooks and screw eyes.

When the porch is to be equipped with a separate roof, the tops of the two side sections should be cut at an angle so that the roof has pitch.

FINISHING THE ATTIC

It is common practice these days for the builder of a house to leave the attic unfinished; but the necessary provisions are often arranged so that the attic can, at some later date, and at the convenience of the home owner, be made into one or more rooms. These "expansion attics," as they are sometimes called, offer a great many possibilities to the home mechanic who is willing to spend a little time, effort, and money to add one or more attractive yet low cost rooms to his house. For example, as the family grows in size, an extra bedroom is a great convenience; or this same space can be used for a quiet study, private sitting room, playroom, or library. And finally, if the attic is large enough a complete and self-contained small apartment can be made out of it. It is worth mentioning at this point that small attractive apartments are always in demand. The rent from such apartments will soon pay for the materials used in construction and the home owner can look forward, after this expense has been paid off, to a steady income which will help bolster up the family budget.

Before the work of finishing the attic begins, however, it is wise to make a complete survey of the space at hand so that every detail may be used to the greatest advantage for the purpose in mind. Local building authorities should be consulted, for if the space is to be used for living quarters, certain regulations as to materials and construction methods must be complied with. For example, some communities demand that there be two methods of exit from a dwelling. If the attic has but one stairway, and this is usually the case, then it may be necessary to build another entrance and exit to the attic.

Some building codes demand that certain types of materials be used for the construction and finishing of the attic and if they are not used, then the apartment will not pass the local building inspection and hence cannot be put up for rental. Also you had better be sure there is no local zoning ordinance against two-family houses, as it would be a shame for you to go to the labor and expense of fixing up a small apartment and then find you could not legally rent it. However, difficulties of that nature will not prevent you from using the space yourself, which is what a home owner would probably want to do anyway in a majority of cases.

There are quite a number of items of this general nature which must be given careful consideration before work begins. But regardless of the minimum requirements of local building codes and regulations, it is to the home owner's own advantage to use only first class materials for the job, no matter how the space is to be used. As a general rule, better grade materials will pay off in longer and better service.

The entire attic need not be utilized at one time. It may be more convenient to construct one room now, a bedroom perhaps, and then add other rooms such as a bath and kitchen at some later date. But if this is to be done, plans should be made

now as to the exact location of these other rooms. It might even be wise to bring up the necessary pipes for the kitchen and bath fixtures and cap them. In that way work in the room finished first would not have to be ripped up later to permit fixtures to be put in.

In case you find it hard to visualize just what might be done about building a small but complete attic apartment, Fig. 1 shows a plan view of such an apartment, with an attic space of about 17 by 37 feet. Remember that you can figure on using only that part of the attic far enough from the eaves so that your side walls

FINISHED ATTIC

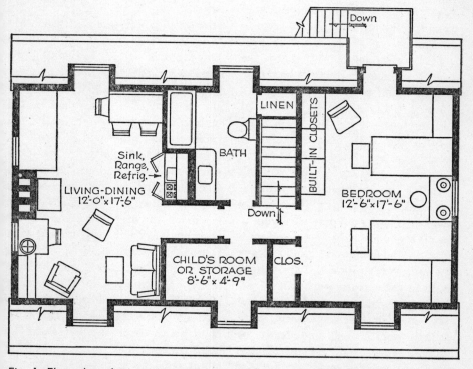

Fig. 1. Floor plan of an attic apartment in which cooking arrangements are reduced to the barest minimum. Five of the projections indicated are for dormer windows and the sixth leads to an outside staircase.

will be 3 or 4 feet high. Measure your attic and make your plans accordingly. In Fig. 1 five small dormer windows and an outside staircase have been built.

Once the plans for the attic space have been completed, then comes the question as to who is to do the work. Naturally, the cheapest method would be for the home mechanic to do the entire job in his spare time, but there are several reasons why this may not be possible. In the first place, many local codes insist that work such as plumbing and wiring be done only by experienced workmen; and in the second place, a job such as adding an extra bathroom requires many special tools, as well as a special knowledge and experience in connection with the subject.

It is very possible that by the time the home mechanic has purchased the necessary equipment, completed his work, and corrected his mistakes made by "trial and error," he will discover that it would have been cheaper to have had the work done by a professional. Barring any restrictions by building codes, the smart plan would seem to be for the home mechanic to do all the work which he feels confident that he can do well, and to leave the more unfamiliar and specialized tasks to the trained workman.

Many home owners have worked out excellent arrangements with skilled workers of one trade or another, whereby the home mechanic does most of the unskilled part of the jobs, while the skilled craftsman drops in only to do the tricky work and to give advice. This is a great saving in time and labor, for during an evening the home mechanic can do the necessary preliminaries, so that on the following day the skilled professional need not waste his time on unskilled tasks but can devote his time to the complicated jobs.

Heating the Attic. A good deal of thought must be given to the matter of how the attic rooms are to be heated during the winter months. If no heating arrangement is made, then the rooms or apartment will be livable for perhaps only half the year —considerable loss in any case.

If the house is heated with warm air, it may be possible as well as practical to install registers in the attic floor or walls, so that warm air from the rooms below will flow up. Another possibility is to install additional hot air ducts with electric fans to force the heated air from the furnace into the attic. For homes heated with steam or hot water, additional radiators and pipes will be required.

But heating the attic by means of the house heating plant depends on whether or not the plant can take on this extra load and still keep all the rooms on the first and second floors comfortable. To answer this question it would be wise to call in a heating engineer or contractor and let him check the capacity of the heating plant. If the furnace is too small to take on the extra load of the attic, then some other method must be used to heat it, or a larger heating plant must be installed. Electric or gas space heaters can be used for heating the attic rooms, and they are convenient as well as clean. However, if electric heaters are to be used, remember that heavy-duty circuit wiring will be necessary to handle a heavy electric load. Gas heaters will require pipes running to the main, and the work of installing them should be done before the attic is completed. In any case, be sure that the necessary provisions are made to heat the attic so that it will be comfortable either for members of the family or for tenants.

Another point that is worth remembering in case the attic apartment is to be rented, is that it is better for the landlord to pay for the heating and to charge a little more rent, than to leave the entire heating problem up to the tenant. But even that is not always true. If electric or gas heaters are installed, you might reason that the power or gas lines for the attic apartment should go through separate meters from those of the rest of the house and the tenant pay the attic heating cost. That would not be exactly accurate as some heat from the lower part of the house will rise to help warm the attic rooms. On the other hand, if the owner pays for the heating, the tenant may turn on gas or electric heaters recklessly and be very wasteful about the fuel burned. So you see no hard and fast rules can be laid down about the best procedure in all cases, so far as heating is concerned.

Attic Plumbing. If the attic is to be finished off as additional rooms for the house, then an attic bathroom is not necessary, although it may prove a great convenience. However, if a separate apartment is to be created, at least a small bathroom is essential.

Probably the best location for the attic bathroom will be directly above one on the floor below. It will be cheaper to run pipes up the shortest distance, naturally, but sometimes there are other considerations. The stairs to the attic may make such a location undesirable or the bathroom below may be too near the eaves. However, a large dormer window might solve the latter problem.

Also, if the house sewage system is taken care of by either a septic tank or cesspool, this equipment may not be large enough to carry the load of another bathroom and kitchen. To handle that problem, either a larger tank would have to be installed or an additional sewer system put in for the attic. In any event it would be most advisable to consult a plumber on plumbing problems before the location of the bathroom and kitchen are definitely decided on.

Another point to be considered is whether the size of the pipes used in the house is large enough to provide the attic with a proper flow of water. Then there is the question of hot water: is the house heater and tank large enough to supply the additional demands of attic rooms? If not, it may be necessary to install a larger heater or a larger tank or both in order to supply planned attic rooms with adequate hot water.

The attic bathroom does not have to take up a great deal of floor space but it should be complete. Attractive bathrooms can be constructed in a space of less than six feet square. See

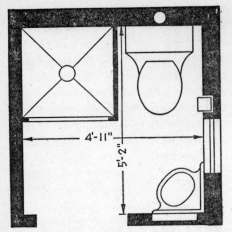

Fig. 2. Floor plan for an attic bathroom less than 6 feet square. Shower, toilet, washbowl and window are indicated.

Fig. 2 for a floor plan of such a bathroom. Installing a shower bath instead of a tub will save space if there is plenty of headroom for it, but on the other hand less headroom is needed over a tub since people seldom stand in one unless there is a shower attached. Also, it is now possible to get tubs considerably smaller than the old-fashioned styles. Your local plumber or plumbing supply house can give you good advice in your plans for a modern, compact, and attractive bathroom.

A kitchen of some kind will be needed for an attic apartment. A kitchen sink involves plumbing so the chances are that the best location for the kitchen would be next to bathroom, as that would simplify the piping. When consulting a plumber about the bathroom, do not forget to mention a kitchen.

Another factor in connection with the kitchen is the cooking range. If a gas range is to be used, pipes will have to be run up from the basement or ground floor. If an electric range is to be installed, a three-wire 230-volt electric system will have to be brought up from the entrance of the service lines to the house. So neither possibility is likely to have any distinct advantage due to installation costs.

Attic Flooring. In many cases, when the house is built, no flooring is laid in the attic, so the first job will be to put down a rough flooring over the joists. Care should be taken during this operation not to step between the joists or drop heavy objects onto the laths and plaster of the ceiling below. To avoid this and still be able to work in comfort, it is wise to have some wide planks available to lay over the joists and form a base on which to move about and work.

Next comes the question of getting building materials up to the attic. It may be possible to carry them up the stairs. Or that may be difficult to do without marring the finish in the hall or stairs below. An alternative method is to hoist the materials up outside and bring them in through an attic window. However, that may be difficult if the windows are small. So another possibility is to measure carefully and cut pieces to smaller size outside or in the cellar and carry the lengths ready to use upstairs.

The rough flooring can be made of tongued and grooved stock intended for this purpose. This will serve as a subflooring and the finish flooring can be put down later when the heavy construction has been completed. It would be a waste of time and money to lay the finish flooring at this time, because it is almost sure to become damaged during the work on the rooms.

Start laying the flooring down the length of one side of the attic. The tongue side of the board should face toward the center of the room. See Fig. 3. When putting down the boards be sure that the end joints between pieces of flooring come over a floor joist. If the joints are not supported by a joist, the flooring at that point may sag or even break when stepped on. The chances are that all the ceiling joists are spaced an equal distance apart and this spacing should be kept in mind when cutting the flooring boards. Make all joints in the rough flooring as tight as possible, and see that the tongue of each board fits well into the groove of the one beside it. Before a board is cut for length, sight along one edge to see if it is badly warped. If this is the case, you had better set it aside and use it for short lengths using only the straight pieces of stock for the longer lengths.

Some difficulty will be experienced in nailing down the first few boards, as the pitch of the roof won't allow much room in which to work. As the

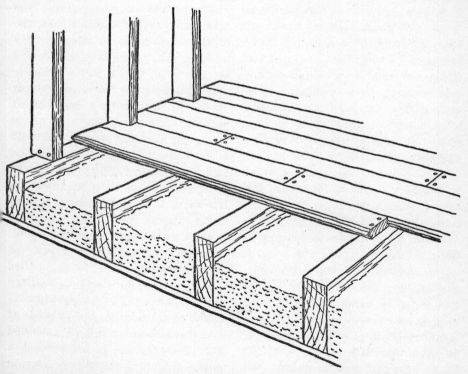

Fig. 3. How to lay an attic floor. Stagger joints, cutting pieces of flooring so that the joints come over joists and are nailed securely. Insulation has been placed between the joists before the floor is laid.

floor progresses, however, and you move out toward the center of the attic, the work will become easier. It may be necessary to rip the last board in order to make it the proper width to fit. When the flooring is all laid, inspect it to make sure that all boards have been properly nailed and that all nails have been driven down. An insufficient number of nails, or nails not driven as far as they will go, will probably cause the floor to squeak later when walked on.

Once the rough flooring has been completed, other materials may be stored in the attic where they will be on hand when needed.

Attic Windows. The chances are that the attic has only two windows, one at each gable, and they are probably rather small ones, hardly satisfactory if the attic is to be used for living quarters. You will likely decide to enlarge these openings, or cut more of them, in order to admit more light. There are many types of windows that can be selected for this purpose, but it will probably be best to pick some of the same general type used throughout the rest of the house, though perhaps smaller in size.

If the window already located in the attic is large enough to provide sufficient ventilation and it is merely a question of desiring more light, this could be secured by installing solid set windows on either side of the window already in place. Solid set windows, such as are used for storm windows, should be the same size as the window you have, and should be cut immediately adjoining

the window you have, so you can reach out to clean the solid-set windows. If more air is desirable, plan on two windows that open with one in between which does not. The foregoing suggestions apply only if your original attic window is 2 by 3 feet or larger. If it is smaller than 2 by 3 feet, you had better plan on replacing it with a larger window or windows.

Windows of many types and sizes can be purchased, ready cut and fitted, from lumber yards and mills. These are complete windows, consisting of sashes, frames, and trim, and should present no great problem to install them.

The opening at the ends of the attic should be cut out to fit the size of the window frame selected. The opening cut in the wall should be somewhat larger than the window frame, so that the frame can be adjusted in the opening and placed absolutely straight.

A portion of the outside wall will have to be cut out and this should be done with care and accuracy. If there are already small windows in the walls, these should be taken out along with the frames and saved for some other purpose. The opening is then enlarged until it is right for the new window.

If there is no opening in the walls, drill holes at the four corners of the section to be removed, and then use a keyhole or compass saw to start the cut. When the cut is large enough a hand saw may be used to finish the job. Do this part of the cutting from the outside.

It will also be necessary to cut out and remove some of the house studding, and the opening should then be framed with double studding and double headers to provide the necessary support. The window frame can then be inserted into the opening, plumbed level and true with wood wedges, and nailed into place. It will be noticed that a groove is cut on the underside of the window sill so that the house siding or shingles can be brought up into the sill. A strip of wood called an apron is then tacked over the joint. The purpose of this arrangement is to prevent rain water blowing along under the sill and getting into the walls.

Next flashing must be put on between window frame and outside wall. How to do this is shown and explained on page 223.

Dormer Windows. In remodeling an attic it may be found that even large windows at the gabled ends do not give the amount of light and ventilation that is required when more than two rooms are to be built. That brings up the possibility of installing one or more dormer windows, samples of which are shown in Figs. 4 to 8. Fig. 5 shows the framework of a pitched roof type dormer and Fig. 4 a picture of the finished job. Fig. 6 shows the framework of the same narrow dormer as viewed from the inside, with part of the roof not shown so the details will be clearer.

Figs. 7 and 8 show the framework and finished view of a flat roof type dormer. Two windows, side by side, could be put in instead of the one as

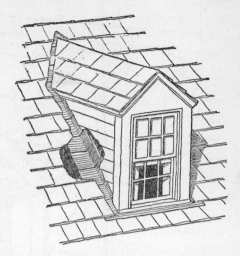

Fig. 4. A dormer window of the pitched roof type with cutouts to show the way copper flashing is put on around the whole dormer.

shown. There is no doubt that dormer windows along the sides of the roof will make any room in the attic more attractive, but it should also be borne in mind that windows of this type will have a decided effect on the outside appearance, even to the point of throwing the general design of the house out of balance. Just how this change will affect the over-all appearance of the house is sometimes difficult for the layman to visualize, and therefore it might be wise to consult an architect on this matter before a final decision is reached.

However, symmetry is a cardinal point to consider, particularly dormers on the front of the house. The wide dormer shown in Fig. 8 would serve well for a bathroom, and would look best in the center of that side of the roof. If you put in the narrow dormer shown in Fig. 4 it might be better to have two of them, equidistant from the ends of the roof.

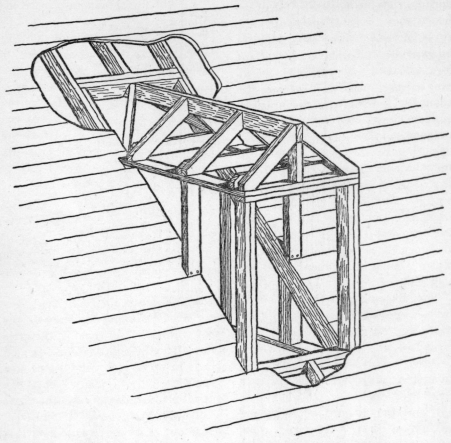

Fig. 5. Framework for a pitched roof type dormer window.

Another point to consider is that the proper construction of a dormer window is a rather sizable undertaking, as it requires the removal of a portion of the roof as well as cutting out some of the roof rafters. It might be safer to have this particular job done by a skilled carpenter. However, if the home mechanic decides to do the job himself, then he should take pains to plan and execute the job in a neat manner.

First of all, remember that most of this work will have to be done while on the roof, so proper scaffolding should be set up so you can work in comfort and safety. And as it will be necessary for the roof to be open for a considerable period of time, the job should be done in warm weather, during a dry spell if possible. In any event, a large sheet of canvas should be on hand for use in covering the opening in case of rain.

Dormer windows can be constructed with either a pitched roof as in Figs. 4 to 6, or with a flat sloped roof as in Figs. 7 and 8. The dormer can be built entirely on a house roof as shown in these pictures, or it can be a continuation of an outside wall. As mentioned before, a dormer with a flat sloped roof can be made large enough to accommodate a bathroom or a small kitchen. Aside from the outside appearances, the size and shape of the dormer will depend on the purpose for which it is intended and the size of the window or windows to be installed.

On examination of Fig. 6 showing the dormer with the pitched roof, it will be noted that the opening in the roof is framed with double rafters. In this respect, when deciding on the width and exact location of the dormer, arrange matters so that the roof rafters will form the two sides. Then double these by spiking rafters

Fig. 6. View of the framework for a pitched roof type dormer window from the inside. Part of the roof has been omitted from drawing to show details of construction.

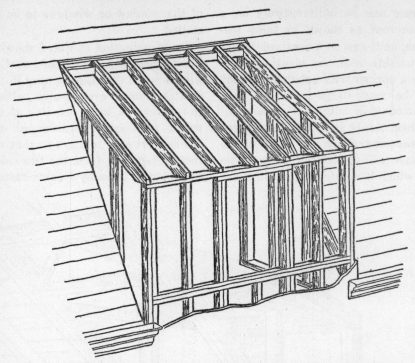

Fig. 7. View of the framework for a sloped roof type dormer window. Notice double studding above space for the window.

of the same size to them. The headers of the opening are also double. The top header is placed at a slight angle that corresponds with the roof pitch while the lower header, which will act as the sill of the dormer, is placed upright, the end rafters being cut at an angle, so that this may be accomplished. The two corner posts at the front of the dormer are double, as is the top plate. Studding forming the sides of the dormer is supported by the double roof rafters on each side. Additional studding runs up from the attic floor to the bottom of these rafters, to form the interior wall of the dormer. The studding broken by the rafters should be in the same line. It will be seen, after studying

the interior view of the dormer, Fig. 5, that it will be necessary to determine in advance where the walls of the attic rooms are to be placed, before these interior studs can be set in position. The studding is not nailed directly to the attic floor but is attached to a 2 x 4 inch sole plate which is nailed to the flooring. The sole (or sole plate) is the horizontal member which bears the studs of the partition.

The dormer with the flat-sloped roof, Figs. 7 and 8, presents something less of a construction problem than the pitched-roof type. Here again the opening for the dormer should be framed with double rafters and headers. Studding forming the sides of the dormer can be set on top of the rafters, as was the case with the pitched-roof dormer, or can be extended unbroken from the attic floor, running on the inside of the roof rafters.

After the dormer has been framed it can be covered with either tongue-and-groove sheathing, or a type of composition board used for this same purpose.

Because of the construction and location of a dormer window it is very important that it be properly flashed to prevent water leaking through the seams. Fig. 3 shows the method of flashing this type of work.

Use copper flashing or some other type that will not rust. When the flashing has been installed the roofing and siding can be applied.

Louvers. One last major change must be made in the outside walls of the attic before work on the attic rooms can begin. This is the installation of louvers at the gable ends to prevent condensation of water vapor on the attic roof and to make the rooms more comfortable during hot weather. The louver should be installed at each gable end of the attic as near the roof peak as possible. See Fig. 9. Louvers can be purchased or made so that they will not allow

Fig. 8. View of finished dormer window of the sloped roof type.

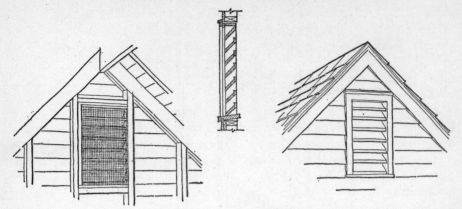

Fig. 9. Three views of a louver, which permits ventilation but keeps out rain and snow. Screen on the inside will keep out insects.

rain or snow to enter but will allow the free passage of air. The louver should also be provided with screening to keep insects out of the attic.

The size of the opening required will depend upon the number of square feet of insulated area in the attic, and also on the temperature that can be expected during the average winter. This information can be obtained from the concern where the insulation for the attic is purchased.

Insulating the Attic. If the attic rooms are to be comfortable in both summer and winter, they must be properly insulated. Fig. 10 shows how this can be done with least trouble. Blanket type insulation is shown but other types of insulation can be applied in much the same manner. Notice that the insulation does not run from the eaves to the peak of the roof but instead is brought across just above the ceiling. This is done so that there will be a dead-air space between the insulation and the top of the roof. The attic space being

finished off should be insulated on all sides. It does no good to insulate an attic room on the top and three sides and put no insulation between that room and an unfinished part of the attic.

If the attic has been provided with collar beams or ceiling joists running between opposite roof rafters, then these can be used as a base on which to attach the insulation, and they will also serve as a base for the room ceiling material. If there are no such beams they will have to be installed at this point, and they should be placed at the height that the room ceiling is to be. However, they must be placed at least two feet below the highest point of the roof to provide the necessary dead-air space.

As the only load which these collar beams or ceiling joists will have to carry will be the weight of the insulation and the ceiling material, they can be made of 2 x 4 inch stock unless the span happens to be very great, in which case it would be best to use 2 x 6 inch lumber, so that there will be no chance of the ceiling sagging. The ceiling rafters should run between each set of opposite roof rafters, and should be set on edge to provide the maximum amount of support. The ceiling joists can be rafters, first mark on the rafters the exact location where the joist is to be fastened. Then cut a joist so that it can be placed between opposite rafters and let the ends of the joist extend an inch or so beyond the

Fig. 10. Insulation of attic rooms. Notice that there is blanket type insulation above the ceiling, along the roof rafters, outside the walls, and under the floor. That under the floor should have been put in place when the house was built.

attached to the rafters with an oblique butt joint, but as this joint depends upon nails alone for its strength, it would be wise to reinforce it by nailing short lengths of 2 x 4 inch stock on the sides.

To get the proper angle for cutting the ends of the joists so that they will fit tightly against the inner edge of the rafters. Put the joist up into position and attach it to the rafter with nails driven in only part of the way. Mark each end of the joist along the angle formed where it meets the rafter. Take down the joist and cut along those lines. Put the rafter up in place again to check the measurement. The two surfaces should come together in a tight fit. If this is the case, try the joist between other rafters, and if it fits properly in all cases, use it as a pattern to cut the rest of the joists.

All of the ceiling joists can be put up in this manner, except those which occupy a spot intended for a wall partition. The top plate of the wall partition must run between rafters; and as there will be need of a joist on each side of the partition to fasten the ceiling, some other arrangement must be made for nailing

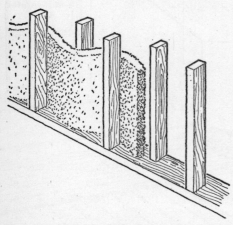

Fig. 11. Method of insulating one room from another. Stagger the studding and the walls do not have to be so thick as otherwise.

up the joists. What can be done is to spike odd lengths of 2 x 4 inch stock to the side of the rafters, so the joists can be attached on each side, leaving a surface the middle wide enough to attach the top plate—about 3⅝ inches. By moving the joists in this manner there will be a slight difference in the distance between them, but as this difference will be smaller, rather than greater, it will not cause

trouble as far as the insulation and ceiling material are concerned.

Once all the ceiling joists are in place, little difficulty should be encountered in applying the insulation. This material can be purchased in standard widths to fit between the rafters and joists, or, in the event that the distance between these members is not standard, extra wide insulation can be purchased and cut to size. As the joists have been placed the same distance apart as the rafters (except in the case of the partition) it is possible to use one long strip of insulation, from one eave to the other.

The insulation is held in place by nails or other fasteners driven through a flat on each side of the insulation and into the sides of the rafters and joists. Follow the manufacturer's directions as to what size fastener should be used and how far apart they should be spaced. The insulation at the gable ends of the attic will run down between the vertical house studding, from ceiling joists to floor. The dormer window must be insulated also. If only one side of the insulation has been covered with waterproof paper, make sure that in each instance this faces toward the inside of the room and is not placed against, or facing, the wall or roofing.

Wall Construction. The next step is to put up the necessary studding to form the walls of the attic rooms. As a base for this studding a 2 x 4 inch sole should be laid down along each side of the attic. The distance the sole is from the roof eaves will determine the height of the vertical walls of the rooms. It would be unwise to make these walls too short as this space would be difficult to utilize in a room. Walls of four feet are about right in many cases. This is not only a useful height for the room, but if small doors are placed in the wall at regular intervals, the space between the wall and the roof eaves can be used as a general storage bin.

When the distance of this wall from the eaves has been decided the sole should be set down so that it is an equal distance from the roof eaves along its entire length. Nail this in place, spacing the nails so that they will go through the rough flooring and into the attic floor joists. Studding is now required between the sole and the rafters. Take a plumb line and drop it from the side of one rafter to the sole. Mark on the sole where the line comes, and then stand a piece of studding on this line and let it come up a little beyond the lower edge of the rafter. Check the position of the studding with a level or square to be sure that it is upright, and then, holding the piece steady, mark with a pencil the angle formed on the studding where it crosses the lower edge of the rafter. Cut the piece of studding along this line and put it into position between the rafter and the sole. If it fits correctly it can be nailed in place at both ends, toeing the nails in. Before this is done, however, it would be a good idea to try this piece of studding between other rafters and the sole. If it should fit correctly at all

points, then use it as a pattern to cut the remaining studs.

One point that should be borne in mind while doing any framing is the conservation of materials. Wallboard, plywood, and insulating material are usually made to fit a standard size framing. This may be either 16 inches or 24 inches on center. If studding, for example, were placed 26 inches on center, it would mean that a piece of wallboard of the standard width of 4 feet (48 inches) would require additional studding at seam, because the regular studding was spaced too far apart. The same holds true for insulating material which is made to fit snugly between members of standard size framing, but which will have to be cut down if the studs are too close together.

Another item that is worth remembering is to try to take advantage of standardization wherever possible. Wallboard and plywood generally come in widths of 4 feet and 8 feet in length, or 12 feet in some cases. With a little planning beforehand, it is often possible to arrange the framing of a room and its size so that you can use many complete sections of material, instead of wasting time cutting them down to size and having a lot of small pieces left over. If the vertical wall of the attic room is four feet high, it will be possible to use one entire section of wallboard with no cutting whatsoever. Naturally, a room cannot be completely planned and built to meet all standards of building materials, but often if enough thought is given to all points of the problem in advance, details can be worked out to reduce effort and waste to a minimum.

On the other hand it may be difficult, or impossible, to get large pieces of material, 4 feet x 8 or 12 feet, up to the attic by small windows or around turns of the stairways. In that case your material will have to be cut before bringing it upstairs, but remember to measure and cut it so that it can be nailed to the studs properly.

Now, if the studding and the ceiling joists have been correctly installed to the rafters so that all are in the same line, we should find, when it comes to installing the wallboard on the ceiling and walls, that the joints between sections of wallboard will line up in a regular pattern and not be staggered.

Before nailing the wallboard permanently in place it will be wise to have the electric wiring, discussed a little later in this section, attended to. That will save pulling down walls or cutting into them.

Partitions. The next step is to divide the attic space into the required number of rooms by means of partitions.

At this stage it is a good idea to sit down and recheck your floor plan to be sure it is the most convenient and efficient arrangement possible. The addition of a dormer window may be the deciding factor in changing the location of a room.

Check to make sure that the stairs will lead up to a living room or kitchen, avoiding a bedroom if pos-

Fig. 12. A door hung in proper position. The hinges are on the other side.

sible. Of course, if the apartment consists of only one room plus kitchen and bath, you may not have much choice.

Preventing Sound Transmission. Before taking up the actual framing of the wall partitions, it would be well to consider ways and means of preventing sound transmission, either between rooms in the attic, or between attic and house proper.

Sound waves in the air can be absorbed by the use of special insulation which is applied and finished in much the same fashion as wallboard. On the other hand, the actual wall partitions will act as sound conductors, and that calls for special construction. The usual method is to build two separate walls with a heavy building felt placed between them. The thickness of such a wall can be reduced by staggering the wall studding, as is shown in Fig. 11. The effectiveness of this arrangement depends upon the fact that the two walls are completely independent of each other. Of course, this method of construction doubles the amount of material required for single walls.

If there are to be any doors in the partition walls, then it is a good idea to have them on hand so that the frames in the partition can be built to fit the door, instead of constructing the frame, only to find that a door of that particular size is not available, or that you must purchase an oversize door and spend considerable time cutting it down to the correct size. Fig. 12 shows a completed door.

The actual framing of the partition should not be difficult. The wall will be made up of 2 x 4 inch studding, running between the sole that is attached to the floor and the plate that runs between the roof rafters. The necessary steps were taken when the ceiling joists were put up, so that the partition plate can be nailed to the rafters. All that needs to be done now is to cut this plate to size, mitering each end at an angle, so that it will fit against the edges of

the rafters. The plate is attached with the broad surfaces facing up and down. The bottom of the plate should be flush with the bottom of the ceiling joists on either side.

Set the sole of the partition in place and measure the distance from it to the bottom of the ceiling joists. Use this measurement for cutting the studding that will run between the sole and the plate. The plate of the partition will run only the same distance as that of the ceiling joists, while the sole will run the entire distance of the partition. The studding at each end of the wall will run up from the sole and is nailed to the rafters. The plate can be put into position and secured by nailing it at the ends to the rafters, and then driving nails through the joists into it. The full-length wall studding can then be attached to the sole by driving nails up through the bottom of the sole, into the bottom of the studding. The studding should be placed 16 inches on center. Brace the vertical studding so that it is upright and then lift the assembly up and move it into position so that the top of the studding will be directly under the plate, which will make the entire framework plumb. The sole can then be nailed to the floor and the studding spiked to the plate. The short studding between the sole and the rafters is now measured, cut, and nailed in place. Openings for doors in the partition should be framed with double studding.

Closet and Storage Space. Some provision should be made during framing for closets and other storage areas. The space between the eaves of the roof and the sides of the attic rooms can be used for general storage space, or recessed cabinets may be built with shelves, or you can construct a built-in chest with drawers.

Fig. 13. Built-in cupboards and drawers are an ideal way to use space in an attic apartment near the eaves where the ceiling is too low for the space to be useful in any other way.

Fig. 13 shows how attractive these can be. You make an attic bedroom larger since you don't need so much moveable furniture. But of course such storage space is close to the floor and will not serve too well for some articles, or for clothes and garments which you wish to hang up.

It would be well to construct at least one full-sized closet that runs to ceiling height. The top of it can be provided with shelves and used for storage. Closets should be framed in the same fashion as the walls and other partitions. Studding around the closet doors should be double.

Ventilation for Bathroom and Kitchen. It may not be possible, even by the addition of extra windows, to locate the bathroom and kitchen where there will be outside windows. In that case exhaust fans can be used to pull the air out of those rooms, allowing fresh air to be drawn in from other parts of the apartment. The exhaust fan is placed in an opening cut through the outside wall, and should be provided with a louver, which can be closed from the inside when the fan is not in operation, to prevent cold air from coming in.

The wiring for the fan should be permanent, and current to the fan should be governed by a conveniently located wall switch. If it is impossible to locate the fan in the room so that it is in an outside wall, then it can be located elsewhere and ducts used to connect it.

The Attic Electric System. When the job of framing the attic has been completed, thought should be given to an adequate electrical system. Just how much of a task this will turn out to be will depend upon what provisions, if any, were made for attic wiring when the house was built. A considerate builder, who realizes that sooner or later the attic space will be converted into rooms, will see to it that adequate wiring and circuits are installed at the same time that the house is wired. It should go without saying that this calls for little added expense or effort when the house is being built.

But if no provisions were made for attic wiring then, it will be necessary for the home mechanic to have wires run up from the main fuse box, through the wall spaces and perhaps under the flooring.

If there is no wiring whatever in the attic, then it would be best to call in an electrician and have the required number of additional circuits brought up from the point where the service lines enter the house. The job of installing additional circuits may require a larger or additional fuse box and major changes in wiring. When this work is being done the electrician should be given a full understanding of the electrical needs of the attic in both the immediate and distant future, so that he can connect up a system that will be adequate, containing enough circuits and outlets. As mentioned earlier, if the attic is to be heated with electric space heaters, or if an electric kitchen range is to be installed, special wiring will be required.

Remodeling the Attic Electric System. Assuming that the attic has been wired to some extent, it may be possible for the home mechanic to make the few minor changes necessary to cover present needs. But before such work is begun, the home mechanic should check with his local building authorities to see if there is any ordinance which forbids his doing this work. In many localities electrical work of this kind can be done legally only by a licensed electrician. In other places, the work must be checked over by an inspector before it can be put into operation.

If there is no code controlling this special work, and the home mechanic feels that he has the ability to do the job neatly and safely, he should follow the recommendations for adequate electrical wiring as set forth in the National Electrical Code. A copy of this code can be had by sending 15 cents to the National Board of Fire Underwriters, 85 John Street, New York, N. Y. Read the code thoroughly before you begin work.

The job of remodeling the attic wiring may consist only of removing an outlet box for a fixture, freeing some of the cable and moving the box to some other location. However, it may be necessary to use longer cables in connection with this work, and because cables cannot be spliced except at light, switch, and junction boxes, either a longer cable must be substituted for the short one, or additional outlets of some type installed. Then again, it may be necessary as well as possible to install additional outlets, such as fixtures, to the existing attic circuits, provided, of course, that these additional outlets will not overload the circuits. (You might refer back to the section on ELECTRICITY starting on page 180.)

Types of Wire. There are many different types of wire used for interior electrical work. Two kinds which meet the approval of many codes for exposed or concealed interior wiring in dry locations, are nonmetallic sheathed cable and armored cable. Nonmetallic sheathed cable (see Fig. 14) consists of two or more wires, each independently insulated, and then covered with a tough heavy outer fabric. This is an inexpensive material and is easy to work with because of its flexibility, and the fact that no special tools are required other than those found in the average home tool kit.

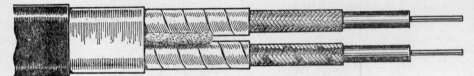

Fig. 14. Nonmetallic sheathed cable used in interior house wiring.

The other type of wiring often found in residential work is armored cable, shown in Fig. 15. This is sometimes called by the trade name "BX Cable." It consists of two or more insulated wires, covered with heavy paper and incased in a flexible steel jacket. The steel jacket provides considerable protection for the wires from possible injury to their insulation, but as the metal covering is not waterproof it should be used only in dry locations. Special cable, with an interior covering of lead, is used for wiring in damp locations.

The two wires inside either the nonmetallic sheathed cable or the armored cable, will have different colored insulation. The wire with the black insulation will be the live or hot wire, while the one with the white insulation or insulation with a white tracer running through it, will be the ground wire. When making connections to wires be sure that the black wire is attached to the black, and the white to the white.

This will hold true in almost every case—except when a two-wire cable is run to a switch from a fixture. In that case, the white wire of the cable running to the switch is spliced to the black wire from the source of current, and the black wire on the cable from the switch is connected to the black wire of the fixture. The wiring must always be arranged so that the switch breaks the flow of current through the black or hot wire, while the white or ground wire goes directly to the fixture and is never interrupted. Fixtures are provided with different colored terminal screws. The white or silver colored screw is for the white wire, and the brass or gold colored is for the black.

If the black and white wires were hooked up at random throughout the electrical system, it would mean that there would be current flowing to a fixture in spite of the fact that the switch was in the "off" position. Such a situation could cause serious trouble if there were a short circuit.

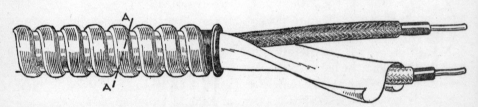

Fig. 15. Armored cable, generally called "BX Cable," used in interior house wiring. The line "A"—"A" shows the proper angle at which to cut the flexible steel jacket with a hack saw. Cut carefully so as to not damage the insulation.

Outlet boxes and switch boxes for use with nonmetallic sheathed cable or armored cable are made to standard design, so that not only can the cable be attached to them easily and securely but also to allow the fixture or switch cover plate to be attached.

An outlet box, such as is shown in Fig. 16, must be used at each point where there is an electrical connection. Wires cannot be spliced at any point except inside an outlet box. These boxes, made of metal, are insurance against a short circuit in the connections; short circuits are the cause of many fires. The boxes must be mounted securely to the framework of the walls. Where an outlet box comes between studding, special hangers can be used to hold the box in place. Boxes, as shown in Fig. 16, are provided with metal cover plates which are to be screwed on tight after the wiring has been completed.

Before any actual wiring is begun, it would be well for the home mechanic to consult a catalogue of electrical fittings and equipment at his local electrical shop, so that he can select the size and type of fittings best suited to his needs.

Outlet boxes and other boxes for switches and the like, are provided with "knockouts" so that wires and cables can be brought into the box. These "knockouts" are incomplete circular cuts made in the sides and bottom of the box. A sharp rap with a screwdriver or other tool will force out the round piece of metal leaving the proper size hole. Mount the box solidly with screws through holes provided for that purpose in the bottom of the box. Mount it onto a 2 x 4 or 1 x 4 inch piece of scrap lumber which you have nailed between two pieces of studding. Then remove only the number of "knockouts" necessary for the wires or cables that are brought into the box.

Nonmetallic sheathed cable or armored cable can be attached to the box so that they will be mechanically secure, by means of special clamps such as shown in Fig. 16. These clamps are fitted over the ends

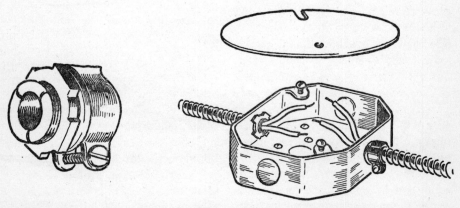

Fig. 16. An outlet box, right, and outlet box clamp. Each cable entering a box should be secured to it by a clamp. Box should be screwed firmly to wooden support.

of the cable and are secured to it by tightening up a screw. The other end of the clamp is threaded and this is pushed through the hole in the box. A bushing is then slipped over the threads, and after this a nut is run on and tightened. The sides of this nut are notched so that it can be tightened with a screwdriver.

When connecting wires to terminal screws on fixtures and switches, remove only enough insulation from the wire ends to allow it to go around the terminal screw once. Be sure that the wire goes around the screw in the same direction that the screw rotates when it is tightened. Only one wire should be used on each terminal screw. If it is necessary to have another wire at this same point, use fixtures made for this purpose, which have two terminal screws on the same side. Wire ends used for connection to terminal screws or splicing must be completely clean of insulation, and the connection must be mechanically secure. In case of splices, the splice should be soldered.

The size of wire to be used for the attic wiring will be governed by the size used elsewhere in the house. A No. 14 wire is considered as the minimum size allowed for interior wiring, but with the increased use of electrical appliances, many homes are wired with the heavier No. 12 to carry the additional load. Needless to say, a No. 14 should not be spliced onto a heavier size wire.

Cutting Armored Cable. Armored cable can be cut satisfactorily with a hack saw, but some practice may be necessary, as it is very important

not to let the saw teeth damage the insulation around the wires. The cut should be made about 8 inches from the end of the cable so that there will be enough uncovered wire exposed for splicing and making connections. To make the cut with a saw, do not cut directly across the cable, but rather, hold the saw at an angle of about 60 degrees to the cable. See Fig. 15. Work slowly and cut through the metal jacket only—not through the paper. When the blade has cut through the metal, the free end of the cable can be twisted and pulled off. The cutting will leave a ragged edge on the end of the cable and this might damage the wire insulation. So a small fiber bushing known as an anti-short bushing is slipped over the end of the cable to insulate the wires from the outside steel jacket.

Fig. 17. A clamp or strap for fastening sheathed cable.

The outer insulation on nonmetallic sheathed cable can be removed with a knife, but care must be taken to not let the knife blade damage the inner insulation around the wire.

Cable can be run through holes bored in the studding and joists, or it can follow the wall and ceiling structure. If there is any possibility that the cable could be mechanically damaged, it should be provided with a running board—a strip of wood secured in place and serving as a base for the cable.

Nonmetallic sheathed cable can be secured to the walls and other framing by means of special straps or clamps such as is shown in Fig. 17. Straps should be placed at least every 4¼ feet and within at least 12 inches of outlet boxes. Armored cable can be attached with a similar strap or with large staples designed for this work. Staples can be installed faster than straps but they cannot be used on nonmetallic sheathed cable as there is danger that the sharp points of the staples might damage the wire insulation. The steel jacket protects armored cable from that danger.

In working with any type of wire or cable, sharp bends should be avoided as they can damage the insulation around the wires.

Extending or Adding Outlets. Before starting to add an additional outlet recheck to make sure that this will not overload that circuit. Overloading is explained on page 186.

Be sure that the current is off in that circuit before handling wires.

The first step in the job will be to locate the approximate position for the new fixture. After that work back along the attic wiring to find out where the extension can be tapped into the source. A tap can be made at a junction box, switch box, or outlet box, provided that the box does not already contain the maximum number of wires set forth in the National Electrical Code. Under no circumstances should a splice be made directly into the wires unless a junction box is first installed, so that the splice can be made inside the box.

Usually a light fixture or a wall outlet provides a convenient place to tap into, but there are a few considerations that must be understood before this can be done. In the first place, there are several ways that light or wall fixtures can be wired.

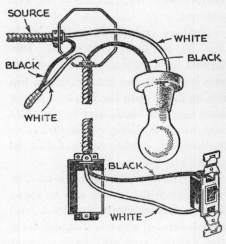

Fig. 18. Wiring for an electric light and wall switch.

Fig. 18 shows one method, where the white wire from the supply (the ground or neutral wire) is connected to the white wire on the fixture. The black wire from the supply is interrupted by a wall switch so that when the switch is open no current will flow to the fixture. If the cable for the new outlet were to be spliced in at the fixture to the white wire, the outlet on this line would be controlled by the switch provided for the first fixture. This might not be a very convenient arrangement.

In a case of this kind it will be necessary to go back to the switch and take the supply of current for the new fixture off the hot side of the switch, tapping onto the black to white spliced wire shown at the left of the picture in Fig. 18. Connect the white line of the new fixture to the white line in junction box. If this is done we shall have an uninterrupted supply of current to the new fixture, regardless of the position of the wall switch.

If there is no wall switch, as in Fig. 19, the light fixture being controlled by a pull chain or other device built into the fixture, then a tap can be made onto the black or power line. Connect black wire to the black and white to white, solder and tape. Splices are explained in detail on page 191.

There are certain hook-ups used in wiring in which a tap can be made from a fixture controlled by a wall switch located at some distance from the fixture, and still have current

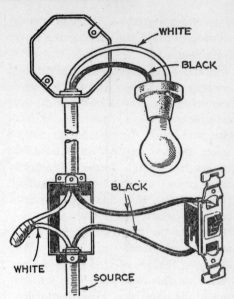

Fig. 20. Another method of connecting an electric light and wall switch.

going to the new outlet regardless of the position of the switch. In this hook-up the cable coming from the power supply is brought to the fixture outlet box. The white wire of the supply cable is spliced to the white wire of the fixture. The black wire of the supply cable is spliced to the white wire in the cable that runs to the switch. The black wire in this switch cable is connected to the black wire of the fixture. Now, if the cable to the new fixture were to be connected so that its white wire was spliced in with the other two white wires already spliced, and the black wire were connected to the splice between the supply black wire and the switch cable white wire, then current to the new fixture would not be interrupted by the switch.

After the wires have been spliced, the cable can be run to the desired

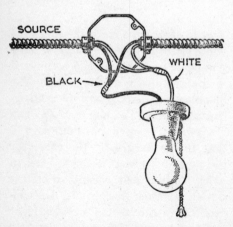

Fig. 19. Wiring for an electric light operated by a pull cord or similar means.

location for either a light fixture or a wall outlet. If a wall outlet is to be installed, no switch may be required, but if a fixture is to be used then a switch should be installed at some convenient point on the wall.

There are several ways of connecting the switch with the cable to the light fixture. It may be possible to work the switch into the lines as shown in Fig. 20. Notice that the black wires are connected to the switch, while the white wires are spliced together. The black, or hot wires, are always the ones to be broken by the switch. An arrangement of this type can only be used when the switch can easily be located somewhere along the run of the cable. It may be more convenient as well as more practical to place the switch at some distance from the cable running to the fixture, and in that case a hook-up such as is shown in Fig. 18 can be used. This is the same as the connection that was used on the fixture which was tapped for supply. It will be noted in this hook-up that the rule mentioned previously, about

always connecting black to black and white to white has apparently been disregarded in this case, for the black wire from supply has been connected to the white wire to the switch. This is permissible under the code provided that the black return wire from the switch is connected to the black fixture wire.

Three-Way Switches. It is often very convenient to be able to control a light fixture from switches located at either of two different points. For example, the light fixture at the head of the attic stairs should be wired up so that it can be turned on and off by means of a switch located at the top of the stairs or a switch at the bottom.

For this particular hook-up three-way switches as well as cable containing three instead of the usual two wires must be used. The third wire in the cable is colored red.

There are several combinations for wiring the switches and fixture, and these will depend upon where the source of power comes in, as well as upon the location of the switches

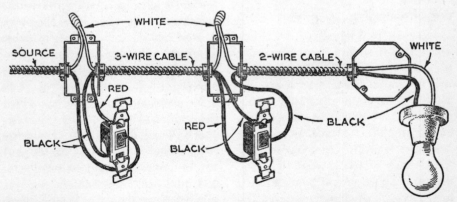

Fig. 21. How to connect a three-way switch, such as is used to provide a light over a stairway with switches at both top and bottom of the stairs.

with respect to the fixture. Fig. 21 shows a hook-up in which the supply comes into one of the switches. The white wire from the supply is connected to the white wire in the three-wire cable. The black wire of supply is connected to the common terminal on switch A. The black and red wires of the three-wire cable are attached to the other two switch terminals, and at the corresponding terminals on switch B. The black wire in the cable to the fixture is then attached to the common terminal on switch B, and the white wire of fixture cable is spliced to the white wire of the three-wire cable.

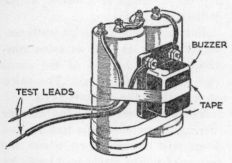

Fig. 22. Method of connecting buzzer and batteries for testing electric wiring.

Testing the System. Before the system is completed or put into operation, it should be given a complete test so as to be sure that there are no short circuits or loose connections. The job of testing can be done with two dry cells and a bell or buzzer similar to the one used for testing a signaling system. See Fig. 22. Switches should be at the "on" position. There should be no current in the system during these tests. Remove all bulbs and outlet plugs.

Take the two leads from the testing bell and battery and touch one to the black wire of the system and the other to the white wire. If the bell rings, then there is a short circuit somewhere in the line. This must be located and fixed at once. The next step is to attach one wire of the testing equipment to the black wire of the system, and the second wire of the testing equipment to the other end, or terminal point, of the black wire of the system, either at the fixture or wall outlet. If the wire has been properly installed the bell will ring. Do the same with the white wire.

The actual installation of fixtures should not be done at this time as they will be in the way when the wall and ceiling materials are put up. Mention of that will be made later in the proper place.

Installing the Walls and Ceiling. Once the basic electrical wiring is completed, the work of finishing off the walls and ceilings of the rooms can be undertaken. Again we assume that if plumbing is to be installed, the pipes have been run up from the floor below so it will not be necessary to tear out sections of wall to bring in pipes. The actual plumbing fixtures cannot, of course, be put in place until the walls are up, but some provision should be made for the washbowl if it is to be the type that is hung on the wall. The bathroom fixtures, washbowl, toilet, and tub or shower, should be purchased and on hand, even though not yet connected, so that you can measure them and make sure that you will not put your walls where the fixtures will not fit.

There are several materials which can be used for the walls and ceiling. Plaster is one, but this usually calls for a professional plasterer, as the proper mixing and application of plaster is not an accomplishment with which the home mechanic is likely to be very familiar. It probably would be better for him to use material such as wallboard, plasterboard, or plywood, which can be handled with saw and hammer, and if properly applied, will give good results.

There are many brands and grades of wallboard on the market. By all means get one of the better kind, as it will be easier to put on and will not be so liable to break.

When purchasing wallboard, secure all the necessary information from your dealer as to the recommended method for filling the seams between sections, and also find out whether sizing is necessary before painting. The usual method of dealing with seams is to either cover them over with strips of wood lath, or fill them with a special cement and reinforce the cement with a perforated or wire-mesh tape. A seam treated in this manner can be painted or papered over with good results.

But this requires that a space of about ⅛ inch or so be left between sections, so that there will be room for the cement. If the seams are to be covered with wood laths then it is important to have the wall and ceiling seams line up wherever possible.

A room filled with irregularly spaced seams on wall and ceiling is difficult to decorate.

An inexpensive grade of plywood can be used for the walls and ceiling, and this can be painted or papered. But plywood with an attractive grain can be used as paneling, receiving no finish other than staining or waxing. If a room is to be paneled in plywood, it may be found that covering both walls and ceiling in this manner is not to your liking; in that case the ceiling can be covered with some other material and painted, or the lower half of the walls can be paneled and the upper portions painted or papered.

Information regarding the application of plywood paneling is given in the next section of this book on REMODELING THE BASEMENT.

The same general procedure will apply when doing the job in the attic except that, due to wall studding and ceiling joists, it will not be necessary to provide furring.

If a room is to be finished in wallboard, then the ceiling should be covered first. This may be difficult for one person to accomplish alone, as it requires getting the large sheet into position, and then holding it in place while nails are driven in. If no helper is available, the task can be done by one person by constructing a large T. Make it out of 1 x 4 inch stock, with the cross arm, or top of the T, the same width as the wallboard, and the upright an inch or two higher than the ceiling of the room. This T can be used to lift and support one end of the wallboard, while the other end is held, moved into the correct position, and nailed. The size and spacing of the nails used should be in accordance with the directions provided with the wallboard or learned from the dealer. Be sure to use enough nails to keep the ceiling from sagging.

The sections going up along the sidewalls do not present so much difficulty. The main point there is to be sure that the sections are properly supported and that they are plumb. Drive in nails close to the edge of the wallboard, so that they can all be covered with the wood lath which is only 2 inches or so in width.

Bring the wallboard as close as possible to openings such as door and windows. By doing so you reduce the size of the trim necessary around those areas to cover up the joint. Obviously, if the wallboard is brought only to within three or four inches of the opening, wide pieces of trim will be required.

In some cases it will be possible to cut a hole in the wallboard, where a light or other fixture is to be placed, before the wallboard is nailed into position. If this is done, check the distance carefully so that the hole will correspond exactly with the outlet box in the studding. If the hole is too far to one side, or is cut too large, the finish plate of the fixture will not completely cover opening.

In the bathroom and kitchen it is desirable that the walls and ceilings have a smooth surface which can be cleaned easily. There are several materials which can be used for this purpose and which can be applied directly over the wallboard. Tileboard, linoleum, metal tiles or oilcloth will serve and either one can be easily installed. As they will require a base, walls of wallboard should be put up first. Then cover the entire walls with the selected material, or cover only the lower half of the walls and paint the top half and the ceiling with enamel. Do not use a water soluble paint in either the bathroom or kitchen.

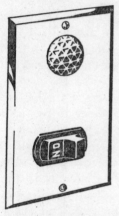

Fig. 23. An electric wall switch panel.

Once the walls and ceilings have been completed, the electric fixtures and switch panels can be installed. Holes are cut through the wallboard, if this was not done before the boards were nailed in place, and the electric wires are connected to the fixtures. Remember to have the electric current shut off, at least from the attic, before working around any of these wires. Each fixture is then connected by screws to the outlet box. In the case of switches, panels should be attached to the box so as to give a neat and finished appearance. See Fig. 23.

Fig. 24. An attic room with built-in desk, bookcase, and divan. There is storage space under the divan. The low ceiling above the desk is sufficient for anyone sitting at the desk.

The next step is to put down some kind of finished flooring. It is a poor policy to leave the subflooring uncovered for it will be hard to keep clean and is unattractive. A wide variety of materials can be used. A hardwood floor can be laid—as has been explained on pages 232 to 240 —or plain linoleum, tile designs or other coverings can be used. If the subfloor is quite rough and not especially tight, it would be wise to cover it with building paper and lay sheets of plywood on it, so as to secure an even and tight base on which to lay the flooring material. Floors for the kitchen and bathroom should be of a kind that will stand hard usage and can be easily cleaned.

When the flooring is down, the plumbing fixtures and kitchen equipment of the permanent type (stove, sink, cupboards, etc.) should be installed. It is assumed that the necessary pipes have been put in, so that it should not be necessary to do any additional cutting into the walls or flooring.

Doors. The rooms are now ready for the finished woodwork and trim. Doors are hung in the frames as explained on pages 278 to 282. It will also be necessary to place wood trim around windows, doors, and baseboards, covering the joints between the walls and floor. If there is to be any built-in furniture in the attic, this should be constructed before the trim goes on. Built-in furniture, such as bookcases and shelves, kitchen cabinets, window seats, and even beds, can be made with no great amount of extra effort or expense, and doing this will save just that much when it comes to furnishing the attic. See Fig. 24. An attic apartment is small and having certain pieces of furniture permanently located will give more room for other things. Keep this built-in furniture along simple lines and it will blend well with almost any style of extra pieces that may be used.

Trim. Wood trim in stock designs can be purchased at most lumber yards, or if you want something a little different from what they have, it can be milled out to order at a slight additional cost. It is recommended that the trim used be of a moderately simple design, and, unless the home mechanic possesses special tools as well as special skill, the joints for fitting the trim together should be made as simple as possible. The miter joint can be used for most of such work, and miter joints are easy to cut in a homemade miter box such as is shown on page 360. The width of the trim required will depend, to a large extent, on how close the wallboard has been fitted to the openings in the wall.

Trim should be cut carefully with a fine-toothed saw, and tacked loosely in place so that the other members of the assembly can be likewise installed, and the entire job checked for accuracy of measurements and cuts before it is finally nailed secure.

While we all like to think that studding and other framing we have put up is all plumb and level, it often proves to be otherwise; so be sure to use a level to check the posi-

Fig. 25. Completed attic apartment living room built in accordance with the floor plans shown in Fig. 1. Note dormer window at right. The kitchenette planned in Fig. 1 is just outside of this picture.

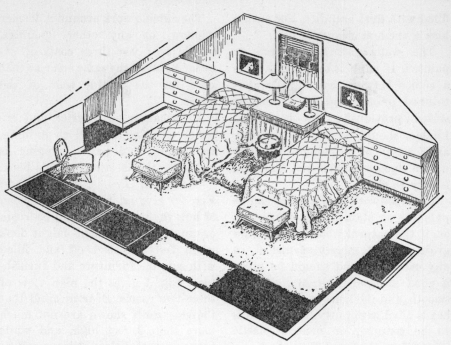

Fig. 26. Completed anc furnished attic apartment bedroom built in accordance with the floor plans shown in Fig 1, except that the outside stairway door is not shown. The two chests could be built into the side walls.

tion of a piece of trim before it is nailed in place. Your eye is not always infallible. Sometimes you can correct previous slight errors before you nail the trim. Nailing should be done with finishing nails, placed in inconspicuous places on the wood when possible, and countersunk slightly with a nail set, so that their heads will be below the wood surface. After the first coat of paint those holes can be filled with putty.

The baseboard covering the joint between the walls and floor should be about 6 inches high and can be nailed to the wall studding. A strip of quarter round molding can then be nailed along the bottom of the baseboard making a rounded joint that will be easy to clean and will not collect dust and dirt.

If the floor is covered with linoleum or some other material of this type, which may need replacing in the future, let the linoleum come right up to the baseboards, and then cover the seam with the quarter round. This will make a tight joint and when the linoleum is removed for replacement, only the quarter round will have to be taken up, and this can be replaced when the new flooring is laid.

Painting and Decorating. Before any painting is done, the attic rooms should be given a thorough cleaning. It will be difficult, if not impossible, to do a good painting job in rooms filled with dust and dirt. For such a task a vacuum cleaner is best.

The walls can be papered or painted. If paint is selected, there is a choice between calcimine, water-thinned paints, and oil paints. As stated previously, the bath and kitchen should be painted with enamel, a type of oil paint which dries with a smooth surface and therefore is easy to clean.

The woodwork in the rooms can be painted, or stained and varnished, or, if the natural wood coloring and grain is right, merely varnished. In any case the wood should be given a good sandpapering so that it is smooth, and the holes caused by nail-heads filled with putty, if the wood is to be painted, or neutral plastic filler, if stained and varnished.

The floors, if they are of wood, can be either painted, varnished, or shellacked.

The outside work around a dormer window, or any other openings, should be given three coats of exterior paint of the same color as that used for the outside trim of the house.

Information on interior and exterior painting, as well as staining, varnishing, and paper hanging is given in other sections of this book.

Completed Rooms. Fig. 25 and Fig. 26 give an artist's conception of how the living room and bedroom of an attic apartment might look when fully finished off and filled with suitable furniture and furnishings. Fig. 1 gives the plan view of these two rooms. Bear in mind that the side walls shown are not much more than 3 feet high, and while space with such low ceilings can be made useful, it has definite limitations, and cannot be used for every purpose.

REMODELING THE BASEMENT

The basement in many homes is pretty much wasted space. It usually contains a few items of household equipment such as the furnace and hot-water heater, and perhaps serves as a general storage place for various odds and ends, but generally only a fraction of the total basement area is fully utilized. So in many cases it would be quite possible for the home mechanic to turn a good portion of this space into useful and attractive rooms.

The usual manner of finishing a basement is to make it into a game or recreation room, but it is just as feasible to use some of the space for a second living room, study, library, or hobby room. So it might be well to consider turning part of the basement into quarters which some of the family can use and enjoy frequently instead of merely fixing up a room to be used when parties are given. However, a game room may be the sort of room most wanted, where a little extra noise would not be so likely to disturb children or other members of the family who have gone to bed early.

In approaching the job of remodeling there is also the utilitarian angle. For example, unless there is a tool shed or an oversize garage, a portion of the basement should be set aside for garden tools and similar equipment. A wheelbarrow, lawn mower, garden hose and reel, lawn furniture and things of this sort require ample storage space which should be located, when possible, near the outside basement door. Some of these things merely need dry storage space during a portion of the year, chiefly during the winter, and can be confined to a relatively small space if hooks and shelves are provided. Screens and storm windows need space but seldom at the same time. Sleds, skis, bicycles, and other recreational equipment must have a place where they can be stored conveniently, and that place generally turns out to be the basement. Many housewives put up their own preserves, jellies and canned goods, and these should have a cabinet with adequate shelf space. More and more homes are acquiring deep-freeze units, and these often cannot be placed in the kitchen; they naturally go in the cellar as the next best place. In some cases space is needed in the cellar for the home laundry. If any member of the family is an amateur photographer, naturally he or she will want a room in the basement for a darkroom.

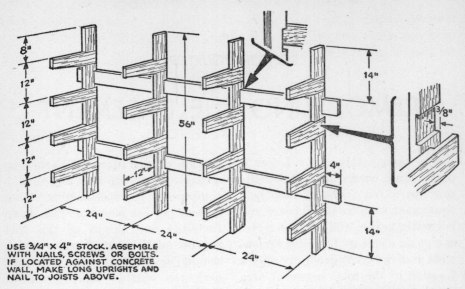

USE 3/4" X 4" STOCK. ASSEMBLE
WITH NAILS, SCREWS OR BOLTS.
IF LOCATED AGAINST CONCRETE
WALL, MAKE LONG UPRIGHTS AND
NAIL TO JOISTS ABOVE.

Fig. 1. A lumber storage rack which will prove very useful to the home mechanic for storing lumber of different sizes so that it is readily available.

And last, but not least, the home mechanic will want a place for his workbench, tools, and some space in which to store wood or other building materials. Fig 1 indicates how to build a lumber storage rack which will not take up very much room but which will conveniently take care of quite a bit of lumber. When remodeling a cellar or refinishing an attic it is much better and more economical to figure carefully what will be needed and to buy a substantial amount of lumber at one time rather than to keep trotting to the lumber yard every other day for another stick of wood.

Through careful planning and the efficient use of ceiling height shelves, overhead racks, and hooks, it is possible to utilize almost every square inch of basement storage space and thus provide a greater area for a recreation room or other purpose. In fact, without such planning and some remodeling, with the articles usually found in cellars just dumped there helter-skelter, one might think the basement was filled too full to put in anything else.

The cost of remodeling a basement can run anywhere from a few dollars to several thousands. And so the first step is to decide exactly how much money can be spent at this time. Do not make the mistake of trying to stretch an inadequate budget by using inferior-grade materials. It is much better to finish off merely half of the available space with good materials and let the rest of the area stand as it is until some later date. For example, a lavatory of some sort in the basement is a great convenience, but it is a rather expensive addition. If to complete the installation of the plumbing fixtures would mean running way over the budget, there is no harm in setting aside sufficient space for it and letting it wait. Later on bring in the pipes and have the fixtures connected.

Before any choice of materials for the basement is made, the home mechanic should consult the men of his local lumber yard, explain his plans, state the amount of money he has available, and let them help him in deciding what type and grade of materials he can best use.

Eliminate Dampness. The most important requirement for a remodeled basement is that it be absolutely waterproof. There is only one sure way of knowing whether or not the basement walls, floor, and seams between the floor and walls are tight, and that is by inspecting them at frequent intervals during the year. A basement which is dry eleven months out of the year, but leaks during excessively wet weather in the fall or spring, is not suitable for remodeling until that condition has been corrected. Various methods of correcting a damp basement are given on pages 206 to 210.

You should first try to determine from which direction the dampness comes. Perhaps only one wall of the four is at fault. Perhaps water from downspouts on one side of the house is settling down next to the foundation. Piping this water well away from the house or grading the soil down and away from the house on that side may be sufficient to stop the cellar dampness. Water is per-

fectly willing to run downhill along the top of the ground rather than soak into the ground. If the land slopes so that water has to run toward the house, it has nowhere to go but to soak in next to the foundation. If these simple measures of grading do not work, then the more elaborate methods for waterproofing a wall described on page 208 should be undertaken.

It should be remembered, however, that a damp basement does not necessarily indicate that there are leaks in either the walls or floor. Dampness may be due to the condensation of water vapor when air strikes the cold masonry. If this is the case, then the moisture can be taken care of by proper ventilation and the use of insulation around the basement walls.

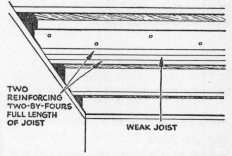

TWO REINFORCING TWO-BY-FOURS FULL LENGTH OF JOIST WEAK JOIST

Fig. 2. Method of reinforcing weak joists or strengthening joists so that supporting posts can be removed. Use large bolts to hold the three timbers together.

Preparing the Basement for Remodeling. Often there are beams or posts in the basement running from the floor to the ceiling to help support the first floor joists. These posts may make it difficult to plan and utilize the basement area to best advantage, and so they should be removed and some other method used to provide the necessary support for the first floor. This can sometimes be done by installing larger and heavier first floor joists and by reinforcing those you have. See Fig. 2 where 2 x 4s have been bolted in place on either side of the original 2 x 6 or 2 x 8 joist. Use good-sized bolts and put them in every 2 feet or less. Another method of providing additional support is to install a steel beam or girder that rests on top of the basement wall and provides support for all the joists. However, the installation of such a beam is a task better left to a contractor. See Fig. 3.

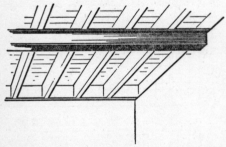

Fig. 3. A steel beam or girder resting on the basement walls and supporting all the first floor joists.

Or you may have a beam supporting the joists which is in turn supported by a post in the center of the basement. That post may be directly in the way of your plans for remodeling. Perhaps you could replace it with two posts nearer the walls where they would not be so much in the way. The combination jack and steel post shown on page 235 and described on page 234 will suggest a way to install adequate support.

Another problem often encountered in the basement is that the walls have been covered with plaster applied directly to the masonry. This plaster will soon deteriorate from dampness either picked up from the masonry wall or from condensation and therefore it should be removed.

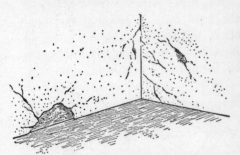

Fig. 4. What generally happens to plaster on a concrete basement wall. It cracks and chips off after a few years.

See Fig. 4. This can be done with a hammer and cold chisel.

Any cracks or holes in the masonry of the basement walls should be filled and the inside surface washed or brushed clean. A complete inspection should be made of all the woodwork in the basement to make sure that none of it has been attacked and damaged by rot or termites. Fig. 5 shows a section of house sill and

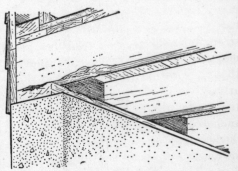

Fig. 5. House sill and joist attacked by dry rot or termites. If permitted to go on the joist will sag and then the floor will sag or squeak.

floor joist that has been so affected. If there are any squeaks in the first floor these should be taken care of now before the basement ceiling material goes up and covers the floor joists.

Basement Stairs. The steps from the first floor to the basement are often rough and unfinished, but what is worse is that they are sometimes too steep and open risers make them

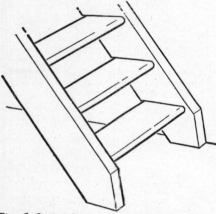

Fig. 6. Stairs that are not safe for frequent use, particularly guests in high heels and party dress.

dangerous. And very frequently the stairs are rather poorly lighted. In many cases the stairs are not structurely sound. If the steps are not too steep, or not in too bad condition, it may be possible to fix them up so that they will be at least safe if not attractive. The first task is to inspect them carefully to see that they are anchored securely at the top and that the bottom of the stringers (or sides) sit level on the basement floor. Figs. 6 and 7 show the difference between unsafe and safe stairs. The safe stairs have risers and a hand rail.

Fig. 7. Stairs that are safe, with risers in place and a solid handrail.

Fig. 8 shows how boards can be nailed across from one stringer to the other to close the risers. Nail a cleat to the under side of the stair tread and then nail the riser to that and to the back of the stair tread below. That is better than merely nailing through the stringers.

A good solid handrail can be made out of 2 x 4 inch stock, planed and sanded smooth so that there will be

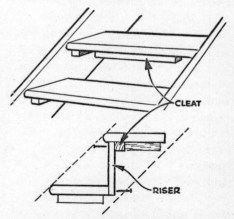

Fig. 8. How to cover open risers on stairs. Nail risers to cleats under treads and to the back of the treads below.

no danger from splinters. If the old stairs are in generally poor condition and too steep, then it would be better to install a new set. Directions for building a rough flight of stairs have been given on pages 291 to 293, but such stairs may not fit in very well with the future plans for the basement. It is one thing to get along with rough stairs when they are used mostly by someone going down to tend the furnace, and it is something entirely different when they are to be used by guests going to and from a basement party or recreation room. It might be preferable to buy stairs from a lumber yard. They generally carry stairs in stock with treads, risers, and stringers all cut and fitted, so that it is merely a matter of assembling them. The experienced home mechanic should have no great difficulty in putting those units together. Basement stairs should be at least three feet wide.

The location of the stairs should be considered. Of course, the top of the flight is probably settled, the stairs have to start where they do, but the point where they end could be changed. The stairs may go straight down and end in the middle of the basement, thus handicapping the layout of basement rooms. So you might be able to change their course, start them down a few steps as before, have a landing, and then continue at a 90° angle from the direction of the top stairs.

Rearranging the Household Equipment. To save space for other purposes it is wise to concentrate household equipment usually found

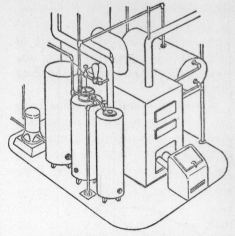

Fig. 9. Equipment grouped together around a furnace, namely, water pump, water supply tank, hot water heater, hot water tank, and automatic stoker.

in the basement into one area. This includes the furnace, hot water heater, water softener (if any), and, in rural areas, the water pump and storage tank. If it is possible to get all of this equipment to one section of the cellar, then it can be partitioned off so as to be out of sight. A partition also helps keep ashes and coal dust out of the rest of the basement.

Moving the heating plant is usually either too expensive or impractical an undertaking because it must be connected into a chimney, but it is often quite possible to move the other pieces of equipment to the same area as that occupied by the furnace. See Fig. 9 for an illustration of those assembled pieces of equipment.

If the home mechanic decides to do this work of moving the plumbing equipment himself, then he should first do a little planning so that the house will be without water for the shortest possible time. Or he might pick a day when the other members of the family are going to be away most of the day. All the necessary pipe should be on hand as well as the tools which will be required for cutting and joining pipe, and any fittings that will be needed. If the hot water heater is fired by gas or electricity, the proper concern should be notified so that they can send a man over in the morning to disconnect the heater and then back again in the afternoon to reconnect it.

Mount the Water Pump. In the case of a water pump, if you have one, it is a good plan to mount it on a solid concrete base when it is moved to the new location. By providing a base to which the pump can be anchored, vibration will be reduced and there is less chance of pipe joints working loose. Another advantage is that the base will keep the pump off the floor and perhaps prevent it from being damaged.

The area on the basement floor to be occupied by the base should be roughened up with a cold chisel so that the new concrete will bond to the old. Clean the area and wet it down before pouring the fresh concrete. A form for the concrete base can be made out of odd scraps of lumber. The best way to attach the pump to the base is to sink machine bolts head first into the fresh concrete, leaving enough of the threaded end above the surface to fit through the holes in the metal base of the pump and motor and so take the

nuts. Accurate measuring is necessary.

Fig. 10 shows a method of placing the bolts so that they will line up with the holes in the pump. Nail boards together to form sides of the form as shown in Fig. 10. Select two inch-thick boards to go across the top. Set water pump on one board and drill down through the holes in the base of water pump through the board underneath. Do same with other board at other end of pump. Nail template marked "A" in place. Very carefully measure and place

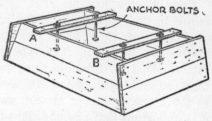

Fig. 10. Form for making a concrete base on which to mount a water pump and motor. Heads of long machine bolts are to be anchored in the concrete.

template B the right distance from template A, so that the holes in the water pump base will line up, and nail template B in place. Insert bolts and screw on nuts as shown in Fig. 10.

Mix concrete, one part Portland cement, 2¾ parts sand, and 4 parts gravel, and fill the form. After the concrete has set, remove nuts, knock off templates A and B, and, if you have measured accurately, the pump and motor can be put in place and bolted down by putting on the nuts.

Before any of the fixtures are disconnected, their water supply should be turned off and the fixture drained.

In the case of the hot water tanks and water supply tanks the water can be drained out by opening the faucet at the bottom of the tank. But before this is done, either open faucets on the house fixtures or disconnect one of the pipes running out of the top of the tank. If this is not done, a partial vacuum will be built up inside the tank when the water starts to drain out and this will prevent a complete draining.

Be sure that the heating element is off before draining the water out of a hot water tank.

Once all the fixtures have been moved to their new location, the job of connecting them back into the system can be begun. The type of pipe selected for extending existing lines should be the same as that used in the house plumbing system, and it is important that any additions to

Fig. 11. A stock and die for threading pipe.

existing pipes be the same size as the original lines.

Cutting and Threading Galvanized Iron Pipe. If galvanized pipe is to be used, then some provision must be made for cutting and threading the various lengths of pipe required for the extension work. Pipes can be cut and threaded at plumbing and hardware stores for a slight additional charge per pipe, but this will require very accurate measuring on the part of the home mechanic if the threaded pipes are to fit perfectly when it comes to assembling. In the long run it would probably be better to rent a pipe

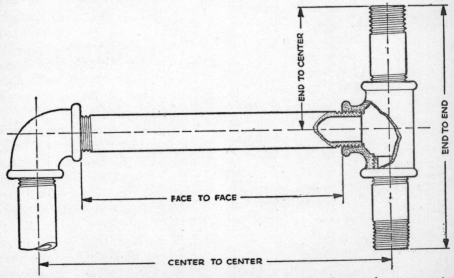

Fig. 12. The correct way to measure pipe is to get your right distance from one center to another, then measure fittings, get distance face of one fitting to face of the other and then add proper amount for the thread engagements.

cutter and the proper size stock and die (see Fig. 11), and cut and thread the pipe right on the job. In that way if you make an error in cutting one piece of pipe you can compensate for it when you cut the next piece of pipe, whereas if your pieces are all cut beforehand, it may be impossible to fit them together.

Before a length of pipe is cut you should measure the distance between the two points it is to connect. Consult Fig. 12. Find the distance from the end or face of one fitting to the face of the other. However, each end of the pipe will be threaded and screwed into a fitting of one kind or another, and allowance must be made for that unexposed portion of the pipe. If, for example, the distance between the faces of two fittings is exactly 14 inches and you are using ¾ inch pipe, then it should be cut 15 inches long to allow ½ inch of thread at each end to screw into the fitting.

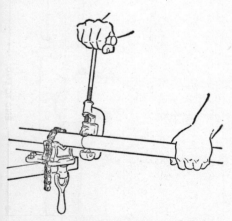

Fig. 13. Using a pipe cutter to cut pipe. The pipe is held firmly in a pipe vise, constructed so that it will not flatten the pipe or damage it.

After measuring and marking the pipe, fasten it in a vise, and make the cut with a pipe cutter. Fig. 13 shows this being done. The pipe is secured in a pipe vise, which grips the pipe on all sides equally. An ordinary vise with its two jaws might flatten the pipe slightly. The pipe cutter has a handle which, when turned, either increases or decreases the distance between the cutting jaws. The cutting wheel of the cutter should be placed over the exact mark on the pipe where the cut is to be made. Tighten up on the cutter handle until the wheel bites into the pipe. Make one revolution around the pipe so that the cut is started straight. Turn the handle so that the cutter makes a deeper bite and then apply oil over the cutting wheel. Make a half turn around the pipe with the cutter in this position and then tighten up on the handle for the next half revolution. Continue in this fashion until the pipe is cut through. A hack saw is not a satisfactory tool to use in cutting galvanized pipe because it is difficult to get a perfectly straight cut with the saw, and unless the cut is straight, proper threading will be impossible.

Threading. Threads are cut with a special die that is held in a stock. Naturally the die must correspond in size to the pipe that is to be threaded. To be sure that the threads are started perfectly square, a guide bushing is used to center the die exactly on the pipe. During the cutting process, oil should be applied over the die. Press the die against the pipe and turn slowly in a clockwise direction. After the die begins to cut, turn it back a fraction of an inch after each half turn to allow bits of metal to break off. After the pipe has been threaded, the inside should be reamed out to remove the metal burr left by cutting. This is taken off by means of a reamer that will fit in a hand brace. Be sure that this burr is removed for it will reduce the flow of water through the pipe if left on.

Fig. 14. Copper tubing which can be bent and is thus easier to install than pipe.

Be sure that the threads are clean and straight for if they are not it will be impossible to get a leak proof joint. In any case, it is a good idea to coat the external threads of each connection with pipe compound or dope before fitting so that the joint will be absolutely watertight. Galvanized pipe is assembled or connected with a stilson or pipe wrench. Two wrenches will probably be required in most cases, one to hold the pipe and the other to hold the fitting.

Cutting and Fitting Copper Tubing. In some homes copper tubing is used for the plumbing system. This kind of pipe can be assembled in two different ways. One method is with flared fittings and the other is with soldered fittings. The two kinds or grades of tubing in general use are "K" and "L." "L" tubing is used for interior work, while the somewhat heavier grade of "K" tubing is used for outside work and heavy duty jobs. See Fig. 14. Copper tubing can be bent whereas galvanized pipe requires elbow fittings.

Of the two methods used in making up or connecting copper tubing, the flared method is probably the easier of the two and requires the

less amount of special equipment or skill. However, when correctly done, soldered connections are less likely to spring leaks.

Special fittings called "Flared Fittings" the same size as the tubing, will be required for this method of assembly, as well as a "Flaring Tool," such as is shown in Fig. 15, which is the proper size. Copper tubing can be cut with a hack saw, but care must be taken, if the tubing is held in a vise while cutting, not to tighten the jaws of the vise so much that you flatten the tubing. Make the cut straight and then ream out the burr on the inside of the tubing. Remove one of the slip nuts from the fitting and place it over the end of the tubing. The threaded opening of the nut should face the end of the tubing. Be sure to do this before flaring the tubing. Then center the flaring tool at the end of the tubing

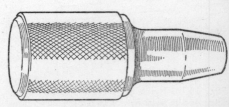

Fig. 15. A flaring tool used for flaring copper tubing.

and strike it with a hammer until the copper tubing spreads out flush with the outside edge of the flaring tool. Fig. 16 shows tubing that has been flared. The beveled edge of the fitting is then centered into the flared end of the tubing and the slip nut brought up and screwed back to the fitting. Then the same thing is done to the other piece of tubing. Fig. 16 shows one side already assembled and the other ready to be.

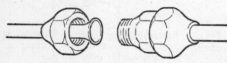

Fig. 16. A flange fitting connecting two pieces of copper tubing. The left hand piece of tubing has been flared as you can see.

Soldered Joints. The other method of joining copper tubing and fittings is with a soldered joint. (See Fig. 17.) This assembly calls for fittings that have no internal or external threads but are made just large enough in diameter so that they can be slipped over the tubing. After the tubing has been cut and reamed, the end should be cleaned with emery cloth or steel wool until it is bright. The same thing must be done to the

inside of the fitting, (see Fig. 18) because any dirt or grease on the metal parts to be joined will prevent the solder from taking hold. Once the

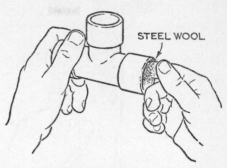

Fig. 18. Cleaning the inside of a fitting preparatory to soldering it to copper tubing. Dirt or grease inside the fitting would prevent solder from taking hold.

surfaces are clean, a light film of flux is applied to the inside of the fitting and to the outside of tubing, as shown in Fig. 19, and the fitting is then slipped in place. Turn the fitting back and forth a few times so that the flux will be well distributed over all the surfaces that are in contact with each other. The fitting must next be heated with a blow torch as

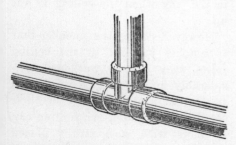

Fig. 17. A soldered joint on copper tubing. The next five pictures show the steps in making such a joint.

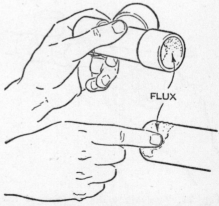

Fig. 19. Applying a light film of flux to the inside of the fitting and the outside of the copper tubing before soldering.

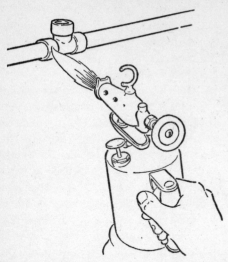

Fig. 20. Heating fitting and tubing with a blowtorch before applying solder.

it will be necessary to heat the fitting for each operation, the completed joint should be covered with wet cloth. This will prevent the solder from melting at this point while the other end of the fitting is being heated. The manner of wrapping on cloth is shown in Fig. 22.

Fig. 22. Protecting two soldered joints with damp cloths before heating the fitting so as to solder a third joint.

shown in Fig. 20 until it is hot enough to melt solder and cause it to flow up into the small seam between the tubing and the fitting. Wire solder is applied to the edge of the fitting, as is shown in Fig. 21, and is continued to be fed until it is no longer drawn into the seam.

It is often necessary to make two soldered joints at one fitting and as

Certain types of fittings used for solder joints have a small hole at the ends, and the wire solder is fed into the hole instead of at the edge.

While work of rearranging the equipment is under way, the necessary pipes and wires should be installed, when possible, so that they will not interfere with any future plans for finishing off the ceiling and walls. For example, if a pipe must run across the ceiling, it is often possible to cut notches in each joist, so that the pipe can be recessed up into the beam where it will not be in the way when the ceiling it put up.

However, you must remember that if notches are cut in the ceiling joists, they will be weakened considerably and should be reinforced to prevent any possibility of their sagging. This job of reinforcing can be done with steel straps placed along the edge of the joists, as is shown in Fig. 23, or with 2 x 2 inch

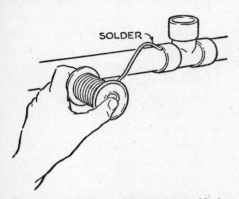

SOLDER

Fig. 21. Applying solder to joint. If the fitting and tubing have been properly heated, solder will be drawn in until the seam is completely filled.

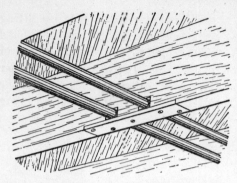

Fig. 23. Method of recessing pipes up into a beam so that a ceiling can be put up. The steel strap not only supports pipes but also restores strength to the beam which was weakened by cutting notches for the pipes.

lumber running the length of the joists and spiked to each side.

Any valves, faucets, or other fittings in the plumbing and heating system that are to be accessible at one time or another should be located, when possible, in some spot outside the room to be finished off. If this cannot be done then, when it comes time to cover the ceiling and walls, openings will have to be made so that these fittings can be reached without effort.

Covering the Furnace. Sometimes it happens that the furance is located in the approximate center of the basement and this presents a considerable problem. One method of getting around it is to screen the furnace, using the same general type of construction that you are going to use for the rest of the finished room. Thus, if the basement is to be finished in a ship motif, the screen around the furnace can be made to resemble the pilot house of a ship, or a cabin, complete with blind portholes and brass ships fittings. If it

is necessary to build around a furnace, remember to leave enough room inside the structure so that the furnace can be cleaned and overhauled when necessary.

Also, be sure that there are enough openings so that the heating plant will get an adequate supply of fresh air. No heating plant will operate efficiently unless it has a proper amount of fresh air so as to allow combustion of the fuel. For this same reason, if the furnace is to be partitioned off in a room with other mechanical equipment, either have an outside window opening into this space, or leave openings of some type in the partition wall for a supply of fresh air.

Of course another method of procedure when the furnace is in the center of the basement, is to leave it there and arrange everything on one side of the basement, thus leaving the other half to be finished off.

However, some modern, automatic heating equipment is now designed so that it can be left uncovered in a basement recreation room without detracting from the appearance of the room to any great degree. This equipment is covered with heat resistant paint, and due to its compactness will not be particularly conspicuous.

Another problem that must be worked out in connection with oil- or coal-burning heating equipment is where to store the fuel. No difficulty is presented in the case of a gas furnace, as here there is only a pipe running outside to the gas main. The fuel-supply tank for an oil burner can be inside or outside the basement. If the tank is inside, then it may be possible to move it to some other location in the basement, or to have it placed outside. In any event, the job of moving the tank and extending the oil pipes should be left to an oil-burner serviceman.

Coal Bins. Regardless of whether a coal furnace is hand fired or has an automatic stoker, it is desirable to have an ample supply of fuel near at hand, and still keep the basement free of dust and ashes.

The ideal location for such a bin would be outside and underground. A portion of the basement wall would serve as one side of the bin, with a hole at the bottom so that coal would be available in the basement. The bin should be provided with a removable top on the outside so that it could be easily filled. If the furnace is fed by an automatic stoker, such as is shown in Fig. 24, the bin must be positioned so that the coal

screw enters at the bottom of the bin and draws coal directly from this point. That eliminates the necessity of hand-filling a small hopper on the stoker at frequent intervals.

If the bin cannot be located outside, then it can be constructed in the basement out of wood or concrete blocks. Some thought should be given when locating the bin to ease of delivering the coal by coal truck. The general practice in most homes is to have a small window and hope that the coal company can manage to chute the coal in down a removable chute. The home mechanic might consider building a permanent coal chute similar to that pictured in Fig. 25. A sheet of metal or wire screen is used as a core to keep the concrete incline from cracking under the impact of a sudden deluge of coal. A metal cover fits tightly into a metal frame at the top, thus preventing water from entering the cellar that way. The width of the chute would

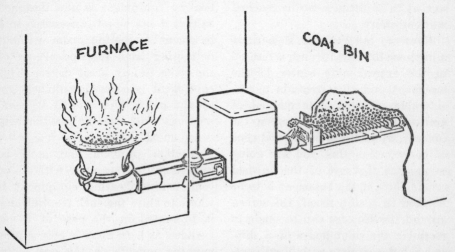

Fig. 24. A modern mechanical coal stoker installed so that the coal is fed directly from the coal bin, thus eliminating all coal shoveling.

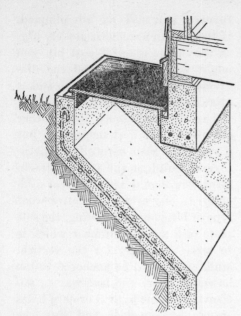

Fig. 25. A built-in coal chute and its metal cover to keep out rain or snow.

of the basement, but if the bin is made air tight, ventilation will have to come from outside. The glass in the coal bin window can be replaced by a louver. However, if a coal chute is installed, a louver will have to be put into the wall next to it.

The size of bin will depend upon the type of fuel being used, the size of the furnace, and the amount of space you want to devote to coal storage. A ton of anthracite will require 37 cubic feet of space, while a ton of bituminous occupies about 46 square feet. A ton of coke requires 65 cubic feet of storage space.

After deciding on the size and location of the bin the first step is putting up a ceiling. Use plywood or wallboard or plasterboard and nail it to the ceiling joists. If the bin is so big that a single piece would not cover the ceiling, or is too unwieldy to handle, two or more pieces can be used, but be sure to have them join at the center of a joist so that both

be about two feet but of course will be governed by the size of the metal cover, which should be purchased before further plans are made. Such a chute is not essential, to be sure, but in making improvements and changing the existing coal bin, if a chute is to be added it should be built before a new bin is constructed. Fig. 26 shows a mechanical coal chute that you can buy and install in the basement wall in place of a window.

Naturally the bin should be placed so that the basement wall will serve as a back to the bin. In remodeling a basement you should plan to make the coal bin tight so that coal dust will not spread. That may impose another problem. If you use soft coal, the bin will require ventilation. Formerly it got that from the rest

Fig. 26. A mechanical coal chute that can be purchased and installed in the basement wall in place of a window.

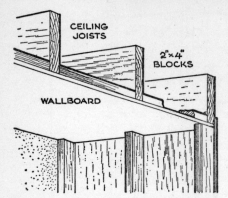

Fig. 27. A dust-proof ceiling is one of the first steps in building a coal bin.

pieces can be nailed securely to the joist. Fig. 27 shows a dustproof ceiling. Notice that 2 x 4 inch supports or blocks have been nailed between the joists along the inside limits of the bin.

Sole Plates. The next step is to attach sole plates to the basement floor. Here the procedure may vary slightly depending on the type of furnace, and style of bin planned. If there is an automatic stoker, Fig. 28 shows the style of coal bin you might wish to build, and the diagrams show how to make the stoker attachment.

The diagrams may look rather complicated at first inspection, but if you study them carefully preparatory to building the stoker attachment, you should have no great difficulty. In any event, no matter what type of bin you are building, the sole plate of 2 x 4 inch lumber which is to serve as a base for the vertical studding, should be anchored to the basement floor. The best way to anchor the soles is to drill or chip holes in the cement floor and sink the heads of long machine bolts in these holes and fill in around the bolts with cement. Have your 2 x 4 inch soles drilled to take the bolts and use them as sort of a template while the

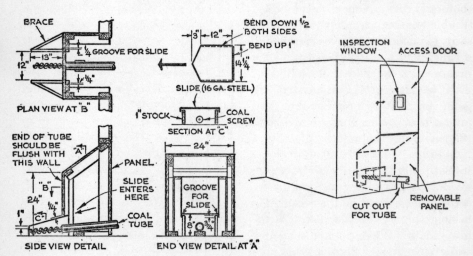

Fig. 28. Method of constructing a stoker attachment for inside of coal bin. Note that bottom part of the Access Door is a removable panel, and only the top part of that door will swing open on hinges, so that one would have to climb up about three feet in order to step into the coal bin.

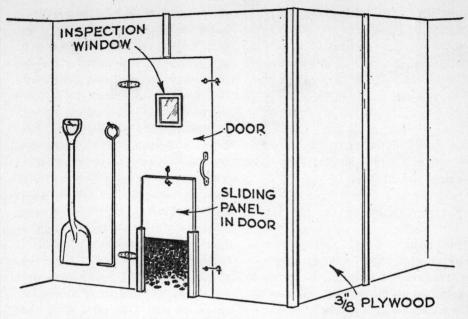

INSPECTION WINDOW

DOOR

SLIDING PANEL IN DOOR

3"/8 PLYWOOD

Fig. 29. Type of coal bin for a hand-fired furnace, using outside basement walls for two of the four sides. The sliding panel in door should not be open as far as shown when the bin is full of coal.

cement is hardening. Do not tighten nuts on the bolts until the cement is thoroughly dry. Going to so much trouble to anchor the sole plates may seem unnecessary but the weight of a full bin of coal exerts tremendous pressure at the base of a coal bin wall, and there is little point in going to great pains to make a bin air tight and then have coal spring it open a little later.

Studding should be spaced at 16 inches on center and run from the sole to the ceiling. An opening for an access door should be framed at the bottom on one side. The sides of the bin should be covered with tongue and groove lumber, tightly fitted and nailed securely. Boards with knot holes or other flaws of that sort are not satisfactory for this purpose be-

cause dust will get through the openings. Bottoms for bins that are to be used for coal stokers will vary according to the type of coal screw. Information on that subject can be obtained by writing to the manufacturer of the stoker, or by asking your local dealer. The bin shown in Fig. 26 should have a sloping bottom so that you would not have to climb in to move the last ton of coal closer to the stoker screw.

Construction of a bin for a hand-fired furnace is somewhat similar. Fig. 29 illustrates such a bin. Here you may have a sliding panel at the bottom of the access door, with a hook to hold it open. When the furnace is not in operation the panel can be closed. For the sides of any bins it is best to use tongue and groove lumber, tightly fitted and securely nailed. It is safer to put this on the inside of the studding, but as that will detract from the appearance of the bin and cut down on the capacity, you can put it on the outside of the studding if you use plenty of nails. In Fig. 29 ⅜ inch plywood is indicated and trim is used to cover seams and add strength. This gives a neat appearance.

If there are two kinds of coal-burning appliances in the house, using different sizes of coal, then a partition should be constructed through the center of the bin and arrangements made for two outside openings to fill the bin, and two access doors on the inside.

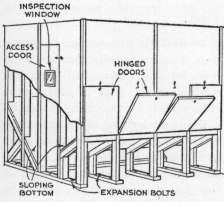

Fig. 30. A coal bin with a sloping bottom and four hinged doors. With rough partition inside bin two sizes of coal can be stored.

Fig. 30 shows a slightly different sort of bin, with a sloping bottom so that coal will slide down as used and always be available at certain points. Instead of one access door there are four and you could always reach any coal left in the bin through one of the four doors. If this type of bin is built, the sole plates held by expansion bolts are put in differently. 1 x 4 inch lumber will do for sole plates instead of 2 x 4 inch. With this type of bin two sizes of coal can be kept easily by having a rough partition inside the bin. Scrap lumber of almost any kind can be used for such an inside partition. Sloping bottoms can be made either of concrete or wood. In the bin shown in Fig. 30 the slope at the back could be made of concrete but it would be easier to make the slope above the hinged doors of wood. With the type of bin shown in Fig. 29 you could have sloping bottoms of cement on three sides to slide the coal toward the panel in the door.

A helpful arrangement for opening the coal bin window without going inside and perhaps scrambling over coal, is shown in Fig. 31. It would also be convenient if that part of the bin next to the window has a sloping bottom.

Basement Plumbing Equipment. It may be necessary to leave a portion of the basement for the home-laundry equipment. (See Fig. 39.) The laundry room does not have to be very large in this age of auto-

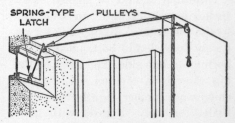

Fig. 31. Method of attaching pulley so coal bin window can be opened or shut without entering the bin.

matic washing machines, driers, and ironers, but it should be well lighted, and ventilated by either natural or artificial means. If it is possible the washing machine should have an outlet connected into the house sewer line, and hot and cold water pipes brought to it, so that the mess and bother of filling and draining the machine with lengths of rubber hose will be eliminated. If possible, you can try to locate the laundry so as to take advantage of the floor drain in the basement if there is one.

As mentioned earlier, in remodeling a basement it is a good plan to install toilet facilities if that is at all practical, or at least to allow space for such installation at a future date. Such fixtures will not only be a convenience in the basement, but may help to alleviate a possible shortage of plumbing facilities throughout the rest of the house. Generally speaking, it is not necessary here to plan a complete bathroom. The usual procedure is to install what is often called a "half-bathroom" or "powder room" consisting of a toilet, wash basin, and perhaps a dressing table.

Because of the absence of bathtub or shower, a room of this sort can often be located under the basement stairs in space that is otherwise wasted or useful only for storage purposes. However, before any definite plans are made for such plumbing in the basement, a plumber should be consulted to determine whether or not the plan is feasible, and if so, where such a room had best be located in order to take advantage

of the existing plumbing. It might be that the sewer line for the house runs along the basement ceiling or the walls, in which case it would be impossible to connect any basement fixtures to it because these fixtures would be lower than the sewer line. In such a case the only alternative would be to install an independent sewer system for the basement plumbing, and that might be too expensive to seem desirable.

Heating the Basement. If the basement rooms are to be comfortable throughout the entire year, then provision must be made so that they are properly heated during the winter months. A well constructed and properly insulated furnace will not give off very much heat to its surroundings unless it happens to be of a design intended for that purpose. For the most part, it is best to discount heating the basement from the furnace proper, and turn to other methods for warmth. As far as hot water or hot air heating systems go, the radiators or registers can be hung from the basement ceiling so that they will be higher than the furnace, and thus operate properly. See Fig. 32 and Fig. 33. If this is

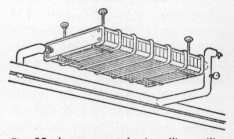

Fig. 32. Arrangement for installing ceiling radiator in basement so that it will be above the furnace and heat properly.

not practical, they can be installed elsewhere, and if lower than the heating plant, fans or pumps can be used to force the hot water or warm air into circulation. Steam radiators will have to be hung from the ceiling or not used at all. In making plans to heat the basement by the central heating plant, it is

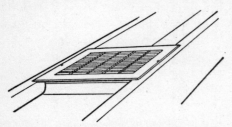

Fig. 33. Arrangement for installing ceiling register so as to heat the basement with hot air.

assumed that the plant is of sufficient size to take on this extra load without a loss of efficiency that might make the rest of the house uncomfortable or difficult to heat. If, for some reason, the central heating plant cannot be used, then electric or gas space heaters can be used. These need not prove particularly expensive to operate as basement rooms need not be heated except when in use.

When making changes in the heating system, try as far as possible to get the pipes out of the way in the same manner as was used for the plumbing pipes. If you have a hot air system, rectangular hot air ducts can be fitted between the ceiling joists as is shown in Fig. 34, and will require less depth than the round pipes usually found on old-fashioned hot-air heating systems.

Windows. Most basements are not very well provided with windows. This is because the ground outside is usually at about the same level as the top of the basement walls, and also, until these last few years, basements were not used for much more than storage purposes and thus there was no need to provide them with many windows.

The first step in getting proper ventilation and natural lighting into the basement is to make the most of the few windows you already have. In many cases bushes and shrubs outside the house prevent very much sunlight or air from reaching the windows. Naturally such bushes and shrubs should be removed and any other obstructions around the window taken away.

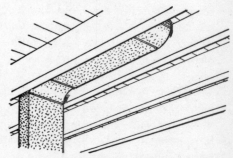

Fig. 34. Rectangular air ducts for conveying hot air will fit in well between joists and occupy less space than round pipes.

Some types of basement windows are not designed to be opened and these should be replaced with windows that can be opened and closed if they face a part of the basement that is going to be finished off into a room. (If a solid window merely confronts an area that is going to be used for storage, there is no need to

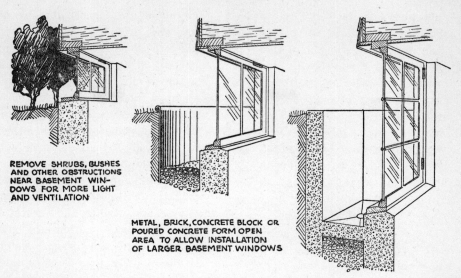

REMOVE SHRUBS, BUSHES AND OTHER OBSTRUCTIONS NEAR BASEMENT WINDOWS FOR MORE LIGHT AND VENTILATION

METAL, BRICK, CONCRETE BLOCK OR POURED CONCRETE FORM OPEN AREA TO ALLOW INSTALLATION OF LARGER BASEMENT WINDOWS

Fig. 35. Basement windows, and methods of providing more light. Areaways or wells are necessary if the bottom of the window is below the level of the ground. The center drawing shows a metal areaway and a pebble bottom. Drawing at right has poured concrete sides and a concrete drain with pebbles underneath.

replace it.) The old window can be removed by chipping away the mortar around the frame with a cold chisel. Clean out the opening and secure the new frame in place with cement mortar. Some basement windows have to be kept sealed tight to prevent water from entering around the seams. In a situation of that sort it is possible to install areaways or wells around the outside of the windows so that they can be opened without water coming in. See Fig. 35. Through the use of deep areaways it is often possible to install longer windows and thus provide many times more light and air than the usual shallow basement window will admit.

The first step in installing an areaway is to dig out the ground around the window to the necessary depth. If the bottom of the areaway is to

be of concrete, the top of the concrete should be about 6 inches below the bottom of the window sill and should be given a slight pitch so that water will flow to and down a drain pipe that has its opening at the bottom of the areaway. See right hand drawing in Fig. 35. If gravel and pebbles are to be used as the bottom of the areaway, as in the central drawing, then the pit should be dug deep enough to permit 18 inches or more of these materials to be poured in.

The three sides of the areaway can be made out of poured concrete, bricks or concrete blocks. Metal areaways can be purchased from building supply-houses; these are attached to the foundation wall with expansion bolts. The walls of a poured concrete areaway should be about 8 inches thick, and should be made with a mixture of 1 part Portland cement, 2½ parts clean, fine sand, and 3½ parts clean gravel.

Sometimes basement windows are so far above the floor that the average person cannot open or close them without standing on a bench or ladder. In that case some device should be installed so that they can be opened and closed easily. Various devices which do this are on sale at supply houses and can be attached without great difficulty.

It is important that the basement be properly ventilated, for not only will stale air make basement rooms uncomfortable but proper ventilation will help prevent condensation on walls and the floor.

If it is impossible to get the proper amount of air circulation by means of windows, then it will be necessary to install an exhaust fan such as is shown in Fig. 36. If there is a bathroom of any kind in the basement which does not have a window opening outside, it should be provided with an exhaust fan. The same holds true for a laundry room if there is one.

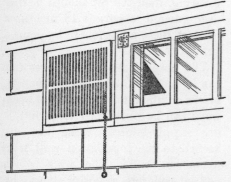

Fig. 36. An exhaust fan installed to provide additional ventilation in the basement.

Basement Fireplace. Among the more radical improvements that can be made in the basement during the remodeling is the installation of a fireplace. Almost every home owner would like to have such an addition to his game room or basement library, but certain factors must be taken into account before any definite plans for construction are decided.

If a fireplace is to operate properly, it must have its own flue and chimney. This chimney can run up inside the house so that the fireplace can be built up from the basement floor, but this calls for some major changes in the house construction because the chimney must be free of any and all structural members of the house. The chimney can also be on the outside of the house, and that presents fewer complications. Of course considerable excavation will have to be made along one portion of the foundation wall, so that a base for the fireplace can be set on about the same level as the basement floor. It will also be necessary to cut an opening in the foundation wall. If it so happens that the ground on which the house is built slopes to one side, so that the basement floor is on about the same level as the ground outside, then the job of building a fireplace at that side of the basement will be considerably easier. In such a case it would be necessary to remove only enough soil to set down a base for the fireplace.

Many home mechanics have built their own fireplaces and have had good results. For those who contemplate building one in the basement, it would be wise to consult with an architect first, and let him decide whether or not the planned fireplace is feasible. It is advisable to have a contractor cut through the foundation, as the job will require special tools, special knowledge, and the use of heavy reinforcing beams of some sort to compensate for that portion of the wall that has been removed.

Another interesting possibility, which can be put to good use when one side of the basement floor is level with the ground outside, is to remove a portion of the wall and replace it with either a large picture window or a wall made of glass blocks. As neither of these materials can support a load over than its own weight, the opening in the wall will have to be reinforced in the same manner used for the fireplace opening.

Miscellaneous Basement Repairs. Before the actual work of building the basement rooms begins, there are a few small details that should be checked. For instance, all pipes and fittings which will be covered by the walls or ceiling material should be inspected for signs of leaks or weak points that might cause a leak in the near future. Pipes and fittings that appear to be in poor condition should be replaced. All pipes should be properly supported so that they will not vibrate or sag. Pipes will vibrate from the momentum of the water flowing through and in time this movement will cause leaks around fittings. Sags in steam pipes will cause the system to pound when steam is coming up. Cold water pipes should be insulated to prevent condensation of moisture that might damage the final room decorations. Hot water and heating lines should be insulated to prevent heat loss.

Basement Pipes. It was suggested earlier in this section that, when possible, pipes running across the ceiling should be recessed into the joists (as shown in Fig. 23) so that they will be covered by the ceiling material. However, sometimes it is not possible to do this without going to a considerable expense, and in that case, the ceiling material will have to go above the pipes. When it comes time to paint and decorate, paint the exposed pipe the same color as the surface in back of it, so that the pipe will not be too conspicuous. Do not make the usual mistake of painting exposed pipes gold or some other bright color, as this will only make them stand out.

When large pipes such as a heating main or sewer line run across the ceiling it is possible to cover them with a wooden box. This can be made out of heavy plywood or 1 inch stock wide enough to cover the pipe. It can be finished-off to resemble an old hand-hewn beam by gouging the surface with a wood chisel and then staining it. Additional false beams can be made and spaced at regular intervals along the ceiling or wall so that the finished work looks natural and in keeping.

If there are a great many pipes running along the ceiling and if there is enough head room in the basement, a false ceiling can be constructed under the pipes. As this ceiling will not have to support any weight other than the ceiling material, 2 x 4 inch joists can be used and then thin plywood.

Building Partitions. The partitions can be made with a wood frame that is later covered with wallboard or plywood. The frame for such a partition will consist of a 2 x 4 inch sole, to form the bottom of the wall. It should be anchored to the concrete basement floor with expansion bolts. A 2 x 4 inch plate is spiked to the basement ceiling joists to form the top of the partition. Vertical studding is run between sole and plate, and is spaced 16 inches on center. All vertical studding should be plumb, and doubled around door and window openings.

When building a partition to ceiling height it must be remembered that this will reduce the normal circulation of air throughout the basement. As basement rooms will require ample fresh air, if they are not to become damp and musty, some type of opening should be installed in each wall. These openings can be windows or louvers, anything to allow air to circulate.

If a partition wall is built for the purpose of concealing some object that is only a few feet high, such as a modern furnace, then it may be advisable to build only a half-wall. A wall of this sort, just high enough to hide the object back of it, will make the basement appear larger than it actually is. This arrangement is useful if the size of the recreation room has been reduced considerably to allow for necessary storage space.

These considerations of a half-wall assume that the house is heated by oil or gas. If heated by coal, air tight partitions will be desirable or necessary between the heating unit and any finished off rooms. However, there are certain conditions where a half-wall will be sufficient.

Such a wall does not have to be built in the conventional manner. It can be made of bricks, concrete blocks, or even glass blocks. By building the wall a little deeper than necessary, it will serve as a bookshelf or cabinet. Building with bricks has been discussed in another part of this book, on pages 43 to 47. Glass blocks can be laid with cement mortar, or by using wooden strips and wooden wedges. The advantage of the wooden strips and wedges method of construction is that the wall can be taken down easily and all the materials used again under different circumstances. Blocks of this type are available at most building supply-houses and lumberyards, and come with the manufacturer's directions regarding installation.

Of course, individual circumstances sometimes make other materials or procedures satisfactory. For instance, a sturdy wooden bookshelf fastened to the basement floor would make a satisfactory section of wall. A basement library could be built with all the walls made of full length, ceiling to floor bookshelves, thus avoiding the necessity and cost of putting up any wall partitions.

Basement Walls. Concrete and masonry foundation walls can be finished in several ways. They can be painted, preferably with a Portland-cement paint which will not be damaged by moisture or the action of the lime in the masonry. But merely painting the walls is not always satisfactory, due to the possibility of condensation of moisture on their surface; furthermore, they do not always absorb sounds. It is probably better in the long run to cover the walls with wallboard or plywood. Regardless of which type of material is selected, it is necessary first to line the walls with furring strips, so that there will be a base to which the wall covering can be nailed, and also to prevent the wallboard or plywood coming into direct contact with the masonry. The small dead-air space between the wall covering and the masonry walls will act as insulation so that there will be no moisture collecting on the surface of the finished wall.

Furring strips may be 2 x 2 or 2 x 4 inch lumber. If the furring can be placed against solid masonry at all points and still remain plumb and true, then the lighter 2 x 2 inch stock can be used. However, if there are any recessed portions of the wall, so that the furring will not be supported along its entire length by the wall, then it would be better to use the heavier 2 x 4 inch pieces. If there is any indication that the walls or the floor are damp at any time during the year, the furring, as well as the lumber used for the wall partitions, should be treated with a wood preservative to prevent rotting. Preservatives of this kind are available and many will also prevent damage

by termites. These preservatives can be applied by brush by the home mechanic, but it is better to purchase wood which has already been treated with the preservative at the mill, or lumberyard, because special equipment is used there to force the preservative into all the wood fibers and not just brush it over the surface.

One strip of furring should be put down at the base of the wall and another run along the top. Vertical strips are then placed between the top and bottom and attached to the masonry walls with special nails. These vertical strips should be spaced 16 inches on center. Furring must, of course, be used around all openings in the walls for doors and windows. It will also be needed around such things as plumbing and heating valves, gas meters, and the like, which could not be moved to some other location but must remain in the part of the basement that is to be finished. What can be done about such things is to build cabinets with doors around them so that when it is necessary to read a meter or turn on or off a valve it can be done with the least inconvenience. But doors should bear large signs painted in white so that strangers can locate them in a hurry if necesary to shut off gas or water or electricity in case of an accident or emergency.

It will not be necessary to use any furring on the ceiling, as the joists will serve as a base for the ceiling material. The only exception there will be in the case of a partition wall running directly under a joist. In such case it will be necessary to nail a strip of 2 x 2 inch board along each side of the joist to serve as a base on which to nail the ceiling material.

Basement Wiring. After the partitions and furring are in place, any necessary changes in the basement wiring can be made. The information on electric wiring in the section on FINISHING THE ATTIC will probably cover all problems found in basement wiring. One advantage in adding new circuits to the basement is that the main fuse box is usually located there. This will make it possible for an electrician to add whatever number of circuits that may be needed for the proper lighting of the basement, without running wires up through the walls and under floors.

When improving the basement electrical system, be sure to provide a light half-way down the basement stairs and install a three-way switch so that the light can be turned on or off either from the top or the bottom of the stairs. Most basements are provided with a minimum of lights by the builder, perhaps only one near the heating plant. Sometimes this is provided with a switch upstairs so that the light can be turned on before you go downstairs to the basement. As long as the basement was all open and free of partitions, that one light in the basement served to illuminate the stairs enough to use them safely, but once you begin putting up walls in the basement you need a light over the stairs, not only to see to use them safely but also to enable you to find your way to turn on other basement lights.

FASTEN SMALL SCREW-CAP JARS UNDER SHELVES FOR EASY LOCATION OF SCREWS, NAILS, BOLTS, ETC.

Fig. 37. Method of storing small articles so that they can be found quickly and easily.

All exhaust fans used in basement rooms should be permanently wired and provided with wall switches. Special care should be given to see that the home laundry is provided with heavy duty circuits, for equipment such as electric driers and ironers require thousands of watts, too heavy a load for the average interior lighting circuit.

And if ducts are required for any of the exhaust fans, such ducts should be installed at this time.

The home mechanic naturally will see to it that his workbench is provided with sufficient lighting and that enough outlets are located near his workbench to handle various power tools. Information on building a workbench has already been given earlier in this volume, on pages 23 to 29, and a workshop room can be finished off as simply or elaborately as the home mechanic desires. Fig. 37 shows a handy way to store nails or screws or other small parts, using the under side of a shelf. Fig. 38 shows a compact and fully equipped tool box.

Covering the Walls and Ceiling. When it comes to covering the walls and ceiling there are several possible choices of materials. The obvious one

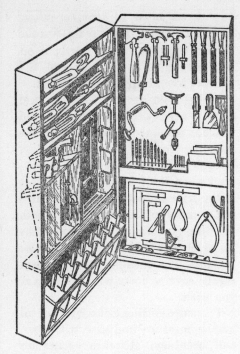

Fig. 38. A Compact tool cabinet.

is wallboard, and this will make a durable and attractive finish. A somewhat more attractive and expensive finish may be had by using plywood paneling. An acoustic type of wallboard for the ceiling has much in its favor, especially if the room being finished is to later contain machinery which would make a noise that might be disturbing. If ordinary wallboard or plywood is used on the ceiling it is best to put some sort of insulation between the ceiling joists so that sound originating in the basement will be absorbed and not pass to the rooms above. The insulation used for this purpose can be the same as that used to prevent the transmission of heat. This treatment should be used for basement rooms such as the workshop and laundry where mechanical noise is likely to be made. It is well to have it also over a game or recreation room if there is a billiard table or other such equipment. On the other hand, if you plan a basement library, insulation may be desirable for the reverse reason, to muffle noise from above.

The necessary information on the installation of wallboard has been given in the preceding section on FINISHING THE ATTIC and so here we will deal only with the installation of plywood paneling.

Plywood paneling comes in a wide selection of rare and beautiful woods. Most lumberyards have sample pieces on hand so that the home mechanic can examine the entire selection before he makes a final choice. Paneling is not to be painted, of course, but it can be stained, waxed, or varnished. If a painted surface is desired, then a wallboard or cheap grade of plywood should be used. The standard-size panel is 4 feet wide and 8 feet high. The cost per square foot for the paneling will vary according to the kind of wood that is used for the finish surface.

Once the wood has been selected the next step is to plan how the panels may be arranged for both balance and economy. It might be a good idea to make a scale drawing of each wall that is to be covered so that the panel arrangements can be worked out easily and accurately. In making up such drawings, the openings for windows and doors should be indicated, and you should also put in all dimensions. Do not just figure on the large areas and forget the small ones around doors or below windows.

Probably the easiest way to install the paneling is to have all seams run vertically. This will probaby give a better appearance as well. As it is seldom found that the width of a wall will be divisible by an even number of panels, some of the panels will have to be cut down in width. Suppose your wall is 15 feet wide and your panels are 4 feet wide. It would not look well to have three full width panels and then one 3 feet wide. It would be better to take 6 inches off each of the two end panels, so that the final result will be well balanced. Or if the wall is 11 feet wide, put a 3 foot panel in the center and full width ones at either end.

There are several ways to take care of the seams between sections of paneling. A simple V-joint is easily obtained and will give good results. If a butt joint is used, then the sections should be spaced a fraction of an inch apart and the seam covered with a strip of molding in the same manner used for wallboard.

Another point that must be considered and decided is how the corners are to be treated. Possibly the least complex method would be to bring the two sections of plywood forming the corner to within about ½ inch of each other and then cover the opening or seam with a strip of molding. Another method would be to make a butt joint without any additional molding being used. That calls for very careful cutting as the

two pieces must fit together along the entire length of the seam. Special corner molding can be used; if so, this is put in place first and the panels brought up tight against it.

If the trim around windows and doors is not yet on or can be removed without too much difficulty, then the paneling can be brought in close enough so that the edges will be covered when the trim is replaced. But if the trim cannot be removed without danger of marring the wood, then the paneling should be brought up as close to the edge of the trim as possible. The ensuing joint or seam can be covered later with molding if you wish.

To insure getting tight joints at all points, measure and saw with care and accuracy. Mistakes earlier in this work can be covered up, but when you get to the paneling there isn't anything to go over that.

To eliminate the possibility of any moisture from the masonry wall damaging the plywood the furring should be covered with waterproof paper or the back side of the plywood should be painted with asphalt paint.

The ceiling should be installed first and when that work has been completed, the walls can go on. Handle the sheets of plywood with the same care recommended for wallboard. To provide additional support for the paneling glue should be used as well as nails to attach it to the furring. The glue used for this work should be the kind recommended by the maker of the plywood and the size and spacing of nails should be done in accordance with the manufacturer's directions. This information can be obtained from the lumberyard. Special molding is available to cover the joint between wall and ceiling.

Basement Floors. When it comes to finishing the floor of the recreation room, the home mechanic has a wide choice of materials. First, the floor can be painted with a regular floor enamel. However, that type of finish can be used only over an absolutely dry surface. To test the floor for possible dampness, cover it with a piece of linoleum or tar paper weighted down and leave it on the floor for 24 hours. If, at the end of that time when the linoleum is removed, there are no damp spots under it, the floor is safe for painting.

In the case of a new house, dampness in the floor is not necessarily a sign that the floor is not watertight. It takes some time for all the water in new concrete to evaporate and so the floor should be left unfinished for additional drying and tests made for dampness at a later date.

The next step in painting a floor with an oil paint is to neutralize the lime in the concrete. This is done by mopping on a solution of 4 pounds of zinc sulfate to a gallon of water. Apply this solution liberally and let it stand for 48 hours. Then flush the surface of the concrete with fresh water to remove the crystals left by the solution and allow the concrete to dry out. When dry, the surface may be painted.

Special paints have been designed, with a rubber or synthetic base, which are especially suitable to be applied to a concrete surface as they will not be damaged by the lime or dampness in the material. You can very likely obtain these at your local paint or hardware store.

Linoleum, rubber tile, cork tile, and asphalt tile may also be used as a floor finish in the basement provided the floor is free from dampness. Flooring materials such as these have to be attached to the concrete with a special mastic.

Another possibility for the floor is to use regular hardwood flooring. The first step to this job is to set down and attach strips of wood called sleepers to the concrete, to form a base to which the flooring can be nailed. These sleepers should be 2 x 3 inch or larger in size, and spaced 16 inches on center or less. Before putting the sleepers down they should be treated with a wood preservative. After they are in place and secured to the concrete, waterproof paper should be set over them to keep any dampness away from the wood flooring. The flooring is then nailed down, spacing the nails carefully so that they will go into the wooden sleepers. Additional information on laying hardwood floors may be found in the section on HARDWOOD FLOORS on page 293 and on pages 393 and 394.

There are some kinds of hardwood flooring (sometimes called parquet floors, and explained on page 239) that come in square sections and are fastened to the concrete with a mastic similar to that used for composition tiles and linoleum.

Because the concrete basement floor provides a good solid base, concrete or ceramic tile may be set down with little extra effort. The first task in this case is to mix a grout of cement and water, and apply it to the area that is to be covered. Before this grout is hard, a mixture of one part cement and three parts sand, with enough water added to make it a workable plastic, is applied to the floor. This coat should be at least ¾ inch thick and of course should be of equal depth over the entire area.

Another point that it is quite important to observe carefully is to mix only as much mortar as you can cover with tile before the mortar sets, a period of about 30 minutes. Dust a light coating of dry cement over the mortar and place the tiles in position after dampening them. Be careful to make sure that each tile is level and on the same plane as the others. A small crack about ⅛ inch wide is left between tiles. That crack is to be filled, after the mortar bed has set, with a mixture of one part cement to one part sand. Force this filler into the seams between the tiles, level off the surface, and then wipe the tiles clean before the filler hardens.

As soon as the basement floor has been completed, doors can be hung and the trim, including the baseboard, can go on. The procedure for attaching hinges and locks and hanging doors has been explained on pages 278 to 284.

Other Basement Rooms. The treatment of walls, ceilings, and floors of the other basement rooms will vary considerably. So far as the room containing the furnace and other allied mechanical equipment is concerned, the masonry walls can be left uncovered unless there is considerable condensation on them, in which case they too should be covered. The ceiling and walls should be covered with a type of wallboard that has definite, fire-resistant qualities. The floor may be left unfinished unless it collects too much dust. If so, it should be painted so as to make sweeping easier.

Basement Darkroom. The main requirement for the basement darkroom is that it be light proof. This can be accomplished by using trim over any exposed seams and by using felt weather stripping around the door if necessary. However, making it light proof is likely to also make it air proof and ventilation is necessary. Windows or louvers are entirely unsuitable as they let in light. Perhaps the easiest method of supplying air would be to have some stovepipe painted black on the inside and curved so that light would not penetrate. Two such openings would be wanted, one as an inlet and the other as an outlet, and the latter might need a small fan attached to dispel fumes of photographic chemicals.

Another requirement of a darkroom is a water supply and drain, and of course electrical outlets will be needed. If the home mechanic is also the amateur photographer, he

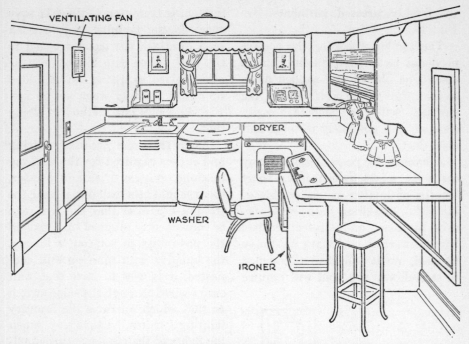

VENTILATING FAN

DRYER

WASHER

IRONER

Fig. 39. A neatly equipped basement laundry, with tubs, washing machine, dryer, ironer, ironing board, shelves, radio, closets, and ventilating fan.

will know from his study of photographic handbooks and magazines just what he prefers in running water facilities, electric connections, shelves and benches. If the photographer is another member of the household, let him or her describe what is needed.

The darkroom floor should be finished with tile or linoleum, something on which chemicals can be spilled and wiped up without damage to the floor. Cement or concrete are not too satisfactory.

Still another point that should have some consideration is dust, for dust has a bad effect on films and lens. Be sure that a ventilation inlet does not open on a part of the basement open to coal dust or ashes. Per-

haps the air inlet should have a cover to shut it when the darkroom is not in use.

Basement Laundry. When finishing the floor of the basement laundry tile will probably be found to be about the best material, for tile will not be damaged in any way by surface moisture and can be easily cleaned and dried. The walls and ceiling should be covered with wallboard which should be painted with an enamel wallpaint so that the surface will not be damaged or stained by water, and it will be easy to wipe clean. If pressing and ironing are to be done in this room, then ample shelf-space will be needed for the finished flatwork and a rack of some kind will be very useful for hanging up freshly pressed garments. See Fig. 39.

The lumber used for the shelves need not be of high quality, but it should be planed and sanded down so that after it has been painted, the surface will be smooth, easily cleaned, and not likely to catch and hold dust.

A hanger for pressed clothes may easily be made by attaching short lengths of lumber on either side of the room, attaching hooks or screw-eyes to them, and stretching steel wire between them. Heavy cord may be used, but it will have a tendency to stretch and sag, and will require

Fig. 40. How to install an ironing board so it will fold up out of the way. False panels give an attractive appearance when folded.

tightening from time to time. To save space in the laundry it is a good plan to attach the ironing board to the wall, either with hinges or some other device, so that it can be folded up out of the way when not in use. Fig. 40 shows one method of doing that.

Aside from the necessary wiring and outlets required for the washing machine, electric drier and presser, there should be a wall outlet near the ironing board so that the iron can be conveniently plugged in. To avoid the possibility of someone's leaving the laundry with the iron still connected, it is wise to have that wall outlet wired through the same switch as that which operates the laundry lighting fixtures. In that way, when the lights of the room are turned off, electric current to the iron will certainly be discontinued.

Storage Room and Vegetable Bin. The main requirement for the room that is to serve as the storage place for canned goods and other preserves, and possibly for a deep-freeze unit, is that it contain ample shelf-space and a light. It would be wise perhaps to enclose the shelves either with a cloth curtain or plywood doors, so that the items on the shelves will not become dust-covered. Fig. 41 shows fairly complete details for building such a storage room.

If the room is to be used as a cold cellar and vegetable bin, then it should be well insulated from the rest of the basement if it is to serve that purpose. This can be done by using insulating boards for the walls and ceiling of the room, or by using regular wallboard and filling the space between walls and above the ceiling with some kind of insulation, either dry fill, batt, or blanket type. This pipe can be provided with a damper so that the amount of cold air entering the bin may be regulated to prevent the air inside from

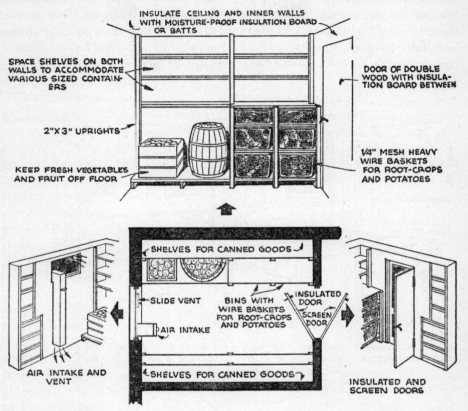

INSULATE CEILING AND INNER WALLS WITH MOISTURE-PROOF INSULATION BOARD OR BATTS

SPACE SHELVES ON BOTH WALLS TO ACCOMMODATE VARIOUS SIZED CONTAINERS

DOOR OF DOUBLE WOOD WITH INSULATION BOARD BETWEEN

2" X 3" UPRIGHTS

KEEP FRESH VEGETABLES AND FRUIT OFF FLOOR

1/4" MESH HEAVY WIRE BASKETS FOR ROOT-CROPS AND POTATOES

SHELVES FOR CANNED GOODS

SLIDE VENT

BINS WITH WIRE BASKETS FOR ROOT-CROPS AND POTATOES

INSULATED DOOR

SCREEN DOOR

AIR INTAKE

SHELVES FOR CANNED GOODS

AIR INTAKE AND VENT

INSULATED AND SCREEN DOORS

Fig. 41. Floor plan and arrangement for a compact storage room and vegetable bin.

To provide the necessary amount of cold, fresh air for the vegetable bin, some arrangement will be needed to bring in air from outdoors. This can be done by running stove pipe through an opening such as a window (perhaps by removing one pane of glass) at the top of the outside wall. The pipe should extend to within a few inches of the bin floor.

becoming so cold that the contents of the bin might freeze. An outlet will be necessary as well, and this should open near the top of the bin to allow the warm air inside to pass out.

Basement Bathroom. The walls and ceiling of a basement bathroom or lavatory should have a smooth surface that can be easily cleaned.

There are several materials which would serve satisfactorily but all need a base of some kind. So it is best to put up wallboard first. Then tileboard, linoleum, metal tiles, or oilcloth can be put on, either over the entire wall or over only the bottom half, painting the top half in that case with oil enamel. The floor

a bar, but also be equipped to act as a lunch counter, so that simple meals or snacks can be cooked and served directly from it, thus eliminating the need of running back and forth to the upstairs kitchen. So if the home mechanic has a yen to sometimes play chef he can build a place where he will be more or less free to do so.

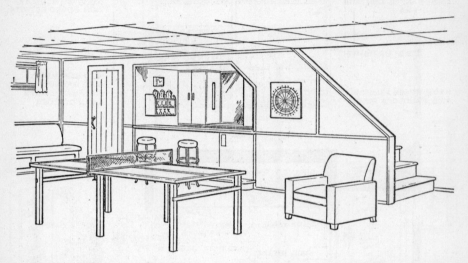

Fig. 42. A basement recreation room with a small bar built in under the stairs. Instead of the table tennis or ping pong table one could have a pool or billiard table or other game equipment as desired.

may be finished with any of the materials suggested for the main basement room, but wood is less desirable than most of the other alternatives mentioned.

Installing a Basement Bar. When a basement room is finished for use as a game or recreation room, an attractive bar or lunch counter will be a pleasing addition. This may range from a simple, portable kind to the more elaborate type pictured in Fig. 42. It may serve not only as

A bar like the one in Fig. 42 would not be too difficult to construct.

The bar is built from a base of 2 x 4 inch lumber anchored to the basement floor. The framework is made from the same-size stock, or lighter materials may be used if they are properly braced. The front of the bar is covered with plywood, and a door can be installed to allow access to the back of the bar. The opening for such a door will require additional framing, and the door should be accurately fitted so that while it will open and close easily, there will not be any wide seams or cracks to mar the appearance of the bar. You can use spring-loaded hinges for the door so that it will open either in or out and then return to a closed position of its own accord.

The top of the bar is covered with tongue and groove boards, but these

leum along the back wall and cover the corner where the two pieces of linoleum join with metal trim.

Shelves for glasses can be hung securely to the wall at the end of the bar as shown or elsewhere. You can have a cupboard for dishes if desired. The space under the bar counter can be used for bottles, full or empty.

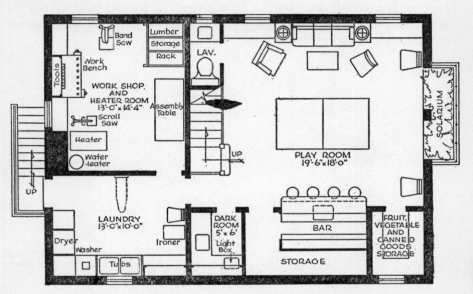

Fig. 43. Floor plan of basement showing how many special rooms can be fitted in with careful planning. An oil or gas burning furnace is marked "Heater."

serve merely as a base for a linoleum counter-top. The edges of the linoleum are covered with metal trim attached to the wood base with wood screws.

All wooden surfaces of the bar should be painted with enamel to provide a hard durable surface and one that can be easily cleaned.

The serving counter of the bar has a wooden base and is covered with linoleum. Also run a strip of lino-

There is almost no limit to the amount of equipment that can be installed on the service counter of the bar. You can make it as simple or fancy as you choose. A hot plate for cooking hamburgers and other snacks should be wired in with BX cable and there should be additional outlets for electric coffee pot, drink mixers, and other gadgets of that sort. An insulated container for ice can be installed, and a small sink with running water will be found to be a great convenience.

The home mechanic interested in building a really complete home bar would do well to visit a store dealing in new and used restaurant, bar, and soda fountain equipment, and purchase such items as suit his fancy, available space, and pocketbook, and incorporate them into his basement bar.

Fig. 43 shows floor plans for a very elaborate basement and demonstrates how many useful rooms could be fitted in. Note that the laundry is located next to the outside stairs to be convenient for hanging clothes outside to dry. Also note that the food storage room is located at the opposite end of the cellar from the heating unit. It is not expected that the average home mechanic will desire or be able to fix up quite as elaborate a layout as this, but he may want to finish off some useful rooms.

BUYING A HOUSE

With few exceptions, buying a house is the largest single purchase that the ordinary family ever makes. The cost of even a relatively small home can run above ten thousand dollars, and while this cost may be spread out over a period of many years, the fact remains that the sum involved is a comparatively large one. The future homeowner therefore, should do his best to make sure that every one hundred cents of his money is getting a dollar's worth of house.

Few of us have the specialized training it takes to know if a house is properly constructed and whether or not it will be in need of constant repairs. There are, however, trained specialists in this field, such as architects, building engineers, and house appraisers, who, after examining the property, can give a very good estimate of its actual worth. It is suggested, therefore, that before signing the final purchase papers, you consult one of the above mentioned specialists. They will charge a fee and while it may seem high, no money you ever spend will bring you greater value.

Because these specialists are expensive, however, the potential home buyer may save himself some money if he makes a preliminary examination of the house first, in order to determine whether it is worth while to have a specialist come out for an appraisal. In other words, it would be foolish to pay a man fifty dollars to tell you a house was not any good if you already knew it was so.

The purpose of this section, then, is to give a few pointers on what to look for in a house, so that you will be at least qualified to determine whether or not the house warrants future consideration.

Location of House. The first point you want to consider is the location of the house. Is it in a good neighborhood surrounded by other homes, or is it on the edge of a noisy business district? If the house is in a residential district, you will pay extra for the pleasant surroundings and therefore you should investigate to see if there are any local ordinances which regulate building in the particular section and which protect you from a sudden decrease in property value.

Then you should give some consideration to transportation, shopping districts and schools. A home beyond regular transportation facilities will be a white elephant unless you have a car, and the cost of a car must then be added to the price of the property, at least in your own mind. One other point you should look into is taxes. Excessively high taxes, which are found in some residential sections, must be considered, not on just a yearly basis, but what the total sum will be in ten or twenty years. This amount may be close to the original purchase price of the house.

The House in General. If possible, try to select a house that not only suits the needs of your family now, but can be expanded should the size of the household increase. Unfinished attics afford the cheapest means of expanding a house, providing there is sufficient head room to allow at least one comfortable room to be constructed. If there is no attic, or it is not large enough, then the only way of expanding the house will be by constructing additional rooms. To decide how feasible this will be, you should consult an architect and check the city building ordinances to see what regulations there are regarding property improvements.

Architectural style is something that the future homeowner will have to decide completely for himself. One point to remember, however, is that brick and stone houses will not require expensive exterior painting as will a house with wood siding.

Inspecting the House. A good place to start inspecting the way a house has been built is in the basement. As you go down into the cellar, notice if there is a damp musty odor. If the house is newly constructed, the poured foundations will contain a lot of water which takes many months to evaporate. But if the house is several years old, then you can assume that the dampness is caused either by condensation on the masonry or by leaks in the walls and floors. The point to keep in mind here is that you are paying for the basement. If it can be redesigned as an attractive den, playroom, or even a home workshop, well and good. But if it is forever going to be damp and musty, then it must be written off as a complete loss as far as livable quarters are concerned, and you will pay extra for a lot of waste space. Another point is that if the basement is constantly damp, some of this dampness and the accompanying odor are bound to get into the rest of the house.

The Foundations. Examine the foundations and basement walls carefully because they will tell you a great deal about how well the house was built. If the walls are made of poured concrete or cement blocks, look for large structural cracks. These usually indicate that the house has done, and may still be doing, considerable settling. If this settling continues, doors and windows will stick, plaster walls and ceiling will crack, floors may buckle and it might be necessary at some later date to jack the house back into proper position. Do not be too concerned with small hairline cracks in the walls. These may be due to several factors and are not as a rule of a serious nature. If the walls are made of concrete blocks, take a penknife or a nail and scrape along some of the mortar joints. If the mortar can be scraped out easily, you might make a note of this fact. Poor quality mortar in bricks or concrete work will allow the wall to leak and may require a complete relaying before the condition is cured.

It might be worth mentioning at this point that a house must not be judged and appraised on just one or two points. It is the overall picture that counts, so make a note of any discrepancy you find and then, when your inspection is finished, add these up to see what you have. No house is perfect and there will be minor flaws in the best of them, but if there are flaws all the way from basement to attic it can then be assumed that the place was jerry-built by someone more interested in cutting construction costs then in building a good house. Such a house is not worth the time and expense of a specialist. So mak^r notes of everything you find that is out of order and use the total of these discrepancies on which to base your final appraisal.

Inspect the basement floor to see if it is damp or if the concrete is sandy and tends to chip off easily. *Joists and Sills.* Now start the inspection of the exposed woodwork in the basement. This will usually consist of the sills and the basement ceiling joists, provided the ceiling is not covered. Take a penknife and stick it into the sills at various points. If the blade goes into the wood easily, it is a pretty fair indication that the wood is not solid. This might be due to termites or dry rot. In either case it would be well to do further investigating. After you are satisfied with the condition of the sills, look at the ceiling joists. These joists should be of 2 x 8 inch or 2 x 10 inch lumber. If the ceiling area is small, 2 x 6 inch timbers can be used, but the general rule is to use something heavier. If the joists are not large enough to stand the load from the floor above, you will continually be faced with the problem of sagging and weak floors. Another point to keep in mind is that if good stout joists were used on the first floor, the chances are that the entire frame of the house was constructed along the same lines—solid and heavy timber throughout. If, however, undersized joists were used on one floor, it may be assumed that undersized lumber was used wherever possible. There are, of course, local city ordinances and building codes regulating the quality and size of materials for use in building, but some communities do not have these laws and in others they are not too well enforced. In the long run it is always best to make sure for yourself. One last item about sills and joists: check to see how the sill and joists are joined. Sometimes this joint is made by cutting out a large section of the joist where it fits onto the sill. It stands to reason that if four inches are cut out of a ten-inch joist you are only getting what corresponds to a six-inch joist.

Look for bridging between the joists. These are strips of wood or metal nailed in a crisscross fashion between the joists. The bridging should run down the approximate center of the ceiling. Bridging is used so that a load on one part of the floor will be distributed among several joists, and also to keep the joists absolutely perpendicular, where they are capable of withstanding the greatest strain. Bridging takes time to install, as each piece of wood must be cut and fitted between the joists. If there is no bridging it can be assumed that the builder was looking for ways and means to save both time and money. If it was saved here, it was probably saved in several other places likely cause you future troubles.

The Heating Plant. Before you leave the basement, give the heating plant a few minutes of your time. Examine the overall picture first. Is the furnace clean on the outside, free of rust with insulation in good condition, or is it dirty, covered with dust, soot and rust with cracked or no insulation whatever? If the furnace has a boiler, look for any signs of leaks which will be indicated by rust around fittings, sections of the boiler, and on the insulation. If the heating plant is a warm air type, notice how many ducts are present and to which portion of the house they extend. A point to keep in mind about warm air furnaces is that while the pipeless type will keep a small one story

building comfortable, it usually fails to do so when you have more than one story or even many rooms on the ground floor.

After these points have been considered, check to see how the furnace is fired. If it is a coal burning type, you should remember that this will require attention about twice a day from some member of the family or household. An alternative measure is to hire someone for the heating season to tend the furnace. Coal will have to be stored in a bin either in the basement or outside, ashes will have to be removed, and there is almost sure to be some dust and dirt in the basement as a result. If the furnace is automatically fired, either by a coal stoker or an oil burner, check the make of these mechanisms and their general appearance. The next thing you want to find out is who services this type of burner. The reason for this is that no matter how well built an automatic burner is, it will require some servicing and replacing of parts. The newer the model of your stoker or burner, the less delay you will probably have in securing new parts.

The last item in connection with the heating plant is the chimney. The construction and the condition of the chimney will have a tremendous effect on how well the heating plant operates, so give this structure a thorough examination. Flaws in chimney construction were outlined in Section Six.

Floors and Stairs. The first items for checking on the ground floor are the floors themselves. Note if the floor sags or groans. Now walk around to see if there are numerous squeaks. These may not necessarily be a sign that the floors are poorly constructed, but worn and squeaky floors do not add to the value of a house by any means. Look for cracks between floor boards, sections of the floor that are warped, and large gaps between baseboard and the flooring. These usually indicate that the wood was green when it was put down.

Walk up the main stairway, putting your entire weight on each stair as you go up. If there are no squeaks you can be fairly sure that the stairs are well constructed, because it is virtually impossible to build a poor flight of stairs and not have them creak under weight. Check the handrail or bannister by pulling or pushing it to see whether or not it is strong enough to hold a person who suddenly loses his balance. In regard to stairs, you should also have noticed as you came from the basement whether these stairs were solidly built and not too steep. Many home accidents are due to basement stairs having either been flimsily built or built on too steep an incline.

Walls and Ceilings. The interior walls and ceilings are usually covered with plaster. The most common failing of plaster is cracking and this can be due to any number of things. The chief cause of large cracks in plaster is that the house has settled. These usually cannot be repaired effectively until the settling process has stopped. Old plaster will sometimes be covered with hairline cracks, and these can usually be taken care of when painting or papering. Plaster which has not been properly applied or has become damp will pull away from the laths and you should be on the lookout for this condition. Examine the walls and ceilings for stains from water. These are usually on the outside walls and are the result of leaks in the house roof or siding. If you find these marks, make a note to check and find out if the leak that caused the trouble was ever repaired. Water stains on the ceiling may be the result of a leak in the roof or outside wall, or it may be from a leaky pipe running through the ceiling. To repair such a leak will generally involve either ripping up the floor above or tearing out the ceiling, either remedy being an expensive undertaking.

Wallboard is another medium for interior walls and ceilings. The chief thing to look for here is the way in which the sections of wallboard have been jointed. If the joint has been filled properly with a special cement and tape, then there will be little difficulty in finishing the wall in either paint or paper. If, however, no method was used to obtain a smooth joint, and there is an open seam between wallboard sections, then it may be virtually impossible to ever decorate the room attractively as long as these badly jointed sections of wallboard remain.

Windows and Doors. The best way to find out about how well the windows and doors work is to try them. Lift the windows up and push them down to see how easily they operate. One or two sticking windows may be due to paint or some other minor item, but if all or most of the windows operate poorly and cannot be moved without considerable strain, then you can fairly safely assume that the frames are out of plumb and it will be a difficult job to get them in alignment again. If the window frame is made out of green lumber, the window is bound to stick as the frame begins to warp.

Slam a few doors to see if the walls shudder and vibrate. A good solid wall and door frame will absorb all or most of the shock of a slamming door without excessive vibrations. Check and see if the door latches shut properly and if it can be locked. Common sense will tell us that one or two doors may be out of line so that the latch and lock do not operate properly, but if most of the doors fail to work properly it is a sign of either poor workmanship or poor materials.

Hardware. There is a tremendous amount of hardware in the average house and few of us notice how much it can add or detract from the appearance of a room. Solid brass is usually regarded as the best material for household hardware, for aside from its pleasing appearance, it lasts indefinitely. There is a considerable amount of brass-plated hardware used and it will only last for a relatively short time. After that, the brass wears off and the metal underneath begins to rust. Solid brass hardware, throughout the house, is a

good indication that the builder was interested more in quality than in saving himself the immediate output of a few extra dollars. Actually, because of its lasting qualities, solid brass is the more economical in the long run.

The Plumbing System. Plumbing is of a major importance in the selection of a house and should be given considerable thought. Unless there is an almost unlimited supply of fresh pure water, efficient modern housekeeping is impossible. The first thing, then, is to find out where the fresh water supply comes from. If it comes from a city main you have no further worries except, perhaps, insufficient pressure—a problem to be taken up later. With a home having its own well with pump and tank to supply the plumbing fixtures, you should find out whether the well is a shallow or artesian one. Shallow wells are easily polluted and they have the bad habit of going dry during a drought. Another point is that while shallow wells served the purpose fifty years ago when the Saturday night bath was still in vogue, they often go completely dry when the strain of daily baths and the family washing is thrown on them. Artesian wells, as a rule, provide an ample water supply but they are known to dry up. Whatever the source of the water may be, take a sample and have it analyzed by a chemist. You will not only find out if the water is pure for drinking purposes but you will also learn its mineral content, whether it is hard, and what it will do to pipes.

If the water is very hard you may have to install a water softener to remove some of the minerals.

Sewerage. Once you are informed on the water supply, find out about sewage disposal. City sewer systems will relieve you of this worry, but rural homes usually have their own sewage disposal system in the form of a cesspool or septic tank. Find out which is used for the house and its location. More than one new home-owner has spent a small fortune trying to locate a cesspool or septic tank somewhere on the property.

Regarding the kind of pipe used for interior plumbing—it is generally agreed that brass and copper pipe will give almost unlimited years of service, but this will depend somewhat on the mineral content of the water and the particular type of brass pipe used. Do not, therefore, pass judgment on the pipe until you have had the water analyzed and know what metal is best for the water. As mentioned before, under normal circumstances, brass and copper will last indefinitely while galvanized iron will rust in time and have to be replaced.

The hot water heater is another important point. If the heater is automatic, either coal, oil, gas, or electric, you need not be concerned, as these heaters will keep your water at an even temperature with little or no effort on your part. If the heater is hand fired with no automatic controls, you should know that aside from the attention the heater will need, there is always the possibility of the water being over-heated. This can cause annoyance and even a bad scalding to members of the family. This kind of hot water heater is another one of the small points that does not necessarily condemn a house, but does not add to its livability. Examine firebox and connections if the heater is aged.

The final test of any plumbing system is whether or not the water comes out of the faucets when you want it. Turn on all the faucets in the house and see what kind of pressure you get in the upstairs bathroom. If you have a good system there will be very little difference between the pressure in the kitchen and the upstairs bathroom. If the pressure in the bathroom is low or even nil, it usually indicates either that the pipes are full of rust and mineral deposits, thus cutting down the volume of water; that the service pipe from the water main to the house is not large enough; or that the city pressure is not great enough. In any case, if you purchase the house, it will be your problem and up to you to solve. One last point on plumbing, and that is bathroom facilities. Many large families require more than one bathroom and as relatively few houses possess more than one, the general scheme is to take an unused room and transform it into a second bathroom. Do not be too cavalier about building an additional bathroom until you have checked with an architect, because if the bathroom is going to require a lot of piping and remodeling it can run into many hundreds of dollars.

The Electrical System. Few homes, if any, contain up-to-date electrical wiring. This is because each year more and more electrical appliances appear on the market, and what might have been adequate wiring a few years ago is now outdated. In homes built twenty or thirty years ago, the scarcity of circuits and outlets is practically on the scale of a major drought. So do not put too much stress on wiring, but rather figure on spending a little money to have the present system brought up-to-date.

Exterior of House. Brick, stone, stucco, asbestos, and wood are the usual materials for fashioning the outside walls of a house, although aluminum can now be added to this list. In the case of brick and stone, you should inspect the mortar joints at random points to see that the mortar is solidly packed and does not crumble or flake away. Another thing to look for are signs of efflorescence, or a white crust on the bricks. This is caused by moisture in the wall, and while in the case of a new house it might be due to water used in making the mortar, in an old house it usually means that the wall is leaking at some point.

Concerning all stucco walls you should look for large cracks and points where the stucco is bulging. This may be a sign that the laths in back have given way or rusted out.

Wood siding is about the most common material for exterior walls. It will require painting every few years, but other than that it serves very well and will not require much upkeep. Check over the surface to see if the paint is peeling or blistering. If this is the case over the entire surface, you can assume that the paint job was poorly done, and the paint will have to be completely removed before a good job can be done. Take a penknife and test the wood to see if it is solid and not rotting. Inspect the lower portion of the outside wall and porch for rot and signs of termites (see TERMITES).

The Roof. As was the case with outside walls, many different materials can be used for roofing. Wood shingles or composition shingles are very satisfactory but in time will have to be replaced. Aluminum and asbestos shingles will last indefinitely and because they are fireproof will bring down the fire insurance rate on the house. If you notice that a number of shingles have slipped out of place you should do a little further investigating, as this indicates poor materials or workmanship. Check the flashing used on the roof and other portions of the house and see what metal it is made of. Copper flashing will last indefinitely but galvanized iron will rust in time if not kept painted.

HOMEOWNER LIABILITY

Many homeowners do not realize that they can be, and very frequently are, held responsible by the law for any injury sustained by a person while on their premises. For example, assume a deliveryman, visiting the house on legitimate business, was to trip on a loose board of the porch and break his leg. He has every right to sue the homeowners for damages and all the chances are in his favor that the court will award him a substantial sum to cover medical expenses and loss of his salary while recovering. This seems perfectly reasonable except that the award might be far beyond what the homeowner could afford. In this case, he would have to raise the money in some manner, even if it required taking out a mortgage on his house or even selling it. Some of the court awards for persons who have lost the sight of one eye or have been permanently incapacitated in some other manner have run into the tens of thousands, a figure that the average homeowner could never cover, short of drastic measures.

As an added hazard there are many dishonest persons who will claim they suffered certain injuries while on the homeowner's premises when in reality they did not. It might be possible for the homeowner to disprove these claims, but it would require time, expense, and the services of a lawyer.

Another point the homeowner should remember is that in many cases, should a child trespass on the premises and receive injury, the homeowner may be sued.

It is not our purpose to pass on the justice of these laws but only to point out to the homeowner their existence. As for a solution on the part of the property owner, this is best accomplished by means of special insurance that covers the homeowner in case someone is injured while on his property. This type of insurance is on the same principle as the insurance you take out on your car to pay damages in the event you have an accident or injure someone. With home insurance, if someone is hurt and sues you, the insurance company does the worrying and the paying. If the insurance company feels that the claim is not justified, then they do the necessary investigating to prove that the claimant is a fraud.

The only alternative, other than insurance, is to keep your property in as good a state of repair as is possible. Do not let anyone get hurt because of your negligence in not fixing a step, keeping the ice off the walk or leaving an uncovered hole in the lawn.

HANDYMAN HINTS

CANE-CHAIR BOTTOMS. Turn the chair upside down and wash the underside of the cane seat with a sponge and hot water so that it is well soaked. Add soap to the water if the cane is dirty. Set the chair so that it can dry in the air; provided the seat is not broken it will tighten and be as firm and taut as when new.

CONCERNING ASHES. Before cleaning out the fireplace for the summer, sprinkle damp tea leaves over the ashes. This procedure will keep much dust from getting out into the room. Do not throw wood ashes away. Mixed with your garden soil they will sweeten the earth.

HARDWOOD FLOORS. When your hardwood floors become scratched and dirty, scrub them with scouring powder, dry well, and rub in linseed oil and turpentine, mixed in equal parts, and let dry. (Never put oil-soaked rags away without washing them. If these are confined where air cannot circulate through them, spontaneous combustion is apt to occur.) The following day the floors may be washed and polished. To keep them in good condition use a lamb's-wool wax mop.

CONCERNING MOTHS. To destroy moths in carpets, lay a wet cloth on the carpet, then rub a hot flatiron over it. The water in the cloth will be converted into steam which will permeate the carpet beneath, thereby destroying the life of the grub. If every once in a while, dry salt is sprinkled on the carpet before sweeping, cleaning will be more effective; and inasmuch as insects do not like salt, enough will remain on the carpet to prevent their lighting upon it. Before going on a vacation, lay a few moth balls next to the felts in the piano before closing it; this will discourage moths from moving in. Wipe clothes closet floors occasionally with a cloth slightly moistened with turpentine—it is an effective "stay away" sign to moths.

VARNISH FOR TOOLS. An excellent varnish for tools is made by combining 2 oz. of tallow with 1 oz. of resin. Melt these ingredients together and strain, while hot, to remove any spots which may be in the resin. Apply a slight coat to your tools with a brush; this will serve as a resistant to rust for a long time.

TO MARK TOOLS. Tools may be easily marked with your name by the following means: Wrap a lump of beeswax in an old piece of thin silk and tie up the ends of the cloth to serve as a handle. Warm the steel of the tool to the point where the beeswax, when rubbed across it, will melt and deposit a good coating of wax on the metal. Let this cool until hard, and then with a graver, or some other thin point, mark your name through the wax to the steel. Now apply a mordant composed of equal parts of nitric acid and water. A feather or thin camel's hair brush may be used for this purpose, but the acid must not be allowed to touch any other part of the tool except where the wax has been applied. After a few moments wash off the acid thoroughly, then warm the metal so that with a soft rag the wax will wipe off easily. (Be extremely careful with nitric acid, as it burns the skin, eats away cloth, and does other serious damage if not controlled. It must be kept in glass-stoppered bottles labelled *Poison,* and stored out of the way. *Antidotes:* Chalk, whiting, carbonate of soda, carbonate of magnesia in water, milk and white of egg and olive oil, and very thick limewater).

BIRDHOUSES. When you make these, do not make a great number, unless you have extensive grounds around your home. Birds, as a rule, do not care to have their nests close together. Remoteness is more to their liking. You can watch them from afar and have just as much pleasure observing their ways. The little wren-box may be placed near the house, perhaps; and the wire mesh that you arrange to hold suet can be tied on a branch nearby, because birds will go almost anywhere for suet. Once you put up a birdhouse do not touch it again during the season.

COAL CONTROL. When you find that the coal in the bin is disappearing too fast into the yawning mouth of the furnace door, try this idea. Get out the watering can that you perhaps use around the flowers during the summer, and into this pour a gallon of water in which a half-pound of washing soda has been dissolved. Sprinkle this over the coal *a few days before burning,* and you will find that the coal will last longer and also give off more heat.

Another bit of good practice for the handyman is to have a box conveniently placed at the foot of the cellar stairs. In this keep a pair of canvas gloves and a pair of old rubbers that can be slipped on easily. Use both of these while tending the furnace, and drop them both in the box as you start upstairs. By this practice you save tracking the dust of the coal and ashes that are always between the furnace and the coalbin onto the kitchen linoleum or to the rugs of the house.

COOL HOUSE IN SUMMER. Early in the morning arrange for a cross ventilation on the lower floors, also in the attic where you can place an electric fan about three feet away from one of the attic windows and facing it. Let the attic door remain open. Soon the hot air from the ceilings of the rooms downstairs, as well as the cool air from outdoors, will be drawn up through the house and out the attic windows. At about ten o'clock when cool, fresh air is in the lower rooms and the attic "hothouse" air has been drawn off, shut off the fan and close the attic door. Then close all windows except those on the shady side of the house, and you will have comfort during the day. When the sun ceases to shine on the windows in the afternoon, open the windows for a free circulation of air.

DOORS THAT RATTLE. At night, when a strong wind causes a bedroom door to rattle, thus disturbing your sleep, tie a strip of cloth around the outside doorknob, then bring it around and tie it to the knob inside the room. When you close the door, the rattle will cease. (However, come the week end, get at the real seat of the trouble).

INEXPENSIVE LINOLEUM. When buying inexpensive linoleum, take the long view—get one or two extra yards. When you lay the covering, look toward the spots that get the most wear, such as those before the stove and sink. From the extra yardage cut squares that will match the pattern and carefully tack these over the most-used places. It should not be difficult to accomplish this so that the squares will not be noticed. When these become worn, take them off. With this procedure you double the wear of the linoleum; and if you want to lengthen its life still more, give it a coat of waterproof varnish.

GLASS JARS. Wide-mouthed glass jars, such as those containing jellies and jams, that come from the grocery stores, make wonderful containers for screws, hooks, small nails, and many odds and ends that are used by the handyman when he is doing an odd job. Keep the tops that screw on, then you can turn the jar about and quickly see whether or not the "odds" or the "ends" are present. A shelf of these for "ready reference" is one of the time-savers of the workbench. Having located the item wanted, pour the contents of the jar onto a newspaper, pick out your piece, and as quickly shoot the remainder of the contents back into the jar by making a trough of the newspaper.

WINDOW CORDS. A much longer life will be given the window cords of your home if you dust the cords twice a year and rub them with a well-greased rag. With this treatment they will be less apt to break, because friction will be greatly reduced; and the raising and lowering of the windows will be made much easier.

VARNISH NOTES. If varnish does not flow properly—seems sticky— thin it by setting the can in a pan of warm water, and it will soon have a workable consistency. Never place it on the stove. If you thin it with turpentine the gloss will be destroyed.

CONCERNING CHIMNEYS. If the soot in the chimney catches fire, put it out by throwing salt on the hearth fire; slightly damp salt is more effective than dry. At the same time set something flat against the chimney breast. The burning soot will soon be smothered.

Before you do any paperhanging in your home, be sure to clean the chimneys; otherwise, when autumn comes and the furnace is started, you may have to clean the new paper.

Hard-coal soot is compact and heavy. During the dampness of the summer season the soot very often drops to the bottom of the chimney where it can be cleaned out through an opening at the base of every properly constructed chimney. If any soot remains on the sides, it may be removed by means of a brick tied to the end of a long rope and worked up and down the chimney.

Another way to clean chimneys is to place a piece of zinc on the hot coals of the kitchen stove or furnace. The vapors that rise from this will clear away the soot by chemical decomposition.

PAINTING TIPS. Paint slowly and see that the paint is evenly spread. A thin coat allowed to dry thoroughly before a second coat is applied is the proper procedure.

Do not use enamel on either woodwork or furniture in a room where the temperature is above 68 degrees Fahrenheit, if you can possibly avoid it.

When painting steps, paint every other one, and when these are thoroughly dry, paint the remaining ones. In this way you can use the steps without injury.

Before repainting screens, clean them with gasoline or benzine. This will remove the dirt more effectively than water. (No lighted matches or cigarettes around the gasoline, however).

Paint that blisters on the exterior of a building does so, usually, on account of dampness. Too often the wood has not been allowed to dry before the paint was applied. Blistered paint should be burned off with a blowtorch; this requires an experienced master-hand.

Dried paint spots on windows can be removed easily by an old safety-razor blade. Use one of the many blade holders on the market. Wash the glass afterwards with water in which there is a little ammonia.

Stubborn paint-marks on clothing will yield to a mixture of turpentine and ammonia. Rub this well into the cloth before cleaning.

When finished painting, clean your brushes thoroughly in turpentine and hot soapsuds. Do not delay if you want the brush in good condition the next time you wish to use it. Do not use strong alkaline or acid solutions. Don't dry brushes fast—nor must they remain wet longer than necessary. Hang them up to dry and you will prolong their life.

Shellac brushes should be washed in denatured alcohol and then in hot soapsuds.

If paint brushes are stiff through disuse, boil them in vinegar for about ten minutes, and they will be made soft and pliable.

A good brush may be put in turpentine or water overnight, between usings, but do not let it remain there.

If one of your paint brushes becomes too worn to do good work, do not discard it; use it for dusting the interstices of ornately-carved woodwork and other hard-to-dust pieces. It will get into places that are hard to reach with a dust-cloth.

SPOTS AND STAINS

Fingermarks. (1) On painted woodwork, rub with cloth that has been dipped in kerosene; (2) on varnished furniture, remove by rubbing with sweet oil; (3) on oiled furniture, rub with kerosene.

Ink Spots. If you wish to remove these from wood, mix equal parts of linseed oil and vinegar and apply the mixture lightly to the spots.

Grease Spots. To remove these from floors, sprinkle with dry soda and pour boiling water over the soda. Let this remain a short while, then scrub with hot soap and water and the spots will disappear.

Varnish Stains. Remove these from clothing by rubbing with a sponge dipped in turpentine.

Match Scratches. These may be removed from white paint by rubbing a half-cut lemon over the damaged spot, to be followed by a moist cloth dipped in whiting powder.

Stains on Sink. Fruit and vegetable stains on the sink may be removed thus: Prepare a paste containing equal parts of baking soda and chlorinated lime. To this add enough boiling water to form a thin paste; spread the mixture on the discolora-

tions in the sink, and allow it to remain a while. You will also save plumbers bills if once or twice a month you run baking soda through the sink trap, after greasy food.

PAPER STICKING TO VARNISH. If paper sticks to table tops or any other varnished surface, it can easily be removed by first applying drops of oil to the paper. Let this soak in, then with a cloth rub the paper gently, when it will come off, and the spot to which the paper adhered will scarcely show a mark.

HEAT-PROOF TABLE TOP. First, remove the old finish. Mix one-third turpentine and two-thirds linseed oil, shake well, and rub into the wood using an old, soft, clean cloth. After a thorough application, rub the surface dry. Hot dishes will not leave marks on this kind of finish.

WINDOW GLASS. Broken and cracked window glass can be patched with cellulose tape. While this makes an effective patch, the glass should be replaced as soon as possible.

USEFUL MAGNET. A small magnet or magnetic screwdriver is a handy little tool for retriving screws and nuts that drop in inaccessible places. A magnet can also be used to test whether hardware is of solid brass or iron that is brass plated. The magnet will adhere to the plated material but not to the solid brass.

REGISTER SCREEN. A piece of wire screening placed under warm air registers will prevent items falling down into the ducts or furnace. This is particularly useful if there are children in the house.

REMOVING CEMENT. Hard cement can be removed from bricks by letting it soak for a few minutes in a solution of 1 part muriatic acid to 10 parts water. This will soften the cement so that it can be scraped off. Flush the acid away with plenty of fresh water and take care not to get the solution on the hands or in the eyes.

QUICK STORM DOOR. Screen doors can be converted into moderately efficient storm doors by covering the wire screening with translucent wire cloth. Tack the translucent cloth to the door frame, using a sufficient number of tacks so that it will not be torn off in a high wind. Use masking tape around the edges to make a tight joint. When the weather becomes warm it is a simple matter to remove the tape, pull out the tacks, and roll up the wire cloth to be used against next winter.

CHRISTMAS LIGHTS. The color of Christmas tree lights can be restored by wiping the glass with alcohol and dipping the bulb in lacquer. Hang the bulb up by the metal base until the lacquer is dry. Do not let lacquer get on the metal base.

A NOTE ON BIRDS. It is often possible to keep birds off a roof by placing a number of toy snakes on various portions of the roof.

DUST FROM REGISTERS. The amount of dust coming through a warm air register can be reduced considerably by removing the register and putting a piece of cheesecloth over the opening. Replace the register and it will hold the cheesecloth in place. In time the cloth will become so dirty that it must be removed and either washed or replaced with a new piece.

REPAIRING ANDIRONS. When andirons burn through, they can often be repaired by slipping a piece of pipe over the two ends, thus forming a sleeve.

CLEANING GLAZED SURFACES. Do not use harsh abrasive cleaning powders on glazed brick or tile, as the finish may be damaged. Use soap and water and, if necessary, a scratchless cleaning powder.

CHIMNEY COVERING. A piece of wire mesh placed over the chimney will prevent rodents and birds from using this opening as an entrance into the house, and will also keep large sparks from the fireplace from possibly setting fire to the roof.

CLEANING ELECTRICAL APPLIANCES. Use a soft brush for cleaning an electric toaster. Never try to wash the toaster or any other electrical appliance of this type in water.

CARPENTER ANTS. Carpenter ants found inside a house can be destroyed by locating the nest and spraying it with carbon tetrachloride. Kerosene may also be used, but this is inflammable.

BASEMENT DRAINS. During heavy rains, water will sometimes come into the basement through the basement floor drain. This can be prevented by having a length of pipe threaded so that it can be screwed into the floor drain.

FURNACE PIPES. It is a good idea to remove the insulation from warm air furnace pipes during the summer months to prevent the pipes from rusting.

CONCRETE STEPS. Concrete steps that are exposed to the weather are best left unpainted. The dampness in the concrete will destroy any oil paints and cement and water paints will soon be worn away.

CONCERNING MARBLE. Stains on marble can often be removed by wiping with a cut lemon. Smoke stains can be wiped away with a cloth and carbon tetrachloride.

PAINTING A SOIL PIPE. The preservative coating on most soil pipes inside the house will destroy an oil paint unless the pipe is first covered with aluminum paint. After this is dry the pipe can be successfully painted.

AN IMPORTANT CHECK. Make it a habit to check the exterior of the house after a heavy storm to see if any gutters, shutters, flashing, or even siding have pulled loose.

DEODORIZER. A piece of charcoal makes a very good deodorizer for refrigerators.

WATERPROOF CEMENT. Litharge and glycerin mixed together into a smooth thick paste will make an excellent waterproof cement for any number of home repair jobs. Allow the cement to harden overnight. This is a good way to replace plastic or bone handles on knives or forks.

CRACKED CHINA. Cracked china can often be saved by boiling the piece in milk for half an hour or so.

LEAKY BRICK WALL. In brick veneer construction on the outside of a house, a small space is left between the bricks and the house sheathing. If the brick wall leaks, water will get into this space and possibly get past the sheathing and spoil the inside plaster. The most effective treatment is to find the leaks in the wall and repair them, but until this is done drill small holes through the brick mortar joints at the base of the wall. These holes should slant up so that water behind the wall will drain outside.

FROZEN LOCKS. Never use boiling water to thaw out a frozen lock, as the water will rust the lock mechanism. Use matches, a candle, or other dry heat.

CLEANING AN IRON. The surface of an electric iron can be cleaned with steel wool. Use a very fine grade only for this job.

WEIGHTS AND MEASURES

LINEAR MEASURE

12 inches	....	1 foot
3 feet	....	1 yard
5½ yards	....	1 rod
40 rods	....	1 furlong
8 furlongs	....	1 mile
5280 feet	....	1 mile

SQUARE MEASURE

144 sq. in.	....	1 sq. ft.
9 sq. ft.	....	1 sq. yd.
30¼ sq. yd.	....	1 sq. rod
160 sq. rods	....	1 acre
640 acres	....	1 sq. mile

1 acre, if measured in a perfect square, is a lot measuring 208⅔ feet on a side.

CUBIC MEASURE
(VOLUME)

1728 cu. in.	....	1 cu. ft.
27 cu. ft.	....	1 cu. yd.

Special Measurements:

1 cord .... 128 cu. ft.
Used in measuring wood for fuel. The legal dimensions of a cord of wood are 8 x 4 x 4 feet.

1 board foot .... $\frac{1}{12}$ cu. ft.
Or 144 cu. in. A board foot measures 1 ft. x 1 ft. x 1 in.

1 perch .... 24¾ cu. ft.
Used in measuring stone or brick. A perch measures 16½ ft. long, 1½ ft. wide, 1 ft. high.

DRY MEASURE

2 pints	....	1 quart
8 quarts	....	1 peck
4 pecks	....	1 bushel

LIQUID MEASURE

4 gills	....	1 pint
2 pints	....	1 quart
4 quarts	....	1 gallon
31½ gallons	....	1 barrel
2 barrels	....	1 hogshead

WEIGHT MEASURE

16 ounces	....	1 pound
100 pounds	......	1 hundredweight
20 hundredweight	....	1 ton

One ton of 2000 pounds (based on the 100-lb. hundredweight) is called a *short* ton. One ton of 2240 pounds (based on the 112-lb. or English hundredweight) is called a *long* or *gross* ton.

THE METRIC SYSTEM

The metric system of weights and measures, which originated in France about 1790, is based upon a decimal division (by tens); all the units in the system are based on or are derived from the *meter,* which is calculated to be one ten-millionth part of the distance from the equator to the pole. The meter is equal to 39.37 U.S. inches, or about 3 feet 3⅜ inches.

Denominations in the metric system progress regularly by tens, and Latin and Greek prefixes indicate the part of, or multiple of, the meter involved in each denomination. Thus, the Latin *milli-*(one thousandth); *centi-*(one hundredth); *deci-*(one tenth), when used in *milli*meter, *centi*meter, *deci*meter, mean one thousandth, one hundredth, and one tenth of a meter respectively. Similarly, the Greek prefixes: *deca*meter (10 meters); *hecto*meter (100 meters); *kilo*meter (1000 meters); *myria*meter (10,000 meters). The names of the units of area, capacity, and weight, follow the same system of prefixes. Of these, the millimeter, centimeter, meter, and kilometer, are in most common use.

LINEAR MEASURE

10 millimeters .... 1 centimeter
10 centimeters .... 1 decimeter
10 decimeters .... 1 meter
10 meters .... 1 decameter
10 decameters ...... 1 hectometer
10 hectometers .... 1 kilometer
10 kilometers ...... 1 myriameter

Equivalents:

1 millimeter (mm) .. .0394 in.
1 centimeter (cm) ... .3937 in.
1 decimeter (dm) ... 3.937 in.
1 meter (m) .... 39.37 in.
1 decameter .... 393.7 in.
1 hectometer .... 328 ft. 1 in.
1 kilometer (km) .... .62137 mile*
1 myriameter .... 6.214 miles
* Or 3280 ft. 10 in.

SQUARE MEASURE

100 sq. mm. .... 1 sq. cm.
100 sq. cm. .... 1 sq. dm.
100 sq. dm. ..... 1 sq. m. (centiare)
100 sq. m. .... 1 sq. deca. (are)
100 sq. deca... 1 sq. hecto. (hectare)
100 sq. hecto. .... 1 sq. km.
While the preceding units are used in the measurement of length and surface, the *are*—which equals 100 square meters—is the basic unit in measuring land.
100 centiares .... 1 are
10 ares .... 1 dekare
10 dekares .... 1 hectare

Equivalents:

1 sq. mm. .... .00155 sq. in.
1 sq. cm. .... .155 sq. in.
1 sq. m. .... 10.764 sq. ft.*
1 sq. km. .... .3861 sq. mile
1 centiare .... 1550 sq. in.
1 are .... 119.6 sq. yd.
1 hectare .... 2.471 acres
* Or 1.196 sq. yd.

CUBIC MEASURE
(VOLUME)

1000 cu. mm. .... 1 cu. cm.
1000 cu. cm. .... 1 cu. dm.
1000 cu. dm. .... 1 cu. m.

Equivalents:

1 cu. mm. .... .000061 cu. in.
1 cu cm. .... .0610 cu. in.
1 cu m. .... 35.314 cu. ft.
1 cu m. .... 1.3079 cu. yd.

DRY AND LIQUID MEASURE

10 millileters (ml) .... 1 centileter
10 centileters (cl) ..... 1 decileter
10 decileters (dl) .... 1 liter
10 liters (l) .... 1 decaliter
10 decaliters (dal) .... 1 hectoliter
10 hectoliters ..... 1 kiloliter (kl)

Equivalents:

1 ml. .... 1 cu. cm.
1 cl. .... 10 cu. cm.
1 dl. .... 1 cu. dm.
1 dal. .... 10 cu. dm.

METRIC	DRY	LIQUID
1 cl. ....6102 cu. in..		338 oz.
1 dl. ...6.102 cu. in..		.845 gill
1 l. .... .908 qt.		1.0567 qt.
1 dal. .. 9.08 qt.		2.64 gal.

WEIGHT MEASURE

10 milligrams (mg) .. 1 centigram
10 centigrams (cg) .... 1 decigram
10 decigrams (dg) .... 1 gram
10 grams (g) .... 1 decagram
10 decagrams .... 1 hectogram
10 hectograms .... 1 kilogram
10 kilograms (kg) ... 1 myriagram
10 myriagrams .... 1 quintal
10 quintals (q) .... 1 tonneau (t)

Equivalents:

1 gram .... .03527 ounce
1 decagram ...... .3527 ounce
1 hectogram ..... 3.527 ounces
1 kilogram ...... 2.204 pounds
1 quintal .... 220.46 pounds
1 tonneau .... 1 metric ton
(2204.6 lbs)

TEMPERATURE

Temperatures in the United States are most often measured on the Fahrenheit scale. Water, on this scale, will freeze at 32 degrees and boil at 212 degrees. The Centigrade scale, used in more precise and scientific measurement, is graduated in such a manner that water will freeze at 0 degrees and boil at 100 degrees. The interval between boiling and freezing, therefore, is conveniently divided into one hundred degrees.

The handyman will sometimes find it necessary to convert a temperature reading from Centigrade to Fahrenheit, or vice versa, and the conversion is easily done according to the following formulas.

To convert Centigrade degrees to Fahrenheit, *multiply* by 1.8 and *add* 32. To convert Fahrenheit degrees to Centigrade, *subtract* 32 and *divide* by 1.8. The addition or subtraction of 32 is necessary in each case because of the fact that 0 degrees C. corresponds to 32 degrees F.

GEOMETRIC FORMULAS

The formulas given below will often be of use to the handyman. He may, for example, want to know the area of a plot of ground, the capacity of a water tank or an oil drum, the number of square feet of floor space in a room. The proper use of these formulas will give the information

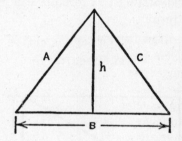

Triangle. To find the area of a triangle, multiply the length of the base (b) by the length of the altitude or height (h) and divide the result by 2.

$$A = \tfrac{1}{2} (b \times h)$$

There is another way to find the area of a triangle, when the lengths of all three sides are known. You can use this method, for instance, to find the area of a triangular plot of land. Add the lengths of the three sides (a, b, and c) together and divide the total by 2. This is expressed in the formula

$$s = \tfrac{1}{2} (a + b + c)$$

Then, subtract the length of each side from s, multiply these results together with s, and extract the square root of the product.

$$Area = \sqrt{s(s-a)(s-b)(s-c)}$$

As an example, assume the lengths of the sides of the triangle to be 5, 7, and 8 feet long. By the first formula, s would equal

$$\tfrac{1}{2}(5+7+8)=10$$

The second formula would then appear like this:

$$Area = \sqrt{10(10-5)(10-7)(10-8)}$$

Calculating this formula will give the result:

$$\sqrt{10 \times 5 \times 3 \times 2} = \sqrt{300} = 17.32 \text{ sq. ft.}$$

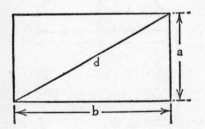

Rectangle. The angles formed by the corners of a rectangle are all right angles (measuring 90 degrees), but the sides—except in a square— are not all of equal length. A *square* is a kind of rectangle, but all its sides are equal in length.

To find the *perimeter* (distance around) of a rectangle, add the lengths of the four sides together.

$$P = 2(a+b)$$

To find the *area* of a rectangle, multiply one side by the adjacent side.

$$Area = a \times b$$

The length of the diagonal (d) of a rectangle can always be found by taking the square root of the sum of the squares of the length and width.

$$d = \sqrt{a^2 + b^2}$$

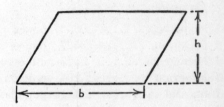

Parallelogram. The parallelogram resembles a rectangle except that the angles formed by the corners are all oblique (more or less than 90 degrees). Strictly speaking, the rectangle and square are special forms of the parallelogram, since opposite sides are parallel. To find the perimeter of a parallelogram, add the lengths of the four sides, as in a rectangle.

To find the area of a parallelogram, multiply the length of the base (b) by the perpendicular distance from the base to the opposite parallel side, called the altitude (h).

$$Area = b \times h$$

Rhombus. A rhombus is an equilateral parallelogram; that is, the lengths of all four sides are equal.

To find the area of a rhombus, multiply the length of the base (b) by the altitude (h), or perpendicular distance to the opposite parallel side, as in a parallelogram.

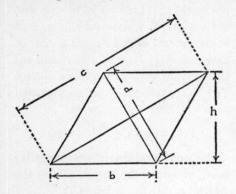

Another method is to measure the lengths of two diagonals (c and d) drawn between opposite corners and divide their product by 2.

$$\text{Area} = \tfrac{1}{2}\,(c \times d)$$

Trapezoid. The trapezoid differs from the figures described thus far in that it has only one pair of opposite sides parallel. The perimeter of a trapezoid is found by taking the sum of the four sides.

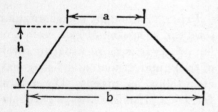

To find the area of a trapezoid, multiply one-half the sum of the lengths of the two parallel sides (a and b) by the height (h).

$$\text{Area} = \tfrac{1}{2}\,(a + b) \times h$$

Trapezium. The trapezium, most irregular figure of those which are discussed, has no opposite sides

parallel. The perimeter of the trapezium can be found in the same manner as the other quadrilateral (four-sided) figures.

To find the area is more difficult. This can best be done, when the lengths of all four sides are known, by drawing the trapezium to scale, drawing a diagonal between two opposite corners, and measuring the diagonal according to the same scale. This will divide the figure into two triangles, and the area of each can be found by using the formula

$$\text{Area} = \sqrt{s(s-a)(s-b)(s-c)}$$

This formula and its use will be found under *Triangle.* After the areas of both triangles have been found, it is simply a matter of adding these together to obtain the area of the trapezium.

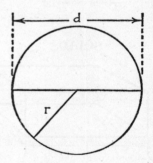

Circle. When working with a circle, it is necessary to know certain of its characteristics and parts. A circle, by definition, is a closed line every point on which is equidistant from the center. The *circumference* is the distance around the circle. The *radius* is the distance from the center to any point on the circumference, or the line so drawn. The *diameter* is the length of a line drawn between two points on the circumference and passing through the center. The diameter is always twice as long as the radius. You will also have to know the constant factor *pi*—represented as π—which is equal to 3.1416.

The circumference of a circle is equal to *pi* times the diameter (*d*) or, since the radius (*r*) is half the diameter,

$$C = 2\pi r$$

The area within a circle is found by multiplying the square of the radius by π.

$$\text{Area} = \pi r^2$$

This may also be expressed—since the radius is one half the diameter—as

$$\text{Area} = \tfrac{1}{4}\pi d^2$$

SOLIDS

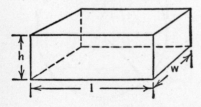

Rectangular Solid. With this figure we come to the measurement of solid figures, such as boxes, pails, blocks, and tanks. A rectangular solid, as distinguished from other solids, has 6 faces and 12 edges. All the faces are rectangular in shape, and all the edges are perpendicular to the faces which they meet. The following procedure is necessary to find the area.

The area of a rectangular solid is the sum of the *lateral area* (area of the sides) and the area of the top and bottom. With dimensions *l*, *w*, and *h*, the lateral area is equal to $2lh + 2wh$, or $2(lh + wh)$. The area of the top and bottom combined is $2lw$. The total area can then be expressed as $2lh + 2wh + 2lw$, or as

$$\text{T.A.} = 2(lh + wh + lw)$$

To find the volume of a rectangular solid, multiply the length (*l*) by the width (*w*) by the height (*h*)

$$V = l \times w \times h$$

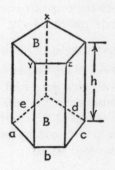

Prism. Although a rectangular solid can be spoken of as a rectangular prism, it is more usual to speak of triangular, trapezoidal, hexagonal, etc., solids as prisms. The lateral faces of a prism are always parallelograms; that is, they have opposite sides parallel. The edges of these faces may or may not be parallel to the top and bottom of the prism, and the bases (top and bottom) may be triangular, square, trapezoidal, etc., in shape.

Find the area of a prism in two operations, as in a rectangular solid. First, find the lateral area, or area of the sides, by multiplying the height (h) by the length of each side and adding the results.

$$\text{L.A.} = h(a + b + c + \ldots)$$

Since the total lengths of the sides equal the perimeter (distance around) of the base, the formula can be expressed more simply as

$$\text{L.A.} = p \times h$$

It remains to find the area of the base, and the method used will depend upon the shape of the base. If it is triangular, use the formula for the area of a triangle; similarly for a trapezoid, square, etc. In the illustration, the base is a pentagon (five sides). Draw lines from X to Y and from X to Z, dividing the base into three triangles, and find their combined area.

After finding the area of the base, expressed as B, double it (since there are 2 bases), and the *total* area of the prism will be

$$\text{T.A.} = ph + 2B$$

To find the volume of a prism, multiply the area of the base (B) by the height (h).

$$\text{V} = B \times h$$

Cylinder. Many common objects are in the form of a cylinder, such as tubes, pipes, cans, tanks, etc., and the handyman will often want to know their area or capacity.

The area of a cylinder is the sum of the lateral area and the areas of the bases. The lateral area is the product of the circumference and the height (h). π is 3.1416. The radius

(r) is one half the diameter of the cylinder.

$$\text{L.A.} = 2\pi r \times h$$

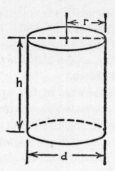

The area of each base is equal to πr^2, and the total area of the cylinder is therefore $2\pi rh + 2\pi r^2$ or T.A. $= 2\pi r(h + r)$.

The volume of a cylinder is the product of the area of the base multiplied by the altitude (h).

$$\text{V} = \pi r^2 \times h$$

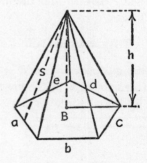

Pyramid. Any figure, one of whose faces is a polygon (four or more sides) and whose other faces are all triangles having a common vertex, or terminating point, is a pyramid. In a regular pyramid, the lateral faces will all be isoceles (two sides equal in length) triangles—except in the case where the base is an equilateral (all sides equal) triangle. In this case, the lateral faces will also be equilateral triangles. This figure is called a *tetrahedron*.

It is necessary to know the slant height (s) of the pyramid, and this can be taken as the altitude of any of the lateral faces.

The lateral area of the pyramid is equal to one half the product of the perimeter of the base and the slant height. Since the perimeter (p) is equal to the sum of the lengths of the lateral faces, the formula can be given as

$$L.A. = \tfrac{1}{2}ps$$

where $p = a + b + c + \ldots$ The total area is the sum of the lateral area plus the area of the base (B). As in a prism, the shape of the base determines the method for finding its area. In the illustration, the base is a pentagon. See *Prism* to find the area of such a figure.

$$T.A. = \tfrac{1}{2}\,ps + B$$

The volume of any pyramid is equal to one third the area of the base multiplied by the altitude (h).

$$V = \tfrac{1}{3}\,Bh$$

Frustum of Pyramid. If a part of a pyramid, including the vertex, is cut off by a plane parallel to the base, the part remaining is called the frustum. There are many objects which are shaped like a frustum of a pyramid, such as a concrete foundation pillar or a feed hopper in the shape of a frustum of a square pyramid.

In a frustum, the lateral faces are in the form of trapezoids (*which see*). The slant height (s) is therefore the altitude of one of the trapezoidal faces. To find the area of the frustum of a pyramid, you must first know the lateral area. This is equal to one half the sum of the perimeters of the bases multiplied by the slant height. The perimeter of the upper base is equal to the sum of the upper lengths of the trapezoidal faces ($a_1 + b_1 + c_1 + \ldots$); the perimeter of the lower base is found in a similar manner ($a_2 + b_2 + c_2 + \ldots$).

$$L.A. = \tfrac{1}{2}s(p_1 + p_2)$$

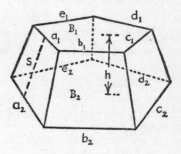

Next, find the areas of the bases—the method depending on their shape. The total area will then be the sum of the lateral area and the areas (B_1 and B_2) of the bases.

$$T.A. = \tfrac{1}{2}s\,(p_1 + p_2) + B_1 + B_2$$

To find the volume of the frustum of a pyramid, use the following formula, h being the perpendicular distance between the bases.

$$V = \tfrac{1}{3}h\,(B_1 + B_2 + \sqrt{B_1 B_2})$$

Cone. A cone can be defined as a solid figure having a circular base and terminating in a vertex. A funnel has a conical shape, and coal and sand are often piled in the shape of a cone.

The total area of a cone is one half the product of the circumference and the slant height plus the area of the base.

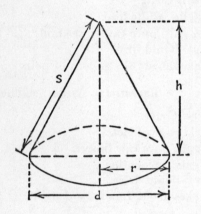

The circumference of a circle is equal to $2\pi r$, where r is the radius of the base and π is 3.1416. This is the lateral area of the cone. The area of the base equals πr^2. The total area of the cone is therefore $\frac{1}{2}(2\pi r)s + \pi r^2$, or, more simply

$$\text{T.A.} = \pi r(s + r)$$

The volume of a cone is equal to one third the product of the area of the base and the altitude (h).

$$V = \tfrac{1}{3}(\pi r^2 h)$$

Frustum of Cone. A frustum of a cone (see *Frustum of Pyramid*) is also a rather common shape. Buckets are in this category, as well as lampshades and other objects in regular home use.

The area of the frustum of a cone is equal to the lateral area plus the areas of the bases. The lateral area is one half the product of the slant height (s) and the sum of the upper and lower circumferences.

$$\text{L.A.} = \tfrac{1}{2}s(2\pi R + 2\pi r)$$

The area of the lower base is πR^2 and the area of the upper base is πr^2. The total area then is equal to $\frac{1}{2}s\,(2\pi R + 2\pi r) + \pi R^2 + \pi r^2$.
This formula can be stated more simply as

$$\text{T.A.} = \pi[(R + r)s + R^2 + r^2]$$

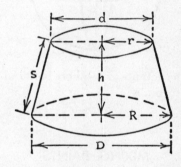

The volume of a frustum of a cone is found by the formula

$$V = \tfrac{1}{3}\pi h(R^2 + r^2 + Rr)$$

where R and r are the radii of the lower and upper bases respectively and h is the perpendicular distance between them.

Sphere. Any round, solid object can be called a sphere, such as an orange or a baseball, but a more formal definition is that a sphere is a solid bounded by one continued curved surface every point of which is equally distant from the center of the sphere.

To find the area of a sphere, determine the length of the radius. One method is to measure the circumference of the sphere. Since the circumference is equal to $2\pi r$, the radius r will then be $\dfrac{C}{2\pi}$. The area of the sphere can then be found by the formula

$$A = 4\pi r^2$$

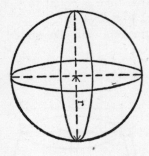

The volume of a sphere is found in the formula

$$V = \tfrac{4}{3}\pi r^3$$

MIXING PAINTS

The following tables indicate the proportions to use when mixing your own paint for use inside or outside the house. Follow directions carefully and remember that thorough mixing is essential to good paint.

EXTERIOR PAINT

New Wood

First Coat:
100 lbs. white lead
4 gals. pure raw linseed oil
2 gals. pure turpentine
1 pt. liquid drier
Makes slightly more than 9 gallons of paint.

Second Coat:
100 lbs. white lead
1½ gals. pure raw linseed oil
1½ gals. turpentine
1 pt. liquid drier
Makes a little more than 6 gallons of paint.

Third Coat:
100 lbs. white lead
3¼ gals. pure raw linseed oil
1 pt. liquid drier
Makes about 6½ gallons of paint.

REPAINTING WOOD

First Coat:
100 lbs. white lead
3 gals. pure raw linseed oil
2 gals. turpentine
1 pt. liquid drier
Makes about 7 gallons of paint.

Second Coat:
100 lbs. white lead
3¼ gals. pure raw linseed oil
1 pt. liquid drier
Makes about 6 gallons of paint.

BACK PAINTING

Painting the rear or unexposed part of the wood.
100 lbs. white lead
3¼ gals. pure raw linseed oil
1 pt. liquid drier
Makes about 6 gallons of paint.

INTERIOR WOODWORK

New Woodwork

First Coat:
100 lbs. white lead
3 gals. pure raw linseed oil
2 gals. turpentine
1 pt. liquid drier
Makes over 8 gallons of paint.

Second Coat:
100 lbs. white lead
1½ gals. turpentine
½ pt. liquid drier
¾ gal. varnish
Makes about 5½ gallons of paint.

Third Coat:
100 lbs. white lead
1¾ gals. turpentine
½ pt. liquid drier
⅛ gal. varnish
Makes about 5 gallons of paint.

OLD WOODWORK

First Coat:
100 lbs. white lead
1½ gals. turpentine
½ pt. liquid drier
¾ gal. varnish
Makes about 5½ gallons of paint.

Second Coat:
100 lbs. white lead
1¾ gals. turpentine
½ pt. liquid drier
⅛ gal. varnish
Makes slightly over 5 gallons of paint.

PAINTING PLASTER

New Plaster

First Coat:
100 lbs. white lead
3 gals. pure raw linseed oil
1¼ gals. pure turpentine
1 pt. liquid drier
2 gals. varnish
Makes over 9 gallons of paint.

Second Coat:
100 lbs. white lead
1½ gals. pure turpentine
½ pt. liquid drier

¾ gal. varnish
Makes over 5½ gallons of paint.

Third Coat (Flat):
100 lbs. white lead
1¾ gals. pure turpentine
½ pt. liquid drier
⅛ gal. varnish
Makes 5 gallons of paint.

Third Coat (Semi-Gloss)
100 lbs. white lead
1½ gals. pure turpentine
¼ pt. liquid drier
1½ gals. varnish
Makes over 6 gallons of paint.

Old Plaster

First Coat:
100 lbs. white lead
1½ gals. pure turpentine
½ pt. liquid drier
¾ gal. varnish
Makes over 5 gallons of paint.

Second Coat:
Either third coat (flat or semi-gloss) used for painting new plaster.

STANDARD LUMBER SIZES

The following tables indicate the gross footage of unfinished lumber and the footage of finished lumber, of various grades. Lumber is ordered according to the rough size, but actual dimensions of the boards vary with the type and grade.

In the table, *Common* indicates a grade of board which may have three or four sound knots but at least two thirds of one side clear. *Clear* is board free of knots, pitch pockets. etc.

Shiplap boards are rabbeted on the edges so that they form a half lap joint when laid alongside each other. *T & G* indicates tongued and grooved lumber. *S4S* means that the board has been surfaced on all four sides.

FLOORING

Size	Overall
1 x 3	$25/32$ x $25/8$
1 x 4	$25/32$ x $31/2$
1 x 6	$25/32$ x $57/16$
$5/4$ x 3	$17/16$ x $25/8$
$5/4$ x 4	$17/16$ x $31/2$
$5/4$ x 6	$17/16$ x $57/16$
$6/4$ x 3	$21/16$ x $25/8$
$6/4$ x 4	$21/16$ x $31/2$
$6/4$ x 6	$21/16$ x $57/16$

FIR, SPRUCE, HEMLOCK BEVEL SIDING

Size	Overall
$1/2$ x 4	$11/32$ x $31/2$
$1/2$ x 5	$11/32$ x $41/2$
$1/2$ x 6	$11/32$ x $51/2$
$1/2$ x 8	$11/32$ x $71/4$
$1/2$ x 10	$11/32$ x $91/4$
$3/4$ x 8	$15/32$ x $71/4$
$3/4$ x 10	$15/32$ x $91/4$
$3/4$ x 12	$15/32$ x $111/4$

CASING AND BASE

Size	Overall
1 x 3	$3/4$ x $25/8$
1 x 4	$3/4$ x $31/2$
1 x 4	$3/4$ x $35/8$
1 x 5	$3/4$ x $41/4$
1 x 5	$3/4$ x $41/2$
1 x 6	$3/4$ x $51/2$
1 x 8	$3/4$ x $71/4$
1 x 10	$3/4$ x $91/4$

ORDINARY LUMBER

Rough Size	Common S4S
1 x 1	$25/32$ x $25/32$
1 x 2	$25/32$ x $15/8$
1 x 3	$25/32$ x $25/8$
1 x 4	$25/32$ x $35/8$
1 x 5	$25/32$ x $45/8$
1 x 6	$25/32$ x $55/8$
1 x 7	$25/32$ x $65/8$
1 x 8	$25/32$ x $71/2$
1 x 9	$25/32$ x $81/2$
1 x 10	$25/32$ x $91/2$
1 x 11	$25/32$ x $101/2$
1 x 12	$25/32$ x $111/2$
2 x 2	$15/8$ x $15/8$
2 x 3	$15/8$ x $25/8$
2 x 4	$15/8$ x $35/8$
2 x 5	$15/8$ x $45/8$
2 x 6	$15/8$ x $55/8$
2 x 7	$15/8$ x $65/8$
2 x 8	$15/8$ x $71/2$
2 x 9	$15/8$ x $81/2$
2 x 10	$15/8$ x $91/2$
4 x 4	$35/8$ x $35/8$
6 x 6	$51/2$ x $51/2$

Rough	Clear S4S	Common Shiplap or T & G
(1x1)	$25/32$ x $25/32$	
(1x2)	$25/32$ x $15/8$	
(1x3)	$25/32$ x $25/8$	$25/32$ x $21/2$
(1x4)	$25/32$ x $31/2$	$25/32$ x $31/2$
(1x5)	$25/32$ x $41/2$	$25/32$ x $41/2$
(1x6)	$25/32$ x $51/2$	$25/32$ x $51/2$
(1x7)	$25/32$ x $61/2$	$25/32$ x $61/2$
(1x8)	$25/32$ x $71/4$	$25/32$ x $71/2$
(1x9)	$25/32$ x $81/4$	$25/32$ x $81/2$
(1x10)	$25/32$ x $91/4$	$25/32$ x $91/2$
(1x11)	$25/32$ x $101/4$	$25/32$ x $101/2$
(1x12)	$25/32$ x $111/4$	$25/32$ x $111/2$
(2x2)	$15/8$ x $15/8$	$15/8$ x $11/2$
(2x3)	$15/8$ x $25/8$	$15/8$ x $21/2$

(2x4)	$1\frac{5}{8}$ x $3\frac{1}{2}$........	$1\frac{5}{8}$ x $3\frac{1}{2}$
(2x5)	$1\frac{5}{8}$ x $4\frac{1}{2}$........	$1\frac{5}{8}$ x $4\frac{1}{2}$
(2x6)	$1\frac{5}{8}$ x $5\frac{1}{2}$........	$1\frac{5}{8}$ x $5\frac{1}{2}$
(2x7)	$1\frac{5}{8}$ x $6\frac{1}{2}$........	$1\frac{5}{8}$ x $6\frac{1}{2}$
(2x8)	$1\frac{5}{8}$ x $7\frac{1}{4}$........	$1\frac{5}{8}$ x $7\frac{1}{2}$
(2x9)	$1\frac{5}{8}$ x $8\frac{1}{4}$........	$1\frac{5}{8}$ x $8\frac{1}{2}$
(2x10)	$1\frac{5}{8}$ x $9\frac{1}{4}$.......	$1\frac{5}{8}$ x $9\frac{1}{2}$
(4x4)	$3\frac{5}{8}$ x $3\frac{5}{8}$........	$3\frac{5}{8}$ x $3\frac{1}{2}$
(6x6)	$5\frac{1}{2}$ x $5\frac{1}{2}$........	$5\frac{1}{2}$ x $5\frac{1}{2}$

GLOSSARY

ABRASIVE. Material such as sandpaper, pumice, and emery, used for polishing, sanding, and grinding.

ACOUSTICS. Having to do with the transmission of sound through air and building materials.

ACROSS THE GRAIN. At right angles to the run of the wood grain.

ADJACENT. Close to, next to.

AGGREGATES. The materials, sand and gravel, mixed with Portland cement to produce concrete.

AIR DRY. Lumber that has been allowed to season in the air rather than in a kiln.

AIR POCKET. In concrete, a cavity in a concrete mass.

AIR SPACE. The area between the inner and outer wall. Any cavity.

ALL LENGTHS. Lumber cut in many different lengths.

ALL WIDTHS. Lumber cut in different widths.

AMPERE. Unit used to measure the rate of flow of electrical current.

ANCHOR. To secure one object to another; a device used to attach two objects together.

ANGLE IRON. A piece of iron or metal in the shape of a right angle; used in carpentry and brickwork to reinforce a joint.

APRON. The molding or casing under a window sill.

AQUASTAT. A control device used to regulate the temperature of the hot water supply when heated by the furnace.

ARCHITRAVE. Wood casing or trim.

AREA. The total surface of a floor or wall.

ARMORED CABLE. Electric wires encased in metal.

ARRIS. The sharp point formed by two surfaces joining, such as the corner of a board.

ASBESTOS. A fireproof mineral.

ASBESTOS PAPER. Heavy paper which will not burn and is a poor conductor of heat.

ASBESTOS SHINGLES. Roof or siding shingles made of Portland cement and asbestos.

ASHLAR. A type of stonework.

BABBITT. A soft metal used for bearings.

BACK PAINTING. Painting the back side or unexposed surface of lumber to prevent the wood from absorbing moisture.

BACK PUTTY. A thin layer of putty placed between the glass and the rabbet of the window.

BACKSAW. A fine-toothed saw with thin blade, reinforced with a steel back, used for chamfering, mitering, etc. Also called a tenon saw.

BALLISTERS. The vertical posts on stair railing.

BALLOON FRAME. Type of house framing used in modern building wherein relatively light lumber is used.

BALL PEEN HAMMER. A hammer with a rounded face used in metalwork.

BASEBOARD. The molding used to cover the joint between the floor and wall. Sometimes, it is called skirting.

BATTEN. A small strip of wood.

BEADING. Small wood molding used for decorative purposes.

BEAM. A heavy timber used in house and building construction.

BELLY. To bulge out.

BENZINE. A liquid used in painting for cleaning brushes and sometimes for thinning.

BEVEL. To cut on a slant, so that the angle formed is not a right angle.

BIBB. A faucet with the nozzle threaded so that a hose can be attached.

BISECT. To cut into two parts.

BLEEDING. The liquid in wood working to the surface.

BOARD FOOT. Unit of measuring lumber. Theoretically, a board measuring 1 square foot on the surface and 1 inch thick, it is usually 144 sq. in., scant, and $1\frac{3}{16}$ in. thick.

BOND. The method or pattern used when laying bricks.

BOND STONE. In masonry, stones used to tie a wall together.

BRAD. A small nail.

BREAKING JOINTS. In masonry, staggering the mortar joints.

BRICK COURSE. A layer of bricks.

BRICK VENEER. A thin layer of bricks used as a finish.

BRIDGING. Small diagonal braces between studding or joists.

BROWN COAT. The second coat of either plaster or stucco.

B. T. U. BRITISH THERMAL UNIT. A unit used to measure heat, equal to the amount of heat required to raise the temperature of 1 pound of water 1 degree F.

BUCKLE. To heave up, lift or warp.

BUILDING CODES. Local laws or ordinances regulating various phases of construction work.

BUTTER. In masonry, to apply mortar to a brick.

BX CABLE. Electric wires in flexible metal covering used extensively in the home electrical system.

CALCIUM CHLORIDE. A chemical that absorbs moisture from the air, used for drying out damp rooms. Also used for melting snow and ice.

CAP. The cement finish as used on top of a brick wall or chimney.

CARBON TETRACHLORIDE. A noninflammable cleaning and degreasing agent, also used in some types of fire extinguishers.

CASEMENT WINDOWS. Windows with the sash hinged to open like a door.

CASING. The wood trim around doors and windows.

CAST IRON PIPES. Soil pipes made of cast iron used for the sewage system.

CAULK. To fill a crack or seam with oakum or caulking compound.

CAULKING COMPOUND. A soft plastic used for caulking, which does not set hard but can be painted.

CEILING JOISTS. Lumber used as supports for the ceiling.

CEMENT. An adhesive for binding objects together. Also Portland cement as used in concrete.

CEMENT PLASTER. A mixture of Portland cement and sand used as a finish coat.

CHAMFER. To cut off a corner to form a bevel. To cut a groove or channel in. Also, the surface formed when the angle made by adjacent faces of a piece of timber, masonry, metal, etc., is cut away.

CHECK VALVE. A valve used in plumbing to prevent a reverse flow of water in a pipe.

CINDERS. Ashes from coal used as fill or mixed with cement to produce cinder blocks.

CLAPBOARD. Boards with one edge thicker than the other, used for house exterior siding.

CLINCH. To bend over.

CLINCH NAIL. Nails made of soft metal for clinching.

CLOCKWISE. To turn in the same direction in which the hands of a clock move.

COLLAR BEAM. A piece of lumber running horizontally between two rafters to provide additional support.

COMMON BOARDS. Boards one inch thick and up to 12 inches wide. Also, a grade of lumber. See Table of Standard Lumber Sizes.

COMMON BRICKS. Ordinary red bricks of standard size.

COMPASS SAW. A saw with narrow, tapering blade used to cut curves, circles, and fine cuts. See Fig. 9, Section 1.

CONCRETE. A mixture of Portland cement, sand, gravel, and water.

CONCRETE PAINT. A mixture composed of cement, water, and coloring matter, for use on concrete and cement surfaces. Any paint formulated for use on concrete or cement.

CONDUIT. A pipe carrying electric wires.

COPING. In masonry, the top finish of a wall.

COPING SAW. A saw with an extremely narrow blade which can be turned in the frame to saw at various angles. See Fig. 8, Section 1.

CORNICE. Usually, the portion of a wall directly under the eaves.

COUNTER FLASHING. Flashing applied over flashing.

COUPLING. In plumbing, a device used to join sections of pipe or hose.

COURSE. In masonry, a layer of bricks. Also a layer of shingles.

CREOSOTE. Wood or coal tar used as a wood preservative.

CROWNING. To raise the center of a flat surface so that water will drain off.

DADO. A rectangular, flat-bottomed grove cut in wood.

DADO JOINT. A joint made by cutting a tongue on the end of one member to fit into a dado cut in the other member.

DADO PLANE. A plane used to cut dados or grooves; a narrow rabbet plane.

DDT. Dichlorodiphenyl trichlorethane. A strong insecticide.

DECALCOMAINAS. A device used to transfer decorative designs onto painted surfaces.

DENATURED ALCOHOL. In painting, a a liquid used for thinning shellac.

DEW POINT. Temperature at which moisture in air condenses.

DIMENSION STUFF. Lumber 2 inches thick and up to 12 inches wide.

DORMER WINDOW. A window built into the side of a roof.

DOUBLE HUNG WINDOW. A window consisting of an upper and lower sash in a frame.

DOUBLE STUDDING. Two pieces of studding spiked together to form the openings for doors and windows.

DOWEL. A round piece of wood.

DOWEL JOINT. A joint made by gluing a dowel into two pieces of wood.

DRY ROT. A decay of wood usually caused by alternative dryness and dampness.

DRY WELL. A hole in the earth filled with stones or gravel used to collect water from house roof.

D. S. GLASS. Double strength glass used for glazing large windows.

EAVES. Portion of roof extending beyond walls.

EFFLORESCENCE. A white crust appearing on bricks caused by mineral salts.

EMERY PAPER. An abrasive paper used on metal.

END-MATCH LUMBER. Boards with the ends tongued and grooved as well as the sides.

ENGLISH BOND. A bond or pattern used in brickwork.

ESCUTCHEON. The metal plate on doors around the knobs and keyhole.

EXCAVATE. To dig out.

EXPANSION BOLT. A bolt designed for anchoring in masonry.

EXPANSION JOINT. Open joints between sections of concrete to allow for expansion and contraction.

EXTERIOR. The outside or outer surface.

FACE. The front, as the face of a wall or the face of a brick. The exposed portion.

FELT PAPER. Heavy paper used in construction work to deaden sound and for insulating purposes.

FERRULE. The metal portion of a paint brush at the base of the bristles.

FIELD STONES. Rough, uncut local stones.

FILLER. In painting, a material used to fill the wood pores. Also gravel or cinders used as a base for laying concrete.

FINISH. The final surface when completed.

FIRE BRICK. Special bricks, used in fireplaces and furnaces, that withstand heat.

FIRE CLAY. A special heat-resisting cement used to bond fire bricks.

FIREPROOF. A material that will not burn.

FIRE RESISTANT. A material that will resist fire but is not absolutely fireproof.

FIRE STOP. A piece of studding used in wall construction to prevent fire from rising through the air space between inner and outer wall.

FLAGSTONES. Stone or concrete slabs used for walks. These can be made by the handyman.

FLASHING. Strips of metal used to make exterior house joints watertight.

FLOW OUT. In painting, the ability of some paints to dry without brush marks.

FLUSH. A flat or even surface.

FLUX. A composition used in soldering to clean the metal and help the solder to flow.

FOOTING. The lower portion of a foundation that rests on the ground. The base.

FRENCH DOOR. A door with panes of glass used instead of wood panels.

Frost Line. The depth to which the earth freezes.

FURRING. Strips of wood nailed to masonry walls to serve as a base of laths or wallboard.

GABLE. The triangular portion at the end of a building.

GALVANIZED. To coat a metal with zinc to prevent rusting.

GALVANIZED NAILS. Zinc-coated nails for use when exposed to weather.

GIRDER. A large beam.

GLASS BLOCKS. Translucent or transparent blocks of glass used in building.

GLAZED BRICKS. Bricks with a glazed surface.

GLAZING. The process of putting a pane of window glass into the sash.

GRADE. The slope or pitch of the ground.

GRAIN. The lines in wood caused by the annual growth.

GRAVEL. Small stones used in making concrete or used as fill.

GREEN LUMBER. Lumber that has not been properly seasoned.

GROUT. A thin cement mortar used for pointing.

HANGER. An iron support used for attaching beams.

HARDWARE. The metal work in a house, such as hinges, locks, etc.

HARDWOOD FLOORS. Floors made out of hardwoods, such as oak and maple, as opposed to those made of softwoods.

HEAD. The top portion of a door or window opening.

HEARTH. The portion of a fireplace that extends into the room.

HOT WIRE. An electric wire with current passing through. A live wire.

INSULATION. Any material that is a poor conductor of heat or electricity.

INTERIOR. The inside of a house or building.

JACK. A mechanism used for lifting heavy objects.

JAMB. Casing or sidepost of a doorway.

JOINT. To fit two pieces of material together.

JOIST. The timber used to support or frame a floor or ceiling.

KEYHOLE SAW. A keyhole saw resembles a compass saw (which see) but has an even more narrow and tapering blade. It is designed for cutting out keyholes and for other fine work.

KILN DRIED. Wood that has been seasoned in a kiln oven rather than in the air.

KNUCKLES OF A HINGE. The rounded portion of a hinge plate that takes the hinge pin.

LATH. Thin strips of wood 4 feet long nailed to studding as supports for plaster. Also can be wire mesh or composition plaster board.

LEADER. The pipe from the gutter to the ground; a downspout.

LIGHT. A plane of glass in a window sash.

LOAD BEARING WALL. A wall that supports additional weight besides its own.

LOUVRE. An opening with boards set at an angle across it to provide ventilation but prevent rain from entering.

MASKING TAPE. A tape with an adhesive on one side used for painting and decorating. The tape can be removed without damage to a painted surface.

MASTIC. A type of composition cement used for linoleum and asphalt flooring.

MATCHED BOARDS. Boards cut with tongue and groove.

MILDEW. A fungus growth.

MITER JOINT. A joint made by cutting each piece of wood at, usually, a 45-degree angle.

MOLDING. Wood that has been milled into special shapes and designs for use as trim.

MORTAR. A mixture of cement and sand used for bonding bricks and stone.

MORTICE. A hole cut into a piece of wood to receive a tenon or tongue shaped at the end of another piece of wood. The resulting fit is called a mortice and tenon joint. Also MORTISE.

MURIATIC ACID. Hydrochloric acid used for cleaning concrete.

NATURAL FINISH. Wood that is left with the natural coloring.

NOVELTY SIDING. Wood siding cut into special designs.

OAKUM. A hemp fiber used for caulking.

ON CENTER. From center to center.

ORANGE SHELLEC. Shellac with natural coloring.

OUT OF PLUMB. Not plumb; in other words, not level or vertical.

PARALLEL. Running side by side in the same direction.

PARAPET. A small low wall.

PARTING STRIP. A thin strip of wood nailed between the upper and lower sashes in a double hung window.

PARTITION. An inside wall, as between two rooms.

PERPENDICULAR. A line running at right angles to another line, such as a wall to a floor. A vertical line.

PICTURE MOLDING. Special molding attached to the walls and from which pictures are hung. Can be either wood or plaster.

PIGMENT. In painting, the material in the paint that provides the color.

PITCH. The slope of a surface, such as a roof or the ground.

PIT SAND. Sand taken directly from the pit.

PLANK. A heavy board.

PLATES. Usually the 2 x 4 inch timbers running horizontally on the top of wall studding.

PLATE GLASS. Heavy glass used for large areas, such as store display windows.

PLUMB. To be in a perfectly upright position.

POINTING. Filling joints in masonry with mortar and striking, or troweling, the joint with the point of the trowel to give a finished appearance. Also, the material used for pointing.

PUMICE STONE. A finely ground stone used for polishing.

PUTTY. A plastic made of powdered whiting and linseed oil.

RABBET. A groove cut in wood along the edge, particularly to receive the edge of another piece of wood and form a rabbet joint.

RABBET PLANE. A plane used for cutting rabbets on the edges of timber and also for cutting grooves in wood.

RADIUS. The distance from the center of a circle to the outside edge.

RAFTER. The board used to support the roof.

RAKE JOINT. Type of mortar joint between bricks. The mortar is raked out of the joint to a certain depth before it sets.

RASP. A coarse file used mainly for filing rough surfaces. Like files, rasps are classified from *rough* to *smooth*.

REBATE. A groove or channel cut in wood. A rabbet.

RED LEAD. A paint primer used on metal.

REINFORCED CONCRETE. Concrete that is strengthened internally by the use of steel bars or heavy wire mesh.

RELATIVE HUMIDITY. The ratio of the amount of moisture present in the air to the maximum amount possible at a given temperature.

RISER. The board that forms the front of the stair step.

ROTTENSTONE. A fine abrasive powder used for polishing furniture.

R.P.M. Revolutions per minute.

ROUGH LUMBER. Lumber that has not been surfaced or dressed.

RUBBLE. Rough stone construction.

RUST. A reddish coating on iron caused by oxidation.

SADDLE BOARD. Boards nailed along the ridge of a roof.

SASH. Portion of the window that moves and holds the panes of glass.

SASH WEIGHT. Metal bar attached to end of window sash cord and used to balance sash.

SCANTLING. Small pieces of dimension lumber. Often applied to 2 x 4's and 2 x 6's.

SHEATHING. Boards nailed over rafters or studding to serve as a base for roofing or siding.

SHIM. A strip of material used to fill a small space.

SHIPLAP. Boards cut along the edge in such a fashion that when nailed alongside one another they form a half-lap joint.

SHRINK. To become smaller due to the loss of moisture.

SIDING. The boards used as the exterior walls.

SILEX. Finely ground quartz used as a filler.

SILL. The wood portion of a house that rests on the foundations.

S. S. GLASS. Single strength glass used in ordinary window panes.

SIZE. A coating applied to plaster or wallboard before paint or paste to prevent uneven absorption.

SKIRTING. Trim used between floor and walls. The baseboard.

SMOKE CHAMBER. Portion of a fireplace directly over the damper.

SOIL PIPE. Pipe used for the sewer system.

SOLDER. An alloy of tin and lead having a low melting point, used for joining metal.

SOLDIER COURSE. In brickwork, bricks set on edge.

STENCIL. A pattern used in painting.

STILE. The side frames of a panel door.

STOOL. The inside sill of a window frame.

STOCK SIZES. Lumber cut to standard sizes.

STRAP HINGE. A heavy hinge used on large doors.

STRAIGHTEDGE. A board with a straight side used for measuring and drawing.

STRINGERS. The sides of a flight of stairs. Also called the carriages.

STRUT. Timber used as brace or support, such as framing. Pieces resisting pressure.

STUDDING. The uprights of a wall. The 2 x 4 inch stock used to frame the sides of a building.

SUBFLOOR. The rough floor under the finish floor.

SURFACE LUMBER. Lumber that has been dressed or smoothed.

SWEATING. Condensation of moisture vapor on a surface.

TANG. Portion of metal tool that fits into handle.

TEMPLATE. A pattern cut out of paper, cardboard, or a similar material. Also, a short piece of timber put under a girder or other beam for added strength. A beam over an opening, such as a doorway.

TENON. Tongue or lip cut on a piece of wood to fit into a mortice.

TENON SAW. See Backsaw.

THICKNESS. In lumber, the distance between the two broad surfaces.

T-HINGE. A hinge shaped like the letter T.

THRESHOLD. A piece of wood or metal under a door.

THROAT. Opening at top of fireplace into chimney where damper is located.

THUMB SCREW. A type of screw that can be tightened by hand.

TIMBER. Lumber over 4 inches thick.

TIN SNIPS. Shears used for cutting thin metal.

TOE NAILING. Nails driven in at angle.

TRANSFORMER. An electrical device used to reduce voltage.

TRIM. Wood used around openings such as doors and windows.

TRISODIUM PHOSPHATE. A strong non-soapy cleaning substance.

TURPENTINE, GUM. Liquid used in painting. The distilled gum from yellow pine trees.

TURPENTINE, WOOD. Liquid extracted from pine wood waste by distillation or by solvents.

VALLEY. The intersection of two roofs of different angles or pitch.

VEHICLE. In painting, the liquid with which the paint pigment is mixed so that it can be brushed on a surface.

VENEER. A thin layer of wood glued to a wood base.

VITRIFIED SOIL PIPE. Hard-baked clay pipe used for outside sewer lines.

VOLT. Unit for measuring electrical pressure.

WAINSCOTING. Wood attached to the lower portion of an interior wall.

WATER TABLE. Molding at bottom of the wall to deflect water from the base of the wall.

WELDING. A method of attaching pieces of metal by means of intense heat.

WHITE LEAD. A paint pigment.

WIDTH. In lumber, the distance across the grain on the broadest surface.

WINDOW FRAME. The portion of the window that holds the sashes.

WINDOW SILL. The bottom of a window frame.

ABBREVIATIONS

A.D. Air dried

Av. Average

Av.L. Average length

Av.W. Average width

Bgs. Bags

Bbl. Barrel

Bd.Ft. Board foot

Bdl. Bundle

Cu.Ft. Cubic foot (feet)

Cu.In. Cubic inch (inches)

Cu.Yd. Cubic yard (yards)

d. Penny. Used as unit of measurement of nail sizes.

Dia. Diameter

Dim. Dimension(s)

D.M. Dressed and matched

D.S. Double strength

Fahr. (F.). Fahrenheit

Ft. Foot or feet. Also expressed as '

Gal. Gallon

H.P. Horsepower

In. Inch or inches. Expressed as "

Lin. Lineal. Linear

Lgth. Length

M. Thousand

Manuf. Manufacturer

No. Number

Nt.Wt. Net weight

Oz. Ounce(s)

Sq. Square

Std. Standard

S1E. Surfaced one edge (lumber)

S2E. Surfaced two edges

S1S1E. Surfaced one side and one edge

S2S1E. Surfaced two sides and one edge

S4S. Surfaced four sides

Tbr. Timber

T&G. Tongued and grooved

Wt. Weight

Wth. Width

x. Times or by

Yd. Yard(s)

INDEX

C

D